THE OFFICIAL PRICE GUIDE TO

Antiques and Other Collectibles

BY

GRACE McFARLAND

FIRST EDITION

HOUSE OF COLLECTIBLES
ORLANDO, FLORIDA 32811

Dear Collector,

I have attempted to prepare a price guide to antiques and collectibles that is both entertaining and informative.

The prices and listings herein are a compilation of many months of research. There are undoubtedly subjects and listings which could have been added to make this guide more complete. The publishers and I welcome mail from you with suggestions for the second edition.

Write to me in care of THE HOUSE OF COLLECTIBLES, 773 Kirkman Road, No. 120, Orlando, Florida, 32811.

Sincerely,

grace McFarland

Grace McFarland

Published by the: House of Collectibles, Inc.
                  773 Kirkman Road, No. 120
                  Orlando, FL 32811

Printed in the United States of America

Library of Congress Catalog Card Number: 78-67961

ISBN: 0-87637-340-6

THE OFFICIAL PRICE GUIDE TO

Antiques and Other Collectibles

TABLE OF CONTENTS

ACKNOWLEDGEMENTS

For help in the preparation of this book, the author wishes to thank the following: Carrousel Midwest, Dale Sorenson, North Lake, WI; Clocks and Things, Cindy and Joseph Fanelli, New York, NY; Abe Kessler Appraisal Service, Queens Village, NY; Central Florida Depression Glass Club, Ruby L. Davis, Pres., Orlando, FL; Les and Susan Gould, Orange, NJ; Movieworld, Los Angeles, CA; L. H. Selman Ltd., Santa Cruz, CA; Pelican Publishing Co., Gretna, LA; Bill Feeny Antiques, Latrobe, PA; Charles Colt, New York, NY; George S. James, Washington, DC; Alfred J. Young, Police Academy Museum, New York, NY; Kruse Auction Co., Auburn, IN.

PHOTOGRAPHIC RECOGNITION

Coverand color section courtesy of:

©Copyright Sotheby Parke Bernet, Inc., New York, NY and
©Copyright PB Eighty-Four, New York, NY

Black and white photographs on pages 12, 31, 63, 122, 130, 137, 141, 157, 179, 243, 247, 266, 274, 277, 280, 281, 284, 286, 293, 309, 317, 343, 349, 416, 418, 419, 421, 428, 430, 433 courtesy of:

©Copyright Sotheby Parke Bernet, Inc.,
Agent Editorial Photocolor Archives, Inc., New York, NY

Black and white photographs on pages 72, 115, 248, 307 courtesy of:

©Copyright PB Eighty-Four, New York, NY

Black and white photograph on page 14 courtesy of:

©Copyright Sotheby Parke Bernet, Inc., Los Angeles, CA

Pattern glass illustrations courtesy of:

Bob Batty, Author of *A Complete Guide to Pressed Glass,*
Pelican Publishing Co., Gretna, LA

INTRODUCTION

This edition of *the Official Price Guide to Antiques and Other Collectibles* is intended to acquaint the public with the quickly increasing vast array of antiques, curios and collectibles, which are available in antique shops, flea markets, yard sales and even the attics of America. The emphasis is on American antiques but some items of European and Oriental origin are included because of their availability and popularity with American collectors.

The antiques and collectibles market has drastically changed over the past few years. Mass-marketing techniques have been applied to the selling of old things, periodicals and books have proliferated, and prices at auctions have become big news even in metropolitan newspapers. For these reasons, price guides are invaluable aids to new collectors, dealers and others involved in the business. Remember, however, that a price guide is never more than a *guide to prices which have been paid;* there is no way to fully anticipate what tomorrow's prices will be.

We are not in the business of selling antiques and collectibles. The editor and publishers have endeavored to make this price guide as accurate and up-to-date as possible and to include as many of the newer collectibles as possible. *We do not buy, sell or appraise antiques* and as our only desire is to inform and educate, we again caution you that the prices contained within this guide are subject to changes depending on geographical location, type of sale (auction, shop, small dealer, yard sale) and even the time of year during which sales occur.

Remember that dealers as well as collectors use this price guide. The collector uses it to determine (1) how much to pay for something and (2) how much to ask for it if a dealer or another collector wants to buy. The dealer looks at these prices with a different eye; he wants to buy items for a price which is anywhere from 25% to 50% off the listed price and sell them for the listed price. This is important information for collectors and a collector should not feel that a dealer is cheating him by buying for less than the price listed in the guide.

Finally, our advice to you is that although price guides tend to be treated as bibles, you should never be afraid to tell a dealer who backs up his price by asserting "it's in the book", that factors such as condition, color, personal appeal and so on make you unwilling to pay the book price for a particular item. In this way everyone will profit in the long run and collectors and dealers will learn the most important lesson: each piece should first be judged by itself, stand on its own merits, and be priced according to its relationship to similar pieces.

WHAT IS THE DIFFERENCE BETWEEN ANTIQUES AND COLLECTIBLES?

According to the United States Tariff Act of 1930, antiques are "works of art (except rugs and carpets made after the year 1700), collections in illustration of the progress of the arts, works in bronze, marble, terra cotta, parian, pottery, or porcelain, artistic antiquities, and objects of art of ornamental character or educational value which shall have been produced prior to the year 1830." Customs officials of the Department of the Treasury interpret this to mean that anything made 100 years before the importation date is an antique. Many dealers, collectors, authors and other experts commonly use the term "antique" to include all items of intrinsic value, rarity, and fitting commonly or widely-accepted ideas of beauty and worth. For this reason, many fine objects made a scant 50 years ago are considered "Antiques" by some. On the other hand, particularly in the field of furniture, some experts claim that only furniture made before 1830 is antique.

A collectible is generally described as any object which because of its significance in popular culture, regardless of "beauty" or rarity, and regardless of intrinsic value, possesses value, nevertheless, to collectors. Examples of collectibles are plastic Art Deco items, ashtrays, matchbooks, comic books, comic character toys, Avon and Jim Beam bottles, Buffalo china, Depression glass, carnival glass, and memorabilia of movies, world's fairs, world wars, etc.

HOW TO JUDGE CONDITION

Condition is often the major determinant of the price of an antique or collectible. In this price guide *all prices quoted are for items in good or better condition* unless otherwise noted. The commendable tendency of most collectors is to buy the best they can at any given time and to expect to "trade up."

The following examples demonstrate what you should look for and expect of any item advertised or sold in "good condition."

Glassware: no cracks, chips, flaws; no repairs or ground-off edges; no mis-matched lids or saucers; no mis-matched color.

Ceramics: no badly scratched or rubbed-off glaze; no chips or cracks; some crazing allowed. Handles, spouts, knobs, lids all present and original and not repaired.

Textiles: no tears, holes or rips in any area but edges (and that only on very old pieces); unfaded and no severe raveling. Textile fragments are quite acceptable, because so many pieces of lace and embroidery are removed from clothing.

Paper: clean, legible, unstained, unfoxed, untorn. Slight damage along fold lines is acceptable. Edges should not have been trimmed (from posters, prints, postcards, etc.) to fit a frame; old prints should not have been recently "hand-colored."

Woodenware: no major cracks, chips or splits; only minor warping. Wood should be in original finish, not stripped, scraped and varnished with polyurethane.

Metalwares: no dents, no obtrusive solder repairs; should have original lids, spouts, handles. Metals meant to be plated (for example nickel-plated brass) should be in original state, not buffed so as to remove the plating.

Mechanical toys, banks: in good working order with original paint in unchipped, unflaked, unretouched condition.

Lamps: no cracks, chips, major flaws; mechanical parts should function; all parts should be present and original; shades should be original although chimneys can be replaced.

Guns: good working order, legible engraving, reasonably good finish; no missing parts; metal should not have been wire-brushed.

Clocks and watches: good working order; complete and clean; works and case original; clear glass can be replaced but reverse-painted glass should be original; dial or face unchipped and unstained.

Furniture: original finish, legs, arms, brasses and hardware; no major cracks, warps, breaks or loss of veneer.

REPRODUCTIONS & FAKES

Over the years, a great many objects have been reproduced and faked. Mechanical banks, glasswares, ceramics, furniture, political campaign items, toys, weathervanes and Art Nouveau jewelry have been duplicated from original molds or plates, or their style has been approximated. Many reproductions are well-done and some are difficult to tell them from the original. Reproductions are sometimes a form of collectible in themselves but only rarely are not as valuable or desirable as the original, *and they never will be* (examples are Wallace Nutting furniture repros, or the 1920s and 30s repros of sandwich glass). It is often pointed out that even a good piece of reproduction 19th Century furniture, for example, is reduced to second-hand furniture the minute you take it home. Reproductions should *not* be represented or priced as originals. Fakes are reproductions from which the maker's marks have been removed and to which have been added scuffing, scratching and distressing intended to fool the unwary.

The best protections against acquiring a reproduction or a fake are studying your field, using books, museums and private collections and buying only from reputable and knowledgeable dealers. Reputable, ethical dealers stand behind what they sell and will give you a detailed bill of sale or a buy-back guarantee.

FINDING DEALERS & INFORMATION

To find local dealers check the yellow pages under "Antiques." You may also visit antiques shows, flea markets, auctions and conventions, or you can enjoy the thrill of detection by attending yard or tag sales, and by going to thrift and second-hand stores.

The following publications not only are sources of information on the history of various antiques and collectibles and trends in the field, they also contain dealer ads and ads of private individuals who either want to sell or want to buy. You can place your own want ads in many of them for a reasonable fee.

American Art & Antiques
1515 Broadway
NYC, N.Y. 10036

American Collector
P.O. Box A
Reno, Nevada 89506

The Magazine ANTIQUES
551 Fifth Avenue
NYC, N.Y. 10017

Antiques & The Arts Weekly
Newtown Bee
Bee Publishing Co.
Newtown, Conn. 06470

Antique Collecting
(American Antique Collector)
P.O. Box 327
Ephrata, Pa. 17522

Antique Collector
Chestergate House
Vauxhall Bridge Road
London SW1V 1HF

Antiques Journal
P.O. Box 1046
Dubuque, Iowa 52001

Antique Monthly
P.O. Drawer 2
Tuscaloosa, Alabama 35401

Antique Trader
P.O. Box 1050
Dubuque, Iowa 52001

Antiques World
P.O. Box 990
Farmingdale, N.Y. 11737

The Clarion,
America's Folk Art Magazine
49 West 53rd St.
NYC, N.Y. 10019

Collectibles Monthly
P.O. Box 2023
York, Pa. 17405

Collector Editions Quarterly
170 Fifth Ave.
NYC, N.Y. 10010

Hobbies
1006 S. Michigan Avenue
Chicago, Ill. 60605

Maine Antiques Digest
P.O. Box 358
Waldoboro, Maine 04572

National Antiques Courier
P.O. Box 500
Warwick, Md. 21912

The New York-Pennsylvania Collector
c/o Wolfe Publications
4 S. Main St.
Pittsford, N.Y. 14534

Nineteenth Century (Forbes)
60 Fifth Avenue
NYC, N.Y. 10011

Ohio Antique Review
72 North St.
P.O. Box 538
Worthington, Ohio 43085

Political Collector
503 Madison Avenue
York, Pa. 17404

Joel Sater's Antiques News
P.O. Box B
Marietta, Pa. 17547

Spinning Wheel
Fame Avenue
Hanover, Pa. 17331

HOW TO USE THIS PRICE GUIDE

The contents have been arranged alphabetically. Some of the larger categories such as glassware, pottery and porcelain, toys and furniture have been grouped together and sub-divided for easy reference into narrower collecting specialties. *An exhaustive index is to be found at the end of the book.* Appearing beside each listing is a check box to enable you to keep an accurate inventory of items which you own, as well as their condition. You may show the condition of an object by placing one of the following marks in the check box.

◻ Poor to fair   ◻ Good   ⊟ Fine   ⊠ Excellent or mint

ADVERTISING GIVEAWAYS

Advertising giveaways were big business in times past, before mechanical advertising came into being. They were graphically illustrated, colorful and often amusing. They are truly an example of the ingenuity of the American businessman.

Price Range

CALENDARS

☐ Comfort, Mother and Child, 1910	25.00	35.00
☐ Gordon R. Cloes Real Estate, girl and dog in car, 1946	10.00	15.00
☐ Gordon R. Cloes Real Estate, girl in sheer gown, 1946	10.00	15.00
☐ Harsford's, Child in bobsled, framed under glass, 1893	40.00	50.00
☐ Mrs. Dinsmore's Balsam, Mother and Child, 1901	30.00	40.00
☐ Santa Fe R.R., "The Chief Is Still The Chief"	20.00	30.00

CLOCKS

☐ Canada Dry Sport Cola, 13" x 18"	22.00	28.00
☐ Cat's Paw, 14" Dia.	40.00	60.00
☐ Coca Cola, "Please Pay When Served"	55.00	85.00
☐ Coca Cola, round metal	30.00	50.00
☐ Dr. Pepper, diamond shape	40.00	60.00
☐ Pepsi The Light Refreshment, wrought-iron, 18" Dia.	30.00	45.00
☐ Pepsi, square with new logo	20.00	30.00
☐ Seven Up, round, brass color metal	25.00	35.00
☐ Vantage Cigarettes, 12" dia., battery	20.00	30.00

SIGNS

☐ Anheuser Busch, Lite up, plastic, picture of man and woman, 18" x 24"	20.00	30.00
☐ Budweiser, lite up, plastic with bottle, 5" x 12"	10.00	15.00
☐ Budweiser, cardboard cutout of two black men riding a bicycle built for two	4.00	6.00
☐ Burgermeister Burgie, lite up, brunette lounging near pool, 12" x 15"	18.00	25.00
☐ Camel Cigarettes, cardboard, blond woman, dated 1941, 20" x 11"	10.00	15.00
☐ Carta Blanca Beer, lite up bar sign	20.00	30.00
☐ Call Again Cigars 5¢, cardboard fan hanger, 5" Dia. . .	2.50	3.50
☐ Coca Cola, "Drink Coca Cola in Bottles", Red tin disc 15" Dia.	25.00	30.00
☐ Coca Cola, "Join The Friendly Circle," 1954, ...	20.00	30.00
☐ Coors Beer, lite up, lake and mountain scene	20.00	30.00
☐ Dr. Meyer's Foot Soap, cardboard, many hands holding bars of soap, 7" x 10"	3.00	5.00
☐ Dutch Masters Cigars, tin oval with picture of 6 Dutch Masters, 11" x 9"	4.50	5.50
☐ Ethyl, gas pump, porcelain, 8" Dia.	20.00	30.00
☐ Falstaff Beer, lite up, logo in gold, 20" x 23"	25.00	30.00
☐ Fire Chief Gasoline, glass panel, 12" x 4"	4.00	8.00

Price Range

SIGNS

☐ Hood Tires, tin, man wearing uniform and flag, 15" x 9"	8.00	12.00
☐ L & N R.R., Marked General Motors Loco., framed print, 16" x 14"	20.00	30.00
☐ Michelob Beer, lite up, cash register sign	18.00	25.00
☐ Model Tobacco, tin with colorful man, 4" x 12"	20.00	30.00
☐ Narragansett Lager, gold and silver letters on red, 20" x 10"	60.00	80.00
☐ National Bohemian Beer, lite up, Mr. Boh and says "Exit", 12" Dia. 1940's	45.00	60.00
☐ Olympia Beer, lite up, sailboat scene, 41" x 15"	45.00	55.00
☐ Olympia Gold, cardboard, 12" x 10"	2.00	3.00
☐ Old Milwaukee Beer, plastic, Victorian style lady, 15" x 22"	14.00	20.00
☐ Pabst Blue Ribbon, blackboard, bartender, 1950's	14.00	18.00
☐ Parking 30 Minutes, metal, 12" x 18"	6.00	10.00
☐ Rheingold Beer, lite up bar sign	14.00	18.00
☐ Schaefer Beer, wood barrel, 14" x 16"	18.00	25.00
☐ Sprollins Odorless Mothproof, cardboard, 14" x 16"	4.00	8.00
☐ Sky Chief Gasoline, glass panel, 12" x 4"	4.00	8.00
☐ State Auto Insurance, porcelain and enamel, 3" x 4"	14.00	18.00
☐ Woo Chong Import Co., paper, oriental women and art objects, 21" x 31", c.1920	25.00	35.00

THERMOMETERS

☐ Antifreeze, 30" L	25.00	35.00
☐ Carstairs, "Join The Carstairs Crowd," round	20.00	30.00
☐ Coke, bottle shape, 27"	45.00	55.00
☐ Coke, gold Bottle shape, 7"	14.00	18.00
☐ Coke, oval Bottle shape, 27"	40.00	50.00
☐ Coke, "Things Go Better With Coke," 17½" D	14.00	18.00
☐ Hires, bottle shape, 27"	35.00	45.00
☐ Nesbits, bottle shape, 27"	35.00	45.00
☐ Pepsi, "Have A Pepsi," 27"	20.00	30.00
☐ Royal Crown Cola, 27"	30.00	40.00
☐ Winston Cigarettes, plastic, 10"	18.00	25.00

TRAYS

☐ Beck's Brewing, buffalo, 13" Dia., 1950's	14.00	18.00
☐ Billy Baxter, big red bird, 12" Dia., 1920's	30.00	40.00
☐ Coca Cola, hostess, 1936	45.00	65.00
☐ Coca Cola, springboard girl, 1939	40.00	60.0
☐ Coca Cola, girl with menu, 1950	20.00	30.00
☐ Coca Cola, Santa Claus, 1973	12.00	20.00
☐ Genessee 12 Horse Ale, horse team, 13" Dia.	30.00	40.00
☐ Miller High Life, girl on moon, 1940's, 13" Dia.	40.00	50.00
☐ Piel's Beer, N.Y., Bert & Harry Piel, 13" Dia., 1957	14.00	20.00
☐ Schmidt's Brewing, Philadelphia, tiger's head and crest, 13" Dia., c. 1950	8.00	15.00

TRAYS

Price Range

- [ ] Valley Forge Beer, Washington's Headquarters, 12" Dia., c. 1940 .... 30.00 40.00
- [ ] World's Fair 1964, unisphere, 12" Dia. 6.00 10.00

ALMANACS

Early settlers of the 18th and 19th centuries used almanacs as a guide for everyday life. Crops were planted and harvested according to the moon phase. Social activities were guided by these books. Almanacs printed 1880-1900's are not rare. The price range for most is $5-$15.

All prices shown are for good condition.

- [ ] 1776—North American Almanack. S. Sterns 35.00 38.00
- [ ] 1783—New England Almanack. Bickerstaff......... 30.00 35.00
- [ ] 1791—Hartford Almanack. Strong 25.00 29.00
- [ ] 1794—New England Almanack. Daboll 20.00 23.00
- [ ] 1796—Hartford Almanack. Strong 20.00 23.00
- [ ] 1797—Hagerstown Almanack. First Edition 80.00 85.00
- [ ] 1799—Leapyear Issue Farmer's Almanack 20.00 23.00
- [ ] 1805—New England Almanack. Daboll 25.00 30.00
- [ ] 1808—New England Almanack. Daboll 15.00 20.00
- [ ] 1808—Farmer's Almanac. V.B. Bates 25.00 30.00
- [ ] 1810—New England Almanack. Daboll 25.00 30.00
- [ ] 1812—Law's Boston 10.00 15.00
- [ ] 1813—New England Almanack. Daboll 20.00 25.00
- [ ] 1815—New England Almanack. Daboll 20.00 25.00
- [ ] 1816—New England Almanack. Daboll 20.00 25.00
- [ ] 1818—New England Almanack. Daboll 18.00 20.00
- [ ] 1820—New England Almanack. Daboll 18.00 20.00
- [ ] 1828—Ontario Almanack. Abner Loud. Canandaigua . 15.00 20.00
- [ ] 1829—Western Almanack 15.00 20.00
- [ ] 1834—Poor Richard's Almanack 15.00 20.00
- [ ] 1837—Anti-Slavery Almanack. New England 25.00 30.00
- [ ] 1843—Presbyterian Almanack 8.00 10.00

ALMANACS

	Price	Range
☐ 1848—Farmer's Almanack. Boston	8.00	10.00
☐ 1850—Town & Country Almanack	8.00	10.00
☐ 1851—National Comic Almanack	8.00	10.00
☐ **1895—Ayer's American Almanack**	9.00	12.00
☐ 1855—True Americans Almanack	35.00	50.00
☐ 1867—Western Almanack. Perkins	10.00	15.00
☐ 1869—Hagerstown Town & Country Almanack	5.00	10.00
☐ 1871—Farmer & Mechanics Almanack. Scovill	7.00	10.00
☐ 1871—Miners Almanack. Pittsburgh	6.00	10.00
☐ 1872—Tarrytown Almanack	6.00	10.00
☐ 1874—United States - Almanack. Hostetter	5.00	10.00
☐ 1880—Hagerstown Almanack. Gruber	5.00	10.00
☐ 1881—Humans and Horses	6.00	10.00
☐ 1885—Presto-Fertilizer Co.	3.50	5.00
☐ 1886—Mandrahe Bitters Almanack	5.00	10.00
☐ 1887—Kendall Doctor at Home	6.00	10.00
☐ **1888—Williams & Clark Fertilizers, colored cover**	7.00	10.00
☐ **1888—Wright's Pictorial Family Almanack**	5.00	10.00
☐ **1895—"The Life Book" Boston D. Sarsaparilla**	8.50	10.00
☐ 1895—Ayers American Almanack	5.00	7.00
☐ 1897—Home Almanack	4.00	6.00
☐ 1900—Barker's Guide/Cookbook	8.00	10.00
☐ 1902—Ladies Birthday Almanack	5.00	7.00
☐ 1902—Swamp Root	3.50	5.00
☐ 1908—Diamond Dye #6	8.00	10.00
☐ 1911—Dr. Ayer's (German)	6.00	8.00
☐ 1912—Ranson's	5.00	7.00
☐ 1912—Royster's	4.00	6.00
☐ 1915—Dr. Ayer's (American Health)	4.00	6.00
☐ 1917—Ladies Birthday Almanack	5.00	7.00
☐ 1919—Poor Richard's Almanack	4.00	6.00
☐ 1923—Hood Farm	4.00	6.00

AMERICAN EAGLES

As a symbol for America, the eagle has been used by countless designers and craftsmen for everything from candlesticks and coverlets to uniform buttons and cheesecloth labels. Some collectors are fascinated by the many forms on which are found interpretations of the eagle and, with other American symbols such as Miss Liberty and Uncle Sam, an interesting motif or topical collection can be formed.

☐ Carved and Gilded Plaster, wings upstretched, perched on green painted mound. 28" H x 39¼" L	200.00	250.00
☐ Carved and Painted Wood Figure, coxcomb and legs painted orange-yellow, body and wings painted blue-green, 10" H x 18" L	2500.00	3000.00
☐ Carved and Painted Wood Figure, grasping American shield, arrows in its talons, 14½" H x 44½" L	500.00	700.00

EAGLES

Price Range

- [ ] Carved and Painted Wood Figure, upraised wings, wood stand, 6½" H 210.00 260.00
- [ ] Carved Pine Figure, open beak, perched on an orb, 14" H x 22" L 450.00 650.00
- [ ] Carved Wood Figure, perched on an orb, 44½" H x 30" W 900.00 1200.00
- [ ] Carved Wood and Gesso Figure, perched on a rockwood, 29" H x 39" L 2000.00 2600.00
- [ ] Cast Iron, perched, grasping flowers, 30" H x 64" L ... 1600.00 2000.00
- [ ] Cast Iron snow eagle 12.00 20.00
- [ ] Cast Iron, spread-winged, perched on an orb, 47" L ... 600.00 700.00
- [ ] Head, carved and painted, yellow and red, 24" L 900.00 1200.00
- [ ] Painted and Molded Papier-Mache, spread-winged, black, 19½" H x 44" L 75.00 125.00
- [ ] Painted Sign, 19th century, oil on metal, spread-winged, perched on U.S. shield 650.00 850.00
- [ ] Tie Pin, eagle on globe, advertising J.I. Case 15.00 20.00

ANIMATION FILM ART

Cels is the name given to the animated drawings rendered on clear "celluloid". They are used in the production of all animated cartoons. Even though thousands of these cels are necessary in the production of cartoons, relatively few of them reach the market place.

ORIGINAL CELS FROM DISNEY FILMS

	UNFRAMED	
	Portfolio	Cels
[ ] "Cinderella"	1200.00	360.00
[ ] "Lady And The Tramp"	1200.00	360.00
[ ] "Mickey Mouse"	1350.00	400.00
[ ] "Pinocchio"	1380.00	420.00
[ ] "Snow White"	1380.00	420.00

	FRAMED	
[ ] "Robin Hood" (except below)	130.00	140.00
Robin Hood character only	140.00	155.00
Little John character only	140.00	155.00
[ ] "Winnie The Pooh" (except below)	140.00	155.00
Winnie The Pooh Character only	155.00	175.00
[ ] "Rescuers"	130.00	140.00
Evinrude character only	140.00	150.00
Orville character only	140.00	150.00
[ ] "Jungle Book"	130.00	145.00
Sherkon character only	135.00	155.00
Baloo character only	140.00	155.00
Baloo and any character	140.00	155.00
[ ] "Pete's Dragon"	130.00	140.00

ORIGINAL COMIC STRIPS   Price Range

☐ Dailys	170.00	185.00
☐ Sundays	220.00	240.00

POSTERS

☐ "Fantasia"	18.00	22.00
☐ "Snow White"	10.00	14.00

ARROWHEADS

Arrowheads very often have obtained their names from geographical locations. Projectile points that are of fine workmanship, substantial size or scarce substances command higher prices.

☐ Agate Basin, 7000 BC, 2-6"	20.00	25.00
☐ Aqua Plano, 7000 BC, 3-6"	25.00	30.00
☐ Avonlea, 8000 BC, 1-2"	1.00	1.50
☐ Brewerton Eared, 4000 BC, 1-2"	1.00	1.50
☐ Calf Creek, 4000 BC, 1½-3"	10.00	14.00
☐ Candy Creek, 1000 BC, 2-2½"	5.00	8.00
☐ Coosa, 500 BC, 1-2"	1.00	1.50
☐ Dalton, 8000 BC, 1¼-3"	10.00	14.00
☐ Delhi, 1200 BC, 1½-3½"	2.00	4.00
☐ Eden Valley, 7000 BC, 3-6"	20.00	25.00
☐ Etley, 2000 BC, 5-9"	20.00	25.00
☐ Grand, 500 BC, 1-2"	2.00	4.00
☐ Hamilton, 500 AD, 1-2"	3.00	4.00
☐ Hardin, 2000 BC, 2½-7"	5.00	7.00
☐ Hell Gap, 7000 BC, 2-5"	8.00	12.00
☐ Kent, 1000 BC, 1½-3"	1.00	2.00
☐ Keota, 1200 AD, ½-1½"	1.00	2.00
☐ Lost Lake, 6000 BC, 2-3½"	6.00	8.00
☐ Matamoros, 500 AD, ¾-1½"	1.00	2.00
☐ Milanville, 5000 BC, 1-2½"	10.00	14.00
☐ Mountain Fork, 3500 BC, 1-2"	.75	1.25
☐ Palmer, 6000 BC, 1-2½"	2.00	4.00
☐ Quad, 8000 BC, 1½-4"	10.00	12.00
☐ Ross, 500 AD, 5-15"	30.00	40.00
☐ Searcy, 5000 BC, 2¼-4"	10.00	12.00
☐ Starr, 1600 AD, 1¼-2¼"	1.00	2.00
☐ Suwanee, 7000 BC, 2-3"	6.00	8.00
☐ Swan Lake, 3000 BC, 1-1½"	.50	1.00
☐ Thebes, 5000 BC, 3-7"	15.00	18.00
☐ Trinity, 2000 BC, 1-2¼"	1.00	2.00
☐ White Springs, 5000 BC, 1½-2½"	1.00	2.00

ART DECO

Art Deco is essentially a design movement, named for an important exhibition in Paris in 1925, called l'Exposition Internationale des Arts Decoratifs. However, the show came at least five years after the movement was underway, and today we call the 20's and 30's the period of Art Deco. Influenced by the same cultures as Cubism and artifacts from ancient Egypt and North and Central America—all characterized by abstract and zigzag designs. There is some time overlap with the Art Nouveau period, but the major differences are characterized by the "modernist" look of Art Deco; The range of Art Deco collectibles is great — from plastic bracelets to custom-designed glass vases.

LAMP, *Chrome/Glass, 4 Legged Tiered Octagonal base, Signed, 22"H, c.1930* ...... 1400.00 - 2000.00

FIGURE, WOMAN IN COSTUME *Ivory/Bronze, 12"H, c.1925* .. 900.00 - 1000.00

Price Range

☐ Ashtray, Bronze and onyx figural, onyx bowl with flower head supporting a ballerina, inscribed Lorezl, c1925, 12¾" H	800.00	1000.00
☐ Bar Pin, Platinum, diamond, jade and onyx with white gold clasp, c1925	800.00	1000.00
☐ Bowl, Frosted birds and bowl, inscribed Lalique	120.00	160.00
☐ Bronze, Ivory figure of a young woman, onyx base, Bessie Callender, c1930, 17" H	900.00	1200.00
☐ Bronze, Pierette and a Pierrot, green, marble base, inscribed, Lorenzl, c1925, 16¾" H	1200.00	1600.00
☐ Brooch, Black onyx with 32 small diamonds and 1 large weighing 1.50	4200.00	4600.00
☐ Cabinet, Harewood, Nickel plated chrome, curved door with five shaped drawers, c1930, 3'11" H x 13½" W	800.00	1000.00
☐ Candlesticks by Jensen, c1925, pair	700.00	800.00
☐ Centerpiece, Bronze and marble, dish and base made of marble with two bronze giraffes, 19"	325.00	425.00

ART DECO

☐ Cigarette Case, Gold and enamel, black enamel on
the front, back and sides, green on top, 3" L 2600.00   3000.00

☐ Cigarette Case, Silver and blue enamel 170.00   190.00

☐ Clock, Desk, jade and enamel, square form, blue
enamelled hands and black Roman numerals,
Cartier, 1¼" H 2200.00   3000.00

☐ Clock, Glass and chrome-plated bronze, chrome face,
black glass and chrome base, c1930, 8¾" H 275.00   425.00

☐ Compact, Black with diamond corners, black enamel
link chain attached to finger ring 950.00   1150.00

☐ Dancer, Exotic silvered figure, marble base, inscribed
Fayral, c1925................................. 550.00   750.00

☐ Dancer, Gilt-Bronze nude figure with outstretched
arms supporting a drapery, inscribed A. Kelety,
c1930, 14½" H 700.00   1000.00

☐ Dancer, Swaying, inscribed CJR Colinet,
c1925, 18½" H 600.00   700.00

☐ Footstool, Upholstered and aluminum, designed by
Deskey, c1931................................. 400.00   600.00

☐ Lapel Watch, Black onyx panel, pin has rose-cut
diamonds, platinum and gold watch, Dreicer & Co. ... 1300.00   1600.00

☐ Lights, Wall, Brass and glass, half cylindrical form
with upper and lower brass band enamelled in black,
c1925, 13" H 225.00   325.00

☐ Plant Stand, Wrought-iron and marble, French c1925,
39" H x 14¾" D................................ 550.00   850.00

☐ Rack, Hall, Lacquer and brass, mirror plate, brass
holders, black support, French, c1930, 5'1" H 375.00   475.00

☐ Ring, Platinum, Cabochon sapphire and 6 baguette
diamonds 1600.00   2000.00

☐ Ring, Platinum, Diamond and ruby, wide band 450.00   650.00

☐ Ring, Ruby center panel, Diamond sides, Van Cleef
and Arpets, c1935............................. 2600.00   3200.00

☐ Table, Glass top, three lucite legs, c1940,
26" H x 36" D................................. 450.00   650.00

☐ Vanity with large mirror 1000.00   1200.00

☐ Vase, Cameo glass, frosted body, bulbous neck,
straight rim overlaid in blue, 9" H 160.00   220.00

☐ Vase, Cameo glass, Le Verre Francais, trumpet form,
yellow and orange overlaid in orange to deep
purple with flowers and leafage, France,
c1925, 18-1/8" H 225.00   325.00

☐ Vase, Pottery, Band of flowers, Longwy, c1925 ...... 175.00   225.00

☐ Woman, Silvered and gilt-bronze figure riding on
elephant, onyx and marble base, French, c1925, 24" .. 1400.00   1800.00

☐ Young Sailor, Bronze and ivory, inscribed BRONZE,
plinth inscribed A. Jorel, Early 20th Century, 9" H 350.00   450.00

ART NOUVEAU

The period of Art Nouveau decorative arts and fine arts ranges from the last fifteen years or so of the 19th century, to the second decade of the 20th. The name derives from an 1895 opening of a design shop in Paris, the name of which was L'Art Nouveau. Two of the most important aspects of Art Nouveau are asymmetry and femininity, and there is a wide use of maidens with flowing hair, flowers, scrolls, tendrils, snakes and anything else with sinuous curves. Art Nouveau objects, particularly fine jewelry, are in great demand today.

BELGIAN MAHOGANY DINING ROOM SUITE *(Entire 8 Pcs.)*
...... 2800.00 - 3400.00

	Price Range	
☐ Basket, Silver, four flower molded feet, calla lily handles, Austrian, Maker's Mark R. O., c1900, 14" L	500.00	600.00
☐ Bell, Bronze, Curtsying woman in gown, inscribed P. Tereszczuk, c1900 2½" H	225.00	300.00
☐ Bookends, Reclining nude female figure on rocky base, inscribed S. Morani, c1914, 7½" L............	100.00	150.00
☐ Bronze Busts, Brown and green patinas, inscribed Gruber, late 19th Century, 5" H, pair	500.00	600.00
☐ Brooch, Gold Egyptian goddess, outspread wings and serpent tail, Austrian, Maker's Mark M.L., c1920, 2-1/8"	375.00	450.00
☐ Brooch, Gold eagle with outstretched wings, open beak, and curled talons, French, c1910, 2¼"	400.00	475.00

ART NOUVEAU

	Price Range	
☐ Clock, Desk type, Nude nymph, metal case	60.00	90.00
☐ Dining Room Suite, Buffet, table sideboard and five chairs, Belgian, c1900	2800.00	3400.00
☐ Figure of Justitia, Bronze, Figure in robe on marble base, inscribed Mausch/Paris, 11¼" H	450.00	550.00
☐ Flask, Lovers on the Beach, Sterling Silver, c1900	110.00	160.00
☐ Girl, Gilt-Bronze and Ivory Figure, playing musical instrument, black marble base, French, c1910, 9½" ..	775.00	875.00
☐ Knife, Paper, Bronze, Peacock with tail trailing into the body, bust portrait of a young woman and lily blossoms, inscribed HWH and 10CB, c1900, 12" L	200.00	275.00
☐ Knives and Forks, Fruit, Silver, Whiplash motif, 19 of each, German, c1900	175.00	250.00
☐ Lamps, Cameo Glass, Forest lake scene, Shade signed Daum Nancy, c1900, 17" H	3200.00	3600.00
☐ Lamp, Glass and Wrought-Iron, Mustard, russet and deep blue, Muller Freres, c1900, 21¾" H	500.00	600.00
☐ Lamp, Bronze Oil, Maiden in robe on circular base, canaster on swivel mount, inscribed Renaa, c1910, 11¼" H	150.00	225.00
☐ Lamp, Three Light Lily, Glass and Bronze, circular base, shade inscribed L.C.T., c1899, 13" H	1400.00	1800.00
☐ Lamp, Woman's head, Bronze base, glass shade, amber on yellow ground, 16" H	300.00	375.00
☐ Mirror, Hand with woman's head and flowing hair, flowers and swans, sterling silver, Unger Bros., c1900	90.00	140.00
☐ Mirror, Vanity, Brass, c1900	50.00	75.00
☐ Pendant and Chain, Gold, Opal and diamond, dragonfly with two diamonds at base, Alion & Co., c1910, 1¾"	1400.00	1800.00
☐ Pitcher, Silver-mounted glass, Bulbous form, lip and handle decorated with flowers and tendrils, Gorham Co., c1900, 10-3/8" H	75.00	125.00
☐ Plant Stand, Hammered brass, Wrought-iron and glass bead, straight legs, lower shelf, Viennese, c1910, 35½" H x 25¾" W	175.00	275.00
☐ Table, Writing, Carved Oak, inlaid leather top, inscribed L. Majorelle, c1900, 5'10-3/8" x 2'5"	1100.00	1600.00
☐ Tray, Bread, Pewter with daisies and dragonfly, base inscribed Kayserzinn, 10-3/8" L	110.00	160.00
☐ Tray, Girl watching sunrise, Bronze, inscribed Maxim, 5"L...	140.00	200.00
☐ Tray, Pin, Female head, Hair flowing into lily pads, inscribed J. Angles, c1900, 9¼" D	775.00	900.00
☐ Urn, Bust of Woman on gold, Vienna, 8" H	80.00	120.00
☐ Vase, Bronze with four beetles, Brown patina, inscribed Ch. Thienot, c1900, 5¼" H	150.00	200.00
☐ Vase, Bronze, Tapered cylindrical with four dragonflies forming handles, inscribed H.E. T., c1900, 10" H .	175.00	275.00

ART NOUVEAU

	Price Range	
☐ Vase, Cameo Glass, Cranberry and mauve, inscribed Galle c1900, 5¼" H	375.00	475.00
☐ Vase, Enamel Cameo Glass, Russet, mustard, and dark green on brown and mustard ground, Daum Nancy, c1900, 5" H	275.00	375.00
☐ Vase, Girl with Doves, German, c1900, 12" H	210.00	260.00
☐ Vase, Pottery, Cherry blossoms in shades of white, iron red, tan, and brown, sea blue at base, Rookwood, c1883, 9" H	600.00	1000.00
☐ Vase, Pottery, Forest scene, Dolphin handles enameled in gilt, Amphora, c1920, 7¼" H	375.00	575.00
☐ Vase, Pottery, Iridescent with tendrils and leafage, amber green and red glaze, French, c1900, 6½" H ...	150.00	200.00
☐ Woman, Bronze and Ivory Bust of Young Egyptian, dark brown patina, inscribed P. Tereszczuk, 19th Century, 5-1/8" H..............................	300.00	400.00
☐ Woman, Bronze, Dancing in Classical Costume, brown patina, German, c1900, 12" H	275.00	375.00

AUTOGRAPHS

Autographs are signatures, and are usually collected by people for their historic interest. The best kind of autographs are actually those found on documents, letters, music scores and other items of interest, rather than those which are collected on a piece of paper by the so-called "autogaph hounds" who dash about from stage door to stage door, especially in New York, gathering signatures. Some people specialize in musicians, aviators, literary figures, U.S. Presidents, and some seek elusive signatures for all the original signers of the Declaration of Independence, or of the Constitution. Many of the prices given here are for signed documents of considerable importance. The signatures alone would bring much less.

HOMER WINSLOW *(1856-1910)*

ERNEST HEMINGWAY
(1899-1961)

BERNARD SHAW *(1856-1950)*

ARTIST	Price Range	
☐ Corot, Camille (1796-1875)	60.00	80.00
☐ Degas, Edgar (1834-1917)	250.00	350.00
☐ Gainsborough, Thomas (1727-88)	300.00	450.00
☐ Homer, Winslow (1836-1910)	75.00	125.00
☐ Picasso, Pablo (1881-1973)	200.00	300.00
☐ Remington, Frederick (1861-1909)	275.00	375.00
☐ Reynolds, Sir Joshua (1723-92)	350.00	600.00
☐ Van Gohh, Vincent (1853-90)	2500.00	3500.00

CIVIL WAR

☐ Burnside, Ambrose (1860's)	75.00	100.00
☐ Davis, Jefferson (1880's)	500.00	800.00
☐ Jackson, Stonewall (1860's)	1000.00	2000.00
☐ Miles, Nelson A. (1860's)	50.00	75.00
☐ Stanton, Edwin M. (1860's)	50.00	100.00

COMPOSERS

☐ Beethoven, Ludwig Van (1770-1827)	3500.00	5500.00
☐ Bizet, George (1838-75)	150.00	250.00
☐ Chopin, Frederic (1810-49)	1000.00	1500.00
☐ Donizetti, Gaetano (1797-1848)	250.00	350.00
☐ Mendelssohn, Felix (1809-47)	175.00	275.00
☐ Schubert, Franz (1797-1828)	5000.00	6000.00
☐ Wagner, Richard (1813-83)	1000.00	1500.00

LITERARY

☐ Austin, Jane (1775-1805)	1000.00	1500.00
☐ Byron, Lord (1788-1824)	1500.00	2500.00
☐ Cooper, James Fenimore (1789-1851)	300.00	600.00
☐ Dickens, Charles (1812-70)	200.00	500.00
☐ Frost, Robert (1874-1963)	350.00	UP
☐ Hemingway, Ernest (1899-1961)	750.00	1250.00
☐ Scott, Sir Walter (1771-1832)	125.00	225.00
☐ Shaw, G. B. (1856-1950)	150.00	200.00
☐ Stevenson, Robert Louis (1850-94)	225.00	350.00
☐ Thomas, Dylan (1914-53)	400.00	800.00
☐ Twain, Mark (1835-1910)	800.00	1200.00
☐ Whittier, John Greenleaf (1807-92)	75.00	175.00
☐ Wilde, Oscar (1856-1900)	300.00	400.00
☐ Wolfe, Thomas (1900-38)	300.00	600.00
☐ Wordsworth, William (1770-1850)	150.00	200.00

U.S. PRESIDENTS

☐ Adams, John (1735-1826)	2000.00	3000.00
☐ Buchanan, James (1791-1868)	150.00	250.00
☐ Eisenhower, Dwight D. (1890-1969)	200.00	300.00
☐ Jackson, Andrew (1767-1845)	1000.00	2000.00
☐ Kennedy, John F. (1917-1963)	750.00	1500.00
☐ Polk, James K. (1795-1849)	1000.00	1500.00
☐ Roosevelt, Theodore (1858-1919)	200.00	300.00
☐ Taylor, Zachary (1784-1850)	1000.00	1500.00
☐ Wilson, Woodrow (1856-1924)	300.00	400.00

AUTO AND AUTOMOBILIA

The first automobile came into being during the turn of the century. Since over 3,500 different models have been built all over the world collectors accumulate not only whole cars but all the various parts of the cars (wheels, horns, engine parts, etc.) In this section we have given you just a representative listing on automobile collectibles. For further information on collector cars, please refer to our book THE OFFICIAL PRICE GUIDE TO COLLECTOR CARS by the Kruse Auction Company.

All prices are for automobiles in excellent condition.

CHEVROLET DELUXE ROADSTER, 1931 . . . . 7500.00

	Price Range	
☐ Abbot. Detroit Automobile, 1918, 8 cyl., 5-passenger . .	8000.00	9000.00
☐ American Underslung. 1909, excellent	9000.00	9500.00
☐ Auburn. 1903, excellent	11000.00	12000.00
☐ Audi. 1928, 8 cyl., excellent	15000.00	16000.00
☐ Buick. 1942, Limited, Fireball 8 cyl., Limousine	7000.00	7800.00
☐ Buick. 1947, Roadmaster, 8 cyl., Sedan	4000.00	4500.00
☐ Buick. 1949, Roadmaster, 8 cyl., Convertible Coupe . .	8000.00	8800.00
☐ Buick. 1950, Estate Wagon, 8 cyl.	4700.00	5000.00
☐ Buick. 1957, Roadmaster, V-8, Convertible	2100.00	2800.00
☐ Buick. 1959, Electra, V-8, Convertible	3000.00	3500.00
☐ Buick. 1959, La Sabre, V-8, Station Wagon	2250.00	2850.00
☐ Buick. 1964, Riviera, V-8, 2-door Hardtop	2900.00	3400.00

AUTOS
Price Range

- ☐ Buick. 1966, Riviera GS, V-8, 2-door Hardtop 2000.00   2400.00
- ☐ Buick. 1969, Wildcat, V-8, Convertible 2500.00   3100.00
- ☐ Cadillac. 1950, V-8, 2-door Hardtop 3000.00   3500.00
- ☐ Cadillac. 1951, Fleetwood 60 Special, V-8, Sedan 3250.00   3800.00
- ☐ Cadillac. 1952, Coupe de Ville, V-8, 2-door Hardtop ... 3650.00   4200.00
- ☐ Cadillac. 1954, Eldorado, V-8, Convertible 5000.00   5600.00
- ☐ Cadillac. 1957, Eldorado, V-8, Brougham 6500.00   7200.00
- ☐ Cadillac. 1959, Eldorado, V-8, Brougham 5500.00   6100.00
- ☐ Cadillac. 1960, Fleetwood Special 60, V-8, 4-door
  Hardtop 3000.00   3500.00
- ☐ Cadillac. 1964, Coupe de Ville, V-8, 2-door Hardtop ... 1750.00   1950.00
- ☐ Cadillac. 1966, El Dorado, V-8, Convertible 2500.00   2900.00
- ☐ Cadillac. 1976, El Dorado, V-8, Convertible 16000.00   22000.00
- ☐ Carbide Brass Running Board and Tank 150.00   175.00
- ☐ Chevrolet. 1950, Belair, 6 cyl., Hardtop 2000.00   2400.00
- ☐ Chevrolet. 1951, Styleline Dix., 6 cyl., Convertible 3200.00   3800.00
- ☐ Chevrolet. 1952, Deluxe, 6 cyl., Convertible 3200.00   3800.00
- ☐ Chevrolet. 1953, Corvette, 6 cyl., Convertible 12500.00   13000.00
- ☐ Chevrolet. 1953, Belair, 6 cyl., Sports Coupe 2000.00   2600.00
- ☐ Chevrolet. 1954, Corvette, 6 cyl., Convertible 10000.00   11000.00
- ☐ Chevrolet. 1954, Belair, 6 cyl., Sport Coupe 2500.00   2850.00
- ☐ Chevrolet. 1955, Corvette, 265 V-8, Convertible 12000.00   18000.00
- ☐ Chevrolet. 1955 Belair, 265 V-8, Convertible 3900.00   4400.00
- ☐ Chevrolet. 1956, Nomad, 265 V-8, Station Wagon 4200.00   4800.00
- ☐ Chevrolet. 1956, Belair, 265 V-8, 4-door Sedan 1500.00   1750.00
- ☐ Chevrolet. 1956, Belair, 265 V-8, Convertible Coupe ... 3600.00   4200.00
- ☐ Chevrolet. 1956, Corvette, 265 V-8, Convertible 6500.00   7100.00
- ☐ Chevrolet. 1956, Belair, 265 V-8, 2-door Sport Hardtop . 2650.00   2900.00
- ☐ Chevrolet. 1958, Belair, 283 V-8, 4-door Hardtop 1500.00   1800.00
- ☐ Chevrolet. 1959, Belair, 230 6 cyl., 4-door Sedan 1000.00   1350.00
- ☐ Chevrolet. 1961, Corvair, 6 cyl., Coupe 1800.00   2000.00
- ☐ Chrysler. 1949, Town & Country, V-8, Convertible 5950.00   6450.00
- ☐ Chrysler. 1951, NY Highlander, V-8, Club Coupe 2500.00   2850.00
- ☐ Chrysler. 1953, Imperial, V-8, 2-door Hardtop 4500.00   5050.00
- ☐ Chrysler. 1954, New Yorker, V-8, 2-door Hardtop 2700.00   3300.00
- ☐ Chrysler. 1956, Windsor, V-8, Sedan 1500.00   1800.00
- ☐ Chrysler. 1957, New Yorker, V-8, 4-door Sedan 2000.00   1350.00
- ☐ Chrysler. 1958, Imperial, V-8, 2-door Hardtop 2750.00   2900.00
- ☐ Chrysler. 1959, New Yorker, V-8, 2-door Hardtop 2000.00   2300.00
- ☐ Chrysler. 1962, Imperial Crown, V-8, 2-door Hardtop .. 3000.00   3500.00
- ☐ Chrysler. 1970, 300-Hurst, 440 V-8, 2-door Hardtop ... 3500.00   4000.00
- ☐ De Soto. 1951, Custom 4 Door, 6 cyl., Sedan 3300.00   3600.00
- ☐ De Soto. 1952, Model S-17, V-8, 4-door Sedan 1950.00   2450.00
- ☐ De Soto. 1955, Fireflite, V-8, 4-door Sedan 1750.00   1950.00
- ☐ De Soto. 1957, Adventurer, V-8, Hardtop 3500.00   3900.00
- ☐ De Soto. 1958, Fireflite, V-8, 4.8 Litre, Convertible 3200.00   3700.00
- ☐ De Soto. 1958, V-8, 2-door Hardtop 2200.00   2450.00
- ☐ De Soto. 1959, Fireflite, V-8, Convertible 3000.00   3500.00
- ☐ De Soto. 1960, Fireflite, V-8, Convertible 2800.00   3300.00

AUTOS

	Price Range	
☐ De Soto. 1961, Adventurer, V-8, 2-door Hardtop	2000.00	2400.00
☐ De Soto. 1962, Adventurer, V-8, 2-door Hardtop	2250.00	2600.00
☐ De Soto. 1942, 4-door, excellent	2600.00	2850.00
☐ Dodge. 1957, Royal Lancer, V-8, 2-door Hardtop	2250.00	2600.00
☐ Dodge. 1958, Royal Lancer, V-8, 4-door Sedan	1800.00	2200.00
☐ Dodge. 1959, Royal Lancer, V-8, 4-door Sedan	1500.00	1900.00
☐ Dodge. 1963, Polara, 361 V-8, 2-door Hardtop	1750.00	1950.00
☐ Dodge. 1966, Charger, V-8 Hemi, Coupe	3500.00	4100.00
☐ Dodge. 1970, Charger, V-8 Hemi, 2-door Hardtop	4500.00	5200.00
☐ Dodge. 1975, Challenger, 440 V-8, Convertible	3200.00	4000.00
☐ Ford. 1925, Model T, 4 cyl., 2.9 Litre, Roadster	4250.00	4600.00
☐ Ford. 1926, Model T, 4 cyl., Touring Car	4800.00	5300.00
☐ Ford. 1927, Model T, 4 cyl., Roadster	4800.00	5300.00
☐ Ford. 1928, Model A, 4 cyl., 2-door Sedan	4500.00	5100.00
☐ Ford. 1929, Model A, 4 cyl., Phaeton	9700.00	11500.00
☐ Ford. 1930, Model A, 4 cyl., Roadster	6700.00	7400.00
☐ Ford. 1931, Model A, 4 cyl., Roadster Deluxe	13500.00	16500.00
☐ Ford. 1932, Model B, 4 cyl., Pick-up Truck	4800.00	5400.00
☐ Ford. 1940, Standard, V-8, Station Wagon	10500.00	18500.00
☐ Ford. 1940, Super, 8 cyl., 3.3 Litre, 4-door	6500.00	7200.00
☐ Ford. 1947, Sportsman, V-8, Convertible coupe (Woodie)	13000.00	20000.00
☐ Ford. 1949, Customline, V-8, Convertible	4500.00	4900.00
☐ Ford. 1952, Sunliner, V-8, Convertible Coupe	2750.00	3200.00
☐ Ford. 1943, Sunliner, V-8, Convertible Coupe	2900.00	3450.00
☐ Ford. 1956, Fairlane, 312 V-8, 2-door Station Wagon	2750.00	3400.00
☐ Ford. 1956, Fairlane, 312 V-8, Crown Victoria (roof)	6800.00	7400.00
☐ Ford. 1957, Country Squire, 312 V-8, Station Wagon ..	2500.00	2800.00
☐ Ford. 1958, Fairlane 500 Skyliner, 353 V-8, Retractable Hardtop	3500.00	4100.00
☐ Ford. 1959, Galaxie Skyliner, 352 V-8, Convertible	3600.00	3900.00
☐ Ford. 1959, Galaxie Skyliner, 352 V-8, Convertible	3500.00	3800.00
☐ Ford. 1961, Falcon Futura, 170 6 cyl., 2-door Sedan ...	1500.00	1900.00
☐ Ford. 1962, Galaxie 500 XL, 390 V-8, Convertible	2500.00	2850.00
☐ Ford. 1964, Galaxie 500 XL, 427 V-8, 2-door Hardtop ..	3500.00	4000.00
☐ Ford. 1965, Fairlane Sport, 289 V-8, 2-door Hardtop ...	2500.00	2900.00
☐ Ford. 1965, Falcon Ranchero, 289 V-8, Pick-up Truck ..	2250.00	2650.00
☐ Ford. 1965, Mustang GT, 289 V-8, Convertible	3500.00	4100.00
☐ Ford. 1965, Mustang GT-2 + 2, 289 V-8, Coupe	2950.00	3400.00
☐ Ford. 1967, Shelby GT-350, 289 V-8, Coupe	3750.00	4300.00
☐ Ford. 1968, Shelby GT-500, 428 V-8, Convertible	4500.00	5200.00
☐ Ford. 1973, Mustang, 351 V-8, Convertible	3500.00	4100.00
☐ Franklin. 1910, Touring Car, 4 cyl., Model G	3750.00	7500.00
☐ Franklin. 1919, Sport Touring Car, 6 cyl.	3400.00	6800.00
☐ Franklin. 1923, Sedan, 2.5 hp.	2000.00	4000.00
☐ Franklin. 1925, Coupe, 2-door	2100.00	4200.00
☐ Franklin. 1930, Rumble Seat Coupe, 6 cyl.	5000.00	10000.00

AUTOS

	Price	Range
☐ Franklin. 1931, Sedan, V-12, Model 17, 4-door	4500.00	9000.00
☐ Franklin. 1932, Sedan, V-12, 5 Ps	4500.00	9000.00
☐ Franklin. 1933, Sedan, 6 cyl., Olympic	4500.00	7000.00
☐ Lincoln. 1950, Cosmopolitan, V-8, Convertible	6500.00	7200.00
☐ Lincoln. 1951, Lido, V-8, 2-door Coupe	3900.00	4300.00
☐ Lincoln. 1952, Cosmopolitan, V-8, 4-door Sedan	2900.00	3400.00
☐ Lincoln. 1954, Capri, V-8, 2-door Hardtop	3650.00	4400.00
☐ Lincoln. 1955, Capri, V-8, Coupe Hardtop	2300.00	2900.00
☐ Lincoln. 1956, Premier, V-8, 6 Litre, 4-door Sedan	3000.00	3500.00
☐ Lincoln. 1956, Continental Mark II, V-8, 2-door Hardtop	10000.00	11000.00
☐ Lincoln. 1957, Continental Mark II, 8 cyl., Convertible .	13500.00	14000.00
☐ Lincoln. 1958, Mark III, V-8, Convertible	4500.00	5800.00
☐ Lincoln. 1959, Mark IV, V-8, 4-door Sedan	2500.00	3300.00

AUTOMOBILIA

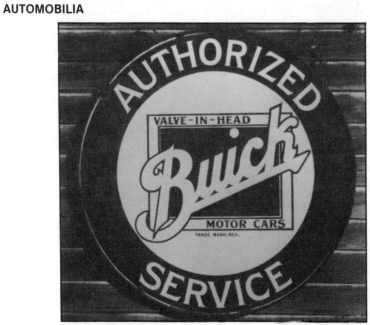

BUICK DEALER SIGN . . . . 150.00 - 200.00

☐ Audel's "Guide to Automobiles". 1915	40.00	50.00
☐ Auto Accessories Book. 1912, Willis Inc., N.Y., N.Y. . .	15.00	20.00
☐ Book on "How to Build Automobiles" by Bubler. 1914	50.00	60.00
☐ Brass Headlamps for 1915 Cadillac	175.00	200.00
☐ Button from Ford Motors. Pin back, 1930's	10.00	12.00
☐ Clear Glass Packard Vase. Grapes and birds	30.00	35.00
☐ Clock. Key wind type, 8-day movement working condition	45.00	50.00
☐ Coil from Model "T" Ford	6.00	8.00
☐ Duster for Man. Silk, excellent condition	45.00	55.00

AUTOMOBILIA

	Price	Range
☐ Duster for Woman. Silk, excellent condition	60.00	65.00
☐ Fan. Used for defrosting (Dodge Bros.), 1936	10.00	12.00
☐ Ford Tire Pump. Working condition	25.00	30.00
☐ Gear Shift. Amber glass in color	9.00	11.00
☐ Green Book of Automobiles (1922). 1st Volume	15.00	20.00
☐ Grill from 1934 Ford	120.00	130.00
☐ Headlamps from Model "T" Ford. Black enamel, pair .	100.00	125.00
☐ Hood Ornament from Dodge (chrome Ram)	16.00	20.00
☐ Hood Ornament from Lasalle (enameled)	6.00	8.00
☐ Hood Ornament. Head with long hair, molded white glass	180.00	200.00
☐ Horn. Brass, from 1909 Klaxon	60.00	65.00
☐ Horn. Bulb type, brass, single twist (1916)	115.00	125.00
☐ Horn. Hand model, "Klaxon" imprinted	25.00	30.00
☐ Hub Cap from Buick. Brass, 3½"	15.00	20.00
☐ Lamp for Driving. Made of brass	100.00	115.00
☐ Lamp from Ford. 10" x 15", made from brass and tin, electric	175.00	200.00
☐ License Plate. Kansas, 1933	10.00	12.00
☐ License Plate. Michigan, 1916, good condition	35.00	45.00
☐ License Plate. Ohio, 1922, good condition	45.00	55.00
☐ License Plate. Pennsylvania, 1908	40.00	50.00
☐ Mercury Brass Hood Ornament (1927)	35.00	45.00
☐ Motor Meter from 1915 Dodge	50.00	60.00
☐ Motor Meter from 1916 Boyce	45.00	55.00
☐ Oil Can. "Ford" written in script	8.00	10.00
☐ "Ooaga" Horn. Electric auto lite, 12"	30.00	35.00
☐ Packard Handbook for Super Eight Sedan (1948)	30.00	35.00
☐ Putman Automobile Handbook (1918)	15.00	20.00
☐ Radiator Cap. Chevrolet, brass	6.00	8.00
☐ Radiator Cap. Dodge, 1930-35	18.00	20.00
☐ Radiator Cap. Ford, brass	6.00	8.00
☐ Radiator Cap from Ford Model "T",brass	10.00	12.00
☐ Radiator Cap. Maxwell, brass	8.00	10.00
☐ Radiator Cap from Pontiac. Indian Head nickel plated over brass (1930)	40.00	50.00
☐ Radiator Emblem Plate. Willy's-Overland, enameled ..	15.00	20.00
☐ Radiator Ornament for Buick. Made of blue glass	35.00	40.00
☐ Showroom Banner. Reads: "Oakland Six—$875.00". Wool, blue with yellow lettering, 48" x 8"	60.00	70.00
☐ Spark Plug. Ford, 1911	20.00	25.00
☐ Steering Wheel from Durant. Wood and brass, made in 1920's	50.00	60.00
☐ Stock Certificates from Hudson and Nash	7.00	8.00
☐ Willy's Allstate. 4 or 6 cyl., excellent	3200.00	3400.00
☐ Wrench. Imprinted with "Ford, U.S.A.," adjustable ...	8.00	10.00

BANKS

MECHANICAL BANKS

These banks were first produced by hardware and tool plants as new products after the Civil War. They remain as one of the most popular and sought after memorabilia and collector items. They have been used for advertising promotion pieces by banks, insurance companies, investment firms, etc.

The best known manufacturers are Stevens of Cromwell, Connecticut; Ives Blaklee Co. of Bridgeport, Connecticut; and Hubley of Lancaster, Pennsylvania. They are generally made of iron, painted bright and attractive colors, and perform a mechanical movement on deposit of a coin.

A dealer offer of approximately 40% of the stated retail value would be very fair for banks in good condition.

EAGLES AND EAGLETS 300.00

LIBERTY BELL, *Iron* 70.00

MECHANICAL
* (reproduced item)

		Price
☐	Afghanistan	700.00
☐	"Always did 'spise a mule". Darky on bench	300.00
☐	"Always did 'spise a mule". Darky Riding Mule *	320.00
☐	Artillery, Block House *	300.00
☐	Artillery, 8-sided Block House	1050.00
☐	Atlas	700.00
☐	Bamboula Bank	310.00
☐	Bank Teller	1800.00
☐	Bad Accident	400.00
☐	Bear, Standing on Hind Legs	285.00
☐	Bird on Church Roof	530.00
☐	Bonzo	820.00
☐	Bowery Bank	2500.00
☐	Bowling Alley	2500.00
☐	Boy Scout	925.00
☐	Boy on Trapeze *	400.00
☐	Boys Stealing Watermelons	625.00
☐	Breadwinner	2500.00
☐	Buffalo *	300.00

MECHANICAL

	Price
☐ Bull and Bear	1250.00
☐ Cabin *	175.00
☐ Called Out	1750.00
☐ Calumet Bank, Tin	140.00
☐ Camel	130.00
☐ Camera, Kodak	2250.00
☐ Cannon, U.S. and Spain	1200.00
☐ Cat Jumping for Mouse	2500.00
☐ Cat and Mouse *	360.00
☐ Chandlers	340.00
☐ Chief Big Moon	550.00
☐ Child's Bank	280.00
☐ Chimpanzee	1700.00
☐ Chinaman with Cue, Tin	810.00
☐ Chinaman Reclining	610.00
☐ Chocolat Menier, Tin	120.00
☐ Circus	2550.00
☐ Circus Ticket Taker *	550.00
☐ Clown Bank, Tin	240.00
☐ Clown Bust	1600.00
☐ Clown and Dog, Tin	1250.00
☐ Clown n Globe	250.00
☐ Cow, Kicking *	1000.00
☐ Columbia Magic	130.00
☐ Confectionary Store	1600.00
☐ Creedmore *	275.00
☐ Crescent Cash Register	310.00
☐ Cupola Bank	825.00
☐ Dapper Dan	375.00
☐ Darktown Battery *	400.00
☐ Dentist *	1000.00
☐ Dime Saving	260.00
☐ Dinah and the Fairy	1500.00
☐ Dog, Speaking	275.00
☐ Trick Dog on 6-piece Base	300.00
☐ Trick Dog, Modern	200.00
☐ Dog on Base * (lost)	325.00
☐ Dog on Turntable	185.00
☐ Dinah *	275.00
☐ Eagle and Eaglets *	300.00
☐ Electric Safe	325.00
☐ Elephant and Clowns	500.00
☐ Elephant, Modern *	100.00
☐ Elephant Howdah with Man	300.00
☐ Elephant, Jumbo, on Wheels	500.00
☐ Elephant, 3 Stars *	250.00
☐ Feed the Kitty	820.00
☐ Football—Calamity	800.00

MECHANICAL

		Price
☐	Fortune Teller, Safe	625.00
☐	Fowler, Hunter and Bird	1850.00
☐	Freedman's Bureau, Chest	675.00
☐	Frog on Lattice Base	140.00
☐	Frog and Serpent, Tin	5100.00
☐	Frogs, 2 Bulls	380.00
☐	Frog on Rock	170.00
☐	Frog on Stump	180.00
☐	Gem *	170.00
☐	Giant	1750.00
☐	Giant in Tower	3100.00
☐	Girl in Chair with Dog	1375.00
☐	Girl Skipping Rope	3150.00
☐	Globe on Arc	125.00
☐	Goat, Little Billy	1025.00
☐	Goat, Butting (Miniature)	400.00
☐	Guessing Bank	860.00
☐	Gem Small Dog-House	175.00
☐	Girl Skipping Rope	2300.00
☐	Goat, Frog and Old Man *	900.00
☐	Halls, Excelsior	100.00
☐	Hillman Coin Target	1475.00
☐	Hindu with Turban *	600.00
☐	Hold the Fort *	920.00
☐	Home	275.00
☐	Home, Tin-Printed	185.00
☐	Hoop-La	320.00
☐	Humpty Dumpty *	195.00
☐	Independence Hall Tower	95.00
☐	Indian Shooting Bear *	410.00
☐	Japanese Ball Tosser, Tin	3750.00
☐	Joe Socko Novelty	310.00
☐	John Bull's Money Box	2750.00
☐	Jonah and the Whale in Boat *	500.00
☐	Kick Inn	425.00
☐	Kiltie	575.00
☐	Leap Frog *	700.00
☐	Liberty Bell	310.00
☐	Lighthouse	450.00
☐	Lion Hunter	860.00
☐	Lilliput, Halls	200.00
☐	Lion and Monkeys *	230.00
☐	Little Hi Hat	625.00
☐	Little Joe *	175.00
☐	Locomotive Bank	85.00
☐	Magician *	560.00
☐	Mammy and Child	650.00
☐	Mason and Hod Carrier	600.00
☐	Mickey Mouse, Tin	1300.00

MECHANICAL

		Price
☐	Mikado	4200.00
☐	Minstrel, Tin	170.00
☐	Minstrel, Cross Legged	475.00
☐	Monkey & Organ Grinder, Modern	115.00
☐	Monkey and Parrot	500.00
☐	Monkey and Cocoanut	600.00
☐	Monkey with Tray, Tin	340.00
☐	Mosque	375.00
☐	Motor Bank	3400.00
☐	Mule and Barn *	350.00
☐	Mule Bucking (Miniature) *	485.00
☐	Music Bank. Tin	465.00
☐	National Bank	450.00
☐	New Bank	260.00
☐	Novelty	200.00
☐	Organ Bank. Cat and Dog	350.00
☐	Organ Bank, and Monkey, Tiny	340.00
☐	Organ Grinder and Bear	1200.00
☐	Owl, Moves Head	110.00
☐	Owl, Slot in Book	140.00
☐	Owl, Slot in Head	250.00
☐	Panorama	1000.00
☐	Patronize the Blind	1300.00
☐	Pelican with Rabbit	520.00
☐	Piano *	1790.00
☐	Picture Gallery	1800.00
☐	Professor Pug Frog *	1800.00
☐	Paddy and Pig *	460.00
☐	Pegleg Beggar *	650.00
☐	Pelican	740.00
☐	Pig, Bismarck	625.00
☐	Pig in Highchair	300.00
☐	Pony — Trick Pony *	285.00
☐	Presto, Small Building	130.00
☐	Pump and Bucket	550.00
☐	Punch and Judy *	450.00
☐	Rabbit, Small	245.00
☐	Rabbit, Tall	300.00
☐	Rabbit and Cabbage	200.00
☐	Rival	5550.00
☐	Rooster	225.00
☐	Sailor Saluting. Tin	620.00
☐	Sambo	410.00
☐	Savo. Tin	130.00
☐	Seek Him Frisk	7600.00
☐	Sentry Bugler. Tin	510.00
☐	Shoot That Hat Bank	3100.00
☐	Signal Cabin. Tin	400.00
☐	Stollwerck, Small. Tin	175.00

MECHANICAL

		Price
☐	Sweet Thrift. Tin	175.00
☐	Santa Claus at Chimney *	310.00
☐	Scotchman. Tin	230.00
☐	Sewing Machine	1550.00
☐	Shoot and Chute	3750.00
☐	Squirrel and Tree Stump	510.00
☐	Stump Speaker	425.00
☐	Tabby Bank	250.00
☐	Tammany *	150.00
☐	Tank and Cannon	310.00
☐	Teddy and the Bear *	465.00
☐	Thrifty Animal Bank. Tin	190.00
☐	Tiger. Tin	810.00
☐	Time is Money	1850.00
☐	Tommy	1550.00
☐	Two Ducks in Pond	615.00
☐	Uncle Remus *	1000.00
☐	Uncle Sam *	360.00
☐	Uncle Tom *	300.00
☐	Viennese Soldier	2600.00
☐	Volunteer	215.00
☐	Watch	360.00
☐	William Tell *	450.00
☐	Wireless	225.00
☐	World's Fair Bank *	340.00
☐	Zoo	575.00

STILL

Still banks are made of iron, white metal, tin, glass, pottery or plastic. A slot was provided to insert the coin and most have a trip door for retrieving coins. These banks, while not scarce, are still difficult to locate in mint or fine condition. Good will mean no chips or breaks, paint bright, but not shiny.

* (reproduced item)

☐	Building Bank No. 370	68.00
☐	Building Bank, Large, No. 411	35.00
☐	Building Bank, Small, No. 305	30.00
☐	Baseball Player No. 10 *	95.00
☐	Bear, Sitting or Standing, No's. 330 & 329	50.00
☐	Beehive, Bear Robbing Hive, No. 169	100.00
☐	Billiken "Good Luck" No. 48	50.00
☐	Boy Scout, 6" High, No. 14	68.00
☐	Buffalo, Small, No. 208	50.00
☐	Buster Brown & Dog No.2	106.00
☐	Camel, Standing, Small, No. 202	100.00
☐	Cat, Sitting, Bow Tie, No. 244	60.00
☐	Clock, Grandfather, No. 222	65.00
☐	Clock, "Time is Money", No. 225	42.00
☐	Cow No. 200	50.00

STILL

		Price
☐	Cradle with Baby, No. 231	95.00
☐	Deer, Antlers, No. 195	45.00
☐	Deer, Large, No. 196	70.00
☐	Dog, Shepherd	55.00
☐	Dog & Tub No. 392	65.00
☐	Dog, St. Bernard, No. 104 *	65.00
☐	Dolphin No. 6	310.00
☐	Donkey & Saddle No. 197	62.00
☐	Donkey & Saddle No. 198	60.00
☐	Duck, Large No. 322	45.00
☐	Duck, Red & Blue, No. 325	55.00
☐	Columbia Dome Building	52.00
☐	Elephant with Howdah No. 68	70.00
☐	Elephant on Tub No.55 *	65.00
☐	Football Player No. 12	150.00
☐	Frog on Lattice No. 402	48.00
☐	Gas Stove, York, No. 139	60.00
☐	General Pershing No. 312	85.00
☐	Globe, Earth	42.00
☐	Gollywog No. 3	90.00
☐	Hansel & Gretel, Cigar Box	65.00
☐	"Home Savings Bank"	55.00
☐	Horse, Black Beauty, No. 82	52.00
☐	Horse, Prancing, Rearing, Standing, No's. 70 & 87	65.00
☐	Independence Hall	60.00
☐	Indian Head, 2 Sides, No. 291	62.00
☐	Indian, Standing, No. 39	85.00
☐	Junior Safe No. 350	46.00
☐	Kitten with Ribbon No. 335	40.00
☐	Lion, Spread Legged, No. 92	48.00
☐	Lion, Small, No. 94	55.00
☐	Lion, Standing, Large, No. 89 *	75.00
☐	Lunch Pail	50.00
☐	Mail Box No. 116, No. 128 *	42.00
☐	Money Bag No. 295	310.00
☐	Mutt & Jeff, Gilt, No. 13	100.00
☐	Negro No. 42	50.00
☐	Negro, 2 Faces, No's. 43 & 44	60.00
☐	Old South Church	60.00
☐	Owl No's. 203 & 104	65.00
☐	"Pass Around the Hat"	70.00
☐	Pig No. 173, No. 184 *	45.00
☐	Pig, "Thrifty", No. 175 *	50.00
☐	Policeman, Irish, No. 8 *	78.00
☐	Policeman, Standing *	70.00
☐	Presto, Still, No. 427	28.00
☐	Puppy, "Fido", No. 337	36.00
☐	Radio, Crosley, No. 141	40.00
☐	Refrigerator, General Electric, No. 237	55.00

STILL

		Price
☐	Rhino No. 252	155.00
☐	Rooster, Standing, No. 186	90.00
☐	Safe, Royal Safe, Deposit	55.00
☐	"Security Safe Deposit", Combination	56.00
☐	Soldier, W.W. I, No. 15	78.00
☐	Steamboat, Iron "Arcade"	78.00
☐	Street Car No. 164	235.00
☐	Teddy Roosevelt No. 309	100.00
☐	Zeppelin No. 171	60.00

BARBED WIRE

Every barbed wire collector gets awfully tired of hearing "What! you collect barbed wire?!!" They know, and you will too if you start to collect it, or join one of the active collectors clubs, that barbed wire is fascinating, and a tangible symbol of the settling of the Western ranges. There are hundreds of styles and types. One especially interesting type is called the "obvious," made with larger-than-usual barbs so that it would be obvious to cattle and they wouldn't be injured. Keep in mind that nothing less than 18"—a "stick"—of barbed wire will do if you're a collector.

Single Round with 2 Points

☐	Gunderson, 1881	2.00	5.00
☐	Half-hitch, 1877	2.50	4.00
☐	Mack's Alternate, 1875	9.00	12.00
☐	"Two Point Ripple Wire"	4.00	6.00
☐	L. E. Sunderland No-Kink, 1884	.50	1.00

Double Round with 2 Points

☐	Baker's half-round barb	.75	1.25
☐	"Forked Tongue"	3.00	6.00
☐	J. D. Curtis "Twisted Point"	1.00	1.50
☐	Glidden Barb on both lines	3.00	5.00
☐	Kangaroo Wire	2.00	4.00

Ribbon Wire

☐	Cast Iron Buckthorn	5.00	8.00
☐	Allis' Flat Ribbon Barb	12.00	18.00
☐	Brinkerhoff's Ribbon Barb	2.00	3.00
☐	"Open Face" by Brinkerhoff, 1881	6.00	9.00
☐	F. D. Ford Flat Ribbon, 1885	3.00	6.00
☐	John Hallner's "Greenbriar", 1878	1.00	3.00
☐	Harbaugh's Torn Ribbon, 1881	5.00	8.00
☐	Kelly's Split Ribbon, 1868	15.00	30.00
☐	Kelmer Ornamental Fence, 1885	12.00	16.00
☐	Scutt's Smooth Ribbon	10.00	15.00

BASEBALL CARDS

The most valuable baseball card is a cigarette card picturing Pittsburg Pirate shortstop Honus Wagner, issued around 1910. This was 24 years after the introduction of baseball cards so, obviously, age isn't the deciding factor. Wagner, a non-smoker, did not want his name associated with cigarettes. He threatened to sue the manufacturer if the card was not pulled off the market. It was, but not before a few had leaked into circulation. Their value has been variously stated at between $500 and $2000. The highest actual sale was for $1500. This is *many times* more than any other card is worth. 25 specimens are known to exist at present.

General guide to values:

PRE-1900. Usually $5 to $25. The most valuable pre-1900 cards are those issued by Gypsy Queen and Old Judge cigarettes (average $15-$25). The Old Judge are large in size and attractive. When these cards carry genuine signatures of the players their values are much higher.

1900-20. Enormous quantities of cards were issued in this period. In just one year, 1910, there were more than 500 "white border" cards, not only of major but minor league players. Most "white borders" bring under $1. Rarer cards of the era were those of Ramly, Turkey Reds, and Hassan Triple Folders. Value of the Ramly is around $10 per card, the Hassan $4. Also valuable ($10 each) are the Fatima "team cards," with team portraits rather than individual players. A complete set of 16, for the 16 big-league teams (there were fewer teams in those days), brings $300 in good condition. These date to 1913. "Gold Border" cards are common and cheap, usually under $1.

1920 on. The values of post-1920 cards range from 1¢ (for current Topps bubblegum cards) to $30 or more for scarce specimens, such as the 1949 Bowman Pacific Coast League. Prior to the Dodgers and Giants moving to California in 1958, the Pacific Coast was an "open" league — that is, higher than Triple A — and had many star players. The Topps 1950 "Current Stars," fairly recent major league cards, bring $20. But this is the exception, not the rule, as a result of low printings. Most cards of this vintage are worth much less. For example the regular Topps cards of 1955 have a value of 20-75¢. *Complete sets* of current Topps cards sell for around $20.

Baseball Cards priced individually, not by sets	Price Range	
☐ American caramel cards, 1908, 1910	3.00	5.00
☐ Boucher's gold coin cigarette "Triple Headers"	4.00	6.00
☐ Cracker Jack cards, 1914, 1915	5.00	12.00
☐ Hassan Cigarette"Triple Headers"	4.00	6.00
☐ Mecca Doublefolders, early 20th C	4.00	6.00
☐ Old Judge cigarette sepia cards, 19th C	3.00	20.00
☐ Tatoo-Orbit gum cards, 1933 Hall of Famers	8.00	10.00

BASKETS

Baskets are increasingly popular collectibles. It is still possible to find a rare basket at yard sales, in basements and attics, but often they are not in very good condition. Indian and Shaker baskets are particularly in demand.

POMO COILED, *Rosette Motif, Shell Beads/Feathers,*
7½" Dia. . . . . 950.00 - 1000.00

	Price	Range
☐ American Indian, Diameter 10"	130.00	180.00
☐ Apache Burden Basket 2½" x 2½"		20.00
☐ Apache Coiled Storage Basket, round body, dark brown with geometric motifs. Height 12½"	700.00	900.00
☐ Apache Coiled Storage Basket, round body, flaring rim, dark brown with animals and human figures. Height 16¾"	700.00	900.00
☐ Apache Coiled Basket, flat base, dark brown with snowflake motif. Diameter 8-3/8"	300.00	400.00
☐ Caushatta effigy baskets; pine cones & needles:		
crawfish, 9" x 6½"		20.00
crab, 6" x 5"		20.00
alligator, 9" x 2¾"		18.00
turtle, 6½" x 3"		18.00
☐ Cheese Basket	40.00	50.00
☐ Cheese Shaker, round. Diameter 12"	200.00	250.00
☐ Hopi Coiled Basket, rectangular body in brown, orange and yellow raincloud and thunder motif. Diameter 5-5/8"	100.00	150.00
☐ Papago Coiled Basket, body woven in dark brown with bands of swastikas. Diameter 11-5/8"	225.00	275.00
☐ Pima Coiled Basket, flat base, flaring body, dark brown with pattern of human figures. Diameter 11¼"	250.00	350.00
☐ Pima Coiled Basket, shallow, dark brown with crosses in the field. Diameter 9¼"	75.00	125.00
☐ Sewing Basket, Wicker	65.00	75.00
☐ Southwest Coiled Storage Basket, flat base, dark brown with arrow motifs. Height 27"	725.00	825.00
☐ Splint, oval, w/wooden handles		150.00

BASKETS

	Price Range	
☐ Splint, back pack		150.00
☐ Splint, back pack		62.00
☐ Split oak buttocks, basket		50.00
☐ Split oak buttocks, large		95.00
☐ Splint, cheese basket, round		120.00
☐ Tlingit Twined Spruce Root Basket, cylindrical body, pale yellow bands with orange zig zag decoration. Dia. 5"	350.00	450.00
☐ Tulare Coiled Basket, flat base, rounded sides, rattlesnake bands in black and reddish brown. Diameter 14½"	1200.00	1300.00
☐ Washo Coiled Trinket Basket, red, blue, black and green on white ground. Diameter 4¼"	100.00	150.00
☐ Yokut Coiled Circular Tray, brown with rattlesnake band. Diameter 18¼"	400.00	500.00

BEER CANS

The world's first beer can was a flat-top made by the American Can Company, Greenwich, Connecticut, and sold be the Krueger Brewing Co. of New Jersey, in 1935. They have been produced in various sizes, shapes, colors, and trademarks. Active competition between the can makers contributed greatly to the production and design. There are many active beer can collecting clubs engaged in trading, buying and selling.

PUNCH TOP   CONE TOP

12 OZ. PULL-TAB CANS

	Price
☐ Al Light Pilsener. Aluminum, red, off-white, brown & gold	.50
☐ Alpen Glen. Aluminum, red, white, green & silver	1.10
☐ Andeker. Gold, black & red	1.00
☐ Arrow 77. Red, white, black & gold	1.50
☐ Aspen Gold. Blue, white, gold & silver	1.20
☐ Ballantine Premium. Aluminum, gold, silver, red & black	1.00
☐ Becker's. Red, white & blue	1.00
☐ Black Label. Red, white & black	1.00
☐ Brewers Best Premium Bavarian. Red, white, green & copper	2.00

12 OZ. PULL TAB CANS   Price

- ☐ Budweiser Lager. Red, white & blue 1.00
- ☐ Burger Premium. Red, white & gold 1.50
- ☐ Bush Bavarian. Aluminum, red, white, blue & black 1.00
- ☐ Canadian Ace Draft Premium. Red, white, woodgrain, black & silver . . 1.00
- ☐ Circle Light Premium. Red, white & black 1.00
- ☐ Colt 45 Malt Liquor "1973/74 Warriors". Red, white, blue, gold & silver 2.50
- ☐ Corona Extra. Red, white, blue & gold 50
- ☐ Dawson Ale. Aluminum, green, white & silver .50
- ☐ Dixie Light. White, green & gold 45
- ☐ Drewerys. Red, white, gold & black 1.00
- ☐ Dubois. Red, white, black & grey 2.00
- ☐ Dubois Busweiser Premium. Gold, white & black 3.00
- ☐ Duke. Red, white, black & gold 1.50
- ☐ El Rancho Light. Yellow, red, green & gold 1.50
- ☐ Esslinger Premium. Red, white & black 50
- ☐ Falstaff Premium. Aluminum, red, white, blue, yellow, silver, brown & gold 1.00
- ☐ Fisher Light Premium. Red, white, silver & gold 1.00
- ☐ Fox Head Bock Draft. Brown, white & gold 1.00
- ☐ Gamecock Ale. Red, white, green & black 3.00
- ☐ Genesee "Light Cream Ale". Green, white, black & silver 1.00
- ☐ Gettleman. White, brown & tan 1.00
- ☐ Geyer's Lager. Red, white, yellow, black & brown 1.00
- ☐ Gluck Pilsener. Red, white, yellow, black, gold & silver 50
- ☐ Golden Brew Premium. Blue, white & gold 50
- ☐ Grand Union Premium. Red, white, orange & blue 50
- ☐ Heibrau Premium. Blue, white, black, green & gold 1.00
- ☐ Hi-En Brau. Brown, white, gold, green & silver 1.50
- ☐ Holihan's Pilsener. Red, white, black & gold 1.00
- ☐ Hop'N Gator. White, brown, black & yellow 50
- ☐ Hudepohl "14K". Red, white, black & gold 1.00
- ☐ Imperial. Red, white, gold & yellow 1.50
- ☐ Iron City. Red, white, black & gray. 1960 World Series Pittsburgh 1.00
- ☐ Iron City. Red, white, black & gray. 1971 World Series Pittsburgh 1.00
- ☐ Iron City. Red, white, black & gray. Stanley Cup Champions Pittsburgh 1.00
- ☐ Iron City. Red, white, black & gray. Baseball World Champions Pittsburgh 1.00
- ☐ Iron City. Red, white, black & gray Super Bowl Winners Pittsburgh 1.00
- ☐ Iron City. Red, white, black & gray. NBA Champions Pittsburgh 1.00
- ☐ Iron City. Red, white, black & gray. Steelers 1.00
- ☐ Kingsbury Light. White, red & blue 1.00
- ☐ Koehler Lager. Red, white & silver 50
- ☐ Light. White, blue, red & gold 50
- ☐ Lite. Blue, white & gold 1.00
- ☐ Lucky Bock. White, gold & green 2.00
- ☐ Mein. Multi-colored 1.00

12 OZ. PULL TAB CANS   Price

- [ ] Mickey's Malt Liquor. White, orange, green & silver .... .50
- [ ] Miller Ale. Red, white, green & gold .... .50
- [ ] Milwaukee's Best. Orange, brown & white 1.00
- [ ] Muhlheim Draft. Red, white, black & gold 1.50
- [ ] Mustang. Red, white, gold & black 2.00
- [ ] Narragansett Lager. Red, white, gold & green 1.00
- [ ] National Bohemian Lager. Aluminum, red, white, gold & silver 1.00
- [ ] National Bohemian Light. Multi-colored 5.00
- [ ] Oconto Premium. Red, white, blue & gold 1.00
- [ ] Oertels '92. Red & white 1.00
- [ ] Old Bohemian Light. Red, white & gold 1.00
- [ ] Old Dutch. Red, white & silver 1.50
- [ ] Old Dutch. Red, white & gold 1.50
- [ ] Old German Premium Lager. Red, white & blue 1.00
- [ ] Old Heidel Brau Lager. Red, white & blue .... .50
- [ ] Olde Frothingslosh. Orange, white, black & gray 1.00
- [ ] Ortlieb's. Red, white, black & silver 1.00
- [ ] Ortlieb's Draught. Red, white & blue 1.50
- [ ] Pabst Bock. Red, white, blue & silver 1.00
- [ ] Pearl Premium Light. Multi-colored 1.00
- [ ] Pfeiffer Premium. Red, white, black & gold 1.00
- [ ] Pickett's Premium. Red, white & blue .... .50
- [ ] Piels Light Lager. Red, white & silver aluminum 1.00
- [ ] Primo. Blue, white, gold & black .... .50
- [ ] Prizer Extra Dry Premium. Red, white, silver & brown 1.00
- [ ] Rahr's All Star. Red, white & silver 2.50
- [ ] Raineir Light. Red, white & gold 1.00
- [ ] Raineir Light. Red, white, gold, silver & aluminum 1.00
- [ ] Schaefer Draft. Red, white & silver .... .50
- [ ] Schell's. Black, orange & white 1.50
- [ ] Schlitz. Silver, white, blue & brown aluminum .... .50
- [ ] Schlitz Stout. Blue, white, black & silver aluminum .... .50
- [ ] Schmidt Draft. Multi-colored. Black bear over strip mine 1.50
- [ ] Schmidt Draft. Multi-colored. Collie with sheep 1.50
- [ ] Schmidt Draft. Multi-colored. Elk 1.50
- [ ] Schmidt Draft. Red, white, yellow & black 1.00
- [ ] Schmidt Light. Red, white, black & gold 1.00
- [ ] Seven-Eleven Premium. Copper, red, white, silver & black 1.00
- [ ] Silver Peak. Blue, silver & white 1.25
- [ ] Spearman Ale. Red, white & green 2.50
- [ ] Static Fair Premium. Blue & silver 7.50
- [ ] Stoney's Pilsener. Red, white, silver & gold .... .50
- [ ] Swinger Malt Liquor. Red, white, blue & silver 3.00
- [ ] Tavern Pale Dry. Red, gold, blue, silver & white 1.00
- [ ] Tudor Ale. Red, white, gold & green 1.00
- [ ] Utica Club Cream Ale. Red, white, green & gold aluminum .... .50
- [ ] Van Dyke Export. Blue, white, gold & black 2.50
- [ ] Velvet Glow Pale Dry. Red, white & gold 1.00
- [ ] Walter's Light. Red, white & black 1.00

12 OZ. PUNCH-TOP CANS
Price

- [ ] ABC. Red, white & blue 4.10
- [ ] ABC. Red, white & silver 5.00
- [ ] Ace Pilsner. White, blue & gold 5.00
- [ ] Acme. Red, silver & black 4.20
- [ ] Adler Brew. Cream, gold, red & green 2.50
- [ ] All American. Red, white, blue & silver 5.00
- [ ] Arrow 77. Red, white, silver & black 2.50
- [ ] Atlantic. Multi-colored 6.00
- [ ] Augustines. Red, white, blue & gold 2.60
- [ ] Ballantine's Ale. Green, gold & black 2.50
- [ ] Ballantine's Light Lager Beer. Copper, white & brown 2.50
- [ ] Banner Extra Dry. Red, white & blue 3.00
- [ ] Best Premium. Red, white, copper & brown 3.20
- [ ] Big State. Brown, red & white 5.50
- [ ] Blatz Bock. Tan, white, brown & gold 3.00
- [ ] Blatz Pilsner. Red, white, black & gold 2.50
- [ ] Blue 'N Gold. Blue, white & gold 4.50
- [ ] Brau Haus Premium Lager. Multi-colored 5.10
- [ ] Brew 52 Light Lager. Red, white & black 5.10
- [ ] Brew 102 Pale Dry. Red, white & yellow 4.00
- [ ] Budweiser Bock. Red, gold, white & green 6.00
- [ ] Budweiser Lager. Red, white & blue 3.00
- [ ] Bull Dog. Red, white & green 4.00
- [ ] Bull Dog Ale. Red, white & green 3.00
- [ ] Bullfrog. Silver, white & green 5.00
- [ ] Busch Lager. Red, white, green & gold 5.00
- [ ] Busch Bavarian. Blue, white, green, black & brown 2.00
- [ ] Canadian Ace Bock. White, black, silver & woodgrain 5.00
- [ ] Chief Oshkosh. Multi-colored 2.50
- [ ] Cold Brau. Red, white, blue & silver 3.00
- [ ] Corona. Gold, white, red, black & yellow 3.00
- [ ] Crystal Rock Pilsener. Blue, white & gold 3.50
- [ ] Drewerys Extra Dry. Red, silver & black 4.50
- [ ] Drewerys Old Stock Ale. White, black & silver 3.50
- [ ] Dutch Lunch. Black, silver & gray 5.00
- [ ] Eastside. Red, white, blue & gold 4.00
- [ ] Edelweiss Bock. Brown, red, gold, white & yellow 5.50
- [ ] Edelweiss Light. Red, white, black & tan 3.00
- [ ] English Lad. Multi-colored 6.00
- [ ] Erin Brew. Gold, red, white & green 4.00
- [ ] Falls City. Red, white, black & gold 3.50
- [ ] Fehr's. Red, white, black & gold 3.50
- [ ] Fisher Premium. Red, white, blue & gold 2.50
- [ ] Fox Brew. Blue, white, green, yellow & purple 3.50
- [ ] Fox Deluxe. Red, white, black & gold 5.00
- [ ] Fox Head 400. Gold, brown, red & tan 3.50
- [ ] Fox Head Lager. Red, black, gold, tan & yellow 4.00
- [ ] Fox Head Malt Liquor. Red, yellow, white, black & gold 4.50
- [ ] Friars Ale. Brown, white & yellow 4.50

12 OZ. PUNCH TOP CANS
Price

- ☐ GB Dark Bock. Red, white, black & silver 6.00
- ☐ Genesee 12 Horse Ale. Green, white & black 4.00
- ☐ Gettelman. Brown, white & gold 2.00
- ☐ Gluck's. Red, white, blue & gold 3.00
- ☐ Goebel Bock. Red, white, black & silver 6.00
- ☐ Goebel Luxury. Red, white, gold & black 3.50
- ☐ Goetz Premium. Blue, white, tan & gold 2.50
- ☐ Gold Label Pale Dry. Red, white, black & gold 3.50
- ☐ Golden Glow. Blue, silver & gray 4.00
- ☐ Golden Glow Ale. Red, tan, silver, black & green 4.00
- ☐ Great Falls Select. Red, white, black & gold 2.50
- ☐ Great Lakes Premium. Red, white & blue 3.00
- ☐ Gunther Premium Dry. Red, white, black & brown 3.00
- ☐ Happy Hops Lager. Red, white, yellow, blue & gold 6.00
- ☐ Heileman's Old Style. Multi-colored 3.00
- ☐ Hi Brau. White, gold & maroon 3.00
- ☐ Huel's Bock. Red, white, yellow, gold & brown 6.00
- ☐ Iroquois. Red, white & silver 3.00
- ☐ Jordan. Gold, white & black 5.50
- ☐ Karl's K. Red, white, yellow & brown 4.50
- ☐ Keg. Red, white & yellow 3.00
- ☐ King's Premium. Blue, white, silver & gold 2.50
- ☐ Kingsbury Pale. Red, white, blue & gold 2.50
- ☐ Krueger. Red, black, gold & silver 6.00
- ☐ Krueger Premium. Red, white, black & gold 3.00
- ☐ Lone Star. Red, white, blue & brown 3.50
- ☐ Lubeck. White, purple, black & gold 5.00
- ☐ Lucky Lager. Red, tan & gold 3.50
- ☐ Meister Brau. Red, white & gold 4.00
- ☐ Meister Brau Bock. White, gold, brown & red 3.00
- ☐ Meister Brau Draft. Gold, white, black & woodgrain 2.50
- ☐ Miller High Life. Red, white, blue, green, gold & silver 2.50
- ☐ Milwaukee's Best. Blue, white & brown 3.50
- ☐ Monarch. Red, white, gold & black 3.00
- ☐ Narragansett Ale. Brown, red, white & gold 3.00
- ☐ Nectar Premium. White, silver, black, gold & blue 4.00
- ☐ Northern. Yellow, brown, white & green 2.50
- ☐ Oconto Premium. Red, white, blue & gold 3.00
- ☐ Old Crown Ale. Tan, gold & black 4.50
- ☐ Old Dutch. Multi-colored 3.50
- ☐ Old German Lager. Black, silver & white 3.50
- ☐ Old Style Lager. Red, white, green, black, gold & brown 2.50
- ☐ Old Tankard Ale. Red, black & silver 5.00
- ☐ Old Tavern Premium Lager. Multi-colored 4.50
- ☐ Old Vienna. Red, silver & white 5.00
- ☐ Pabst. Blue, white & silver 3.50
- ☐ Pabst Blue Ribbon Bock. Yellow, green, blue & silver 5.00
- ☐ Pearl. Tan, red, white & gold 3.50
- ☐ Pearl Lager. White, red, gold & blue 3.00

12 OZ. PUNCH TOP CANS   Price

- [ ] Pearl Lager. Multi-colored 2.50
- [ ] Peels Light Lager. Red, white & silver aluminum 2.50
- [ ] Prager. Red, white, black & gold................................4.50
- [ ] Prior Lager. Red, white, green & black.........................4.00
- [ ] Rahr's. Red, white & silver 3.50
- [ ] Raineir. Gold, red, silver, white & purple 3.50
- [ ] Raineir Old Stock Ale. Gold, orange, black, green & white...........3.50
- [ ] Regal Pale. Red, white, blue & gold 2.50
- [ ] Reserve. Blue, white, gold & black 3.00
- [ ] Rheingold. Red, yellow, blue, green & woodgrain..................3.00
- [ ] Ruppert. Purple, white & woodgrain.............................3.50
- [ ] Salzburg Eastern. Red, white & gray 3.00
- [ ] Schaefer Lager. Red, black, gold & light woodgrain................3.50
- [ ] Sheridan Premium. Red, white & gold 2.50
- [ ] Southern Select. Gold, white & red 5.50
- [ ] Special Brew. Red, silver & black 5.00
- [ ] Star Model. Red, white, blue & silver 4.00
- [ ] Sterling Ale. Green, red, brown, cream & silver...................6.00
- [ ] Storz Gold Crest. Red, white, brown, gold & silver.................4.00
- [ ] Tahoe. Blue, green, yellow, white & red 6.00
- [ ] Tavern Pale. Red, tan & gold....................................3.50
- [ ] Tivoli. Red, white, black, gold & silver 3.50
- [ ] Tudor Ale. Green, white & gold..................................3.00
- [ ] Tudor Bock. Red, white, gold & green 5.50
- [ ] Tudor Premium. Red, white & blue...............................3.00
- [ ] Utica Club Pale Ale. Red, white, yellow & gold 3.50
- [ ] Valley Forge. Red, white & blue 3.50
- [ ] Viking. White, gold & red..6.00
- [ ] Walter's Bock. Red, white, brown & green 3.50
- [ ] Walter's Pilsener. Red, white, black & gold 3.50
- [ ] Western Gold Lager. Purple, silver & white 4.00
- [ ] Weidemann Fine. Red, white, black & gold 2.50
- [ ] Windsor Premium. Blue, white & silver 3.00
- [ ] Wisconsin Gold Label. Gold, white & silver.......................3.00
- [ ] Yusay Pilsen. Red, white & blue 3.50

STANDARD CONE TOPS

- [ ] ABC. Blue, gold, white & red.....................................22.00
- [ ] Aero Club Pale Select Beer. Gold, blue, white & red 27.00
- [ ] Altes Lager Beer. Green, gold, black & red 30.00
- [ ] Apache Export Ale. Copper, white & black 26.00
- [ ] Atlantis Ale. Red, gold, white & black 27.00
- [ ] Augustines Beer. Red, white, yellow, gold & blue 18.00
- [ ] Barbarossa. Multi-colored 24.00
- [ ] Berghoff 1887. Black, orange, yellow & white 20.00
- [ ] Beverwyck Beer. Green, white & gold 24.00
- [ ] Blackhawk Topping Beer. Yellow, red, black & white 23.00
- [ ] Blatz Ale. Yellow, brown, white & black 23.50
- [ ] Blatz Milwaukee Beer. Blue & white...............................28.00
- [ ] Blue Bonnet Extra Pale Beer. Multi-colored 26.00

STANDARD CONE TOPS
Price

- [ ] Bruck's Jubilee Beer. Blue, gray & red 22.50
- [ ] Bubs Beer. White, red, gold & black 18.00
- [ ] Buckeye Beer. Multi-colored. 20.00
- [ ] Canadian Ace Ale. White, silver, red, black & woodgrain 20.00
- [ ] Carling Red Cap Ale. Green, black & cream 22.00
- [ ] Century Lager Beer. Red, white, blue, gray & black 28.00
- [ ] Champagne Velvet. Red, white, cream, copper & red 17.00
- [ ] Clyde Cream Ale. Cream, red & black 25.00
- [ ] Copper Club Pilsner Beer. Green, white & copper 22.50
- [ ] Cremo Beer. Blue, white, gold & black 24.00
- [ ] Dawson's Master Ale. Yellow, orange, black & red 25.00
- [ ] Diehl. Gold, black & white 15.00
- [ ] Dubois Export. White, red, gold & black 25.00
- [ ] Duquesne Pilsner Beer. White, gold, red & blue 22.00
- [ ] Eastside. Red, white, blue & gold 14.00
- [ ] Ebling. Silver, red & black 16.00
- [ ] Ebling Ale. Silver, green & black 16.00
- [ ] Edelweiss Light Beer. Red, white, black & gold 19.00
- [ ] Falls. Red, white, yellow, gold & black 16.00
- [ ] Falstaff. Brown, white, green yellow, black & red 10.00
- [ ] Fehr's. White, red, black & silver 15.00
- [ ] Fort Pitt Pale Ale. Green, red, black, white, green & gold 25.00
- [ ] Fort Pitt Special Beer. Red, white, gold & black 24.00
- [ ] Fort Schuyler. Red, white, gold & black 15.00
- [ ] Fountain Brew Beer. Green, yellow, white & black 22.00
- [ ] Fox Deluxe Beer. Gold, white, brown & red 20.00
- [ ] Free State. Red, white, blue & gold 16.00
- [ ] Gam. White, gold & black 25.00
- [ ] Gettelman. Gold, brown, white & red 21.00
- [ ] Gipps Amberlin Beer. Cream, red, white, green, gold & black 24.00
- [ ] Glueck's. Red, white, silver & brown 14.00
- [ ] Gold Medal Beer. Copper, brown & white 22.00
- [ ] Gold Crest. Red, white, blue & gold 24.00
- [ ] Gotham Fine Beer. Red, white, gray & gold 27.50
- [ ] Grain Belt Beer. Red, black, white & gold 16.00
- [ ] Gus' Premium Topper Beer. Black, red & white 24.00
- [ ] Haas. Red, white, black & gold 24.00
- [ ] Hanley's Extra Pale. Gold, white & purple 24.00
- [ ] Hauenstein. Red, white, black, gray & gold 14.00
- [ ] Heidel-Brau. Orange, green, white & gold 14.00
- [ ] Hoosier Beer. Red, white, black & gold 26.00
- [ ] Horton Old Stock Ale. Brown, black, gold & cream 25.00
- [ ] Hudepohl. Red, white, blue & silver 14.00
- [ ] Iron City Beer. Red, white & black 24.00
- [ ] Iroquois. Multi-colored 24.00
- [ ] Jax Pilsner Style Beer. Blue, orange & white 24.00
- [ ] Kato. Gold, black, red, yellow & white 16.00
- [ ] Kato Lager Beer. Silver, black & red 18.00
- [ ] Kessler. Red, white, blue, silver & black 16.00

STANDARD CONE TOPS Price

- ☐ Koehler Select. Blue, gold, black & white 25.00
- ☐ Koehler's Beer. Red, white, black & gold 25.00
- ☐ Koenig Brau Premium Beer. Red, white, gold & black 22.00
- ☐ Kuebler Pale Beer. Red, black, white & silver 24.00
- ☐ Leinenkugel's. Red, white, black & silver.........................15.00
- ☐ Leisy's Light Beer. Blue, cream & gold 24.00
- ☐ Life Staff Pale Lager Beer. Red, black & gold 25.00
- ☐ Maier. Red, white & black 14.00
- ☐ Maier Gold Label Ale. Green, gold & silver 24.00
- ☐ Maier Export Beer. Red, blue & silver 24.00
- ☐ Milwaukee Club Beer. Brown & cream 22.00
- ☐ Milwaukee Club Beer. Gold, silver, black & yellow 21.00
- ☐ Monarch Beer. Red, white, black & gold 24.00
- ☐ Monterey Beer. Blue & white 26.00
- ☐ Muehlebach's. Green, white, red & gold 16.00
- ☐ Namar Premium Beer. Red, white, blue & gold 24.00
- ☐ National Bohemian Pale Beer. Black, yellow, red & white 22.00
- ☐ Neuweiler's. Gray, tan, brown, black & silver 9.50
- ☐ Neuweiler's Cream Ale. Blue, orange, white, gold & black 22.00
- ☐ Northern Beer. Multi-colored 18.00
- ☐ Northern Beer. Brown, green & yellow 18.00
- ☐ Oertels '92. Black, silver, red & blue 16.00
- ☐ Old Dutch Brand. Black, brown, red, gold & white.................24.00
- ☐ Old Export. Red, white & purple 21.00
- ☐ Old German. Red, white, blue & yellow 10.00
- ☐ Old Shay. Cream, red, black & gold 24.00
- ☐ Old Style Lager. Multi-colored 14.50
- ☐ Old Topper Golden Ale. Green, yellow, white & black 22.00
- ☐ Old Topper Snappy Ale. Black, white, brown & yellow 20.00
- ☐ Old Timer Premium Beer. Red, white, gold & black 24.00
- ☐ Olde Virginia. Red, white, blue, green & gold 14.50
- ☐ Old Vienna. Red, white, black & gold 26.00
- ☐ Pacific Lager Beer. Blue, green, white & black 26.00
- ☐ Peerless Beer. Red, white & gold 22.00
- ☐ Peerless Extra Premium. Red, white, green & gold 20.00
- ☐ Peel's Special Light Beer. Red, gold, black & cream...............25.00
- ☐ Prima. Red, white, blue & gold 24.00
- ☐ Rainier Old Stock Ale. Red, white, green & black 22.00
- ☐ Rainier Special Export. Red, white & black 22.00
- ☐ Rainier Club Extra Dry. Red, white, black & silver 22.00
- ☐ Red Ribbon Beer. Red, white, silver & black 28.00
- ☐ Red Top Ale. Red, black, gold & yellow 25.00
- ☐ Red Top Extra Pale Beer. Red, white, gold & black 24.00
- ☐ Regal. Brown, gold, red & white 18.00
- ☐ Rhinelander. Green, white, black & gold 24.00
- ☐ Rich Brau. Gold, black, red & white 25.00
- ☐ Rocky Mountain. Red, white, black & silver 17.00
- ☐ Royal. Red, white, black & yellow................................26.00
- ☐ Royal Bohemian. Red, white, blue & gold 16.00

STANDARD CONE TOP

Price

- [ ] Royal Pilsner Beer. Red, yellow & black 25.00
- [ ] Schell's "Deer Brand". Red, blue, gold & cream 24.00
- [ ] Schlitz. White, brown, blue & copper 14.00
- [ ] Schlitz Lager. White, brown, cream & blue 22.00
- [ ] Schmidt's. Red, white, gold & black 22.00
- [ ] Schmidt's City Club. Red, white & yellow 14.00
- [ ] Schmidt's First Premium. Red, white, blue, green, black & pink 15.00
- [ ] Schmidt's of Philadelphia. Silver, cream, gold, red & black 28.00
- [ ] Seven Eleven. White, red, gold & black 28.00
- [ ] '76 Ale. Red, black, green & cream 26.00
- [ ] Sierra. Gold, yellow, white, blue & silver 14.00
- [ ] Stag. Red, white, black & gold 15.00
- [ ] Steinerbru. Red, gold, black & cream 28.00
- [ ] Stock Ale by Croft. Red, gold & cream 26.00
- [ ] Sun Valley. Blue, white & yellow. 28.00
- [ ] Tacoma Pale Beer. Blue, white & brown 28.00
- [ ] Tavern Beer. Multi-colored 25.00
- [ ] Trophy. Red, white, gold & black 28.00
- [ ] Tube City. Red, white, gold & black 26.00
- [ ] Utica Club. Red, white & gold 27.00
- [ ] Van Merritt. Green, white, red & black 28.00
- [ ] V.R. Light Mellow. Red, white & black 28.00
- [ ] Walter's Pilsner. Green, white, gold & black 24.00
- [ ] Washington Pilsner. Red, white, blue & gold 28.00
- [ ] W. Virginia Special Export Beer. Red, white, blue & gold 24.00
- [ ] White Tap. Red, white, blue & gold. 28.00
- [ ] White Seal. Red, white, gold & black 26.00
- [ ] Weidemann Bohemian. Red, white, gold & black 26.00
- [ ] Wooden Shoe. Red, white & blue 26.00
- [ ] Yuengling. Red, white & gold 26.00

BELLS

Bells were known many thousands of years ago in the Far East and in South America. They were introduced in Europe over 1500 years ago. Bells are used to summon, warn, mark rejoicing or mourning, or to record time. Most working bells are made of bronze, brass, bell metal, iron or silver. Glass and china bells are, for the most part, either decorative or are part of the new wave of limited edition, made-to-be-collected items.

	Price Range	
[ ] Brass Bell. Stork	25.00	30.00
[ ] Brass Clapper Bell	90.00	105.00
[ ] Brass Dinner Bell	3.00	8.00
[ ] Brass Musical Chime Bell	25.00	30.00
[ ] Brass Bell. Wooden handle, 6"	10.00	15.00
[ ] Brass Bell. Wooden handle, 7"	20.00	25.00
[ ] Brass Bell. Wooden handle, 8"	20.00	22.00
[ ] Brass Bell. Wooden handle, 4"	5.00	8.00

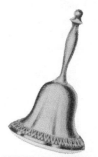

SHIP'S BELL, *1845*

SHIP'S BELL, *Dolphin*

AMBER GLASS BELL

BELLS

	Price Range	
☐ Brass Bell. Wooden handle	10.00	14.00
☐ Bronze Bell. Angel holder	85.00	90.00
☐ Cast Iron Bell. Mechanical	115.00	125.00
☐ China Bell. Cobalt, 5"	40.00	45.00
☐ China Bell. German, clown painted on	60.00	65.00
☐ Chinese Brass Gong Bell. 9"	30.00	40.00
☐ Church Bell. Solid brass, single tier	90.00	105.00
☐ Church Bell. Solid brass, triple tier	140.00	175.00
☐ Conestoga. Graduated on strap (4), brass	150.00	200.00
☐ Cow Bell. Iron ring with strap attachment	20.00	30.00
☐ Cow Bell. Leather collar	6.00	10.00
☐ Cow Bell Clapper	18.00	25.00
☐ Cutter-type Bell. Iron strap (3)	60.00	75.00
☐ Dinner Bell. Crystal	35.00	50.00
☐ Dinner Bell. Enamel on metal	40.00	50.00
☐ Dinner Bell. Nickel	8.00	10.00
☐ Dinner Bell. Ornate sterling silver	50.00	60.00
☐ Dog Bells. 4" high sculptured handles (pair)	45.00	75.00
☐ Door Bell. Abbe's patent double strike	18.00	30.00
☐ Door Bell. Brass	40.00	50.00
☐ Elephant Bell. Brass	32.50	40.00
☐ Elephant Bell. Cloisonne	50.00	100.00
☐ Fire Alarm Bell	30.00	40.00
☐ Glass Bell. Amber, all glass	90.00	100.00
☐ Glass Bell. Bristol, 11½"	90.00	100.00
☐ Glass Bell. Bristol wedding bell, 14"	120.00	125.00
☐ Glass Bell. Carnival	12.50	15.00
☐ Glass Bell. Cranberry glass, clear handle	130.00	145.00
☐ Glass Bell. Clear dark green	70.00	85.00
☐ Glass Bell. Cut glass including handle	120.00	135.00
☐ Glass Bell. Nailsea bell, solid glass handle, loops and swirls in color	175.00	200.00
☐ Venetian Glass Bell. Ruby red, enamel decoration	75.00	85.00
☐ Venetian Glass Bell. Latticino, 4¼" high, pink	135.00	150.00

BELLS

	Price	Range
☐ Venetian Glass Bell. Goose bell	15.00	20.00
☐ Hand Bell. Brass	75.00	100.00
☐ Hand Bell. Brass with decorations	60.00	75.00
☐ Hand Bell. Brass with wooden handle	65.00	100.00
☐ Iron Cow Bell	10.00	15.00
☐ Iron Dinner Bell	95.00	100.00
☐ Iron Farm Bell	200.00	225.00
☐ Iron Sleigh Bell	35.00	50.00
☐ Lady Sculptured Bell. 4" high	125.00	150.00
☐ Majolica Bell. Dog	30.00	36.00
☐ Mass Bell. Solid brass	65.00	75.00
☐ Mission Bell. Min. clapper	50.00	75.00
☐ Mission Bell. Spanish	75.00	100.00
☐ Pewter Sterling Bell	18.00	20.00
☐ Pressed Glass Bell. Smokey	3.00	5.00
☐ School Bell. Metal, wooden handles, small	50.00	75.00
☐ School Bell. Metal, wooden handle, large	65.00	85.00
☐ School Bell. 5"	40.00	45.00
☐ School Bell. 6½"	60.00	70.00
☐ School Bell. 8¼"	75.00	90.00
☐ School Bell. 9½"	80.00	90.00
☐ School Bell. Bronze 20" iron yoke. Jones & Hitchcock, 1856	—	950.00
☐ Sheep Bell	40.00	50.00
☐ Ship Bell. Brass, 1845	175.00	200.00
☐ Ship Bell. Brass dolphin	175.00	200.00
☐ Sleigh Bells. Leather strap of 17 bells	150.00	200.00
☐ Sleigh Bells. Leather strap of 20 bells	225.00	250.00
☐ Sleigh Bells. Iron string of 25 bells	250.00	275.00
☐ Sleigh Bells. Brass string of 25 bells	200.00	225.00
☐ Soldier. Roman	30.00	50.00
☐ Sterling Silver Bell. Woman	110.00	115.00
☐ Pewter Sterling	18.00	20.00
☐ Pressed Glass Bell. Smokey	3.00	5.00
☐ Town Crier. Long with wooden handle	80.00	100.00
☐ Trolley Car. 8" diameter	55.00	75.00
☐ Turtle. German mechanical	60.00	75.00

BICYCLES

Olad High-Wheeler bicycles were popular during the 1800's and 1890's. Since they were produced in great quantities they are readily easy to find and fun to ride too. From these evolved the bicycle as we know it today. As bicycling becomes more popular, and it is, the demand for the collectible bicycle increases — look for values to increase, also.

BICYCLES

	Price Range	
☐ Bone Shaker, 1850	1600.00	2000.00
☐ Chainless bike, 1853	130.00	190.00
☐ Columbia chainless, 1856	200.00	250.00
☐ Spring fork bike, 1862	600.00	700.00
☐ Eagle Hi-Wheeler with brake, 1865	3000.00	3500.00
☐ Buggy Spoked Triangle pedal Hi-Wheel Bike, 1866 ...	525.00	650.00
☐ Eagle 50 inch Hi-Wheeler, 1872	2000.00	2500.00
☐ 50 inch Hi-Wheeler, 1878	1200.00	1600.00
☐ Tricycle 3-wheel Tandem Columbian Bike, 1888	3000.00	3600.00
☐ Two Wheeler, 1896	300.00	400.00
☐ 56 inch High-Wheeler, 1898	650.00	750.00
☐ Columbia Bike Hi-Wheeler, 1901	1200.00	1600.00
☐ Two Wheeler Bike, 1914	100.00	150.00
☐ Tandem Bike, 1914	225.00	300.00
☐ Scooter, foot, 1927	175.00	225.00

BOOKS

Books date back before the age of handwriting when symbols were chiseled into stone tablets. Later vellum and papyrus leaves were used and rolled into scrolls, bound in wooden boards or etched on stone. It wasn't until about 1450 that Gutenberg developed the printing press which made books available in quantity to more people. Listed here is a very small sample of the millions of books available to collectors. For further information and listings, you may refer to *The Official Guide to Old Books,* by William Rodger.

☐ Alcott, Louisa M., *Little Women,* Boston, 1869	100.00	125.00
☐ Allen, Col. Ethan, *Reason, The Only Oracle of Man,* New York, 1836, 2nd Edition	70.00	75.00
☐ American Bibles, New York, 1822, pocket size	55.00	80.00
☐ Audubon, John J., *The Birds of America,* London, 1827-38, "elephant folio", 37" high	250000.00	350000.00
☐ Bierce, Ambrose, *Shapes of Clay,* San Francisco, 1903	130.00	145.00
☐ *Boston Massacre,* short narrative of the horrid massacre in Boston. Boston, 1770	1000.00	1300.00
☐ Buchanan, James, *Sketches of the History, Manners and Customs of the North American Indians,* New York, 1824	90.00	125.00
☐ Burroughs, Edgar Rice, *Jungle Tales of Tarzan,* Chicago, 1919	65.00	75.00
☐ Clemens, Samuel Langhorne ("Mark Twain"), Hartford, 1876. Some bindings in cloth, some leather .	500.00	2000.00
☐ Corry, John, *The Life of George Washington,* New York, 1807	135.00	165.00
☐ Darwin, Charles, *Expression of Emotions in Man and Animals,* London, 1872, First Edition	80.00	100.00
☐ Dickens, Charles, *A Christmas Carol,* New York, 1844	40.00	60.00
☐ Dickinson, Emily, *Poems,* 3rd series, Boston, 1896. 1st issue has "Roberts Brothers" stamped on spine ..	225.00	250.00

BOOKS

	Price	Range
☐ Disney, Walt, *Who's Afraid of the Big Bad Wolf,* Philadelphia, 1933	55.00	65.00
☐ Ellsworth, H.W., *Teacher's Guide to Ellsworth's New System of Practical Penmanship,* New York, 1864	35.00	45.00
☐ Faulkner, William, *The Hamlet,* New York, 1940, black cloth cover	225.00	250.00
☐ Fitzgerald, F. Scott, *The Great Gatsby,* New York, 1925, green cloth cover	110.00	125.00
☐ Ford, Paul, *Bibliography of Benjamin Franklin,* Brooklyn, 1889	110.00	120.00
☐ Frost, John, *History of the State of California,* Auburn, 1853	55.00	70.00
☐ Griffith, G.W.E., *My 96 Years in the Great West,* Los Angeles, 1929	30.00	45.00
☐ Hart, Charles Henry, *A Biographical Sketch of His Excellency, Abraham Lincoln, Late President of The United States,* Albany, 1870	110.00	160.00
☐ Hemingway, Ernest, *For Whom the Bell Tolls,* New York, 1940, light tan cloth cover	105.00	155.00
☐ Henderson, W.A., *A Modern Domestic Cookery and Useful Receipt Book,* Boston, 1844	110.00	125.00
☐ Hitchcock, Nevada D., *The Record War-Time Cookbook,* Philadelphia, 1918	8.00	10.00
☐ Holmes, Oliver Wendell, *Dissertations,* Boston, 1836	80.00	100.00
☐ Irving, Washington, *The Rocky Mountains,* Philadelphia, 1837	130.00	165.00
☐ James, Henry, *Traveling Companions,* New York, 1919, green cloth cover	90.00	110.00
☐ Kelmscott Press, 1895, *The Life and Death of Jason,* by William Morris	350.00	400.00
☐ Kipling, Rudyard, *Abaft the Funnell,* New York, 1909	35.00	45.00
☐ Longfellow, Henry Wadsworth, *Tales of a Wayside Inn,* Boston, 1858	40.00	55.00
☐ Mitchell, Margaret, *Gone With The Wind,* New York, May 1936	120.00	170.00
☐ Nebraska Ned, *Buffalo Bill and his Daring Adventures in the West,* Baltimore, n.d.(1913), 192 pp., soft bound	125.00	135.00
☐ Newton, Isaac, *Universal Arithmetick, or, A Treatise of Arithmetical Composition and Resolution,* London, 1728	55.00	80.00
☐ Nightingale, Florence, *Notes on Hospitals,* Third Edition, London, 1863	80.00	100.00
☐ Reidesel, Madam, *Letters and Memoirs Relating to the War of American Independence,* 1827	110.00	125.00
☐ Rodier, Paul, *The Romance of French Weaving,* New York, 1931	18.00	25.00
☐ Scott, Sir Walter, *The Lady of the Lake,* London, 1863	110.00	125.00
☐ Seligman, G.S. & Hughes, E.T., *Domestic Needlework,* London, 1926	110.00	120.00

BOOKS

Price Range

- [ ] Shakespeare, William, *Shakespeare's Comedies, Histories and Tragedies,* London, 1685 .... 5000.00 7500.00
- [ ] Siringo, Charles A., *A Texas Cowboy,* Chicago, 1885 .. 300.00 500.00
- [ ] Soyer, Alexis, *Modern Housewife,* New York, 1866 ... 30.00 35.00
- [ ] Standish, Burt L., *Frank Merriwell's Tact,* New York, n.d.(1910), soft bound 12.00 15.00
- [ ] Steinbeck, John, *The Grapes of Wrath,* New York, 1940, two volumes, cloth with leather spine 160.00 175.00
- [ ] Stowe, Harriett Beecher, *Uncle Sam's Emancipation,* Philadelphia, 1853 .... 85.00 100.00
- [ ] Studen, J.H. & Jasper, T., *The Birds of North America,* Columbus, Ohio, 1878, 2 volumes 225.00 260.00
- [ ] Thackeray, William M., *The Four Georges,* New York, 1860 .... 110.00 125.00
- [ ] Triplett, Frank, *The Life, Times and Treacherous Death of Jesse James,* Chicago, 1882 .... 350.00 550.00
- [ ] Vale Press. Blake, William, *The Book of Thel,* Songs of Innocence and Songs of Experience, n.d. (1897) ... 70.00 90.00
- [ ] Walton, Izaak, *The Complete Angler,* London, 1842 ... 115.00 140.00
- [ ] Wilder, Thornton, *The Angel that Troubled the Waters,* New York, 1928, signed, Ltd. 40.00 65.00
- [ ] Wilkins, John, *The Mathematical and Philosophical Works of the Right Reverend John Wilkins, Late Lord Bishop of Chester,* London, 1708 .... 150.00 165.00
- [ ] Williams, Tennessee, *The Glass Menagerie,* New York, 1945 .... 75.00 110.00

BIBLES

- [ ] American Bible, Trenton, New Jersey, 1791 .... 550.00 1000.00
- [ ] American Bible, Brooke County, Virginia, 1826 ...... 550.00 800.00
- [ ] Ashendene Press' 20th C Book of Ecclasiasticus 300.00 500.00
- [ ] Bible in English, London, E. Whytechurche, 1553 .... 800.00 1300.00
- [ ] Biblia Latina, Venice, Nicolaus Jenson, 1479 .... 800.00 1000.00
- [ ] John Field's Bible, mid-1600's, woodcuts 35.00 50.00
- [ ] Nonesuch Press 5-volume Bible, 1924-27 .... 75.00 140.00
- [ ] 19th C Miniature Bible 45.00 55.00

CHILDRENS' BOOKS

- [ ] Abbott, Jacob, *Marco Polo's Travels & Adventures.* Boston, 1848 .... 25.00 35.00
- [ ] Alcott, Louisa M. *Little Women.* Boston, 1869 .... 25.00 35.00
- [ ] Aldrich, Thomas Bailey. *The Story of a Bad Boy.* Boston, 1870 .... 225.00 275.00
- [ ] Alger, Horatio. *Ragged Dick.* Boston, 1868 .... 700.00 800.00
- [ ] Andersen, H.C. *The Snow Queen.* London, Routledge, n. d., 1890 .... 4.00 6.00
- [ ] Belson, Mary. *The Orphan Boy.* London, 1812 .... 10.00 15.00
- [ ] Caroll, Lewis. *Alice's Adventures in Wonderland.* London, 1865. Rare 10,000.00 12,500.00
- [ ] Caroll, Lewis. *Sylvia & Bruno.* London, 1889 .... 75.00 100.00
- [ ] Carroll, Lewis. *Through the Looking-Glass & What Alice Found There.* London, 1872 .... 150.00 200.00

CHILDREN'S BOOKS

	Price	Range
☐ Carroll, Lewis. *The Hunting of the Snark.* London, 1876	150.00	200.00
☐ Disney, Walt. *The Adventures of Mickey Mouse, Book I.* Philadelphia, 1931	500.00	750.00
☐ Disney, Walt. *Who's Afraid of the Big Bad Wolf.* Philadelphia, 1933	75.00	125.00
☐ Field, Eugene. *Little Willie.*	20.00	25.00
☐ Graham, Kenneth. *Fun o' the Fiar.* London, 1929	25.00	30.00
☐ Greenaway, Kate. *Kate Greenaway's Book of Games.* London, n. d., 1889	100.00	140.00
☐ Harris, Joel Chandler. *The Story of Aaron.* New York, 1896	30.00	40.00
☐ Harris, Joel Chandler. *Uncle Remus, His Songs & His Sayings.* N. Y., 1881	300.00	350.00
☐ Howells, William Dean. *A Boy's Town.* N. Y., 1890	20.00	30.00
☐ Lear, Edward. *A Book of Nonsense.* London, 1861	225.00	275.00
☐ Lofting, Hugh. *The Story of Dr. Dolittle.* N. Y., 1923	12.00	18.00
☐ Milne, A. A. *Winnie-the-Pooh.* London, 1926	125.00	150.00
☐ Phillips, E. O. *Birdie & Her Dog.* London, 1885	15.00	20.00
☐ Potter, Beatrix. *The Pie & The Patty-pan.* London, 1905	75.00	100.00
☐ Potter, Beatrix. *The Tale of Peter Rabbit.* London, n. d., 1901	475.00	525.00
☐ Potter, Beatrix. *The Tailor of Gloucester.* N. p., n. d., London, 1902	275.00	325.00
☐ Potter, Beatrix. *The Tale of Benjamin Bunny.* London, 1904	60.00	90.00
☐ Ray, Joseph. *Ray's Arithmetic, First Book ... For Young Learners.* Cincinnati, n. d., 1857	15.00	25.00
☐ *Rhymes for the Nursery.* Boston, n. d., 1837	15.00	25.00
☐ Richard, Laura E. *Captain January.* Boston, 1898	20.00	25.00
☐ Sewell, Anna. *Black Beauty.* Boston, n. d., 1890	60.00	75.00
☐ Southey, Robert. *The Story of the Three Bears.* London, 1837	75.00	100.00
☐ Stockton, Frank R. *The Adventures of Captain Horn.* New York, 1895	10.00	15.00
☐ Watson, Henry C. *The Yankee Tea Party.* Philadelphia, 1851	15.00	20.00
☐ Webster, Jean. *Daddy Long Legs.* New York, 1912	50.00	70.00
☐ Wiggin, Kate Douglas. *The Story of Patsy.* Boston, 1890	10.00	15.00

COOKBOOKS

	Price	Range
☐ *Archdeacon's Kitchen Cabinet.* Chicago, 1876	30.00	40.00
☐ Barrows, Anna. *Principles of Cookery.* Chicago, 1910 .	14.00	18.00
☐ Blot, Pierre, *What to Eat & How to Cook It.* N. Y., 1865 .	35.00	50.00
☐ Blot, Pierre, *Hand-Book of Practical Cookery.* N. Y., 1868	18.00	24.00
☐ Brooks, R. O., *Vinegars & Catsup.* N. Y., 1912	8.00	12.00
☐ Brown, Susan Anna, *The Invalid's Tea-Tray.* Boston, 1885	14.00	18.00

COOKBOOKS

Price Range

☐ Clark, Imogen, *Rhymed Receipts for Any Occasion.*
Boston, 1912 .... 15.00 20.00
☐ Cornelius, Mrs., *The Young Housekeeper's Friend.*
Boston & N. Y., 1846 .... 125.00 150.00
☐ Carson, Juliet, *The American Family Cookbook.*
Chicago, 1898 .... 30.00 50.00
☐ Croly, Mrs. J. C., *Jennie June's American Cookery
Book.* N. Y. 1870. .... 30.00 40.00
☐ *Dainty Dishes for Slender Incomes.* N. Y., 1900 ...... 15.00 20.00
☐ Decker, John W., *Cheese Making.* Wisconsin, 1909 ... 25.00 35.00
☐ *Dining & Its Amenities.* "By a Lover of Good Cheer."
N. Y., 1907 .... 20.00 30.00
☐ *Favorite Cook Book.* N. Y., 1891 .... 14.00 18.00
☐ Gillette, Mrs. F. L., *White House Cook Book.*
Chicago, 1889 .... 70.00 80.00
☐ Henderson, W. A., *Modern Domestic Cooker &
Useful Receipt Book.* Boston, 1844 .... 120.00 135.00
☐ Hilliard, Thomas M., *The Art of Carving.*
Detroit, n. d., 1899 .... 8.00 14.00
☐ Hurtzler, Victor., *The Hotel Francis Cook Book.*
Chicago, 1919 .... 10.00 15.00
☐ Hitchcock, Nevada D., *The Record War-Time Cook
Book.* Philadelphia, 1918 .... 8.00 14.00
☐ Heug, H., *New Book of Designs for Cake-Bakers,* etc.
N.p., 1893 .... 18.00 25.00
☐ Kirwan, A. V., *Host & Guest.* London, 1864 .... 18.00 25.00
☐ King, Chas. H., *Cakes, Cake Decorations & Desserts*
Philadelphia, 1896 .... 25.00 30.00
☐ *Kitchen Directory & American Housewife.* N. Y., 1844.
Softbound 50.00 75.00
☐ Kitchiner. Wm., *The Cook's Oracle.* Boston, 1822 .... 75.00 100.00
☐ Lambert, Mrs. Almeda., *Guide for Nut Cookery.*
Battle Creek, Michigan, 1899 .... 90.00 100.00
☐ Langdon, Amelie., *Just for Two.* Minneapolis, 1907 ... 7.50 10.00
☐ Leslie, Miss, *Directions for Cookery.* Philadelphia,
1863. 59th edition 15.00 20.00
☐ Lincoln, Mrs. D. A., *Boston School Kitchen Text-Book.*
Boston, 1887 .... 20.00 25.00
☐ Lockhart, Marion., *Standard Cook Book for All
Occasions.* N. Y., 1925 .... 7.50 10.00
☐ MacDougall, A. F., *Coffee & Waffles.* N. Y., 1927 ..... 7.50 10.00
☐ MacKenzie, Colin, *MacKenzie's Five Thousand
Recipes.* Philadelphia, 1825 .... 125.00 150.00
☐ Muckenstrum, Louis, *Louis' Every Woman's Cook
Book.* Boston & N. Y., 1910 .... 12.50 15.00
☐ *National Cook Book,* "By a Lady of Philadelphia."
Philadelphia, 1855. Fifth edition 100.00 150.00
☐ Nelson, Harriet S., *Fruits & Their Cookery.* N. Y. 1921 . 10.00 15.00
☐ Nicol, Mary E., *366 Dinners.* By "M.E.N." N. Y., 1892. ... 15.00 20.00

COOKBOOKS

	Price	Range
☐ Norton, Caroline T., *The Rocky Mountain Cook Book.* Denver, 1903	25.00	35.00
☐ Owens, Mrs. F., *Cook Book & Useful Household Hints.* Chicago, 1883	20.00	25.00
☐ Parloa, Maria, *The Appledore Cook Book.* Boston, 1878	25.00	35.00
☐ Paul, Mrs. Sara T., *Cookery from Experience.* Philadelphia, 1875	25.00	50.00
☐ Pereira, J., *A Treatise on Food & Diet.* N. Y., 1843	30.00	40.00
☐ Poindexter, Charlotte M., *Jane Hamilton's Recipes.* Chicago, 1909	15.00	20.00
☐ Poole, H. M., *Fruits & How to Use Them.* N. Y., 1890	12.50	15.00
☐ Randolph, Mary, *The Virginia Housewife, or Methodical Cook.* Washington, D. C., 1830	350.00	500.00
☐ Ranholfer, Charles, *The Epicurean.* N. Y., 1900	35.00	50.00
☐ Rees, Mrs. Jennie Day, *The Complete Cook Book* Philadelphia, 1900	5.00	10.00
☐ Rice, Louise, *Dainty Dishes from Foreign Lands.* Chicago, 1911	10.00	15.00
☐ Robinson, Mrs. H. M., *The Practical Cook Book.* N. Y., 1864	35.00	50.00
☐ Ronald, Mary, *Century Cook Book.* N. Y., 1895	25.00	35.00
☐ Rorer, Sarah Tyson, *Mrs. Rorer's Cakes, Icings & Fillings.* Philadelphia, 1905	15.00	20.00
☐ Rundell, Maria E., *A New System of Domestic Cookery.* Boston, 1807	150.00	200.00
☐ Sala, Geo. A., *The Thorough Good Cook.* N. Y., 1896	50.00	75.00
☐ Scott, Mrs. Anna B., *Mrs. Scott's North American Seasonal Cook Book.* Philadelpia, 1921	15.00	20.00
☐ *Secrets of Meat Curing & Sausage Making.* Chicago, 1911	30.00	50.00
☐ Senn, C. Herman, *The Book of Sauces.* Chicago, 1915	5.00	10.00
☐ Shute, Miss T. S., *The American Housewife Cook Book.* Philadelphia, 1878	30.00	35.00
☐ Simonds. J., *The American Book of Recipes.* Boston, 1854	35.00	50.00
☐ Southworth, May E., *101 Chafing-Dish Recipes.* San Francisco, 1904	15.00	20.00
☐ Stanford, Martha P., *The Old & New Cook Book.* New Orleans, 1904	75.00	100.00
☐ Stanton, Mrs. Florence, *The Practical Housekeeper.* Philadelphia, 1901	25.00	50.00
☐ *Table Talk's Illustrated Cook Book.* Philadelphia, 1901	25.00	50.00
☐ Taylor, Jennie, *The Surprise Cook Book.* N. Y., 1889	7.50	10.00
☐ Tilden, Joe, *Joe Tilden's Recipes for Epicures.* San Francisco, 1907	25.00	35.00
☐ Tschirky, Oscar, *The Cook Book by "Oscar" of the Waldorf.* Chicago, 1896	35.00	50.00

COOKBOOKS

Price Range

☐ Tyree, Marion Cabell, *Housekeeping in Old Virginia.* Louisville, 1890	50.00	75.00
☐ Wallace, L. H., *The Modern Cook Book.* N. Y., 1912 ...	10.00	15.00
☐ Ward, Artemas, *The Encyclopedia of Food.* N. Y., 1923	100.00	150.00
☐ *What Shall We Eat?* N. Y., 1868	20.00	25.00
☐ Wheeler, Eliza Ann, *The Frugal Housekeepers Kitchen Companion.* N. Y., 1848	25.00	35.00
☐ White, Mrs. Peter A., *The Kentucky Cookery Book.* Chicago, 1891	50.00	75.00
☐ Wilson, Mrs. Mary A., *Wilson's Cook Book.* Philadelphia, 1920	25.00	35.00
☐ Ysaguirre & LaMarca. *Cold Dishes for Hot Weather.* N. Y., 1896	7.50	10.00

DETECTIVE FICTION

☐ Boothby, Guy, *A Bid for Fortune.* N. Y., First Am. edition	20.00	30.00
☐ Boothby, Guy, *Curse of the Snake.* London, 1902	15.00	20.00
☐ Chandler, Raymond, *The Big Sleep.* London, 1939	25.00	30.00
☐ Chandler, Raymond, *The Little Sister.* London, 1949	12.50	18.00
☐ Chandler, Raymond, *The Simple Art of Murder.* London, 1950	10.00	15.00
☐ Chandler, Raymond, *Spanish Blood.* Cleveland/New York, 1946	25.00	35.00
☐ Christie, Agatha, *Easy to Kill.* N. Y., 1939. First Am edition	12.50	18.00
☐ Christie, Agatha, *Hercule Poirot's Christmas* London, 1939	12.50	18.00
☐ Christie, Agatha, *The Hollow.* London, 1946	12.50	18.00
☐ Christie, Agatha, *A Murder is Announced* N. Y., n. d. (1950)	12.50	15.00
☐ Christie, Agatha, *The Mysterious Mr. Quinn* London, 1930	25.00	35.00
☐ Christie, Agatha, *Taken at the Flood* London, 1948 ...	15.00	25.00
☐ Collins, Wilkie, *The Moonstone.* London, 1868. Three vols. Violet cloth. Rare. The first detective story in the English language in book form.		1250.00
☐ Doyle, Sir Arthur C., *The Adventures of Sherlock Holmes.* London, 1892-4. Two vols. Blue cloth	200.00	250
☐ Doyle, Sir Arthur C., *The Adventures of Sherlock Holmes.* N. Y., n. d. (1892). Blue cloth. Not the first issue	18.00	25.00
☐ Doyle, Sir Arthur C., *My Friend the Murderer.* N. Y., n. d. (1893)	18.00	25.00
☐ Doyle, Sir Arthur C., *The Memoirs of Sherlock Holmes.* London, 1894. Dark blue cloth	200.00	225.00
☐ Doyle, Sir Arthur C., *The Hound of the Baskervilles.* London, 1902. Red cloth.	400.00	500.00
☐ Doyle, Sir Arthur C., *The Return of Sherlock Holmes.* London, 1904. Dark blue cloth.	300.00	350.00

DETECTIVE FICTION

	Price	Range
☐ Doyle, Sir Arthur C., *Sir Nigel.* London, 1906.	125.00	150.00
☐ Doyle, Sir Arthur C., *The Croxley Master.* N. Y., 1907 . .	250.00	300.00
☐ Doyle, Sir Arthur C., *The Poison Belt.* N. Y., 1913	25.00	35.00
☐ Doyle, Sir Arthur C., *The Case Book of Sherlock Holmes.* London, n. d. (1927). Red cloth.	100.00	125.00
☐ Fleming, Ian, *Casino Royale.* London, 1950	20.00	30.00
☐ Fleming, Ian, *Diamonds are Forever.* London, 1956 . . .	10.00	15.00
☐ Fleming, Ian, *Dr. No.* London, 1958	10.00	15.00
☐ Fleming, Ian, *Goldfinger.* London, 1959	10.00	15.00
☐ Gardner, Erle Stanley, *The Case of the Howling Dog* N. Y., 1934	10.00	15.00
☐ Queen, Ellery, *The Adventures of Ellery Queen.* London, 1935.	20.00	25.00
☐ Sayers, Dorothy L., *Begin Here.* London, 1940	10.00	15.00
☐ Sayers, Dorothy L., *Busman's Honeymoon.* London, 1937.	10.00	15.00
☐ Sayers, Dorothy L., *Gaudy Night.* London, 1935	15.00	25.00
☐ Sayers, Dorothy L., *In the Teeth of Evidence.* London, 1939.	20.00	25.00
☐ Sayers, Dorothy L., *Murder Must Advertise.* London, 1933.	10.00	15.00

BOTTLES

Bottle-collecting is growing in popularity because of the variety available, and the intrigue of the hunt. Many collectors actually go on bottle digs—like archaeologists—and find their choicest examples on the sites of old city dumps. Other types of collectible bottles are those which were manufactured in interesting figural shapes to appeal to collectors; examples of these are Avons and various whiskey bottles. For information, please consult our *Official Price Guide to Bottles, New and Old,* by Dot and Carlo Sellari.

AVON

Avon began as the California Perfume Company in 1886. In 1926 the name Avon was used and in 1939 the company became Avon Products, Inc. They are made in varied shapes and filled with cosmetic products.

	Price	Range
☐ Abraham Lincoln Decanter, 1971	2.00	3.00
☐ After Bath, Refreshers, 1964	3.00	4.00
☐ After Shave, 1951	3.00	5.00
☐ After Shave, 1964 4-A	8.00	10.00
☐ After Shower, 1959	25.00	60.00
☐ Aladdin's Lamp, 1971	6.00	8.00
☐ All Purpose Bottle, 1937	10.00	20.00
☐ Alpine Flask, 1966	35.00	50.00
☐ American Beauty Fragrance Jars, footed	80.00	100.00
☐ American Ideal Perfume, 1 oz., CPC	85.00	110.00
☐ American Ideal Talc, 1917, 3½ oz. CPC	70.00	120.00
☐ Angel, Golden, 1968	3.00	6.00
☐ Atomizer Set CPC White Rose, 1908	100.00	and up
☐ Attention Set, 1957	12.00	35.00
☐ Baby Set, CPC Powder & Toilet Water	100.00	175.00
☐ Bandoline Hair Dressing, CPC 1915	40.00	50.00
☐ Bath Seasons, 1967	3.00	5.00
☐ Bath Urn, 1971	2.50	4.50
☐ Beauty Basket, 2 bottles, 1947	20.00	65.00
☐ Bird of Paradise, bird shaped bottle, 1970	7.00	9.00
☐ Boxing Gloves, plastic bottles, 1960	12.00	24.00
☐ Bright Night Cologne, 1954	10.00	15.00
☐ Buttons -N- Bows Cologne with bow on neck, 1963	4.00	8.50
☐ Captain's Choice, green after-shave bottle	4.50	8.00
☐ Casey's Lantern, 1966	8.00	18.00
☐ Charisma, Circle of Pearls, set 1957	20.00	55.00
☐ Close Harmony, barber bottle, 1963	10.00	25.00
☐ Cologne Mist, ribbed bottle, 1968	2.00	4.00
☐ Cotillion Deluxe, 3 bottle set boxed, 1953	32.00	65.00
☐ Cotillion Duo, 2 bottle set boxed, 1964	10.00	16.00
☐ Country Gardens, jar with ribbon, 1971	2.50	4.50
☐ Courtship Perfume, 1938	20.00	50.00
☐ Crystal Cologne, 1966	2.00	5.00
☐ Daisies Won't Tell Cologne with white cap, 1957	3.00	7.00
☐ Daisies Won't Tell Deodorant, 1963	2.50	4.50
☐ Elegante Cologne, swirl bottle, 1957	8.00	12.00
☐ Elegante Excalibur, 1969	4.00	7.00
☐ Fair Lady, 4 bottle set, 1940	75.00	90.00
☐ Fashion Figurine, Old Time Costume Bottle, 1971	3.50	6.00
☐ Field Flowers, Umbrella, 1971	3.00	5.00
☐ First Edition Gift Set, 1967	8.00	10.00
☐ Flowertime Set, 2 bottles boxed, 1949	20.00	40.00
☐ Flowertime Talc, 1949	8.00	17.50
☐ Fox Hunt, 1966	8.00	15.00
☐ Garden of Love Perfume, plastic handle, 1940	11.00	16.00

AVON

	Price	Range
☐ Gardenia Perfume, gold cap, 1940	40.00	60.00
☐ Gentlemen's Selection, 1970	2.00	3.00
☐ Greek Warrior, blue and silver warrior head bottle	7.00	12.00
☐ Hair Lotion, Avon label, 1957	4.00	8.00
☐ Happy Times, 3 piece set, 1951	20.00	45.00
☐ Heartfelt, 2 piece set boxed, 1964	20.00	30.00
☐ Here's My Heart, Lady Slipper, bottle with bow, 1970	9.00	12.00
☐ Here's My Heart, perfume, ½ oz., 1948	100.00	150.00
☐ Icicle, 1967	4.00	5.00
☐ Island Lime, straw-wrapped bottle, 1966	2.00	4.50
☐ Jardin d'Amour Perfume, 1954	100.00	150.00
☐ Jasmine Bath Salts, black top, 1946	10.00	20.00
☐ Just Two, tall faceted bottles	20.00	45.00
☐ King Pin, bowling pin bottle, 1969	3.00	5.00
☐ Lavender Fragrance Jar, CPC 8 oz. jar	100.00	150.00
☐ Liberty Bell, bell shape bottle, 1971	2.00	4.00
☐ Lily of the Valley Perfume, CPC 7 dram.	70.00	85.00
☐ Little Champ, 1967	2.00	4.00
☐ Lucy Hays Perfume, small bottle, 1936	20.00	40.00
☐ Luscious Perfume, small bottle, 1950	8.00	12.00
☐ Mallard, duck shape bottle, 1967	6.00	8.50
☐ Marness Cologne, round bottle, 1955	10.00	20.00
☐ Occur, One I Love, 3 bottle set, 1957	25.00	50.00
☐ Packard Roadster, antique car shape, 1970	4.00	6.00
☐ Persian Wood, cologne mist, 1956	4.50	9.00
☐ Pony Express, horse & rider bottle, 1971	2.00	5.00
☐ Quaintance Perfume, 3 dram in box, 1949	50.00	75.00
☐ Rapture Perfume Oil bottle, 1964	6.50	8.50
☐ Rapture Perfume Rocker bottle, 1960	4.50	8.50
☐ Rapture Rhapsody, set with tray, 1964	10.00	25.00
☐ Riviera Cologne, gold top, 1968	3.00	6.00
☐ Royal Orb, round bottle with orb top, 1965	10.00	30.00
☐ Saddle Kit, 3 piece set with "cowskin" box, 1970	14.00	18.00
☐ Skin So Soft, glass bottle, 1962	8.00	10.00
☐ Skin So Soft, urn bottle, gold top, 1965	8.50	12.00
☐ Somewhere Perfume, 1 oz., 1961	60.00	75.00
☐ Somewhere Perfume Oil, glass, 1964	6.00	12.00
☐ Sparkler, Christmas bulb bottle, 1968	5.00	6.00
☐ Sparkling Burgundy, set, 1957	40.00	60.00
☐ Spicy Cologne Plus, square bottle, 1965	4.00	10.00
☐ Spring Goddess, 3 piece set, 1957	40.00	50.00
☐ Swinger, golf bag & clubs bottle, 1969	6.50	12.00
☐ Tail Winds, after shave bottle, 5 oz., 1971	2.00	4.00
☐ To A Wild Rose, bath oil bottle, 1953	8.50	15.00
☐ To A Wild Rose Perfume, 1 oz. square top, 1959	50.00	100.00
☐ To A Wild Rose Town Pump, old pump bottle, 1968	2.50	4.50
☐ Unforgettable Beauty Dust, 1965	3.50	6.50
☐ Unforgettable Cologne Mist bottle, 1965	2.00	4.00
☐ Unforgettable Valet Set, 2 pieces with box, 1949	16.00	32.00

AVON

	Price	Range
☐ Unforgettable Western Choice, steer horns with gold tips, 1967	16.00	22.00
☐ Weather or Not, barometer shape bottle, 1969	4.00	7.00
☐ Wild Rose Set, body powder and cologne, 1951	10.00	20.00
☐ Wishing Cream Lotion, milk glass, 1963	3.00	4.00
☐ Young Hearts "Honey Bun" 2 piece set, 1954	11.00	22.00
☐ Young Hearts Set, bubble bath cologne talc, 1954	22.00	45.00

BARBER

These bottles are by far the most attractive and are prized for their artistic value. They were made of clear, colored, and milk glass and used primarily for dispensing after shave lotion and witch hazel.

	Price
☐ Amethyst, white flowers, gold leaves	75.00
☐ Art Nouveau design	60.00
☐ Blue-green, 8½" with label	18.00
☐ Bohemian floral enamel design, 8½"	65.00
☐ Camphor White "Witch Hazel"	72.00
☐ Chartruese, enameled design, 8½"	65.00
☐ Clear with enameled flowers	24.00
☐ Cut glass, pewter top	30.00
☐ End-of-Day, white on amber	65.00
☐ Flowers on white satin	75.00
☐ Green checkered	63.00
☐ Green imprinted glass, bulb-shaped	65.00
☐ Hobnail amber, 8"	45.00
☐ Hobnail Vaseline	85.00
☐ Honey amber, floral design, pewter spout	68.00
☐ Honey amber, quilted pattern, porcelain stopper	85.00
☐ Lime green, 8", 19th century	60.00
☐ Mary Gregory, amethyst with girl, 1900's	185.00
☐ Milk glass, white, 9", sunken label	17.00
☐ Milk glass, white, unembossed	15.00
☐ Milk glass, white, stenciled, 9"	25.00
☐ Milk glass, white, hexagonal base	55.00
☐ Milk glass, white, "Water"	20.00
☐ Opalescent swirl, 9"	75.00
☐ Opaque, 8"	45.00
☐ Milk Glass, pink, 8½"	50.00
☐ Purple Slag, 8"	82.00
☐ Red, 3½"	16.00
☐ Sapphire blue with brown thumbprint	95.00
☐ Satin glass, 10¼", white loops on cranberry, pewter stopper	165.00
☐ Spanish lace in cranberry	75.00
☐ Stars & Stripes, 1890's	75.00
☐ Tiffany style	160.00
☐ Wedgwood, three colors, embossed, classical scenes	695.00

BEAM

In 1953 the James Beam Distilling Company designed a decanter for the Christmas season. This first issue was a fabulous success and was the start of the many variety "Beam" bottles. Most of the bottles are produced in fine regal china.

	Price Range	
☐ Alaska (1958), star-shaped bottle, turquoise blue and gold, Regal china, 9½" high	80.00	90.00
☐ Agnew Elephant (1970), political	1600.00	2000.00
☐ Arizona (1968-69), scene of canyon, Regal china, 12" high	4.00	6.00
☐ Baseball (1969), Centennial	7.00	9.00
☐ Bing Crosby National Pro-Am (1970-73), replicas of Crosby hat, pipe and golf club	18.00	25.00
☐ Blue Jay (1969), bird in sky-blue with black and white markings	8.00	15.00
☐ Blue Cherub (1960) (Executive)	150.00	200.00
☐ Blue Fox (1967), Trophy	9.00	13.00
☐ Blue Gill (1974), Trophy	9.00	13.00
☐ Bohemian Girl (1974), Regal china	18.00	25.00
☐ Cardinal (1968), Kentucky cardinal	30.00	50.00
☐ Cardinal (1973), female	14.00	21.00
☐ Cats (1967), trio of cats, Regal china, 11½" high	10.00	15.00
☐ Churchhill Downs (1969-70), 95th Anniversary	7.00	10.00
☐ Clear Bourbon Crystal (1967), glass specialty	4.00	7.00
☐ Cleopatra Yellow (1962), glass specialty	15.00	18.00
☐ Coffee Warmer (1954), glass specialty	16.00	23.00
☐ Colorado (1959), light turquoise with pioneers	45.00	60.00
☐ "Dancing Scot", glass specialty	11.00	20.00
☐ Doe (1963), pure white neck markings, Regal china, 13½" high	25.00	35.00
☐ Doe, English (1959), pink speckled	600.00	650.00
☐ Dog, English Setter (1959)	60.00	72.00
☐ Dog (1959), long-eared Setter dog, Regal china, 15½" high	65.00	85.00
☐ Duck (1957), green Mallard, Regal china, 14½" high . .	35.00	55.00
☐ Eagle (1966), Regal china, 14½" high	15.00	20.00
☐ Elephant and Donkey (1960), political	24.00	32.00
☐ Fiesta Bowl (1973), genuine Regal china, football player	10.00	15.00
☐ First National Bank of Chicago (1964), blue circular bottle	2750.00	3500.00
☐ Fish (1957), sailfish, Regal china, 12¼" high	35.00	55.00
☐ Florida Shell (1968-69), two colors, Regal china, 9¾" high	5.00	9.00
☐ Football Hall of Fame (1972), stopper shaped like half of a football, 9¾" high	8.00	16.00
☐ Fox (1965), bushy tailed fox, Regal china, 12¼" high .	35.00	55.00
☐ Golden Chalice (1961), grey blue body with gold accents	70.00	100.00

BEAM

	Price	Range
☐ Grey Cherub (1958), checkered design, 12" high	300.00	375.00
☐ Grand Canyon (1969)	12.00	21.00
☐ Great Dane (1976)	16.00	17.00
☐ Grecian (1956)	3.50	5.25
☐ Germany Bottle—Weisbaden (1973), Regal china	8.00	12.00
☐ Hannah Duston (1973)	12.00	22.00
☐ Harrolds Club (1957), Man in a Barrel, 14¾" high	400.00	525.00
☐ Harvey's Wagonwheel (1969)	5.00	12.00
☐ Harold's Club V.I.P. (1967), Customer Special	59.00	70.00
☐ Harold's Club Covered Wagon (1974)	19.00	23.00
☐ Idaho (1963), shape of Idaho state, Regal china, 12¼" high	70.00	85.00
☐ Jackalope (1971), Regal china, 14" high	12.00	20.00
☐ Jackalope (1972), Regal china	22.00	30.00
☐ Jug, Oatmeal (1966)	35.00	42.00
☐ Kansas (1960-61), leather thong, Regal china, 11¾" high	70.00	85.00
☐ Katz Cat (1967), yellow, Customer Specialties	20.00	30.00
☐ Katz Cat (1968), black, Customer Specialties	8.00	14.00
☐ Kentucky Black Head—Brown Head (1967), Regal china, 11½" high	12.00	22.00
☐ London Bridge (1971)	23.00	28.00
☐ Manitowac Submarine (1970), Trophy	9.00	15.00
☐ Mark Anthony (1962)	20.00	24.00
☐ Majestic (1966), royal blue decantur, 14½" high	40.00	50.00
☐ Marbled Fantasy (1965), decantur on marble base....	80.00	95.00
☐ Nebraska (1967), round bottle, Regal china, 12¼" high	10.00	15.00
☐ Nebraska Football (1972), Bob Devaney, head coach, 8¾" high...............................	6.00	12.00
☐ Nevada (1964), circular bottle, Regal china, 12¼" high	60.00	75.00
☐ New Hampshire (1967-68), shape of the state, Regal china, 13½" high	8.00	12.00
☐ New Jersey (1963-64), Regal china, pyramid shaped, 13½" high.......................	70.00	85.00
☐ North Dakota (1964), Regal china, 11¾" high	95.00	120.00
☐ Ohio (1966)	12.00	19.00
☐ Olympian (1960), glass specialty	5.00	10.00
☐ Oregon (1959), green-tone bottle, 8¾" high	40.00	50.00
☐ Pearl Harbor Memorial (1972), stopper is an American eagle, 11½" high.....................	10.00	18.00
☐ Penny the Poodle (1970), grey Trophy	5.00	10.00
☐ Poodle (1970), grey & white, Regal china, 12" high....	14.00	20.00
☐ Prestige (1967), resembles flower basket, 11" high ...	20.00	35.00
☐ Ram (1958), Regal china, 12½" high	180.00	220.00
☐ Redwood (1967), Regal china.....................	12.00	18.00
☐ Robin (1969), olive grey, Regal china, 13½" high	8.00	16.00
☐ Royal Gold Round (1956), classic shape, 12" high	135.00	160.00

BEAM

Price Range

- [ ] St. Louis Statue (1972), St. Louis on horseback, 13¼" high .... 18.00 · 28.00
- [ ] Santa Fe (1960), 350th anniv. of city, 10" high 200.00 300.00
- [ ] Slot Machine (1968), grey, Regal china 5.00 12.00
- [ ] Smoked Crystal Genie (1964) 5.00 15.00
- [ ] Tavern Scene (1959), Executive 80.00 95.00
- [ ] Texas Rabbit (1971), Trophy 8.00 16.00
- [ ] Tiffany (1973) 10.00 18.00
- [ ] U.S. Open (1972), Pebble Beach, CA Golf Tournament, 10½" high 15.00 18.00
- [ ] Uncle Sam Fox (1971), Club 10.00 15.00
- [ ] Woodpecker (1969), Regal china, 13½" high 7.00 15.00
- [ ] West Virginia (1963), 1863 Centennial 180.00 200.00
- [ ] Wyoming (1965), Regal china, 12" high 70.00 85.00
- [ ] Yosemite (1967) 10.00 14.00
- [ ] Yuma Rifle (1968), Regal china 6.00 14.00

BITTERS

Bitters bottles are prized by collectors because they came in a range of sizes and shapes. They were generally filled with remedies for stomach and digestive disorders.

- [ ] Abbott's Bitters, round, amber, machine made 8.50 10.50
- [ ] African Stomach Bitters, round, amber 40.00 80.00
- [ ] American Stomach Bitters, oval clear glass, 9" high .. 22.00 32.00
- [ ] Atwood's Quinine Tonic Bottles, rectangular, aqua, 8½" high................................. 44.00 54.00
- [ ] Atwood's Jaundice Bitters, aqua, 12-sided, 6¼" high . 5.50 8.50
- [ ] Angostura Bark Bitters, figural bottle, amber, 7" high . 40.00 50.00
- [ ] Bavarian Bitters "Hoffheimer Brothers", amber, 9½" high 75.00 100.00
- [ ] Big Bill Best Bitters, amber, 12" high, embossed ..... 100.00 and up
- [ ] Bourbon Whiskey Bitters, amber, 9" high 60.00 80.00
- [ ] Brown's Aromatic Bitters, oval, aqua, 8¼" high 60.00 80.00
- [ ] Burdock Blood Bitters, square, machine made, aqua . 6.00 12.00
- [ ] Carpathian Herb Bitters, amber, 8½" high 60.00 80.00
- [ ] Carter's Liver Bitters, oval, amber, 8 5/8" high 85.00 95.00
- [ ] Clarke's Giant Bitters, rectangular, aqua, 6¾" high .. 35.00 55.00
- [ ] Dandelion XXX Bitters, rectangular, clear, 7¾" high . 40.00 70.00
- [ ] Doyle's Hop Bitters, square, light amber, "1872", 9½" high 20.00 50.00
- [ ] Dr. Flint's Quaker Bitters, rectangular, "Providence, R.I.", aqua, 9 5/8" high 20.00 50.00
- [ ] Golden Seal Bitters, square, amber, 9" high 80.00 100.00
- [ ] Granger Bitters, 3 different Anchor sizes, flask bottles, 7 7/8" high 8.00 22.00
- [ ] Hall's Bitters, barrel-shaped, pale amber, dark amber, 9½" high 100.00 150.00
- [ ] Dr. Henley's California Bitters, sky blue, W. Frank & Sons, Pittsburgh, Pa.................. 40.00 60.00

BITTERS

Price Range

- [ ] Hops and Malt Bitters, cabin-type bottle,
  yellow amber, 9 5/8" high 60.00   90.00
- [ ] Iron Bitters, square, "Brown Chemical Co.",
  8 5/8" high 15.00   30.00
- [ ] Kennedy's East India Bitters, square, clear
  glass, 9" high 35.00   55.00
- [ ] King Soloman Bitters, Seattle, Wash.,
  rectangular, amber, 8½" high 75.00   95.00
- [ ] Lincoln Bitters, rectangular, labeled, clear
  glass, 9 3/8" high 10.00   20.00
- [ ] Litthauer Stomach Bitters, gin shape bottle,
  milk glass, 9¼" high 90.00   100.00
- [ ] McKeever's Army Bitters, round, drum shape,
  amber, 10½" high 350.00   500.00
- [ ] Nightcap Bitters, multi-sided bottle, clear
  glass, 9 3/8" high 60.00   80.00
- [ ] O'Leary's 20th Century Bitters, square,
  amber, 8½" high 75.00   95.00
- [ ] Oriental Tonic Bitters, amber, 10" high .... 65.00   and up
- [ ] Paine's Celery Compound Bitters, rectangular,
  amber, 8" high 5.00   14.00
- [ ] D. Planett's Bitters, iron pontil, aqua, 9¾" high 50.00   85.00
- [ ] Penn's for the Liver Bitters, square, amber, 8½" high . 50.00   60.00
- [ ] Red Cloud Bitters, square, "Taylor & Wright",
  green, 9½" high 80.00   100.00
- [ ] Red Jacket Bitters, square, "Bennet & Pieters",
  amber, 9½" high 50.00   70.00
- [ ] Royal Pepsin Stomach Bitters, rectangular,
  amber, 9" high 65.00   85.00
- [ ] Sanborn's Laxative Bitters, rectangular, labeled,
  clear glass, 10" high 10.00   20.00
- [ ] Schroeder's Bitters, Kentucky, CWC bottom, amber .. 150.00   200.00
- [ ] Dr. Skinner's Sherry Wine Bitters, rectangular,
  "So. Reading, Mass.", aqua, pontil, 8½" high 60.00   90.00
- [ ] Dr. Stoever's Bitters, square, "Kryer & Co.",
  amber, 9" high 50.00   80.00
- [ ] Tufts Tonic Bitters, rectangular, labeled,
  aqua, 9" high 10.00   14.00
- [ ] Old Dr. Townsend's Celebrated Stomach Bitters,
  handled jug, light amber, 8¾" high .... 110.00   and up
- [ ] Peter Vierling's Blood Purifying Bitters, square,
  amber, 10" high 60.00   90.00
- [ ] West India Stomach Bitters, square, amber,
  "St. Louis, Mo.", 10" high 45.00   70.00
- [ ] Yazoo Valley Bitters, amber, 8¾" high 40.00   60.00
- [ ] Zoeller's Stomach Bitters, rectangular bottle
  amber, 9½" high 60.00   80.00

HISTORICAL FLASKS

Flasks have been collected continuously for almost a century and are the prestige items of bottle collecting. They have been most sought after and continue to skyrocket in price. Because flasks have maintained and gone up in value the market has been flooded with replicas. Novices will do well to consider trading with a reputable dealer.

	Price Range	
☐ Washington & Eagle Flask—pint size, aquamarine. Bust of Washington	200.00	250.00
☐ Washington & Jackson Flask—pint size, olive amber. Bust of Washington in uniform; Jackson in uniform on reverse side	100.00	150.00
☐ Log Cabin Flask—pint size, aquamarine. Cabin with 13 stars above; reverse has barrel with the words "Hard Cider"	310.00	500.00
☐ Jackson & Eagle Flask—quart size, aquamarine. Bust of Jackson; reverse has spread eagle on arrows.	210.00	320.00
☐ Jenny Lind—pontil, aqua, 10½" tall	38.00 and up	
☐ Franklin & T.W. Dyott Flask—pint size, aquamarine. Bust of Franklin; reverse has "T.W. Dyott, M.D."	110.00	160.00
☐ Lafayette & DeWitt Clinton Flask—pint size, olive amber. Bust of Lafayette; reverse has "DeWitt Clinton"	290.00	350.00
☐ Railroad Flask—pint size, yellow amber. Horse and loaded cart lengthwise, "Success to the Railroad"	160.00	210.00
☐ Washington—prune color, pontil, 10½" tall	90.00 and up	
☐ Sailor Bottle—amber, 7½" tall. Dancing sailor	55.00 and up	
☐ Union—aqua, 7½" tall. Ball and cannon	75.00 and up	

INK

Many commercial ink bottles were manufactured to be used as inkwells and as bottles in which ink could be sold. In recent years the advent of the ball-point pen made these bottles rather extinct and an attractive collectible.

☐ Arnold, P. & J., 9½" high	8.50	12.50
☐ Barrel teakettle inkwell, 3¼" high, colbalt blue	375.00	450.00
☐ Boat shape, 2½" long	8.00	12.00
☐ "C. Crolius," stoneware inkwell. 2 3/8" x 3 1/4" blue glaze over gray	800.00	1000.00
☐ Carter's, cobalt	6.00	12.00
☐ Carter's, green, cone-shaped	4.00	8.00
☐ Carter's "Violet Ink", round, 1882	4.00	8.00
☐ Carter's "Black Letter Ink," cone-shaped	8.00	12.00
☐ Carter's "For Fountain Pens," square bottle	2.00	4.00
☐ Caw's "New York," aqua, 2¾" high	4.00	8.00
☐ Cross Pen Company, aqua, 2¾" high	18.00	28.00
☐ "De Halsey Patente" ink bottle, 3¼"	200.00	375.00
☐ Earles Ink Company, tan, 6 1/8" high	6.00	12.00
☐ Edison Ink Company, clear, 2 7/8" high	2.00	6.00
☐ "Farley's Ink" bottle, deep olive amber, 1 7/8" x 1 3/4".	200.00	250.00
☐ George Ohr printing press inkwell, yellow and green pottery, 5" high	200.00	275.00

INK

	Price	Range
☐ George Ohr tiger's head inkwell, bright blue pottery ..	300.00	375.00
☐ Greenwood's, clear, 1½" high	4.00	6.00
☐ Hooker's, aqua, 2" high	10.00	20.00
☐ "J. & I.E.M." turtle ink bottle, 1 3/4" x 2 1/8", cobalt ...	250.00	350.00
☐ "Hover Phil" ink bottle, 2¼" light green	125.00	175.00
☐ Igloo ink bottle, 2", sapphire blue	200.00	275.00
☐ Johnson Ink Company, dark green, 5 7/8" high	20.00	30.00
☐ "Josiah Jonsons" fountain inkwell, brown & gray pottery	200.00	235.00
☐ Keene Marboro St., 3-mold inkwell, 2 1/4" x 2 5/8", black	1400.00	2000.00
☐ L.E. Waterman Company, clear glass, machine made, with label	2.00	5.00
☐ Mille fioreGlass, paper weight base of bottle	40.00	60.00
☐ Mount Vernon Glass Works, sapphire blue, 3-mold inkwell, 1¾" high	2000.00	2750.00
☐ National Surety Ink, clear glass, 9" high	4.00	8.00
☐ Parker, diamond shape, cobalt glass, 2½" high	10.00	20.00
☐ "Pitkin" type-ringed inkwell, 1¼" high, live green	425.00	475.00
☐ S.S. Staffords, qt. bottle with spout, aqua, cobalt blue	8.50	15.50
☐ Square Ink Bottles, amethyst, aqua, cobalt blue, 2½" high	2.00	4.00

MILK

The interest in milk bottles has been rather recent. Early bottles, before waxed cardboard discs were pressed into the top, are very hard to find. More recent types of milk bottles are also likely to grow in value since they are being substituted with paper and plastic containers.

☐ A.G.S. & Co., clamp top, 1898	25.00	50.00
☐ Alpine Milk Co., quart	2.00	5.00
☐ Birch Creek Dairy, pint, applied label, 1930's	2.00	4.00
☐ Borden Condensed Milk, tin top, ribbed, 1900	5.00	10.00
☐ California Dairies, ½ pint, round	2.00	4.50
☐ Carnation, quart, round "Carnation"	2.00	4.00
☐ Crystal Milk Jar, round, embossed "W T & Co."	55.00	and up
☐ Damascus Creamery, pint round, amethyst	3.00	6.00
☐ Empire Dairy, ½ pint, round	2.00	6.00
☐ Fairmont, pint, round	2.00	6.00
☐ Florida Universal Store Bottle, pint, clear	2.00	6.00
☐ Grandview Dairy, quart, round	2.50	4.50
☐ Hazelwood, ½ pint, round, yellow tint	2.00	4.00
☐ Hi Grade, quart, round	2.00	4.00
☐ Juniper Valley Dairy Co., quart, round	3.00	5.00
☐ Mayflower Milk, quart, square, applied label	2.00	4.00
☐ Meadow Brook Dairy, quart, round	2.50	4.50
☐ Meadowview Dairy, quart, square	4.50	6.50
☐ Milk for Health, quart, square, amber	4.00	8.00
☐ Milk for Infants, round, tin top	30.00	and up

MILK

	Price	Range
☐ One Quart, round, quart	2.00	4.00
☐ Peoples Dairy, quart, round, applied label, amber	20.00	30.00
☐ Pure Milk Nature Food, pint, round	2.00	4.00
☐ Riviera Dairy, quart, round "Cream Top"	4.50	6.50
☐ Salem Store Bottle, quart, round	2.00	4.00
☐ Standard Dairy, quart, square	2.00	4.00
☐ Sunny Brook Dairy, quart, square, amber	2.00	4.00
☐ Thatchers Dairy, quart, round, 1884	10.00	20.00
☐ To Be Washed And Returned, pint, round	2.00	4.00
☐ Turner Centre Creamery, round machine made, circa 1903	50.00	and up

PERFUME

☐ Atomizer, with etched roses	30.00	40.00
☐ Chelsea, Berry scent bottle	4000.00	4400.00
☐ Chelsea, Gold-mounted, tulip bottle	4400.00	4800.00
☐ Gollywog, Original box	18.00	25.00
☐ Pressed Glass, Bulbous, facet. stopper, 5½" H......	45.00	60.00
☐ Steuben Rosaline Bottle	240.00	280.00

POISON

☐ "Be Careful," Embossed, amber, 8"	20.00	30.00
☐ "Poison," Amber, 8"	16.00	20.00
☐ "Poison," Embossed, ribbed, cobalt, 8"	50.00	70.00
☐ Quilted Pattern, Cobalt blue, 10".................	20.00	25.00
☐ Skull and Crossbones, Embossed, amber, 8"........	18.00	22.00
☐ "The Owl Drug Co.," Cobalt blue, 10"	60.00	80.00

WHISKEY

Within the past decade modern, annual, and commemorative issues of many decorative and collectors items have been produced. This trend has moved into bottle collecting. Hundreds of new figurals have been produced to satisfy this demand.

Ballantine Bottles

☐ Duck	10.00	14.00
☐ Seated Fisherman	14.00	18.00
☐ Golf Bag	10.00	14.00
☐ Scottish Knight...............................	10.00	14.00
☐ Zebra	12.00	16.00

Bols Bottles

☐ Ballerina	14.00	16.00
☐ Dutch Girl	18.00	22.00
☐ Elephant	8.00	12.00
☐ Tea Pot, Delft	10.00	14.00

Borghini Bottles

☐ Cat...	4.00	6.00
☐ Cherubs with Mirror	8.00	12.00
☐ Dog	14.00	16.00
☐ Horse Head..................................	14.00	16.00
☐ Old Ford	8.00	10.00

Borghini Bottles   Price Range

- [ ] Peasant Girl 8.00   10.00
- [ ] Penguin 8.00   12.00
- [ ] Rooster 4.00   6.00
- [ ] Santa Maria 8.00   10.00

J.W. Dant Bottles

- [ ] Alamo 6.00   8.00
- [ ] Boeing 747 .... 14.00   18.00
- [ ] Boston Tea Party 4.00   8.00
- [ ] Bourbon 3.00   6.00
- [ ] Chukar Partridge 8.00   14.00
- [ ] Eagle 8.00   14.00
- [ ] Fort Sill Centennial 8.00   12.00
- [ ] Mountain Quail.............................. 8.00   12.00
- [ ] Patrick Henry 8.00   14.00
- [ ] Prairie Chicken 8.00   12.00
- [ ] Ruffed Grouse 8.00   12.00
- [ ] Speedway 500............................... 6.00   10.00
- [ ] Tea Party................................... 3.00   6.00
- [ ] Woodcock................................... 8.00   12.00
- [ ] Wrong Way Charlie.......................... 20.00   30.00

Ezra Brooks

- [ ] Alligator 14.00   18.00
- [ ] Arizona 7.00   15.00
- [ ] Big Bertha.................................. 14.00   18.00
- [ ] Bird Dog 10.00   16.00
- [ ] Cable Car 8.00   12.00
- [ ] Dice 6.50   8.50
- [ ] Elk 10.00   16.00
- [ ] Golden Eagle 10.00   20.00
- [ ] Historical Flasks—Set of 4 .... 8.00   16.00
- [ ] Indian Hunter 10.00   14.00
- [ ] Jack of Diamonds............................ 7.00   10.00
- [ ] Killer Whale 22.00   28.00
- [ ] Liberty Bell 10.00   14.00
- [ ] Maine Lobster............................... 25.00   30.00
- [ ] Mr. Merchant................................ 12.00   16.00
- [ ] Oil Gusher 8.00   12.00
- [ ] Panda Bear 8.00   12.00
- [ ] Pirate 8.00   10.00
- [ ] Queen of Hearts 7.00   9.00
- [ ] Reno Arch 8.00   10.00
- [ ] Sea Captain 10.00   14.00
- [ ] Silver Dollar 8.00   12.00
- [ ] Ski Boot.................................... 12.00   14.00
- [ ] Telephone 8.00   10.00
- [ ] Ticker Tape 10.00   12.00
- [ ] Vermont Skier 10.00   16.00

Ezra Brooks

	Price	Range
☐ Western Rodeos	14.00	20.00
☐ Whiskey Flasks	4.00	6.00
☐ Zimmerman's Hat	12.00	22.00

Garnier Bottles

☐ Aladdin's Lamp	12.00	22.00
☐ Alfa Romeo	4.00	8.00
☐ Apollo	12.00	16.00
☐ Bacchus	10.00	15.00
☐ Bellows	14.00	18.00
☐ Bullfighters	14.00	18.00
☐ Candlestick	20.00	30.00
☐ Cardinal	14.00	18.00
☐ Clown with Tuba	18.00	22.00
☐ Eiffel Tower	18.00	24.00
☐ Fiat 500, 1913	12.00	16.00
☐ Giraffe	12.00	20.00
☐ Hunting Vase	12.00	20.00
☐ Indian	14.00	20.00
☐ Jockey	14.00	20.00
☐ Locomotive	12.00	16.00
☐ Paris Taxi	25.00	35.00
☐ Pheasant	15.00	20.00
☐ Policeman	8.00	12.00
☐ Sheriff & Indian	8.00	12.00
☐ Trout	14.00	18.00
☐ Violin	8.00	12.00

Luxardo Bottles

☐ Bacchus	16.00	20.00
☐ Candlestick, alabaster	25.00	30.00
☐ Cellini Vase	28.00	34.00
☐ Coffee Carafe	18.00	24.00
☐ Dolphin Figural	35.00	65.00
☐ Duck, green	30.00	40.00
☐ Owl, onyx	35.00	40.00
☐ Puppy	28.00	34.00
☐ Silver Brown Decanter	22.00	28.00
☐ Squirrel	32.00	36.00
☐ Venus	16.00	20.00

Wild Turkey Bottles
Austin Nichols

☐ Wild Turkey #1	250.00	365.00
☐ Wild Turkey #2	175.00	285.00
☐ Wild Turkey #3	120.00	155.00
☐ Wild Turkey #4	110.00	135.00
☐ Wild Turkey #5	35.00	40.00
☐ Wild Turkey #6	25.00	35.00

BOXES

Boxes are one of the most useful collectibles, as something can be put in each one of them. Women, especially, are said to love collecting boxes, and certainly all the women I know—including myself—have more than a handful. The prices are based on materials (naturally, precious materials cost the most), age, size and uniqueness.

WALNUT DESK BOX   250.00 - 300.00

	Price Range	
☐ Bible Box, Carved oak, mid 1600's, English	425.00	475.00
☐ Book-Shaped Box, Inlaid, large	60.00	80.00
☐ Book-Shaped Box, With name and dated 1861	300.00	350.00
☐ Book-Shaped Box, Pennsylvania German, painted wood	30.00	50.00
☐ Book-Shaped Box, Inlaid colored wax hearts, stars . .	15.00	20.00
☐ Box, Wilcox, quadruple plate, scrolls, pointer dogs, lock lion's paw feet, 9" x 5" W	175.00	200.00
☐ Bride's Box, 19th Century, German or Pennsylvania German, oval	100.00	150.00
☐ Cigarette Box, "Wavecrest," cream, blue, white, pink forget-me-nots, word "Cigarettes," 4" H	250.00	300.00
☐ Cigarette Box, Cloisonne, cylindrical, unmarked	60.00	100.00
☐ Cigarette or Chocolate Box, brass, Princess Mary, WW1, with Mary, and names of Allies around lid	35.00	45.00
☐ Cigar Box, Coromandel with brass fittings, mid 19th Century	175.00	225.00
☐ Collar Box, Man's, with drawor, black with red lining .	6.00	10.00
☐ Cutlery Box, Triple compartments, walnut, 10" x 16" .	55.00	65.00
☐ Dresser Box, Orange plush with molded celluloid trim, all tools intact	20.00	30.00
☐ Glove Box, Coromandel, gilt brass with green stones inlaid	60.00	90.00
☐ Jewelry Box, Plated silver (replated,) cherubs playing, 8" x 6" x 3"	100.00	150.00
☐ Jewel Casket, Simpson, Hall & Miller silverplate, round on pedestal with 3 cupids with wings, finial another cherub	100.00	150.00

BOXES

	Price Range	
☐ Jewel Box, Jenning Bros. ormolu, scenes of lovers, children in relief, pink plush lining, 2½" H	20.00	30.00
☐ Jewel Box, Pairpont "Wavecrest," 9" diam.	700.00	800.00
☐ Jewel Box, "Wavecrest," ormolu mounts, square shape, 7" x 7" x 5" H	400.00	450.00
☐ Lacquer, Octagonal, yellow with Oriental designs, early 1800's	275.00	325.00
☐ Lap Desk, Brass inlaid, walnut, 15" W	130.00	180.00
☐ Leather Box, Pressed design	12.00	18.00
☐ Lectern Box, Carved, painted, with carved book on top, (from Stewart Gregory Folk Art Auction)		17,500.00
☐ Lunch Box, Tin, Art Deco design, nursery characters	40.00	50.00
☐ Pantry Box, Scandinavian Bentwood	100.00	140.00
☐ Pantry Boxes, 5 graduated, round, painted, all	150.00	200.00
☐ Pantry Box, 10", varnished	20.00	30.00
☐ Pantry Box, 2-fingered round, small size	100.00	140.00
☐ Pantry Box, 3-fingered oval, painted red (possibly Shaker)	125.00	175.00
☐ Pantry Box, Oval, 2-fingered, c1820	125.00	150.00
☐ Patch Box, Royal Bayreuth tapestry, 5 sheep on lid, 2½" x 1½", gray mark	130.00	170.00
☐ Snuffbox, Mauchline ware, boxwood, 3½" W	50.00	75.00
☐ Snuff Box, Horn, acorn-shaped, screw-on top, 1¾" L	25.00	35.00
☐ Snuff Box, Pewter	35.00	45.00
☐ Snuff Box, Treenware, 2¾" Diam.	15.00	22.00
☐ Stamp Box, Sterling with enameled lid, chair and finger ring	25.00	35.00
☐ Stationary Box, Late 19th Century, walnut with brass and ivory decoration, 7" H	110.00	160.00
☐ Tea-Caddy, Marguetry, English, c1780	525	600.00
☐ Tea-Caddy, Imitation tortoise shell, early 1800's, green, English	225.00	275.00
☐ Tool Box, Oak	25.00	35.00
☐ Tool Box, Child's, 1930, with tools	40.00	50.00
☐ Tramp Art Wall Boxes, Small	30.00	45.00
☐ Wall Box, Open top, painted brown, 19th Century	150.00	200.00
☐ Writing Box, Oak, 18th Century, English, 13½" W	125.00	175.00

BUTTONS

On the whole, buttons are inexpensive on the collector market, the vast majority — including old ones and those of handsome or unusual design — selling under $5. Many bring less than $1, while quite a few, as any browser in antiques shops should know, can be picked out of "25 ¢ each" boxes. For a button, $20 is a high price, equivalent perhaps to a postage stamp that sells for $20,000.

What influences the price of a button? Material, craftsmanship, oddity, age, and its appeal to collectors — this last factor being a rather indefinable one.

BUTTONS

Obviously, a gold button will automatically be valuable because of the metal. The same is true of silver. But even materials not intrinsically valuable, such as glass, can make for valuable buttons because their appeal *as materials* happens to be stronger among buyers. Collectors of glass also collect glass buttons. There are not many collectors of plastic.

Originality is a prime point so far as design goes; not in design *motif* but in the handling of motif. Buttons depicting flowers are plentiful enough, but a flower design imaginatively worked is sure to interest button buffs and command a decent price. Never forget that button collecting is largely a topical hobby (faces on buttons, animals on buttons, etc.), and that really bizarre motifs which fall outside the realm of a collected "topic" may be scarce but have a hard time finding buyers.

	Price Range	
☐ Black Glass, cameo head	8.00	12.00
☐ Brass, angry rooster	6.00	10.00
☐ Brass, cherubs with cornucopia and goat	2.75	3.75
☐ Brass disc, bridge and river scene, black and white	60.00	90.00
☐ Ceramic, bird, black and white	20.00	30.00
☐ Cloisonne, birds flying, brass, black and white with red background	60.00	90.00
☐ Enamel, woman at fountain	45.00	65.00
☐ Gold plated, dragon	4.00	6.00
☐ Pewter, owl's head	1.75	2.50
☐ Pierced brass, Little Red Riding Hood	10.00	16.00
☐ Porcelain, cherub catching butterflies, pink, black and white	12.00	20.00
☐ Porcelain, flowers and butterfly, 18th C.	16.00	22.00
☐ Porcelain, pasture scene with children	22.00	30.00
☐ Silver, Bacchus, God of Wine, etched design	20.00	30.00
☐ Stamped brass, two children fighting and pulling hair	18.00	25.00
☐ Stamped brass, two mice	22.00	30.00
☐ Steel with floral design	1.50	2.25
☐ Victorian, figure, black glass disc	7.00	10.00
☐ Wedgwood, blue and white figure, 18th C.	170.00	210.00

CANES & WALKING STICKS

Everyone, no matter what his occupation or his social status, had a cane or walking stick during the 19th century. Violin masters had special canes which concealed a 2" wide violin! As if that wasn't enough, other canes were made which concealed music stands. Any gadget cane is worth much more than a simple decorative one.

☐ Amethyst, Cut glass handle	160.00	190.00
☐ Bamboo, Curved handle	8.00	10.00
☐ Blown Glass, Green	60.00	75.00
☐ Dog's Head, Fox Terrier, painted & carved wood	195.00	200.00
☐ Dog's Head, Wood with brown eyes	20.00	25.00
☐ Dog's Head, Glass eyes	18.00	20.00

CANES & WALKING STICKS

Price Range

- ☐ Ivory, Carved hound's head 30.00   35.00
- ☐ Ivory, Carved clenched hand 150.00   300.00
- ☐ Monkey, Hand carved........................... 80.00   100.00
- ☐ Mother-of-Pearl and Gold...................... 50.00   70.00
- ☐ Parade Cane, china clown head 18.00   20.00
- ☐ Umbrella, Wood case 90.00   100.00
- ☐ Walking Stick, Gold head...................... 80.00   90.00
- ☐ Walking Stick, Sterling........................ 25.00   30.00

CAROUSEL ANIMALS

The collecting of carousel animals depicts one of the most unusual areas of collectibles. These beautiful, hand-carved and sculptured creations are true examples of a lost art.

PHILADELPHIA TOBOGGON, CARRETTA
.... 2500.00 - 3000.00

- ☐ Armitage Hershell Jumpers, track type, no holes through horse, 1890 .... 700.00   800.00
- ☐ Carmel Borrelli, 60 x 50 .... 2600.00   3200.00
- ☐ Carmel Borrelli, 54 x 56 .... 3200.00   4000.00
- ☐ Carmel Borrelli, 49 x 49 .... 2200.00   3000.00
- ☐ Carmel Borrelli, Stander 3000.00   4000.00
- ☐ Dentzel Jumping Mare, Pittsburgh, PA Carrousel 2000.00   3000.00
- ☐ Metal Ilions, Jumper off kiddie machine, 36" 175.00   250.00
- ☐ Muller, Medium stander, 71" 1800.00   2500.00
- ☐ Muller Dentzel, Parrots on back of saddle, 79" 3600.00   4000.00
- ☐ Parker, Large flowers with jewel centers 950.00   1300.00
- ☐ Parker Jumper, Super sweet horse 800.00   1000.00
- ☐ Parker Style Aluminum Horse, 52 x 29 .... 325.00   375.00
- ☐ Spillman, Flag on side, 66" 850.00   1150.00
- ☐ Spillman, Nice flowing mare, shield, 66" 850.00   1150.00
- ☐ Trojan Jumper, 66" 600.00   700.00

Courtesy: Carrousel Midwest, Dale Sorenson, North Lake, WI.

CARTOON ART

Cartoon art has a fascination all its own. Many early cartoons still hold the same interest for people of all ages. Listed below are a few of the famous and rare examples of cartoon art.

	Price Range	
☐ Bode, Vaughn. "Dr. Peeper" page	350.00	375.00
☐ Bald, Ken. "Dr. Kildare" daily....................	20.00	25.00
sunday....................................	35.00	40.00
☐ Caniff, Milton. "Steve Canyon" daily	100.00	150.00
☐ Capp, Al. "Lil'l Abner" daily	75.00	100.00
sunday....................................	150.00	175.00
☐ Crane, Roy. "Buz Sawyer" daily..................	150.00	175.00
☐ Disney, Walt. "Mickey Mouse" daily	85.00	100.00
☐ Fisher, Bud. "Mutt & Jeff" daily..................	300.00	350.00
☐ Fredericks, Fred. "Mandrake" daily	35.00	50.00
☐ Gray, Harold. "Little Orphan Annie" daily	300.00	325.00
☐ Kelly, Walt. "Pogo" daily	275.00	350.00
☐ Lehti, John. "Tarzan" daily	50.00	75.00
☐ Lank, Leonard. "Mickey Finn" daily	200.00	250.00
☐ Messmer, Otto. "Felix the Cat" sunday	225.00	250.00
☐ Sagendorf, But. "Popeye" daily..................	75.00	100.00
sunday....................................	125.00	150.00
☐ Schulz, Charles. "Peanuts" daily	210.00	250.00
sunday....................................	375.00	400.00
☐ Smith, Al. "Mutt and Jeff" daily..................	50.00	100.00
sunday....................................	85.00	125.00
☐ Tobin, Don. "Little Woman" daily	30.00	50.00
☐ Van Buren, Raeburn. "Abbie an' Slats" daily	125.00	150.00
☐ Wunder, George. "Terry" dialy...................	45.00	75.00
☐ Young, Chic. "Blondie" daily	65.00	100.00

CASH REGISTERS

Probably one of the most interesting and decorative collectibles are old cash registers. Introduced in the 1880's, they are still found easily and command substantial prices if found in good condition.

☐ National, Brass................................	400.00	450.00
☐ National, Brass, Floor model with drawers	1000.00	1200.00
☐ National, Brass, Ornate	350.00	400.00
☐ National, Brass with marble	300.00	325.00
☐ National, Brass and mahogany	360.00	390.00
☐ National, size 313, 1912, 17" high, sales up to $1	550.00	600.00
☐ Monitor, No. 1A, oak with decal, pat'd 1900	275.00	300.00
☐ National, embossed nickel plated lockbox, 6" x 6¾" x 6¾"	150.00	175.00
☐ National, No. 13, 1898	500.00	525.00
☐ Premier Junior	300.00	325.00

CATS

We all have heard of so-called eccentric ladies with 17 cats, but there are lots of collectors of things in the cat motif—and they often have hundreds of objects. Ceramics, precious metals, wood, glass, cloth—all are materials used by artisans for making cat figures.

	Price Range	
☐ Cookie jar, stoneware, Chessie, 22" H	39.00	45.00
☐ Painting, oil, primitive of white cat, 1920's	20.00	25.00
☐ Fairy lamp, gray & white kitten, blown green eyes, 3½" H	35.00	40.00
☐ Bookend, Art Deco brass, copper & chrome, arched-back, heavy	12.00	15.00
☐ Mirror frame, 3 cats playing around mirror	65.00	75.00
☐ Pillow, needlepoint, folk art grey/white cat	20.00	35.00
☐ Postcard, animated cat, Arthur Thiele	5.00	25.00
☐ Still bank, cat on tub, 4" H	75.00	100.00
☐ Toy, wind-up cat chasing rat, German, c1910	80.00	90.00
☐ Toy, wind-up meowing cat, plush-covered, turn-of-the century, works, but plush in poor condition	25.00	35.00
☐ Postcard, embossed cat & dog on pillow	5.00	10.00

CHALKWARE

Chalkware is supposed to be "poor man's Staffordshire." By that is meant Staffordshire figures of animals and people and birds, which were used as mantle ornaments througout the 19th Century. Chalkware is rather like plaster, and was cast in molds and painted, and sold for pennies. Chalkware is not to be confused with cast plaster figures given away as prizes at carnivals and fairs in the last 40 years or so, although even those are becoming collectible in their own right.

☐ Bank, Black Dog with glass eyes.................	40.00	45.00
☐ Bookends, Pirates, painted. Pair	40.00	45.00
☐ Boy, Reading Books. 10½" H	85.00	100.00
☐ Cat, 4½" H	140.00	160.00
☐ Cat, 6½" H	130.00	160.00
☐ Dancing Lady, 14" H.............................	15.00	30.00
☐ Dog, 8½" H.....................................	110.00	130.00
☐ Dog, 11½" H....................................	230.00	260.00
☐ Dove, Green with blue wings. 12" H	190.00	220.00
☐ Eagle, Spread. 9½" H	280.00	310.00
☐ Horn of Plenty, 14" H	15.00	30.00
☐ Indian, Cigar Store, reclining. 23" H	190.00	220.00
☐ Lamb, Grey Body. 8½" H	260.00	290.00
☐ Owl, 12" H	165.00	195.00
☐ Pigeon, 10" H	120.00	140.00
☐ Rabbit, Sitting. 8" H	140.00	160.00
☐ Sheep, Mother with babies. 7" H	180.00	210.00
☐ Shepherd, German. 17½" H	60.00	80.00

CHALKWARE   Price Range
- [ ] Squirrel, 10" H.................................. 160.00   180.00
- [ ] Stag, Rectangular base. 15" H 230.00   260.00
- [ ] Gnome, German, 1930's, 11" H .... 18.00   —
- [ ] Indian, reclining, c1920, 26" x 13" .... 35.00   —
- [ ] Bank, apple with red cheeks .... 25.00   —
- [ ] Charley McCarthy, 15" H .... 17.50   —
- [ ] Black boy w/watermelon, 4" H .... 10.00   —

CHESS SETS

Chess is the game of kings and paupers, and both can collect chess sets too, though many sets are extremely costly. Chess sets are made of all kinds of precious materials, as well as leather, wood, and ceramics. Also collectible to a certain extent—although not according to the die-hard old-timers—are single pieces. You might specialize in rooks or knights or any other piece which takes your fancy.

- [ ] Chess Set, Royal Dux porcelain, Genghis Khan & entourage, white, cobalt blue, gold 480.00
- [ ] Chess Set, Ivory, carved. 6" H 375.00   400.00
- [ ] Chess Set, Ivory, Red and White 130.00   150.00
- [ ] Chess Set, Ivory Inlaid, Italian 1880's, hand carved pieces 470.00   540.00

CHRISTMAS TREE ORNAMENTS & LIGHTS

Chances are you have at least one very old Christmas tree glass ornament in your decoration box. It has survived, amazingly, for at least 75 winters, and while the lacquer may be slightly chipped, and maybe a bent paperclip is now stuck in the neck, it still has a place of pride on the tree each year. Such an ornament might be worth as much as $25 or so, depending on subject and condition. Also quite collectible are Christmas tree lights—even if they no longer work. The most collectible of these are the blown glass ones made in molds in Occupied Japan during the 1940's. Comic characters, animals and snowmen are all available.

- [ ] Light, Andy Gump, Milk Glass 10.00   12.00
- [ ] Light, Bear with Guitar, Milk Glass 10.00   12.00
- [ ] Light, Blue Bird, Milk Glass 4.00   6.00
- [ ] Light, Clown, Milk Glass 10.00   14.00
- [ ] Light, Elephant, Milk Glass 6.00   10.00
- [ ] Light, Fish, Milk Glass 5.00   8.00
- [ ] Light, Gingerbread Man 8.00   10.00
- [ ] Light, Humpty Dumpty, Milk Glass 6.00   10.00
- [ ] Light, Lantern 2.00   4.00
- [ ] Light, Puss In Boots, Milk Glass 15.00   20.00
- [ ] Light, Santa, Painted 10.00   14.00
- [ ] Light, Snowman, Milk Glass 10.00   14.00

CHRISTMAS TREE ORNAMENTS & LIGHTS

Price Range

☐ Light Zeppelin with Flag	8.00	10.00
☐ Ornament, Ball, Amber	16.00	20.00
☐ Ornament, Ball, Canary, Blown Glass	12.00	16.00
☐ Ornament, Bear w/Muff, Blown Glass	40.00	45.00
☐ Ornament, Child, Milk Glass	6.00	10.00
☐ Ornament, Clown Head, Blown Glass	35.00	40.00
☐ Ornament, Football Player, Milk Glass	12.00	16.00
☐ Ornament, Girl, Blown Glass	30.00	35.00
☐ Ornament, Heart, Blown Glass, Large	15.00	18.00
☐ Ornament, Icicle, Glass	14.00	18.0Q
☐ Ornament, Santa, with Plaster Face	10.00	14.00
☐ Ornament, Swan, Blown Glass	8.00	12.00

CIRCUS MEMORABILIA

If you always wanted to join the circus, but couldn't bring yourself to do it, perhaps a collection of circus memorabilia would suffice. Paper items are by far the most collectible category, but this doesn't mean that some people (with more room than most of us) don't collect wagons, carvings, and perhaps even Big Tops. A few circus wagons have been discovered by diligent searchers in the Midwest being used as chicken coops!

☐ Band Wagon, Horse drawn	375.00	425.00
☐ Book, *Dr. Dolittle's Circus* by Hugh Loftring, New York, 1924	80.00	110.00
☐ Booklet, Walter L. Main circus, 8pp, color, wraps	12.50	15.00
☐ Broadside handbills, 1920's, illus., 10 x 28	15.00	20.00
☐ Courier, "Illustrated News," P.T. Barnum, 1897, 16pp	37.50	50.00
☐ Herald or handbill, Sparks Circus, 1921, 28" l	12.50	15.00
☐ Poster, P.T. Barnum & Co., Lake Front, Chicago, Monday, July 19th	15.00	20.00
☐ Poster, Clyde Beatty, Training Lions and Tigers, 1930	70.00	90.00
☐ Poster, Dale's Animal 3-ring circus	10.00	15.00
☐ Poster, Adams Forepaugh Sells circus, pictures Aurora Zoaves, Mint Condition	45.00	60.00
☐ Program, Ringling Bros., Barnum & Bailey, 1948	9.00	12.50
☐ Program, Hagenbeck-Wallas	15.00	20.00
☐ Sheet Music, Children At The Circus, 1909	20.00	30.00
☐ Sheet Music, When It's Circus Day Back Home, 1917	20.00	30.00
☐ Song Book, Barnum & London Musical Album, large size	22.50	30.00
☐ Stationery, Sparton Bros., ornate, unused	2.50	5.00
☐ Tickets, Hunts Bros., 1940's, illus. w/clown, large	100 for 6.00	
☐ Wagon, Wood and tin with scene of circus on wagon, 17½" L	90.00	140.00
☐ Toy, Circus train, tin, 1950's, 8 pieces	100.00	125.00
☐ Toy, Clown, Wooden, hinged	60.00	90.00
☐ Toy, Lion Cage, Driver and lions	110.00	160.00

CIVIL WAR MEMORABILIA

During the 3rd quarter of the 19th century we were involved in what was the bloodiest war of all time. From 1861-1865 our great ancestors fought bravely and in doing so freed slaves and gave our country a new sense of decency. The Civil War years produced some of the most desirable antiques in today's market place. Essentially all the collectibles listed here are dated from 1861-1865.

U.S. CALVARY HAT
. . . . 75.00 -100.00

UNION INFANTRY DRUM
. . . . 300.00 - 400.00

	Price Range	
☐ Ammunition Pouch. Black leather (U.S. Arsenal)	60.00	70.00
☐ Badge. For helmet, sheild with eagle	20.00	25.00
☐ Bayonet and Scabbard. From .58 caliber rifle.	65.00	75.00
☐ Bayonet. For U.S. 45-70 rifle	40.00	50.00
☐ Bayonet. With brass plate	65.00	75.00
☐ Belt Buckle. With "U.S." insignia	25.00	35.00
☐ Boots. From cavalry	130.00	140.00
☐ Buckle. From Navy, brass with anchor	135.00	140.00
☐ Button. From Confederate jacket	25.00	30.00
☐ Canteen. From Union Army, with strap	40.00	50.00
☐ Canteen. From Union Army	50.00	60.00
☐ Canteen. Made of tin	140.00	150.00
☐ Cartridge Box. Brown leather	40.00	50.00
☐ Cavalry Boots	145.00	150.00
☐ Chin Straps. From officer's hat	18.00	20.00
☐ Doctor's Bag. Black leather	275.00	300.00
☐ Enlistment Papers. Fully endorsed, from Union Army .	30.00	35.00
☐ Gloves. From officer's wardrobe (leather).	75.00	85.00
☐ Holster. For rifle	75.00	85.00
☐ Horse Bit	55.00	65.00
☐ Knife. Bowie with ivory handles	95.00	105.00
☐ Knife and Tool Combination	18.00	20.00
☐ Leggings. Black leather	120.00	130.00
☐ Mess Kit. Ivory handles, in case	40.00	50.00
☐ Revolver. 36 cal., Navy Colt (1861)	800.00	1000.00
☐ Ribbon (1861-1865). Blue-gray in color with banner around Loneorn's head reading "With Malice Toward None With Charity For All"	60.00	70.00
☐ Sword. Confederate-made with Ivory grip	350.00	375.00
☐ Sword. From Union Cavalry with shield	175.00	200.00
☐ U.S. Musket (1861). Navy Colt	800.00	1000.00

CLOCKS

All prices given are for timepieces in guaranteed working condition, assuming that cases, hands, labels, dials, decorated glass and hardware are original. Most clock or watch collectors can evaluate the extent of repair necessary to put a timepiece in proper working condition.

*Courtesy: Clocks and Things, Joseph Fanelli
New York, NY.*

COTTAGE

CALENDAR

GRANDMOTHER

GRANDFATHER

OCCIDENTAL

CLOCKS — ACORN (1847-1850)
Manufactured, probably exclusively, by the designer J. C. Brown of Forestville Manufacturing Co., Bristol, Connecticut, in the years 1847-1850. The Acorn is one of the American classic clocks and prices have risen rapidly.

All prices shown are for clocks in fine working condition.

Price Range

☐ Acorn — Shelf or mantel clock with sidearms, 8 day time & strike double fuzee movement, mahogany case. "J. C. Brown Esq." home painted on glass tablet. Wind holes at 4 & 8, 26" high. This is the original model Acorn 4000.00   5500.00

☐ Forestville Clock Company, J. C. Brown, circa 1848, wood fuzee powered movement. Star, leaf and scroll design on front tablet. Plain dial, wind holes at 4 & 8. Approximately 26" high. With sidearms 3200.00   3800.00

☐ Forestville Manufacturing Co., 8 day time & strike wooden fuzee movement, mahogany case. Classic Greek Revival. "Merchants Exchange Philadelphia" painted on front tablet. Musical lyre and leaf motif on dark background around dial. Wind holes at 4 & 6, 26" high. With sidearms 3800.00   4500.00

☐ Plain dial Standard Acorn. Wood fuzee 8 day movement, time & strike. Painting of "State House-Hartford" on front tablet. Winds at 4 & 6, 26" high 3000.00   3500.00

☐ Standard Acorn — J. C. Brown. Floral motif dial. Fuzee movement, time & strike. Winds at 4 & 8. No sidearms, acorns on wooden base. Clock is 26" high . 2200.00   2600.00

☐ Intermediate Acorn, "Square Bottom", 8 day fuzee, time and strike movement. Front tablet — etched leaf motif. Plain dial, "porthole" shows movement. Wind holes at 3 & 9, approximately 24" high, heavy sidearms 1800.00   2400.00

☐ Final Acorn type — circa 1850. Fuzee brass 8 day movement. "Square Bottom", no arms, etched leaf motif on tablet, plain face, wind holes at 3 & 9 . . . . 1200.00   1600.00

CLOCKS — ALARM (1878-1916)
☐ American Alarm, Parker Clock Co., circa 1890's, nickel case, one day movement, time, alarm. Alarm bell is base of clock. 55.00   70.00

☐ Ansonia — "Bee". Nickel case, 1 day time, 2 inch dial   45.00   55.00

☐ Ansonia — "Bee". Nickel case, 1 day time, bell on top, 5" high 65.00   80.00

☐ Ansonia — "Trolley". 1 day time, alarm bell on top . . .   75.00   95.00

☐ Ansonia — "Striking Doll" Alarm Clock. Cast iron Cherub sits on top and strikes alarm bell with hammer. Nickel case, 1 day time, circa 1880 . . . . 225.00   250.00

☐ Ansonia — "Locomotive". Cast iron train, clock set into boiler front, "cow catcher" base, 1 day time, "Pat. April 23, 1878" 185.00   250.00

CLOCKS — ALARM (1878-1916)   **Price Range**

☐ Darche Electric Clock Company. "Get-up" alarm, cast iron base and structure, circa 1910, battery operated alarm, 8¾" high 100.00 125.00

☐ Electric Alarms, various makers, circa 1910 .... 25.00 75.00

☐ Sessions Clock Co., Forestville, Conn. — "Columbia", 1 day time, gold gilt bell, case and bezel 45.00 60.00

☐ New Haven Clock Co. — "Tatoo Alarm". 1 day time, 4" bronze metal gong on back, 15 minute intermittent alarm 65.00 80.00

☐ Seth Thomas — circa 1890's. Embellished heavy cast bronze case. Second and alarm dial on face, 9½" high 85.00 125.00

☐ Seth Thomas — "Lodge". House shaped clock. Gilt front, 1 day time and alarm, 7" high 100.00 135.00

☐ Western Clock Co. — "Westclox" Baby Ben — 1915. Black face, luminous numbers and hands 25.00 35.00

☐ Western Clock Co. — "Westclox" Big Ben — 1910, plain and luminous dial, each 60.00 80.00

☐ Wm. L. Gilbert Clock Co. — "Hello". Nickel case, 1 day movement, 2 top bells. Carriage type clock, with handle. Circa 1898, 9" high 65.00 75.00

☐ Wm. L. Gilbert Clock Co. — "Belfry". Liberty Bell "under shed", 11" high, Liberty Bell is the alarm, circa 1898 .... 125.00 150.00

☐ Parker Clock Co., Conn. Two alarm bells, on engraved cast iron base under clock 70.00 90.00

CLOCKS — BANJO (1802-1968)

Patented in 1802 by Simon Willard. This beautiful and unique design is still being produced today. The name is derived from the case which is shaped like banjo. The most valuable are those made from 1810-1830 and signed. All Banjos regardless of date have risen in value and collectibility.

☐ William Cummens (Apprentice to Simon Willard), Roxbury, Mass. 1812, 34" high. Original reverse painting of "Pennsylvania Capitol" by Charles Bullard. Brass sidearms, acorn finials, wind hole at 2 .... 4000.00 5000.00

☐ Brewster F. Ingraham — Banjo, Boston, Mass. Circa 1850. 8 day time, spring driven movement with pendulum. Mahogany case, brass sidearms 750.00 900.00

☐ Aaron Willard — Boston, Mass. Circa 1810, mahogany case, 34" long, eglomise panel and door (reverse painting on glass), landscape or seascape. Brass sidearms, acorn finial, winds at 2 .... 4000.00 5000.00

☐ Simon Willard — "S. Willard's Patent" on eglomise glass door. Mahogany case, brass sidearms and bezel. Circa 1804, 40" long. "Geometric" and floral motif on front panel and door. Acorn finial (brass or gilded wood)* 5500.00 8500.00

CLOCKS — BANJO (1802-1968)

Price Range

☐ E. Howard & Co. — Boston, Mass. Weight driven Banjo (Banjo Regulator), 8 day time only, no sidearms. Case — mahogany or rosewood with or without second dial. Size can vary from 29" to 56" 2000.00   5000.00

☐ Curtis & Dunning — Concord Mass. Circa 1820, square bottom, 8 day time and strike. Eglomise panel with "PATENT", and sea battle, War of 1812, on door. Brass and bezel and sidearms. Fluted wooden pendant. Made by Lemuel Curtis, designer of the Girandole Clock 5500.00   7000.00

☐ Federal Mahogany Banjo — New England. Circa 1830, a drum clock, gilt acorn finial, eglomise panel — patriotic motif, base panel — "Constitution and Guerriere" — War of 1812 sea battle, 39½" high. Brass sidearms, gilt-wood bracket 1850.00   2500.00

☐ E. Ingraham Co. — "Treasure", 8 day pendulum movement, mahogany case, 39" high, 2 rod strike, silver plated dial. Eagle finial. Stenciled "Pirate Treasure" picture on door, Arabic numerals, 1920 . . . .   300.00   375.00

☐ Seth Thomas Banjo. "Geometric and floral" stenciled front, mahogany case, brass sidearms, eagle finial, Arabic numerals, circa 1940 . . . .   250.00   325.00

☐ William King Lemist — Roxbury, Mass. Apprentice to Simon Willard. Eglomise glass panel and door. Center piece — frigate under full sail. Enameled and gilded front. Dial inscribed "Made by William Lemist — 1812". Mahogany case 34" high, gilt acorn finial 4000.00   4800.00

CLOCKS — BEE HIVE (1840-1855)

A Connecticut shelf clock, cased in the shape of a rounded gothic arch. Average dimensions, 18½" high, 11" wide, 4" deep. Made in the late 1840's. Many manufactured into the early 20th century.

☐ Ansonia Clock Co. — Ansonia, Conn. Bee Hive, or Round Gothic, 8 day Alarm and strike Clock. Set alarm ring on face of clock. Rustic gold leaf scene painted on glass door 175.00   250.00

☐ J.C. Brown — Bristol, Conn. Rippled front mahogany veneer on pine case. Spring wound 8 day movement. Brass alarm set ring on dial, "3 ball" hands. Painted and stenciled glass door 325.00   375.00

☐ Chauncey Jerome (on label). Rosewood case, stencil decorated front and glass door, 8 day alarm, set ring on dial, "spade hands", 19" high, circa 1852 . . . .   400.00   500.00

CLOCK — BLACK (1880-1920)

☐ Ansonia — "Boston". Classic Greek front, bronze columns on black enameled iron clock, 8 day half-hour strike, gong, visible escapement, 11" high 125.00   165.00

CLOCK — BLACK (1880-1920)   Price Range

- [ ] Ansonia — New York. Black wooden case with engraved flowers on front. Top is flat. Gilt metal scrolled feet, 6½" dial. 10½" high x 18" long 125.00 150.00
- [ ] Wm. L. Gilbert — "Windsor". Enameled iron, gilt trimmings, 9½" high, 8 day ½ hour strike, flat top, porcelain dial, gilt lion heads with rings, 5" dial...... 115.00 145.00
- [ ] Ingraham — "Gypsy — Imitation Marble Clock" (made of wood). 5" dial, flat top, real marble insets at base of columns, 8 day half-hour strike, gong, movement, 10" high x 16¾" long. Gilt side ornaments and feet 145.00 185.00
- [ ] E. Ingraham — "Florence". Imitation French marble (made of wood) and Ormolu, bracket clock, 8 day ½ hour strike, gong, 20" high, 10" wide. Elaborate gilt metal trim, 5" dial 125.00 175.00
- [ ] New Haven — "Harcourt". Enameled iron, flat top, 8 day ½ hour strike, gong, porcelain dial. Gilt legs, trim, bezel 130.00 185.00
- [ ] New Haven — "Brandon". Enameled wood flat top, 8 day, ½ hour strike, gong, gilt dial legs and trim, 11" high 115.00 135.00
- [ ] New Haven — "Monarch". Enameled black wood case, gilt trim, legs and bezel, 8 day ½ hour strike, gong. Marbleized columns and inserts, 6" dial, 12" high x 17" long 125.00 175.00
- [ ] Sessions Clock Co. Enameled black wood case. Gilt arched columns, "Greek" statues, side ornaments and feet, 8 day ½ hour strike, gong 125.00 185.00
- [ ] Waterbury — "Palmetto". Black enameled iron clock, with "classic" seated bronze figure 175.00 250.00
- [ ] Waterbury Clock Co. — "Pomona". Flat top polished marbleized wood, green gilt trimmings, 8 day ½ hour strike, gong. 17" long, 11½" high, gilt lion side ornaments 125.00 175.00
- [ ] French — Black marble mantel clock, 8 day time & strike movement. Porcelain dial with visible escapement 185.00 350.00

CLOCKS — CALENDAR (1860-1873)

- [ ] E. Ingraham Co., Bristol, Conn. Short drop, octagon, oak case, 8 day movement, 8" dial with calendar, 19" high, center wind hole, circa 1890 .... 300.00 400.00
- [ ] E. Ingraham & Co., Bristol, Conn. Figure 8 wall calendar clock. Round head and bottom. B. B. Lewis day and month calendar mechanism, 30" high, circa 1880 750.00 900.00
- [ ] E. Ingraham Co., Bristol, Conn. Wall regulator with calendar. Oak case, 8 day time strike. Spring driven wall calendar clock. 38" x 17" x 4¼" 325.00 425.00

CLOCKS — CALENDAR (1860-1873)

☐ Ithaca — "Parlor" Calendar. Ornate carved black walnut case, black dials, white Roman numerals on time, Arabic on calendar. Pendulum bob is crystal glass. 8 day time, strike movement, 20" high 2200.00 2800.00

☐ Ithaca — Calendar shelf clock, 24" high, oak case, burl walnut inserts, 8 day time, strike. Clear "porthole: in calendar shows pendulum bob, month and day windows 575.00 850.00

☐ Ithaca — Calendar, oak case, 8 day time strike, "half-moon" window in calendar shows pendulum bob. Month & day windows in calendar, arch top with finial, 26" high 575.00 850.00

☐ B. B. Lewis — Wall & Shelf Calendars — Spring or weight driven. Clock mechanism made by various companies. Day of week shown by hand at dial center. Month and day indicated by 2 hands on calendar (lower) dial. Clocks made starting in 1862 . . . . 550.00 3000.00

☐ New Haven Clock Co. — Short drop octagon calendar. Oak case, 12" face wall-clock, 8 day time strike, 22" high, circa 1875 . . . . 325.00 375.00

☐ Seth Thomas — Plymouth Hollow, Conn. "Perpetual Calendar" shelf clock, 4 sided top, 8 day strike, oak case, 20" high. "Patent February 15, 1848", day and month windows 700.00 900.00

☐ Wm. L. Gilbert Clock Co., Winsted Conn. "Oriental". Ornate carved walnut case, parlor clock, 8 day strike, gong, calendar, black glass door with floral stencil, windows show day and month, 27" high, 15" high 550.00 650.00

CLOCKS — CARRIAGE

Carriage, or Travel Clocks were popular from 1870 to 1910. They were used both as Travel and Mantle Timepieces. Many are still found with original leather travel cases.

☐ French Gilt 8-day Clock 400.00 550.00

☐ French Grand Sonnerie 8-day with repeat. This clock strikes the hours and quarters at each quarter 2000.00 2600.00

☐ American Waterbury Time, strike and repeat, ca. 1890 275.00 375.00

☐ Very Ornate French Clock, circa 1870 . . . . 500.00 600.00

☐ French Architectural Style Quarter Strike and Repeat 1000.00 1250.00

☐ Plain French Time and Alarm 200.00 275.00

☐ French Clock with hand-painted enamel panels, perpetual 1500.00 3000.00

☐ Miniature Waterbury 125.00 175.00

☐ Miniature 8-day Silver Swiss with hand enamel 375.00 600.00

☐ French Clock with oval sides, hour strike and repeat . 1200.00 1800.00

☐ Fancy French Quarter Strike and Repeat, engraved overall 1500.00 2000.00

CLOCKS — CONNECTICUT SHELF (1835-1890)   **Price Range**

☐ Ansonia Clock Co. — "Crystal Palace Clock", circa 1880. Gilt metal figures of Early American soldier & fisherman on base. Open weighted pendulum. Glass dome on many varieties 300.00   400.00

☐ Ansonia, Conn., circa 1851. Small shelf 30 hour strike with alarm. Painted glass door with floral or game motif. Rosewood case with flat top, 16" high 175.00   225.00

☐ Ansonia Clock Co., "Occidental", circa 1875-78. Ornate carved walnut case, classic carved head on arch. 8 day time and strike movement. Etched & stenciled floral design with "ANSONIA" on glass front door tablet. Height 24", dial 6" 250.00   300.00

☐ Ansonia Clock Co., circa 1860. Flat top shelf clock, 16½" high. Gothic rosewood case, 1 day time & strike. Floral stencil on glass door panel 165.00   225.00

☐ J. C. Brown — Forestville Mfg. Co., Bristol, Conn., circa 1850. "OG" type wooden case inlaid with Mother-of-Pearl, and scrolled bronze decorations. Brass 8 day movement is weight driven. Gilt decorated glass door tablet. Winds at 4 & 7 . . . .   350.00   400.00

☐ J. C. Brown — Standard Sharp Gothic type steeple . . .   300.00   425.00

☐ J. C. Brown — Twin Steeple Round Gothic 400.00   550.00

☐ Chauncey Jerome, New Haven, Conn. — "Barnum", circa 1852. "OG" type rosewood cae, 15" high, 30 hour time & strike movement. Glass front door tablet with geometric star motif 200.00   265.00

☐ Waterbury Porcelain Clock — "Parlor #88, circa 1898. China cased 8 day, ½ hour strike, gong movement. Elaborate roccoco gilded case, 13" high with floral motif. Porcelain dial with gilt bezel 175.00   300.00

☐ Wm. L. Gilbert Clock Co., Winsted, Conn. — "Star Round Top", circa 1875. Eight day time, strike, alarm, spring wound. Alarm set ring on dial 125.00   195.00

☐ Wm. L. Gilbert Clock Co., Winsted, Conn. — "Column Weight", circa 1875. Hollow gilt side columns direct weights. Thirty hour time and strike brass movement. "OG" entablature (molding) on flat top of clock. Scalloped opening on dial shows movement. Decal glass tablet of songbird on limb. Height 25" x 15½" wide 165.00   275.00

☐ E. Ingraham & Co., Bristol, Conn. — "Doric", circa 1880. Rosewood case, 16" high, 8 day time & strike brass movement. Round dial and glass door stenciled with floral motif. Wood rosettes centered 185.00   225.00

☐ E. Ingraham & Co., Bristol, Conn. — "Venetian", circa 1880. Round top rosewood case, 18" high with 8 day time & strike brass movement. Round dial and glass door with stenciled floral motif 185.00   250.00

CLOCKS — CONNECTICUT SHELF (1835-1890)   **Price Range**

☐ "Utah", "Iowa", etc., circa 1890. Elaborate "Jig-saw" oak case with curlecue wood inserts. Glass door front with elaborate stencil, 8 day ½ hour strike, gong, movement. Height 23" with a 6" dial. This type of clock made in dozens of varieties 175.00   285.00

☐ Seth Thomas, Plymouth Hollow, Conn. — "Cathedral", circa 1880. Black cast iron case with towers and statues and painted front. 30 hour time and strike movement. Pendulum bob shows through. .   165.00   200.00

☐ Seth Thomas, Plymouth Hollow, Conn., circa 1825. Spread eagle crest on walnut case. White painted dial, floral spandrels. Eglomise door panel depicts "Independence Hall-Philadelphia" surrounded by eagle and floral border. Side colonettes stenciled, 34½" high x 17½" wide 850.00   950.00

☐ Seth Thomas, Plymouth Hollow, Conn., circa 1830. Inlaid mahogany and curly maple case, oblong top with "OG" frieze. White painted dial with floral spandrels. Eglomise panel depicts a balloon ascension. Applied side columns, height 25" x 15" wide 375.00   425.00

CLOCKS — CONNECTICUT WALL (1800-1900)

☐ E. Ingraham & Co., Bristol, Conn. — "Ionic", circa 1860. Round drop "Figure 8", clear glass drop door (also with design on glass). Brass 8 day time & strike movement. Wood rosettes centered on drop. Single wind hole 375.00   500.00

☐ E. Ingraham & Co., Bristol, Conn. — "Walnut or Gilt Gallery". Round gallery 8 day spring wound time & strike movement in heavy round case. Diameter ranges from 10" to 20" 200.00   500.00

☐ E. Howard & Co., Roxbury, Mass. "Round Gallery", circa 1850-1860. Gilt wood frame, 8 day time & strike movement. Wind holes in center and at 12. Diameter of case — 29" 600.00   800.00

☐ Chauncey Jerome, New Haven — "Gallery 8 Day Time-Piece", circa 1860. Spring wound brass movement. Round gilt frame case, 22" diameter, single center wind hole 400.00   550.00

☐ Wm. L. Gilbert Clock Co., Winsted, Conn. — "Octagon Lever", circa 1875. Heavy walnut case. Thirty hour time & strike movement. "Patent Lever Escapement" and second dial on 8" diameter face. Wind hole at 3 . .   225.00   285.00

☐ Seth Thomas, Thomaston, Conn. — "Drop-Octagon" with 3 sided 12" drop. Black painted glass door shows pendulum bob through window. Wind holes at 5 & 7 . .   350.00   425.00

☐ Seth Thomas — "Umbria", circa 1898. Hooded oak case, pediment with finial on arch. Clear glass door, regulator pendulum and scale. 8 day time & strike movement, second dial on face. Height 40½", dial 8", wind holes at 4 & 8 . . . .   575.00   750.00

		Price Range
CLOCKS — CONNECTICUT WALL (1800-1900)		

☐ Seth Thomas — "Post Office Clock", circa 1890. Oak, walnut, or cherry case. Clear glass door, regulator pendulum. 8 day weight driven movement. Second dial on 12" face, 34" high 600.00 750.00

CLOCKS — COTTAGE (1836-1916)

☐ Seth Thomas — Plymouth Hollow, Conn. "Albert". Circa 1898. Arch top walnut case. 8 day time & strike movement. Eagle decal on glass door. Height 16½", dial 6", wind holes at 4 & 8 . . . . 150.00 200.00

☐ Seth Thomas — Plymouth Hollow, Conn. Rosewood case, three sided top. 30 hour time & strike & alarm movement, alarm ring on dial. Star motif stencil on door, 12" high, 6" dial 150.00 200.00

☐ Wm. L. Gilbert Co. — Winsted, Conn. "Rose Cottage Time". Circa 1875. Flat top rosewood case. Thirty hour time, strike, alarm. Wind holes at 4 & 10, alarm set ring on dial. Floral stencil on glass, 9 7/8" high x 7 3/4" wide 150.00 200.00

☐ Jerome & Co. — Philadelphia. Circa 1852. "Prince Albert". Flat top mahogany case, 30 hour time & strike brass movement. Rustic scene on glass door. Height 15" 185.00 225.00

CLOCKS — GIRANDOLE (1815-1818)

☐ J. L. Dunning — Concord, Mass. Circa 1810-1830. Mahogany case, 45" high, stained pine acanthus leaf base and panels. Gilt eagle finial. "Porthole" shows pendulum bob. Wind hole at 2 . . . . 5000.00 7000.00

☐ Lemuel Curtis — Concord, Mass. Circa 1814-1818. Designer and creator of the "Girandole". Ornate gilding and carving on case. Mythological or patriotic motif on front. Convex glass 22000.00 30000.00

CLOCKS — GRANDMOTHER (1770-1815)

☐ Nathaniel Hamlin — Augusta, Maine, circa 1814. Break arch dial signed on face. Wind holes at 3 & 9. Oak case 44" high . . . . — 7500.00

☐ Thomas Clagett — Newport, R.I., circa 1770-1880. Scrolled arched dial with 2 finials. Two part base. Etched 2 tone Roman numeral face. 61" high (tallest Grandmother) . . . . — 5500.00

☐ Noah Ranlet, Gilmanton, New Hampshire, circa 1776-1790. Fretwork arched hood with 3 brass finials. Arabic numerals on dial. Carved skirt on base . . . . — 5800.00

☐ Caleb Leach — Plymouth, Mass., circa 1776-1790. Arched hood, 3 brass finials. Signed face with second and day dials. Height 4' 7" . . . . — 6000.00

☐ Reuben Tower — Hanover, Mass., circa 1810-1820. Cherry wood case stained to imitate mahogany, with elaborate fretwork arch and wood finials. Floral motif on spandrels and dial . . . . — 4200.00

CLOCKS — GRANDMOTHER (1770-1815)   Price Range

☐ B. Youngs — Schenectady, New York, circa 1760. Flat
top straight sided oak case. Round dial with Arabic
numerals, single wind hole at 6. 36" high x 11" wide . .   —   4200.00

CLOCKS — GRANDFATHER (1738-1870)

☐ Joseph Doll, circa 1800-1810. Inlaid American eagle &
shield over lower door. Fan inlays at base corners of
cherry wood case. "Whitestails" on hood. Moon
phase dial in arch. Hour, minute, and day hands on
dial. . . . .   —   5800.00

☐ William Clagett — Newport, Rhode Island, circa 1740.
Flat top case with molding. Square signed dial with ¼
hour marks, "ringed" key wind holes. Burl walnut
veneer on door and base . . . .   —   7500.00

☐ Gawin Brown — Boston, Mass., circa 1766. Hooded
pine case "Japanned" and grained, 3 brass finials on
hood. Brass signed dial (on "boss"), with second dial
and day window. Height 90", with 12" dial . . . .   —   8200.00

☐ Philip Brown — Hopkinton, New Hampshire, circa
1820. Cherry wood case, fretwork hood with 3 brass
finials. White signed enamel face with floral spandrels. Arabic numerals on minute ring, Roman
numerals on hour ring. Height 86" . . . .   —   5200.00

☐ William Cummens (apprentice to Simon Willard), circa 1805-1815. Perforated fretwork hood with 3 brass
finials. Mahogany case with fan inlays. Hemisphere
dial arch with moon phase dial. Signed face with se-
cond dial and day window . . . .   —   8500.00

☐ Issac Doolitle — New Haven, Conn. Flat top molded
hood, 3 brass finials. Engraved brass dial with brass
spandrels, signed and dated "1745" on boss. Arched
window in case door. Height 90½" . . . .   —   5200.00

☐ Christian Forrer — Lampeter, Pennsylvania, circa
1750. Engraved and signed brass dial, brass spandrels. Flat top hood, straight oak case with
"port-hole" window (for pendulum bob) in door. Brass
one day single weight movement. Height 84", 10½"
dial. . . . .   —   0000.00

☐ Jacob Ely — Mannheim, Penn., circa 1805. Arched
"Whitestails" hood, 3 brass ball finials. Hemisphere
dial with moon phases, second dial and day window
and sweep second hand. Inlaid walnut case, 100"
high x 19" wide . . . .   —   5800.00

☐ Benjamin Willard — 1743-1808 — Grafton, Mass. With
"105" on dial. 88" high with "209" . . . .   —   8500.00

☐ Simon Willard — White iron dial with moon and calen-
dar, mahogany case, Federal inlay, circa 1799 . . . .   —   14500.00

☐ Paine Wingate — Haverhill, Mass. White dial, circa
1817 . . . .   —   5200.00

	Price Range	
CLOCKS — GRANDFATHER (1738-1870)		
☐ Silas Hoadley — Riley Whiting 30 hour — wooden works	800.00	950.00
☐ Ithaca — 8 day spring — oak or mahogany — glass door, circa 1870-1910	550.00	800.00
CLOCKS — FRENCH		
☐ FRENCH "Banjo" mantel clock. "Vincenti C. France." 8 day time and strike. Gilded wood case with brass feet, side arms and finial. 21 inches high. Shaped like banjo clock	250.00	325.00
☐ FRENCH tall clock. "Morbier" movement. 8 day time strike and alarm. Repeats hour strike with first strike on bell. Repeat on gong. Weight driven. Ornamental brass bezel and pendulum. Vertical rack and snail. Porcelain dial. Without case	450.00	600.00
☐ FRENCH gold wall clock. 4½" circular porcelain dial decorated with garland, gold filigree hands, gilt metal motif on case in form of ribbons and bows. 8 day movement	375.00	500.00
☐ FRENCH Gothic clock. Mahogany case with satin wood inlay, 15-day movement. Chimes & strikes	250.00	325.00
☐ FRENCH Havilland Roccoco China case. Deep green floral design with gold trim. American. 8 day works	75.00	250.00
☐ FRENCH Majolica mantel clock. Wine colored with gold decor. Fretted brass dial under beveled glass door. 12 inches high, 7 inches wide, 8-day movement	250.00	375.00
☐ FRENCH clock metal cased, bronzed, time & strike, 3 classical style cameo adornments, Roman numeral dial on red porcelain disk, 18 inches high	225.00	300.00
☐ FRENCH mantel clock. Battery operated. Movement with pendulum, mahogany case. Bulle, France	150.00	225.00
☐ FRENCH Tiffany mantel clock. 8 day time and strike. Marble case with brass trim. Tiffany & Co., N.Y. on dial	375.00	450.00
☐ FRENCH mantel clock. 8 day time and strike. Matching candelabras case and candelabras are onyx with ormolu trim	400.00	525.00
☐ FRENCH Louis XVI mantel clock under glass dome. "Ate Duminil, Paris." 15 day time and strike. Mahogany case with ormolu trim and four columns. Mahogany inlaid base. Original dome and base	600.00	800.00
☐ FRENCH swinging doll clock. "Farcotbte, C.D.E., Paris." 8 day time only. Pendulum doll in swing moving forward and backward. Ormolu ball. Case alabaster and brass. Under glass dome. Price according to size	550.00	800.00
☐ FRENCH swinging ball clock. 8 day time only. White metal figure, female, classic. Price according to size	550.00	1200.00
☐ FRENCH statue clock, 1895, green onyx & gilt, Joan D'Arc figure finial, hour & ½ hour bell. Brown & green onyx back. Porcelain flowered dial	350.00	450.00

CLOCKS — FRENCH   **Price Range**

☐ FRENCH statue clock, 1889, pompeian red marble, bronzed figure of Mozart as boy with violin, gilt, feet, porcelain & bronze dial, hour & ½ hour bell 375.00   500.00

☐ FRENCH statue clock, 1890, Louis XV style, Homme D'Lettres. Bronzed metal case, marble base, 18 inches high. Black marble dial, intaglio Roman numerals, beveled crystal front and clear crystal cover 375.00   500.00

☐ FRENCH black marble clock, porphyry & urn & finial. Brass lion heads side, brass lion feet front, crystal door front, brass pierced door on back, time and strike   200.00   275.00

☐ FRENCH Empire clock, circa 1810. Open brass pendulum, black wood case, four columns, brass ormolu. Ornately embossed brass dial with black Roman numerals, 20 inches high, time & strike 550.00   700.00

☐ FRENCH black marble, 1890, Grandpierre Fils, Paris, time & strike, escapement. On dial face Romanesque style, black marble & brass dial, intaglio Roman numerals, 16 inches wide, 9 inches high 325.00   400.00

☐ FRENCH tall case clock with "Morbier" movement. 8 day time and strike. Repeats hour strike. Vertical rack and snail striking. Simulated light gridiron pendulum. Oak case 94 inches high. Glass door. Carved hood front of large flower basket 800.00   1200.00

☐ FRENCH regulator. Pin wheel escapement. 8 day time only. Boxed movement. Simulated gridiron lyre pendulum. Porcelain dial sweep second hand. Single weight. Overall height 53 inches.
Without case 750.00   950.00
With ornate case 1500.00   2500.00

☐ FRENCH mantel clock with matching candelabras. 8 day time strike. Brass spring driven movement. Black marble, ormolu and cloissone case. Japy Freres & Co. with touch mark 800.00   1200.00

☐ FRENCH swinging clock. 8 day time only. Ball and pendulum swings from arm of woman operating drill press. Clock was gift to a chairman of Labor Board, Paris, France 750.00   900.00

☐ FRENCH swinging clock. 8 day time only. White metal figure clock. Pendulum has crystal disk and thermometer 600.00   750.00

☐ FRENCH Louis XV bracket clock. 15 day time and strike. Brass movement. Case "Bouelle" with ormolu trim. Circa 1780 . . . .   2200.00   3000.00

French clocks made prior to 1800 may still be found in the American Antiques market. The originals are rapidly increasing in value. Copies of these "LOUIS" style clocks were made in the mid-1800's. While the copies have value, they should not be sold, or bought, as the originals. Caution is the byword.

CLOCKS — LOOKING GLASS & TRANSITION (1820-1840)   **Price Range**

☐ Barnes, Bartholemew Co. — Bristol, Conn., circa 1835. Triple decker. Gilt floral splat, floral face. Country scene on center tablet 400.00   550.00

☐ E. G. Bartholemew — Bristol, Conn., circa 1828. Single door — painted rustic scene on tablet. Stenciled splat & columns fruit & flower motif. 30 hour standard wood movement, weight driven 375.00   500.00

☐ Basset & Gibbs — Litchfield, Conn., circa 1830. Miniature Looking Glass clock. Arabic numerals on face. Fruit basket stenciled splat. Height 24" 500.00   625.00

☐ Rodney Brace — Northridgewater, Mass., circa 1820. Flat, heavy columns. 30 hour wood movement — weight driven. Mirror in door. 24" high 500.00   625.00

☐ Birge Mallory & Co. — Bristol, Conn., circa 1840. 3 decker with painted center tablet. Carved gilt floral splat. Mirror in bottom door. Brass rolling pinion movement — 30 hour. VERY RARE 950.00   1150.00

☐ Ephraim Downs — Bristol, Conn., circa 1825. Claw feet, pineapple finials. Arabic numerals on dial. Glass tablet with country scene. Eagle stencil splat. Standard 30 hour movement 475.00   550.00

☐ C. & L. C. Ives — Bristol, Conn., circa 1830-40. Elaborate carved splat. Floral motif on dial embossed spandrels. Center mirror tablet. Bottom tablet has painted country scene 475.00   550.00

☐ Dyer, Wadsworth & Co. — Augusta, Georgia, circa 1838. Triple decker. Gold gilt carved eagle splat, black chapter ring dial, white numerals. Floral center tablet. Country scene on bottom tablet 550.00   625.00

☐ E. K. Jones — Bristol, Conn., circa 1835. Simple carved splat on half columned case. Arabic numerals on dial, floral spandrels. Mirror tablet door. Weight driven wood movement 325.00   450.00

☐ Munger & Benedict — Auburn, N. Y., circa 1820. Empire type, mirror door. Flat top, "twist" side columns. Arabic numerals on dial. Brass weight driven movement 575.00   625.00

☐ Munger & Pratt — Ithaca, New York, circa 1830. Scrolled splat, "leaf" carved side columns, mirror door. 30 hour wood movement — weight driven. 36" high 400.00   550.00

☐ Spencer Hotchkiss & Co., circa 1830. Triple decker clock. Gilt carved floral splat. Mirror center tablet. Second dial on face, carved brass weight driven movement. 31" high 575.00   650.00

☐ Spencer Hotchkiss & Co., circa 1835. Triple decker clock. Gilt carved floral splat. Mirror center tablet. Eight day brass weight driven movement, 31" high . . .   550.00   625.00

CLOCKS — LOOKING GLASS & TRANSITION (1820-1840) Price Range

☐ Eli Terry — Broken arch splat, with shielded eagle painted insert. Floral painted dial and spandrels. Arabic numerals. Stenciled columns. Door tablet painted with country scene. 30 hour standard weight driven movement. Height 25" 625.00 800.00

☐ Jerome & Darrow — Bristol, Conn., circa 1830. Two decker clock. Painted and carved eagle splat. Turned side columns. Scene of domed mansion on glass tablet. Floral spandrels and second dial on face 525.00 625.00

☐ Wells Forbes — Bristol, N.H., circa 1842. Scrolled splat, flat side columns. White painted dial, gilded spandrels. Painted door panel — 2 Federal mansions in landscape, floral stencil surround. Height 31" x 15½" wide 375.00 475.00

CLOCKS — LYRE (1822-1825)

More ornate form of banjo. The fronts of the cases have some type of a carved leaf motif.

☐ Albert Phipps, circa 1829. Ornate white & gilt case, base & bracket. Gilt eagle finial, single wind hole at 2. Height 44" .... — 4000.00

☐ Lemuel Curtis (Originator of the Girandole) — Concord, Mass. Shelf Lyre, mahogany "Lighthouse" case. 30" high. Wind hole at 2, 6" dial .... — 6500.00

☐ Aaron Willard, Jr. — Boston, Mass., circa 1830. Plain type lyre. Mahogany case carved acanthus leaves, plain face and pendant, acorn finial. Winds at 2, 36" high .... — 6800.00

☐ Sawin & Dyar — Boston, Mass., circa 1822. "Stringed" Lyre (over glass), carved gilt case on plain base & pendant. Spread eagle finial .... — 5500.00

CLOCKS — MASSACHUSETTS SHELF (1800-1830)

☐ Nathan Hale — Chelsea, Vermont, circa 1800-1820. Purple glass front with floral motif. Wayside scene on base panel. Pierced splat with brass finials. Signed on dial and front, height 34" x 13" .... — 7800.00

☐ A. Willard — Boston, Mass., circa 1800-1810. Pierced fretwork hood, 2 brass acorn finials. "Kidney shape" metal dial .... — 13500.00

☐ Simon Willard — Roxbury, circa 1790-1800. "Kidney-shape" glass door. Flat top mahogany case, 30" high. Long fluted columns on base. "Simon Willard, Roxbury" engraved on dial plate .... — 18500.00

☐ John Sawin — Boston, Mass., circa 1830. Flat top hood shelf alarm clock. Decorated tablet, mirror base. Signed dial, wind holes at 2 and 8:50, "barbed arrow" hands. Height 30" x 14" wide.................... — 8200.00

CLOCKS — MASSACHUSETTS SHELF   **Price Range**

☐ David Wood — Newburyport, Mass., circa 1800. Hooded fretwork arch, 3 brass finials. Mahogany panelled case with brass fittings. Square dial with floral spandrels. Country lake painting in broken arch. Single wind hole at 2 .... — 11500.00

CLOCKS — OG (1800-1918)

Manufactured from 1825 to 1918. Name derived from S-like curved molding on door. Three sizes of OG alarm clocks:

    A. Seth Thomas — 16" 30-hour spring movement.
    B. Waterbury Clock Company — 19" spring movement.
    C. Terry & Andrews (1842-1850) Bristol, Conn. One day weight movement.

☐ Ansonia Brass & Copper Company — Ansonia, Conn., circa 1850-60. 30 hour brass, spring wound time, strike & alarm, 18" high. Floral spandrels and alarm ring on face. Flower stencil glass door 150.00 180.00

☐ Ansonia Clock Company — Ansonia, Conn., circa 1855. Walnut veneered case, 26" high. Floral stencil on glass door 115.00 150.00

☐ Brewster & Ingraham — Bristol, Conn., circa 1850. Time & strike 30 hour movement. Oak case, floral motif etched on glass door, 24" high 115.00 150.00

☐ Daniel Pratt, Jr. — Reading, Mass., circa 1840. Weight driven time, strike & alarm. Floral spandrels on face. Eagle & flag motif stenciled on glass door 150.00 225.00

☐ J. C. Brown, Forestville Mfg. Co., circa 1850. Walnut veneer case, 30 hour time, strike & alarm. Weight driven movement. Rustic scene on glass door, 26" high 115.00 150.00

☐ Chauncey Jerome — Bristol, Conn., circa 1830-40. Basic OG case with "picture frame" flat molding. Face inscribed "Made by C. Jerome, Bristol, Ct. U.S.A." 30 hour brass weight driven movement, mirror glass door 175.00 225.00

☐ Jerome & Company — New Haven, Conn. Standard OG 135.00 160.00

☐ Silas Hoadley — Plymouth, Conn. Arabic numerals & floral spandrels on dial. Makers name embossed on wind hole grommets. 30 hour brass movement 26" high 175.00 225.00

☐ Wm. S. Johnson — N.Y.C., circa 1860. 30 hour brass weight driven movement. Extra hand on dial to indicate movement, 20" high 175.00 225.00

☐ C. S. Sperry — Pearl St., N.Y., circa 1830. "Flat OG" (no "S" Molding). Wood movement, weight driven. Frosted glass tablet & lyre motif 150.00 180.00

☐ Seth Thomas. 30 hour alarm brass movement 115.00 150.00

CLOCKS — OG (1800-1918)   **Price Range**

☐ Seth Thomas — Thomaston, Conn., circa 1898. "OG Weight". Walnut veneered case, 25" high. 8 day weight driven time & strike movement. Whooping crane stencil in oval on glass dome 150.00   225.00

☐ Smith & Goodrich — Bristol, Conn., circa 1850. Miniature OG, 15" x 8¾". One day fuzee, spiral gong, alarm movement. Floral motif glass tablet 325.00   400.00

☐ Waterbury Clock Co. — Waterbury, Conn., circa 1850. Spring wound alarm movement, 30 hour, 18½" x 12", 3¾" dial 115.00   165.00

CLOCKS — PILLAR AND SCROLL (1818-1895)

America's first mass produced shelf clock. The original design was by Eli Terry.

☐ Jacob D. Custer — Norristown, Pa., circa 1845. Broken arch with painted basket of flowers. Pine case mahogany veneer. 38" high. Arabic numerals, second dial, and "NORRISTOWN PATENT" on face 4200.00   5500.00

☐ Ephraim Downs — Bristol, Conn., circa 1820. Mahogany veneered pine case, 3 brass urn finials. Floral spandrels. Eglomise* door panel with painted country scene. Height 32" 1200.00   1500.00

☐ Erastus Hodges — Torrington, Conn., circa 1820. Veneered case 28" high. One day wood movement. Arabic numerals and floral spandrels on dial. Rustic Eglomise* scene on glass door panel 1200.00   1500.00

☐ Ansel Merrel — Vienna, Ohio, circa 1828. Arabic numerals and floral spandrels on dial.............. 900.00   1250.00

☐ Mark Leavenworth — Waterbury, Conn., circa 1830. Miniature Pillar & Scroll 22½" high, with 3 brass finials. Arabic numerals on face with floral spandrels. Eglomise* front panel. VERY RARE 2200.00   3000.00

☐ Norris North & Company — Waterbury, Conn., circa 1820. Large East & West movement. Escape wheel, inside plates. Winding arbors 3¾" apart. Weight travels in center, bell on top. VERY RARE................. —   3200.00

☐ Seth Thomas, circa 1895. Brass 8 day movement 400.00   475.00

☐ Seth Thomas — Plymouth, Conn., circa 1818. Mahogany veneered 30" high case. Floral spandrels and face. Eglomise rustic scene door panel. "Porthole" shows off-center pendulum bob 1500.00   2000.00

☐ E. Terry & Sons — Plymouth, Conn., circa 1825-35. Mahogany veneered pine case, 31" high, 3 brass urn finials. Gilt spandrels and Roman numerals 1400.00   2000.00

☐ Eli Terry — Plymouth, Conn., circa 1818. Mahogany veneered pine case, 29" high, 3 brass finials. White painted face with floral spandrels. Arabic numerals (hour & minute), outside escapement. Eglomise* country scene door panel. Pendulum bob "porthole" . 1800.00   2500.00

*Eglomise — Reverse painted on glass.

CLOCKS — STEEPLE (1800-1938)

Clocks topped with spires. Elias Ingraham, of Bristol is credited with the design. There are four sizes of Steeple Clocks: (1) Sub-Miniature, Ansonia, 10½" high. (2) Miniature, Waterbury Clock Co., 14¾" high. (3) Standard Seth Thomas, 20" high. (4) Steeple on Steeple Elisha Manross, 24" high.

Price Range

☐ Ansonia Clock Company — Ansonia, Conn., circa 1898. Sharp Gothic standard steeple. 30 hours brass time, strike & alarm, spring movement. Floral stencil glass panels 185.00   275.00

☐ Brewster & Ingraham (Elias Ingrahams Company), circa 1845. Sharp Gothic twin steeple. Oak case 16" high, with 8 day time & strike brass movement 425.00   750.00

☐ Chauncey Jerome — New Haven, Conn., circa 1850. Sharp Gothic standard steeple. Eight day time & strike fuzee movement. Eagle & ribbon stencil panel. Height 20" x 12" wide 275.00   375.00

☐ Birge & Fuller — Bristol, Conn., circa 1844-48. Standard steeple on steeple. Wagon Spring (J. Ives patent) or fuzee movement. Veneer case 27½" high. Design stenciled on case and base doors. "Porthole" in dial shows movement 3000.00   3750.00

☐ Forestville Mfg. Co., circa 1850. Round gothic twin steeple, ripple finish. "President's House" (White House) painted on tablet. 8 day spring 550.00   700.00

☐ J. C. Brown — Forestville, Conn., circa 1845. Sharp Gothic ripple front ("pie crust") case, 15½" high. Tablet with painted view of Forestville 550.00   650.00

☐ Terry & Andrews — Bristol, Conn., circa 1842-50. Sharp Gothic twin steeple with veneered case. White painted dial Eglomise* panel transfer — printed with "Independence Hall". Height 19½" 550.00   625.00

☐ Waterbury Clock Co. — Waterbury, Conn., circa 1880. Miniature Steeple, 14" high. Mahogany veneered case. Stenciled clear door shows pendulum 275.00   375.00

☐ Wm. L. Gilbert Co. — Winsted, Conn., circa 1850-1860. "Winsted Gothic Extra". Sharp Gothic standard steeple. Round dial in maple veneer door. Oval glass panel shows pendulum bob. Height 17¼" x 10½" wide . . . .   —   225.00

*Eglomise — **Reverse painted on glass.**

CLOCKS — WALNUT (1880-1916)

Walnut and Oak Clocks are similar in every way other than the woods. All prices shown are for fine-working condition.

☐ W. L. Gilbert Co. — Walnut eight day shelf clock. "Classic" carved head center. 24" x 14½", 5½" dial .   175.00   250.00

☐ Ingraham — Walnut eight day alarm clock. Elaborate carved splat. "Bird" stencil on glass door, 24" x 16", 5" dial 175.00   250.00

CLOCKS — WALNUT (1880-1916)

Price Range

☐ Wm. Gilbert Co. — Winsted, Conn. Black walnut case. "Bird" motif stencil, 19" x 10½", 4¾" dial 175.00   250.00

☐ Ingraham — "Liberty" Walnut 8 day. "Classic" head on case. 20½" x 13¼", 5" dial 425.00   575.00

☐ Ingraham — "New York". Walnut 8 day time & strike, elaborate carved case, stenciled door, 23" x 14", 6" dial 225.00   300.00

☐ F. Kroeber — New York City. Black walnut 8 day shelf clock. Small square glass door, cut crystal pendulum bob, 21" x 14½", 5" dial 500.00   600.00

☐ New Haven Clock Co. — Walnut 8 day alarm shelf clock. "Wheat" stencil glass door. 20" x 13", 5" dial . .   175.00   250.00

☐ New Haven Clock Co. — Adjustable scale on pendulum, 8 day clock, 20½" x 14¼", 5" dial 175.00   275.00

☐ George Owen — Winsted, Conn., circa 1880. Walnut case. "Kidney" dial & clear glass door, 23" x 14", 5" dial 225.00   275.00

☐ Seth Thomas — "Oxford", Walnut elaborate carved case. 8 day time, strike & alarm movement. Thermometer in center of splat, 22½" x 14", 6" dial 225.00   300.00

☐ Seth Thomas — "Fargo", Walnut case 8 day strike & alarm. 22" x 13", 6" dial 225.00   300.00

☐ Waterbury Clock Co. — "Nelson", Walnut 8 day movement. "Bird" stencil on glass door. 22" x 13½", 6" dial   200.00   250.00

☐ E. N. Welch Mfg. Co. — Black walnut miniature 30 hour alarm. Clear glass door. 21" x 13", 5" dial 225.00   275.00

☐ Waterbury Clock Co. — "Tampa", Walnut Calendar shelf clock. 8 day calendar & strike. Thermometer and barometer on side of door. 22" high, 6" dial 400.00   550.00

*Any "WALNUT" with calendar movements are worth double.

CLOCKS — OAK

All have glass fronts, most with floral, geometric or patriotic motifs and stenciled or painted on the fronts.

☐ Oak Clock with time and strike 175.00   225.00
☐ Oak Clock with time and strike and calendar* 350.00   575.00
☐ Political and Military carved oak clocks. Admiral Dewey, Admiral Schley, Admiral Sampson, President McKinley, President Roosevelt 300.00   375.00

* Any "OAK" clocks with calendar movements are worth double.

CLOCKS — SHIP CLOCKS

☐ Seth Thomas — Round metal cased 8-day double spring drive with a lever balance wheel movement. 6¼" diameter 200.00   250.00

☐ Seth Thomas — 30-hour Ships Bell Clock with metal case, bell below, strikes ships bell, not the hour 375.00   500.00

☐ Chelsea — Boston, Mass. Ship Strike, round bronze case. Circa 1900 (still made today) 250.00   950.00

CLOTHING

It's a lucky thing that people used to save their clothing (and that is a hint that you, too, should save for future collectors!), because out-of-fashion costume is a hot collectible today. The fashion for soft, feminine white clothes in the mid-70's, sent everyone to their attic, hoping—and often finding—sellable or wearable examples. Vests, coats, tuxedos, shawls, handbags—all are potentially valuable.

	Price Range	
☐ Apron, Ruffled Bottom	6.00	10.00
☐ Bonnet, Gingham with Button	28.00	32.00
☐ Boy's Sailor Suit, 3-piece wool	25.00	30.00
☐ Camisole, Victorian	20.00	25.00
☐ Cape, Seal	35.00	40.00
☐ Child's Dress, embroidered white cotton, 1910	25.00	30.00
☐ Coat, Coonskin, c1920	190.00	220.00
☐ Coat, Cutaway, c1880	40.00	50.00
☐ Coat, Lady's Sealskin, c1940	100.00	130.00
☐ **Coat, Man's morning w/tails**	25.00	30.00
☐ Coat, Man's Black Velvet Opera, c1910	100.00	120.00
☐ Dress, 2-piece Velveteen	35.00	45.00
☐ Dress, Black Embroidered Silk, c1890	75.00	100.00
☐ Dress, Black & White Tafetta, c1870	25.00	30.00
☐ Dress, Early 1800's	30.00	35.00
☐ Dress, 1880's, 2-piece, black silk & brocade	350.00	400.00
☐ Dress, White, Lace trim	80.00	100.00
☐ Dress, White Silk Wedding, 1880's	125.00	130.00
☐ Dress, Wine Velvet	25.00	30.00
☐ Dress, Sheer Wool Stripe, 1850	30.00	40.00
☐ Handbag, Beaded, Multicolored	55.00	75.00
☐ Handbag, Beaded, Drawstring, Multi-color & Black	24.00	30.00
☐ **Handbag,** beaded, black, top expands, c. 1900	30.00	50.00
☐ **Handbag,** crocheted, drawstring top, c. 1900	20.00	30.00
☐ **Handbag,** embroidered on velvet, c. 1880	80.00	100.00
☐ **Handbag,** embroidered silk and gold, c. 1890	75.00	90.00
☐ **Handbag,** enameled clasp top, c. 1910	40.00	60.00
☐ Handbag, Mesh, Sterling Silver	80.00	100.00
☐ Handbag, Lucite, 1940's-50's	10.00	40.00
☐ Handkerchief, White Silk	20.00	25.00
☐ Hat, Opera, Black Silk	45.00	75.00
☐ Hat, black bonnet, silk, c. 1820	40.00	50.00
☐ Hat, bonnet, straw and silk bow, c. 1890	25.00	40.00
☐ Hat, ladies' straw with plum black, c. 1890	80.00	90.00
☐ Hat, ladies' straw cloche, c. 1920	20.00	30.00
☐ Hat, men's straw panama, c. 1890	75.00	85.00
☐ Hat, men's top, beaver grey silk band, c. 1870	100.00	120.00
☐ Hat, men's top, felt wool, c. 1850	90.00	100.00
☐ Hat, men's top, collapsible, c. 1890	100.00	125.00
☐ Hats, 1940's, Felt, some w/feathers	5.00	10.00
☐ Neck Piece, Fox or Mink	25.00	30.00

CLOTHES

	Price Range	
☐ Pantaloons, Victorian	15.00	20.00
☐ Parasol, White Linen	55.00	75.00
☐ Robe, Gold and Black Silk	15.00	20.00
☐ Shawl, Tapestry, Czech., 64" x 64", fringed	30.00	40.00
☐ Shawl, Fringed Design	55.00	75.00
☐ Shawl, Spanish Silk, 51" square	75.00	85.00
☐ Shawl, Turkish Embroidered, 7' x 1'4"	150.00	225.00
☐ Skirt Hoop	20.00	25.00
☐ Suit, Swallowtail, 1900's	75.00	95.00

COCA COLA COLLECTIBLES

The most popular soft drink in the world has another claim to fame. The Coca Cola Company has always maintained an imaginative and successful campaign to promote its products, and over the years many of these items have become highly desirable collectibles. Coca Cola collectibles continue to attract interest at an astonishing pace in the collector marketplace. Coke has managed to keep pace with the moods and events of our times. Many hobbyists feel the history of Coke advertising and promotions have directly mirrored the growth culture of a nation. The Duster girl in her vintage auto represented Coca Cola at the turn of the century on trays, bookmarks, and calendars. She was soon followed by the Flapper of the Roaring 20's, who in turn gave way to the U.S. Army Nurse Corps when both Coke and the United States knew that patriotism was the order of the day.

Although the older items in particular are the most valuable (especially pre World War II), it pays to be aware that later items continue to attract attention and are likely to increase in value. New Coca Cola promotions are being conceived at this time. It's great fun collecting nostalgia pieces of yesterday, while at the same time keeping a sharp eye on the Coke collectibles of tomorrow.

ROOSTER TRAY,
c. 1957 .. 75.00 - 100.00

TAKE HOME CARTON,
c. 1939 ...... 30.00 - 50.00

PLASTIC SIGN,
9"Dia. . . 20.00 - 25.00

COCA COLA COLLECTIBLES

	Price Range	
☐ Ashtray. Aluminum, 1955	2.00	4.00
☐ Ashtray and Match Holder. 1940	170.00	185.00
☐ Ashtray. Metal, 1963	3.00	4.00
☐ Ashtray. Mexican, painted aluminum	2.00	3.00
☐ Ashtray. Picture of Atlanta plant	15.00	18.00
☐ Ashtray. Set of card suites, 1940	50.00	55.00
☐ Ball Point Pen with Telephone Dialer	5.00	7.00
☐ Blotter. "Delicious and Refreshing", 1904	9.00	12.00
☐ Blotter. Duster Girl in auto, 1904	9.00	12.00
☐ Blotter. "Icy Style COLD Refreshment", 1939	6.00	8.00
☐ Blotter. "Restores Energy and Strengthens Nerves", 1906	8.00	10.00
☐ Blotter. Santa Claus with children, 1938	6.00	7.50
☐ Blotter. Sprite with bottle-top hat, 1953	3.00	4.00
☐ Blotter. Sprite with bottle-top hat, 1956	2.00	3.00
☐ Book Cover, 1951	5.00	7.00
☐ Book Mark. Coke Can, 1960	8.00	10.00
☐ Book Mark. Hilda Clark, 1899	135.00	150.00
☐ Book Mark. Hilda Clark, 1900	130.00	145.00
☐ Book Mark. Little Girl with Bird House, 1904	150.00	170.00
☐ Book Mark. Lillian Russel, 1904	75.00	85.00
☐ Book Mark. Owl on Perch, 1906	95.00	105.00
☐ Book Mark. Valentine, 1899	100.00	120.00
☐ Book Mark. Victorian Lady	160.00	185.00
☐ Bottle Holder Protector, paper envelope, 1932	5.00	7.00
☐ Bottle Holder Protector, 6 bottle type, 1933	35.00	40.00
☐ Bottle. Amber glass, 1905	20.00	25.00
☐ Bottle. "Best by a Dam Site", 1936	35.00	50.00
☐ Bottle. Circa 1905, light green	10.00	13.00
☐ Bottle. Circa 1915, applied paper label	35.00	40.00
☐ Bottle. Display 20 in., 1923	100.00	115.00
☐ Bottle. Donald Duck, 7 oz., painted	4.00	8.00
☐ Bottle. Double diamond, amber glass, 1905	20.00	30.00
☐ Bottle. Fountain syrup type, 1900-1920	65.00	85.00
☐ Bottle. Gold Dipped 50th Anniversary, 26 oz.	6.00	10.00
☐ Bottle. Israil Exposition, 1975	6.00	10.00
☐ Bottle. Miniature perfume	25.00	40.00
☐ Bottle. Nine inches tall, 1902	15.00	20.00
☐ Bottle. Oklahoma 1903-1967 Presentation	65.00	75.00
☐ Bottle. Turkey, embossed four sides	15.00	25.00
☐ Calendar. American Birds, 1959	—	10.00
☐ Calendar. Bathing Beauty, 1930	—	95.00
☐ Calendar. "Betty", 1914	—	300.00
☐ Calendar. Boy with Dog, 1931	100.00	125.00
☐ Calendar. Boy with Fishing Pole, 1937	80.00	100.00
☐ Calendar. Coca Cola Girl, 1910	900.00	950.00
☐ Calendar. Flapper Girl, glass in hand, 1926	550.00	600.00
☐ Calendar. Garden Girl, 1920	70.00	90.00
☐ Calendar. Girl at Party, 1925	60.00	70.00

COCA COLA COLLECTIBLES

Price Range

☐ Calendar. Girl with Record in Hand, 1968	6.00	10.00
☐ Calendar. "Grisilda", 1905	250.00	300.00
☐ Calendar. Hilda Clark, 1900	450.00	500.00
☐ Calendar. Knitting Girl, 1919	100.00	130.00
☐ Calendar. Lady at Desk, 1899	750.00	800.00
☐ Calendar. Lady with Tennis Racket, 1891	740.00	800.00
☐ Calendar. Lady with Roses, 1902	600.00	650.00
☐ Calendar. Lillian Nordica with bottle, 1904	850.00	875.00
☐ Calendar. Modern Image Dancing, 1970	3.00	4.50
☐ Calendar. Old Man with Boat, 1936	100.00	115.00
☐ Calendar. Pearl White, 1916	220.00	250.00
☐ Calendar. Snowman and Girl, 1958	10.00	12.00
☐ Calendar. Two Models, 1912	275.00	300.00
☐ Calendar. U.S. Army Nurse Corp., 1943	25.00	30.00
☐ Calendar. Victorian Lady Cloth Replica, 1972	8.00	10.00
☐ Calendar. World War I Girl, 1917	200.00	220.00
☐ Calendar. 1973 reproduction of 1899 Valentine, 1973 .	10.00	15.00
☐ Carrier. First paper carton, 1924	25.00	30.00
☐ Carrier. Foil-covered carton, 1941	15.00	20.00
☐ Carrier. July Fourth 6-box wrapper, 1935	35.00	50.00
☐ Carrier. Santa Claus carton, 1931	20.00	25.00
☐ Carrier. Vendor's holder, 1940	60.00	75.00
☐ Carrier. Wooden take home type, 1940	17.00	24.00
☐ Carrier. Yellow wooden, 1939	20.00	25.00
☐ Case. Miniature, display type, 24 bottles	3.00	4.00
☐ Case. Miniature, plastic bottles & case, 1973	3.00	4.00
☐ Case. Miniature, 28 bottles, gold finish	30.00	35.00
☐ Case. Shipping type, 1906	120.00	130.00
☐ Case. Wooden, 24 bottle type, 1924	5.00	7.50
☐ Car Bottle Holder. 1950	15.00	20.00
☐ Cigarette Case. Frosted glass, 50th Anniversary 1936	90.00	110.00
☐ Cigarette Lighter. Aluminum, 1963	7.00	10.00
☐ Cigarette Lighter. Coke bottle shape, 1940	5.00	8.00
☐ Cigarette Lighter. Coke can, 1950	25.00	30.00
☐ Cigarette Lighter. Music box plays "Dixie"	18.00	25.00
☐ Cigarette Lighter. Musical, 1960	28.00	35.00
☐ Clock. Brass mantle type, 1954	85.00	105.00
☐ Clock. Dome style, 1950	175.00	190.00
☐ Clock. Electric brass wall model, 1915	240.00	300.00
☐ Clock. Hilda Clark Celluloid desk clock, 1901	1800.00	1950.00
☐ Clock. Ideal Brain Tonic, 1893	2000.00	2200.00
☐ Clock. Leather Boudoir, 1919	200.00	240.00
☐ Clock. Pendulum wall style, 1893	900.00	1050.00
☐ Clock. Re-issue of Betty, 1974	50.00	70.00
☐ Clock. Small Boudoir style, 1915	240.00	260.00
☐ Clock. Spring operated wall style, brass pendulum ...	300.00	350.00
☐ Clock. Walnut wall model, 1960	215.00	240.00
☐ Crock. Fountain dispenser, hand painted, 1890	1400.00	1650.00
☐ Cuff Links. Bottle cap, 1954	7.00	10.00

COCA COLA COLLECTIBLES

	Price Range	
☐ Cuff Links. Blue pearl	70.00	85.00
☐ Cuff Links. Gold burnish links & tie clip, 1952	12.00	16.00
☐ Cuff Links. Salesman's sterling silver links and tie tack, 1930	50.00	60.00
☐ Cuff Links. Sterling silver, 1923	45.00	55.00
☐ Flashlight. Bottle shaped plastic	3.00	4.00
☐ Glass. 5¢ with arrow, 1905	120.00	145.00
☐ Glass. Flair type, 1900	175.00	185.00
☐ Glass. Flair Lip, 1923	30.00	40.00
☐ Glass. Fountain type with syrup line, 1900	50.00	60.00
☐ Glass. Fountain type, no syrup line	7.00	10.00
☐ Glass. Home promotion type, red & white	1.00	2.00
☐ Glass. Pewter, 1930	70.00	80.00
☐ Glass Globe. Leaded, 1928	2850.00	3100.00
☐ Ice Pick and Opener. 1940	7.00	10.00
☐ Key Chain. Amber replica bottle with brass chain, 1964	5.00	7.00
☐ Key Chain. Car key style, 1950	25.00	30.00
☐ Key Chain. Red with gold bottle, 1955	15.00	25.00
☐ Key Chain. 50th Anniversary Celebration, 1936	10.00	15.00
☐ Lamp. Bottle shape, 1920	800.00	975.00
☐ Lamp. Leaded glass chandelier, Tiffany design, 1910	3800.00	4200.00
☐ Mirror. Cameo design, 1905	8000.00	8300.00
☐ Mirror. Fountain type, 1900	1400.00	1800.00
☐ Mirror. Trademark inscription, 1900	2800.00	3100.00
☐ Mirror. Pocket-size, "Bathing Beauty", 1918	275.00	290.00
☐ Mirror. Pocket-size, "Betty", 1914	100.00	120.00
☐ Mirror. Pocket-size, "Coca Cola Girl", 1909	125.00	145.00
☐ Mirror. Pocket-size, "Coca Cola Girl", 1911	120.00	140.00
☐ Mirror. Pocket-size, "Drink Coca Cola 5¢", 1914	250.00	275.00
☐ Mirror. Pocket-size, "Elaine", 1917	150.00	160.00
☐ Mirror. Pocket-size, "Enjoy Thirst", 1930	75.00	90.00
☐ Mirror. Pocket-size, "Garden Girl", 1920	250.00	275.00
☐ Mirror. Pocket-size, "Juanita", oval, 1905	185.00	200.00
☐ Mirror. Pocket-size, "Lillian Russel", round, 1904	70.00	80.00
☐ Mirror. Pocket-size, oval, 1903	130.00	150.00
☐ Mirror. Pocket-size, "Relieves Fatique", 1906	150.00	180.00
☐ Mirror. Pocket-size, "St. Louis Exposition", 1904	100.00	110.00
☐ Mirror. Pocket-size, "St. Louis Fair", 1904	130.00	145.00
☐ Milk Glass Light Fixture. 1920	750.00	850.00
☐ Milk Glass Light Shade. 1920	375.00	400.00
☐ Note Pad. Celluloid covered, 1902	75.00	95.00
☐ Opener. Bone handle knife, 1908	130.00	150.00
☐ Opener. Nashville Anniversary, 1952	50.00	65.00
☐ Opener. Skate key style, 1935	35.00	45.00
☐ Opener. "Starr X", 1925	2.50	4.50
☐ Opener. Stationary wall model, 1900	20.00	25.00
☐ Paperweight. Coca Cola gum, 1916	75.00	85.00
☐ Paperweight. Coke cooler music box, 1951	40.00	55.00

COCA COLA COLLECTIBLES

Price Range

☐ Paperweight. "Coke is Coca Cola", 1948	70.00	90.00
☐ Paperweight. Hollow glass, tin bottom, 1909	250.00	275.00
☐ Pen. Baseball bat, 1940	20.00	30.00
☐ Pencil Box. 1930	20.00	35.00
☐ Pencil Holder. Celluloid, 1910	125.00	135.00
☐ Pencil Holder. Miniature ceramic, 1960	65.00	75.00
☐ Pencil Holder. Tin, 1925	4.00	6.00
☐ Pencil Sharpener. Plastic, 1960	5.00	10.00
☐ Pencil Sharpener. Red metal, 1933	12.00	16.00
☐ Playing Cards. Airplane Spatter, 1942 (deck)	10.00	12.00
☐ Playing Cards. Coca Cola Girls, 1909 (deck)	50.00	60.00
☐ Pocket Secretary. Leather bound, 1920	30.00	40.00
☐ Postcard. "All Over the World", 1913	105.00	120.00
☐ Postcard. Duster Girl driving car, 1906	90.00	100.00
☐ Postcard. Girl with picture hat, 1909	25.00	30.00
☐ Postcard. Horse and delivery wagon, 1900	120.00	140.00
☐ Postcard. Men in speedboat, 1913	95.00	110.00
☐ Postcard. Picture of bottling plant, 1905	110.00	130.00
☐ Postcard. School teacher at blackboard, 1913	85.00	95.00
☐ Postcard. Truck carrying cases of Coke, 1913	125.00	145.00
☐ Postcard Set. Dick Tracy series, 1942	135.00	155.00
☐ Poster. "Bathing Beauty", 1918	400.00	425.00
☐ Poster. "Betty". 1914	250.00	270.00
☐ Poster. "Early Display with Young Lovers", 1891	450.00	480.00
☐ Poster. "Flapper Girl", 1929	150.00	170.00
☐ Poster. "Florine McKinney", 1936	35.00	45.00
☐ Poster. "Girl in Hammock", 1900	425.00	450.00
☐ Poster. "Hilda Clark Cuban", 1901	300.00	325.00
☐ Poster. "Soldier and Girl", 1943	25.00	30.00
☐ Radio. Coke bottle shaped, 1930	300.00	340.00
☐ Radio. Coke can shaped, 1971	12.00	18.00
☐ Radio. Coke cooler shaped, 1949	135.00	150.00
☐ Radio. Crystal radio set, 1950	95.00	105.00
☐ Radio. Transistor, vending machine shaped, 1963	55.00	75.00
☐ Sign. "Betty", tin, 1914	500.00	700.00
☐ Sign. Bottle tray, tin, 1900	300.00	340.00
☐ Sign. "Coca Cola Girls", cardboard, 1922	75.00	85.00
☐ Sign. Coke bottle, tin	95.00	110.00
☐ Sign. "Elaine", tin, 1917	475.00	500.00
☐ Sign. "Hilda Clark", paper, 1900	250.00	280.00
☐ Sign. "Hilda Clark", tin, 1904	275.00	295.00
☐ Sign. "Lillian Russel", oval, tin, 1904	750.00	800.00
☐ Toy. Bank—bottle cap, 1950	12.00	16.00
☐ Toy. Bank—vending machine, 1948	20.00	25.00
☐ Toy. Bean bag, 1971	20.00	26.00
☐ Toy. Boomerang, 1940	38.00	45.00
☐ Toy. Coke truck, 1930	125.00	140.00
☐ Toy. Coke truck, 1945	60.00	80.00
☐ Toy. Comic book, 1951	70.00	85.00

COCA COLA COLLECTIBLES

	Price Range	
☐ Toy. Darts, 1940	60.00	80.00
☐ Toy. Hot rod, 1971	18.00	24.00
☐ Toy. Kite—American Flyer, 1930	180.00	190.00
☐ Toy. Marbles, 1950	40.00	58.00
☐ Toy. Model plane, 1950	35.00	45.00
☐ Toy. Red & white Coke car	30.00	40.00
☐ Toy. Tic-tac-toe game, 1940	75.00	85.00
☐ Toy. Train set (Lionel), 1974	95.00	105.00
☐ Toy. Volkswagen van, 1950	20.00	30.00
☐ Toy. Whistle, 1945	5.00	8.00
☐ Toy. Yo-yo, 1955	3.00	6.00
☐ Tray. "Bathing Beauty", 1930	95.00	115.00
☐ Tray. "Betty", 1912	80.00	95.00
☐ Tray. "Betty", oval, 1914	70.00	85.00
☐ Tray. Ceramic "Change Receiver", 1900	490.00	510.00
☐ Tray. "Coca-Cola Girl", oval, 1909	95.00	115.00
☐ Tray. "Elaine", 1917	45.00	60.00
☐ Tray. "Farm Boy with Dog", 1931	90.00	110.00
☐ Tray. "Flapper Girl", 1923	65.00	80.00
☐ Tray. "Frances Dee", 1933	18.00	25.00
☐ Tray. "Girl at Party", 1925	60.00	75.00
☐ Tray. "Girl in the Afternoon", 1938	38.00	45.00
☐ Tray. "Girl with Fox Fur", 1925	65.00	85.00
☐ Tray. "Girl with French Menu", 1950	65.00	80.00
☐ Tray. "Girl with Umbrella", 1957	60.00	75.00
☐ Tray. "Hilda Clark", 1904	240.00	270.00
☐ Tray. "Johny Weismuller & Maureen O'Sullivan", 1934	160.00	180.00
☐ Tray. "Juanita", round, 1905	140.00	165.00
☐ Tray. "Olympic Games", 15" x 11", 1976	10.00	15.00
☐ Tray (serving). Plastic, 1971	45.00	60.00
☐ Tray. Replica of "Duster Girl", 1972	25.00	40.00
☐ Tray. "Sailor Girl", 1940	25.00	40.00
☐ Tray. "Saint Louis Fair", oval, 1904	155.00	185.00
☐ Tray. "Santa Claus", 15" x 11", 1973	20.00	30.00
☐ Tray. "Soda Fountain Clerk", 1927	70.00	85.00
☐ Tray. "Springboard Girl", 1939	40.00	55.00
☐ Tray. "Summer Girl", 1921	80.00	110.00
☐ Tray. T.V. tray, candle design, 1972	18.00	25.00
☐ Tray. T.V. tray, Thanksgiving motif, 1961	18.00	25.00
☐ Tray. "Topless", 1908	460.00	490.00
☐ Tray. "Two Girls at Car", 1942	32.00	40.00
☐ Tray. "Vienna Art Nude", 1905	190.00	220.00
☐ Tray. "Western Bottling Co.", 1905	85.00	100.00
☐ Wallet. Coke bottle emblem, 1915	70.00	80.00
☐ Wallet. Coca Cola script, 1922	85.00	95.00
☐ Wallet. Embossed coin purse, 1906	140.00	155.00

COINS

A factor in determining the value of a coin is the "condition" or state of preservation. In almost all coins, and especially in rare or "key" coins, the better condition or grade, the more desirable the coin. A "key" coin in strictly uncirculated (brand new) condition may bring a hundred times the price of the same date coin in poor condition.

Code abbreviations:

ABP — Average Buy Price
V. FINE — Very Fine
EX. FINE — Extra Fine
UN — Uncirculated

For more concise information on coin collecting please consult our publication *The Official Blackbook Price Guide of United States Coins* which is published annually.

SMALL CENTS — INDIAN HEAD, 1859-1909

The metalic content of the coin was changed in 1864 to 95% copper and 5% zinc and tin, weight reduced to 48 grains. The coin then produced was thinner than the preceding cents, and the color was different. The first 1864 cents did not have the designers initial "L" on the headress ribbon. Later in the year, the letter did appear on a limited quantity. The initial is on all Indian cents for following years.

James B. Longacre the designer of the Indian cent was born August 11, 1794. It was supposed for years that he had used his small daughter as a model for it. It is generally conceded now that he modelled the Indian cent after Roman-Greek statuary in his collection.

INDIAN CENT
obverse / reverse

DATE	Mintages	ABP	G-4 Good	F-12 Fine	EX-40 Ex.Fine	MS-60 Unc.	Proof
☐ 1859 36,400,000		2.00	3.00	9.00	50.00	300.00	600.00
☐ 1860 20,566,000		2.00	3.00	7.00	20.00	90.00	450.00
☐ 1861 10,100,000		4.00	7.00	15.00	30.00	100.00	450.00
☐ 1862 28,075,000		1.50	2.75	5.00	18.00	80.00	400.00
☐ 1863 49,840,000		1.50	2.75	5.00	15.00	90.00	500.00
☐ 1864 Copper Nickel . . . 13.740,000		3.00	5.00	11.00	30.00	100.00	525.00
☐ 1864 Bronze . . . 39,233,714		1.50	3.00	6.50	20.00	55.00	700.00
☐ 1864 L on Ribbon		10.00	25.00	60.00	100.00	295.00	7500.00
☐ 1865 35,429,286		1.10	2.25	5.25	18.00	45.00	225.00

SMALL CENTS — INDIAN HEAD, 1859-1909

DATE	Mintages	ABP	G-4 Good	F-12 Fine	EX-40 Ex. Fine	MS-60 Unc.	Proof
☐ 1866	9,826,500	8.00	15.00	23.00	60.00	125.00	300.00
☐ 1867	9,821,000	8.00	15.00	23.00	60.00	125.00	300.00
☐ 1868	10,266,500	8.00	15.00	21.50	50.00	125.00	300.00
☐ 1869	6,420,000	12.00	20.00	52.00	110.00	270.00	375.00
☐ 1869 over 8		40.00	55.00	175.00	400.00	1000.00	—
☐ 1870	5,275,000	7.00	17.00	42.00	80.00	175.00	300.00
☐ 1871	3,929,500	15.00	25.00	50.00	100.00	200.00	300.00
☐ 1872	4,042,000	18.00	30.00	70.00	125.00	250.00	375.00
☐ 1873	11,676,500	3.00	6.50	15.00	37.50	80.00	200.00

NICKELS — LIBERTY HEAD, 1883-1912

The Liberty Head nickel first appeared in 1883. They were the work of Charles E. Barber, Mint engraver. The design in low relief is considered to be one of the best issued by the United States.

The reverse has a large Roman numeral "V", and first issues did not have the word "CENTS". These "centless" nickels were sometimes gold-plated and passed as five dollar gold pieces. Later, in the same year, they were re-engraved to include the words "CENTS" at the bottom, and "E PLURIBUS UNIM" high above in the wreath.

The 1913 Liberty Head nickel is one of the most celebrated coins in the United States. No one, not even experts, has learned how and by whom the coins were made. The U.S. Mint denies making them, and they were not authorized by Congress. Five pieces were made, however, and they are all accounted for. Counterfeits are known to exist.

LIBERTY NICKEL
obverse / reverse

☐ 1883							
no cents .	5,479,519	.90	1.75	2.50	6.00	30.00	250.00
w/cents . .	16,032,983	1.70	4.25	9.00	20.00	55.00	175.00
☐ 1884	11,273,942	1.80	4.25	8.75	17.00	55.00	175.00
☐ 1885	1,476,490	40.00	100.00	175.00	250.00	400.00	500.00
☐ 1886	3,330,290	17.00	27.00	45.00	75.00	160.00	250.00
☐ 1887	15,263,652	1.00	2.75	5.50	12.00	55.00	175.00
☐ 1888	10,720,483	2.50	4.50	8.50	13.50	55.00	175.00
☐ 1889	15,881,361	1.25	2.25	5.00	12.00	55.00	175.00
☐ 1890	16,259,272	1.00	3.50	5.75	13.00	55.00	175.00
☐ 1891	16,834,350	.80	2.35	5.00	12.00	55.00	175.00
☐ 1892	11,699,642	.75	2.00	5.00	12.00	55.00	175.00
☐ 1893	13,370,195	.75	1.75	4.50	12.00	55.00	175.00
☐ 1894	5,413,132	1.00	3.75	8.00	14.50	65.00	175.00

NICKELS — LIBERTY HEAD, 1883-1912

DATE	Mintages	ABP	G-4 Good	F-12 Fine	VF-20 V.Fine	EX-40 Ex.Fine	MS-60 Unc.
☐ 1895	9,979,884	.75	1.75	4.25	11.00	55.00	175.00
☐ 1896	8,842,920	.65	1.80	7.00	14.00	125.00	160.00
☐ 1897	20,428,735	.40	1.00	2.50	11.00	125.00	160.00
☐ 1898	12,532,087	.45	1.00	2.50	11.00	125.00	160.00
☐ 1899	26,029,031	.45	1.00	2.75	9.50	125.00	160.00
☐ 1900	27,255,995	.35	.45	1.50	20.00	125.00	160.00
☐ 1901	26,480,213	.35	.45	1.50	20.00	125.00	160.00
☐ 1902	31,480,579	.35	.45	1.50	20.00	125.00	160.00
☐ 1903	28,006,725	.35	.45	1.50	20.00	125.00	160.00
☐ 1904	21,404,984	.35	.45	1.50	20.00	125.00	160.00
☐ 1905	29,827,276	.35	.45	1.50	20.00	125.00	160.00
☐ 1906	38,613,725	.35	.45	1.50	20.00	125.00	160.00
☐ 1907	39,214,800	.35	.45	1.50	20.00	125.00	160.00
☐ 1908	22,686,177	.35	.45	1.50	20.00	125.00	160.00
☐ 1909	11,590,526	.35	.45	2.00	20.00	125.00	160.00
☐ 1910	30,169,353	.35	.45	1.50	20.00	125.00	160.00
☐ 1911	39,559,372	.35	.45	1.50	20.00	125.00	160.00
☐ 1912	26,236,714	.35	.45	1.50	20.00	125.00	160.00
☐ 1912D ...	8,474,000	.50	.80	5.00	35.00	375.00	—
☐ 1912S	238,000	13.00	22.00	35.00	85.00	675.00	
☐ 1913* Not a regular mint issue — 5 known, SUPERIOR SALE 1978 200,000.00.							

DIMES — MERCURY DIMES, 1916-1945

This dime was designed by A.A. Weinman. Though commonly called the "Mercury Dime", the obverse is a representation of Liberty. The wings crowning her cap symbolize liberty of thought. The reverse design shows a fasces of sticks with an axe protruding and a bunch of laurel. This coin looks very much like a Denarius of Rome in 100 B.C.

MERCURY DIME
obverse / reverse

☐ 1916	22,180,000	.55	.75	1.35	2.50	4.75	26.00
☐ 1916D...	264,000	175.00	200.00	400.00	500.00	750.00	2000.00
☐ 1916S...	10,450,000	.80	1.75	4.75	6.25	10.00	50.00
☐ 1917	55,230,000	.55	.65	1.25	1.75	3.50	26.00
☐ 1917D ..	9,402,000	.75	1.50	6.50	10.50	20.00	150.00
☐ 1917S...	27,330,000	.55	.65	1.50	3.00	6.00	68.00
☐ 1918	26.680,000	.55	.65	3.25	7.50	14.00	70.00
☐ 1918D...	22,674,800	.55	.75	4.00	6.50	15.00	125.00
☐ 1918S...	19,300,000	.55	.75	2.00	4.00	9.50	95.00
☐ 1919	35,740,000	.55	.65	1.25	3.00	5.00	50.00

DIMES — MERCURY DIMES, 1916-1945

DATE	Mintages	ABP	G-4 Good	VG-8 V.Good	F-12 Fine	EX-40 Ex.Fine	MS-60 Unc.
☐ 1919D ...	9,939,000	.60	1.25	6.00	14.00	27.00	195.00
☐ 1919S...	8,850,000	.60	1.25	6.00	13.00	25.00	220.00
☐ 1920	59,030,000	.55	.65	1.25	2.00	3.50	25.00
☐ 1920D...	19,171,000	.55	.75	2.50	4.00	8.50	90.00
☐ 1920S...	13,820,000	.55	.75	2.00	4.00	8.50	90.00
☐ 1921	1,230,000	6.00	12.00	42.50	80.00	280.00	1200.00
☐ 1921D ..	1,080,000	11.00	19.00	55.00	100.00	60.00	1100.00
☐ 1923	50,130,000	.55	.65	1.00	1.50	3.00	25.00
☐ 1923S...	6,440,000	.55	.95	3.50	6.75	15.00	175.00
☐ 1924	24,010,000	.55	.65	1.00	1.75	3.75	50.00
☐ 1924D ..	6,810,000	.55	2.50	8.00	10.00	28.00	200.00
☐ 1924S...	7,120,000	.55	2.50	8.00	10.00	28.00	200.00

QUARTERS — STANDING LIBERTY, 1916-1930

The designer of this series, Hermon A. MacNeil, used the full figure of Liberty for the obverse design. On the left arm is a shield which is upraised in the attitude of protection. The right hand holds an olive branch of peace. The reverse design is the flying eagle. In 1917, the eagle was placed higher on the coin and three stars were placed under it.

The design theme is militant, reflecting the sentiments of a nation prepared for war yet yearning for peace.

STANDING LIBERTY QUARTER
obverse / reverse

☐ 1916	52,000	250.00	350.00	450.00	600.00	1200.00	2000.00
☐ 1917	8,792,000	3.00	6.00	7.00	10.00	55.00	200.00
☐ 1971D ...	1,509,200	4.00	8.00	10.00	12.00	55.00	210.00
☐ 1917S....	1,952,000	4.00	8.00	10.00	12.00	55.00	275.00

STARS UNDER EAGLE:

☐ 1917	13,880,000	1.85	3.75	5.00	8.00	30.00	125.00
☐ 1917D ...	6,224,400	2.75	6.50	11.50	15.00	30.00	125.00
☐ 1917S....	5,552,000	3.50	9.00	14.00	18.00	30.00	125.00
☐ 1918	12,240,000	1.75	3.50	5.50	8.50	30.00	125.00
☐ 1918D ...	7,380,000	3.00	7.50	10.00	13.50	29.00	125.00
☐ 1918S....	11,072,000	1.75	4.00	6.00	9.00	30.00	125.00
☐ 1981S							
over 7	11,072,000	150.00	200.00	285.00	450.00	1250.00	6200.00
☐ 1919	11,324,000	2.00	5.00	6.50	10.00	50.00	125.00
☐ 1919D ...	1,944,000	12.50	23.50	35.00	42.00	110.00	325.00

QUARTERS — STANDING LIBERTY, 1916-1930

DATE	Mintages	ABP	G-4 Good	F-12 Fine	EX-40 Ex.Fine	MS-60 Unc.	Proof
☐ 1919S....	1,836,000	13.50	22.00	35.00	47.00	105.00	350.00
☐ 1920.....	27,860,000	1.25	3.00	4.25	5.75	20.00	125.00
☐ 1920D ...	3,586,400	4.25	9.50	14.00	25.00	55.00	165.00
☐ 1920S....	6,380,000	1.75	6.50	8.50	12.00	29.00	125.00

HALF DOLLARS — LIBERTY WALKING, 1916-1947

On this magnificent coin, symbolic Liberty strikes a new pose as she carries the olive branches of peace, while striding toward the dawn of a new day. The designer is A.A. Weinman, whose initials AW appear under the tip of the wing feathers.

**WALKING LIBERTY
HALF DOLLAR**
obverse / reverse

DATE	Mintages	ABP	Good	Fine	Ex.Fine	Unc.	Proof
☐ 1916.....	608,000	6.50	11.00	25.00	70.00	275.00	—
☐ 1916 D on obv .	1,014,000	3.50	6.50	16.00	60.00	175.00	—
☐ 1916 S on obv..	508,000	15.00	25.00	55.00	150.00	450.00	—
☐ 1917.....	12,292,000	2.75	3.00	4.50	14.00	55.00	—
☐ 1917 D on obv .	765,400	3.50	6.50	22.00	75.00	225.00	—
☐ 1917 D on rev ..	1,940,000	2.75	3.25	11.00	59.00	250.00	—
☐ 1917 S on obv..	952,000	4.00	7.00	24.00	125.00	360.00	—
☐ 1917 S on rev ..	5,554,000	2.75	3.00	5.50	32.00	175.00	—
☐ 1918.....	6,634,000	2.75	3.00	5.00	35.00	225.00	—
☐ 1918D ...	3,853,040	2.75	3.00	7.00	65.00	375.00	—
☐ 1918S....	10,282,000	2.75	3.00	5.00	32.00	150.00	—
☐ 1919.....	962,000	2.75	5.00	15.00	135.00	650.00	—
☐ 1919D ...	1,165,000	2.75	4.50	15.00	195.00	1500.00	—
☐ 1919S....	1,552,000	2.25	4.25	14.00	200.00	2000.00	—
☐ 1920.....	6,372,000	2.75	2.50	5.00	25.00	175.00	—
☐ 1920D ...	1,551,000	2.75	3.50	9.00	115.00	1200.00	—
☐ 1920S....	4,624,000	2.75	3.25	7.00	60.00	1150.00	—
☐ 1921.....	246,000	18.00	27.00	60.00	350.00	1800.00	—
☐ 1921D ...	208,000	35.00	52.00	85.00	425.00	2150.00	—
☐ 1921S....	548,000	5.50	9.00	25.00	800.00	8000.00	—
☐ 1923S....	2,178,000	2.75	3.00	6.00	85.00	885.00	—

HALF DOLLARS — LIBERTY WALKING, 1916-1947

DATE	Mintages	ABP	G-4 Good	F-12 Fine	EX-40 Ex.Fine	MS-60 Unc.	Proof
☐ 1927S	2,393,000	2.75	3.00	5.00	42.00	335.00	—
☐ 1928S	1,940,000	2.75	3.00	5.00	47.00	475.00	—
☐ 1929D ...	1,001,200	2.75	3.50	7.00	39.00	225.00	—
☐ 1929S	1,902,000	2.75	3.00	5.00	29.00	225.00	—
☐ 1933S	1.786,000	2.75	3.00	5.00	20.00	275.00	—

SILVER DOLLARS — LIBERTY HEAD OR "MORGAN"
1878-1904, AND 1921

This silver dollar was designed by George T. Morgan. It was first issued in 1878. The Liberty Head dollar is also known as the "Bland" dollar after the Bland Silver Bill of 1878 which called for the new design.

MORGAN DOLLAR
obverse / reverse

DATE	Mintages	ABP	Ex.Fine	Unc.	Proof
☐ 1878					
7 Tail Feathers	416,000	7.50	10.00	30.00	3000.00
8 Tail Feathers	750,000	7.00	9.00	22.00	775.00
7 over 8 Tail Feathers		7.50	15.00	29.00	—
☐ 1878CC	2,212,000	7.00	13.00	32.50	—
☐ 1878S	9,774,000	7.00	8.50	11.50	—
☐ 1879 14,807,100	7.00	8.50	13.00	2000.00
☐ 1879CC	756,000	42.00	8.50	850.00	—
☐ 1879 O.................	2,887,000	7.00	8.50	15.00	—
☐ 1879S	9,110,000	7.00	8.50	10.00	—
☐ 1880 12,601,355	7.00	48.00	12.50	1800.00
☐ 1880CC	591,000	25.00	52.00	75.00	—
☐ 1880 over 79CC		28.00	75.00	150.00	—
☐ 1880 O.................	5,305,000	7.00	8.50	27.50	—
☐ 1880S	8,900,000	7.00	8.50	9.00	—
☐ 1881	9,163,975	7.00	8.50	13.00	1800.00
☐ 1881CC	296,000	30.00	52.00	75.00	—
☐ 1881 O.................	5,708,000	7.00	8.50	10.50	—
☐ 1881S	12,760,000	7.00	8.50	9.25	—

COMBS

For centuries beautiful and decorative combs have adorned milady's hair. These ornate combs were originally designed to serve as jewelry pieces.

	Price Range	
☐ Bakelite, back comb w/coral, 5" L, c. 1880	80.00	90.00
☐ Celluloid, side comb, Victorian, c. 1880	20.00	25.00
☐ Celluloid, back comb, Art Nouveau, c. 1900	40.00	50.00
☐ Celluloid, back comb, feather design, c. 1930	90.00	100.00
☐ Celluloid, back comb, rhinestones, c. 1940	60.00	75.00
☐ Celluloid, hair pins, rhinestones, c. 1930	15.00	20.00
☐ Celluloid, back comb, Art Deco, c. 1920	50.00	60.00
☐ Tortoise, hair pin, Art Nouveau, c. 1910	30.00	40.00
☐ Tortoise, back comb, coral, 6" L, c. 1880	150.00	175.00
☐ Tortoise, back comb, 7½" L, c. 1840	100.00	125.00
☐ Tortoise, back comb, English, rhinestones, c. 1890	125.00	150.00
☐ Silver, back comb, rhinestones, 5" L, c. 1890	125.00	150.00

COMIC BOOKS

The comic book evolved, obviously, from the newspaper comic strip. Indeed, all the early comic books were nothing but reprints of old newspaper strips collected and bound in soft covers. It wasn't until the appearance of *Detective Comics* in 1937 that any original material was used. A year later Superman made his debut in *Action #1*, and the comic book business was assured of success. *Detective #27* introduced Batman, Timely countered with The Human Torch, Captain America and The Submariner, Fawcett came up with Captain Marvel and his family, and the race for the most unique superhero was under way. It continues to this day.

As An Investment

Comic books, like any commodity, become valuable when the demand exceeds the supply. There are more comic book fans and collectors now than ever before — and a goodly number of the Golden Age Comic books can be collected as speculation. If kept preserved carefully, and for a long enough period of time, certain select comic books can be very lucrative as long term investments.

"Number Ones" First Issues

On the following pages is a comprehensive listing of "NUMBER ONES", the first issues of a given comic book series. They also serve as indicators to the values of other books in the series. When the No. 1 book is high in price most of the other earlier editions are also in this category. Space does not permit complete listing of each book and its value in this section. Those listed here give a good "outline" of the current Comic Book market.

COMIC BOOKS

For a complete book on the subject of all comic books, space books and their current values, a copy of *The Official Price Guide to Comic and Space Books* is recommended.

© William M. Gaines

© E. C. Publications, Inc.

© 1950 Harvey Publishing

COMIC BOOKS (1933 TO DATE) "NUMBER ONES" FIRST ISSUES

	Very Good	Mint
☐ Abbott and Costello Comics #1	6.00	10.00
☐ Action #1	4500.00	7000.00
☐ Adventure #1	200.00	400.00
☐ Adventure #48 (Hourman)	200.00	300.00
☐ Air Fighters	55.00	90.00
☐ Alice in Wonderland	4.00	6.00
☐ All American (Hop Harrigan & Scribbly)	120.00	180.00
☐ All Good Comics	8.00	12.00
☐ All Funny Comics	6.00	9.00
☐ All Hero	80.00	120.00
☐ All Select (Vol. 1)	150.00	250.00
☐ All Sunrise Comics	2.00	3.00
☐ All Winners (Vol. 1)	300.00	500.00
☐ All Winners (Vol. 2)	120.00	200.00
☐ All Your Comics	6.00	9.00
☐ All Your Comics (25¢ issue)	6.00	12.00
☐ Amazing	60.00	100.00
☐ Amazing Fantasy #15	200.00	300.00
☐ Amazing Man	100.00	150.00
☐ Amazing Spiderman	220.00	330.00
☐ American Air Forces	5.00	8.00
☐ America's Best	60.00	100.00
☐ America's Greatest	140.00	230.00
☐ Anarcho, Dictator of Death	12.00	18.00
☐ Animal Antics	5.00	8.00
☐ Animal Comics	200.00	300.00

COMIC BOOKS

	Very Good	Mint
☐ Animal Fables	20.00	30.00
☐ Animated Movie-Tunes	3.00	5.00
☐ Annie Oakley	6.00	9.00
☐ Archie	80.00	100.00
☐ Archie Annual	12.00	20.00
☐ Army & Navy Comics	15.00	25.00
☐ Arrow	50.00	80.00
☐ Atoman	13.00	20.00
☐ Atomic Comics	5.00	8.00
☐ Atomic Thunderbolt	5.00	8.00
☐ The Avengers	80.00	120.00
☐ Aviation Cadets	4.00	6.00
☐ Bang-Up Comics	50.00	75.00
☐ The Barker	4.00	6.00
☐ Bill Barnes Comics	24.00	36.00
☐ Bingo Comics	3.00	5.00
☐ Black Cat Comics	30.00	50.00
☐ Blackstone Comics	5.00	8.00
☐ Black Swan Comics	5.00	8.00
☐ Black Terror	50.00	75.00
☐ Blazing Comics	6.00	10.00
☐ Blue Beetle	5.00	8.00
☐ Blue Bolt	120.00	175.00
☐ Blue Circle Comics	6.00	9.00
☐ Blue Ribbon Comics	22.50	35.00
☐ Bee-29 The Bombardier	3.00	4.00
☐ Bomber	10.00	15.00
☐ Book of Comics (25¢)	6.00	9.00
☐ Boy Commandos	120.00	180.00
☐ Brave & The Bold	60.00	100.00
☐ Buck Rogers	5.50	9.00
☐ Bulletman	120.00	180.00
☐ Buz Sawyer	7.00	10.00
☐ Buzzy	4.00	6.00
☐ Calling All Girls	4.00	6.00
☐ Calling All Kids	2.00	3.00
☐ Camera Comics	3.00	4.50
☐ Camp Comics	40.00	60.00
☐ Cannonball Comics	4.00	6.00
☐ Captain Aero Comics	25.00	40.00
☐ Captain America #1	1200.00	2000.00
☐ Captain America 100	1.25	2.00
☐ Captain Battle	40.00	60.00
☐ Captain Battle, Jr.	20.00	30.00
☐ Captain Fearless Comics	25.00	40.00
☐ Capt. Marvel Adventures	1200.00	1800.00
☐ Capt. Marvel, Jr.	150.00	250.00
☐ Capt. Marvel (Marvel Series)	1.00	1.50
☐ Captain Midnight	60.00	100.00

COMIC BOOKS	Very Good	Mint
☐ Catman	50.00	80.00
☐ Challengers of The Unknown	30.00	50.00
☐ Champion	35.00	55.00
☐ Circus of Fun Comics	2.00	3.00
☐ Cisco Kid Comics	6.00	9.00
☐ Classics Illustrated #1 (First Edition)	120.00	180.00
☐ Colossus	35.00	55.00
☐ Columbia, Gem of The Comics	10.00	15.00
☐ Color (Dick Tracy)	110.00	175.00
☐ Comedy	60.00	100.00
☐ Comic Capers	3.00	5.00
☐ Comic Cavalcade	130.00	200.00
☐ Comic Land	4.00	6.00
☐ Comics for Kids	3.00	4.00
☐ Comics On Parade (Tarzan by Hal Foster)	100.00	150.00
☐ Coo Coo Comics	4.00	6.00
☐ Corliss Archer	14.00	21.00
☐ Crack Comics	200.00	300.00
☐ Crash Comics	50.00	80.00
☐ Crime and Punishment	50.00	80.00
☐ Crime Exposed	3.00	5.00
☐ Crime Fighters	1.25	1.85
☐ Crime Reporter	6.00	10.00
☐ Crime Smasher	4.00	6.00
☐ Crimes by Women	6.00	10.00
☐ Crown Comics	4.00	6.00
☐ Cryin' Lion	1.50	2.00
☐ Crypt of Terror #17	120.00	180.00
☐ Curly Kayoe	4.00	6.00
☐ Cyclone Comics	30.00	50.00
☐ Dandy Comics	20.00	30.00
☐ Daring Mystery	500.00	800.00
☐ Daredevil (1st Series)	400.00	600.00
☐ Daredevil (Marvel)	25.00	40.00
☐ Detective Comics (1937)	400.00	600.00
☐ Detective #27	2500.00	4000.00
☐ Debbie Dean Comics	3.50	5.00
☐ Devil Dogs	8.00	12.00
☐ Dick Tracy Monthly (Dell)	10.00	15.00
☐ Dime Comics	6.00	10.00
☐ Dixie Dugan	6.00	10.00
☐ Doc Savage	100.00	150.00
☐ Doctor Solar	2.50	4.00
☐ Doll Man	110.00	175.00
☐ Dolly Dill Comics	1.50	2.00
☐ Don Fortune	4.00	6.00
☐ Don Winslow of The Navy	25.00	40.00
☐ Donald Duck—Color #4	1000.00	1500.00
☐ Dotty Dripple	2.00	3.00

COMIC BOOKS

	Very Good	Mint
☐ Double Life of Private Strong	15.00	25.00
☐ Durango Kid	40.00	60.00
☐ Dynamic Comics	25.00	40.00
☐ Eagle Comics	40.00	60.00
☐ Eerie Comics	130.00	200.00
☐ Egbert	4.00	6.00
☐ Ella Cinders and Blackie	16.00	24.00
☐ Ellery Queen	6.00	10.00
☐ Elmo	2.75	4.00
☐ Everybody's Comics	6.00	10.00
☐ Exciting Comics	50.00	80.00
☐ Exposed Crime	2.50	3.50
☐ The Face	20.00	30.00
☐ Famous Funnies (July 1934)	250.00	400.00
☐ Famous Stories	10.00	15.00
☐ Fantastic Comics	60.00	100.00
☐ Fantastic Four	300.00	500.00
☐ Fat and Slat	20.00	30.00
☐ Felix The Cat	50.00	75.00
☐ Feature	100.00	150.00
☐ Fight Comics	70.00	105.00
☐ Fighting Yank	60.00	90.00
☐ Flash Gordon—Four Color	200.00	300.00
☐ First Love	1.50	2.50
☐ Flame Comics	100.00	150.00
☐ Flash (1st Series)	400.00	600.00
☐ Flash (2nd Series)	60.00	100.00
☐ The Fly	12.00	20.00
☐ Forever People	4.00	6.00
☐ Four Color	15.00	25.00
☐ Four Favorites	40.00	60.00
☐ Frankenstein Comics	12.00	20.00
☐ Frisky Fables	2.00	3.00
☐ Frontine Combat	55.00	90.00
☐ Front Page	8.00	12.00
☐ Funland Comics	1.50	2.50
☐ The Funnies	60.00	100.00
☐ Funny Animals	10.00	15.00
☐ Funny Book	2.50	4.00
☐ Funny Folks	5.00	7.50
☐ Funny Frolics	1.50	2.50
☐ Funnyman Comics	10.00	15.00
☐ Funny Stuff	6.00	10.00
☐ Funny World	2.75	4.00
☐ Future	30.00	50.00
☐ Future World	2.00	3.00
☐ Gangbusters	6.00	10.00
☐ Gangsters Can't Win	2.00	3.00
☐ Gay Comics	12.00	20.00

COMIC BOOKS

	Very Good	Mint
☐ Gem Comics	5.00	7.50
☐ Gene Autry Comics	60.00	100.00
☐ "Georgie" Comics	3.50	5.00
☐ Ghost Rider (1st Series)	35.00	52.00
☐ Ghost Rider (2nd Series)	30.00	45.00
☐ Gift Comics	150.00	225.00
☐ G.I. Combat	3.00	5.00
☐ Giggle Comics	4.00	6.00
☐ Golden Lad	12.00	20.00
☐ Goofy Comics	3.00	5.00
☐ Great Comics (1941)	5.00	8.00
☐ Great Comics	5.00	8.00
☐ Green Hornet	100.00	150.00
☐ Green Lama	30.00	50.00
☐ Green Lantern (1st)	150.00	250.00
☐ Green Lantern (2nd)	30.00	50.00
☐ Green Mask	50.00	80.00
☐ Grit Grady Comics	4.00	6.00
☐ Ha Ha Comics	4.00	6.00
☐ Hap Hazard Comics	3.00	5.00
☐ Happy Comics	3.00	5.00
☐ Hawkman	3.00	5.00
☐ Henry	6.00	9.00
☐ Heroic	60.00	100.00
☐ Hi-Ho Comics	2.75	4.00
☐ Hi-Jinx	2.00	3.00
☐ Hi-Lite Comics	7.00	10.00
☐ Hit Comics	250.00	400.00
☐ Hollywood Comics	5.00	7.50
☐ Homer Cobb	10.00	15.00
☐ Hoppy the Marvel Bunny	4.00	6.00
☐ House of Mystery	12.00	20.00
☐ Horse Feathers Comics	12.00	18.00
☐ Hulk	130.00	200.00
☐ Humdinger	3.50	5.00
☐ Human Torch	600.00	1000.00
☐ Humor Comics	2.00	3.00
☐ Humphrey Comics	3.50	5.00
☐ Ibis	60.00	100.00
☐ Ideal Comics	8.00	12.00
☐ Incredible Hulk 102	3.50	5.00
☐ Incredible Hulk Fiction (30)	35.00	40.00
☐ Iron Man	5.00	8.00
☐ It Really Happened	3.00	5.25
☐ Jackpot Comics	80.00	125.00
☐ Jaguar	3.00	5.00
☐ Jamboree Comics	1.50	2.50
☐ Jeep Comics	2.00	3.00
☐ Jimmy Olson	60.00	100.00

COMIC BOOKS

	Very Good	Mint
☐ Jingle Jangle Comics	30.00	50.00
☐ Jing-Pals Comics	2.00	3.00
☐ Joe Polooka (Vol. 1)	15.00	25.00
☐ Joe Polooka (Vol. 2)	8.00	12.00
☐ Joker	60.00	100.00
☐ Journey Into Mystery	40.00	60.00
☐ Juke Box Comics	8.00	12.00
☐ Jumbo	300.00	500.00
☐ Jungle Comics	115.00	175.00
☐ Jungle Girl	45.00	67.50
☐ Junie Prom Comics	2.50	3.50
☐ Junior Miss	5.00	7.50
☐ Justice League of America	30.00	50.00
☐ Kamandi	2.00	3.00
☐ Key Comics	4.00	6.00
☐ Kiddie Kapers	.70	1.00
☐ Kid Eternity	13.00	20.00
☐ Kid Komics	110.00	175.00
☐ King Comics	225.00	350.00
☐ The Killers	10.00	15.00
☐ Kitty	2.00	3.00
☐ Ko Komics	4.00	6.00
☐ Koko and Kola	2.00	3.00
☐ Komic Kartoons	3.00	4.50
☐ Komik Pages	4.00	6.00
☐ Krazy Komics (1st Series)	8.00	12.00
☐ Krazy Komics (2nd Series)	20.00	30.00
☐ Krazy Krow	2.00	3.00
☐ Krazylife Comics	1.50	2.50
☐ Laffy-Daffy Comics	1.30	1.90
☐ Lance O'Casey	6.00	10.00
☐ Land of The Lost	15.00	25.00
☐ Latest Comics	2.00	3.00
☐ Lawbreakers Always Lose	1.50	2.00
☐ Leading	120.00	180.00
☐ Little Lulu—Four Colors	50.00	80.00
☐ The Living Bible	4.00	6.00
☐ The Lone Ranger	25.00	40.00
☐ Looney Tunes	.30	.50
☐ Lucky Comics	4.00	6.00
☐ Lucky "7" Comics	5.00	7.50
☐ Mad	100.00	150.00
☐ Mad Hatter	5.00	7.50
☐ Magic Comics	50.00	75.00
☐ Major Hoople Comics	10.00	15.00
☐ Major Victory Comics	12.00	20.00
☐ Manhunt!	12.00	18.00
☐ Man of War	40.00	60.00
☐ Marmaduke Mouse	3.35	5.00

COMIC BOOKS	Very Good	Mint
☐ Mary Marvel	57.50	85.00
☐ Marvel Family	60.00	100.00
☐ Marvel Mystery	5600.00	9300.00
☐ Mask Comics	8.00	12.00
☐ Master	275.00	400.00
☐ Medal of Honor Comics	4.00	6.00
☐ Merry Comics	1.50	2.50
☐ Merry-Go-Round Comics	5.75	8.00
☐ Mighty Mouse Comics	10.00	15.00
☐ Military	300.00	500.00
☐ Millie The Model	14.00	21.00
☐ Miracle Comics	25.00	40.00
☐ Miss America	50.00	80.00
☐ Miss Fury	225.00	350.00
☐ Mr. District Attorney	6.00	10.00
☐ Mr. Miracle	2.50	4.00
☐ Molly O'Day	13.00	20.00
☐ Monkeyshines Comics	2.75	4.00
☐ Moon Girl	30.00	50.00
☐ Moon Mullins	6.00	9.00
☐ More Fun	250.00	400.00
☐ More Fun (52)	1300.00	2000.00
☐ Mopsy	6.00	9.00
☐ Movie Comics (1st Series)	100.00	150.00
☐ Murder, Inc.	8.00	12.00
☐ Mutt and Jeff	50.00	75.00
☐ Mystery Men Comics	100.00	150.00
☐ Mystic (Vol. 1)	400.00	600.00
☐ Mystic (Vol. 2)	30.00	50.00
☐ Namora	40.00	50.00
☐ Napoleon and Uncle Elby	20.00	30.00
☐ National Comics	200.00	300.00
☐ Navy Heroes	4.00	6.00
☐ Nellie The Nurse	2.75	4.00
☐ New Book of Comics	100.00	150.00
☐ New Gods	2.50	4.00
☐ Nickel Comics	130.00	200.00
☐ Nutty Comics	2.00	3.00
☐ Nyoka	40.00	60.00
☐ "O.K." Comics	30.00	45.00
☐ Oaky Doaks	20.00	30.00
☐ Okay Comics	12.00	20.00
☐ Our Army At War	13.00	20.00
☐ Our Flag	80.00	120.00
☐ Our Gang	130.00	200.00
☐ Outlaws	1.50	2.50
☐ Ozzie and Babs	2.00	3.00
☐ Pageant of Comics (Mopsy)	6.00	9.00

COMIC BOOKS

	Very Good	Mint
☐ Patches	2.75	4.00
☐ Panic	10.00	15.00
☐ Patsy Walker	14.00	21.00
☐ Penny	4.00	6.00
☐ Pep	150.00	250.00
☐ Peter Pat	12.00	18.00
☐ Peter Rabbit	16.00	24.00
☐ Phantom (Harvey Hits #51)	10.00	15.00
☐ Picture News	5.00	7.50
☐ Picture Stories From The Bible (Old Test.)	8.00	12.00
☐ Picture Stories From The Bible (New Test.)	8.00	12.00
☐ Police Cases (Authentic)	3.35	5.00
☐ Planet	150.00	250.00
☐ Plastic Man	120.00	180.00
☐ Police Comics	300.00	500.00
☐ Popeye	60.00	90.00
☐ Pop-Pop Comics	2.75	4.00
☐ Popular Comics	100.00	150.00
☐ Power Comics	5.00	7.50
☐ Powerhouse Pepper	70.00	105.00
☐ Prize Comics	45.00	70.00
☐ Public Enemies	1.00	1.50
☐ Punch and Judy	4.00	6.00
☐ Punch Comics	30.00	50.00
☐ Puppet Comics	2.00	3.00
☐ Puppetoons	8.00	12.00
☐ Puzzle-Fun Comics	10.00	15.00
☐ Raggedy Ann & Andy	40.00	60.00
☐ Rangers	50.00	80.00
☐ Real Fact Comics	6.00	10.00
☐ Real Funnies	5.00	7.50
☐ Real Heroes	4.00	6.00
☐ Real Screen Funnies	18.00	27.00
☐ Real Sports Comics	2.00	3.00
☐ Red Band Comics	6.00	10.00
☐ Red Circle Comics	5.00	8.00
☐ Red Dragon	20.00	30.00
☐ Remember Pearl Harbor	6.00	9.00
☐ Ribtickler	2.75	4.00
☐ Romance Trail	6.00	9.00
☐ Romantic Adventures	3.00	4.50
☐ Romantic Picture Novelettes	5.00	7.50
☐ Roundup	2.75	4.00
☐ Samson	2.50	4.00
☐ Sea Hound	5.00	7.50
☐ Sensation Comics	200.00	300.00
☐ Seven Dead Men	4.00	6.00
☐ Seven Seas Comics	14.00	21.00
☐ Shadow Comics	115.00	175.00

COMIC BOOKS	Very Good	Mint
☐ Shazam	1.50	2.50
☐ Showcase #1	60.00	100.00
☐ Sheena	80.00	120.00
☐ Ship Ahoy	4.00	6.00
☐ Silly Tunes	4.00	6.00
☐ Silver Streak	225.00	350.00
☐ Silver Streak #7 (Daredevil Battles Claw)	200.00	300.00
☐ Skyman	30.00	50.00
☐ Sky Sheriff	5.00	7.50
☐ Slam-Bang Comics	50.00	80.00
☐ Smash Comics	60.00	100.00
☐ Smilin' Jack	30.00	45.00
☐ Snappy Comics	3.00	4.00
☐ Sparkler (Sparkman)	60.00	90.00
☐ Sparkler (Jim Hardy)	16.00	24.00
☐ Sparkling Stars	6.00	9.00
☐ Sparkman	13.00	20.00
☐ Sparky Watts	12.00	18.00
☐ Special Agent	2.50	3.50
☐ Special Comics	140.00	210.00
☐ Special Edition Comics (Capt. Marvel)	550.00	850.00
☐ Spectre 1	2.50	4.00
☐ Speed Comics	60.00	100.00
☐ Spirit	40.00	60.00
☐ Spook Comics	2.00	3.00
☐ Spooky Mysteries	3.00	4.50
☐ Sport Comics	5.00	8.00
☐ Sport Stars	3.00	4.50
☐ Spotlight Comics	12.00	18.00
☐ Spunky	4.00	6.00
☐ Spy Smasher	130.00	200.00
☐ Star Comics	27.50	45.00
☐ Star-Spangled	100.00	150.00
☐ Startling Comics	80.00	120.00
☐ Star Studded Comics	8.00	12.00
☐ Steve Canyon	20.00	30.00
☐ Steve Roper	3.00	5.00
☐ Strange Adventures	30.00	50.00
☐ Strange Tales	50.00	80.00
☐ Stuntman	80.00	100.00
☐ Sub-Mariner (2nd Series)	4.00	6.00
☐ Super Duck Comics	10.00	15.00
☐ Supermouse	4.00	6.00
☐ Super Rabbit	5.00	7.50
☐ Supersnipe	10.00	15.00
☐ Sub-Mariner (1st Series)	4.00	6.00
☐ Superworld Comics	40.00	60.00
☐ Superboy	150.00	250.00
☐ Super-Magic Comics	40.00	60.00

COMIC BOOKS	Very Good	Mint
☐ Superman #1	1700.00	2750.00
☐ Suspense Comics	8.00	12.00
☐ Sweet Sixteen	3.00	4.50
☐ Saint, The	20.00	30.00
☐ Science Comics	3.00	4.00
☐ Scoop Comics	33.00	40.00
☐ Scream Comics	2.00	3.00
☐ Taffy Comics	2.75	4.00
☐ Tailspin Tommy	16.00	24.00
☐ Tales of Suspense	30.00	50.00
☐ Tales to Astonish	30.00	50.00
☐ Tarzan (1948)	60.00	100.00
☐ Tarzan (Single Series #20)	200.00	300.00
☐ Teen Titans 1	4.00	6.00
☐ Tegra, Jungle Empress	20.00	30.00
☐ Terrific Comics	8.00	12.00
☐ Tessie The Typist	15.00	25.00
☐ Texan Comics	4.00	6.00
☐ Three Ring Comics	2.00	3.00
☐ Thrilling Comics	50.00	80.00
☐ Thunder Agents	3.00	5.00
☐ Tick Tock Tales	2.75	4.00
☐ Tiny Tot Tales	16.00	24.00
☐ Tip Top	130.00	200.00
☐ TNT Comics	4.00	6.00
☐ Tom Mix Western	27.50	35.00
☐ Top-Notch Comics	100.00	150.00
☐ Top Secrets of F.B.I.	4.00	6.00
☐ Top Spot Comics	5.00	7.50
☐ Topsy-Turvy Comics	2.00	3.00
☐ Tor	50.00	75.00
☐ Tough Kid Squad	160.00	240.00
☐ Tower of Shadows	1.50	2.00
☐ Toyland Comics	4.00	6.00
☐ Toy Town Comics	2.00	3.00
☐ Treasure Comics	5.00	7.50
☐ True Comics	8.00	12.00
☐ True Life Secrets	2.00	3.00
☐ Tubby—Color #381	14.00	21.00
☐ Uncle Sam	100.00	150.00
☐ Uncle Scrooge #386	160.00	240.00
☐ Underworld	3.50	5.00
☐ United Comics (Fritz Ritz)	5.00	7.50
☐ U.S. Agent	3.50	5.00
☐ U.S.A. Comics	450.00	700.00
☐ U.S. Jones	60.00	90.00
☐ Variety Comics	6.00	10.00
☐ Vault of Horror #12	130.00	200.00
☐ Vic Flint	2.75	4.00

COMIC BOOKS	VeryGood	Mint
☐ Vic Jordan	3.00	4.50
☐ Victory Comics	60.00	100.00
☐ Vic Verity	4.00	6.00
☐ Walt Disney Comics & Stories	1400.00	2250.00
☐ War Comics	12.00	18.00
☐ War Heroes (1940)	5.00	8.00
☐ Warlock	2.00	3.00
☐ Weird Comics	60.00	100.00
☐ Weird Fantasy (13)	130.00	200.00
☐ Weird Science (12)	140.00	225.00
☐ Weird Science Fantasy (23)	40.00	60.00
☐ Western Bandit Trails	4.00	6.00
☐ Wham Comics	25.00	40.00
☐ Whirlwind	30.00	50.00
☐ Whiz 2	2750.00	4500.00
☐ Wilbur Comics	10.00	15.00
☐ Wild West	8.00	12.00
☐ Winnie Winkle	12.00	18.00
☐ Witty Comics	2.75	4.00
☐ Wonderworld Comics	130.00	200.00
☐ Wonder Woman	200.00	300.00
☐ World Famous Heroes	10.00	15.00
☐ World's Best (Finest)	360.00	540.00
☐ Wow	80.00	120.00
☐ X-Men	40.00	60.00
☐ Yankee Comics	27.50	45.00
☐ Yellow Claw	12.00	18.00
☐ Yellowjacket Comics	14.00	21.00
☐ Young Allies	230.00	400.00
☐ Young King Cole	3.50	5.00
☐ Young Life	2.40	3.60
☐ Young Romance	10.00	15.00
☐ Ziggy Pig	4.00	6.00
☐ Zip Comics	120.00	180.00
☐ Zoo Funnies	1.50	2.00
☐ Zoot (2)	8.00	12.00

COMIC CHARACTER SPIN OFFS

It's doubtful that there is any one who hasn't been charmed and delighted with the magic of Walt Disney's creativity. It may be that your favorite character is the spunky Mickey Mouse, the shy, gentle Bambi, or the loving Snow White and her mischievous Seven Dwarfs.

These and many other Disney inspired Superstars are among the most loved entertainers of our time. The great success of the Disney ventures led to an immense number of items that were marketed over the years. Such items now enjoy status as highly desirable collectibles.

BUCK ROGERS,
Ingraham, c. 1935   400.00 - 500.00

DRUM SET . . . . . 525.00 - 550.00

COMIC CHARACTER SPIN OFFS

The many figurines, dolls, toys, household items, and Disney signature pieces of all varieties continue to show marked gains in values. Increasing numbers of collectors are being drawn to the Disneybilea and are establishing it as a stable and profitable collector area. Many of America's most popular comic characters have been taken off the printed page or the animated movie screen and made three-dimensional.

	Price
☐ Alarm Clock. Mice on second hand	250.00
☐ Album Mickey Mouse Picture	72.00
☐ Baby Spoon and Fork. Mickey Mouse, silverplate, 1930	25.00
☐ Bank. Donald Duck	30.00
☐ Bank. Dumbo, ceramic c. 1949	25.00
☐ Bank. Papier mache Mickey Mouse	25.00
☐ Bank. Red tin post office, Mickey Mouse	40.00
☐ Bank. Waste paper basket, Minnie Mouse	35.00
☐ Bisque Figurines. Mickey and Minnie, Japan	35.00
☐ Book. Disney's Art	58.00
☐ Book. Bambi, 1949	8.00
☐ Book. Caveman Island, Mickey Mouse	15.00
☐ Book. Donald Duck Comic, 1955	5.00
☐ Book. Mickey and Friends, 1939, Disneyville	15.00
☐ Book. Mickey's Adventures, 1931	12.00
☐ Book. Mickey and The Pirates Submarine	8.00
☐ Book. Mickey and The Scared Jewels, 1936	10.00
☐ Book. Mickey and The Seven Ghosts	15.00
☐ Book. Mickey in the Foreign Legion	16.00
☐ Book. Mickey's Library of Games	35.00
☐ Book. Mickey The Mail Pilot	12.00
☐ Book. Mickey's Big Little Book	11.00
☐ Book. Mickey's Silly Symphonies	10.00
☐ Book. Pinnocchio Coloring and Store, 1939	30.00
☐ Book. Recipes from Mickey, 1930's	29.00

COMIC CHARACTER SPIN OFFS

	Price
☐ Book. Walt Disney Storyland, 1964	28.00
☐ Bowl. Red Beetleware, Mickey Mouse	18.00
☐ Box. Mickey Mouse pencil	20.00
☐ Bracelet. 12 character, gold finish	19.00
☐ Bracelet. Seven Dwarfs, silver plate	18.00
☐ Brochure. Disneyland opening day, 1955	25.00
☐ Bubble Pipe. Mickey Mouse, W. D. P.	8.00
☐ Buckle. Hand-painted silver Mickey	12.00
☐ Building Set. Mickey Mouse, 1957	20.00
☐ Button. Mickey Mouse, Pin Back	50.00
☐ Camera. Donald Duck	35.00
☐ Candy Container. Disney Dwarf, papier-mache	35.00
☐ Car. Wind-up Mickey Tin Roadster	45.00
☐ Case. Donald and Mickey pencil	22.00
☐ Celluloid. 1938 Practical Pig Cartoon	400.00
☐ Ceramic Figurines. Donald Duck and three nephews, 1943	65.00
☐ Chair. Canvas Beach Micky	120.00
☐ Charm. Mickey Mouse, 1"	10.00
☐ Child's Plate. Divided. Donald Duck	35.00
☐ Christmas Ornament. Tree lights	100.00
☐ Clock. Mickey, animated	15.00
☐ Clock. Mickey, electric	42.00
☐ Container. Mickey, candy	52.00
☐ Cookie Jar. Dumbo turnabout	35.00
☐ Creamer. Buster Brown	38.00
☐ Cup. Baby's Mickey, silver, 1934	60.00
☐ Cup. Elsie the Cow	16.00
☐ Cup. Mickey, silver, 1934	40.00
☐ Cutouts. Snow White, 20 pieces, c. 1937	35.00
☐ Decoder Pin. Orphan Annie, radio premium, 1940	15.00
☐ Dish. Snow White, tin, 1937	12.00
☐ Doll. Bashful Dwarf, masked face, 1930	40.00
☐ Doll. Bashful Dwarf, bisque	28.00
☐ Doll. Doc Dwarf, rubber	25.00
☐ Doll. Donald Duck First National Bank	58.00
☐ Doll. Donald Duck, Disney, bisque	20.00
☐ Doll. Dopey Dwarf, 1938, painted face	45.00
☐ Doll. Dopey Dwarf, stuffed	25.00
☐ Doll. Ginger in Musketeer outfit	30.00
☐ Doll. Grumpy Dwarf	90.00
☐ Doll. Happy Dwarf, rubber	18.00
☐ Doll. Happy Dwarf, stuffed	24.00
☐ Doll. Mickey Clown, cloth, wood & celluloid	90.00
☐ Doll. Mickey, Japanese Model	35.00
☐ Doll. Mickey, 3"	10.00
☐ Doll. Mickey, rubber	30.00
☐ Doll. Minnie Mouse, Japanese	30.00
☐ Doll. Minnie Mouse, rubber	20.00
☐ Doll. Mother Goose, bisque	25.00

COMIC BOOK SPIN OFFS   Price

- [ ] Doll. Pinocchio, vinyl head 19.00
- [ ] Doll. Pluto, rubber 6.00
- [ ] Dolls. Set of Mickey, Minnie & Pluto, 1933 .... 28.00
- [ ] Dolls. Snow White and Seven Dwarfs 40.00
- [ ] Drummer. Mickey Mouse toy, windup 115.00
- [ ] Figure. Fantasia, c. 1940 .... 25.00
- [ ] Figurine. Bambi, 1949 .... 20.00
- [ ] Figurine. Dopey 20.00
- [ ] Figurine. Hippo from Fantasia 12.00
- [ ] Figurine. Jimminey Cricket..................... 15.00
- [ ] Figurine. Joe Carioca 8.00
- [ ] Figurine. Mickey, black rubber 30.00
- [ ] Figurine. Minnie and mandolin.................. 15.00
- [ ] Figurine. Pinocchio........................... 15.00
- [ ] Figurine. Miniature Seven Dwarfs (each) 15.00
- [ ] Figurine. Sleeping Beauty 15.00
- [ ] Figurine. Snow White 15.00
- [ ] Figurine. Show White with Seven Dwarfs 145.00
- [ ] Figurine. Three Little Pigs..................... 37.00
- [ ] Figurine. Wicked Cat.......................... 15.00
- [ ] Fork. Donald Duck, stainless 3.00
- [ ] Fork. Mickey Mouse, stainless.................. 3.00
- [ ] Game. Donald Duck, 1938, Board Game 22.00
- [ ] Gloves. Spin and Marty, western 5.00
- [ ] Gravy Boat. Mickey and Minnie 28.00
- [ ] Gumball Machine. Mickey Mouse 375.00
- [ ] Guitar. Mousegetar Junior 34.00
- [ ] Hairbrush. Donald Duck 15.00
- [ ] Handcar. Mickey and Minnie (Lionel) 250.00
- [ ] Handcar. Mickey, keywound (Lionel) 270.00
- [ ] Handpuppet. Minnie Mouse, 10", 1950's 22.00
- [ ] Handpuppet. Pinocchio, rubber head 15.00
- [ ] Hot Water Bottle. Donald Duck 24.00
- [ ] Ironing Board. Snow White, tin 50.00
- [ ] Jack-in-Box. Donald Duck...................... 20.00
- [ ] Jar. Cookie, Donald Duck 15.00
- [ ] Jar. Cookie, Mickey and Minnie 55.00
- [ ] Juggler Trick. Popeye, c. 1929 .... 27.00
- [ ] Kit. Nurse, Mickey Mouse, 1940 .... 25.00
- [ ] Lamp. Donald Duck............................ 70.00
- [ ] Lamp. Mickey Mouse cowboy 45.00
- [ ] Lead Figures. Maggie & Jigs 55.00
- [ ] Lunchbox. Mickey the Firefighter 20.00
- [ ] Machine. Bubble gum, Mickey 15.00
- [ ] Mask. Minnie, paper, 1932 .... 19.00
- [ ] Mickey and Minnie Windup. Tin 420.00
- [ ] Pull Choo Choo 1 .... 45.00
- [ ] Mouse Club Set. Paper 15.00
- [ ] Fire Engine. Rubber........................... 18.00

COMIC CHARACTER SPIN OFFS

Price

☐ Mirror. Mickey Mouse and handbag	8.00
☐ Mug. Patriots—Mickey & Pluto	25.00
☐ Ornament. Snow White	12.00
☐ Pail. Three Pigs, tin, candy	55.00
☐ Paperdolls. Dagwood	8.00
☐ Paperdolls. Snow White & Seven Dwarfs	50.00
☐ Paperweight. Mickey with American flag, iron	14.00
☐ Pencil Box with Ruler. Mickey Mouse	20.00
☐ Pencil Box. Minnie Mouse, Dixor, 1934	45.00
☐ Pencil Sharpener. Donald Duck	12.00
☐ Pin. Mickey Mouse, enameled, 1935	48.00
☐ Pin. Superman, Kelloggs PEP, premium	15.00
☐ Pinocchio. Wooden doll, 1974	74.00
☐ Pitcher. Tweetie Bird	15.00
☐ Planter. Alice in Wonderland	15.00
☐ Planter. Bambi and Thumper	15.00
☐ Planter. Mickey Mouse	25.00
☐ Plate. Mickey & Minnie, plastic	30.00
☐ Platter. Mickey & Minnie	30.00
☐ Projector. Mickey Mouse Club Films	40.00
☐ Pull Toy. Ferdinand the Bull	60.00
☐ Puppet. Donald Duck Astronaut	12.00
☐ Puppet. Mickey Mouse, hand puppet	10.00
☐ Puzzle. Donald Duck	15.00
☐ Roly Poly Toy. Mickey Mouse	15.00
☐ Rubber Bathing Cap. Donald Duck	7.00
☐ Rubber Figure. Mickey Mouse, c. 1930	45.00
☐ Rug. Mickey and Minnie in airplane	150.00
☐ Rug. Mickey and Minnie ice skating	150.00
☐ Salt & Pepper Shakers. Donald Duck, china	14.00
☐ Salt & Pepper Shakers. Dick Tracy and Junior	22.00
☐ Sheet Music. Snow White, c. 1937	8.00
☐ Storybook. Mickey Mouse, c. 1931	40.00
☐ Stove. Orphan Annie, hob shelf missing	38.00
☐ Straws. Mickey Mouse, 1940	8.00
☐ Tea Set. Donald Duck, full set	60.00
☐ Tea Set. Mickey and Musical Instruments, full set	50.00
☐ Teeth. Mickey English unauthorized cloth	75.00
☐ Toby Mug. Jiminey Cricket, plastic with moving eyes	18.00
☐ Toothbrush Holder. Mickey and Pluto	85.00
☐ Toothbrush Holder. Three Pigs	60.00
☐ Watch. Mickey Mouse, Ingersoll/Sears	35.00
☐ Watering Can. Tin, Donald Duck, 1938	20.00
☐ Watchband. Enameled links, Mickey design	35.00
☐ Watch. Pocket, Mickey Mouse, 1933	180.00
☐ Watch. Snow White, strap band	75.00
☐ Windup Toy. Bambi, applied eyes	18.00
☐ Wood Blocks. Mickey Mouse, 18 blocks box, 1935	75.00
☐ Wristwatch, Mickey Mouse, 1928	50.00
☐ Vase. Bambi, china	11.00

CORKSCREWS

With the invention of corks used to seal wine in a bottle also came the invention of the corkscrew. Throughout the centuries hundreds of various devices were made to extract these corks from bottles. The most simple designs still remain the most efficient. However, many are decorative and very expensive.

	Price Range	
☐ American Folding Corkscrew, 6" L, c. 1900	15.00	20.00
☐ Animal Design, Steel, 5" L, c. 1880	10.00	15.00
☐ Buffalo Horn, Steel, 8" L, c. 1840	25.00	30.00
☐ Genuine Bone Handle, Steel, 6" L, c. 1900	15.00	20.00
☐ Hand Carved Horn, with brush, 8" L, c. 1870	50.00	60.00
☐ Hand Carved Wood Handle, Steel screw, 6" L, c. 1880	20.00	25.00
☐ Hand Lever Spring Loaded, 5" L, c. 1910	15.00	20.00
☐ Iron Corkscrew, 6" L, c. 1900	25.00	30.00
☐ Lunds Corkscrew, 5" L, c. 1870	20.00	25.00
☐ Magic Lever, 5" L, c. 1840	50.00	60.00
☐ Plier Style, All steel, 7" L, c. 1880	20.00	25.00
☐ Pocket Style, 2" L, c. 1890	10.00	15.00
☐ Turned Wood Handle, Steel, 6" L, c. 1900	15.00	20.00
☐ Screw Style, All Steel, 5" L, c. 1870	40.00	50.00
☐ Stag Horn, Steel, 6" hand carved, c. 1880	75.00	80.00
☐ Steel Ring, Collapsible, 3" L, c. 1870	20.00	25.00
☐ Steel Ring Handle and Screw, 5" L, c. 1880	20.00	25.00
☐ Sterling Silver Eagle Head Corkscrew, 5" L, c. 1870 . .	100.00	120.00
☐ Wire Cutter With Brush, c. 1870	30.00	35.00

COVERLETS

Coverlets are bed-coverings woven on a loom. Some were done on a loom at home—these are most often done in two strips which were sewn together. Sometimes fringe was then added. Jacquard looms, with a punched card which signaled the loom when to raise and lower wires which would alter the pattern, made intricate coverlet-weaving fairly simple. Jacquard attachments could be put on old draw looms, but most jacquard coverlets were commercially made. The colors in which coverlets are found are blue, brown, red, green, yellow, and white. Occasionally black and scarlet appear. Designs are geometric, floral, figural, patriotic, symbolic, etc., and the name of the maker is often woven into one or more corners, along with a date. Sometimes the name is the owner—the person for whom the coverlet was made— and the symbol, such as a lion or an eagle, of the weaver was put in the corner with the owner's name.

☐ Black and White, Flowers, Birds	275.00	325.00
☐ Blue and White, Geometric Design, Double Woven Wool	100.00	125.,00
☐ Blue and White, Handloomed, 1840's	150.00	190.00
☐ Butterflies, Blue, 6' x 6'	50.00	70.00
☐ Double Woven, Indigo and Cream	240.00	270.00

COVERLETS

Price Range

☐ Jacquard Woven, Red, Eagle Motif, signed	250.00	300.00
☐ Jacquard Woven, Red, Green and White, Single Panel, Oak-Leaf and Flower Design	200.00	275.00
☐ Jacquard Woven, Red, Tan, Ivory, Eagle Motif, "Independence, Virtue, Liberty"	800.00	900.00
☐ Jacquard Woven, Red and White, Single Panel, Floral Motif	280.00	380.00
☐ Jacquard Woven, Red and White, Single Panel, Lilies and Floral Sprays, signed	12500	200.00
☐ Jacquard Woven, Red, White and Blue, Exotic Birds Feeding their Young	625.00	825.00
☐ Jacquard Woven, Red, White and Blue, Single Panel, Star and Flower Motif	180.00	200.00
☐ Jacquard Woven, Red, White and Green, Single Panel, Flowers, Star, Spread Winged American Eagle	180.00	210.00
☐ Jacquard Double Woven, Blue and White, Rosettes, Leaves, Snowflakes	350.00	400.00
☐ Silk Quilted, "Pillar Stripe," Yellow and White, Vine with Pink and White Fruit.......................	175.00	275.00
☐ Woven, Crewel Pattern.........................	275.00	300.00

COWBOY GEAR

Collectibles of the old west are extremely popular. One important segment is cowboy gear. His unique dress and tools of his trade hold interest for everyone. His saddle is a good example of this era. Since it was one of the most durable items of his gear, they can be found more readily than other parts of his dress.

☐ Boots, depending on condition	75.00	250.00
☐ Chaps, leather, good condition, c. 1880	150.00	250.00
☐ Colt, single action, Army revolver, .38 cal. to .45 cal., c. 1880	200.00	600.00
☐ Hats, beaver fur, c. 1880	200.00	300.00
☐ Holster and belt, western style, c. 1880	100.00	250.00
☐ Lariat, rawhide, c. 1880	100.00	200.00
☐ Lariat, rope, c. 1890	60.00	150.00
☐ Saddle, early western style, c. 1840	200.00	400.00
☐ Saddle, calvary style, c. 1860	150.00	300.00
☐ Saddle, Colorado, western, c. 1880	200.00	400.00
☐ Saddle, Texas, western, c. 1890	150.00	300.00
☐ Spurs, plain, iron small rowels, c. 1880	75.00	100.00
☐ Spurs, plain, army issue, c. 1880	60.00	100.00
☐ Whip, quirt leather, rawhide, c. 1880	50.00	100.00
☐ Winchester, 1876 model rifle, 40 to 50 cal., c. 1876 ...	400.00	800.00
☐ Winchester, 1886 model rifle, 45 to 50 cal., c. 1886 ...	300.00	700.00
☐ Winchester, 1894 model rifle, 25 to 38 cal., c. 1894 ...	150.00	400.00

CRÉCHES
(MINIATURE NATIVITY SCENES)

Miniature manger scenes are used at Christmas to depict the birth of Christ. During the eighteenth century, craftsman from all over Europe produced as many kinds of crèches as their own imagination would allow. Here are but a few examples that exist.

Price Range

☐ American, wood & painted plaster, 6 pc. set, c. 1920 .	40.00	50.00
☐ French, hand painted, angel 12", single pc., c. 1875 . .	250.00	300.00
☐ French, hand painted, wooden, 12 pc. set, c. 1890 . . .	200.00	250.00
☐ German, ceramic, 12 pc. set, c. 1900	75.00	100.00
☐ German, hand carved, 14 pc. set, c. 1880	100.00	125.00
☐ Guatamalan, hand carved, 15 pc. set, c. 1900	75.00	90.00
☐ Mexican, hand painted clay, 18 pc. set, c. 1920	75.00	90.00
☐ Mexican, red clay, 10 pc. set, c. 1910	60.00	80.00
☐ Polish, hand carved, wood, nativity scene, one piece, c. 1890	100.00	125.00

DANCE MEMORABILIA

☐ Isadora Duncan, 8" x 10" b/w photo by Arnold Genthe, signed and inscribed, papier mache molded frame, good condition	375.00	425.00
☐ Isadora Duncan, 8" x 10" b/w photo, dancing pose, wearing Greek-style costume, not signed	50.00	60.00
☐ Isadora Duncan, 8" x 10" b/w photo, full face, signed in purple ink, c. 1924	250.00	300.00
☐ Isadora Duncan, 5" x 4" photo, partially hand colored, signed, rare	180.00	200.00
☐ Isadora Duncan, three pen-and-ink drawings, one signed by her, brief notes scribbled by her	—	500.00
☐ Isadora Duncan, holograph letter, signed, financial matters (17 lines)	150.00	175.00
☐ Isadora Duncan, poster advertisement, 22" x 30", large photographic illustration	215.00	230.00
☐ Isadora Duncan, photo by Arnold Genthe, b/w, re printed from the original negative, unsigned	60.00	80.00
☐ Martha Graham, program from dance recital, Los Angeles, signed by her, cover wrinkled, c. 1948	20.00	30.00
☐ Martha Graham, scrapbook containing 23 photos, 4 letters, numerous clippings	—	300.00
☐ Martha Graham, program from recital, Los Angeles, c. 1948	20.00	30.00
☐ Martha Graham, holograph letter w/original stamped envelope	120.00	130.00

DANCE MEMORABILIA

POSTERS IN GENERAL. The value of dance (ballet, classical etc.) posters representing major companies and/or noted stars can be gauged roughly as follows, excepting in the case of a great superstar such as Isadora Duncan:

American dance poster	pre-1900,	$50-$100
American dance poster	1901-1920,	25- 50
American dance poster	1921-1940,	20- 35
American dance poster	after 1940,	10- 25

Foreign posters are generally more colorful and tend to command higher prices, especially in the places of origin. French posters are, overall , the most highly sought and most expensive. But seldom does any dance poster reach as high as $200.

DECOYS

Most people think of ducks when they think of decoys, but there are also frog, fish, owl, goose and crow decoys, all of which are collectible. People collect by carver and by type and by species and by flyway (the flying path taken by certain groups of species during migration). Decoys are made of everything from woven reeds (ancient Amerind type) to painted canvas-over-wood to combinations of naturally-occuring roots and branches to well-carved wood. Condition is important—particularly of paint. But beware of decoys in mint condition—too often they are recent ornamental decoys, meant for the den mantlepiece, not the reedy swamp.

HEN AND DRAKE PINTAILS, *by Lem Ward* . .   4500.00 - 5000.00   Price Range

☐ Black Duck, August Mock Drake, c. 1900	150.00	175.00
☐ Black Duck, Dan English	460.00	500.00
☐ Black Duck, Handcarved, c. 1900	60.00	80.00
☐ Brant, Carved Cedar	200.00	300.00
☐ Brant, Mason's	150.00	175.00
☐ Canadian Goose, Hurley Conklin	525.00	625.00
☐ Canadian Goose, L. Parker	200.00	225.00
☐ Coot, Benjamin J. Schmidt	130.00	160.00
☐ Drake, Red-Breasted Merganser, H. Conklin	130.00	160.00
☐ Duck, Pacific Northwest	25.00	30.00
☐ Fish, 4½"	30.00	35.00
☐ Fish, Carved and Painted, 19th Century. Pair	220.00	320.00

DECOYS

	Price	Range
☐ Golden Eye	55.00	65.00
☐ Golden Plover	55.00	65.00
☐ Great Blue Heron, Sheet Metal, Painted	275.00	350.00
☐ Gull, With Iron Weight, J. W. Carter	1800.00	2400.00
☐ Hen Mallard, Ward Brothers, c. 1920	110.00	210.00
☐ Lesser Yellowlegs, dated 1896	200.00	300.00
☐ Mallard, Papier-Mache	12.00	16.00
☐ Mallard Drake, Cork	16.00	20.00
☐ Owl, 19th Century	175.00	200.00
☐ Pintail Drake, Carved Cedar	200.00	250.00
☐ Pintail Duck, Green Beak	40.00	45.00
☐ Pintail Hen and Drake, L. T. Ward. Pair	2200.00	3000.00
☐ Plover, Black-Bellied, Elmer Crowell	1000.00	1500.00
☐ Red-Headed Duck, Cork	160.00	180.00
☐ Ruddy Duck Hen, L. T. Ward	120.00	140.00
☐ Snipe	30.00	35.00
☐ Swan, c. 1900	410.00	450.00

DOLLS

The interest in doll collecting that has developed over the past few years has been phenomenal. It has become one of the largest and most popular hobbies in the United States. Doll clubs and shows are springing up all over the country. From simple rag figures to extremely ornate china dolls, these former playthings now command increasingly higher prices.

JENNIE LIND

JUMEAU

DOLLS   Price

☐ African Fertility Doll. Handcarved 30.00
☐ Alexander (Madame) Sonja Henie. Original blonde wig,
   dressed, 15" 122.50
☐ A.M. Baby Doll. Blue eyes, open mouth, Bisque head,
   composition body & wig, 18" 250.00
☐ A.M. bisque head Oriental baby. Brown eyes, painted hair,
   jointed composition body, dressed, 16" 575.00
☐ A.M. bisque head girl. Open mouth, chunky body, dressed 35½ " .   280.00
☐ Belton. Blue paperweight eyes, human hair wig, closed
   mouth, dressed, 12" 375.00
☐ Biedermeier china doll. Original body, dress
   made in Austria 1890, 24" 200.00
☐ Bisque doll. Closed mouth, kid body, eyebrows, 22" 250.00
☐ Bisque doll. Jointed body, human hair wig, 23" 225.00
☐ Bye-lo Baby. Bisque head marked "Grace S. Putman," blue eyes
   cloth body, dressed, 11½ " 390.00
☐ Charlie Chaplin. Composition head, closed mouth, molded hair,
   cloth body, Louis Amberg & Son, 1915, original clothes, 15" 400.00
☐ Chase (Martha). Stockinet girl, dressed, 30½ " 210.00
☐ China head lady. Blonde hair, dressed, 24" 180.00
☐ China head lady. Molded hair, smiling face, dressed, 28" 325.00
☐ China head Jenny Lind. China arms and legs, dressed, 26" 350.00
☐ Deanna Durbin. Composition, dressed, 17" .250.00
☐ Effanbee. Negro girl, painted eyes, molded hair, ball jointed,
   composition body, dressed, 14" 150.00
☐ Fanny Brice. Composition, original clothes, 12" 165.00
☐ Florodora (A.M.). Bisque head girl, brown eyes, wig, dresses, 16" . .125.00
☐ French Fasion Doll. Blue eyes, blonde wig, 16" 400.00
☐ French Character Doll. In period costume, 20" 650.00
☐ Frozen Charlotte Doll. Alice in Wonderland 400.00
☐ Frozen Charlie, blonde or brunette, 15" tall 375.00
☐ Frozen Negroe arms close to body, 3½ " tall 50.00
☐ Fulper pottery head baby. Blue sleep eyes, dressed, 17" 185.00
☐ Gebruder Heubach. Boy toddler, 7½ " 300.00
☐ Gebruder Heubach. Bisque head character baby, intaglio eyes,
   painted hair, undressed, 8½ " 150.00
☐ German Fashion Doll. Blue eyes with short blonde wig, bisque
   head, composition body, "K*R", 24" 450.00
☐ Gibson Girl. Blonde hair, unclothed, marked "Brack" 350.00
☐ Gibson Girl. Brown eyes, original wig, unclothed 275.00
☐ Grave Dolls. Peruvian Chan Chan, 16th c.   30.00
☐ Handwerk & Henrich. Jointed body, blue/movable eyes, bisque
   head, made in Germany, 18" 185.00
☐ Half-figure Doll. w/whisk broom, Germany, glass 30.00
☐ Happy Fats Girl. Bisque Firl, original label, 4" 150.00
☐ Hummel Children. Swivel heads, closed mouths, molded
   hair, dressed, 12" (pair) 145.00
☐ Jennie Lind. Black hair, silk dress with jacket 600.00
☐ Jumeau Doll. Brown eyes, original clothing, 18" 400.00

DOLLS

Price

- [ ] Jumeau Doll. Composition body, brown paperweight eyes, marked "Tete Jumeau", circa 1907, 25" 750.00
- [ ] Jumeau Doll. Brown eyes and blonde mohair wig, closed mouth, marked "Tete Jumeau", 17" 900.00
- [ ] Jumeau Doll. Portrait type, bisque head, marked "E.J." 950.00
- [ ] Jumeau, (Screaming), Automation, bisque 8500.00
- [ ] J.D. Kestner. Brown eyes (glass), open-close mouth, bisque head, dressed, 18" 140.00
- [ ] J.D. Kestner bisque head girl. Brown eyes, human hair wig, bisque arms, dressed, 18" 160.00
- [ ] J.D. Kestner kid body with bisque lower arms and fingers. Closed mouth, swivel neck and inset blue eyes 425.00
- [ ] Kathy Kruse Doll. Painted eyes, cloth body, 20" 85.00
- [ ] Kewpie Doll. Traveller with suitcase, 3½" 145.00
- [ ] Kewpie Doll. Made in Japan, unclothed, 12" 75.00
- [ ] Kewpies, signed Rose O'Neill, German, 4" H, elbows on knees, hand cupping chin, chalkware 8.00
- [ ] Kewpie Doll. Tall bisque, hand-painted features, 5" 85.00
- [ ] Kley & Hahn bisque head baby. Brown eyes, open mouth with teeth and molded tongue, jointed composition body, dressed, 26" 400.00
- [ ] Lenci Girl. All felt, dressed, 22" 150.00
- [ ] Miss Knot. Jointed peg wooden, black hair, 9" 250.00
- [ ] Mickey and Minnie Mouse Dolls. Wooden bodies (pair) 95.00
- [ ] Moon Mullins Doll. Comic strip character, bisque 45.00
- [ ] Martha Washington Doll. Parian and bisque parts, signed and dated 1847, 20" 300.00
- [ ] Paper Mache Doll. Blonde sausage curls, dressed ....,.......150.00
- [ ] Parian Doll. Boy wearing pants and shirt, very rare, circa 1820, 18" .850.00
- [ ] Parian Doll. Girl wearing long gown, circa 1850, 24" 400.00
- [ ] Parian Girl Doll. Blonde, painted eyes, period clothing, 1870 ......400.00
- [ ] Pierotti. Wax, rooted hair, blue glass eyes, detailed fingers and toes 475.00
- [ ] Pincushion Doll. China, mkd. Germany 30.00
- [ ] Schoenhut Doll. Walking type, waxed covered wood 200.00
- [ ] Schoenhut Sailor. With original military costume 160.00
- [ ] Schoenhut, sleep-eye, new wig, repainted head, body and head marks still visible, 17" Tall 175.00
- [ ] Shirley Temple Doll. Blue eyes, open mouth, 27" 160.00
- [ ] Simon & Halbig bisque head girl. Brown sleep eyes, pierced ears, brown human hair wig, jointed composition body, dressed, 20½" ..250.00
- [ ] Steiner (Edmund U.) bisque head girl. Cloth body, bisque forearms, dressed, 27" 250.00
- [ ] Steiner (Herm) bisque head baby. Cloth body, 5" head 105.00
- [ ] Tall Gladdie Boy. Composition body 270.00
- [ ] Tall German Character Doll. Dressed as Admiral, 12" 260.00
- [ ] Tall Character Doll. Blue eyes, jointed limbs 165.00
- [ ] Tall German Character Baby. Glass eyes, jointed, marked "K & H", 22", circa 1880 ....250.00
- [ ] Tall Character Doll. Campbell Kid. Composition body, 12" 75.00

DOLLS

		Price
☐	Wood Felix the Cat. Jointed and painted, 8½"	90.00
☐	Wax. Paperweight blue eyes, molded boots, 20"	220.00
☐	Wax Doll. Black wig, composition arms and legs, 20"	220.00

DOLLS — ANTIQUE

		Price Range	
☐	Armand Marseille 23". "My Dearie"	210.00	250.00
☐	Armand Marseille 20". Open mouth, kid body	110.00	150.00
☐	Bilton 15". Sockethead, wood, composition body	390.00	425.00
☐	Bru 18". Sockethead, bisque shoulder & lower arms	2000.00	2750.00
☐	Cameo 13". Kewpie, all composition	50.00	80.00
☐	China 13½". Black hair with flowers	190.00	225.00
☐	Denamur 15". Sockethead, mouth closed	775.00	875.00
☐	Effanbee 14". Ann Shirley	60.00	80.00
☐	Effanbee 18". Susan	45.00	70.00
☐	Fulpher 31". Socket head composition body	300.00	375.00
☐	Gebruder Heuback 12". Sockethead, mouth closed	475.00	550.00
☐	Half Dolls 2¾". Blonde with flowers, Japan	6.00	10.00
☐	Half Dolls 3½". White with checks on dress, Japan	6.00	10.00
☐	Heinrich Handwerch 22". Sockethead	225.00	275.00
☐	Heirback, Ernst 19½" baby	165.00	190.00
☐	Kammer & Reinhardt 17". Sockethead, original wig	675.00	750.00
☐	Kammer & Reinhardt 20". Brown eyes & lashes	310.00	360.00
☐	Kestner 10". Gibson, Germany	600.00	700.00
☐	Kestner 25". Sockethead, Germany	300.00	350.00
☐	Papier Mache 30". Cloth body with blue eyes	385.00	450.00
☐	Rabery & Delphieu 17". Sockethead	775.00	850.00
☐	Rag Dolls 17½". Doll of the 1890's	75.00	125.00
☐	Reinecke, O. 18". Open mouth with two teeth	255.00	300.00
☐	Schmitt & Fils 10". Sockethead, closed mouth	1600.00	2000.00
☐	Schoenaur & Hoffmeister 30¼". Sockethead	110.00	150.00
☐	Schoenhut 16". Wood	200.00	275.00
☐	Scheutzmeister & Puendt 17". Sockethead, baby	210.00	260.00
☐	Simon & Halbig 14". Dark pocket head, Germany	160.00	200.00
☐	Simon & Halbig 20". Sockethead	390.00	450.00
☐	Steiner, Julius N. 10". Sockethead, mache body	500.00	1000.00

DOLLS — MODERN

☐	Lucy Arnez—Rag 27". Plastic face	15.00	25.00
☐	Gene Autry—Terry Lee 16". Button on shirt	140.00	180.00
☐	Beatles—England 5". Hard plastic	30.00	45.00
☐	James Bond "007"—Ideal 12½". Plastic with vinyl arms	27.00	35.00
☐	Captain Kangaroo—19". Cloth with vinyl head	22.00	28.00
☐	Ben Cartwright—American Character 8". Solid vinyl	22.00	30.00
☐	Carole Channing—"Hello Dolly" 11½". Plastic	4.00	6.00
☐	Charlie Chaplin—Rag 17". Painted face	60.00	85.00
☐	Dick Clark—Doll Artist 22". Bisque head with cloth body	150.00	175.00
☐	Marlene Dietrich—Joy Doll 14½". Blue eyes, blonde wig	40.00	60.00
☐	Doctor Doolittle—Mattel 22½". Cloth with vinyl head	15.00	22.00
☐	Judy Garland—Ideal 18". Original dress, open mouth with teeth	75.00	95.00

DOLLS — MODERN

	Price Range	
☐ Betty Grable—21". Blue eyes, blonde mohair wig	40.00	55.00
☐ John F. Kennedy—Kamar 13". Sitting reading newspaper	18.00	26.00
☐ Charlie McCarthy—puppet 30". Plastic head	40.00	60.00
☐ Mary Poppins—Horseman 12". Plastic, rooted black hair	15.00	20.00
☐ Queen Elizabeth—Doll Artist 20"	160.00	190.00
☐ Debbie Reynolds—Valentine 19". Plastic, jointed knees	7.00	10.00
☐ Roy Rogers & Dale Evans—Dutchess 7". Hard plastic. (each)...	4.00	8.00
☐ Scarlet O'Hara—Alexander 14". All composition with black wig......................................	55.00	75.00
☐ Soupy Sales—Knickerbacher 13". Vinyl............	30.00	45.00
☐ Liz Taylor—Doll Artist 15". Cloth body, bisque head ..	95.00	120.00
☐ Shirley Temple—Ideal 17". All composition with wig .	45.00	70.00
☐ Tiny Tim—18". Cloth	15.00	22.00
☐ Twiggy—Mattel 11". Blue eyes	8.00	12.00
☐ Flip Wilson—"Geraldine" 16". Cloth	20.00	25.00

DOLLHOUSES

The most expensive dollhouses are definitely those which were made by some identifiable company. Unfortunately, this tends to make people — at least new collectors — ignore the finely-crafted and exquisite hand-made dollhouses, which grandfathers made for grand-daughters, and which have been passed down through generations. Prices for these hand-made houses are quite low — usually under $100.00

☐ Dollhouse. Bliss, 13"	145.00	165.00
☐ Dollhouse. Lithographed, c. 1930	70.00	90.00
☐ Dollhouse. Tootsietoy	25.00	30.00
☐ Dollhouse. Tudor Style, Schoenhut	285.00	315.00
☐ Dollhouse. Walt Disney, 6-room, metal	50.00	—
☐ Small German dollhouse, embossed paper railing on second floor, unfurnished, c. 1900	—	300.00
☐ English dollhouse, four rooms with staircase, two fireplaces, orig., late c. 1800	800.00	900.00
☐ Dollhouse, fireplaces in all rooms, simulated carved shingles, stucco exterior, late c. 1920	700.00	800.00
☐ French chateau-style dollhouse, windows on three sides, working door, c. 1890	600.00	700.00
☐ German dollhouse, curtained windows, attic, steps leading to front door, c. 1800	1400.00	1500.00
☐ German castle in ½" to 1' scale, modeled after a late gothic castle, c. 1875	2000.00	3000.00

DOLLHOUSE FURNITURE

Small scale furniture was made (and is still being made) for furnishing dollhouses. Everything from petite toilets to tiny candlesticks is available. The listings below are all for old dollhouse furniture.

	Price
☐ Stove, tin kitchen, w/utensils 11"H	$100.00
☐ Broom holder, tin, w/brooms & dust pan	45.00
☐ Dining table, golden oak, scale 1' to 1"	60.00

DOLLHOUSE FURNITURE

	Price
☐ Bowfront chest, Tynietoy, scale	50.00
☐ Hepplewhite sofa, Tynietoy, scale	60.00
☐ Bathtub, tin, paint worn, 2½" L, late 19th c.	20.00
☐ Victrola, 4-legs, painted wood, 4½" H	45.00
☐ Rope bed, 15½" L x 10½" W, ticking mattress & pillow	25.00
☐ Bedroom suite, 4 pieces: chairs, bureau	35.00

PAPER DOLLS

They may not have 3-dimensional substance, but children and collectors are as devoted to paper dolls as to more life-like dolls. The early ones from turn-of-the-century children's magazines, and even earlier ones made by such companies as Willimantic Thread (see below) are most desirable. And those in uncut condition, still imprisoned on their sheets of paper, are more select than cut items.

	Price Range	
☐ Annie Oakley	7.50	10.00
☐ Betsy McCall	1.00	1.50
☐ Betty Field	14.00	20.00
☐ Captain Marvel	12.00	16.00
☐ Dolly Dimple	5.00	8.00
☐ Elizabeth Taylor	15.00	18.00
☐ Esther Williams	12.00	16.00
☐ Flying Captain Marvel	4.00	6.00
☐ Jolly Hane	8.00	10.00
☐ Katzenjammer Kids	7.00	10.00
☐ Little Miss Sunbeam	18.00	22.00
☐ Mary Poppins	5.00	7.00
☐ Our Gang	48.00	58.00
☐ Palmer Cox, Brownies, Irishman, Scotsman, etc., 1888	35.00	50.00
☐ Princess Elizabeth	22.00	28.00
☐ Rabbit Family	7.00	10.00
☐ Raggedy Ann	16.00	20.00
☐ Sandy and Candy	4.00	6.00
☐ Teddy Bear	34.00	40.00
☐ Tricia Nixon	6.00	10.00
☐ Twiggy	6.00	10.00
☐ Wacs and Waves	14.00	18.00
☐ Willimantic Thread Co., uncut pair, Boy & Girl, 4" tall, with 28 articles of dress, 1885		55.00
☐ Winsome Winnie	38.00	45.00

DOGS

Probably even more popular among motif collectors than cats are dogs. The tendency is, however, for dog collectors to specialize by breed — be it dachshunds, terriers, whatever. Some of the most unique and interesting dog figures are not really recognizable breeds; these are the folk art dog carvings and modelings of wood and clay.

DOGS
	Price
☐ Beagles, 2, painting, primitive contemporary folk artist	65.00
☐ Bulldog, cast iron, spotty paint	30.00
☐ Cocker Spaniel, cast iron, full body........................	22.00
☐ Dachshund, terra cotta, glazed, 5½" H	40.00
☐ Dachshund, Puppies in Knapsack, Vienna bronze, 1" H	85.00
☐ English Pug, cast iron, full figure, 6½" x 9"	40.00
☐ Great Dane, porcelain, Hutschenreuther figurine, 7½" H	165.00
☐ Greyhound, paperweight, Belleek, 3rd black mark, 7" H	570.00
☐ Hunter & Dog, porcelain, Czechoslovakian, 7½" H	140.00
☐ Old English Sheep, Royal Dux, c. 1945	35.00
☐ Rose Quartz, w/base, 2" H	38.00
☐ Spaniel, sewer tile	175.00
☐ Terriers, 3 in a basket, Doulton	22.50
☐ Wirehaired Terrier, Vienna porcelain, show dog position, 4¾" x 4½"	40.00
☐ Wirehaired Terrier, Vienna bronze, onyx base	135.00
☐ Wooden Dog, painted, curled in sleep, very primitive, 19th century .	175.00
☐ Wooden Spotted Dog, primitive carving, 20th century	38.00

DOOR STOPS

Door stops are unusual figures usually of brass or iron, used primarily as their name indicates, but also as decorations for the home.

☐ Airedale Dog. Iron	30.00
☐ Bull. Iron...	30.00
☐ Bulldog. Iron	30.00
☐ Pointer. Iron	32.50
☐ Scottie Dog. Iron	32.50
☐ Terrier Dog. Iron...	32.50
☐ Boxer. Iron	27.50
☐ Cocker. Iron	32.50
☐ German Shepherd	45.00
☐ Cat. Black. Iron	27.50
☐ Cat. Black. Iron with green eyes	32.50
☐ Cockatoo. Iron	25.00
☐ Court Jester & Animal.....................................	50.00
☐ Dogs. Large. Iron	45.00
☐ Dolly with Toy. Iron	40.00
☐ Elephant..	25.00
☐ Fiddler & Violin. Cast iron.................................	30.00
☐ Flowers in Basket. Solid Brass.............................	50.00
☐ Fox. Brass	65.00
☐ Frog. Solid Bronze.......................................	85.00
☐ Horses. Iron	50.00
☐ Kitten, Iron	35.00
☐ Lamb. Black. Cast iron	42.50
☐ Lion. Large iron	45.00

DOOR STOPS

	Price
☐ Little Red Riding Hood & The Wolf. Iron (pr.)	75.00
☐ Parrot. Cast iron	30.00
☐ Pointer. Iron	32.50
☐ Snooper. Iron	55.00
☐ Windmill. Iron	32.50
☐ Wolf. Iron	40.00

EGGS

Eggs are a symbol of eternal life, all over the world — so it is easy to see why eggs have come to be a symbol for Easter. The range for collectors is very great — everything from Faberge charms to painted wooden eggs from Russia.

(right) SILVER/SHADED ENAMEL RUSSIAN EASTER EGG .... 400.00 - 600.00

(left) ENGRAVED OSTRICH EGG .... 400.00 - 600.00

	Price Range	
☐ Art Glass Egg, Iridescent, large, Vanderbelt	30.00	40.00
☐ Box, China painted with flowers and birds, hinged lid, brass fittings, 9½" L	120.00	160.00
☐ Easter Candy Container, Papier mache, egg being drawn by rabbit, 4" L	10.00	15.00
☐ Easter Egg, Baby chick, Goebel, 1978	10.00	18.00
☐ Easter Egg, Dove on cover, Wedgwood, 1977	50.00	70.00
☐ Easter Egg, Glass, undecorated, large, set of 4	35.00	45.00
☐ Easter Egg, Porcelain, Royal Bayreuth, 1979	22.00	30.00
☐ Easter Egg, Porcelain with floral decoration, Furstenberg, 1974	15.00	25.00
☐ Easter Egg, Silver and enamel, lilies and forget-me-nots, Faberge, by Ruckert, c. 1900	11,000.00	12,500.00
☐ Jewel Case, Mother-of-pearl, gilded metal, egg "wheelbarrow"	60.00	75.00

EYEGLASSES

One would be amazed as to the changes eye-wear has seen over the centuries. Since the thirteenth century eyeglasses have been in use. The earliest examples that can be found today are from the 1800's. Be on the lookout — the rare pieces in good condition command higher prices.

	Price Range	
☐ Harold Lloyd, bone frame, c. 1920	50.00	60.00
☐ Lorgnette, English, gilded, c. 1840	100.00	125.00
☐ Lorgnette, mother-of-pearl, c. 1800	60.00	70.00
☐ Lorgnette, sterling silver, c. 1840	125.00	150.00
☐ Lorgnette, tortoise shell, c. 1800	100.00	125.00
☐ Monocle, gold frame, silk cord, c. 1800	40.00	50.00
☐ Pinch, spectacles, hard rubber, c. 1860	40.00	60.00
☐ Pinch, spectacles, wire frame, c. 1920	40.00	50.00
☐ Pinch, spectacles, Art Deco, wire frame, c. 1930	40.00	50.00
☐ Quizzing, monocle, gold & silver, c. 1800	75.00	85.00
☐ Scissor, gold plated, ornate, c. 1880	75.00	85.00
☐ Spectacles, steel framed w/ties, c. 1800	90.00	100.00
☐ Spectacles, steel framed, wire temples, c. 1800	90.00	100.00

FANS

Fans are a most decorative and interesting item. They rate high as collectible because of the wide variety of beautiful designs. While being very useful, a fan was also looked upon as something decorative—a piece of jewelry, etc. Fans have been in use for many centuries.

☐ Advertising, lithographed late 19th century	5.00	10.00
☐ Black net, with sequins	12.00	16.00
☐ Bride's, lace, hand painted	15.00	20.00
☐ Brise, gilded, painted with 3 vignettes, loop	115.00	125.00
☐ Child's brise, painted, ribbon and floral design	50.00	55.00
☐ Cockade, silver and cut steel pique, middle quizzing glass	250.00	275.00
☐ Feather, small late 19th century	100.00	125.00
☐ Feather, signed Duvelleroy, 19th century	400.00	500.00

FANS

	Price	Range
☐ French, painted, signed Jolivet, 19th century	400.00	500.00
☐ French, carved, painted, signed	50.00	60.00
☐ Garrett snuff, advertising, paper, 1928	8.00	10.00
☐ George Washington & Cherry Smash, lithographed . .	17.00	20.00
☐ Gold edge, pink silk, ebony ribs	25.00	30.00
☐ Hand painted, floral design, wood	12.00	15.00
☐ Horn, carved, painted pansies, blue ribbon	70.00	80.00
☐ Maribou Feathers, satin 20" W, hand painted	70.00	90.00
☐ Oriental, straw, lacquered handle	8.00	10.00
☐ Oriental, silk, with Geisha figure	5.00	7.00
☐ Ostrich plume, tortoise shell sticks	10.00	15.00
☐ Pearl Sticks, sequin design, 8"	25.00	30.00
☐ Puzzle, 4 scenes, 2 way opening	105.00	110.00
☐ Regency, brise, painted, floral design, amber guards .	95.00	100.00
☐ Regency, brise, painted with vase of flowers	30.00	50.00
☐ Satin flower center, carved, ivory sticks	50.00	75.00
☐ Silk, hand painted animal figure and books	25.00	35.00
☐ Silk, hand painted figures and floral designs with original storage container	55.00	75.00
☐ Souvenir centennial, 12" L, historical buildings	50.00	85.00
☐ Wedding, ivory	50.00	60.00

FARM MACHINERY

While a specialized area of collectibles, farm machinery affords one a great opportunity to tinker with the past. These monsters of the soil certainly draw the interest of all those looking upon them. Unique, unusual and interesting are the words best used to describe the following examples of farm machinery.

$187⁰⁰
With Saw Frame

$149⁵⁰
Without Saw Frame,

"It Pays for Itself"

Sattley's Best

Engine Specifications

Power — Guaranteed full horse power at normal speed.

Oiling — Automatic sight feed lubricator supplies oil to piston, cylinder and wrist-pin bearing.

Cooling — Water cooled, ample cooling capacity in every size.

Ignition — Webster oscillating magneto — no wiring or short circuits.

Bore—5 H. P., 5¼ inches; 7 H. P., 6 inches.

Stroke—5 H. P., 7 inches; 7 H. P., 8½ inches.

Type—1-cylinder. Kerosene, with throttling governor. Gasoline—three speed.

☐ AVERY steam engine, 1912, 40 hp. w/full extension wheels	16000.00	18000.00
☐ BAKER steam engine, 1920, 20 hp. single cyl. side mount	3200.00	3500.00

FARM MACHINERY

	Price	Range
☐ CASE tractor, 1927, model "C", 4 cyl., rubber wheels, restored, good condition	750.00	1000.00
☐ CASE tractor, 1931, VAC model, rubber wheels, restored, good condition	350.00	500.00
☐ Deere, John tractor, 1935, model "B", rubber wheels, restored, good condition	400.00	600.00
☐ INTERNATIONAL HARVESTER tractor, 1937, model "H", rubber wheels, restored, good condition	750.00	1000.00
☐ SATTLEY'S timber saw, kerosene engine	1200.00	1400.00
☐ Upright steam saw rig, 10 hp	100.00	1200.00
☐ RUSSELL traction steam machine, 8 hp., restored	3500.00	4000.00

FIREARMS

Factors determining firearm values are demand, rarity and condition. They have been used for protection and pleasure as well as for improper and illegal purposes. They have progressed from the early Flintlocks to the more modern Remington & Winchesters. This section covers the most famous examples of pistols and longarms.

COLT ARMY

COLT BISLEY

PISTOLS:

☐ ALLEN & THURBER, 1840-50, sidehammer target pistol, 34 cal.	200.00	300.00
☐ ALLEN & WHEELLOCK, 1858-65, center hammer pistol, 31 to 38 cal.	150.00	200.00
☐ ALLEN & WHEELLOCK, 1858-61, sidehammer belt revolver, 31 to 34 cal.	300.00	400.00
☐ ETHAN ALLEN, 1840-42, first model pocket rifle 31 cal.	250.00	350.00
☐ ETHAN ALLEN, 1830-40, second model pocket rifle 31 cal.	275.00	375.00
☐ COLT, Army revolver, 1860-73, 44 cal.	600.00	900.00
☐ COLT, automatic pistol, 1905-11, 45 cal.	200.00	800.00
☐ COLT, belt, 1838-40, Paterson revolver 31 to 34 cal. . .	2400.00	2800.00
☐ COLT, Bisley revolver, 1894-1913, 32 to 45 cal.	900.00	1500.00
☐ COLT, Deringer, 1870-90, 41 cal.	200.00	500.00

FIREARMS

	Price Range	
☐ COLT, dragoon revolver, 1847-50, 31 cal.	1000.00	5000.00
☐ COLT, 45 automatic pistol, 1905-11, 45 cal.	200.00	800.00
☐ COLT, 1841, Hartford dragoon revolver, 44 cal.	2000.00	3000.00
☐ COLT, model 1855-70, sidehammer pocket revolver, 28 cal.	200.00	300.00
☐ COLT, Navy revolver, 1850-73, 31 cal.	1000.00	5000.00
☐ REMINGTON, 1863-73, single action, revolver 36 cal. .	200.00	300.00
☐ REMINGTON, 1861-62, Navy revolver, 36 cal.	250.00	350.00
☐ REMINGTON, 1861-62, Deringer, 22 cal.	600.00	700.00
☐ REMINGTON, 1865-88, pocket pistol, 22 cal.	100.00	200.00
☐ REMINGTON, 1866-1935, double Deringer, 41 cal. ...	200.00	400.00
☐ REMINGTON, 1871-88, Army rolling black pistol, 50 cal.	200.00	350.00
☐ REMINGTON, 1918-34, model 51, automatic pistol, 32 cal.	1800.00	2400.00
☐ REMINGTON-BEALES, 1855-70, sidehammer pocket revolver, 31 cal.	250.00	300.00
☐ SMITH & WESSON, 1857-60, first issue revolver, 22 cal.	200.00	250.00
☐ SMITH & WESSON, 1905-09, single shot pistol, 22 cal.	200.00	250.00
☐ SMITH & WESSON, 1882-83, DBL action, third model revolver, 32 cal.	100.00	150.00
☐ SMITH & WESSON, 1913-21, 35 automatic pistol, 35 cal.	175.00	275.00

KRAG BOLT ACTION CARBINE

LONGARMS

☐ ALLEN & WHEELLOCK, 1855-60, breech loader, 36 to 50 cal.	300.00	650.00
☐ ETHAN ALLEN, 1865-71, DBL, barrel shotgun, 10 to 12 gauge.................................	200.00	350.00
☐ COLT, 1837-38, model ring lever rifle, 34 to 44 cal.	3500.00	4000.00
☐ COLT, 1856-59, sporting rifle, 36 cal.	1000.00	1500.00
☐ COLT, 1856-64, revolving carbine, 36 to 56 cal.	1000.00	1250.00
☐ COLT, 1883-95, DBL, barrel shotgun, 10 to 12 gauge ..	250.00	350.00
☐ COLT, 1887-1904, lightning slide action, 22 cal.	250.00	350.00
☐ KRAG BOLT ACTION RIFLE, 1894-96, 30 to 40 cal. ...	150.00	1000.00
☐ KRAG BOLT ACTION RIFLE, 1896-98, 30 to 40 cal. ...	150.00	250.00
☐ KRAG BOLT ACTION & CARBINE, 1896-98, 30 to 40 cal.	200.00	400.00

LONGARMS

	Price	Range
☐ REMINGTON, 1862-65, percussion rifle, 58 cal.	500.00	650.00
☐ REMINGTON BLACK HILLS RIFLE, 1877-82, 45 to 60 cal.	300.00	500.00
☐ REMINGTON-KEENE, 1880-88, bolt action rifle, 45 to 70 cal.	1000.00	1500.00
☐ REMINGTON-HEPBURN, 1883-1907, sporting & target rifle, 22 to 50 cal.	250.00	450.00
☐ REMINGTON-WHITMORE, 1874-82, DBL, barrel shotgun rifle	500.00	600.00
☐ SMITH AND WESSON, 1879-87, 320 revolving rifle, 320 cal.	1500.00	2000.00
☐ SPRINGFIELD FLINTLOCK CARBINE, 1807-10, 54 cal.	1000.00	1500.00
☐ SPRINGFIELD FLINTLOCK MUSKET, 1814-16, 69 cal.	300.00	1200.00
☐ SPRINGFIELD FLINTLOCK MUSKET, 1816-40, 69 cal.	200.00	1000.00
☐ SPRINGFIELD FLINTLOCK MUSKET, 1817-21, 69 cal.	300.00	1500.00
☐ SPRINGFIELD FLINTLOCK MUSKET, 1849-51, 69 cal.	700.00	1000.00
☐ SPRINGFIELD FLINTLOCK RIFLE, 1817-40, 54 cal. . .	750.00	1200.00
☐ SPRINGFIELD HARPERS FERRY FLINTLOCK MUSKET, 1795-1815, 69 cal.	300.00	1500.00
☐ SPRINGFIELD PERCUSSION CARBINE, 1855-56, 54 cal.	800.00	1500.00
☐ SPRINGFIELD PERCUSSION MUSKET, 1844-55, 69 cal.	200.00	400.00
☐ SPRINGFIELD PERCUSSION RIFLE, 1857-61, 58 cal. .	500.00	1100.00
☐ SPRINGFIELD PERCUSSION RIFLE, 1861-62, 58 cal. .	200.00	600.00
☐ SPRINGFIELD PERCUSSION RIFLE, 1863, 58 cal. . . .	250.00	600.00
☐ SPRINGFIELD PERCUSSION RIFLE, 1864-65, 58 cal. .	250.00	500.00
☐ SPRINGFIELD ROLLING BLOCK RIFLE, 1871-72, 50 cal.	200.00	450.00
☐ SPRINGFIELD TRAPDOOR CARBINE, 1880, 45-70 cal.	200.00	400.00
☐ SPRINGFIELD TRAPDOOR CARBINE, 1873-77, 45-70 cal.	400.00	900.00
☐ SPRINGFIELD TRAPDOOR CARBINE, 1888, 45-70 cal.	200.00	400.00
☐ SPRINGFIELD TRAPDOOR RIFLE, 1868-72, 50 cal. . .	200.00	400.00
☐ SPRINGFIELD TRAPDOOR RIFLE, 1870-73, 50 cal. . .	200.00	400.00
☐ SPRINGFIELD 1903 RIFLE, 1903, 30-60 cal.	100.00	1000.00
☐ WINCHESTER HOTCHKISS BOLT ACTION RIFLE, 1879-99, 45-70 cal.	250.00	350.00
☐ WINCHESTER MODEL 1866 RIFLE, 1866-98, 44 cal. . .	1200.00	1500.00
☐ WINCHESTER MODEL 1873 RIFLE, 1873-1919, 32 to 44 cal.	350.00	600.00
☐ WINCHESTER MODEL 1876 RIFLE, 1876-97, 40 to 50 cal.	300.00	450.00
☐ WINCHESTER MODEL 1886-1935, 33 to 50 cal.	300.00	450.00
☐ WINCHESTER MODEL 65 RIFLE, 1933-47, 218 bee to 32 cal.	275.00	400.00
☐ WINCHESTER MODEL 1895 RIFLE, 1896-1931, 30 to 40 cal.	200.00	300.00
☐ WINCHESTER MODEL 1894 RIFLE, 1894-present, 25 to 38 cal.	150.00	300.00

FIRE FIGHTING EQUIPMENT

Every aspect of fire fighting is represented in collections including fire engines which sell for thousands of dollars. Fire marks, made of cast iron, zinc, lead and other metals, were bolted to houses and building to signal rival firefighting companies that insurance was paid up. Caution: many are now being reproduced in lightweight aluminum.

FIRE ENGINES:	Price Range	
☐ AMERICAN LAFRANCE, 1944, Auburn V-12 engine w/ladders, siren, bell unrestored, fair conditon	1000.00	1200.00
☐ AMERICAN LAFRANCE, 1924, 6 cyl., type 75 pumper, restored, good condition	2000.00	2400.00
☐ AMERICAN LAFRANCE, 1917, 6 cyl., type 40 pumper, restored, good condition	14000.00	16000.00
☐ AMERICAN LAFRANCE, 1948, 6 cyl., pumper, restored, fair condition	1200.00	1500.00
☐ CHEVROLET, 4 cyl., 1927, 1-ton, restored, excellent condition	4000.00	4200.00
☐ FORD, 1948, F-6, V-8, equipped unrestored, excellent condition	1800.00	2000.00
☐ FORD, 1947, unrestored, fair condition	1000.00	1200.00
☐ FORD, 1941, 8 cyl., restored, good condition	1500.00	2000.00
☐ SEAGRAVE, 1928, Model "A", 4 cyl., restored, excellent condition	15000.00	18000.00
FIRE MARKS:		
☐ Hands clasped. Germantown National Fire, 1843	135.00	150.00
☐ Hydrant. F. A., 1817, Brass plaque	80.00	100.00
☐ Twentieth century fire marks	25.00	50.00
☐ United Firearms Insurance Co. Iron plaque	60.00	75.00
HELMETS:		
☐ Brass. Eagle finial	185.00	200.00
☐ Firefighter parade helmet. Spike top, army type	110.00	120.00
☐ Handpainted helmet shield. 19th C.	500.00	550.00
☐ Leather, Black embossed with brass eagle, c. 1889	75.00	100.00
☐ Leather. Ornamental parade helmet, 18th C.	650.00	700.00
☐ Leather. Trumpet finlal	110.00	120.00

HELMETS

	Price	Range
☐ Leather. Three corned Gratacap, mid 1800's	1000.00	1500.00
☐ Leather. White, eagle, "Chairns Bros." mtg., mid 19th C.	100.00	125.00

MISCELLANEOUS:

☐ Axe. Nickel-plated head, c. 1850's	175.00	250.00
☐ Bell. Brass, operated by hand crank	225.00	235.00
☐ Bucket. Owner's name inscribed, early 19th C.	850.00	1000.00
☐ Bucket. Leather, decorated with helmet and hatchet .	200.00	225.00
☐ Bucket. Leather, painted	170.00	200.00
☐ Brass Fireman's Belt Buckle, fire engine engraved, 1870's	60.00	75.00
☐ Hose Nozzle. Brass, 12"	15.00	75.00
☐ Trumpet. Nickle plated, "working horn", tall	125.00	150.00
☐ Trumpet. Silver plated with red tassel, engraved "Orig. 1877"	275.00	300.00
☐ Tickets. Fireman's benefits, 19th C.	5.00	7.50
☐ Watercolor & drawing, pumpers, crowd, etc., 19th C. .	375.00	400.00
☐ Watercolor and honor roll	300.00	325.00

FIREPLACE EQUIPMENT

Utensils for starting and tending fires include andirons, bellows, screens, tools, lighters and trammel hooks. They have been built of a variety of material and can be as finely sculptured or as crudely made as the maker wished.

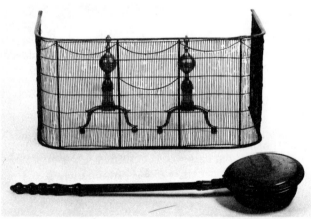

ANDIRONS

	Price
☐ Iron. Carved ball on top, 7" high, circa 1860	150.00
☐ Brass. Federal style, ball tops, spurred arch supports and snake feet, 13" high, pr.	120.00
☐ Brass urn finials on wrought iron knife blade standards, 23" high, pr.	250.00
☐ Cast iron figures of Hessian soldiers, 20th century, 20" high, pr. . . .	55.00
☐ Solid brass. 30" high, circa 1850, pr.	400.00

MISCELLANEOUS: Price

- [ ] Leather. Flowered panel, 16" long 55.00
- [ ] Leather. Flowered panel, 16" long, brass tip 60.00
- [ ] Wood. Metal nozzle, 20" long 55.00
- [ ] Hand-carved mahogany. Leather inset with brass nails, 18" 110.00
- [ ] Coal Hod. Frog style porcelain covered lift top 80.00
- [ ] Coal Hod. Burnished brass, helmet type with scoop 160.00
- [ ] Coal Hod. Copper with iron feet, handle and bail 65.00
- [ ] Coal Hod. Cast iron, green with floral decor, trimmed in gold 135.00
- [ ] Fender. Brass mesh with clowed feet, 50" long 160.00
- [ ] Fender. Iron, 12" high with brass trim 130.00
- [ ] Fender. Brass, 48" long 400.00
- [ ] Grate. Iron with legs, 9" high, 18" long 55.00
- [ ] Hearth Broom. Birch splint, American 175.00
- [ ] Hearth Shovel. Wrought iron, 27" long 15.00
- [ ] Lighter. New England type, brass 45.00
- [ ] Poker. Iron with tooled brass handle, 22½" long 17.50
- [ ] Poker. Iron, 59" long 20.00
- [ ] Screen. Classical Roman design, hinged 3 part 140.00
- [ ] Screen. Laquered, black with gold in Oriental design on stand 425.00
- [ ] Screen. Wood, single panel, floral decor 55.00
- [ ] Tongs. Brass 30.00
- [ ] Tools. Shovel, poker, tongs and holder. Brass 150.00
- [ ] Tool set. 3 pieces in holder 200.00
- [ ] Trammel. Wrought iron with adjustable sawtooth, 48" long 55.00
- [ ] Trammel hook. Forged iron, holds pots, 39" to 60" 100.00

FISHING TACKLE

Useful tools of the past intrigue the sport fisherman. While design and mechanical improvements have developed better fishing reels and rods, the old lures and flies which proved so popular in catching fish can still bring home the limit. All fishermen look with great interest on the tackle used in years past.

	Price Range	
[ ] Casting rod. Split bamboo, 5' straight handle, c. 1800	40.00	50.00
[ ] Casting rod. Tonkin cane, 5½', c. 1900	50.00	60.00
[ ] Casting rod. Heddon split bamboo, 6', c. 1920	75.00	100.00
[ ] Creel Fishing Basket. Wicker w/leather straps, c. 1880	100.00	150.00
[ ] Fish Hooks. Set of 50, c. 1910	10.00	15.00
[ ] Fly Box. Metal, round, c. 1910	20.00	30.00
[ ] Fly Box. Wooden, 6" x 10", c. 1900	50.00	60.00
[ ] Fly Rod. Heddon split bamboo, 9½', c. 1922	60.00	70.00
[ ] Fly Rod. H. L. Leonard, 8½', c. 1890	150.00	175.00
[ ] Fly Rod. H. L. Leonard, 7', c. 1885	300.00	325.00
[ ] Flies. English, set of 12, c. 1880	400.00	425.00
[ ] Reel. English fly, silver, c. 1850	500.00	600.00
[ ] Reel. Meisselbach, fly 3" featherweight, c. 1895	30.00	40.00

FISHING TACKLE

	Price	Range
☐ Reel. Meisselbach, tri-part, c. 1922	30.00	40.00
☐ Reel. Orvis, fly, solid silver, c. 1874	600.00	700.00
☐ Reel. Orvis, fly, c. 1874	100.00	150.00
☐ Reel. Pflueger, level wind, c. 1922	25.00	30.00
☐ Reel. Shakespeare, casting, level wind, c. 1922	25.00	30.00
☐ Reel. Shakespeare, universal, take down, c. 1922	25.00	30.00
☐ Reel. Von Hofe, fly, small, c. 1890	90.00	100.00
☐ Reel. Von Hofe, trolling, c. 1918	100.00	125.00
☐ Rod Case. Wood, 5', brass trim, c. 1880	80.00	100.00
☐ Steel Casting Rod. Wards, w/case, agate guides, 5½', c. 1922	30.00	40.00
☐ Steel Casting Rod. Wards, telescopic 9', c. 1922	25.00	30.00
☐ Tackle Box. Wooden & brass trim, 14", c. 1910	50.00	60.00
☐ Tackle Box. Metal & brass trim, 16", c. 1925	50.00	60.00

FOLK ART

If you haven't met folk art yet, and recognized it as something you love, keep trying. There is really something for everybody. One of the most exciting things about it is that you can buy what you like, and nevermind rules. Folk art, at least in America, usually means the work of Americans, and most American collectors tend to specialize in American work. Look for folk artists in your home town — your aunt, your milkman, your barber, even the chief of police may turn out to be an untutored artist, a painter or carver, who is able to create works of art — nothing like Rembrandt or the latest Pop artist, but full of integrity and charm.

☐ Archuleta sculpture, covered with sawdust & glue, small size	500.00	& up
☐ Bottlecap sculpture, snake	150.00	175.00
☐ Carving, cat in a cage, wood, early 20th C.	65.00	100.00
☐ Carving, eagle, snake, wood, painted, 18" H, early 20th C.	675.00	800.00
☐ Carving, four horses and wagon, w/driver, 20th C.	325.00	350.00
☐ Carving, man in chair, unpainted, 8" H, 1950's	45.00	60.00
☐ Carving, TV cameraman on camera dolly, 1950's	30.00	50.00
☐ Fraktur, part printed, part hand-colored, Victorian frame	40.00	50.00
☐ Mourning picture, embroidery on silk, 16" x 20"	325.00	350.00
☐ Oil on board, little girl in hooded cape, 7" x 9", c. 1820	90.00	100.00
☐ Oil on board, rat terrier w/rat, 19th C.	250.00	300.00
☐ Oil on canvas, apples & book, 8" x 10"	375.00	400.00
☐ Oil on canvas, boy, girl, lamb, mid-19th C.	130.00	150.00
☐ Oil on canvas, fruit & bird, unframed, 24" x 18", c. 1835	500.00	600.00
☐ Oil on canvas, Irish Setter, 16" x 19", framed	300.00	350.00
☐ Portraits, oil, Ammi Phillips, man & woman (pair)		35000.00
☐ Portraits, man & woman (pair), unsigned, 19th C.	325.00	350.00
☐ Portraits, man & woman (pair), unsigned, 33" x 28" framed, 19th C.	300.00	350.00

FROGS

Another motif collection, growing in popularity in the last 10 years or so, despite its improbability, is frogs. Frogs are made in many materials — some of the most desirable are the smallest — the Vienna bronzes. A wide variety of frog objects can be bought in bazaars and shops around the world — everything from raw rubber frogs from Columbia, South America for about 50 cents, to carved wooden frogs in Germany for a couple of dollars.

	Price Range	
☐ Cybis frog, mint condition	265.00	300.00
☐ Jadite frog on leaf, oriental, 2" L	95.00	100.00
☐ Mexican wooden frog, painted & carved, contemporary	11.00	15.00
☐ Pewter, cast, 1" H	5.00	7.50
☐ Planter, large open-back frog, unmarked china	10.00	15.00
☐ Puerto Rican clay frog, green glaze, 1½" H		1.00
☐ Ring, cast silver, finely detailed, garnet eyes	25.00	30.00
☐ Ring, cast silver, set with coral, Mexican	10.00	15.00
☐ Straw, Appalachia, woven like basket, 1930's	25.00	30.00
☐ Vienna bronze frogs, seesaw	275.00	300.00
☐ Vienna bronze, tiny frog on leaf, 1" L	20.00	25.00
☐ Zsolnay, signed, irridescent green	16.00	20.00

FURNITURE

Before buying an expensive piece of furniture it should be checked by a reliable appraiser. It is an ever-changing market and buyer and seller both should take advantage of a professional opinion before experiencing financial disaster.

In this section are listed many distinct styles and types of furniture. The differences between them are sometimes subtle and sometimes quite striking. All dates given are approximate.

Courtesy: Abe Kessler, New York, NY.

PERIODS

JACOBEAN	1603-1665	AMERICAN FEDERAL	1800-1815
RESTORATION	1665-1688	LATE FEDERAL	1835-1880
WILLIAM & MARY	1689-1702	REGENCY	1810-1830
QUEEN ANNE	1702-1714	DIRECTOIRE	1795-1808
CHIPPENDALE	1745-1772	AMERICAN EMPIRE	1815-1845
LOUIS XV	1720-1765	FRENCH	1810-1875
LOUIS XVI	1765-1789	DUNCAN PHYFE	1800-1827
HEPPLEWHITE	1780-1790	EARLY VICTORIAN	1835-1870
SHERATON	1790-1810	LATE VICTORIAN	1870-1900

WALL MIRROR, *Continental Inlaid and Gilded Bilboa*
. . . . 600.00 - 700.00

CORNER CHAIR, *Queen Anne Carved Walnut*
. . . . 2200.00 - 2600.00

PINE LIFT-TOP BLANKET CHEST,
Chippendale Painted and Decorated . . . . 1200.00 - 1600.00

BEDS

Price Range

- [ ] Brass, Late Victorian period, English design 375.00 500.00
- [ ] Brass, Double, Ornate scrollwork 1000.00 1250.00
- [ ] Brass, Single, simple styling, round posts 450.00 500.00
- [ ] Cannonball, Field Bed 125.00 350.00
- [ ] Carved walnut, ornately decorated 225.00 400.00
- [ ] Four Poster, Bamboo-like head and foot pieces 300.00 450.00
- [ ] Four Poster, Maple with and without canopy, c 1800's 500.00 3500.00
- [ ] Iron Beds, (depending on scroll work) 125.00 175.00
  Jenny Lind —
- [ ] Single, walnut 225.00 300.00
- [ ] Double, maple................................ 300.00 350.00
- [ ] Spool, Victorian 100.00 175.00
- [ ] Maple, Field bed 225.00 350.00

BENCHES

- [ ] Church, Pine, 48" long 200.00 300.00
- [ ] Cobbler, Walnut 250.00 300.00
- [ ] Cobbler, Pine, upholstered seat 450.00 500.00
- [ ] Deacon, Spindle back, 8 legs.................... 450.00 500.00
- [ ] Fireside, Pine, scroll design.................... 500.00 600.00
- [ ] Mammy, 6', Green, c 1800's 600.00 700.00
- [ ] Windsor, 9', Bamboo turnings 350.00 400.00

BENTWOOD

The process of bending wood with steam was perfected by Michael Thonet in Vienna in 1856. Bentwood furniture is still being produced by the Thonet firm and several others including the Sheboygan Chair Company, Tidioute Chair Company, and Jacob and Joseph Kohn.

- [ ] Arm, Signed Thonet 200.00 250.00
- [ ] Child's Highchair 150.00 200.00
- [ ] Child's Nursing Rocker 150.00 175.00
- [ ] Child's Rocker, signed Thonet................... 250.00 275.00
- [ ] Cradle in Stand, with top 1300.00 1500.00
- [ ] Hat Rack 275.00 300.00
- [ ] Side, Caned seat............................. 70.00 75.00
- [ ] Side, Wood Seat, signed Thonet 60.00 70.00
- [ ] Stool, Caned Seat............................ 90.00 100.00

CANDLESTANDS

- [ ] Chippendale, Carved and turned walnut dish top 2000.00 3000.00
- [ ] Chippendale, Turned and inlaid cherrywood 400.00 600.00
- [ ] Chippendale, Turned maple and cherrywood 500.00 800.00
- [ ] Federal, Carved mahogany tilt-top 300.00 500.00
- [ ] Federal, Inlaid mahogany Oval-top 3000.00 5000.00
- [ ] Federal, Inlaid mahogany tilting-top 1000.00 1200.00

CANDLESTANDS

	Price	Range
☐ Federal, Inlaid turned cherrywood	750.00	1000.00
☐ Federal, Maple octagonal	300.00	500.00
☐ Federal, Turned cherrywood	—	—
☐ Queen Anne, Turned and painted maple	400.00	600.00
☐ Queen Anne, Turned cherrywood	400.00	600.00
☐ William & Mary, Carved cherrywood two-light, Trestle base	2000.00	3000.00
☐ William & Mary, Turned walnut, rare	4000.00	6000.00
☐ Wrought Iron and walnut adjustable	750.00	1000.00

CHAIRS

	Price	Range
☐ Black Lacquer, Cane, C. 1800's	400.00	425.00
☐ Brace Back Windsor, Side Chair	400.00	550.00
☐ Brace Back Windsor, Arm	850.00	950.00
☐ Captain's, Pine, Side	250.00	275.00
☐ Child's, Arrowback	150.00	200.00
☐ Child's, Captain's	150.00	200.00
☐ Child's, High Chair, Windsor	150.00	200.00
☐ Child's, Ladderback, Red Paint	85.00	90.00
☐ Chippendale, Arm	1750.00	2000.00
☐ Chippendale, Carved walnut side, pair	15000.00	20000.00
☐ Chippendale, Corner	400.00	500.00
☐ Chippendale, Country, 18th Century	500.00	600.00
☐ Chippendale, Side, Cherry	1250.00	1500.00
☐ Chippendale, Side, Upholstered	750.00	1000.00
☐ Chippendale, Wing	9500.00	10000.00
☐ Eastlake, Victorian, Side	100.00	150.00
☐ Eastlake, Victorian, Walnut, Arm	150.00	200.00
☐ Gentlemen's, Carved	350.00	400.00
☐ Hepplewhite, Side Upholstered	750.00	1000.00
☐ Hepplewhite, Side	525.00	700.00
☐ Ladderback, Arm, Cherry	450.00	500.00
☐ Ladderback, Side, Maple	250.00	300.00
☐ Ladderback, Side, Mahogany	350.00	400.00
☐ Parlor, Walnut, upholstered seat & back	500.00	600.00
☐ Pennsylvania, Arrowback	100.00	110.00
☐ Queen Anne, Arm	2200.00	2500.00
☐ Queen Anne, Banister	400.00	500.00
☐ Queen Anne, Corner, Maple	700.00	800.00
☐ Queen Anne, Country, Round feet	350.00	400.00
☐ Queen Anne, Side, Walnut	1500.00	2000.00
☐ Queen Anne, Wing	9500.00	10000.00
☐ Shaker, Ladderback	250.00	300.00
☐ Shaker, Side	450.00	500.00
☐ Shaker, Straight	80.00	100.00
☐ Sheraton, Arm	500.00	750.00
☐ Sheraton, Country	300.00	450.00
☐ Sheraton, Side	375.00	500.00
☐ Victorian, Arm, early	325.00	500.00
☐ Victorian, Arm, Gentleman's	500.00	750.00

CHAIRS

	Price	Range
☐ Victorian, Arm, Ladies	450.00	500.00
☐ Victorian, Side, early	100.00	150.00
☐ Windsor, Fanback	200.00	300.00
☐ Windsor, Side, Bamboo turned, pair	350.00	375.00
☐ Windsor, Side, Bow Back	200.00	250.00

CHESTS

☐ Apothecary, With drawers	250.00	300.00

BLANKET:

☐ Chippendale, Walnut	900.00	1000.00
☐ Curly Maple	950.00	1000.00
☐ Pine, cannonball feet	250.00	275.00
☐ Pennsylvania, red	130.00	150.00
☐ Tiger Maple	1000.00	1200.00

CHIPPENDALE:

☐ Birch	1750.00	2000.00
☐ Cherry	3000.00	3500.00
☐ Mahogany	5000.00	6000.00
☐ Maple	4000.00	4500.00
☐ Walnut	2000.00	3000.00
☐ Commode, Bedside	500.00	750.00
☐ Eastlake, Victorian, drawers	225.00	500.00

HEPPLEWHITE:

☐ Cherry	1000.00	1200.00
☐ Mahogany	1000.00	1250.00
☐ Maple	1250.00	1500.00
☐ Walnut	1000.00	1250.00

SHERATON:

☐ Cherry, inlaid	750.00	1000.00
☐ Mahogany, 4 drawer	1000.00	1500.00
☐ Maple	750.00	1000.00
☐ Walnut	500.00	750.00
☐ Silver Chest, Velvet lined Mahogany	250.00	300.00

CORNER CUPBOARDS

☐ American Mahogany	850.00	1000.00
☐ Chippendale, Maple & Cherrywood	1100.00	1500.00
☐ Chippendale, Pine	1500.00	2000.00
☐ Federal Inlaid, Cherrywood	2000.00	3000.00
☐ Primitive, Pine, carved and painted	600.00	800.00
☐ Queen Anne, Carved, barrel back, Pine	600.00	800.00
☐ Queen Anne, Carved and painted, Pine	600.00	800.00

DESKS

Price Range

AMERICAN:

- ☐ Walnut, Carved, 72" 250.00   350.00
- ☐ Cherry, Slant Front 2000.00   2500.00

CHIPPENDALE STYLE:

- ☐ Flat Top, kneehole 4000.00   4500.00
- ☐ Slant Front, Mahogany 8500.00   9000.00
- ☐ Slant Front, Maple 8500.00   9000.00
- ☐ Slant front, platform 4000.00   4500.00

HEPPLEWHITE STYLE:

- ☐ Bureau Style 1500.00   2000.00
- ☐ Flat Top, Kneehole 2250.00   2500.00
- ☐ Slant Front, Mahogany 2250.00   2500.00

LAP DESKS:

- ☐ Inlaid Wood, velvet lined 100.00   150.00
- ☐ Mahogany, brass hinged 150.00   200.00
- ☐ Walnut, lined, secret compartment 75.00   100.00

ROLL TOPS:

- ☐ Mahogany 600.00   700.00
- ☐ Oak, Brass 500.00   700.00
- ☐ Oak, S Design, 50" 400.00   600.00
- ☐ Oak, Waterfall 700.00   2000.00

SCHOOLMASTER:

- ☐ Kneehole, Mahogany inlay 500.00   600.00
- ☐ Pine and Maple 250.00   275.00
- ☐ Slant Front 200.00   300.00

SHERATON STYLE:

- ☐ Bureau Style 1000.00   1250.00
- ☐ Country, Pine, drawer 1000.00   1250.00
- ☐ Flat Top, kneehole 1000.00   1250.00
- ☐ Slant Front 1250.00   1500.00

VICTORIAN STYLE:

- ☐ Flat Top, kneehole 650.00   800.00
- ☐ Slant Front 650.00   800.00

DRY SINKS

- ☐ Pine, Metal top 375.00   400.00
- ☐ Pine, Painted 325.00   375.00
- ☐ Pine, Primitive, rough condition 125.00   135.00
- ☐ Pine, Refinished 400.00   500.00
- ☐ Walnut, 2 shelves, zinc lined trough 750.00   900.00

KITCHEN UTILITY CUPBOARDS

- ☐ Four compartment storage, beveled glass 350.00   400.00
- ☐ Oval, wall type, oak 50.00   75.00

HIGHBOYS & LOWBOYS
(American Made)

Price Range

CHIPPENDALE
CHERRY

☐ Highboy	15000.00	18000.00
☐ Lowboy	8000.00	10000.00

MAHOGANY

☐ Highboy	18000.00	20000.00
☐ Lowboy	10000.00	12000.00

MAPLE

☐ Highboy	25000.00	35000.00
☐ Lowboy	17500.00	20000.00

WALNUT

☐ Highboy	15000.00	18000.00
☐ Lowboy	5000.00	7000.00

QUEEN ANN STYLE
CHERRY

☐ Highboy	15000.00	18000.00
☐ Lowboy	8500.00	10000.00

CURLY MAPLE

☐ Highboy — Flat Top	8000.00	10000.00
☐ Highboy — Bonnet Top	10000.00	15000.00

MAHOGANY

☐ Highboy	18000.00	20000.00
☐ Lowboy	10000.00	12000.00

MAPLE

☐ Highboy	17500.00	20000.00
☐ Lowboy	8500.00	10000.00

WALNUT

☐ Highboy	15000.00	18000.00
☐ Lowboy	5000.00	7000.00

WILLIAM & MARY
BURLED WALNUT

☐ Highboy, Inlaid	3000.00	4500.00

MAHOGANY

☐ Highboy, Bonnet Top, inlaid	4500.00	6000.00

MAPLE

☐ Highboy, Flat Top	2500.00	3500.00

WALNUT

☐ Highboy, Flat Top, inlaid	2500.00	3000.00
☐ Highboy, Bonnet Top, carved	3500.00	4500.00

LOVESEATS

☐ Art Nouveau Style	350.00	500.00
☐ Eastlake, Victorian, Walnut	400.00	500.00
☐ Empire Victorian, Transitional	500.00	600.00
☐ Louis XVV, Wing back	2500.00	3000.00
☐ Rococo, Victorian, upholstered	600.00	700.00

MIRRORS

	Price	Range
☐ Brass, Figural design	160.00	175.00
☐ Chippendale, Georgian	1500.00	2500.00
☐ Chippendale, Mahogany, English	800.00	1000.00
☐ Chippendale, Walnut	800.00	1000.00
☐ Chippendale, Walnut, wall	500.00	600.00
☐ Convex, Federal period	1250.00	2250.00
☐ Empire Dressing table	400.00	450.00
☐ Empire, Standard	250.00	750.00
☐ English Dressing table	400.00	450.00
☐ Federal, Gilt wood and gesso, eagle	700.00	850.00
☐ Queen Anne, Mahogany, gilted	2500.00	3250.00
☐ Regency, Standard	250.00	750.00
☐ Rococo, Wood, large	1000.00	1200.00
☐ Shaving, Carved	50.00	75.00
☐ Shaving, Mahogany	150.00	175.00
☐ Traveling, Wood inlay	25.00	50.00
☐ Oval, Floor type, oak	275.00	300.00

MUSIC CABINETS

☐ Serpentine Legs, Single door	125.00	150.00
☐ Serpentine Legs, Double door	150.00	175.00

ROCKERS

☐ Arrow Backs, Federal painted and decorated	300.00	400.00
☐ Bamboo, Turned and painted Windsor hoop back	525.00	725.00
☐ Boston, Painted	500.00	650.00
☐ Cane, Back and seat refinished	85.00	105.00
☐ Cherrywood, American, mid 19th Century, yoke top rail, scrolled armrests	150.00	250.00
☐ Boston, Wicker seat	125.00	175.00
☐ Child's, Wood and wicker seat	50.00	70.00
☐ Child's, Turned and black painted wood platform	100.00	150.00
☐ Easklake, Platform	75.00	90.00
☐ Eastlake, Platform fabric seat	350.00	375.00
☐ Federal, Painted and decorated	200.00	250.00
☐ Ladderback, Ornate	400.00	500.00
☐ Victorian, Grecian, restored	200.00	250.00
☐ Victorian, Mahogany, 19th Century	80.00	120.00
☐ Victorian, Walnut, leaf design	250.00	275.00
☐ Walnut Frame, Complete upholstery with tufted back	550.00	650.00
☐ Windsor, Bamboo turning	400.00	600.00
☐ Windsor, Fanback, signed	450.00	600.00

SECRETARIES

☐ Empire, American	700.00	1700.00
☐ Federal	3000.00	3000.00
☐ Hepplewhite	3000.00	5000.00
☐ Regency	1500.00	2500.00
☐ Sheraton	1500.00	3000.00
☐ Victorian	1000.00	3000.00

SIDEBOARDS

	Price Range	
☐ Chippendale, American	10000.00	12000.00
☐ Empire, American	1500.00	2000.00
☐ Hepplewhite	3500.00	4500.00
☐ Regency	1500.00	2000.00
☐ Sheraton	2500.00	4000.00
☐ Victorian	1000.00	1500.00

SOFAS & SETTEES

	Price Range	
☐ American Sofa, Carved Walnut	1800.00	2000.00
☐ Belter Sofa, Rosewood	3500.00	4500.00
☐ Chippendale, Sofa, Mahogany	3500.00	4000.00
☐ Chippendale, Sofa, 6 legs	7500.00	8000.00
☐ Chippendale Settee	3500.00	4000.00
☐ Directoire Sofa	1250.00	3000.00
☐ Directoire Settee	900.00	1000.00
☐ Eastlake Sofa	225.00	275.00
☐ Eastlake Settee	175.00	200.00
☐ Empire Sofa	200.00	300.00
☐ Empire Settee	200.00	300.00
☐ Empire Sofa, Mahogany, French	750.00	1000.00
☐ Empire Settee, French	450.00	600.00
☐ Federal Sofa, Mahogany, carved	600.00	750.00
☐ Federal Settee, Painted, decorated	1200.00	1400.00
☐ Hepplewhite Sofa	3000.00	3500.00
☐ Hepplewhite Settee	1500.00	1700.00
☐ Queen Anne Sofa	6000.00	6500.00
☐ Queen Anne Settee	4000.00	4500.00
☐ Rococo Sofa, Walnut, carved	2700.00	3000.00
☐ Rococo Settee, serpentine back	450.00	550.00
☐ Sheraton Sofa, Mahogany	1750.00	2000.00
☐ Sheraton Settee	950.00	1000.00
☐ Victorian Sofa, Louis XV, Walnut, carved	1200.00	1500.00
☐ Victorian Sofa, Louis XV, Walnut	600.00	700.00
☐ Victorian Sofa, Louis XVI, French	3500.00	4000.00
☐ Victorian Settee, Louis XVI, French	1750.00	2000.00
☐ William & Mary Settee, Upholstered	700.00	800.00
☐ Windsor, Bamboo, Spindle back	1800.00	2000.00

STOOLS

	Price Range	
☐ George II, Mahogany oval	1500.00	2000.00
☐ George II, Walnut stool	2000.00	2500.00
☐ George III, Mahogany feet, carved	400.00	600.00
☐ German Rococo, Gilt-wood	800.00	1000.00
☐ Louis XV Style Painted, pair	250.00	350.00
☐ Regency Rosewood, Piano	200.00	300.00
☐ Rush Seat, Turned and painted	100.00	150.00

TABLES
Price Range

CARD & GAME:

☐ Chippendale, American	5500.00	6000.00
☐ Chippendale, American, carved mahogany turret-top	2500.00	3500.00
☐ Chippendale, English	1750.00	2000.00
☐ Duncan Phyfe Style, Mahogany	750.00	1000.00
☐ Federal, Maple inlay	800.00	1000.00
☐ Federal, Marble inlay	2600.00	3000.00
☐ French Backgammon, Louis XVI	3000.00	3500.00
☐ Hepplewhite, American	—	—
☐ Hepplewhite, English	1250.00	1500.00
☐ Queen Anne Style, English	2600.00	3000.00
☐ Sheraton, American	1250.00	1500.00
☐ Sheraton, English	750.00	1000.00

DROP LEAF:

☐ Birch Gate-Leg, 6 legs, high drop leaf, American	1250.00	1500.00
☐ Birch Gate-Leg, 6 legs, high drop leaf, English	650.00	800.00
☐ Chippendale, American Mahogany	5500.00	6000.00
☐ Chippendale, English	1750.00	2000.00
☐ Empire & Victorian, American	350.00	500.00
☐ Empire & Victorian, English	250.00	400.00
☐ Harvest, Pine 5'	500.00	600.00
☐ Hepplewhite, American	1250.00	1500.00
☐ Hepplewhite, English	500.00	750.00
☐ Queen Anne, American Swing Legs	5500.00	6000.00
☐ Queen Anne, English, Swing Legs	1750.00	2000.00
☐ Sheraton, American	750.00	1000.00
☐ Sheraton, English	500.00	750.00

TILT TOP:

☐ Chippendale, American	2250.00	2500.00
☐ Chippendale, English	1000.00	1200.00
☐ Federal, American	1000.00	1250.00
☐ Federal, English	475.00	600.00
☐ Hepplewhite, American	2250.00	2500.00
☐ Hepplewhite, English	1250.00	1500.00
☐ Pembroke, Mahogany, carved, 28"	450.00	500.00
☐ Queen Anne, American	1250.00	1500.00
☐ Queen Anne, English	500.00	750.00
☐ Regency, American	1000.00	1250.00
☐ Regency, English	475.00	600.00

WORK TABLE:

☐ Cherry with Drawers	400.00	500.00
☐ Empire, Cherry, sewing	450.00	500.00
☐ Empire, Mahogany	350.00	450.00
☐ Mahogany, English	1500.00	2000.00
☐ Maple, American	900.00	1100.00
☐ Victorian, Walnut, sewing	300.00	500.00

OCCASIONAL TABLES:

	Price	Range
☐ American Pine	200.00	250.00
☐ Hepplewhite, American	650.00	800.00
☐ Hepplewhite, English	375.00	400.00
☐ Office, Pine	115.00	125.00
☐ Tea, Mahogany	1750.00	2000.00
☐ Sheraton, American	450.00	500.00
☐ Sheraton, English	350.00	400.00
☐ Victorian, American	250.00	300.00
☐ Victorian, English	200.00	300.00

OAK FURNITURE

Oak furniture gained its popularity because of durability and beauty. Antique oak furniture is still in existence and speaks well of its sturdy construction and design.

BEDS

☐ Cane headboard and footboard, plain style	225.00	250.00
☐ Folding style	450.00	500.00
☐ Footboard with scroll	300.00	350.00
☐ Open panel designs	200.00	225.00

BENCHES

☐ Church, 56" long	300.00	400.00
☐ Church pews, decorated ends, 8' L	45.00	55.00

BOOKCASES

☐ Desk and adjustable shelf combination	300.00	700.00
☐ Five horizontal adjustable shelves, no glass	300.00	700.00
☐ Four horizontal adjustable shelves with glass	275.00	300.00
☐ Large library bookcase with glass front	1300.00	1600.00
☐ Six tiered stacking, Gunn Furniture Co., 1901	450.00	500.00

CHAIRS

☐ Armless, padded seat, no carving, set of 4	200.00	250.00
☐ Armless, wood seat, very ornate, set of 4	300.00	350.00
☐ Barber shop chair, pneumatic	1800.00	2200.00
☐ Ornate back	350.00	400.00
☐ Shaker style, set of 4	225.00	300.00
☐ Single upholstered seat, with arms, square design, set of 4	80.00	160.00
☐ Upholstered seats, 4 armchairs, 2 side	725.00	800.00
☐ Windsor style, set of 4	200.00	225.00

CHESTS

☐ Oak, paneled	400.00	450.00

CHINA CABINETS

☐ Claw style legs, ornate	600.00	800.00
☐ Leaded glass, quartered oak, claw feet	550.00	600.00
☐ Serpentine legs, ornate	800.00	900.00

DESKS

Price Range

☐ Bombay Style, claw feet	225.00	300.00
☐ C-curve, 36"	450.00	550.00
☐ Kneehole	90.00	100.00
☐ Ladies', tall roll-top, glass doors on top shelves, matching chair	3200.00	3800.00
☐ Lapdesk, inkwell	65.00	75.00
☐ Office type, kneehole	250.00	300.00
☐ S-curve, 42", refinished	925.00	1100.00
☐ S-curve, 50", with swivel chair, mint	1175.00	1300.00
☐ Secretary type with beveled glass	1200.00	1500.00
☐ Ŝ Design, 50", rolltop	400.00	600.00
☐ Side-by-side	100.00	150.00
☐ Waterfall, rolltop	700.00	2000.00
☐ Wooton, S-roll	2200.00	2500.00

DRESSERS

☐ Bombay Style, ornately carved	200.00	300.00
☐ Dressing Table, with mirror	150.00	175.00
☐ Square Style, three drawers with mirror	150.00	175.00

DRY SINK

☐ Zinc-lined top	325.00	350.00

FERN OR PLANT STAND

☐ Pedestal or with legs, 28"-29" H	38.00	48.00

HALL RACKS

☐ Claw Feet, large mirror	600.00	650.00
☐ Serpentine Legs, round mirror, one drawer	400.00	450.00
☐ Square Style, ornately carved, paneled back	500.00	550.00
☐ Two piece, double seat bench, ornately carved	500.00	550.00

ICE BOXES

☐ Double Door, refinished	200.00	300.00
☐ Four Door, carved	1000.00	1100.00
☐ "Mascot", brass hardware, refinished, 4' x 2'	375.00	450.00
☐ "Mascot", brass hardware, refinished, 4' x 2'	375.00	450.00
☐ Meat Cooler, walk-in, with inlaid white glass panels, matching counter, 1920's, 10' H x 8' x 6'	14000.00	15000.00
☐ Single Door	150.00	200.00
☐ Six Door, with mirror	400.00	450.00

MIRRORS

☐ Oval, floor type	275.00	225.00
☐ Square, floor type	200.00	225.00
☐ Square, wall type	50.00	75.00
☐ Traveling, wood inlay	25.00	50.00

MUSIC CABINETS

☐ Quartered Oak, hand-carved, single door	150.00	175.00

ROCKERS

☐ Pressed Back	90.00	100.00
☐ Spindled Back	75.00	90.00

SIDEBOARDS

Price Range

☐ Leaded glass doors and sides with mirror	500.00	550.00
☐ Ornate with drawers and mirrors	550.00	600.00
☐ Plain with drawers	250.00	300.00
☐ 4-Drawers and cellavettes	225.00	300.00

TABLES

☐ Library	60.00	200.00
☐ Library, carved lion head supports, claw feet, 2 drawers	875.00	950.00
☐ Library, large round legs, dark finish	125.00	175.00
☐ Occasional	50.00	200.00
☐ Round, egg and dart edges, octagonal base	750.00	825.00
☐ Round, large	300.00	450.00
☐ Round, ornate carvings	700.00	900.00
☐ Round, small	200.00	300.00
☐ Square, large	150.00	200.00
☐ Square, ornate	300.00	400.00
☐ Square, small	75.00	125.00

WARDROBES

☐ Double Door, beveled glass	350.00	400.00
☐ Double Door, without glass	225.00	300.00
☐ Single Door, plain	150.00	200.00

MISSION OAK

☐ G. Stickley, signed, desk and chair, inlaid	14500.00	15000.00
☐ G. Stickley, signed, sideboard	1300.00	1600.00
☐ G. Stickley, signed, spindleback armchair and sidechair	3000.00	3500.00
☐ G. Stickley, signed dowry chest	900.00	1200.00
☐ Limbert Arts & Crafts, Grand Rapids, sideboard	115.00	155.00
☐ Mission Style, unsigned library table, small	215.00	245.00
☐ Morris Chair and footstool	2500.00	3000.00

PAINTED FURNITURE

By painted furniture is meant American painted furniture dating between 1790 and the 1870's. Much furniture was made, particularly in the country, which was intended from the start to be painted. The various techniques use brushes, steel and wooden combs, sponges, crinkled paper, even the sooty flame of a tallow candle. The decorations include plain-painted (1 color, no design), imitation graining (various wood grains imitated), marbleizing (marble imitation), and decorative and imaginary painting (everything from flowers to mermaids). The earlier the piece & bigger it is, the more expensive. A good place for beginning collectors to start is with picture frames, small boxes, single side chairs, etc.

CHAIRS

☐ Highchair, English, Windsor, c. 1810	395.00	450.00
☐ Highchair, salmon, splay leg	275.00	300.00
☐ Hitchcock, set of four	300.00	350.00

CHAIRS

Price Range

- Plank-seat, thumback, yellow, w/stenciled flowers, set of four 900.00 1000.00
- Sidechair, ladderback, 5 slats, green over red, 49" H, 19th C. 350.00 400.00
- Sidechairs, shoulder back, Pennsylvania, set of 6, 1830's 1500.00 2000.00
- Sidechairs, Pennsylvania, green w/stenciled flowers, set of 6, c. 1850's-60's 750.00 1000.00
- Sidechairs, Pennsylvania, balloon back, stenciled, set of 4 .... 325.00 350.00
- Sidechairs, urn back, stenciled on green, set of 6 .... 1000.00 1100.00
- Sidechairs, Federal, rush seats, 6 different townscapes or crest rails, (Gregory Sale), c. 1895 .... 16000.00

CHESTS

- Blanket, scallaped base, green plaid painted 125.00 150.00
- Blanket, 2-drawer, red 450.00 500.00
- Blanket, bracket base, green 300.00 350.00
- Blanket, Connecticut, carved and painted, lift top, top restored, 17th C. 20000.00
- Blanket, lift top, 2-drawer, red 725.00 750.00
- Blanket, lift top, 2-drawer, red, original brasses 400.00 425.00

CUPBOARDS

- Corner, glazed, turned feet, 1 drawer, original hardware, 84" H 3000.00 3400.00
- Corner, grained (Stewart Gregory Folk Art Auction) .. 10000.00
- Tabletop, red 500.00 550.00

TABLES

- Dropleaf, New England, black and red, small 1050.00 1100.00
- Dressing, Federal, yellow, reeded legs (Gregory sale) . 5250.00
- Dressing, New England, grained 350.00 400.00
- Tavern, sawbuck style, scrub tops, pr., 19th C. 225.00 250.00
- Tea, Sheraton style, octagonal top, red plain painted . 350.00 375.00

MISCELLANEOUS

- Bed, hired man's, red 50.00 100.00
- Bench, bucket, Pennsylvania, mustard graining over red, 41" H x 31" W, early 1800's 325.00 350.00
- Candlestand, quatrefoil base, plain painted 225.00 250.00
- Dry Sink, small, plain painted 425.00 450.00
- Graining Combs, 12 wooden handled in box 35.00 50.00
- Hitchcock Settee, children's, w/side chair & arm chair 3800.00 4000.00
- Steel Graining Combs, 5 blued steel, 1890's 16.00 20.00
- Trunk, Norwegian, rosemaeling,1871 .... 375.00 400.00

WICKER FURNITURE

The popularity of wicker furniture has remained high throughout the years. Its light and fresh look adds to the decor attitudes of today. Newly made wicker is styled closely to antique design so please be careful in determining its authenticity.

WICKER FURNITURE

	Price Range	
☐ Baby Carriage, fancy, c. 1900	100.00	125.00
☐ Baby Stroller, fancy, c. 1900	125.00	150.00
☐ Chair, straight, rolled arm and back, c. 1890	90.00	110.00
☐ Chair, straight, wing back, rolle darm, c. 1880	250.00	275.00
☐ Davenport, fan back with cushions, 82", c. 1900	200.00	250.00
☐ Davenport, wing arms and back with cushions, 96", c. 1900	300.00	350.00
☐ Davenport, open high back with cushions, 82", c. 1910	200.00	250.00
☐ Davenport, solid back, round arms with cushions, 96", c. 1910	350.00	400.00
☐ Davenport, open high back, wing arms with cushions, 84", c. 1900	175.00	200.00
☐ Davenport, pointed high back with cushion, 72", c. 1890	240.00	250.00
☐ Davenport, straight sides with cushion back and seat, 72", c. 1900	150.00	200.00
☐ Fern Stand, bamboo legs, 10" x 36", c. 1880	75.00	100.00
☐ Fern Stand, straight legs, 10" x 42", c. 1890	90.00	100.00
☐ Lounge, straight sides with cushion, 25", c. 1900	190.00	220.00
☐ Lounge, set up side with cushion, 96", c. 1900	250.00	350.00
☐ Rockers, fancy high back, wing arms, c. 1890	200.00	250.00
☐ Rockers, straight high back, c. 1880	100.00	125.00
☐ Rockers, straight back, no arms, c. 1880	70.00	90.00
☐ Rockers, wide, rolled arms and back, c. 1890	150.00	175.00
☐ Rockers, wide, rolled back, c. 1880	150.00	175.00
☐ Rockers, wide, rolled back and arms, child's, c. 1875 .	200.00	250.00
☐ Rockers, wing back, wide flat arms, c. 1890	190.00	210.00
☐ Settee, wing arm, 60", c. 1920	125.00	150.00
☐ Settee, bucket back, 60", c. 1910	150.00	190.00
☐ Settee, overstuffed, 72", c. 1900	300.00	350.00
☐ Swing, straight side and back, 72", c. 1890	175.00	200.00
☐ Table, round, wood top, 36", c. 1890	150.00	200.00
☐ Table, sewing, wood top, 18" x 42", c. 1880	175.00	200.00
☐ Table, end, wood top, 18" x 24", c. 1900	100.00	125.00
☐ Table, coffee, wood top, 18" x 36", c. 1900	75.00	100.00

GAMES

Both board games (those played on printed boards or checkered boards), toys such as Tiddly Winks and jacks are all collected.

☐ Around The World With Nellie Bly. Lithograph	70.00	90.00
☐ Backgammon, Black and Red, c. 1880	75.00	95.00
☐ Baseball, Marble, Pinch Hitter	25.00	30.00
☐ Blacks, Wood with Pictures, c. 1900	38.00	45.00
☐ Cards, Original Box, c. 1896	28.00	32.00
☐ Dominoes, Ebony and Ivory, Brass Pegs	48.00	55.00

GAMES

		Price	Range
☐	Fortune's Wheel, Parker Bros., c. 1903	40.00	55.00
☐	Game of Boy Scouts, Parker Bros., c. 1912	22.00	30.00
☐	Game of Snaps, West & Lee, c. 1873	10.00	20.00
☐	Game of Tri-Bang, McLaughlin, c. 1898	28.00	35.00
☐	Little Red Riding Hood, Milton Bradley, c. 1900	28.00	35.00
☐	Mah-Jong Sets, Ivory and Bamboo Tiles in black lac- quered box, c. 1923	75.00	95.00
☐	Mah-Jong Sets, Ivory Tiles	260.00	290.00
☐	Pick-Up-Sticks, Wooden, c. 1937	3.00	6.00
☐	Pinball, Bagatelle, c. 1950	8.00	12.00
☐	Tell It To The Judge, Eddie Cantor, c. 1936	18.00	22.00
☐	Tiddly Winks, Milton Bradley	13.00	16.00
☐	Touring Game, Park Bros., c. 1926	12.00	16.00
☐	What's My Line, c. 1950	6.00	10.00

MARBLES

Some marble collectors add anything that's round and under the size of a golf ball to their marble collections, for if it doesn't have a hole, you know it isn't a bead—but there's no way of knowing if it isn't a marble. Marbles are made of **glass, ceramic, wood and even steel—but steel marbles aren't collectible.**

☐	Bennington, Box of 50	80.00	120.00
☐	Bennington, Light to dark blue, 1½"	8.00	12.00

SULPHIDES

☐	Anteater, 1"	45.00	60.00
☐	Bear, 7/8"	60.00	70.00
☐	Bird, 1¼"	45.00	60.00
☐	Cat, 1¼"	45.00	60.00
☐	Cougar, Standing	60.00	70.00
☐	Cow, 1 5/8"	60.00	70.00
☐	Dog, Large.	50.00	65.00
☐	Dog, Shaggy, 1¼"	60.00	70.00
☐	Horse, Running, 1½"	55.00	70.00
☐	Lamb, 1¾"	60.00	70.00
☐	Lion, Sitting, 6"	60.00	70.00
☐	Rabbit, Running	60.00	70.00
☐	Rooster, 2"	60.00	70.00
☐	Sheep, 2"	70.00	80.00
☐	Squirrol, 1½"	65.00	85.00
☐	Woodpecker, 4"	60.00	70.00

SWIRL

☐	Blue, Red, White, 2"	50.00	60.00
☐	Blue, Green, Yellow, 1½"	50.00	60.00
☐	Cane, 1½"	60.00	70.00
☐	Green, Yellow, Red, 1½"	60.00	70.00
☐	Red, Green, White, 1¾"	65.00	75.00

GLASS

ART GLASS

The Art Nouveau period developed no better expression of the era than did *art glass*. While many European artists were giving birth to Art Nouveau, America was also developing its own followers. American Art Glass craftsmen developed their own techniques and designs. It was not long until the quality of American Art Glass surpassed that of European glass makers. Although the Art Nouveau Period lasted only about 20 years, true examples like those listed below will be treasured and will last forever.

	Price Range	
☐ Atomizer, 5¾" high, Despres'	260.00	300.00
☐ Atomizer, ebony colored, Mueller Freres	260.00	300.00
☐ Bottle, cologne, with silver tip, red & white, Webb	1440.00	1540.00
☐ Bottle, cologne with silver stopper, Webb	800.00	900.00
☐ Bowl, 9½" D x 3¼" H with handles, Aurene	750.00	900.00
☐ Compote, 9", Quezal	320.00	350.00
☐ Dresser Jar, with leaves and vines, Gres'	300.00	400.00
☐ Inkwell, 6", three color, Shneider	325.00	425.00
☐ Jar, crackle design, Marinot	1340.00	1380.00
☐ Pitcher, 4" H, Marinot	1370.00	1390.00
☐ Pitcher, 8", Gres'	390.00	450.00
☐ Pitcher, salt, Aurene	175.00	200.00
☐ Pitcher, enamel, bowl on layered glass, unsigned	425.00	450.00
☐ Rose Bowl, with flowers, unsigned	350.00	400.00
☐ Toothpick Holder, dark flowers, Daum	165.00	195.00
☐ Vase, small, signed Webb, blue & white	1425.00	1500.00
☐ Vase, 5" scenic view, Decourchemont	410.00	450.00
☐ Vase, 5" Citron, carved floral, Webb	1375.00	1450.00
☐ Vase, miniature, three color, Marinot	1200.00	1350.00
☐ Vase, 7", purple with butterfly, Webb	1800.00	2000.00
☐ Vase, 6", blue & white, Webb	1470.00	1520.00
☐ Vase, 4½", footed, elaborate 3 colors	1000.00	1300.00
☐ Vase, 8", yellow glass with applied iris decoration	625.00	725.00
☐ Vase, 16", M.O.P., white on red, Webb	2100.00	2500.00
☐ Vase, white on raisin, deeply carved, 4½"	950.00	975.00
☐ Vase, white on deep yellow, Marinot	1500.00	1800.00
☐ Vase, 12", floral pattern on yellow background, unsigned	775.00	900.00
☐ Vase, lake scene, gold, brown, 11", Daum	1200.00	1350.00
☐ Vase, scene, amber, 18", unsigned	900.00	950.00
☐ Vase, frosted white to green, 10", Quezal	800.00	900.00
☐ Vase, scenic view, 5"	400.00	500.00
☐ Vase, ruby, flowers, Patte De Verre, G. Argy—Rousseau	350.00	500.00
☐ Vase, white cameo leaves on citron, butterfly, 7¼", T. Webb	1800.00	2800.00
☐ Vase, cameo & enamel, crackled amber background, 8", Daum Nancy	900.00	1100.00
☐ Vase, cameo, white flowers on red, 4½", Webb	900.00	1100.00

PLATED AMBERINA BEAKER,
c. 1890 . . . . 1000.00 - 1100.00

WHEELING PEACHBLOW CRUET
AND STOPPER, *c. 1890*
. . . . 550.00 - 600.00

PLATED AMBERINA BOWL,
c. 1890 . . . . 1000.00 - 1500.00

DURAND IRIDESCENT GLASS VASE,
c. 1905 . . . . . . 400.00 - 500.00

QUEZEL IRIDESCENT TRUMPET
VASE, *c. 1900* . . 500.00 - 600.00

TIFFANY IRIDESCENT SHALLOW
BOWL, *c. 1905* . 300.00 - 400.00

TIFFANY IRIDESCENT GLASS VASE,
c. 1905 . . . . . . 700.00 - 800.00

AGATA

Made by Joseph Locke of New England Glass Company, Cambridge, Massachusetts. A single layered shaded opaque glass ranging from deep raspberry at the top to a rich cream at the base, but characterized by irregular splotches of dark grey to black caused by an alcohol treatment in the finishing operation.

	Price Range	
☐ Bowl, finger	900.00	1000.00
☐ Bowl, handle, 4"	1800.00	1900.00
☐ Bowl, raspberry	725.00	750.00
☐ Bowl, sugar	1500.00	1700.00
☐ Celery Dish	1500.00	1650.00
☐ Cruet, 1650	1650.00	1700.00
☐ Pitcher, milk, Akro Agate Handle	3000.00	3500.00
☐ Sugar Bowl	1500.00	1600.00
☐ Toothpick Holder, square top	500.00	550.00
☐ Toothpick Holder	600.00	1000.00
☐ Tumbler, water	700.00	750.00
☐ Vase, fluted rim, 8"	1500.00	2000.00
☐ Vase, lily shape, 8"	1300.00	1400.00
☐ Water Pitcher	2600.00	3000.00
☐ Water Tumbler, deep color, good molting	750.00	800.00
☐ Water Tumbler, molted	600.00	700.00
☐ Whiskey	800.00	875.00

AMBERINA

Amberina process was developed by the New England Glass Co. This process was granted to other major glass companies. In the 1920's Libbey Glass Company produced this beautiful amberina coloration which ranged from deep fuschia to a beautiful amber.

☐ Basket, diamond, handle	110.00	120.00
☐ Basket, green & red	160.00	175.00
☐ Bowl, 8", diamond quilted	200.00	225.00
☐ Bowl, footed thumbprint	140.00	150.00
☐ Butter Dish, covered	325.00	375.00
☐ Candlestick	125.00	150.00
☐ Carafe, 6"	300.00	350.00
☐ Castor, pickle	250.00	285.00
☐ Celery, Fushia, Double Quilt	275.00	295.00
☐ Compote, Fushia, 7"	100.00	125.00
☐ Creamer, diamond applied handle	150.00	165.00
☐ Creamer, inverted thumbprint,	150.00	165.00
☐ Cruet, inverted thumbprint, handle	300.00	325.00
☐ Cups, diamond quilted, reeded amber handle	100.00	125.00
☐ Decanter, thumbprint	200.00	225.00
☐ Finger bowl	135.00	150.00
☐ Fluted bowl	180.00	200.00
☐ Mug, handled	100.00	115.00
☐ Perfume bottle, with atomizer	200.00	225.00
☐ Pitcher, inverted thumbprint, 7"	215.00	250.00

AMBERINA

	Price	Range
☐ Pitcher, water, 11"	225.00	250.00
☐ Pitcher, water, swirled	250.00	275.00
☐ Punch cup	50.00	175.00
☐ Sugar & Creamer, daisy & button	450.00	500.00
☐ Toothpick Holder, Russian cut	165.00	176.00
☐ Tumbler	50.00	125.00
☐ Vase	100.00	500.00

BACCARAT

Famous Baccarat Glass was first made by artistic and talented French craftsmen in 1765. They developed this unique and different quality manufacturing technique that has never been duplicated.

☐ Box, oval, green opalene multi-colored floral	90.00	120.00
☐ Box and Cover, gold etched floral design, 4" x 6", c. 1890	150.00	175.00
☐ Butter Dish, covered blue animal design, c. 1890	40.00	50.00
☐ Candle Holder, single swirl pattern, gold etched, c. 1890	120.00	150.00
☐ Cake Stand, rose tiente swirl covered, c. 1900	100.00	120.00
☐ Cologne Bottle, gold and blue with stopper, 4", c. 1880	150.00	175.00
☐ Decanter, rose tiente swirl, 10", c. 1900	100.00	120.00
☐ Decanter Set, 6 glasses, blue floral pattern, c. 1880 ..	200.00	225.00
☐ Dish, flat, blue, 6", c. 1890	40.00	50.00
☐ Inkwell, covered clear swirl, c. 1900	40.00	50.00
☐ Perfume Decanter, with stopper, rose swirl, c. 1890 ..	50.00	60.00
☐ Perfume Bottle, with stopper, cobalt blue, c. 1900 ...	80.00	100.00
☐ Powder Jar, covered, rose swirl, c. 1890	40.00	60.00
☐ Toothpick Holder, rose swirl, c. 1890	20.00	30.00
☐ Vase, rose tiente swirl with floral, 10", c. 1890	60.00	70.00
☐ Vase, cobalt blue and gold, signed, 12", c. 1890	175.00	200.00
☐ Tray, oval, rose tiente swirl, 12", c. 1890	80.00	100.00

BOHEMIAN

Bohemian glass is named for its country of origin, which is now a part of Czechoslovakia. It was made popular during the Victorian era, but is still produced today. It is an ornate, overlay, or flashed glassware.

☐ Basket, ruby with clear florals, oval	60.00	80.00
☐ Berry Bowl, ruby, vintage, 8 1/2" x 3 5/8"	40.00	60.00
☐ Bottles, perfume, ruby, vintage, 5"	50.00	65.00
☐ Box, powder, ruby, bird & butterfly	90.00	110.00
☐ Butter Dish, ruby, deer & castle	130.00	160.00
☐ Candy Dish, amber, covered	70.00	90.00
☐ Compote, ruby, deer & castle, 8" D x 7" H...........	38.00	45.00
☐ Compote, ruby, vintage pattern, 9"	225.00	250.00
☐ Cordial, green to clear, 6 pieces	175.00	200.00
☐ Cordial Set, green, 7 pieces	150.00	175.00
☐ Decanter, ruby, vintage, 9" high	65.00	85.00
☐ Decanter, vintage, with fluted stopper, 10" high	40.00	50.00

BOHEMIAN

	Price	Range
☐ Decanter, ruby, cut & engraved, 15" high, pair	100.00	140.00
☐ Decanter, ruby, vintage design	165.00	190.00
☐ Door Knobs, ruby	55.00	75.00
☐ Dresser Set, animal design, 5 pieces	225.00	250.00
☐ Dresser Set, leaf pattern, 3 pieces.	45.00	55.00
☐ Goblet, ruby, vintage, knob stem	80.00	100.00
☐ Goblet, amber feet & knob stem, Intaglio cut	55.00	75.00
☐ Goblet, cut & fluted, birds in flight, 6" high.	40.00	50.00
☐ Jar, amethyst, with lid	50.00	75.00
☐ Lamp, cobalt overlay, 12" H.	160.00	180.00
☐ Liqueur Set, ruby, cut florals, 7 pieces	90.00	110.00
☐ Lustre, pair, ruby with enamel flowers	225.00	250.00
☐ Mug, ruby, clear handle, 4½" H.	45.00	55.00
☐ Pitcher, ruby, vintage	130.00	150.00
☐ Pokal & Cover, ruby, deer & castle pattern, 15½" H. . .	180.00	200.00
☐ Sugar Shaker, ruby cut to clear roses with original top	50.00	65.00
☐ Tankard, deep cut panels, applied clear handle,		
5 5/8" H	85.00	105.00
☐ Toothpick Holder, ruby, deer & pine tree pattern	28.00	38.00
☐ Tray, etched glass, yellow	100.00	125.00
☐ Tumbler, blue with white overlay	35.00	65.00
☐ Tumbler, green with white overlay.	35.00	65.00
☐ Tumbler, ruby, bird & castle	30.00	40.00
☐ Tumbler, ruby, vintage	30.00	40.00
☐ Tumbler, ruby; vintage, footed	50.00	60.00
☐ Urn, covered, large, deers.	165.00	190.00
☐ Urn, Intaglio deer & trees, ruby, covered, 14" H	140.00	160.00
☐ Vase, enamel flowers, green	100.00	125.00
☐ Vase, amber and gold leaf design	75.00	100.00
☐ Vase, bud, ruby, etched deer	55.00	75.00
☐ Vase, ruby, wine leaves	45.00	70.00
☐ Vases, pair, green with white overlay	175.00	200.00
☐ Vase, ruby, castle & deer, 5" H	80.00	100.00
☐ Vase, ruby, castle & bird, 10¼" H	120.00	150.00
☐ Vase, deer & trees, amber, 12" H	150.00	180.00
☐ Vase, flowers & bird, ruby, 12½" H	110.00	130.00
☐ Whiskey Set, deer & castle, decanter with 4 shot		
glasses, apricot	130.00	160.00
☐ Wine Set, deer & castle, ruby, decanter with 6 glasses	235.00	265.00

BRISTOL

The broad term Bristol is given by collectors to various types of semi-opaque glasses. It is the product of several glass houses in Bristol, England, where several glass makers are located.

☐ Barber Bottle	25.00	30.00
☐ Bowl, covered punch	170.00	190.00
☐ Box, 3½" H, dark blue	60.00	80.00
☐ Decanters, blue with shield labeled "Rum"	90.00	110.00
☐ Dresser Set, 3 pieces, black with white florals	85.00	105.00

BRISTOL

	Price	Range
☐ Ducks, 10", mouth open forms candlesticks	90.00	120.00
☐ Hand, holding vase	60.00	80.00
☐ Mug, 3¼", "Remember Me"	40.00	60.00
☐ Pitcher, 4" H, "Remember Me" in gold	50.00	70.00
☐ Ring Tree, 3" H, blue	40.00	50.00
☐ Sugar & Creamer, white	140.00	160.00
☐ Tumbler, peasant scene	14.00	18.00
☐ Urn, 19" H, covered, heavy enamel with cupids	170.00	190.00
☐ Vase, 5" H, bird on branch	35.00	50.00
☐ Vase, 7" H, smokey opaline	40.00	55.00
☐ Vase, 10" H, green with enameled florals, pair	65.00	75.00

BURMESE

The process used in making Burmese art glass was accidentally discovered by Fredrick S. Shirley, an employee of the Mt. Washington Glass Co., New Bedford, Massachusetts. The glass was patented in 1885. Most items have no particular pattern, however, some have a ribbed hobnail design.

☐ Basket, 8¼", Mt. Washington	860.00	900.00
☐ Bell, 6" glossy finish	440.00	470.00
☐ Biscuit Jar, handpainted	740.00	770.00
☐ Bowl, 4", filigree around neck	325.00	375.00
☐ Bowl, 8", footed, with decoration	400.00	450.00
☐ Candlestick, diamond with four feet	590.00	640.00
☐ Creamer & Sugar Bowl with wishbone handles	680.00	710.00
☐ Cruet, vinegar, dull finish, 7", light coloring	475.00	525.00
☐ Cup, custard	290.00	320.00
☐ Epergne, single lily in sculptured brass on brown marble base	340.00	370.00
☐ Fairy Lamp, clear base	480.00	520.00
☐ Glass, lemonade, with handle, fair color	220.00	270.00
☐ Holder, toothpick, small, original label tricorn	320.00	390.00
☐ Holder, toothpick, small, acid finish, floral decoration	335.00	400.00
☐ Lamp, fairy, clarke, patent, 5"	280.00	340.00
☐ Nut Dish, 3 feet	345.00	375.00
☐ Pitcher, creamer, 3½", wishbone feet	675.00	775.00
☐ Plate, 5"	315.00	345.00
☐ Plate, 8"	415.00	445.00
☐ Rose Bowl, acid finish, unsigned Webb	285.00	325.00
☐ Sherbet, footed	365.00	395.00
☐ Sugar Bowl, 5½"	740.00	780.00
☐ Toothpick Holder, hat shape	670.00	690.00
☐ Toothpick Holder, acid finish, Mt. Washington	160.00	190.00
☐ Tumbler, 4", fine coloring, Queen's design	470.00	525.00
☐ Tumbler, water, 4", good color	260.00	320.00
☐ Tumbler, glossy finish, Mt. Washington	160.00	190.00
☐ Vase, 4" dull finish	200.00	275.00
☐ Vase, 4" H, ruffled rim, acid finish	165.00	195.00
☐ Vase, 4" swirled ribs, average color	270.00	325.00
☐ Vase, 12½" H, double gourd shape	590.00	640.00
☐ Vase, 18", Grecian decoration with handles	3100.00	3750.00

CAMBRIDGE

Named for its make Cambridge Glass of Cambridge, Ohio. Articles include Crown Tuscanware, black satin and tableware with nude satin lady for stems.

	Price Range	
☐ Ashtrays, 4" seashell	15.00	25.00
☐ Basket, crystal cut	60.00	75.00
☐ Basket, ebony, 8½"	80.00	100.00
☐ Bowl, centerpiece, azurete, 10"	35.00	50.00
☐ Bowl, tulip shaped, amberina	40.00	65.00
☐ Bowl, seashell, with feet	95.00	125.00
☐ Bowl, silver deposit on back, 9"	40.00	65.00
☐ Bowl, square with feet	30.00	50.00
☐ Candelabra, 10", with birds	45.00	60.00
☐ Candle Holder, Crown Tuscan	50.00	60.00
☐ Candlestick, 10", Helio, pair	90.00	125.00
☐ Champagne Glass, nude figure for stem	50.00	65.00
☐ Claret	10.00	12.50
☐ Compote, crystal	35.00	50.00
☐ Cordial, set of six	45.00	65.00
☐ Creamer, crystal souvenir edition	15.00	25.00
☐ Cup, custard	7.00	10.00
☐ Decanter, amethyst	25.00	35.00
☐ Decanter, 12", amber, with stopper	30.00	35.00
☐ Dish, candy covered	24.00	35.00
☐ Dish, soap covered, Helin	25.00	30.00
☐ Dish, seafood, with fish	40.00	45.00
☐ Dish, nut	25.00	45.00
☐ Flower Holder, crystal	30.00	45.00
☐ Goblet, rock crystal	12.00	15.00
☐ Goblet, Roxanne, crystal cut	15.00	20.00
☐ Goblet, Rosepoint, crystal	20.00	25.00
☐ Ice Bucket, ebony	30.00	45.00
☐ Pitcher, water, etched	20.00	25.00
☐ Plates, bread & butter, Rosepoint	5.00	7.50
☐ Plates, cake, 10", handled, amber	20.00	25.00
☐ Plates, dinner, Rosepoint	30.00	35.00
☐ Relish Dish, 5"	25.00	30.00
☐ Relish Dish, 9", 3 pieces	25.00	30.00
☐ Swans, apple green, 3½"	20.00	30.00
☐ Swans, crystal, 3½"	25.00	30.00
☐ Swans, Crown Tuscan, 2½"	20.00	25.00
☐ Tray, Sandwich, etched	15.00	20.00
☐ Tray, black & silver, handles	50.00	75.00
☐ Tumbler, amethyst	5.00	7.50
☐ Tumbler, iced tea, Rosepoint	15.00	20.00
☐ Tumbler, juice, green	5.00	7.50
☐ Tumbler, lemonade	10.00	12.00
☐ Vases, bud, 10"	25.00	30.00
☐ Vases, Crown Tuscan, 12"	45.00	60.00
☐ Vases, bell shape	30.00	45.00
☐ Wine Glass, rock crystal	5.00	7.50

CORALENE

One of the many types of art glass. Satin glass was the base with tiny glass beads affixed in various patterns then fired. Made primarily by the New England Glass Company in the 1880's. Many items are being reproduced today.

	Price Range	
☐ Basket, on peachblow, coral design, in blue MOP	375.00	400.00
☐ Pitcher, wheat motif on satin glass, 8"	275.00	300.00
☐ Toothpick Holder	350.00	375.00
☐ Tumbler, water, MOP blue/white, coral	300.00	325.00
☐ Vase, satin glass, yellow to white	375.00	400.00
☐ Vase, MOP with zig-zag design in yellow beads	400.00	500.00
☐ Vase, apricot satin glass, seaweed design	200.00	250.00
☐ Vase, flowers in blue satin glass, 6¼"	450.00	500.00

DURAND '

Victor Durand, Jr., said to be a descendant of the family which made Baccarat glass, headed the Vineland Glass Works Company which produced this glass in the 1920's and by his father before him.

This glass was of similar quality and beauty to that made by Tiffany.

☐ Bowl, vase 6½" H, blue with white heart	385.00	415.00
☐ Candleholder, 3" H, amber base	185.00	205.00
☐ Compote, 5½" H, cranberry	440.00	480.00
☐ Lamp, umbrella shaped shade, 30"	1540.00	1580.00
☐ Liqueur, blue & white, canary yellow stem	180.00	210.00
☐ Plate, 8" D, feather pattern	315.00	345.00
☐ Vase, 5" H, iridescent emerald green	130.00	160.00
☐ Vase, 7" H, iridescent blue, signed	510.00	550.00
☐ Vase, 12" H, red & clear, "Crackle", signed	765.00	795.00
☐ Wine, 5¾" H, feather pattern	180.00	210.00

GALLÉ

Emile Gallé (1846-1905), the most renowned of the French art glass masters, was born in Nancy, the glass center of France. He began his first glass factory in 1879 and in 1884 gained recognition at an art exposition. This led to his appointment as the headmaster of the glass school at Nancy.

He was able to obtain fascinating artistic new effects by the use of varied colored glass casings upon a base of translucent or transparent glass during the heating process. All of this work was executed in relief as it was first etched out of a mass with acid and then the detail engraved with a wheel.

☐ Atomizer, sable with honey tones, 5¾"	250.00	290.00
☐ Bottle, perfume, frosted gold with violets, 4 1/8"	240.00	270.00
☐ Bowl, blue, white, frosted, purple flowers & leaves, 4"	195.00	225.00
☐ Bowl, green, blue, frosted, boat-shaped, 9½"	290.00	340.00
☐ Bowl, red leaves, yellow ground, Acorns, 3" x 4¼" . . .	370.00	400.00
☐ Box, cameo, covered, gold with purple flowers, 4¼" . .	430.00	470.00
☐ Box, green floral, frosted, diamond shape, 8½" x 5½"	490.00	520.00
☐ Cameo powder box, carved, signed with star, 4½" sq., 2" H	440.00	470.00

GALLÉ

	Price	Range
☐ Cruet, dragon, beetle & butterfly, signed	320.00	350.00
☐ Cup & Saucer, enameled	100.00	120.00
☐ Dish & Cover, clear with enameled grey, red, black & pink, circa 1900, 5" H	340.00	370.00
☐ Lamp, night light, fuchsias, lemon ground with brass fitting	510.00	560.00
☐ Lamp, base, deep maroon leaves, amber, 13½"	520.00	590.00
☐ Pitcher, bird in flight, 3"	160.00	200.00
☐ Pitcher, yellow with grapes, 8" H.................	370.00	400.00
☐ Shot Glass, green thistle cameos, 2½"	190.00	230.00
☐ Toothpick Holder, enameled, multi-colored, signed, 2" H...	120.00	150.00
☐ Tumbler, deep amber, enameled dragon, 2½"	2600.00	3200.00
☐ Vase, cameo overlay, ovoid, iris on white, 7½", signed and label	1200.00	1600.00
☐ Vase, triple overlay cameo, pedestal, landscape, 7"..	1200.00	1600.00
☐ Vase, cameo, carved deep purple design, signed, 3¼" H...	375.00	400.00
☐ Vase, cameo, carved scene, 4 colors, signed, 14" H ..	1300.00	1400.00
☐ Vase, cameo, fruit, leaves & flowers, 10"	840.00	870.00
☐ Vase, cameo, carved red berries & leaves, frosted ground, signed, 3½" H........................	290.00	320.00
☐ Vase, cameo, carved brown florals against pink ground, signed, 5½" high	375.00	425.00
☐ Vase, cameo, carved green river with trees & pink sky, signed, 6½" H	540.00	590.00
☐ Vase, cameo, carved gold, blue & brown trees and mountain, 10" H	575.00	625.00
☐ Vase, cameo, carved pink flowers, beige & green leaves, blue sky, signed, 13½" H	675.00	750.00
☐ Vase, cameo, tapered cylinder, carved scene, signed, 14" H...	1400.00	1500.00
☐ Vase, cameo, carved amber iris, frosted dark ground, signed	450.00	500.00
☐ Vase, dragonfly, 4 colors, 17¼"	1275.00	1375.00
☐ Vase, forest on pink, ferns, tri-petal top, 11½".......	1000.00	1050.00
☐ Vase, gray & amber floral, green foot, frosted, signed, 4½".....................................	500.00	540.00
☐ Vase, praying mantis, crystal & enamel, 5½"	590.00	630.00
☐ Vase, white/green wisteria, pink base & top, 17½"...	410.00	450.00
☐ Vase, cameo, carved purple & green pendant, pink & grey ground, circa 1900, signed	375.00	400.00
☐ Vase, cameo, carved green vines, gold & white frosted ground, signed, 26"	1000.00	1075.00

HEISEY

Heisey Glass was made in Newark, Ohio by the U. H. Heisey Co., in the late 1890's to 1957 when the factory closed. Molds of animal figures were obtained by the Imperial Glass Company of Bellview, Ohio, and reproduced between 1964 and 1967.

Heisey has become the most sought after of the "Depression Glass" genre, and prices are constantly on the increase. All Heisey Glass was marked with a (H) impressed in glass. Many pieces can still be found in thrift shops and garage sales and can be bought reasonably.

	Price Range	
☐ Ashtray, crystalite	25.00	50.00
☐ Ashtray, duck	35.00	50.00
☐ Basket, bow tie pattern, Flamingo	38.00	50.00
☐ Basket, etched butterfly	95.00	125.00
☐ Basket, 10" H, fluete & panel	90.00	120.00
☐ Bon Bon, pink, 5½" x 7"	40.00	50.00
☐ Bookends, figural horse, pair	100.00	150.00
☐ Bowl, berry, butterfly design	45.00	75.00
☐ Bowl, berry, Greek Key	85.00	125.00
☐ Bowl, berry, Provincial	65.00	80.00
☐ Bowl, "Crystalite" pattern with handles	65.00	90.00
☐ Bowl, punch, 12" D, pedastal, fluted	255.00	270.00
☐ Bowl, dessert, Pied Piper	35.00	45.00
☐ Candelabra, 10½" H, 3-light	90.00	140.00
☐ Candle Holder, Lariat pattern	65.00	75.00
☐ Candlesticks, 4" H, crystal etched, pair	75.00	90.00
☐ Candlesticks, Old Sandwich, 6½" H, pair	85.00	125.00
☐ Candlesticks, Empress, Sahara, pair	100.00	150.00
☐ Candy Dish, "Crystalite" pattern with handles	45.00	60.00
☐ Candy Dish, pierced silver rim, "Greek-Key" pattern	45.00	55.00
☐ Carafe	75.00	100.00
☐ Celery, Empress	45.00	50.00
☐ Celery, Greek Key, 12"	55.00	65.00
☐ Celery, Queen Anne, Sahara	55.00	60.00
☐ Celery Dish, "urn" pattern	60.00	70.00
☐ Centerpiece Bowl, orchid	65.00	90.00
☐ Champagne, orchid	18.00	35.00
☐ Champagne, Pied Piper	15.00	20.00
☐ Champagne, Sahara	20.00	25.00
☐ Champagne, clear	6.00	16.00
☐ Cigarette Box, "Crystalite"	45.00	75.00
☐ Cigarette Urn, gold border	45.00	50.00
☐ Cigarette Urn, Ridgeleigh	25.00	35.00
☐ Cocktail Shaker with optional top, Rooster Head (rare)	120.00	150.00
☐ Compote, 9" H, diamond optic in green	60.00	75.00
☐ Creamer, Flamingo	27.00	32.00
☐ Creamer, Waverly	25.00	30.00
☐ Creamer & Sugar, Greek Key	30.00	40.00
☐ Cup & Saucer, Queen Anne	25.00	30.00

HEISEY

	Price	Range
☐ Cup & Saucer, pink	20.00	35.00
☐ Custard Dish, "Waverly" pattern	17.00	24.00
☐ Dessert Berry Bowl & Plates, "Urn" pattern (set)	150.00	200.00
☐ Dessert Plate, "Star" etched bottom (rare)	18.00	& up
☐ Dish, cheese & crackers, Saturn	65.00	90.00
☐ Dish, lemon, Ridgeleigh	27.00	32.00
☐ Goblet, colonial design	15.00	18.00
☐ Goblet, old Sandwich	22.00	30.00
☐ Goblet, Princess Anne, Sahara	22.00	30.00
☐ Goblet, Saturn, Sahara	22.00	30.00
☐ Ice Bucket, colonial design	75.00	90.00
☐ Ice Bucket, ribbed	60.00	90.00
☐ Jar, candy, Greek Key, covered	90.00	120.00
☐ Lemonade Set, pitcher & six glasses	110.00	175.00
☐ Mugs, Old Sandwich	25.00	35.00
☐ Mugs, Pineapple & Gan	28.00	32.00
☐ Perfume Bottle, blue band trimmed in gold	45.00	60.00
☐ Pitcher, colonial, 7¾" H	50.00	75.00
☐ Pitcher, Greek Key, 6¼" H	55.00	75.00
☐ Pitcher, milk, Wedding Band	45.00	75.00
☐ Pitcher, water, emerald green	160.00	200.00
☐ Pitcher, water, eight panels	90.00	120.00
☐ Pitcher, water, Greek Key	110.00	150.00
☐ Plates, colonial, 6"	25.00	35.00
☐ Plates, Fancy Loop, 8"	25.00	35.00
☐ Plates, Flamingo, Empress, 8"	15.00	25.00
☐ Plates, Queen Anne, 7"	30.00	40.00
☐ Powder Jar, colonial, covered with sterling silver top	75.00	120.00
☐ Punch Bowl, Green Key	275.00	325.00
☐ Punch Bowl, Prince of Wales, Plumes, 2 pieces	275.00	325.00
☐ Relish, divided	50.00	75.00
☐ Salt & Pepper, etched, pair	25.00	35.00
☐ Sherbet, colonial	50.00	75.00
☐ Sherbet, fluted	45.00	55.00
☐ Sherbet, Flamingo	27.00	32.00
☐ Sherbet, Greek Key	25.00	30.00
☐ Sherbet, Sandwich	50.00	75.00
☐ Spooner, beaded swag, milk white	50.00	75.00
☐ Sugar & Creamer, "Urn" pattern, pair	45.00	75.00
☐ Syrup, etched	30.00	50.00
☐ Toothpick, beaded swag	45.00	75.00
☐ Toothpick Holder, "Crystolite" pattern	30.00	45.00
☐ Toothpick, fancy loop	45.00	75.00
☐ Tumbler, colonial	15.00	25.00
☐ Tumbler, Ipswich, juice	10.00	15.00
☐ Tumbler, thumbprint in crystal	18.00	22.00
☐ Vase, crystal, 21"	140.00	160.00
☐ Vase, fan, etched, 7½"	50.00	75.00
☐ Vase, etched vine design, 10" H	75.00	90.00

HEISEY

	Price	Range
☐ Whiskey, Coronation, 2½", ounce	17.00	22.00
☐ Wine, colonial, 3 ounce	22.00	26.00
☐ Wine, Tally Ho.................................	40.00	55.00

LALIQUE, RENE

His glass was produced in Paris from the 1890's until his death in 1945, and is marked R. Lalique. Present pieces just bear the name Lalique. A very high quality glass designed in the Art Deco and Art Noveau style. Those pieces signed R. Lalique, of course, commmand much higher prices and are more sought after by collectors.

☐ Ashtray, frosted and clear with lovebirds	40.00	55.00
☐ Atomizer, 5" H, metal top, six nude figures on frosted ground	95.00	140.00
☐ Bottles, brown frosted ground with elegant ladies several positions, 6"...........................	240.00	285.00
☐ Bottles, perfume, square inclined toward middle with woman's profile	90.00	125.00
☐ Bottles, perfume, Art Nouveau, 4½"...............	325.00	375.00
☐ Bottles, perfume, heart shaped	25.00	45.00
☐ Bottles, perfume, square with dome shaped stopper ..	80.00	110.00
☐ Bottles, perfume, shaped like two flowers	40.00	65.00
☐ Bowl, six lovebirds in middle, 8½" D, signed	200.00	250.00
☐ Bowl, irridescent green, 3" H, signed	210.00	280.00
☐ Bowl, cupids and roses, 9" H	50.00	95.00
☐ Bowl, intaglio foliage and birds, 9" D	100.00	145.00
☐ Bowl, dragonfly on the lid, 3" x 2"	40.00	55.00
☐ Box, Grecian women in frosted beige, signed	200.00	245.00
☐ Box, powder, satin finish, 3 dancing nudes, 3½" dia., R. Lalique	225.00	250.00
☐ Box, swan design with lid	75.00	100.00
☐ Clock, wrens on black enameled clock face, Omega, 8"	925.00	1050.00
☐ Decanter, square with bubble design, R. Lalique signature	125.00	175.00
☐ Figurine, bear, signed, 4" H, standing.............	145.00	185.00
☐ Figurine, frosted nude man on a clear base, 8"	240.00	280.00
☐ Figurine, dove with turned head, 2½" H	40.00	60.00
☐ Glass, roosters on raised band, 3"	25.00	55.00
☐ Knife Rest, baby-head on each end, 4"	64.00	85.00
☐ Lamp, clear model of a fish on a wave, shaped bronze stand	1300.00	1800.00
☐ Plaque, flowers and lovebirds on green ground, 7" x 10"	500.00	575.00
☐ Plate, chrysanthemums engraved on clear glass, 15" H	210.00	280.00
☐ Plate, bordered with frosted pansies, 4"............	40.00	65.00
☐ Sugar Shaker, Egyptians on orange frosted ground, signed, 5¼" H......................	175.00	225.00
☐ Tumbler, fish in relief, footed	60.00	85.00

LALIQUE, RENE

	Price	Range
☐ Tray, nudes in relief, 4½" long	70.00	85.00
☐ Vase, Art Nouveau, two cranes on frosted blue ground, 7¼"	325.00	375.00
☐ Vase, "Coq et Plumes", 6", some crazing, R. Lalique .	600.00	950.00
☐ Vase fan design in frosted, signed	200.00	24500
☐ Vase, leaf design in grey, 6½"	525.00	560.00
☐ Vase, nudes on panels, 7½", R. Lalique	900.00	1300.00
☐ Vase, roosters on turquoise, Art Deco, 4½"	300.00	345.00
☐ Vase, rose handles with thorns, brown satin, 7½" ...	215.00	250.00
☐ Vase, seahorses on handles, fish and seaweed figures	145.00	170.00
☐ Vase, snails on frosted ground, 6½"	250.00	310.00

LEGRAS

Legras was a contemporary of Galle', Daum and the other great French masters in the art of Cameo glass. Although a lesser known artist among the collectors of Cameo glass, his work is starting to command prices as high as some of the more familiar designers.

☐ Bowl, acid etched bleeding hearts, 6½"	320.00	340.00
☐ Centerpiece, morning glories, signed, 14"	460.00	490.00
☐ Dish, carved harbor scene with boats, 5" x 5" H	300.00	350.00
☐ Rose Bowl, carved with enameled gold flowers, 4" D x 4½" H	375.00	400.00
☐ Tray, frosted, orange Cameo cuttings, 4¾" x 2¾" ...	180.00	200.00
☐ Vase, Cameo, carved scene of trees & water, signed, 5" H	275.00	300.00
☐ Vase, Cameo, carved & enameled landscape scene, signed 6¼" H	275.00	300.00
☐ Vase, Cameo, carved & enameled orange hounds & trees, signed, 9" H	390.00	420.00
☐ Vase, Cameo, bud, carved fuchsia blossoms & leaf age, signed, 11½" H	250.00	275.00

LIBBEY GLASS

Successor of the New England Glass Co., they produced not only fine cut and intaglio glass but fine art glass. Amberina and animal stemware designed by Nash are perhaps the best known.

☐ Basket, intaglio cut, signed	450.00	550.00
☐ Basket, 7", cut glass with florals and geometrics, signed............................	275.00	325.00
☐ Bowl, cut glass, signed	120.00	175.00
☐ Bowl, 2½" cream colored satin, decorated, signed ...	550.00	650.00
☐ Bowl, punch, etched	35.00	45.00
☐ Candlestick, 6", crystal stem, red feather top, signed, pair..................................	375.00	425.00
☐ Champagne, bear stem	95.00	125.00
☐ Champagne, squirrel stem.......................	85.00	115.00
☐ Cordial, "Vista" Nash series	15.00	20.00
☐ Cup, punch, World's Fair 1893	275.00	350.00

LIBBEY

	Price	Range
☐ Dish, pin, signed	25.00	45.00
☐ Goblet, kangaroo stem	120.00	160.00
☐ Goblet, squirrel	50.00	75.00
☐ Pitcher, 14 tumblers, signed	950.00	1150.00
☐ Plate, "Santa Maria", signed, 7¾" D	190.00	250.00
☐ Salt & Pepper Shakers, "Columbian Expo" 1893, pair	185.00	250.00
☐ Sugar Shaker, with pewter top, 5½" H	290.00	350.00
☐ Syrup Pitcher, with original top, 6" H	290.00	350.00
☐ Tazza, 6" crystal and shades of blue, signed	450.00	500.00
☐ Tumbler, opaque white with green & rust husks, 4"	45.00	65.00
☐ Vase, opaque white with green & rust husks, 4"	75.00	100.00
☐ Vase, 12" corset shaped, amethyst overlay cut to clear, signed	330.00	370.00
☐ Vase, 10" Amberina Jack-in-the-Pulpit, signed Libbey	330.00	370.00
☐ Vase, 16", loving cup with two handles, footed, signed	550.00	650.00
☐ Water Carafe, blue husks with gold	290.00	360.00
☐ Wine, bear stem	55.00	75.00
☐ Wine, "Diana" Nash series	15.00	25.00
☐ Wine, Monkey stem	75.00	100.00

LOETZ

An Austrian art glass made just before the turn of the century, and is similar in appearance to Tiffany glass. Loetz was a contemporary of Tiffany and worked his factory. The blue iridescent peacock feather design is highly prized. Most pieces are not signed, thus "signed Loetz" demands a higher price.

	Price	Range
☐ Atomizer, blue with green & brown design, signed	240.00	270.00
☐ Basket, blue, looped handle, 7"	180.00	220.00
☐ Basket, brides, red with enamel decoration, silver holder	300.00	350.00
☐ Bon Bon Dish, signed, 5½" high	300.00	350.00
☐ Bowl, iridescent green, 8"	75.00	100.00
☐ Bowl, lavender, aqua, signed, 3"	275.00	325.00
☐ Cameo Box, carved blue florals, covered	450.00	500.00
☐ Candlestick, 10", red and green fern decoration, pair	110.00	150.00
☐ Cruet, multi-colored	150.00	200.00
☐ Epergne, four green trumpet lilies and small baskets	250.00	300.00
☐ Inkwell, with brass lid	125.00	175.00
☐ Jar, biscuit, handled	45.00	75.00
☐ Rose Bowl, applied lily pads, 3¾"	275.00	325.00
☐ Syrup, blue & green	175.00	225.00
☐ Tumbler, ornate	50.00	75.00
☐ Vase, 3½" high, blue, Austria signed,	275.00	325.00
☐ Vase, 6" high, blue iridescent, pinched sides, signed	675.00	725.00
☐ Vase, 6½" high, iridescent green & blue, signed	340.00	370.00
☐ Vase, 7" high, feather design, signed	300.00	350.00
☐ Vase, 7" high, iridescent green & blue, signed	140.00	170.00
☐ Vase, 8" high, bronze iridescent, pedestal base	70.00	100.00

LOETZ

	Price Range	
☐ Vase, 8" high, green iridescent	110.00	150.00
☐ Vase, 8¾" high, multi-colored iridescent, signed	325.00	375.00
☐ Vase, 9½" high, silver over olive, signed	450.00	600.00
☐ Vase, 10" high, fine iridescence with heavy silver overlay, signed	850.00	950.00
☐ Vase, 12" high, dark and light blue iridescent	850.00	950.00

LUTZ

This term is usually applied to any piece of finely threaded or striped glass and named after its designer, Nicholas Lutz. Lutz was employed by the Boston and Sandwich Glass Co., where the glass was manufactured in the late 1870's.

☐ Basket, candy cane stripes, 6"	65.00	95.00
☐ Bottle, blue, green & red, 5"	40.00	60.00
☐ Bowls, clear with red, white and green threads, 6¼" .	150.00	175.00
☐ Bowls, finger and plate, red & white filigree striping ..	85.00	115.00
☐ Bowls, finger, rose colored threading, 5"	40.00	70.00
☐ Bowls, finger, & underplate, clear with ruffled edges, pink & white goldstone stripes	65.00	95.00
☐ Compote, sterling with ring handle, 14" high	450.00	500.00
☐ Cup & Saucer, 4" filigree white and light blue	175.00	225.00
☐ Creamer, Lattichinio with blue threads, miniature....	125.00	175.00
☐ Cup & Saucer, Latticinio	50.00	80.00
☐ Ewer, pink ribbons with goldstone, applied handle, miniature..................................	60.00	100.00
☐ Jar, 14" covered, applied decoration, footed, attributed to Lutz	10.00	15.00
☐ Liquer, stripes on clear crystal	80.00	120.00
☐ Pitcher, water, gold threading	300.00	350.00
☐ Plate, spiral green design, 7".....................	100.00	150.00
☐ Sugar & Creamer, blue	225.00	275.00
☐ Tumbler, blue threading........................	75.00	100.00
☐ Tumbler, water, 4", twisted blue and white threading .	150.00	200.00
☐ Tumbler, lavender stripes	250.00	300.00
☐ Vase, 3½", clear with white threads	75.00	100.00
☐ Vase, 8½", pink threads	120.00	160.00
☐ Vase, 12", white and applied bosses, filigree handles .	300.00	350.00
☐ Washbowl and Pitcher Set, wheeling type, some documentation................................	7.00	10.00
☐ Whiskey, Latticinio, pink, gold & white, 2½" high	70.00	100.00

MARY GREGORY

Mary Gregory was an artist hired by the Boston and Sandwich Glass Co. and was responsible for her delightful "children playing" motifs. This glass enameled in white with silhouette type figures is now termed Mary Gregory Glass and is being widely reproduced.

☐ Ale Glass, white enameled girl	38.00	48.00
☐ Ale Mug, figure of girl, hand-painted	25.00	40.00
☐ Atomizer, barefoot boy in knee pants	110.00	140.00

MARY GREGORY

Price Range

- [ ] Barber Bottle, pale green with white enamel decorations and hand-painted figure of young boy on side .. 38.00 60.00
- [ ] Box, with hinged lid, cranberry 115.00 145.00
- [ ] Box, powder, 4" hinged, with cream & red decorations 35.00 50.00
- [ ] Butter Dish, white, enameled decor 120.00 140.00
- [ ] Creamer, white enameled boy 120.00 140.00
- [ ] Decanter, with crystal stopper, 10" high............ 120.00 260.00
- [ ] Jewel Box, white enameled boy holding flowers 220.00 260.00
- [ ] Inkwell, 1¼" square, swirl pattern 10.00 18.00
- [ ] Kerosene Lamps, Ca. 1880, covered squat bowls, pair 115.00 165.00
- [ ] Mug, white enameled boy holding flowers 220.00 260.00
- [ ] Pitcher, water, 8" high, clear with enamel girl 42.00 70.00
- [ ] Pitcher, white enameled boy holding flowers, 8¼" H . 120.00 140.00
- [ ] Pitcher, water, cranberry 170.00 190.00
- [ ] Pitcher, cream, 6½" high, light green, curved handle . 30.00 55.00
- [ ] Plaque, 10" high, young girl in woodland scene 80.00 130.00
- [ ] Stein, 15" high, pale amber glass with tall lid of burnished pewter, hand-painted figure of girl........ 85.00 135.00
- [ ] Sugar Bowl, cream colored with figure of girl........ 16.00 32.00
- [ ] Tumbler, water, 4" high, cream and amber enameling 16.00 32.00
- [ ] Tumbler, amber, white enameled girl, 5" high 80.00 100.00
- [ ] Tumbler, green, white enameled boy, 5" high........ 26.00 36.00
- [ ] Vase, bud, 4¾" high, cranberry.................. 155.00 185.00
- [ ] Vase, 5¼" high, cobalt blue, hand-painted white figure 26.00 42.00
- [ ] Vase, 5½" deep, rich green, with figures of small boy and girl hand-painted on enameled sides, pair....... 70.00 135.00
- [ ] Vase, 7½" high, cranberry...................... 70.00 90.00
- [ ] Vase, 8" high, green with filigree and enameled decorations................................ 68.00 110.00
- [ ] Wine Container, sculptured, rounded bowl with narrow neck and cut stopper, thumbprint pattern 64.00 110.00
- [ ] Wine Decanter, 5" deep, 10½" high, with clear bubble stopper 95.00 115.00

MILLEFIORE

Meaning literally "thousand flowers", Millefiore glass was made by joining colored glass rods into flower formations and fusing into canes before the glass was blown. This technique was developed by the Egyptians in the first century B.C.

- [ ] Bowl, two handles, 3½" high, 2" deep 150.00 200.00
- [ ] Box, covered, 3" high 150.00 200.00
- [ ] Box, covered, 4" high 160.00 210.00
- [ ] Creamer 275.00 350.00
- [ ] Cruet, applied clear handle, 6" high 90.00 140.00
- [ ] Cruet, with cut stopper........................ 285.00 350.00
- [ ] Cruet, with complete millefiore, handle & stopper, 5" high.................................... 170.00 210.00
- [ ] Goblet, colored canes in base, stem & base clear, 7½" high................................... 170.00 220.00
- [ ] Jug, 2½" high................................. 95.00 125.00

MILLEFIORE

	Price	Range
☐ Lamp, 7" miniature with dome shade and base in millefiore	155.00	205.00
☐ Lamp, with matching shade, 15" high	475.00	575.00
☐ Paperweight, 3", crowned all over design, modern	30.00	50.00
☐ Pitcher, applied handle, 2¾" high	90.00	140.00
☐ Pitcher, cream, 4", scattered millefiore on white ground	210.00	260.00
☐ Punch Set, 7 pieces	125.00	175.00
☐ Rose Bowl, ruffled, 6"	115.00	175.00
☐ Salt	75.00	125.00
☐ Toothpick Holder, 4 pinched sider	95.00	145.00
☐ Toothpick Holder, flared rim with flowers	75.00	135.00
☐ Tumbler, 4" high	140.00	180.00
☐ Tumbler, 4", overall millefiore in blues and greens	95.00	145.00
☐ Tumbler, clear, 3½" high	75.00	125.00
☐ Vase, 2¾" high, fluted rim	30.00	60.00
☐ Vase, 3½" high, multi-colored canes in red	90.00	130.00
☐ Vase, 5½" high, blue & green paperweight canes	70.00	110.00
☐ Vase, 7¼" high, two handles	65.00	105.00
☐ Vase, 8", double handled on lavender background (Venetian)	45.00	65.00
☐ Vase, 10", urn shaped, excellent regular pattern	155.00	200.00
☐ Vase, unusual dragonfly design with netting, signed	425.00	475.00
☐ Vase, 8", double handled, millefiore laid in rows	190.00	240.00
☐ Vase, 8", random millefiore on blue background	320.00	380.00

PEACH BLOW

Somewhat of a universal term, "Peach Blow" is used by collectors to describe several varieties produced by more than a half dozen glass companies. Shadings will vary from rose to yellow, blue or white depending on its maker and will vary in layers. Sandwich Peach Blow is one-layered and the English is two-layered. A relative newcomer is a single-layered new Martinsville "Peach Blow".

	Price	Range
☐ Bisquit Jar, enameled & jeweled decor, Mt. Washington, signed	600.00	650.00
☐ Bowl, black-eyed Susans & stems, Mt. Washington	3100.00	3400.00
☐ Bowl, bride's, New Martinsville, 3 3/8" deep	110.00	160.00
☐ Bowl, ruffled edge, Sandwich, 7" deep, 3½" high	190.00	240.00
☐ Bowl, sunburst, ruffled edge, New Martinsville, 4 7/8" deep	110.00	160.00
☐ Carafe, glossy finish, Wheeling	675.00	775.00
☐ Compote, Gunderson, 6" deep	215.00	260.00
☐ Cup & Saucer, raspberry color with white handle, Gunderson	350.00	425.00
☐ Darner, end open, New England	120.00	160.00
☐ Darner, glossy, New England	200.00	275.00
☐ Decanter, amber, Wheeling, 9½"	2500.00	3000.00
☐ Finger Bowl, New England, 5 x 2½"	350.00	400.00
☐ Hat, diamond-quilted pattern, 3" high	120.00	160.00

PEACH BLOW   Price Range

- ☐ Lamp Base, ornate, yellow to cranberry, Wheeling, 9" high 675.00 750.00
- ☐ Muffinier, original metal top, Wheeling, 5½" high 725.00 800.00
- ☐ Pear glossy, New England 275.00 350.00
- ☐ Pitcher, gold enameling of branches & butterfly, Webb, 9½" high 425.00 525.00
- ☐ Pitcher, water, Wheeling 1400.00 1600.00
- ☐ Rose Bowl, New England 550.00 625.00
- ☐ Salt, dip, New Martinsville 50.00 75.00
- ☐ Salt, glossy, Wheeling 225.00 275.00
- ☐ Toothpick Holder, square, New England 450.00 500.00
- ☐ Tumbler, acid, Wheeling 450.00 500.00
- ☐ Tumbler, glossy finish, New England 350.00 400.00
- ☐ Tumbler, wild rose, New England 275.00 325.00
- ☐ Vase, butterfly & blossoms, Webb, 5½" high 320.00 370.00
- ☐ Vase, enameled dragonfly, branches & blossoms, Webb, 5" high 325.00 375.00
- ☐ Vase, glossy, Wheeling, 6" high 790.00 860.00
- ☐ Vase, lily with 3 petals, New England, 7¾" high 685.00 750.00
- ☐ Vase, Mt. Washington, 12" high .... — —
- ☐ Vase, replica of Morgan Vase, glossy, Wheeling, 10" high 1000.00 1500.00
- ☐ Vase, ruffled, Sandwich, 5½" high 120.00 160.00
- ☐ Vase, scalloped rim, Gunderson, 8½" high 245.00 295.00
- ☐ Vase, trumpet-shaped, glossy, New England, 15" high 1100.00 1250.00

RUBENA VERDE

Rubena Verde, a Victorian glass, made by Hobbs, Brockuneir and Company of Wheeling, West Virginia around 1890 is now considered an art glass. It varies in colors from yellow-green to red.

- ☐ Basket, pointed handle & applied cranberry petals, 6" wide, 6¼" high 70.00 100.00
- ☐ Bowl, finger, ruffled rim, 4" 70.00 90.00
- ☐ Bowl, rose, ribbed, 4" x 5" 90.00 110.00
- ☐ Butter Dish, daisy & button, clear base 275.00 300.00
- ☐ Cologne Bottle, applied decorations around base 75.00 100.00
- ☐ Cologne Bottle, blue & white enameled flowers, 3" deep, 7¾" high 110.00 140.00
- ☐ Creamer, applied handle, cranberry to green 120.00 150.00
- ☐ Cruet, shades of red to green 160.00 180.00
- ☐ Epergnes, ruffled with clear glass edge, 3 horns and handing basket, 13" high, 8½" deep 350.00 375.00
- ☐ Mustard Pot, 3" with spoon 110.00 140.00
- ☐ Pitchers, inverted thumbprint, 5½" high 175.00 200.00
- ☐ Pitchers, canary handle, 7" high 250.00 300.00
- ☐ Punch Cup, enamel decor 75.00 100.00
- ☐ Rose Bowl, "Crackle", 5 1/8" deep, 4 3/4" high 100.00 125.00
- ☐ Shot Glass, palm tree, cranberry tree, cranberry to vaseline 25.00 30.00

RUBENA VERDE
Price Range

☐ Sweet Meat Dish, cranberry to vaseline with silver-plate basket holder, 5½" deep, 6" high	85.00	95.00
☐ Toothpick Holder, pinched sides	140.00	180.00
☐ Tumbler, inverted thumbprint, enameled flower	80.00	100.00
☐ Vase, green to cranberry, 4½"	75.00	100.00
☐ Vase, notched & paneled, 7"	75.00	100.00
☐ Vase, trumpet-shaped with 8 scallops, 8¾"	175.00	200.00
☐ Vase, 6-pointed petals, gold scrolls & flowers, 9½" . .	200.00	240.00
☐ Vase, hobnail pattern, 10"	275.00	300.00
☐ Vase, drapery pattern, 11", pair	350.00	400.00
☐ Vase, trumpet-shaped	290.00	340.00

SANDWICH

Many varieties and types of Sandwich glass were produced by the Boston and Sandwich Glass Company and covered a span of over 60 years from about 1824. Today many lacy glass, pattern glass and other types made at any number of glass shops are loosely called "sandwich".

☐ Basket, cranberry, white	175.00	195.00
☐ Basket, sapphire	65.00	75.00
☐ Bottles, cologne, blue	80.00	90.00
☐ Bottles, cologne, yellow	200.00	215.00
☐ Bottles, cologne, purple	100.00	120.00
☐ Bottles, scent, opalescent	100.00	125.00
☐ Bowl, floral design, 8"	40.00	50.00
☐ Bowl, geometric flint, 7"	20.00	25.00
☐ Bowl, lyre & heart, shallow, 9¼"	175.00	195.00
☐ Bowl, oak leaf, 8"	35.00	45.00
☐ Candlesticks, hexagon, flint, amber	160.00	175.00
☐ Candlesticks, hexagon, blue & white, 7¾", pair	500.00	525.00
☐ Compote, deep blue, blown	375.00	400.00
☐ Compote, diamond pattern, flint	160.00	180.00
☐ Compote, flower & loop, flint	160.00	180.00
☐ Dish, colored feathers	130.00	145.00
☐ Dish, amber, floral design	30.00	45.00
☐ Lamps, flint, heart & thumbprint design, 9"	125.00	135.00
☐ Lamps, flint, heart & thumbprint design, whale oil . . .	125.00	135.00
☐ Lamps, amethyst, transparent, 11"	475.00	500.00
☐ Pitcher, syrup, star design	140.00	150.00
☐ Pitcher, tankard type, milk, 6"	80.00	95.00
☐ Pitcher, tankard type, water, overshot ice holder, circa 1865	200.00	250.00
☐ Plates, cornucopia, 8"	90.00	100.00
☐ Plate, peacock eye, 5¼"	35.00	55.00
☐ Plate, Roman Rosette, 7"	44.00	75.00
☐ Plate, vine & harp design, 4"	20.00	35.00
☐ Salt Container, bird, iridescent	150.00	165.00
☐ Salt Container, deep blue, patterned	100.00	120.00
☐ Salt Container, lavender, Royal design	175.00	195.00
☐ Tray, Gothic pattern, 5" x 7"	50.00	65.00

SANDWICH

	Price	Range
☐ Tray, butterfly, 8"	185.00	200.00
☐ Tieback, opalescent, pewter mounts, 4¼", pair	60.00	70.00
☐ Tieback, Rosette, pewter mounts, 4", pair	40.00	50.00
☐ Vases, bird, enameled design, 8½", pair	80.00	90.00
☐ Vases, yellow, 11", pair	300.00	350.00
☐ Vases, lavender, loop, 9", pair	1300.00	1400.00

SATIN (SATIN MOTHER OF PEARL)

Articles made of opaque glass in white or colors that have been treated with acid to form a smooth, dull surface are referred to as "Satin Glass". Many of these pieces are shaded from a darker tone at the top to a lighter shade at the bottom. Blue, orange, and red are some of the colors. Mother of Pearl (M.O.P.) is a special two-layer satin glass. A pattern (diamond-quilting, thumbprint, rain-drop and others) are impressed in the first layer. The second layer traps air in the low places which shows through the finished piece   a pearly iridescence. Usually called M.O.P. Satin Glass, perfected in 1886 by Joseph Webb, an Englishman.

	Price	Range
☐ Basket, M.O.P. looped handle, 6½" high	125.00	175.00
☐ Basket, white & purple, 8"	175.00	225.00
☐ Bobeche, ruffled rim, yellow	18.00	26.00
☐ Bottle, perfume, ruffled edge with stopper	135.00	195.00
☐ Bowl, black with gold trim	225.00	245.00
☐ Bowl, cloverleaf M.O.P. swirl, cased in blue, ribbon crimped edge, 5"	450.00	500.00
☐ Bowl, M.O.P. blue with feet in crystal, 6"	500.00	550.00
☐ Bowl, 3-flower, ribbed, baby blue, 3"	75.00	125.00
☐ Box, covered, diamond-quilted pattern, 5"	145.00	195.00
☐ Butter Dish, diamond-quilted pattern, pink, frosted underplate	245.00	295.00
☐ Collar & Cuff Box, diamond-quilted pattern, pink, signed, 6" x 6".................................	495.00	545.00
☐ Cracker Jar, green with pink floral decor	140.00	190.00
☐ Ewer, blue, overlay, with frosted handle, 10"	270.00	300.00
☐ Ewer, applied handle, blue M.O.P. Herringbone pattern......................................	500.00	550.00
☐ Finger Bowl, pink & blue	145.00	195.00
☐ Jar, powder, covered, green	120.00	140.00
☐ Lamp, peacocks, amber, 13¼"	440.00	480.00
☐ Lamp, "Gone with the Wind", M.O.P. with brass frame	495.00	545.00
☐ Lamp, hanging, red, Regal iris	245.00	295.00
☐ Lamp, peg, pink quilted tank	500.00	575.00
☐ Mustard Pot, white ribbed satin with blue enamel flowers, 3".....................................	120.00	170.00
☐ Pitcher, rose to pink, applied camphor handle, 5"	225.00	235.00
☐ Pitcher, rainbow, soft pink & blues, frosted handle, M.O.P., 10½" high	725.00	825.00
☐ Plate, with painted strawberries, 12"	125.00	135.00
☐ Rose Bowl, blue overlay, flowers, 4"	90.00	140.00
☐ Rose Bowl, pink to white, rough pontil, 6"	140.00	190.00

SATIN

	Price Range	
☐ Rose Bowl, white M.O.P. Venetian Diamond, applied camphor thorn feet, 5½" high	275.00	350.00
☐ Rose Bowl, wine to white, ruffled top, 4"	55.00	75.00
☐ Salt & Pepper, apples	120.00	130.00
☐ Salt & Pepper, enameled floral decor	120.00	160.00
☐ Sugar & Creamer, red with silver trim	390.00	440.00
☐ Sugar Shakers, blue	120.00	160.00
☐ Sugar Shakers, cream shading to blue, silver top	140.00	190.00
☐ Tumblers, apricot, diamond-quilted	140.00	190.00
☐ Tumblers, raspberry, diamond-quilted	100.00	140.00
☐ Tumblers, blue, Herringbone	100.00	130.00
☐ Tumblers, yellow, swirl	120.00	160.00
☐ Vase, pink to deep rose M.O.P., signed Webb, 4½" high, 3¾" wide	170.00	220.00
☐ Vase, diamond-quilted, rainbow, 5 1/8"	725.00	800.00
☐ Vase, diamond-quilted, blue, ruffled top	240.00	280.00
☐ Vase, bud, blue, clear overlay, violets, 3¾"	175.00	225.00
☐ Vase, diamond-quilted, pink, signed Webb	425.00	500.00
☐ Vase, raindrop, rainbow	825.00	900.00

TIFFANY

Louis Comfort Tiffany (1848-1933) scion of the most important family of jewelers in America during the 19th century began his carreer as a painter under the noted American landscape master George Innes (1825-1894) in New York and later with the French orientalist Lem Belly in Paris.

After many visits to North Africa, Tiffany's imagination was fired by the exotic colors, the fascinating forms and textures which combined Roman, Etruscan, Byzantine and medieval works of art, turning his interests toward the decorative in 1879.

Tiffany's Favrille (derived from Old English "fabile"meaning a craft or craftsman) resulted from his fascination with the iridescence that ancient glass developed after being buried for centuries in damp soil. The Tiffany furnaces opened in Corona, Long Island in 1893. There, Favrille pieces were produced both in the classical and in the art nouveau style of plant-like shapes with their affinity for natural forms.

After 1895, Tiffany and his associates began experimenting with enamel and reposse copper. Apples and leaves, dragonflies, flowers and lily pads were the motifs combining iridescent glass and copper boxes. These smaller items are signed "L.C.T." usually accompanied by an identifying number.

☐ Bottle, 18K gold stopper, Rock Crystal	375.00	450.00
☐ Bowl, blue, scalloped, 5" x 2½"	430.00	500.00
☐ Bowl, gold iridescent with flower center, 1½"	325.00	400.00
☐ Bowl, etched leaves on bronze base, 5" high	1945.00	2145.00
☐ Box, cigar, lined with cedar, copper with green glass .	280.00	350.00
☐ Candlesticks, iridescent gold, twisted stems, 7" high, pair	780.00	850.00
☐ Candy Dish, peacock blue, flower form	650.00	725.00
☐ Champagne, hollow stem, 7"	425.00	475.00

TIFFANY

	Price	Range
☐ Compote, iridescent gold, 6½" x 9½" high	750.00	825.00
☐ Finger Bowl & Underplate, gold iridescent, paneled . . .	310.00	370.00
☐ Goblet, pink & green, 9"	450.00	525.00
☐ Lamp, acorn, base & shade, 10" x 19" high	3100.00	3300.00
☐ Nut Dish, iridescent gold with blue highlights, ruffled rim	340.00	380.00
☐ Paperweights, owl	1600.00	2100.00
☐ Pitcher, deep blue, 4¼"	560.00	620.00
☐ Plate, gold iridescent, 6"	560.00	640.00
☐ Plate, pastel lavender, 9" deep	290.00	330.00
☐ Plate, pink with white feather ribbing, 10¼"	375.00	450.00
☐ Salt, ruffled edge	250.00	275.00
☐ Salt, master, gold iridescent	325.00	400.00
☐ Shade, green feather on opalescent, 6"	310.00	370.00
☐ Toothpick Holder, iridescent gold, pinched sides, 1½" high	275.00	325.00
☐ Tumbler, green feathering on clear, numbered, 5"	250.00	300.00
☐ Tumbler, vintage	480.00	540.00
☐ Urn, iridescent gold, numbered, 3¼" high	325.00	400.00
☐ Vase, flower form, gold, green, L.C. Tiffany, Faville, 6"	775.00	875.00
☐ Vase, gold iridescent, green leaf & vine, trumpet, 12" .	1275.00	1375.00
☐ Vase, gold iridescent, bronze base, 13" pair	870.00	970.00
☐ Vase, lotus leaf decor, metal base, 12"	2600.00	2800.00
☐ Vase, molded flowers, 10"	1600.00	1900.00
☐ Wine, engraved vintage, 6"	275.00	325.00
☐ Wine, gold iridescent, L.C.T., 4"	220.00	260.00
☐ Wine, Royal design, gold numbered, 7"	325.00	400.00

VENETIAN

Venetian Glass has been made on the island of Murano in Italy since about 1350. Typical of the work of the 19th and 20th centuries is the fine filigree white and colored twisted spirals. The use of gold and bronze powder in the glass is also typical. It is still being made in a wide range of qualities afford-able to most.

☐ Basket, clear glass, green leaves & flowers	185.00	215.00
☐ Bottle, lavender, flowers with gold stone	80.00	100.00
☐ Bottle, ribbons of white and gold stone, 4" high	70.00	90.00
☐ Bowl, clear with gold foot & edge	70.00	90.00
☐ Bowl, amber to cranberry, applied flowers, crystal base	130.00	160.00
☐ Candlesticks, Dolphin, clear glass with gold, 5"	55.00	75.00
☐ Candlesticks, fruits, applied, 10"	28.00	38.00
☐ Candlesticks, Dolphin, blue fluted top, 6¼", pair	145.00	175.00
☐ Candy Dish, enameled pink roses & green leaves, 6" deep	55.00	75.00
☐ Candy Jar, orchid & blue with enameled pink flowers, 10½" high	75.00	95.00
☐ Card Holder, swans on both sides	40.00	50.00
☐ Champagne, fruit & cherubs	80.00	100.00

VENETIAN

	Price	Range
☐ Champagne, Dolphin stem	80.00	100.00
☐ Compote, two dolphins, gold, ruby with gold flecks ..	80.00	100.00
☐ Compote, red with twisted stem	50.00	70.00
☐ Compote, blue with gold overlay, 10" deep..........	175.00	200.00
☐ Cordial Set, gold & enamel on clear, decanter, tray and eight glasses	190.00	210.00
☐ Cup & Saucer, pink demitasse....................	50.00	70.00
☐ Fingerbowl & Underplate, pink, red, white floral	40.00	50.00
☐ Goblet, Dolphin stem, yellow eyes, 8" high	60.00	75.00
☐ Pitcher, water, enameled blues, bulbous shape	80.00	100.00
☐ Plates, pink, gold sprayed, 7½"	25.00	35.00
☐ Plates, pink, diamond optic	18.00	25.00
☐ Salt, swan, pink body with gold decor	28.00	38.00
☐ Sherbet, green with gold trim....................	75.00	100.00
☐ Vase, gold, green & white, 6" high	60.00	80.00
☐ Vase, pale rose bottom, applied green leaves, 9½" high	135.00	165.00
☐ Vase, ruby with applied clear ring, 10½" high	90.00	110.00
☐ Vase, Dolphin stem, pale rose, 12" high	50.00	70.00
☐ Vase, pink & gold flowers with green vines, inlaid amethyst	145.00	165.00
☐ Wine, cherubs & grapevine, cranberry	55.00	75.00
☐ Wine Set, amber decanter, 11" high, six wines, 5½" ..	265.00	295.00

VERRE DE SOIE

Verre De Soie was made by the Steuben Glass Company under the direction of Frederic Carder around 1905-10. This iridescent type glass was among the finest glassware produced in America. It was discontinued in the 1930's.

☐ Basket, blue handle	140.00	180.00
☐ Bottle, cologne, 7" high	250.00	300.00
☐ Box, powder, sterling lid, engraved flowers	100.00	140.00
☐ Candlestick, stem twisted, 10" high, pair	300.00	350.00
☐ Compote, engraved, signed Hawkes, 5" x 8"	240.00	300.00
☐ Cream & Sugar, engraved, signed Hawkes, set	350.00	400.00
☐ Glass, portrait, etched, signed Hawkes, 6"	70.00	90.00
☐ Goblet	150.00	200.00
☐ Pitcher, 9¾" high	200.00	240.00
☐ Salt, pedestaled, Steuben	80.00	100.00
☐ Sherbets, with underplates, set of 8	450.00	500.00
☐ Vase, Fleur de Lis, Steuben, 3½" x 6"	450.00	500.00
☐ Vase, bulbous base, short neck with 3¼" deep, 7" ...	250.00	300.00
☐ Vase, floral decor with crimped top, 7½"	170.00	210.00
☐ Water Set, decanter, 12½" high, orchids in lavender, set of six matching tumblers	550.00	650.00
☐ Wine, etched flowers and leaves	100.00	150.00

CUT GLASS SWEATMEAT URNS . . . .   125.00 - 200.00

SANDWICH STYLE TOILET BOTTLES . . . .   250.00 - 350.00

CARNIVAL GLASS

The term "Taffeta Glass" was used before what is now known as Carnival Glass. The iridescent color was given in an attempt to imitate Tiffany Glass.

ACORN BURRS — NORTHWOOD

	Price Range	
☐ Berry Set. Master bowl & 4 sauce dishes, purple	250.00	275.00
☐ Berry Set. Master bowl & 6 sauce dishes, marigold . . .	150.00	175.00
☐ Bowl. Berry, purple, 9½" deep	80.00	110.00
☐ Bowl. Red	125.00	150.00
☐ Butterdish. Covered, purple	175.00	200.00
☐ Creamer & Sugar Bowl. Marigold	200.00	240.00
☐ Pitcher (water). Purple	375.00	425.00
☐ Punch Bowl & Base. Ice green	925.00	1000.00
☐ Punch Cup. Marigold	18.00	24.00
☐ Sauce Dish. Purple	15.00	20.00
☐ Spooner. Purple	100.00	125.00
☐ Tumbler. Green	50.00	75.00
☐ Water Set. 6 pieces, green	525.00	575.00

APPLE BLOSSOM TWIGS

☐ Bowl. 6" deep, marigold	12.00	14.00
☐ Bowl. 6¾" deep, frosty white	25.00	30.00
☐ Bowl. 8" deep, white	45.00	50.00
☐ Bowl. 9" deep, peach opalescent	50.00	60.00
☐ Bowl. 9" deep, purple	60.00	70.00
☐ Creamer & Sugar Bowl. Marigold, pair	32.00	38.00
☐ Plate. 9" deep, cobalt blue	130.00	140.00
☐ Plate. 9" deep, purple	175.00	200.00

BASKET — NORTHWOOD

☐ Aqua	145.00	175.00
☐ Green	75.00	100.00
☐ Ice Blue	110.00	150.00
☐ Ice Green	100.00	150.00
☐ Marigold	40.00	70.00
☐ Purple	65.00	95.00
☐ Teal Blue	130.00	160.00
☐ White	85.00	115.00

BIRDS & CHERRIES

☐ Bon Bon Dish. Marigold	40.00	50.00
☐ Bon Bon Dish. Purple	40.00	50.00
☐ Bowl. 8" deep, purple	50.00	60.00
☐ Bowl. 9" deep, green	180.00	220.00
☐ Compotes. Marigold	35.00	40.00
☐ Compotes. Purple	45.00	55.00

BUTTERFLY & BERRY

☐ Bowl. 8" deep, marigold	40.00	60.00
☐ Bowl. 9¾" deep, green, 3-footed	90.00	120.00
☐ Butterdish. Blue, covered	150.00	175.00
☐ Creamer. Purple	60.00	90.00

BUTTERFLY & BERRY

Price Range

	Price	Range
☐ Hatpin Holder. Marigold	675.00	725.00
☐ Sauce Dish. Blue	20.00	25.00
☐ Sugar Bowl. Green, covered	80.00	110.00
☐ Tumbler. Green	60.00	90.00
☐ Vase. 9" high, marigold	20.00	25.00
☐ Vase. Red	225.00	275.00
☐ Water Set. 7 pieces, blue	400.00	450.00

COIN DOT

	Price	Range
☐ Bowl. 7" deep, blue	30.00	35.00
☐ Bowl. 8½" deep, aqua opalescent	70.00	100.00
☐ Bowl. 8½" deep, purple	25.00	35.00
☐ Bowl. 9" deep, marigold	22.00	28.00
☐ Bowl. Red	300.00	350.00
☐ Compote. 6¾" x 4½", peach opalescent	25.00	35.00
☐ Pitcher (water). Marigold	90.00	110.00
☐ Rose Bowl. Green	40.00	50.00
☐ Rose Bowl. Purple	40.00	50.00
☐ Water Set. 7 pieces, marigold	225.00	275.00

GRAPE & CABLE

	Price	Range
☐ Banana Boat. Blue	200.00	225.00
☐ Banana Boat. Ice blue	300.00	315.00
☐ Banana Boat. Marigold	100.00	125.00
☐ Banana Boat. White	250.00	300.00
☐ Berry Set. 7 pieces, purple	225.00	275.00
☐ Bon Bon. 2 handles, blue	40.00	50.00
☐ Bowl. 5" deep, marigold	12.00	16.00
☐ Bowl. 5" deep, red	200.00	250.00
☐ Bowl. 6½" deep, ice blue	60.00	75.00
☐ Bowl. 7" deep, purple	30.00	40.00
☐ Bowl. 7½" deep, marigold	25.00	30.00
☐ Bowl. 8½" deep, footed, green	35.00	45.00
☐ Bowl (ice cream). 11" deep, white	200.00	225.00
☐ Butterdish. Covered, green	175.00	200.00
☐ Candle Lamp. Marigold	525.00	575.00
☐ Candlestick. Blue, one	90.00	110.00
☐ Candlestick. Marigold, pair	100.00	125.00
☐ Card Tray. Green	50.00	76.00
☐ Centerpiece Bowl. Cobalt blue	300.00	350.00
☐ Centerpiece Bowl. Ice green	550.00	600.00
☐ Cologne Bottle. With stopper, green	125.00	150.00
☐ Cologne Bottle. With stopper, purple	200.00	225.00
☐ Compote. Covered, purple	225.00	250.00
☐ Compote. Open, marigold	325.00	350.00
☐ Cookie Jar. Marigold	175.00	200.00
☐ Cookie Jar. White	400.00	450.00
☐ Creamer. Marigold	60.00	70.00
☐ Creamer. Individual size, purple	75.00	100.00
☐ Creamer & Sugar Bowl. Individual size, green, pair	150.00	175.00

GRAPE & CABLE

	Price	Range
☐ Cup & Saucer. Ice blue	325.00	375.00
☐ Decanter. With stopper, marigold	375.00	425.00
☐ Decanter. With stopper, purple	675.00	725.00
☐ Dresser Set. 6 pieces, purple	1000.00	1100.00
☐ Dresser Set. Ice blue	300.00	350.00
☐ Dresser Set. Marigold	125.00	150.00
☐ Fernery. Purple	975.00	1025.00
☐ Hatpin Holder. Amethyst	125.00	150.00
☐ Hatpin Holder. Ice blue	300.00	325.00
☐ Hatpin Holder. Ice green	775.00	800.00
☐ Hatpin Holder. Marigold	125.00	150.00
☐ Nappy. Wit handle, purple	65.00	85.00
☐ Pin Tray. Marigold	150.00	175.00
☐ Pitcher (water). 8¼" high, purple	175.00	200.00
☐ Pitcher (tankard). 9¾" high, marigold	425.00	475.00
☐ Plate. 7½" deep, hand grip turned up, green	50.00	70.00
☐ Plate. 9" deep, marigold	60.00	70.00
☐ Powder Jar. Covered, green	80.00	100.00
☐ Powder Jar. Covered, purple	70.00	80.00
☐ Punch Bowl & Base. 11" deep, green	400.00	450.00
☐ Punch Bowl & Base. 11" deep, white	825.00	875.00
☐ Punch Bowl & Base. 14" deep, marigold	525.00	575.00
☐ Punch Bowl & Base. 17" deep, purple	1600.00	1700.00
☐ Punch Cup. Green	25.00	35.00
☐ Punch Cup. Ice green	55.00	75.00
☐ Punch Set. 14" bowl, base & 6 cups, green	650.00	700.00
☐ Punch Set. 14" bowl, base & 8 cups, marigold	625.00	675.00
☐ Sauce Dish. Ice blue	55.00	75.00
☐ Sauce Dish. White	45.00	60.00
☐ Spooner. Marigold	45.00	60.00
☐ Sugar Bowl. Covered, purple	160.00	180.00
☐ Sugar Bowl. Individual size, marigold	50.00	75.00
☐ Sweetmeat Jar. Purple	175.00	225.00
☐ Tobacco Humidor. Marigold	250.00	275.00
☐ Tumbler. 6 pieces, marigold	125.00	175.00
☐ Water Set. Pitcher & 6 tumblers, green	—	—

GRAPE & GOTHIC ARCHES

	Price	Range
☐ Berry Set. 7 pieces, blue	140.00	170.00
☐ Bowl. Green, large	30.00	40.00
☐ Butterdish. Covered, marigold	80.00	100.00
☐ Creamer. Blue	50.00	60.00
☐ Creamer & Sugar Bowl. Marigold	50.00	70.00
☐ Pitcher. Water, blue	200.00	225.00
☐ Spooner. Marigold	30.00	40.00
☐ Sugar Bowl. Covered, blue	70.00	80.00
☐ Table Set. 4 pieces, blue	350.00	375.00
☐ Tumbler. Blue	30.00	35.00
☐ Tumbler. Green	25.00	30.00
☐ Water Set. 7 pieces, blue	350.00	375.00

	Price	Range
☐ Water Set. 7 pieces, green	475.00	500.00
☐ Water Set. 7 pieces, marigold	200.00	240.00

MAPLE LEAF

☐ Berry Set. 7 pieces, marigold	75.00	100.00
☐ Bowl. Berry, footed, marigold	50.00	75.00
☐ Bowl. Berry, purple	75.00	100.00
☐ Bowl. Ice cream, footed, purple, small	25.00	35.00
☐ Butterdish. Covered, blue	120.00	150.00
☐ Butterdish. Covered, marigold	70.00	90.00
☐ Creamer. Marigold	35.00	45.00
☐ Creamer. Purple	45.00	55.00
☐ Dish (ice cream). 4" deep, marigold	10.00	14.00
☐ Pitcher (water). Marigold	100.00	125.00
☐ Pitcher (water). Purple	225.00	250.00
☐ Sauce Dish. Blue	20.00	25.00
☐ Spooner. Blue	50.00	75.00
☐ Spooner. Marigold	30.00	40.00
☐ Sugar Dish. Covered, green	60.00	70.00
☐ Table Set. 4 pieces, purple	240.00	270.00
☐ Tumbler. Blue	75.00	100.00
☐ Tumbler. Purple	5.0	45.00
☐ Water Set. 7 pieces, purple	375.00	425.00

ORIENTAL POPPY

☐ Pitcher (water). Green	425.00	475.00
☐ Pitcher (water). Purple	650.00	700.00
☐ Tumbler. Green	50.00	60.00
☐ Tumbler. Ice green	180.00	200.00
☐ Tumbler. Marigold	30.00	40.00
☐ Tumbler. White	85.00	95.00
☐ Water Set. 5 pieces, white	850.00	900.00
☐ Water Set. 7 pieces, blue	1350.00	1450.00
☐ Water Set. 7 pieces, purple	775.00	825.00

RASPBERRY

☐ Bowl. 9" diameter, marigold	35.00	45.00
☐ Pitcher (milk). Ice blue	875.00	925.00
☐ Pitcher (milk). Marigold	75.00	85.00
☐ Pitcher (water). Green	175.00	225.00
☐ Pitcher (water). Purple	275.00	325.00
☐ Sauceboat. Green	75.00	100.00
☐ Tumbler. Ice green	475.00	525.00
☐ Tumbler. Marigold	20.00	30.00
☐ Water Set. 7 pieces, green	350.00	400.00
☐ Water Set. 7 pieces, purple	375.00	425.00

STAG & HOLLY

☐ Bowl. 7" deep, footed, blue	50.00	60.00
☐ Bowl. 8" deep, footed, green	65.00	75.00
☐ Bowl. 8" deep, footed, purple	70.00	80.00

STAG & HOLLY

	Price	Range
☐ Bowl. 9" deep, footed, marigold	55.00	65.00
☐ Bowl. 10" deep, blue	225.00	250.00
☐ Bowl. 11" deep, 3-footed, aqua	175.00	225.00
☐ Bowl (nut). Marigold	25.00	35.00
☐ Plate. Footed, marigold, small..................	150.00	175.00
☐ Rose Bowl. Green, large........................	150.00	175.00
☐ Wine. Marigold	16.00	20.00

STRAWBERRY

☐ Berry Set. 7 pieces, purple	125.00	150.00
☐ Bon Bon Dish. 2-handled, blue..................	35.00	45.00
☐ Bowl. 8" deep, marigold	125.00	150.00
☐ Bowl. 8½" deep, purple	55.00	65.00
☐ Bowl. 9" deep, green	60.00	75.00
☐ Bowl. 10" deep, fluted white	75.00	100.00
☐ Epergne. Purple	65.00	76.00
☐ Nappy. 2-handled, red	275.00	300.00
☐ Plate. With grip, 6" deep, marigold	45.00	55.00
☐ Plate. With grip, 7½" deep, green	60.00	70.00
☐ Plate. 9" deep, marigold.......................	55.00	65.00
☐ Plate. 9" deep, purple	75.00	85.00

THREE FRUITS

☐ Berry Set. 7 pieces	170.00	200.00
☐ Bowl. 7" deep, marigold	35.00	45.00
☐ Bowl. 7½" deep, green........................	35.00	45.00
☐ Bowl. 8½" deep, purple	45.00	55.00
☐ Bowl. 8½" deep, white	65.00	75.00
☐ Bowl. 8¾" fluted iron, purple	55.00	65.00
☐ Bowl. 9" deep, green	35.00	45.00
☐ Bowl. 9" deep, marigold	25.00	35.00
☐ Bowl. 9" deep, dome footed, white	75.00	85.00
☐ Bowl. 10" deep, purple	85.00	100.00
☐ Card Tray. 7½" deep, green with hand grip	65.00	75.00
☐ Plate. 9" deep, aqua	450.00	500.00
☐ Plate. 9" deep, green	85.00	100.00
☐ Plate. 9" deep, marigold.......................	60.00	80.00
☐ Plate. 9" deep, purple	65.00	75.00
☐ Plate. Ice blue, opalescent	475.00	525.00

VINEYARD

☐ Bowl. Purple	40.00	50.00
☐ Pitcher (water). Marigold	60.00	70.00
☐ Pitcher (water). Purple	275.00	300.00
☐ Tumbler. Marigold	20.00	30.00
☐ Tumbler. White	100.00	125.00
☐ Water Set. 5 pieces, marigold	150.00	200.00
☐ Water Set. 7 pieces, purple	350.00	400.00

WINDMILL MEDALLION

☐ Bowl. 7" deep, marigold	22.00	26.00
☐ Bowl. 8" deep, marigold, ruffled	15.00	20.00

WINDMILL MEDALLION

	Price	Range
☐ Bowl. 9" deep, marigold, footed	25.00	30.00
☐ Dresser Tray. Oval, green	125.00	150.00
☐ Pickle Dish. Marigold	15.00	20.00
☐ Pitcher (milk). Purple	200.00	225.00
☐ Tumbler. Marigold	15.00	20.00
☐ Tumbler. Purple	45.00	55.00
☐ Water Set. 5 pieces, marigold	90.00	110.00

WINE & ROSES

☐ Pitcher. Marigold	125.00	150.00
☐ Water Set. 6 pieces, marigold	275.00	325.00
☐ Wine. Blue	50.00	60.00
☐ Wine. Marigold	30.00	40.00

ZIG ZAG

☐ Bowl. 9¼" deep, marigold	35.00	45.00
☐ Bowl. 10" deep, ruffled rim, purple	75.00	100.00
☐ Pitcher (water). Blue with enamel decor	125.00	150.00
☐ Pitcher (water). White with enamel decor	175.00	200.00
☐ Tumbler. Purple with enamel decor	25.00	35.00

CUSTARD GLASS

Custard glass was named for its similarity to the color of baked custard and varies to light cream. Most major glass companies produced over twenty patterns. Some were decorated with gold.

☐ Banana Dishes. Chrysanthemum sprig	250.00	275.00
☐ Banana Dishes. Oval, 10"	200.00	225.00
☐ Banana Dishes. Louis XV	150.00	160.00
☐ Berry Bowl. Beaded circle	175.00	195.00
☐ Berry Bowl. Chrysanthemum sprig	150.00	195.00
☐ Berry Bowl. Diamond and roses	40.00	50.00
☐ Bon Bon Dishes	12.00	17.50
☐ Bowls. Floral with feet, 4"	40.00	50.00
☐ Bowls. Louis XV, oval	125.00	150.00
☐ Bowls. Weaved, grape & cable	55.00	60.00
☐ Butter Plates. Chrysanthemum sprig	200.00	250.00
☐ Butter Plate. Flower, panelled	150.00	170.00
☐ Butter Plate. Geneva, covered	125.00	140.00
☐ Butter Plate. Intaglio covered	160.00	175.00
☐ Celery. Chrysanthemum sprig	175.00	200.00
☐ Celery. Winged scroll	175.00	200.00
☐ Compotes. Argonaut shell	90.00	110.00
☐ Compotes. Chrysanthemum sprig	75.00	100.00
☐ Compotes. Intaglio, Northwood	75.00	100.00
☐ Creamer. Chrysanthemum sprig	90.00	110.00
☐ Creamer. Diamond Peg. Souvenir	45.00	55.00
☐ Creamer. Inverted fan & feather	160.00	175.00
☐ Creamer. Louis XV	100.00	110.00
☐ Creamer. Maple leaf	90.00	125.00
☐ Cruet. Chrysanthemum sprig	150.00	175.00

CUSTARD GLASS

	Price	Range
☐ Cruet. Intaglio	150.00	165.00
☐ Cruet. Louis XV	175.00	185.00
☐ Goblets. Beaded swag	65.00	90.00
☐ Goblets. Grape & Gothic	50.00	65.00
☐ Mug. Chrysanthemum sprig	30.00	45.00
☐ Mug. Geneva	50.00	65.00
☐ Mug. Shield	20.00	25.00
☐ Salt & Pepper Shakers. Argonaut shell	300.00	400.00
☐ Salt & Pepper Shakers. Chrysanthemum sprig	45.00	65.00
☐ Salt & Pepper Shakers. Intaglio	40.00	65.00
☐ Sauce Dishes. Beaded swag	40.00	50.00
☐ Sauce Dishes. Chrysanthemum sprig	75.00	95.00
☐ Sauce Dishes. Louis XV, 5"	50.00	65.00
☐ Spooner. Argonaut shell	100.00	150.00
☐ Spooner. Chrysanthemum sprig	100.00	150.00
☐ Spooner. Diamond Peg	75.00	90.00
☐ Spooner. Louis XV	80.00	95.00
☐ Tumbler. Argonaut shell	110.00	125.00
☐ Tumbler. Chrysanthemum sprig	90.00	100.00
☐ Tumbler. Maple leaf	50.00	75.00

CUT GLASS

Cut Glass is usually deeply cut in all-over patterns in heavy lead blanks and has a distinct bell tone when struck. Usually refers to pieces made from 1880 to 1914 during the "Brilliant Period". Made in many shops such as Hawkes, Libby and Dorflinger, some of which marked their pieces with a trademark.

☐ Ashtray, Rectangular	45.00	70.00
☐ Bottles, cordial, pinwheel, bell shaped with original stopper	55.00	75.00
☐ Bottles, Silver overlay	400.00	475.00
☐ Bottles, Dresser, signed Hawkes, Middlesex pattern, 3"x5¾" H	70.00	90.00
☐ Bottles, Whiskey, strawberry diamond & fan with cut stopper, 9½" H		
☐ Bottles, Whiskey, strawberry diamond & fan with cut stopper, 9½" H	65.00	85.00
☐ Bottles, Wine, hobstars, diamond point & fans signed Galt & Bros.	180.00	220.00
☐ Bottles, Whiskey jug, blue cut to clear, bull's eye & notched prism	460.00	500.00
☐ Bowls, pinwheel design, 8"x3"	45.00	60.00
☐ Bowls, Harvard pattern, 8"x3"	105.00	120.00
☐ Bowls, Oval, deeply cut	165.00	195.00
☐ Bowls, Hawkes, hobstars & fans, 8"x3"	130.00	150.00
☐ Bowls, Heavily cut, signed Libbey	245.00	290.00
☐ Bowls, Oval, French, ca 1890	300.00	350.00
☐ Bowls, Finger with plate, rayed star pattern,	30.00	45.00
☐ Bowls, Fruit, pinwheel & feathered fan pattern, 1900's	200.00	250.00
☐ Bowls, Punch, Brazillian pattern, 12" H	525.00	750.00

CUT GLASS

	Price	Range
☐ Bowls, Hobstar, large with stand, 14" H	650.00	850.00
☐ Boxes, Art Nouveau brass and leather	450.00	525.00
☐ Boxes, Cigarette, with ash tray lid	60.00	75.00
☐ Boxes, Dresser, Harvard pattern, intaglio corn flower	50.00	70.00
☐ Boxes, Dresser, Russian pattern, cut buttons on lid &3 applied feet, 5½"x3½" H	165.00	190.00
☐ Boxes, Jewelry, cutting on base, hobstar on cover, 5¾" D	145.00	165.00
☐ Boxes, Jewelry, Florence pattern, sterling silver rims, 6½"x3" H	240.00	280.00
☐ Boxes, Powder, Hawkes signed	250.00	280.00
☐ Bracelet, Heart locket	450.00	525.00
☐ Butterdish, American crystal, 2 pieces, 1900's	275.00	375.00
☐ Butterdish, English, 2 piece, 1900's	135.00	225.00
☐ Candelabra, 4 branch glass, Art Deco	200.00	260.00
☐ Candy dish, English, 1890's	90.00	130.00
☐ Candy dish, American, Clarke	85.00	135.00
☐ Candy dish, Sterling and crystal, Hawkes	135.00	175.00
☐ Carafe, Block & fan	27.50	35.00
☐ Carafe, Diamond & strawberry	170.00	200.00
☐ Carafe, Hobstar and clover	44.00	55.00
☐ Carafe, Pinwheel cut flowers, water	75.00	110.00
☐ Carafe, Prism & Fan	75.00	90.00
☐ Carafe, Russian, starred buttons	280.00	320.00
☐ Carafe, Water, single star pattern	50.00	70.00
☐ Carafe, Water, Harvard cutting, prism stem	90.00	110.00
☐ Carafe, Water, hobstar & notched prism	64.00	75.00
☐ Carafe, Water, pinwheel, crosscut diamond & flasked fan	70.00	85.00
☐ Carafe, Wine, hobstar & fan, sterling collar	100.00	125.00
☐ Cordials, Crystal and silver, pair	750.00	825.00
☐ Cordials, Sterling and blown glass	125.00	175.00
☐ Creamer, Watterford, ca 1930's	38.50	50.00
☐ Cruet, 7½" H, pyramid shape	45.00	65.00
☐ Decanter, 8" H, Harvard cut	80.00	135.00
☐ Decanter, Art Deco, pressed pattern Chrysler Building	90.00	120.00
☐ Decanter, Pineapple cut	90.00	120.00
☐ Decanter, Pineapple fan, brilliant cut	75.00	110.00
☐ Decanter, Stoppered	165.00	190.00
☐ Dish, Bon Bon, Hunt Royal pattern	45.00	65.00
☐ Dish, Bon Bon pedestal dish, pair	450.00	500.00
☐ Dish, Candy, floral, Hawkes	35.00	50.00
☐ Dish, Cheese & Cracker, signed Hoare	300.00	400.00
☐ Dish, Cheese & Cracker, hobstar & strawberry diamond	95.00	115.00
☐ Dish, Cheese, pinwheels	275.00	325.00
☐ Dish, Cheese, diamond, fan, covered	375.00	450.00

CUT GLASS

	Price	Range
☐ Dish, Ice cream, hobstar	395.00	425.00
☐ Dish, Lemon, signed Hawkes	32.00	40.00
☐ Dish, Nut, signed Libbey, pair	270.00	310.00
☐ Dish, Olive, hobstar & comet	36.00	45.00
☐ Dish, Shell, signed Hoare	95.00	120.00
☐ Dish, Signed Omega	45.00	60.00
☐ Dish, Square, Imperial, signed Libbey	170.00	210.00
☐ Dish, 4 sections, strawberry, diamond points	145.00	175.00
☐ Dish, condiment, heavily cut, 1900's	85.00	180.00
☐ Dish, pedestal	270.00	310.00
☐ Figurine, Antique "sevre" cherub group	1200.00	1400.00
☐ Glasses, Etched pair, signed Libbey	100.00	140.00
☐ Glass, Magnifying, ivory handles	1200.00	1400.00
☐ Glass, Magnifying, Art Nouveau, sterling	135.00	170.00
☐ Glass, Magnifying, Mother of Pearl	135.00	170.00
☐ Goblet, panel & prism, cut	40.00	55.00
☐ Goblet, 2 prism, cut signed Hawkes, each	45.00	80.00
☐ Goblet, Spiral pinwheel pattern	27.50	45.00
☐ Inkwell, Crystal	225.00	300.00
☐ Inkwell, Sterling lid, 2" H	25.00	40.00
☐ Inkwell, Silver and crystal	525.00	600.00
☐ Jar, Art Nouveau, lid sterling	37.50	45.00
☐ Jar, Candy, Hawkes, 11"	190.00	240.00
☐ Jar, Cracker, silver top & handle	225.00	260.00
☐ Jar, Ivory temple, pair	4800.00	5000.00
☐ Jar, Powder, Art Nouveau, hobstar & fan	60.00	75.00
☐ Jar, Powder, crystal	70.00	100.00
☐ Jar, Powder, crystal	120.00	165.00
☐ Jar, Powder, sterling lid, 3"x3"	35.00	45.00
☐ Jar, Mustard, signed Webb	50.00	95.00
☐ Jar, Powder, Reine Des Fleurs	70.00	85.00
☐ Jar, Tobacco, sterling top, 7"	125.00	150.00
☐ Jewelry, Antique cross with rubies and diamonds	120.00	160.00
☐ Jug, Whiskey, Clarke	280.00	325.00
☐ Knife Rest, ball ends with diamond cutting	32.50	40.00
☐ Knife Rest, ca 1920's	17.50	32.00
☐ Knife Rest, Hawkes signed	22.50	30.00
☐ Lamp, Table, mushroom shade, 18"	375.00	575.00
☐ Matchstrikes, Antique pair	200.00	250.00
☐ Muffineer, Sterling, cone shaped	24.00	38.00
☐ Nappy	75.00	110.00
☐ Pitchers, Cider, prism & bull's eye, hobstar base 8"H	140.00	170.00
☐ Pitchers, Claret, Encore pattern by Strauss, 12" H	240.00	290.00
☐ Pitchers, Milk, Russian pattern with starred buttons, 5" H	350.00	425.00
☐ Pitchers, Milk, signed Hawkes, deep cutting, 12 point star base, 5½" H	140.00	180.00

CUT GLASS

	Price	Range
☐ Pitchers, Tankard, hobstars, strawberry diamond & fan, 16 point base, 11½" H	120.00	160.00
☐ Pitchers, Water, Harvard pattern, handle double faceted	180.00	240.00
☐ Pitchers, Water, Irvin's white rose pattern, 9" H	170.00	130.00
☐ Pitchers, Water, Millicent pattern, signed Hawkes, 8½" H	180.00	220.00
☐ Pitcher, Water, Maple City Glass Co., signed	185.00	210.00
☐ Plates, Hawkes, signed, hobstar center 6½" D	45.00	65.00
☐ Plates, Hawkes, carnations, 7" D	105.00	130.00
☐ Plates, Hunt's royal pattern, 7" D	50.00	65.00
☐ Plates, 8½" D, hobstars & strawberry diamond around rim, center, 4½" D	40.00	60.00
☐ Plates, 10" D, 12 panels of frosted stars & hobstars	185.00	210.00
☐ Punch Bowl, in 2 sections, flower with star, box pattern	1200.00	1400.00
☐ Platter, Ice Cream, oval Russian art	300.00	360.00
☐ Salt & Pepper shakers, 6" H, pair	22.00	32.00
☐ Syrup, Sterling, Hawkes, dispenser etched crystal	165.00	200.00
☐ Stickpin with opal	90.00	120.00
☐ Stickpin with cameo	135.00	175.00
☐ Stickpin with diamond	90.00	120.00
☐ Stickpin with diamond	125.00	165.00
☐ Stickpin with horseshoe	75.00	100.00
☐ Stickpin with antique cameo	150.00	180.00
☐ Trays, Bread, cane & intaglio florals	80.00	95.00
☐ Trays, Card, starred buttons, Russian pattern	70.00	85.00
☐ Trays, Ice Cream, signed by Hoare, cane, prism 9"x2½" H	165.00	190.00
☐ Trays, Ice Cream, signed by Hawkes, Brazillian pattern 12¼"x8½"	180.00	195.00
☐ Trays, Ice Cream, Corinthian pattern, 14"x8½"	215.00	260.00
☐ Trays, Harvard pattern, with florals & leaves, 11"x6¼" H	90.00	120.00
☐ Trays, Libbey signed, Neols pattern	550.00	600.00
☐ Tumbler, Water, cut all over	9.00	14.00
☐ Vase, Bud, English	50.00	110.00
☐ Vase, Corset style with ribbed etchings	35.00	65.00
☐ Vase, Double handle, 4" H	55.00	80.00
☐ Vase, w/dahlias & leaves, 8" H	115.00	140.00
☐ Vase, English, graceful shape, 16" H	275.00	375.00
☐ Vase, Art Deco	75.00	110.00
☐ Vase, Sterling and crystal vase, Hawkes	270.00	330.00
☐ Vase, Flower, signed Hawkes, 16" H	195.00	250.00
☐ Vase, Flower, signed Webb, wide mouth, 1900's	195.00	250.00
☐ Vase, Grapes & leaves, Libbey 12"	140.00	170.00
☐ Vase, Hawkes, 18"	140.00	170.00
☐ Vase, Intaglio cut, floral & leaf, Libbey	145.00	170.00

CUT GLASS

	Price	Range
☐ Vase, Pedestal, notched & cross cut, 16"	110.00	140.00
☐ Vase, Pinwheel, strawberry diamond & fan, 8"	45.00	65.00
☐ Vase, Sunburst pattern	675.00	725.00
☐ Vase, Trumpet, fluted for, signed Hawkes	120.00	180.00
☐ Vase, Trumpet, pinwheel cut with riffled edging	150.00	190.00
☐ Vase, Trumpet, signed Hawkes	210.00	260.00
☐ Vase, Trumpet, 16"	290.00	325.00
☐ Vase, Verre De Soie, signed Hawkes	115.00	145.00
☐ Wine, Glass cooler	55.00	70.00
☐ Wine, Hawkes	2250.00	2800.00
☐ Wine, Teardrop, Strauss	50.00	65.00
☐ Wine, Rose, Libbey	37.50	44.00

DEPRESSION GLASS

Colored glassware was machine made during the "Depression Years" of the late 1920's and early 1930's. The glass was available in ten cent stores and given away at filling stations, theatres, and used for promotional purposes. There are approximately 150,000 collectors and the popularity is steadily increasing each year. There are over 80 depression glass clubs which sponsor shows with attendance in the thousands.

Of the approximately 100 different patterns and colors produced, rose pink remains the favorite color. Luncheon sets (16 pieces) sold for as low as $1.29. Today, a dinner service, depending on the scarcity of the pattern, may cost from $100.00 to $1000.00 a set. *Courtesy: Ruby Davis, Orlando, Fla.*

ADAMS
Pink—Jeannette Glass Co.

	Price
☐ Bowl. 6"	6.00
☐ Bowl. 10", oval	8.50
☐ Butter Dish	55.00
☐ Cup & Saucer	10.00
☐ Candlesticks (pair)	25.00
☐ Plate. 7¾"	5.00
☐ Plate. 9"	7.00
☐ Platter	8.00
☐ Shakers (pair)	22.00
☐ Sherbet. 3"	22.00
☐ Pitcher. 8"	17.00
☐ Tumbler. 4½"	8.00
☐ Vase. 7½"	50.00

Green color is higher priced.

AMERICAN SWEETHEART
(McBeth-Evans Glass Co.)

☐ Bowl. 6"	4.00
☐ Bowl. 9"	9.00
☐ Bowl (cream soup)	10.00
☐ Creamer	5.00
☐ Sugar	5.00
☐ Plate. 6"	2.00

AMERICAN SWEETHEART

		Price
☐	Plate. 9¼"	6.00
☐	Plate. 11"	8.00
☐	Sherbet. 3"	6.00
☐	Sherbet. 5" (thin)	10.00
☐	Shakers (pair)	35.00
☐	Pitcher. 5¾" (rare)	100.00
☐	Pitcher (juice). 6"	25.00
☐	Pitcher. 8"	22.00
☐	Tumbler. 3"	8.00
☐	Tumbler. 4"	10.00
☐	Tumbler. 9 oz. (ftd.)	12.00
☐	Tumbler (wine). 4"	40.00
☐	Tumbler Goblet. 6"	20.00
☐	Vase. 8"	14.00

BLOCK OPTIC
(Hocking Glass Co.)

Gray and Pink

☐	Bowl. 4"	2.50
☐	Bowl. 8¾"	6.00
☐	Butterdish (round)	22.50
☐	Creamer	4.50
☐	Cup	3.00
☐	Plate. 6"	1.75
☐	Plate. 8"	3.00
☐	Plate. 9"	4.50
☐	Pitcher. 8"	20.00
☐	Shakers (pair)	15.00
☐	Saucer	3.00
☐	Sherbet	2.50
☐	Tumbler (juice)	3.50
☐	Tumbler. 9 oz. (ftd.)	6.00
☐	Tumbler. 10 oz. (ftd.)	10.00
☐	Tumbler (goblet). 6"	10.00
☐	Tumbler. 7¼" (thin)	8.00

BUBBLE
(Hocking Glass Co.)

Light Blue

☐	Bowl. 4"	4.00
☐	Bowl. 4½"	3.00
☐	Bowl. 5½"	4.00
☐	Bowl (soup). 7½"	5.00
☐	Bowl. 8 3/8"	6.00
☐	Cup	2.50
☐	Plate. 6¾"	2.50
☐	Plate. 9¼"	3.00
☐	Plate (grill)	4.50
☐	Platter	6.00
☐	Sugar & Creamer	14.00

CHERRY BLOSSOM
(Jeannette Glass Co.)

Pink	Price
☐ Bowl. 5"	6.00
☐ Bowl (cereal)	10.00
☐ Bowl (soup)	16.00
☐ Pitcher. 7½"	175.00
☐ Pitcher. 8"	150.00
☐ Sherbet	5.00
☐ Tumbler. 4¼"	12.00
☐ Shakers (rare)	125.00

Luncheon sets in red and cobalt blue are rare.

☐ Plate. 8"	60.00
☐ Cup	65.00
☐ Saucer	25.00

DORIC AND PANSY
(Jeannette Glass Co.)

Teal Blue	
☐ Bowl. 4½"	6.00
☐ Bowl. 9"	12.00
☐ Butterdish (rare)	450.00
☐ Creamer (rare)	80.00
☐ Cup	6.50
☐ Plate. 6"	6.00
☐ Plate. 7"	16.00
☐ Plate. 9"	12.00
☐ Shakers. Pair (rare)	350.00
☐ Sugar (rare)	80.00
☐ Saucer	3.50

FLORAL
(Jeannette Glass Co.)

	Price Range	
	Pink	Green
☐ Bowl. 4"	3.50	4.50
☐ Bowl (cream soup)	20.00	150.00
☐ Bowl. 7½"	6.00	8.00
☐ Bowl. 8" (covered)	10.00	12.00
☐ Bowl (oval)	6.00	8.00
☐ Butterdish	45.00	55.00
☐ Candlesticks (pair)	24.00	30.00
☐ Candy Jar	16.00	24.00
☐ Coasters	4.00	6.00
☐ Creamer	5.00	6.00
☐ Cup	4.00	5.00
☐ Plate. 6"	2.50	3.00
☐ Plate. 8"	4.00	5.00
☐ Plate. 9"	6.00	7.50
☐ Platter	5.00	6.50
☐ Pitcher	15.00	20.00

FLORAL

	Price	Range
☐ Pitcher (lemonade). 10¼" (rare).................	100.00	125.00
☐ Saucer.......................................	2.50	3.00
☐ Shakers (pair)	20.00	25.00
☐ Sherbet	4.50	6.00
☐ Tumbler. 4".................................	4.50	6.00
☐ Tumbler. 4¾"...............................	7.00	8.00
☐ Tumbler. 5¼"...............................	15.00	18.00

FLORENTINE II (POPPY)
(Hazel Glass Co.)

Green **Price**

☐ Bowl. 5"	4.00
☐ Bowl. 6"	6.00
☐ Bowl. 8½"	10.00
☐ Butterdish	70.00
☐ Cup...	4.00
☐ Creamer	4.50
☐ Plate. 6"	2.50
☐ Plate. 8½"	3.50
☐ Plate (grill). 10½"	4.00
☐ Platter	6.00
☐ Pitcher	20.00
☐ Saucer	2.00
☐ Shakers (pair)...	20.00
☐ Sherbet	4.00
☐ Sugar	4.00
☐ Tumblers. 4" (flat)	6.00
☐ Tumblers. 5" (ftd.)	10.00
☐ Vase. 6"	10.00

(Yellow prices are higher.)

HOLIDAY
(Jeannette Glass Co.)

☐ Bowl. 5"	3.50
☐ Bowl. 7¾" (soup)..	9.00
☐ Bowl. 8½"	10.00
☐ Bowl. 9½" (oval)	6.50
☐ Bowl. 10¾"	16.00
☐ Butterdish	25.00
☐ Cake Plate (3 legs).......................................	25.00
☐ Candlesticks (pair)	30.00
☐ Cup...	3.50
☐ Plate. 13¾" (round)......................................	30.00
☐ Plate. 9"	3.50
☐ Plate. 6"	2.00
☐ Platter	6.00
☐ Saucer	2.00
☐ Sherbert	4.00
☐ Tumbler. 4" (ftd.)	12.00
☐ Tumbler. 4" (flat)	8.00
☐ Tumbler. 6" (footed).....................................	20.00

NO. 612 (HORSESHOE)
(Indiana Glass Co.)

Green   **Price**

- [ ] Bowl. 4½" 2.00
- [ ] Bowl (cereal). 6" 6.00
- [ ] Bowl. 8½" 2.00
- [ ] Bowl. 10½" (oval) 4.00
- [ ] Butterdish 12.00
- [ ] Candy in Metalholder 8.00
- [ ] Cup 20.00
- [ ] Plate. 8½" 4.00
- [ ] Plate. 9 3/8" 5.00
- [ ] Plate. 11¼" 6.50
- [ ] Pitcher (rare) 170.00
- [ ] Platter 8.00
- [ ] Saucer 2.50
- [ ] Sherbet 6.50
- [ ] Tumbler 4¾" (ftd) 8.00
- [ ] Tumbler 12 ox. (ftd) rare 750.00

IRIS AND HERRINGBONE
(Jeannette Glass Co.)

- [ ] Chrystal
- [ ] Bowl 4½" 3.50
- [ ] Bowl 6" 8.00
- [ ] Bowl 7½" Soup 15.00
- [ ] Bowl 8" 5.00
- [ ] Butterdish 20.00
- [ ] Candlesticks pr. 12.00
- [ ] Candy & Cover 40.00
- [ ] Creamer 4.00
- [ ] Cup 4.00
- [ ] Cup, Demitasse 8.00
- [ ] Saucer 10.00
- [ ] Pitcher 15.00
- [ ] Plate 8" 15.00
- [ ] Plate 11¾" 6.00
- [ ] Saucer 2.50
- [ ] Sherbet 4" 6.00
- [ ] Sugar 3.50
- [ ] Tumbler 4" flat 12.00
- [ ] Tumbler 6" frosted 6.00
- [ ] Goblet 4" Wine 6.00
- [ ] Goblet 7" 9.00

LACE EDGE
(Hocking Glass Co.)
Pink

- [ ] Bowl, cereal 5.00
- [ ] Bowl, 9½" 5.00

LACE EDGE   **Price**

- ☐ Bowl, 10½" 40.00
- ☐ Butterdish 30.00
- ☐ Candlesticks (pair) 50.00
- ☐ Candy & Cover 15.00
- ☐ Cookie Jar 20.00
- ☐ Plate, 7¾" 4.00
- ☐ Plate, 8¾" 4.00
- ☐ Plate Grill 4.50
- ☐ Platter 8.00
- ☐ Tumbler, 5" (ftd) 12.00

MADRID FEDERAL GLASS CO.
Amber

- ☐ Bowl 5" 3.50
- ☐ Bowl 8" 6.00
- ☐ Bowl 9½" 10.00
- ☐ Butterdish 45.00
- ☐ Candlesticks (pr.) 12.00
- ☐ Cookie Jar 20.00
- ☐ Jello Mold 5.00
- ☐ Plate 7½" 5.50
- ☐ Plate 8" 3.50
- ☐ Plate 10½" 12.00

MAYFAIR
(Open Rose)

Pink

- ☐ Bowl 5" 5.00
- ☐ Bowl 7" 8.00
- ☐ Bowl 9", 3 legs (rare) 450.00
- ☐ Bowl 10" 8.00
- ☐ Butterdish 30.00
- ☐ Cookie Jar 20.00
- ☐ Cup 5.50
- ☐ Creamer 8.00
- ☐ Decanter 50.00
- ☐ Plate 8½" 6.00
- ☐ Plate 9½" 15.00
- ☐ Saucor 6.00
- ☐ Sugar 8.00
- ☐ Sugar Lid (rare) 400.00
- ☐ Sherbet 3" 5.50
- ☐ Sherbet 4¾" 25.00
- ☐ Pitcher 6" 18.00
- ☐ Pitcher 8½" 25.00
- ☐ Tumbler 4" 12.00
- ☐ Tumbler 5½" (ftd) 16.00
- ☐ Goblet 4" 30.00
- ☐ Goblet 5½" 20.00

MISS AMERICA
(Hocking Glass Co.)
Pink   Price

☐   Bowl 6" 6.00
☐   Bowl 8" 25.00
☐   Bowl 10" oval 8.00
☐   Bowl cream soup 12.00
☐   Butterdish (rare) 300.00
☐   Cake Plate 15.00
☐   Cup 8.00
☐   Plate 6" 3.50
☐   Plate 8½" 7.00
☐   Pitcher 8" 60.00
☐   Tumbler 4½" 16.00
☐   Tumbler 6¾" 25.00
☐   Goblet 3 oz. 30.00
☐   Goblet 5½" 20.00

PATRICIAN
(Spoke)

Amber

☐   Bowl 6" 6.00
☐   Bowl 8½" 8.00
☐   Bowl cream soup 5.00
☐   Butterdish 45.00
☐   Cookie Jar 35.00
☐   Creamer 4.00
☐   Cup 3.50
☐   Plate 7" 5.50
☐   Plate 9" 3.50
☐   Plate 10½" 4.00
☐   Pitcher 8" 37.50
☐   Sugar & Lid 15.00
☐   Tumbler 4" 8.00
☐   Tumbler 5½" (ftd) 22.50

PRINCESS
(Hocking Glass Co.)

Green

☐   Bowl 4½" 6.00
☐   Bowl 5½" 8.00
☐   Bowl, oval 10.00
☐   Bowl, bat shaped 12.00
☐   Butterdish 55.00
☐   Cake Plate 8.00
☐   Cup & Saucer 6.50
☐   Cookie Jar 20.00

PRINCESS

		Price
☐	Plate 6"	2.50
☐	Plate 8"	4.00
☐	Plate 9"	8.00
☐	Sherbet	5.00
☐	Shakers (pair)	25.00
☐	Pitcher 8"	20.00
☐	Vase	14.00

SHARON
(Federal Glass Co.)

Pink

☐	Bowl 8½"	6.00
☐	Bowl 9½", oval	8.00
☐	Bowl 10½"	10.00
☐	Butterdish	35.00
☐	Cake Plate (ftd)	12.00
☐	Candy Jar	20.00
☐	Cheese Dish (rare)	300.00
☐	Cup	4.00
☐	Creamer	7.00
☐	Plate 6"	3.00
☐	Plate 7½"	6.00
☐	Plate 9½"	6.00
☐	Platter	8.00
☐	Shaker (pair)	25.00
☐	Sugar	6.00
☐	Sugar lid	8.00
☐	Tumbler 4"	10.00
☐	Tumbler 6½" (ftd)	20.00
☐	Pitcher	47.50

MILK GLASS

	Price	Range
☐ Animal Covered Dish, duck, Atterbury, 11" L	175.00	225.00
☐ Basket, Basket Weave, twisted handle, 4"	25.00	35.00
☐ Bell, smoke, fulted rim, 7"	15.00	25.00
☐ Bottles, cologne, Portraite Modallion, 5½"	55.00	75.00
☐ Bottles, dresser, Actress, 11"	45.00	65.00
☐ Bottles, perfume, Germany, 1¾"	7.50	15.00
☐ Bowls, Acanthus leaf, 10" D	75.00	100.00
☐ Bowls, lacy, Edger, 8"	75.00	100.00
☐ Bowls, lattice, 8½"	85.00	125.00
☐ Bowls, scalloped edge, 11"	25.00	45.00
☐ Box, glove, covered 10" x 4"	35.00	45.00
☐ Butter, Apple Blossom	100.00	150.00
☐ Cake Stand, 11" diameter with star in center	95.00	125.00
☐ Candlestick, Crucifix, round base, 10"	25.00	35.00
☐ Celery, Maize	70.00	100.00

MILK GLASS

	Price	Range
☐ Compotes, Atterburg	35.00	50.00
☐ Compotes, raised grapes, pink	15.00	25.00
☐ Creamer, prism	25.00	40.00
☐ Creamer, sawtooth, flint	40.00	60.00
☐ Dish, battleship marked Dewey	40.00	60.00
☐ Dish, cat cover, blue with white head	40.00	60.00
☐ Dish, hand & dove corner, Atterbury	125.00	175.00
☐ Dish, quail cover	35.00	55.00
☐ Dish, woolly lamb cover	150.00	200.00
☐ Egg Cup, birch leaf	20.00	30.00
☐ Goblet, blackberry	25.00	50.00
☐ Goblet, cane	45.00	75.00
☐ Hat, Uncle Sam	25.00	32.50
☐ Match Holder, hen & rabbit	12.00	18.00
☐ Mug, hobnail	22.50	28.50
☐ Mustard Jar, Dutch figures, 4"	35.00	55.00
☐ Pitcher, little boy	75.00	100.00
☐ Pitcher, owl	185.00	225.00
☐ Pitcher, water, pink	45.00	75.00
☐ Plates, battleship Maine	35.00	45.00
☐ Plates, dogs & squirrel	40.00	60.00
☐ Plates, Easter duck	25.00	45.00
☐ Plates, three owls	35.00	55.00
☐ Platter, Rock of Ages	125.00	175.00
☐ Rolling Pin, wooden handles	40.00	60.00
☐ Salt & Pepper, grape	20.00	40.00
☐ Salt & Pepper, rabbits	50.00	75.00
☐ Spooner, swan	25.00	50.00
☐ Sugar Bowls, cat cover	350.00	400.00
☐ Sugar Bowls, Wilde Rose, miniature	30.00	50.00
☐ Sugar Shaker, acorn	30.00	50.00
☐ Sugar Shaker, poppy	30.00	50.00
☐ Syrups, Tree of Life, blue, pewter top	70.00	100.00
☐ Toothpick, monkey & stump	30.00	40.00
☐ Tray, cake, Atterbury	30.00	40.00
☐ Tray, pin, heart shape	4.00	6.00
☐ Tray, World's Fair, St. Louis, 1904	30.00	50.00
☐ Tumbler, black trim	9.00	15.00
☐ Tumbler, cuff with button	28.50	35.00
☐ Tumbler, St. Louis Exposition	10.00	15.00
☐ Vase, gargoyle 8½"	20.00	30.00
☐ Vase, roses, 7"	28.50	35.00
☐ Vase, ruffled top, 9½"	30.00	45.00
☐ Waste Bowl, monkey	125.00	175.00

PATTERN GLASS

Pattern Glass was produced in large quantities after the invention of the pattern glass machine. There are only a representative number here. The early glass was made of lead and had a distinctive bell-tone ring which is the most in demand. Pattern Glass reached its height in popularity in the late 1800's. There are many reproductions and a reputable dealer should be consulted before purchase. Photos Courtesy: Bob Batty, author of
"A Complete Guide to Pressed Glass"

ACTRESS (c. 1872)

	Price Range
☐ Bowl, FTD	15.00- 30.00
☐ Butter plate	65.00- 80.00
☐ Cake dish	80.00- 95.00
☐ Cheese dish, CVD . . .	170.00-185.00
☐ Compote, CVD	120.00-135.00
☐ Dish	30.00- 45.00
☐ Creamer	55.00- 70.00
☐ Goblet	70.00- 85.00
☐ Honey dish, CVD	60.00- 75.00
☐ Marmalade dish	67.00- 82.00
☐ Pinafore pitcher	135.00-170.00
☐ Sauce dish, flat	12.00- 20.00
☐ Sauce dish, FTD	12.00- 20.00
☐ Shakers, S/P	95.00-110.00
☐ Sugar bowl	60.00- 75.00

ALABAMA (c. 1898)

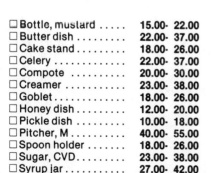

☐ Bottle, mustard	15.00- 22.00
☐ Butter dish	22.00- 37.00
☐ Cake stand	18.00- 26.00
☐ Celery	22.00- 37.00
☐ Compote	20.00- 30.00
☐ Creamer	23.00- 38.00
☐ Goblet	18.00- 26.00
☐ Honey dish	12.00- 20.00
☐ Pickle dish	10.00- 18.00
☐ Pitcher, M	40.00- 55.00
☐ Spoon holder	18.00- 26.00
☐ Sugar, CVD	23.00- 38.00
☐ Syrup jar	27.00- 42.00

ALMOND THUMBPRINT (c. 1890)

	Price Range
☐ Ale tumbler	62.00- 77.00
☐ Butter dish	80.00- 95.00
☐ Celery vase	60.00- 75.00
☐ Champagne glass . . .	60.00- 75.00
☐ Creamer	55.00- 70.00
☐ Compote, CVD	45.00- 60.00
☐ Cordial glass	60.00- 75.00
☐ Creamer	60.00- 75.00
☐ Cruet, FTD	60.00- 75.00
☐ Decanter	55.00- 70.00
☐ Egg cup	27.00- 42.00
☐ Goblet	45.00- 60.00
☐ Pitcher	75.00- 90.00
☐ Punch bowl	140.00-175.00
☐ Shaker, individual . . .	10.00- 18.00
☐ Shaker, large, flat . . .	15.00- 22.00
☐ Sugar bowl	60.00- 75.00
☐ Tumbler	35.00- 50.00

AMAZON (c. 1870)

☐ Bowl	18.00- 26.00
☐ Butter plate	25.00- 40.00
☐ Cake stand	30.00- 45.00
☐ Celery vase	20.00- 30.00
☐ Champagne glass . . .	18.00- 26.00
☐ Claret glass	12.00- 20.00
☐ Compote	12.00- 20.00
☐ Cordial, ruby	18.00- 26.00
☐ Creamer	20.00- 35.00
☐ Goblet	15.00- 22.00

	Price Range
☐ Mug	8.00- 15.00
☐ Pitcher, syrup	25.00- 40.00
☐ Pitcher, W	37.00- 52.00
☐ Sauce dish	8.00- 15.00
☐ Shakers, S/P	22.00- 37.00
☐ Spoon holder	20.00- 30.00
☐ Sugar bowl	25.00- 40.00
☐ Table set, child's	85.00-100.00
☐ Tumbler	12.00- 20.00
☐ Vase	18.00- 26.00
☐ Wine glass	12.00- 20.00

APOLLO (c. 1897)

	Price Range
☐ Butter dish, CVD	30.00- 45.00
☐ Cake stand	25.00- 40.00
☐ Celery, etched	23.00- 38.00
☐ Compote, CVD	42.00- 57.00
☐ Creamer	25.00- 40.00
☐ Egg cup	8.00- 14.00
☐ Goblet	20.00- 30.00
☐ Muffineer, etched	35.00- 50.00
☐ Pickle dish	12.00- 20.00
☐ Pitcher, M	35.00- 50.00
☐ Sauce, flat	5.00- 10.00
☐ Sauce, FTD	10.00- 18.00
☐ Spoon holder	18.00- 26.00
☐ Sugar bowl	30.00- 45.00
☐ Tray, W	27.00- 42.00
☐ Tumbler	10.00- 18.00
☐ Whiskey	18.00- 26.00
☐ Wine jug	12.00- 20.00

ARCHED GRAPE (c. 1870)

	Price Range
☐ Celery vase	37.00- 52.00
☐ Compote, CVD	55.00- 70.00
☐ Cordial	15.00- 22.00
☐ Creamer	37.00- 52.00
☐ Goblet	25.00- 40.00
☐ Pitcher, W	57.00- 72.00
☐ Sauce dish	10.00- 18.00
☐ Spoon holder	30.00- 45.00
☐ Sugar bowl	42.00- 57.00
☐ Tumbler	18.00- 26.00
☐ Wine glass	21.00- 36.00

ARGUS (c. 1870)

	Price Range
☐ Ale, 2 styles	85.00-100.00
☐ Bowl	35.00- 50.00
☐ Butter dish, CVD	70.00- 85.00
☐ Cake stand	80.00- 95.00
☐ Celery vase	55.00- 70.00

	Price Range
☐ Champagne	60.00- 75.00
☐ Cordial glass	22.00- 37.00
☐ Creamer	55.00- 70.00
☐ Decanter, quart	85.00-100.00
☐ Goblet	43.00- 58.00
☐ Lamp, FTD	60.00- 75.00
☐ Mug	75.00- 90.00
☐ Pitcher, W applied handle	175.00-210.00

	Price Range
☐ Sauce dish	20.00- 30.00
☐ Shakers, S/P	50.00- 65.00
☐ Spoon holder	45.00- 60.00
☐ Sugar bowl	70.00- 85.00
☐ Tumbler, jelly	20.00- 35.00
☐ Tumbler, W	27.00- 42.00
☐ Wine jug	45.00- 60.00

ART (c. 1890)

	Price Range
☐ Basket, fruit	45.00- 60.00
☐ Bowl	24.00- 39.00
☐ Butter dish, CVD	37.00- 52.00
☐ Cake stand	40.00- 55.00
☐ Celery vase	30.00- 45.00
☐ Compote, CVD., FTD	43.00- 58.00
☐ Cracker jar	27.00- 42.00
☐ Creamer	30.00- 45.00
☐ Cruet	23.00- 38.00
☐ Dish, banana	
☐ Goblet	27.00- 42.00
☐ Mug	18.00- 26.00
☐ Pickle dish	15.00- 22.00
☐ Pitcher, W	45.00- 60.00
☐ Plate	32.00- 57.00
☐ Relish	8.00- 14.00
☐ Sauce, flat	8.00- 14.00
☐ Spoon holder	20.00- 30.00
☐ Sugar bowl	34.00- 49.00
☐ Tumbler	12.00- 20.00
☐ Vinegar	20.00- 30.00

ASHBURTON (c. 1855)

Price Range

☐ Ale glass	45.00- 60.00
☐ Bitters bottle	45.00- 60.00
☐ Butter plate	110.00-145.00
☐ Celery, plain top	70.00- 85.00
☐ Celery, scalloped top	85.00-100.00
☐ Champagne glass ...	57.00- 72.00
☐ Creamer, rare	155.00-190.00
☐ Decanter, quart	80.00- 95.00
☐ Egg cup, 2 styles	22.00- 37.00
☐ Goblet, straight	55.00- 70.00
☐ Jug, 3 pints.........	115.00-150.00
☐ Lamp..............	85.00-100.00
☐ Mug..............	55.00- 70.00
☐ Sauce dish	20.00- 30.00
☐ Spoon holder	43.00- 58.00
☐ Toddy jar, 2 sizes	240.00-275.00
☐ Tumbler, jelly	23.00- 38.00
☐ Tumbler, W.........	35.00- 50.00
☐ Whiskey	45.00- 60.00
☐ Wine bottle, tumble-up	140.00-175.00

BABY FACE (c. 1870)

☐ Cake stand, large and small	75.00- 90.00
☐ Celery vase	70.00- 85.00
☐ Compote, large and small	115.00-150.00
☐ Cordial	75.00- 90.00
☐ Creamer	105.00-140.00
☐ Lamp..............	90.00-125.00
☐ Pitcher	165.00-200.00
☐ Salt, open	30.00- 45.00
☐ Sauce, flat	22.00- 37.00
☐ Spoon holder	67.00- 82.00

BALL AND SWIRL (c. 1870)

☐ Butter dish	40.00- 55.00
☐ Cake stand.........	23.00- 38.00

Price Range

☐ Celery vase	15.00- 22.00
☐ Compote, CVD and open	37.00- 52.00
☐ Cordial glass	18.00- 26.00
☐ Creamer	24.00- 39.00
☐ Decanter...........	24.00- 39.00
☐ Finger bowl	10.00- 18.00
☐ Goblet............	18.00- 26.00
☐ Mug, large	12.00- 20.00
☐ Pitcher, plain	45.00- 60.00
☐ Pitcher, etched	52.00- 67.00
☐ Sauce, flat	8.00- 14.00
☐ Spoon holder	15.00- 22.00
☐ Sugar bowl	37.00- 52.00
☐ Tumbler	10.00- 18.00
☐ Whiskey, flint	29.00- 44.00
☐ Wine jug	15.00- 22.00

BALTIMORE PEAR (c. 1870)

☐ Bowl	20.00- 35.00
☐ Celery vase	35.00- 50.00
☐ Plate	40.00- 55.00
☐ Sauce, flat	8.00- 14.00
☐ Sauce, FTD, lg./sm. ..	10.00- 18.00
☐ Pitcher, W.........	55.00- 70.00
☐ Spoon holder	27.00- 42.00
☐ Sugar bowl	43.00- 58.00

BAMBOO (c. 1800)

☐ Celery vase	15.00- 22.00
☐ Compote, CVD	35.00- 50.00
☐ Creamer	20.00- 30.00
☐ Dish, oblong........	18.00- 26.00
☐ Pitcher, M.........	30.00- 45.00
☐ Sauce, flat	6.00- 12.00
☐ Shaker, S/P........	20.00- 30.00
☐ Spoon holder	10.00- 18.00
☐ Sugar bowl	20.00- 35.00
☐ Tumbler	15.00- 22.00

BARBERRY (c. 1880)

☐ Bowl	18.00- 26.00
☐ Butter plate	42.00- 57.00
☐ Celery	30.00- 45.00
☐ Compote, high, low ..	45.00- 60.00
☐ Cordial glass	25.00- 40.00
☐ Creamer	40.00- 55.00
☐ Egg cup, berries	22.00- 37.00
☐ Goblet............	21.00- 36.00
☐ Pickle	25.00- 40.00
☐ Pitcher, syrup pewter top	60.00- 75.00

	Price Range
☐ Pitcher, W	55.00- 70.00
☐ Plate	21.00- 36.00
☐ Salt, FTD	18.00- 26.00
☐ Sauce, flat & FTD ...	7.00- 22.00
☐ Spoon holder	27.00- 42.00
☐ Sugar bowl, CVD	50.00- 65.00
☐ Syrup jar	25.00- 40.00
☐ Wine jug	15.00- 20.00

BARLEY (c. 1870)

☐ Butter dish, CVD	25.00- 40.00
☐ Butter, CVD	31.00- 46.00
☐ Cake stand	24.00- 39.00
☐ Celery dish	25.00- 40.00
☐ Compote, CVD	
and open	42.00- 57.00
☐ Cordial glass	15.00- 22.00
☐ Creamer	23.00- 38.00
☐ Goblet.............	20.00- 30.00
☐ Jam jar	25.00- 40.00
☐ Pickles, handles	15.00- 22.00
☐ Pitcher, M	30.00- 45.00
☐ Plate, bread	20.00- 30.00
☐ Platter.............	30.00- 45.00
☐ Sauce, flat and FTD .	10.00- 18.00
☐ Spoon holder	23.00- 38.00
☐ Sugar bowl	27.00- 42.00
☐ Wine jug	18.00- 26.00

BARRED FORGET-ME-NOT
(c. 1883)

Butter dish
☐ Clear..............	22.00- 37.00
☐ Yellow.............	33.00- 48.00
☐ Blue	41.00- 46.00
☐ Green	50.00- 65.00
Cake, large and med	
☐ Clear..............	23.00- 38.00
☐ Yellow.............	35.00- 50.00
☐ Blue	40.00- 55.00

	Price Range
☐ Green	60.00- 75.00
Celery vase	
☐ Clear..............	23.00- 38.00
☐ Yellow.............	30.00- 45.00
☐ Blue	34.00- 49.00
☐ Green	47.00- 62.00
Compote, low	
☐ Clear..............	27.00- 42.00
☐ Yellow.............	47.00- 62.00
☐ Blue	55.00- 70.00
☐ Green	63.00- 78.00
Cordial glass	
☐ Clear..............	15.00- 22.00
☐ Yellow.............	20.00- 30.00
☐ Blue	32.00- 47.00
☐ Green	37.00- 52.00
Creamer	
☐ Clear..............	20.00- 35.00
☐ Yellow.............	25.00- 40.00
☐ Blue	30.00- 45.00
☐ Green	40.00- 55.00
Goblet	

☐ Clear..............	18.00- 26.00
☐ Yellow.............	20.00- 30.00
☐ Blue	25.00- 40.00
☐ Green	37.00- 52.00
Pickle dish	
☐ Clear..............	12.00- 20.00
☐ Yellow.............	20.00- 30.00
☐ Blue	23.00- 38.00
☐ Green	31.00- 46.00
Pitcher, M	
☐ Clear..............	25.00- 40.00
☐ Yellow.............	35.00- 50.00
☐ Blue	40.00- 55.00
☐ Green	55.00- 70.00
Plate	
☐ Clear..............	18.00- 26.00
☐ Yellow.............	30.00- 45.00
☐ Blue	35.00- 50.00
☐ Green	45.00- 60.00
Sauce dish	
☐ Clear..............	6.00- 12.00

	Price Range
☐ Yellow	10.00- 18.00
☐ Blue	12.00- 20.00
☐ Green	15.00- 22.00
Spoon holder	
☐ Clear	20.00- 30.00
☐ Yellow	25.00- 40.00
☐ Blue	30.00- 45.00
☐ Green	45.00- 60.00
Sugar bowl	
☐ Clear	18.00- 26.00
☐ Yellow	30.00- 45.00
☐ Blue	33.00- 50.00
☐ Green	45.00- 60.00
Wine glass	
☐ Clear	12.00- 20.00
☐ Yellow	23.00- 38.00
☐ Blue	30.00- 45.00
☐ Green	37.00- 52.00

BASKET WEAVE (c. 1883)

	Price Range
Butter dish	
☐ Clear	30.00- 45.00
☐ Yellow	40.00- 55.00
☐ Blue	50.00- 65.00
☐ Green	60.00- 75.00
Compote	
☐ Clear	30.00- 45.00
☐ Yellow	47.00- 62.00
☐ Blue	60.00- 75.00
☐ Green	80.00- 95.00
Cordial glass	
☐ Clear	15.00- 22.00
☐ Yellow	20.00- 35.00
☐ Blue	27.00- 42.00
☐ Green	38.00- 53.00
Creamer	
☐ Clear	20.00- 30.00
☐ Yellow	37.00- 52.00
☐ Blue	43.00- 58.00
☐ Green	55.00- 70.00
Cup/saucer	
☐ Clear	20.00- 35.00
☐ Yellow	30.00- 45.00
☐ Blue	33.00- 48.00
☐ Green	40.00- 60.00
Egg cup	
☐ Clear	12.00- 20.00
☐ Yellow	25.00- 40.00
☐ Blue	27.00- 42.00
☐ Green	40.00- 55.00
Lamp	
☐ Clear	25.00- 40.00
☐ Yellow	35.00- 50.00

	Price Range
☐ Blue	40.00- 55.00
☐ Green	55.00- 70.00
Mug	
☐ Clear	12.00- 20.00
☐ Yellow	20.00- 30.00
☐ Blue	23.00- 38.00
☐ Green	37.00- 52.00
Pickle dish	
☐ Clear	10.00- 18.00
☐ Yellow	18.00- 26.00
☐ Blue	20.00- 35.00
☐ Green	33.00- 48.00
Pitcher	
☐ Clear	30.00- 45.00
☐ Yellow	40.00- 55.00
☐ Blue	45.00- 60.00
☐ Green	57.00- 72.00
Plate	
☐ Clear	18.00- 26.00
☐ Yellow	23.00- 38.00
☐ Blue	35.00- 50.00
☐ Green	45.00- 60.00
Sugar bowl	
☐ Clear	25.00- 40.00
☐ Yellow	35.00- 50.00
☐ Blue	45.00- 60.00
☐ Green	55.00- 70.00
Tray, bread	
☐ Clear	22.00- 37.00
☐ Yellow	30.00- 45.00
☐ Blue	45.00- 60.00
☐ Green	55.00- 70.00
Tray, W	
☐ Clear	20.00- 35.00
☐ Yellow	30.00- 45.00
☐ Blue	40.00- 55.00
☐ Green	45.00- 60.00
Tumbler	
☐ Clear	12.00- 20.00
☐ Yellow	20.00- 30.00
☐ Blue	20.00- 35.00
☐ Green	32.00- 47.00

BEADED ACORN MEDALLION (c. 1883)

	Price Range
☐ Butter dish, CVD	25.00- 40.00
☐ Champagne glass ...	27.00- 42.00
☐ Compote, high and low	42.00- 57.00
☐ Creamer	40.00- 55.00
☐ Egg cup	20.00- 30.00
☐ Goblet	22.00- 37.00
☐ Honey bowl	10.00- 18.00

	Price Range
☐ Pickle dish	10.00- 18.00
☐ Pitcher, W.........	35.00- 50.00
☐ Plate	20.00- 30.00
☐ Salt, FTD	15.00- 22.00
☐ Sauce dish	6.00- 12.00
☐ Spoon holder	25.00- 40.00
☐ Sugar bowl	45.00- 60.00
☐ Wine glass	12.00- 20.00

BEADED BAND (c. 1884)

☐ Goblet............	20.00- 35.00
☐ Jam jar	18.00- 26.00

BEADED DEWDROP (c. 1898)

☐ Butter plate, handled large and small ...	55.00- 70.00
☐ Cake plate	40.00- 55.00
☐ Celery vase	40.00- 55.00
☐ Celery tray	32.00- 47.00
☐ Condiment, 4-pc.	60.00- 75.00
☐ Creamer, lg./sm.	42.00- 57.00
☐ Cruet............	18.00- 26.00
☐ Cup/saucer........	20.00- 35.00
☐ Goblet............	40.00- 55.00
☐ Mug..............	32.00- 47.00
☐ Pitcher, W.........	55.00- 70.00
☐ Sauce dish, flat, handled	10.00- 18.00
☐ Shakers, sm./lg......	27.00- 42.00
☐ Spoon holder	20.00- 35.00
☐ Sugar bowl, lg./sm. ..	50.00- 65.00
☐ Toothpick holder	20.00- 35.00
☐ Tumbler	30.00- 45.00
☐ Wine glass	31.00- 46.00

BEADED GRAPE (c. 1880)

Bowl	
☐ Clear	18.00- 26.00
☐ Green	24.00- 39.00
Butter dish	
☐ Clear	43.00- 58.00
☐ Green	67.00- 82.00
Cake stand	
☐ Clear	40.00- 55.00
☐ Green	60.00- 75.00
Celery	
☐ Clear	32.00- 47.00
☐ Green	50.00- 65.00
Compote	
☐ Clear	35.00- 50.00
☐ Green	57.00- 72.00
Cordial glass	

	Price Range
☐ Clear	23.00- 38.00
☐ Green	35.00- 50.00
Creamer	
☐ Clear	40.00- 55.00
☐ Green	70.00- 85.00
Cruet	
☐ Clear	27.00- 42.00
☐ Green	50.00- 65.00
Dish	
☐ Clear	25.00- 40.00
☐ Green	45.00- 60.00
Pickle dish	
☐ Clear	12.00- 20.00
☐ Green	22.00- 37.00
Pitcher	
☐ Clear	45.00- 60.00
☐ Green	85.00-100.00
Platter	
☐ Clear	35.00- 50.00
☐ Green	60.00- 75.00
Shakers, S/P	
☐ Clear	31.00- 46.00
☐ Green	55.00- 70.00
Spoon holder	
☐ Clear	20.00- 35.00
☐ Green	35.00- 50.00
Sugar bowl	
☐ Clear	40.00- 55.00
☐ Green	60.00- 75.00

BEADED GRAPE MEDALLION (c. 1867)

☐ Celery vase	50.00- 65.00
☐ Compote, CVD	55.00- 70.00
☐ Cordial glass	33.00- 48.00
☐ Creamer	70.00- 85.00
☐ Egg cup	24.00- 39.00
☐ Goblet............	27.00- 42.00
☐ Honey bowl	12.00- 20.00
☐ Pickle dish	12.00- 20.00
☐ Pitcher, W.........	85.00-100.00
☐ Plate	18.00- 26.00
☐ Salt and pepper	12.00- 20.00
☐ Sauce dish	10.00- 18.00
☐ Spoon holder	25.00- 40.00
☐ Sugar bowl	45.00- 60.00

BEADED LOOP (c. 1906)

☐ Butter dish	27.00- 42.00
☐ Cake stand.........	32.00- 47.00
☐ Celery vase	27.00- 42.00
☐ Compote	20.00- 30.00

	Price Range
☐ Cordial glass	12.00- 20.00
☐ Creamer	21.00- 36.00
☐ Goblet..............	25.00- 40.00
☐ Mug...............	18.00- 26.00
☐ Pickle dish	15.00- 22.00
☐ Pitcher, W..........	40.00- 55.00
☐ Sauce dish	8.00- 12.00
☐ Salt and pepper	20.00- 30.00
☐ Sugar shaker	18.00- 26.00
☐ Spoon holder	25.00- 40.00
☐ Sugar bowl.........	25.00- 40.00
☐ Toothpick holder	8.00- 16.00
☐ Tray, bread	20.00- 30.00
☐ Tumbler	20.00- 30.00
☐ Wine glass	20.00- 35.00

BEADED TULIP (c. 1894)

☐ Butter dish	35.00- 50.00
☐ Compote, high	34.00- 49.00
☐ Cake stand	43.00- 58.00
☐ Cordial glass	24.00- 39.00
☐ Creamer	20.00- 35.00
☐ Dish, oval	12.00- 20.00
☐ Goblet.............	27.00- 42.00
☐ Jam jar	18.00- 26.00
☐ Lamp..............	24.00- 39.00
☐ Pickle dish	10.00- 18.00
☐ Pitcher, M..........	27.00- 42.00
☐ Pitcher, W..........	40.00- 55.00
☐ Plate, flat	20.00- 35.00
☐ Sauce dish, flat	8.00- 14.00
☐ Spoon holder	24.00- 39.00
☐ Sugar bowl	33.00- 48.00
☐ Tray, W	35.00- 50.00
☐ Wine glass	18.00- 26.00

BELLFLOWER (c. 1850)

☐ Bowl, berry and flat ..	95.00-110.00
☐ Butter dish	75.00- 90.00
☐ Castor bottle	30.00- 45.00
☐ Celery, banded and ribbed top	155.00-190.00
☐ Champagne	95.00-110.00
☐ Compote, CVD and open	155.00-190.00
☐ Cordial glass	75.00- 90.00
☐ Creamer	140.00-175.00
☐ Decanter, qt.	140.00-175.00
☐ Egg cup	40.00- 55.00
☐ Goblet.............	190.00-225.00
☐ Honey	20.00- 35.00
☐ Lamp, marble base ..	140.00-175.00

	Price Range
☐ Mug, applied handle .	110.00-145.00
☐ Pickle dish	95.00-110.00
☐ Pitcher, M..........	440.00-475.00
☐ Pitcher, syrup	240.00-275.00
☐ Pitcher, W..........	240.00-275.00
☐ Plate	60.00- 75.00
☐ Salt, CVD and open ..	140.00-175.00
☐ Sauce dish	20.00- 35.00
☐ Spoon holder	65.00- 80.00
☐ Sugar bowl.........	95.00-110.00
☐ Tumbler	70.00- 85.00
☐ Wine glass	80.00- 95.00

BIRD AND STRAWBERRY (c. 1890)

☐ Bowl, FTD..........	35.00- 50.00
☐ Butter dish	40.00- 55.00
☐ Candy dish	40.00- 55.00
☐ Cake stand	32.00- 47.00
☐ Compote, CVD and open	45.00- 60.00
☐ Creamer	35.00- 50.00
☐ Goblet.............	20.00- 35.00
☐ Pickle dish	40.00- 55.00
☐ Cup	10.00- 18.00
☐ Sauce dish	8.00- 16.00
☐ Spoon holder	18.00- 26.00
☐ Sugar bowl.........	45.00- 55.00
☐ Tumbler	15.00- 22.00
☐ Water set	275.00-310.00
☐ Wine glass	25.00- 40.00

BLACKBERRY (c. 1870)

Bowl	
☐ Clear	22.00- 37.00
☐ Milk Glass	50.00- 65.00
Champagne	
☐ Clear	37.00- 52.00
☐ Milk Glass	60.00- 75.00
Compote	
☐ Clear	75.00- 90.00
☐ Milk Glass	155.00-190.00
Creamer	
☐ Clear	50.00- 65.00
☐ Milk Glass	95.00-110.00
Dish	
☐ Clear	45.00- 60.00
☐ Milk Glass	95.00-110.00
Egg cup	
☐ Clear	35.00- 50.00
☐ Milk Glass	95.00-110.00
Goblet	
☐ Clear	35.00- 50.00

	Price Range
☐ Milk Glass	70.00- 85.00
Honey	
☐ Clear	12.00- 20.00
☐ Milk Glass	35.00- 50.00
Salt	
☐ Clear	23.00- 38.00
☐ Milk Glass	60.00- 75.00
Sauce dish	
☐ Clear	10.00- 18.00
☐ Milk Glass	20.00- 35.00
Spoon holder	
☐ Clear	40.00- 55.00
☐ Milk Glass	70.00- 85.00
Tumbler	
☐ Clear	20.00- 30.00
☐ Milk Glass	33.00- 48.00

BLEEDING HEART (c. 1870)

☐ Bowl	25.00- 40.00
☐ Butter dish	47.00- 62.00
☐ Cake stand	45.00- 60.00
☐ Compote, high, low	
and oval	55.00- 70.00
☐ Cordial glass	23.00- 38.00
☐ Creamer	40.00- 55.00
☐ Dish	10.00- 18.00
☐ Egg cup	25.00- 40.00
☐ Goblet, plain and	
knob stem	27.00- 42.00
☐ Mug	23.00- 38.00
☐ Pickle, oval and	
relish	50.00- 65.00
☐ Pitcher	65.00- 80.00
☐ Plate, cake	55.00- 70.00
☐ Platter	60.00- 75.00
☐ Salt and pepper	20.00- 35.00
☐ Sauce dish	12.00- 20.00
☐ Spoon holder	20.00- 30.00
☐ Sugar bowl	50.00- 65.00
☐ Tumbler	25.00- 40.00
☐ Wine glass	25.00- 40.00

BLOCK AND FAN (c. 1880)

	Price Range
☐ Butter dish	27.00- 42.00
☐ Cake stand	22.00- 37.00
☐ Carafe	35.00- 50.00
☐ Celery vase	20.00- 30.00
☐ Compote dish	20.00- 35.00
☐ Cordial glass	15.00- 22.00
☐ Creamer	21.00- 36.00
☐ Cruet, large and small	30.00- 45.00
☐ Goblet	20.00- 35.00
☐ Jam jar	18.00- 26.00
☐ Lamp	20.00- 35.00
☐ Pickle dish	10.00- 18.00
☐ Pitcher, W	25.00- 40.00
☐ Plate	18.00- 26.00
☐ Sauce dish	10.00- 10.00
☐ Salt and pepper	22.00- 37.00
☐ Spoon holder	18.00- 26.00
☐ Sugar bowl	27.00- 42.00
☐ Tumbler	15.00- 22.00
☐ Wine glass	20.00- 30.00

BROKEN COLUMN (c. 1891)

☐ Basket handle	70.00- 85.00
☐ Bowl, 6 styles	20.00- 35.00
☐ Butter dish	35.00- 50.00
☐ Cake stand	37.00- 52.00
☐ Carafe, W	35.00- 50.00
☐ Celery vase	30.00- 45.00
☐ Champagne glass	50.00- 65.00
☐ Compote, high	
and low	45.00- 60.00
☐ Cracker jar, CVD	70.00- 85.00
☐ Creamer	22.00- 37.00
☐ Cruet	20.00- 30.00
☐ Cup/saucer	25.00- 40.00
☐ Goblet	20.00- 30.00
☐ Jam jar	45.00- 60.00
☐ Pickle dish	10.00- 18.00
☐ Plate	25.00- 40.00

Price Range		
☐ Sauce dish	8.00-	14.00
☐ Shakers	20.00-	35.00
☐ Sugar bowl	95.00-	110.00
☐ Tumbler	18.00-	26.00
☐ Wine glass	40.00-	55.00

BUCKLE (c. 1870)

☐ Bowl	34.00-	49.00
☐ Butter dish	70.00-	85.00
☐ Champagne glass ...	90.00-	105.00
☐ Compote, high		
and low	70.00-	85.00
☐ Cordial glass	45.00-	60.00
☐ Creamer	70.00-	85.00
☐ Dish, sm.	4.00-	12.00
☐ Dish, oval	30.00-	35.00
☐ Egg cup, DBL	30.00-	45.00
☐ Goblet.............	40.00-	55.00
☐ Mug..............	25.00-	40.00
☐ Pickle dish	27.00-	42.00
☐ Pitcher, W........	95.00-	110.00
☐ Salt and pepper	18.00-	26.00
☐ Sauce dish	12.00-	20.00
☐ Spoon holder	45.00-	60.00
☐ Sugar bowl	50.00-	65.00
☐ Tumbler	32.00-	47.00
☐ Wine glass	45.00-	60.00

BUDDED IVY (1870)

☐ Compote, high		
and low	50.00-	65.00
☐ Creamer	43.00-	58.00
☐ Goblet.............	35.00-	50.00
☐ Mug..............	25.00-	40.00
☐ Pickle	10.00-	25.00
☐ Pitcher, W........	45.00-	60.00
☐ Salt and pepper	12.00-	27.00
☐ Sauce dish	8.00-	14.00
☐ Spoon holder	30.00-	45.00
☐ Sugar bowl	40.00-	55.00

BULL'S EYE (c. 1870)

Price Range		
☐ Butter dish	85.00-	100.00
☐ Celery vase	50.00-	65.00
☐ Champagne vase....	70.00-	85.00
☐ Cologne	60.00-	75.00
☐ Compote, high		
and low	70.00-	85.00
☐ Cordial glass	34.00-	49.00
☐ Creamer	70.00-	85.00
☐ Cruet, small	45.00-	60.00
☐ Decanter...........	52.00-	67.00
☐ Egg cup, DBL	49.00-	55.00
☐ Goblet.............	45.00-	60.00
☐ Jar, CVD	55.00-	70.00
☐ Lamp.............	95.00-	110.00
☐ Pickle dish	30.00-	45.00
☐ Salt and pepper	35.00-	50.00
☐ Spoon holder	40.00-	55.00
☐ Sugar bowl	80.00-	95.00
☐ Tumbler	55.00-	70.00
☐ Water bottle	55.00-	70.00
☐ Wine bottle.........	40.00-	55.00

BULL'S EYE WITH DIAMOND POINT (c. 1850)

☐ Bowl	70.00-	85.00
☐ Butter dish	115.00-	150.00
☐ Celery vase	80.00-	95.00
☐ Champagne glass ...	70.00-	85.00
☐ Cologne	74.00-	89.00
☐ Compote, high		
and low	115.00-	150.00
☐ Cordial glass	60.00-	75.00
☐ Creamer	140.00-	175.00
☐ Decanter, pt. & qt.	95.00-	110.00
☐ Egg cup	80.00-	95.00
Goblet glass		
☐ Lemonade	55.00-	70.00
☐ Water	55.00-	70.00
☐ Whiskey, rosette	38.00-	53.00

	Price Range
☐ Honey dish	30.00- 45.00
☐ Mustard jar	60.00- 75.00
☐ Pitcher	140.00-175.00
☐ Sauce dish	20.00- 35.00
☐ Spoon Holder	60.00- 75.00
☐ Sugar bowl	95.00-110.00
☐ Water bottle	120.00-155.00
☐ Wine glass	55.00- 70.00

BULL'S EYE WITH FLEUR-DE-LIS (c. 1850)

	Price Range
☐ Bowl, berry	80.00- 95.00
☐ Butter dish	95.00-110.00
☐ Celery vase	82.00- 97.00
☐ Compote, high and low	95.00-110.00
☐ Cordial glass	45.00- 60.00
☐ Creamer	110.00-145.00
☐ Decanter, pt. & qt.	75.00- 90.00
☐ Goblet	55.00- 70.00
☐ Lamp	110.00-145.00
☐ Pitcher, W	265.00-300.00
☐ Plate	70.00- 85.00
☐ Salt, FTD	35.00- 50.00
☐ Sugar bowl	105.00-140.00

CABBAGE ROSE (c. 1870)

	Price Range
☐ Butter dish	75.00- 90.00
☐ Cake stand	57.00- 72.00
☐ Celery vase	42.00- 57.00
☐ Compote	55.00- 70.00
☐ Cordial glass	29.00- 44.00
☐ Creamer	52.00- 67.00
☐ Egg cup, DBL	20.00- 35.00
☐ Pickle dish	15.00- 22.00
☐ Pitcher	75.00- 90.00
☐ Plate	140.00-175.00
☐ Salt and pepper	15.00- 22.00
☐ Sauce dish	10.00- 20.00
☐ Spoon holder	40.00- 55.00
☐ Sugar bowl	52.00- 67.00
☐ Tumbler	30.00- 45.00
☐ Wine glass	35.00- 50.00

CABLE (c. 1850)

	Price Range
☐ Butter dish	75.00- 90.00
☐ Celery vase	65.00- 80.00
☐ Champagne glass	70.00- 85.00
☐ Compote, high and low	70.00- 85.00
☐ Cordial glass	60.00- 75.00

	Price Range
☐ Creamer	77.00- 92.00
☐ Decanter, pt. & qt.	165.00-200.00
☐ Egg cup	27.00- 42.00
☐ Goblet	50.00- 65.00
☐ Honey	12.00- 20.00
☐ Lamp, marble base	110.00-145.00
☐ Mug	62.00- 77.00
☐ Pitcher, W	240.00-275.00
☐ Plate	45.00- 65.00
☐ Salt and pepper	40.00- 55.00
☐ Sauce dish	12.00- 20.00
☐ Spoon holder	45.00- 60.00
☐ Sugar bowl/creamer	130.00-165.00
☐ Tumbler, FTD	80.00- 95.00
☐ Wine glass	70.00- 85.00

CANADIAN (c. 1870)

	Price Range
☐ Celery dish	30.00- 45.00
☐ Compote, CVD	45.00- 60.00
☐ Cordial glass	20.00- 35.00
☐ Creamer	35.00- 50.00
☐ Goblet	25.00- 40.00
☐ Jam jar	22.00- 37.00
☐ Pitcher, lg./sm.	60.00- 75.00
☐ Plate	25.00- 40.00
☐ Sauce dish	8.00- 14.00
☐ Spoon holder	27.00- 42.00
☐ Sugar bowl	37.00- 52.00
☐ Wine glass	25.00- 40.00

CANE (c. 1875)

	Price Range
☐ Bowl, berry	20.00- 30.00
☐ Yellow	23.00- 38.00
☐ Blue	27.00- 42.00
☐ Green	20.00- 35.00
☐ Bowl, waste	15.00- 22.00
☐ Yellow	20.00- 35.00
☐ Blue	23.00- 38.00
☐ Green	18.00- 26.00
☐ Butter dish	31.00- 46.00
☐ Yellow	40.00- 55.00

	Price Range
☐ Blue	45.00- 60.00
☐ Green	35.00- 50.00
☐ Compote	23.00- 38.00
☐ Yellow	37.00- 52.00
☐ Blue	50.00- 65.00
☐ Green	35.00- 50.00
☐ Cordial	20.00- 35.00
☐ Yellow	30.00- 45.00
☐ Blue	35.00- 50.00
☐ Green	25.00- 40.00
☐ Creamer	20.00- 30.00
☐ Yellow	32.00- 47.00
☐ Blue	43.00- 58.00
☐ Green	35.00- 50.00
☐ Goblet	20.00- 30.00
☐ Yellow	25.00- 40.00
☐ Blue	30.00- 45.00
☐ Green	20.00- 35.00
☐ Jam jar	15.00- 22.00
☐ Yellow	25.00- 40.00
☐ Blue	32.00- 47.00
☐ Green	25.00- 40.00
☐ Pickle dish	12.00- 20.00
☐ Yellow	19.00- 34.00
☐ Blue	23.00- 38.00
☐ Green	20.00- 30.00
☐ Pitcher, W	21.00- 36.00
☐ Yellow	35.00- 50.00
☐ Blue	45.00- 60.00
☐ Green	30.00- 45.00
☐ Sauce dish	8.00- 14.00
☐ Yellow	15.00- 22.00
☐ Blue	18.00- 26.00
☐ Green	12.00- 20.00
☐ Salt and pepper	20.00- 35.00
☐ Yellow	30.00- 45.00
☐ Blue	35.00- 50.00
☐ Green	25.00- 40.00
☐ Spoon holder	18.00- 26.00
☐ Yellow	20.00- 35.00
☐ Blue	30.00- 45.00
☐ Green	18.00- 26.00
☐ Sugar bowl	27.00- 42.00
☐ Yellow	43.00- 58.00
☐ Blue	52.00- 67.00
☐ Green	37.00- 52.00
☐ Tray	23.00- 38.00
☐ Yellow	35.00- 50.00
☐ Blue	45.00- 60.00
☐ Green	30.00- 45.00
☐ Tumbler	15.00- 22.00
☐ Yellow	20.00- 30.00
☐ Blue	25.00- 40.00
☐ Green	20.00- 30.00

CARDINAL BIRD (c. 1870)

	Price Range
☐ Cake stand	32.00- 47.00
☐ Compote, CVD	40.00- 55.00
☐ Creamer	32.00- 47.00
☐ Goblet	30.00- 45.00
☐ Honey dish	10.00- 18.00
☐ Mug	35.00- 50.00
☐ Pitcher	55.00- 70.00
☐ Sauce dish	15.00- 20.00
☐ Spoon holder	32.00- 47.00
☐ Sugar bowl	37.00- 52.00

CHAIN (c. 1880)

☐ Butter dish	37.00- 52.00
☐ Cake stand	20.00- 30.00
☐ Compote, CVD	30.00- 45.00
☐ Cordial glass	20.00- 30.00
☐ Creamer	32.00- 47.00
☐ Dish	12.00- 20.00
☐ Goblet	18.00- 26.00
☐ Pickle dish	18.00- 26.00
☐ Pitcher, W	30.00- 45.00
☐ Plate	12.00- 20.00
☐ Platter, large	20.00- 30.00
☐ Sauce, flat & FTD	12.00- 20.00
☐ Salt and pepper	18.00- 26.00
☐ Spoon holder	23.00- 38.00
☐ Sugar bowl	35.00- 50.00
☐ Wine glass	20.00- 35.00

CHAIN WITH STAR (c. 1880)

☐ Butter dish	30.00- 45.00
☐ Cake stand	20.00- 30.00
☐ Compote, high and low	27.00- 42.00
☐ Cordial glass	18.00- 26.00
☐ Creamer	18.00- 26.00
☐ Dish	15.00- 22.00
☐ Goblet	15.00- 22.00
☐ Pickle dish	10.00- 18.00
☐ Pitcher, W	32.00- 47.00
☐ Plate	20.00- 35.00
☐ Sauce dish	12.00- 20.00
☐ Shakers, S/P	18.00- 26.00
☐ Spoon holder	22.00- 37.00
☐ Sugar bowl	30.00- 45.00
☐ Wine glass	20.00- 30.00

CHAMPION (c. 1880)

☐ Toothpick, green	40.00- 55.00
☐ Water set	45.00- 60.00

Price Range

CHANDELIER (c. 1800)

☐ Bowl, berry and finger	15.00- 22.00
☐ Butter dish	27.00- 42.00
☐ Celery dish	23.00- 38.00
☐ Compote, CVD	
and open	35.00- 50.00
☐ Creamer	20.00- 35.00
☐ Goblet	40.00- 55.00
☐ Pitcher, W	34.00- 49.00
☐ Sauce, flat	10.00- 18.00
☐ Spoon holder	20.00- 35.00
☐ Sugar, CVD	25.00- 40.00
☐ Tray, W	30.00- 45.00
☐ Tumbler	20.00- 30.00
☐ Wine glass	20.00- 35.00

CHECKERBOARD (c. 1880)

☐ Bowl, sm./lg.	10.00- 18.00
☐ Butter dish	20.00- 35.00
☐ Celery dish	10.00- 18.00
☐ Celery vase	18.00- 26.00
☐ Cheese dish	20.00- 30.00
☐ Creamer	18.00- 26.00
☐ Cruet, small	18.00- 26.00
☐ Goblet	12.00- 20.00
☐ Pickle dish	8.00- 14.00
☐ Pitcher, M/W	25.00- 40.00
☐ Plate	12.00- 20.00
☐ Punch cup	6.00- 12.00
☐ Sauce dish	6.00- 12.00
☐ Shakers, S/P	15.00- 22.00
☐ Sherbet dish	8.00- 14.00
☐ Spoon holder	15.00- 22.00
☐ Sugar bowl	20.00- 35.00
☐ Tumbler	10.00- 18.00
☐ Wine glass	6.00- 12.00

CLEAR DIAGONAL BAND (c. 1870)

☐ Butter dish	32.00- 47.00
☐ Celery dish	27.00- 42.00
☐ Compote, high	
and low	33.00- 48.00
☐ Cordial glass	18.00- 26.00
☐ Creamer	30.00- 45.00
☐ Goblet	20.00- 30.00
☐ Jam jar	20.00- 30.00
☐ Pitcher, M	22.00- 37.00
☐ Plate	15.00- 23.00
☐ Platter	35.00- 50.00
☐ Sauce, FTD	8.00- 14.00
☐ Shakers, S/P	23.00- 38.00
☐ Spoon holder	23.00- 30.00
☐ Sugar bowl	32.00- 47.00

Price Range

CLEAR RIBBON (c. 1880)

☐ Butter dish	42.00- 57.00
☐ Cake stand	55.00- 70.00
☐ Celery vase	20.00- 35.00
☐ Compote, large	60.00- 75.00
☐ Creamer	32.00- 47.00
☐ Dish	32.00- 47.00
☐ Goblet	30.00- 45.00
☐ Mug	15.00- 30.00
☐ Pickle	21.00- 36.00
☐ Pitcher	57.00- 72.00
☐ Platter	30.00- 45.00
☐ Sauce dish	8.00- 16.00
☐ Spoon holder	30.00- 45.00
☐ Sugar bowl	40.00- 55.00

CLEMANTIS (c. 1876)

☐ Bowl, berry	15.00- 22.00
☐ Butter dish	34.00- 49.00
☐ Creamer	30.00- 45.00
☐ Goblet	22.00- 37.00
☐ Lamp	20.00- 25.00
☐ Pickle dish	8.00- 14.00
☐ Pitcher, W	37.00- 52.00
☐ Sauce dish	8.00- 14.00
☐ Spoon holder	20.00- 30.00
☐ Sugar bowl, CVD	35.00- 50.00

COLUMBIAN-COIN (c. 1870)

☐ Bowl, berry and finger	80.00- 95.00
☐ Butter plate	110.00-145.00
☐ Cake stand	85.00-100.00
☐ Celery dish	70.00- 85.00
☐ Compote, open	130.00-165.00
☐ Creamer	60.00- 75.00
☐ Cruet	95.00-110.00
☐ Goblet	75.00- 90.00
☐ Lamp	100.00-135.00
☐ Pickle dish	37.00- 52.00
☐ Pitcher, M/W	140.00-175.00
☐ Sauce dish	23.00- 38.00
☐ Shakers, S/P	90.00-105.00
☐ Spoon holder	57.00- 72.00
☐ Sugar bowl	105.00-140.00
☐ Toothpick	55.00- 70.00
☐ Tray, W	90.00-105.00
☐ Tumbler	30.00- 45.00

CORD AND TASSEL (c. 1870)

☐ Butter plate	30.00- 45.00
☐ Cake stand	30.00- 45.00

	Price	Range
☐ Celery tray	27.00-	42.00
☐ Compote, high		
and low	32.00-	47.00
☐ Cordial glass	18.00-	26.00
☐ Creamer	30.00-	45.00
☐ Dish	10.00-	18.00
☐ Egg dish, DBL	12.00-	20.00
☐ Goblet	20.00-	30.00
☐ Lamp..............	30.00-	45.00
☐ Pitcher S/M	40.00-	55.00
☐ Sauce dish	10.00-	18.00
☐ Spoon holder	22.00-	37.00
☐ Sugar bowl	30.00-	45.00
☐ Tumbler	15.00-	22.00
☐ Wine glass	20.00-	30.00

CORDOVA (c. 1890)

	Price	Range
☐ Bottle, perfume	27.00-	42.00
☐ Bowl, CVD, finger		
and open	15.00-	22.00
☐ Butter plate	18.00-	26.00
☐ Cake stand	15.00-	26.00
☐ Celery vase	12.00-	20.00
☐ Compote, CVD		
and open	20.00-	35.00
☐ Creamer	12.00-	20.00
☐ Cruet, small	12.00-	20.00
☐ Pitcher, W/S/M	20.00-	35.00
☐ Cup	6.00-	12.00
☐ Sauce dish	3.00-	9.00
☐ Spoon holder	10.00-	18.00
☐ Sugar bowl	15.00-	22.00
☐ Toothpick holder	8.00-	14.00
☐ Tumbler	8.00-	14.00

COTTAGE (c. 1870)

	Price	Range
☐ Banana dish	18.00-	26.00
☐ Bowl	8.00-	14.00
☐ Butter dish	20.00-	30.00
☐ Cake stand	20.00-	30.00
☐ Celery tray	15.00-	22.00
☐ Compote, low		
and high	25.00-	40.00
☐ Creamer	20.00-	30.00
☐ Cruet, small	10.00-	18.00
☐ Cup/saucer.........	10.00-	18.00
☐ Dish	8.00-	14.00
☐ Goblet.............	12.00-	20.00
☐ Pickle dish	8.00-	14.00
☐ Pitcher, pt. & qt......	18.00-	26.00
☐ Plate	12.00-	20.00
☐ Sauce dish	3.00-	9.00
☐ Salt and pepper	8.00-	14.00

	Price	Range
☐ Spoon holder	12.00-	20.00
☐ Sugar bowl	20.00-	35.00
☐ Tray, W	18.00-	26.00
☐ Tumbler	8.00-	14.00
☐ Wine glass	10.00-	18.00

CROESUS (c. 1897)

	Price	Range
☐ Bowl	45.00-	60.00
☐ Butter dish	80.00-	95.00
☐ Celery tray	50.00-	65.00
☐ Compote, jam	70.00-	85.00
☐ Creamer	60.00-	75.00
☐ Cruet, small	55.00-	70.00
☐ Pickle dish	22.00-	37.00
☐ Pitcher, W..........	85.00-	100.00
☐ Plate	67.00-	82.00
☐ Relish dish	30.00-	45.00
☐ Sauce dish	15.00-	22.00
☐ Shakers, S/P........	35.00-	50.00
☐ Spoon holder	33.00-	48.00
☐ Sugar bowl	80.00-	95.00
☐ Toothpick holder	25.00-	40.00
☐ Tumbler	22.00-	37.00

CROW'S FOOT (c. 1895)

	Price	Range
☐ Butter dish	25.00-	40.00
☐ Cake stand	25.00-	40.00
☐ Celery tray	18.00-	26.00

	Price Range
☐ Compote	27.00- 42.00
☐ Cordial glass	12.00- 20.00
☐ Creamer	20.00- 30.00
☐ Goblet	18.00- 26.00
☐ Pitcher, W/S	25.00- 40.00
☐ Plate	18.00- 26.00
☐ Relish	12.00- 20.00
☐ Sauce dish	8.00- 14.00
☐ Shaker, S/P	20.00- 30.00
☐ Spoon holder	15.00- 22.00
☐ Sugar bowl	20.00- 30.00
☐ Tumbler	12.00- 20.00

CRYSTAL (c. 1860)

	Price Range
☐ Ale glass	20.00- 30.00
☐ Bowl	35.00- 50.00
☐ Butter plate	37.00- 52.00
☐ Celery vase	25.00- 40.00
☐ Champagne glass . . .	27.00- 42.00
☐ Compote	40.00- 55.00
☐ Cordial glass	20.00- 30.00
☐ Creamer	35.00- 50.00
☐ Decanter, pt. & qt. . . .	40.00- 55.00
☐ Egg cup	23.00- 38.00
☐ Goblet	27.00- 42.00
☐ Mug	25.00- 40.00
☐ Pitcher, W	65.00- 80.00
☐ Sauce dish	10.00- 18.00
☐ Spoon holder	23.00- 38.00
☐ Sugar bowl	52.00- 68.00
☐ Tumbler	35.00- 50.00
☐ Wine glass	30.00- 45.00

CRYSTAL WEDDING (c. 1880)

	Price Range
☐ Bowl, berry	34.00- 49.00
☐ Butter dish	34.00- 49.00
☐ Cake stand	45.00- 60.00
☐ Celery vase	23.00- 38.00
☐ Creamer	24.00- 39.00
☐ Dish, CVD	50.00- 65.00
☐ Lamp	27.00- 42.00
☐ Mug	25.00- 40.00
☐ Pitcher, W	45.00- 60.00
☐ Sauce dish	8.00- 14.00
☐ Shakers, S/P	20.00- 35.00
☐ Spoon holder	20.00- 35.00
☐ Sugar bowl	37.00- 52.00
☐ Tumbler	15.00- 22.00

CUPID AND VENUS (c. 1870)

	Price Range
☐ Bowl	50.00- 65.00
☐ Butter plate	70.00- 85.00

	Price Range
☐ Celery tray	37.00- 52.00
☐ Champagne glass . . .	45.00- 60.00
☐ Compote, high and low	52.00- 67.00
☐ Cordial glass	40.00- 55.00
☐ Creamer	35.00- 50.00
☐ Cruet, small	32.00- 47.00
☐ Dish, large and small	20.00- 35.00
☐ Goblet	45.00- 60.00
☐ Jam jar	40.00- 55.00
☐ Mug	25.00- 40.00
☐ Pickle dish	15.00- 22.00
☐ Pitcher, W/M	45.00- 60.00
☐ Plate	34.00- 49.00
☐ Sauce dish	10.00- 18.00
☐ Spoon holder	35.00- 50.00
☐ Sugar bowl	50.00- 65.00
☐ Tray	30.00- 45.00

CURRIER AND IVES (c. 1880)

	Price Range
☐ Butter plate	32.00- 47.00
☐ Cordial glass	15.00- 22.00
☐ Creamer	20.00- 30.00
☐ Cup/saucer	23.00- 38.00
☐ Decanter, qt.	20.00- 35.00
☐ Dish	20.00- 30.00
☐ Goblet	20.00- 30.00
☐ Lamp	20.00- 35.00
☐ Mug	25.00- 40.00
☐ Pitcher, sm./lg.	25.00- 40.00
☐ Plate	20.00- 35.00
☐ Sauce dish	6.00- 12.00
☐ Shakers, S/P	20.00- 30.00
☐ Spoon holder	15.00- 22.00
☐ Sugar bowl	29.00- 44.00
☐ Tray	32.00- 47.00
☐ Wine glass	15.00- 22.00

CURTAIN (c. 1880)

	Price Range
☐ Bowl, berry	8.00- 14.00
☐ Bowl	15.00- 22.00
☐ Butter dish	34.00- 49.00
☐ Cake stand	20.00- 35.00
☐ Celery tray	22.00- 37.00
☐ Compote	40.00- 60.00
☐ Creamer	30.00- 45.00
☐ Goblet	18.00- 26.00
☐ Mug	15.00- 22.00
☐ Pickle dish	18.00- 26.00
☐ Pitcher, W/M	35.00- 50.00
☐ Plate, sq.	18.00- 26.00
☐ Sauce, FTD	10.00- 18.00
☐ Shakers, S/P	18.00- 26.00

	Price Range
☐ Spoon holder	22.00- 37.00
☐ Tray, bread	25.00- 40.00
☐ Tumbler	20.00- 30.00

CUT LOG (c. 1880)

	Price Range
☐ Butter dish	35.00- 50.00
☐ Cake stand	43.00- 58.00
☐ Celery tray	20.00- 35.00
☐ Compote, CVD and open	32.00- 47.00
☐ Cracker bowl	25.00- 40.00
☐ Creamer	20.00- 30.00
☐ Cruet	15.00- 22.00
☐ Goblet	27.00- 42.00
☐ Honey dish	15.00- 22.00
☐ Mug	15.00- 22.00
☐ Mustard dish	10.00- 18.00
☐ Pickle dish	10.00- 18.00
☐ Pitcher, W	35.00- 50.00
☐ Sauce dish	6.00- 12.00
☐ Shakers, S/P	15.00- 22.00
☐ Spoon holder	18.00- 24.00
☐ Sugar bowl	24.00- 39.00
☐ Tumbler	10.00- 18.00
☐ Wine glass	20.00- 30.00

DAHLIA (c. 1880)

	Price Range
Butter plate	
☐ Clear	37.00- 52.00
☐ Blue	45.00- 60.00
Cake stand	
☐ Clear	23.00- 38.00
☐ Green	37.00- 52.00
Champagne glass	
☐ Yellow	50.00- 65.00
☐ Blue	33.00- 48.00
Compote	
☐ Clear	50.00- 65.00
☐ Blue	60.00- 75.00
Cordial glass	
☐ Yellow	50.00- 65.00
☐ Green	40.00- 55.00
Creamer	
☐ Clear	20.00- 30.00
☐ Green	25.00- 40.00
Egg cup	
☐ Yellow	65.00- 80.00
☐ Green	55.00- 70.00
Goblet	
☐ Blue	40.00- 55.00
☐ Green	47.00- 62.00
Mug, large	

	Price Range
☐ Clear	32.00- 47.00
☐ Yellow	60.00- 75.00
Mug	
☐ Blue	30.00- 45.00
☐ Green	37.00- 52.00
Pickle dish	
☐ Clear	15.00- 22.00
☐ Yellow	30.00- 45.00
Pitcher, M	
☐ Clear	30.00- 45.00
☐ Blue	40.00- 55.00
Plate	
☐ Clear	20.00- 30.00
☐ Yellow	40.00- 55.00
☐ Blue	27.00- 42.00
☐ Green	32.00- 47.00
Platter	
☐ Blue	41.00- 56.00
☐ Green	50.00- 65.00
Sauce dish	
☐ Clear	18.00- 18.00
☐ Yellow	23.00- 40.00
Spoon holder	
☐ Clear	20.00- 35.00
☐ Green	35.00- 50.00
Sugar bowl	
☐ Yellow	60.00- 75.00
☐ Green	50.00- 65.00
Wine glass	
☐ Clear	25.00- 40.00
☐ Green	40.00- 55.00

DAISY AND BUTTON WITH CROSS BARS (c. 1888)

	Price Range
Bowl	
☐ Clear	18.00- 26.00
☐ Vaseline	30.00- 45.00
Butter plate	
☐ Clear	23.00- 38.00
☐ Vaseline	42.00- 57.00
Butter dish	

	Price Range			Price Range
☐ Clear	33.00- 48.00		☐ Blue	30.00- 45.00
☐ Vaseline	45.00- 60.00		Butter dish	
Celery Vase			☐ Clear	24.00- 39.00
☐ Clear	30.00- 45.00		☐ Blue	52.00- 67.00
☐ Vaseline	35.00- 50.00		Celery vase	
Compote				
☐ Clear	40.00- 55.00			
☐ Vaseline	60.00- 75.00			
Creamer				
☐ Clear	21.00- 36.00			
☐ Vaseline	33.00- 48.00			
Cruet				
☐ Clear	27.00- 42.00			
☐ Vaseline	47.00- 62.00			
Goblet				
☐ Clear	20.00- 30.00		☐ Clear	20.00- 35.00
☐ Vaseline	31.00- 46.00		☐ Blue	45.00- 60.00
Mug			Creamer	
☐ Clear	18.00- 26.00		☐ Clear	20.00- 30.00
☐ Vaseline	22.00- 37.00		☐ Blue	40.00- 55.00
Pickle dish			Goblet	
☐ Clear	10.00- 18.00		☐ Clear	15.00- 22.00
☐ Vaseline	20.00- 30.00		☐ Blue	37.00- 52.00
Pitcher			Mug	
☐ Clear	21.00- 36.00		☐ Clear	12.00- 20.00
☐ Vaseline	32.00- 47.00		☐ Blue	21.00- 36.00
Sauce dish			Pitcher	
☐ Clear	6.00- 12.00		☐ Clear	35.00- 50.00
☐ Vaseline	12.00- 20.00		☐ Blue	67.00- 82.00
Shakers, S/P			Punch	
☐ Clear	20.00- 30.00		☐ Clear	3.00- 9.00
☐ Vaseline	33.00- 48.00		☐ Blue	18.00- 26.00
Spoon holder			Sauce dish	
☐ Clear	18.00- 26.00		☐ Clear	8.00- 14.00
☐ Vaseline	30.00- 45.00		☐ Blue	15.00- 22.00
Sugar bowl			Spoon holder	
☐ Clear	30.00- 45.00		☐ Clear	15.00- 22.00
☐ Vaseline	41.00- 56.00		☐ Blue	33.00- 48.00
Toothpick holder			Sugar bowl	
☐ Clear	10.00- 18.00		☐ Clear	21.00- 36.00
☐ Vaseline	20.00- 30.00		☐ Blue	50.00- 65.00
Tray			Toothpick holder	
☐ Clear	10.00- 18.00		☐ Clear	10.00- 18.00
☐ Vaseline	20.00- 30.00		☐ Blue	20.00- 35.00
Tray, bread			Tray	
☐ Clear	25.00- 40.00		☐ Clear	25.00- 40.00
☐ Vaseline	35.00- 50.00		☐ Blue	45.00- 60.00
Tumbler			Tumbler	
☐ Clear	12.00- 20.00		☐ Clear	10.00- 18.00
☐ Vaseline	20.00- 30.00		☐ Blue	23.00- 38.00

DAISY AND BUTTON (c. 1887)

Bowl
☐ Clear 12.00- 20.00

Price Range

DAKOTA (c. 1890)

☐ Basket	50.00- 65.00
☐ Butter dish	23.00- 38.00
☐ Bowl, berry	20.00- 30.00
☐ Bowl, finger	18.00- 26.00
☐ Celery vase	23.00- 38.00
☐ Compote	35.00- 50.00
☐ Creamer	23.00- 38.00
☐ Goblet	25.00- 40.00
☐ Jam jar	18.00- 26.00
☐ Mug	15.00- 22.00
☐ Pitcher	45.00- 60.00
☐ Plate	18.00- 26.00
☐ Salt and pepper	22.00- 37.00
☐ Spoon holder	25.00- 40.00
☐ Sugar bowl, CVD	40.00- 55.00
☐ Sugar bowl, etched ..	20.00- 35.00
☐ Tumbler	18.00- 26.00
☐ Wine glass	18.00- 26.00

DEER AND PINE TREE (c. 1860)

☐ Butter dish	53.00- 68.00
☐ Cake stand	65.00- 80.00
☐ Celery vase	45.00- 60.00
☐ Compote, CVD	65.00- 80.00
☐ Creamer	43.00- 58.00
☐ Jam jar	35.00- 50.00
☐ Mug, sm./lg.	30.00- 45.00
☐ Pickle dish	18.00- 26.00
☐ Pitcher	83.00- 98.00
☐ Platter	40.00- 55.00
☐ Salt	12.00- 20.00
☐ Sauce, FTD	15.00- 22.00
☐ Spoon holder	35.00- 50.00
☐ Sugar bowl	55.00- 70.00
☐ Tray, bread	67.00- 82.00

DELAWARE (c. 1899)

Banana
☐ Clear	20.00- 35.00
☐ Cranberry	35.00- 50.00
☐ Green	60.00- 75.00

Bowl, berry
☐ Clear	20.00- 35.00
☐ Cranberry	40.00- 55.00
☐ Green	45.00- 60.00

Butter dish
☐ Clear	33.00- 48.00
☐ Cranberry	90.00-105.00
☐ Green	95.00-110.00

Celery

Price Range

☐ Clear	20.00- 30.00
☐ Cranberry	60.00- 75.00
☐ Green	70.00- 85.00

Creamer
☐ Clear	22.00- 37.00
☐ Cranberry	45.00- 60.00
☐ Green	80.00- 95.00

Cruet
☐ Clear	20.00- 30.00
☐ Cranberry	52.00- 67.00
☐ Green	70.00- 85.00

Pitcher

☐ Clear	30.00- 45.00
☐ Cranberry	95.00-110.00
☐ Green	115.00-150.00

Punch
☐ Clear	10.00- 18.00
☐ Cranberry	25.00- 40.00
☐ Green	30.00- 45.00

Sauce dish
☐ Clear	10.00- 18.00
☐ Cranberry	21.00- 36.00
☐ Green	30.00- 45.00

Spoon holder
☐ Clear	18.00- 26.00
☐ Cranberry	50.00- 65.00
☐ Green	60.00- 75.00

Sugar bowl
☐ Clear	30.00- 45.00
☐ Cranberry	95.00-110.00
☐ Green	115.00-150.00

Toothpick holder
☐ Clear	10.00- 18.00
☐ Cranberry	25.00- 40.00
☐ Green	30.00- 45.00

Tray
☐ Clear	30.00- 45.00
☐ Cranberry	60.00- 75.00
☐ Green	95.00-110.00

Tumbler
☐ Clear	18.00- 26.00
☐ Cranberry	32.00- 47.00
☐ Green	32.00- 57.00

DEW AND RAINDROP (c. 1900)

Price Range

☐ Banana	75.00- 90.00
☐ Bowl, berry	34.00- 49.00
☐ Butter plate	47.00- 62.00
☐ Cordial glass	32.00- 47.00
☐ Creamer	40.00- 55.00
☐ Cup	22.00- 37.00
☐ Pitcher, W.	55.00- 70.00
☐ Sauce dish	10.00- 18.00
☐ Shakers, S/P	35.00- 50.00
☐ Spoon holder	30.00- 45.00
☐ Sugar bowl	50.00- 65.00
☐ Tumbler	27.00- 42.00

DEWEY (c. 1894)

Butter plate
☐ Clear	20.00- 30.00
☐ Yellow	45.00- 60.00
☐ Green	50.00- 65.00

Creamer
☐ Clear	20.00- 30.00
☐ Vaseline	33.00- 48.00
☐ Green	40.00- 55.00

Cruet
☐ Clear	20.00- 35.00
☐ Green	45.00- 60.00

Mug
☐ Clear	30.00- 45.00
☐ Green	60.00- 75.00

Pitcher
☐ Clear	33.00- 48.00
☐ Green	73.00- 88.00

Plate
☐ Clear	20.00- 35.00
☐ Vaseline	35.00- 50.00
☐ Green	45.00- 60.00

Sauce dish
☐ Clear	6.00- 12.00
☐ Vaseline, set	240.00-275.00
☐ Green	18.00- 26.00

Shakers, S/P
☐ Clear	20.00- 30.00
☐ Vaseline	50.00- 65.00
☐ Green	55.00- 70.00

Spoon holder
☐ Clear	20.00- 30.00
☐ Vaseline	18.00- 26.00
☐ Green	40.00- 55.00

Sugar bowl
☐ Clear	20.00- 35.00
☐ Vaseline	40.00- 55.00
☐ Green	50.00- 65.00

Tumbler

Price Range

☐ Clear	18.00- 26.00
☐ Vaseline	27.00- 42.00
☐ Green	32.00- 47.00

DIAMOND POINT (c. 1890)

☐ Bowl	45.00- 60.00
☐ Butter plate	70.00- 85.00
☐ Celery vase	45.00- 60.00
☐ Champagne glass . . .	70.00- 85.00
☐ Compote, high and low	87.00-102.00
☐ Cordial glass	60.00- 75.00
☐ Creamer	80.00- 95.00
☐ Cruet, sm.	70.00- 85.00
☐ Decanter, sm./lg.	70.00- 85.00
☐ Dish	40.00- 55.00
☐ Egg cup	30.00- 45.00
☐ Goblet	43.00- 58.00
☐ Honey	18.00- 26.00
☐ Lamp	115.00-150.00
☐ Mug	40.00- 55.00
☐ Pitcher, sm./lg.	80.00- 95.00
☐ Plate	20.00- 35.00
☐ Salt and pepper	45.00- 55.00
☐ Sauce dish	15.00- 22.00
☐ Spoon holder	50.00- 65.00
☐ Sugar bowl	95.00-110.00
☐ Wine glass	65.00- 80.00

DIAMOND QUILTED (c. 1890)

☐ Bowl	15.00- 22.00
☐ Bowl, waste	10.00- 18.00
☐ Butter dish	30.00- 45.00
☐ Celery vase	22.00- 37.00
☐ Champagne glass . . .	18.00- 26.00
☐ Compote, CVD	40.00- 55.00
☐ Compote, open	23.00- 38.00
☐ Cordial glass	10.00- 18.00
☐ Creamer	20.00- 35.00
☐ Pickle dish	12.00- 20.00
☐ Pitcher, sm./lg.	37.00- 52.00

	Price Range
☐ Sauce, round	12.00- 20.00
☐ Sauce, FTD	15.00- 22.00
☐ Spoon holder	20.00- 35.00
☐ Sugar bowl	30.00- 45.00
☐ Tray	23.00- 38.00
☐ Tumbler	10.00- 18.00
☐ Whiskey	18.00- 26.00
☐ Wine glass	20.00- 35.00

DIAMOND SUNBURST (c. 1860)

☐ Cake stand	21.00- 36.00
☐ Celery vase	15.00- 22.00
☐ Compote	30.00- 45.00
☐ Cordial glass	8.00- 14.00
☐ Creamer	25.00- 40.00
☐ Dish	12.00- 20.00
☐ Goblet	12.00- 20.00
☐ Lamp	20.00- 30.00
☐ Pickle dish	12.00- 20.00
☐ Pitcher	18.00- 26.00
☐ Salt and pepper	12.00- 20.00
☐ Sauce dish	8.00- 14.00
☐ Shakers, pr.	12.00- 20.00
☐ Spoon holder	18.00- 26.00
☐ Sugar bowl	25.00- 40.00
☐ Tumbler	12.00- 20.00
☐ Wine glass	12.00- 20.00

DIAMOND THUMBPRINT (c. 1860)

☐ Bottle	95.00-110.00
☐ Bowl	95.00-110.00
☐ Butter plate	135.00-170.00
☐ Celery vase	165.00-200.00
☐ Cordial glass	185.00-220.00
☐ Creamer	140.00-175.00
☐ Decanter, pt. & qt. ...	110.00-150.00
☐ Honey dish	35.00- 50.00
☐ Mug, handle	95.00-110.00
☐ Sauce dish	20.00- 35.00
☐ Spoon holder	70.00- 85.00

	Price Range
☐ Sugar bowl	150.00-185.00
☐ Tumbler	95.00-110.00
☐ Vase	120-00155.00
☐ Wine glass	140.00-175.00

DOUBLE SPEAR (c. 1880)

☐ Celery vase	25.00- 40.00
☐ Compote, high	35.00- 50.00
☐ Creamer	30.00- 45.00
☐ Dish, deep	18.00- 26.00
☐ Egg cup, DBL	12.00- 20.00
☐ Goblet	18.00- 26.00
☐ Pickle dish	10.00- 18.00
☐ Pitcher, M	35.00- 50.00
☐ Sauce dish	10.00- 18.00
☐ Spoon holder	22.00- 37.00
☐ Sugar/creamer	45.00- 60.00

DRAPERY (c. 1870)

☐ Bowl, CVD	20.00- 30.00
☐ Butter dish	40.00- 55.00
☐ Compote	40.00- 55.00
☐ Creamer	30.00- 45.00
☐ Dish	15.00- 22.00
☐ Egg cup, DBL	10.00- 10.00
☐ Goblet	18.00- 24.00
☐ Pitcher, W	34.00- 49.00
☐ Plate, oval	18.00- 24.00
☐ Sauce dish	6.00- 12.00
☐ Spoon holder	23.00- 38.00
☐ Sugar bowl, CVD	32.00- 47.00
☐ Tumbler	20.00- 35.00

EGG IN SAND (c. 1880)

☐ Cake stand	23.00- 38.00
☐ Compote, high	40.00- 55.00
☐ Cordial glass	12.00- 20.00
☐ Creamer	20.00- 30.00
☐ Goblet, sm.	20.00- 30.00

	Price Range
☐ Pitcher, W/M	25.00- 40.00
☐ Sauce dish	6.00- 12.00
☐ Shakers, S/P	20.00- 35.00
☐ Spoon holder	15.00- 22.00
☐ Sugar bowl, CVD	28.00- 43.00
☐ Tray, bread	20.00- 35.00
☐ Tumbler	12.00- 20.00
☐ Wine glass	12.00- 20.00

EGYPTIAN (c. 1870)

	Price Range
☐ Butter plate	50.00- 65.00
☐ Celery vase	32.00- 47.00
☐ Compote	45.00- 60.00
☐ Creamer	30.00- 45.00
☐ Goblet.............	30.00- 45.00
☐ Honey	12.00- 20.00
☐ Pickle dish	22.00- 37.00
☐ Pitcher	45.00- 60.00
☐ Plate, cake	33.00- 48.00
☐ Platter............	45.00- 60.00
☐ Relish dish	12.00- 20.00
☐ Spoon holder	29.00- 44.00
☐ Sugar bowl	40.00- 55.00

ESTHER (c. 1896)

	Price Range
☐ Bowl, berry	30.00- 45.00
☐ Butter dish, CVD	75.00- 90.00
☐ Celery, clear	15.00- 20.00
☐ Compote, clear	20.00- 30.00
☐ Creamer	12.00- 20.00
☐ Cruet	20.00- 30.00
☐ Dish, cheese, CVD ...	25.00- 40.00
☐ Dish, jelly	55.00- 70.00
☐ Goblet, clear	18.00- 26.00
Pickle	
☐ Clear	9.00- 24.00
☐ Green	23.00- 38.00
Pitcher	
☐ Clear	45.00- 60.00
☐ Green	80.00- 95.00
☐ Plate	30.00- 45.00
Sauce	
☐ Clear	8.00- 14.00
☐ Green	20.00- 35.00
☐ Spoon holder	35.00- 50.00
☐ Sugar, green	63.00- 78.00
☐ Toothpick holder	70.00- 85.00
☐ Tumbler, green	35.00- 50.00
☐ Wine jug	18.00- 26.00

EUREKA (c. 1860)

	Price Range
☐ Butter plate	25.00- 40.00
☐ Champagne glass ...	25.00- 40.00
☐ Compote	60.00- 75.00
☐ Cordial glass	27.00- 42.00
☐ Creamer	42.00- 57.00
☐ Dish, oval	20.00- 30.00
☐ Egg cup	20.00- 35.00
☐ Goblet..............	25.00- 40.00
☐ Plate	30.00- 45.00
☐ Salt shaker, pr.......	15.00- 22.00
☐ Sauce dish	10.00- 18.00
☐ Spoon holder	24.00- 39.00
☐ Sugar bowl	50.00- 65.00
☐ Tumbler	20.00- 35.00
☐ Wine glass	25.00- 40.00

EXCELSIOR (c. 1850)

	Price Range
☐ Bitters bottle	35.00- 50.00
☐ Bowl, CVD and open .	95.00-110.00
☐ Butter plate	80.00- 95.00
☐ Candlesticks, pair ...	100.00-135.00
☐ Celery vase	70.00- 85.00
☐ Champagne glass ...	63.00- 78.00
☐ Claret glass	30.00- 45.00
☐ Compote, CVD	
and open	95.00-110.00
☐ Cordial glass	20.00- 35.00
☐ Creamer	77.00- 92.00
☐ Decanter, pt. & qt. ...	60.00- 75.00
☐ Egg cup, DGL & SGL .	40.00- 55.00
☐ Goblet.............	35.00- 50.00
☐ Lamp..............	115.00-150.00
☐ Pitcher	80.00- 95.00
☐ Salt, FTD	23.00- 38.00
☐ Spoon holder	55.00- 70.00
☐ Sugar bowl	80.00- 95.00
☐ Tumbler	30.00- 45.00
☐ Vase	33.00- 48.00
☐ Wine glass	45.00- 60.00

Price Range

FESTOON (c. 1860)

	Price Range
☐ Bowl, berry, finger and waste	20.00- 35.00
☐ Butter dish	30.00- 45.00
☐ Cake stand	25.00- 40.00
☐ Celery vase	18.00- 26.00
☐ Compote	35.00- 50.00
☐ Creamer	18.00- 26.00
☐ Goblet	20.00- 30.00
☐ Pickle dish	18.00- 26.00
☐ Pickle jar	25.00- 40.00
☐ Pitcher, W	25.00- 40.00
☐ Plate	30.00- 45.00
☐ Sauce dish	5.00- 10.00
☐ Spoon holder	14.00- 20.00
☐ Sugar bowl, CVD	25.00- 40.00
☐ Tray	23.00- 38.00
☐ Tumbler	20.00- 35.00
☐ Wine glass	15.00- 22.00

FINE CUT (c. 1870)

	Price Range
☐ Bowl, finger	14.00- 20.00
☐ Bowl, waste	18.00- 26.00
☐ Butter plate	35.00- 50.00
☐ Celery tray	16.00- 24.00
☐ Compote	40.00- 55.00
☐ Creamer	22.00- 37.00
☐ Cruet, sm.	16.00- 24.00
☐ Goblet	20.00- 35.00
☐ Mustard jar	12.00- 20.00
☐ Pickle dish	8.00- 14.00
☐ Pitcher, W	30.00- 45.00
☐ Plate	18.00- 26.00
☐ Sauce, clear	8.00- 14.00
☐ Shakers, S/P	12.00- 20.00
☐ Spoon holder	20.00- 30.00
☐ Sugar bowl	26.00- 41.00
☐ Tray, bread	18.00- 28.00

FINECUT AND PANEL (c. 1870)

	Price Range
☐ Bowl, CVD	18.00- 26.00
☐ Butter dish	30.00- 45.00
☐ Cake stand	22.00- 37.00
☐ Celery tray	25.00- 40.00
☐ Compote	25.00- 40.00
☐ Cordial glass	12.00- 20.00
☐ Creamer	20.00- 35.00
☐ Goblet	25.00- 40.00
☐ Lamp	45.00- 60.00
☐ Pickle dish	12.00- 20.00
☐ Pitcher, W	29.00- 44.00

	Price Range
☐ Plate	12.00- 20.00
☐ Platter	22.00- 37.00
☐ Sauce dish	5.00- 12.00
☐ Shakers, S/P	20.00- 30.00
☐ Spoon holder	20.00- 35.00
☐ Sugar bowl	29.00- 44.00
☐ Toothpick holder	8.00- 15.00
☐ Tray	12.00- 20.00
☐ Tumbler	12.00- 20.00
☐ Wine glass	20.00- 35.00

FINE RIB (c. 1880)

	Price Range
☐ Bitters bottle	50.00- 65.00
☐ Bowl, CVD, shallow	70.00- 85.00
☐ Butter plate	80.00- 95.00
☐ Castor bottle	18.00- 26.00
☐ Celery vase	60.00- 75.00
☐ Champagne glass . . .	40.00- 55.00
☐ Cordial glass	50.00- 65.00
☐ Creamer	95.00-110.00
☐ Cup	35.00- 50.00
☐ Decanter, bar, qt.	45.00- 60.00
☐ Dish	50.00- 65.00
☐ Egg cup, CVD	60.00- 75.00
☐ Goblet	45.00- 60.00
☐ Honey dish	15.00- 22.00
☐ Jug, W	60.00- 75.00
☐ Lamp	125.00-160.00
☐ Mug	50.00- 65.00
☐ Pitcher, W	155.00-190.00
☐ Plate	45.00- 60.00
☐ Salt and pepper	12.00- 20.00
☐ Sauce dish	15.00- 22.00
☐ Spoon holder	50.00- 65.00
☐ Sugar bowl, CVD	70.00- 85.00
☐ Tumbler, lemonade, water, whiskey	40.00- 55.00
☐ Wine glass	32.00- 47.00

FISHSCALE (Coral) (c. 1880)

	Price Range
☐ Berry dish	45.00- 60.00
☐ Bowl, CVD	20.00- 35.00
☐ Butter plate	35.00- 50.00
☐ Cake stand	25.00- 40.00
☐ Celery vase	20.00- 35.00
☐ Compote, 6 sytles . . .	40.00- 55.00
☐ Creamer	25.00- 40.00
☐ Goblet	24.00- 39.00
☐ Lamp	24.00- 39.00
☐ Mug, sm./lg.	20.00- 35.00
☐ Pickle dish	20.00- 30.00

Price Range

☐ Pitcher, sm./lg......	35.00-	50.00
☐ Plate.............	23.00-	38.00
☐ Sauce, round, square		
FTD............	15.00-	20.00
☐ Sugar bowl.........	20.00-	30.00
☐ Spoon holder.......	25.00-	40.00
☐ Tray, round........	27.00-	42.00
☐ Tumbler...........	18.00-	26.00

FLATTENED SAWTOOTH (c. 1880)

☐ Celery tray.........	30.00-	45.00
☐ Compote, CVD......	60.00-	75.00
☐ Cordial glass.......	35.00-	50.00
☐ Creamer...........	30.00-	45.00
☐ Decanter, qt........	45.00-	60.00
☐ Egg cup...........	24.00-	39.00
☐ Goblet.............	29.00-	44.00
☐ Ice bucket........	40.00-	55.00
☐ Pitcher, W..........	70.00-	85.00
☐ Plate..............	31.00-	46.00
☐ Salt, CVD, FTD		
round, flat........	40.00-	55.00
☐ Spoon holder.......	35.00-	50.00
☐ Sugar bowl.........	40.00-	55.00
☐ Tumbler...........	35.00-	50.00

FLOWER MEDALLION (c. 1910)

☐ Bowl, berry.........	8.00-	14.00
☐ Butter plate........	20.00-	35.00
☐ Celery.............	12.00-	20.00
☐ Compote, CVD sm./lg.	18.00-	26.00
☐ Creamer...........	10.00-	16.00
☐ Decanter, qt........	20.00-	35.00
☐ Goblet.............	10.00-	16.00
☐ Pitcher, M..........	20.00-	35.00
☐ Relish dish.........	6.00-	12.00
☐ Sauce dish.........	2.00-	6.00
☐ Spoon holder.......	8.00-	14.00
☐ Sugar bowl, CVD....	18.00-	26.00
☐ Tumbler...........	5.00-	12.00
☐ Wine glass.........	8.00-	14.00
☐ Wine set, 6 glasses..	95.00-	110.00

FLUTE (c. 1850)

☐ Bitters bottle.......	30.00-	45.00
☐ Candlesticks, pr.....	45.00-	60.00
☐ Champagne glass...	21.00-	36.00
☐ Creamer...........	30.00-	45.00
☐ Cup, FTD..........	18.00-	26.00
☐ Decanter, qt........	40.00-	55.00
☐ Egg cup, DBL.......	15.00-	22.00

Price Range

☐ Goblet.............	20.00-	30.00
☐ Lamp.............	30.00-	45.00
☐ Spoon holder.......	15.00-	22.00
☐ Wine glass.........	15.00-	22.00

FROSTED GLASS (c. 1870)

☐ Bowl, CVD and open.	20.00-	35.00
☐ Butter plate........	40.00-	55.00
☐ Cake stand.........	40.00-	55.00
☐ Celery vase........	45.00-	60.00
☐ Champagne glass...	42.00-	57.00
☐ Claret glass........	23.00-	38.00
☐ Compote, CVD		
and open........	45.00-	60.00
☐ Creamer...........	25.00-	40.00
☐ Cruet, sm...........	45.00-	60.00
☐ Lamp.............	45.00-	60.00
☐ Pickle dish.........	42.00-	57.00
☐ Pitcher, syrup, water.	60.00-	75.00
☐ Plate..............	20.00-	35.00
☐ Shakers, S/P........	40.00-	55.00
☐ Spoon holder.......	22.00-	37.00
☐ Sugar bowl, CVD....	38.00-	53.00
☐ Tumbler...........	18.00-	26.00
☐ Wine glass.........	30.00-	45.00

FROSTED LEAF (c. 1850)

☐ Bottle.............	115.00-	150.00
☐ Butter plate........	95.00-	110.00
☐ Celery vase........	80.00-	95.00
☐ Champagne glass...	165.00-	200.00
☐ Compote, CVD		
and open........	115.00-	150.00
☐ Cordial glass.......	140.00-	175.00
☐ Creamer...........	110.00-	145.00
☐ Decanter, qt........	120.00-	155.00
☐ Egg cup (scarce)....	70.00-	85.00
☐ Salt, FTD..........	30.00-	45.00
☐ Sauce dish.........	20.00-	35.00
☐ Spoon holder.......	70.00-	85.00
☐ Sugar bowl.........	95.00-	110.00
☐ Tumbler...........	115.00-	150.00
☐ Wine glass.........	125.00-	160.00

FROSTED LION (c. 1870)

☐ Butter plate........	90.00-	105.00
☐ Celery.............	80.00-	95.00
☐ Compote, low, high		
oval............	115.00-	150.00
☐ Cordial glass.......	95.00-	110.00
☐ Creamer...........	45.00-	60.00

JEWELRY

clockwise from top

FRENCH SILVER-GILT OIGNON WATCH
(Masson, Paris, Dia. 2¼", c. 1700) . . . . $3,800.00 - 4,400.00
LOUIS XVI GOLD & ENAMEL SNUFF BOX
(Joseph-Etienne Blerzy, Paris, L 3¼", c. 1784) . . . . 9,000.00 - 12,000.00
SILVER-GILT PAIR CASE WATCH
(Nilardi, Stettin, Dia. 2-1/8", c. 1700) . . . . 5,000.00 - 6,000.00
SWISS GOLD, ENAMEL & PEARL WATCH & CHATELAINE
(Dia. 2", L 14", late 18th century) . . . . 9,000.00 - 11,000.00
MINIATURE OF A LADY
(signed & dated, Dia. 2-3/8", c. 1805) . . . . 800.00 - 1,200.00

TIFFANY FAVRILE GLASS & BRONZE NASTURTIUM LAMP
(signed Tiffany Studios, H 31½", dia. 21¾", 1899-1920) . . . $30,000.00 - 40,000.00

FRENCH AUTOMOTON "DANDY"

(H 27½") . . . . $5,500.00 - 6,500.00

VIOLIN *(signed Nicolo Amati, Cremona, L of back 13-13/16", c. 1659)* . . . . $40,000.00 - 50,000.00

LIONEL STANDARD GAUGE TRAIN SET
(engine L 17", passenger L 21½", c. 1930) . . . . $8,000.00 - 9,000.00

EARLY AMERICAN TINWARE
(c. 1820)
top left to right

tray, Dia. 12"
. . . . $600.00 - 800.00
coffee pot H 9"
. . . . . . 1,200.00 - 1,800.00
tray, Dia. 13¼"
. . . . 500.00 - 650.00

center

canister H 8¼"
. . . . . . 300.00 - 400.00
vessels, H 5-3/8"
. . . . . . 300.00 - 400.00

tray, L 12-5/8"
. . . . . . 700.00 - 900.00
coffee pot, H 12"
. . . . . 1,500.00 - 2,000.00
syrup jug, H 4"
. . . . . . 700.00 - 850.00

bottom

document box, H 10", W 9"
. . . . . . 500.00 - 700.00
box, H 11½", L 11"
. . . . . . 1,200.00 - 1,600.00
document box,
H 7-5/8", L 9-7/8"
. . . . . . 600.00 - 800.00

ORIENTAL WOOD, IVORY & LACQUER GROUP
(signed Kokoku, 19th/20th century) . . . . $8,000.00 - 9,000.00

GALLÉ MARQUETRY VITRINE
(bronze mounts, signed E. Galle, H 5′ 3½″, W 26″, c. 1900) . $22,000.00 - 30,000.00

LOUIS XV BOIS SATINE PURPLEWOOD & KINGWOOD PARQUETRY COMMODE

(signed, Migeon H 34½″, W 4′2½″, D 25″, mid-18th century) . . . . $22,000.00 - 26,000.00

CHINESE EXPORT PLATES

left
ORANGE FITZHUGH
(c. 1800-1810)

Dia. 7¾" . . . . $3,600.00 - 4,200.00
Dia. 7¾" . . . . 3,600.00 - 4,200.00
Dia. 9¾" . . . . 2,000.00 - 2,500.00

center

Dia. 10½" . . 3,400.00 - 3,800.00
DEWITT CLINTON
(c. 1796-1810)

L 12¾" . . . 3,600.00 - 4,200.00
L 10" . . . . . 1,800.00 - 2,200.00

right
ORANGE FITZHUGH
(c. 1800-1810)

Dia. 7¾" . . 3,600.00 - 4,200.00
Dia. 7¾" . . 3,600.00 - 4,200.00
Dia. 9-7/8" 1,400.00 - 1,800.00

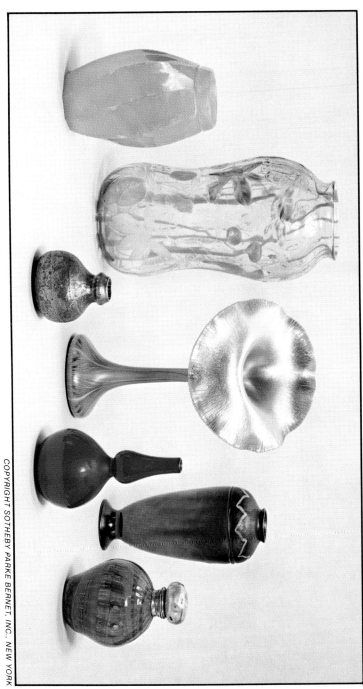

TIFFANY FAVRILE GLASS

(c. 1890-1925) left to right

agate vase, H 7-1/8" .... $3,500.00 - 4,500.00
cameo vase, H 12½" .... 3,800.00 - 4,500.00
cypriote vase, H 3¼" .... 1,400.00 - 2,000.00
quezal vase, H 11¾" .... 2,200.00 - 2,800.00

vase, H 6½" .... $3,800.00 - 4,400.00
vase, H 8¾" .... 1,800.00 - 2,400.00
agate bottle, H 5¾" .... 3,500.00 - 4,500.00

left & right
AMERICAN SILVER PORRINGER (signed Paul Revere I or II, Boston, c. 1750-60) each . . . . $7,000.00 - 8,000.00
center **CHILD'S PORRINGER** (signed Paul Revere II, Boston, c. 1790) . . . . 13,000.00 - 17,000.00

RUSSIAN SILVER GILT & ENAMEL PUNCH SET

(signed N.I.T., H 10-1/8", Dia. 19¼", c. 1910) . . . . $12,000.00 - 16,000.00

GERMAN BI-PLANE (tin & cardboard. L 17½", c. 1910) .... $550.00 - 700.00

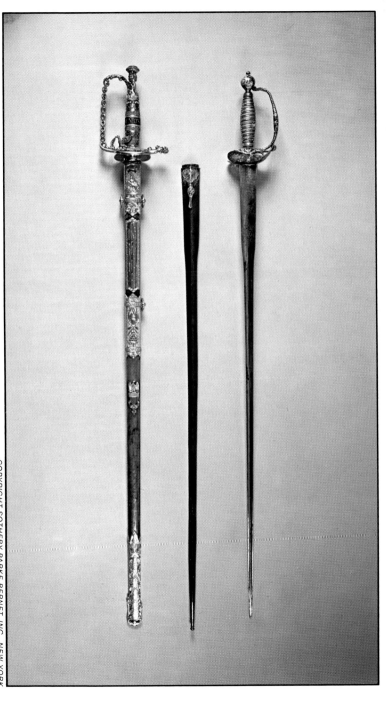

GOLD, DIAMOND, SILVER & ENAMEL SWORD
(presented to Gen. Joseph Hooker, L 40½", c. 1862) . . . . $30,000.00 - 35,000.00

PENS *(top to bottom)*
Parker Lucky Curve #33 Pen *(L 5-5/8″, c. 1910)* $40.00
Parker Lucky Curve Jack Knife Safety #20 Pen *(L 5-3/8″, c. 1918)* 20.00
Parker Lady Pastel Pen *(L 4-5/8″, c. 1930)* 20.00
Parker Lady Pastel Pencil *(L 4-7/8″, c. 1929)* 10.00

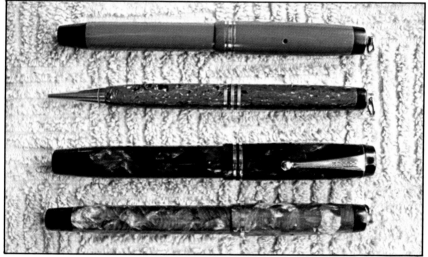

PENS *(top to bottom)*
Parker Lady Duofold Pen *(L 4-3/8″, c.1931)* $30.00
Parker Lady Duofold Pencil *(L 4-7/8″, c. 1932)* 10.00
Parker Duofold Junior Pen *(L 4-3/4″, c. 1931)* 15.00
Parker Lady Duofold Pen *(L 4-7/8″, c. 1930)* 20.00

	Price Range
☐ Egg cup, DBL	65.00- 80.00
☐ Goblet	55.00- 70.00
☐ Honey dish	20.00- 35.00
☐ Jam jar, CVD	95.00-110.00
☐ Lamp	140.00-175.00
☐ Pitcher, W/M/S	140.00-175.00
☐ Relish dish	30.00- 45.00
☐ Salt shaker	80.00- 95.00
☐ Sauce dish	20.00- 35.00
☐ Spoon holder	35.00- 50.00
☐ Sugar bowl	95.00-110.00
☐ Tray, bread	60.00- 75.00
☐ Tumbler, lion head in relief	70.00- 85.00
☐ Wine	110.00-145.00

FROSTED RIBBON (c. 1870)

☐ Bitters bottle	20.00- 35.00
☐ Butter plate	35.00- 50.00
☐ Celery vase	42.00- 57.00
☐ Champagne glass	37.00- 52.00
☐ Compote, high, low and open	110.00-145.00
☐ Cordial glass	27.00- 37.00
☐ Creamer	20.00- 35.00
☐ Egg cup	20.00- 30.00
☐ Pitcher	42.00- 57.00
☐ Salt and pepper	12.00- 20.00
☐ Sauce dish	10.00- 16.00
☐ Spoon holder	30.00- 45.00
☐ Sugar bowl	70.00- 85.00
☐ Tray	25.00- 40.00
☐ Tumbler	27.00- 42.00
☐ Wine glass	35.00- 50.00

FROSTED STORK (c. 1880)

☐ Bowl	37.00- 52.00
☐ Butter plate	60.00- 75.00
☐ Creamer	60.00- 75.00
☐ Goblet	47.00- 62.00
☐ Jam jar	42.00- 57.00
☐ Pitcher	85.00 100.00
☐ Platter	50.00- 65.00
☐ Sauce dish	12.00- 20.00
☐ Spoon holder	45.00- 60.00
☐ Sugar bowl	80.00- 95.00
☐ Tray, bread	40.00- 55.00

GARFIELD DRAPE (c. 1881)

| ☐ Bowl, berry | 34.00- 49.00 |
| ☐ Butter plate | 50.00- 65.00 |

	Price Range
☐ Cake stand	37.00- 52.00
☐ Celery vase	30.00- 45.00
☐ Compote, high, low	50.00- 65.00
☐ Creamer	35.00- 50.00
☐ Egg cup, DBL	18.00- 26.00
☐ Goblet	22.00- 37.00
☐ Honey dish	12.00- 20.00
☐ Pickle dish	14.00- 29.00
☐ Pitcher, W/M	50.00- 65.00
☐ Sauce, FTD, flat	10.00- 16.00
☐ Spoon holder	20.00- 30.00
☐ Sugar bowl, CVD	18.00- 26.00
☐ Tumbler	18.00- 26.00
☐ Wine glass	20.00- 35.00

GRAPE AND FESTOON (c. 1870)

☐ Butter plate	55.00- 70.00
☐ Celery vase	50.00- 65.00
☐ Compote, high, low	60.00- 75.00
☐ Cordial glass	40.00- 55.00
☐ Creamer	47.00- 62.00
☐ Dish, lg.	20.00- 35.00
☐ Egg cup	23.00- 38.00
☐ Goblet	30.00- 45.00
☐ Pickle dish	16.00- 24.00
☐ Pitcher, M	55.00- 70.00
☐ Plate	20.00- 35.00
☐ Salt, FTD	15.00- 30.00
☐ Sauce dish	10.00- 16.00
☐ Spoon holder	20.00- 30.00
☐ Sugar bowl	37.00- 52.00
☐ Wine glass	20.00- 30.00

GRAPE BAND (c. 1850)

☐ Compote, high, low	55.00- 70.00
☐ Cordial glass	30.00- 45.00
☐ Egg cup, DBL	12.00- 20.00
☐ Goblet	16.00- 24.00
☐ Pickle dish	10.00- 16.00
☐ Pitcher, M	45.00- 60.00
☐ Plate	20.00- 30.00
☐ Salt, FTD	10.00- 16.00
☐ Sauce dish	8.00- 16.00
☐ Spoon holder	18.00- 26.00
☐ Sugar bowl	30.00- 45.00
☐ Tumbler	18.00- 26.00
☐ Wine glass	15.00- 22.00

Price Range

GRAPE WITH THUMBPRINT
(c. 1890)

	Price Range
☐ Banana	15.00- 22.00
☐ Bowl	15.00- 22.00
☐ Butter plate	45.00- 60.00
☐ Celery vase	27.00- 42.00
☐ Creamer	40.00- 55.00
☐ Goblet	23.00- 38.00
☐ Pitcher, W/M	52.00- 67.00
☐ Sauce dish	8.00- 14.00
☐ Spoon holder	20.00- 35.00
☐ Sugar bowl	45.00- 60.00
☐ Syrup dish	32.00- 47.00
☐ Tumbler	18.00- 26.00

GRASSHOPPER (c. 1880)

☐ Bowl, CVD	43.00- 58.00
☐ Butter plate	40.00- 55.00
☐ Celery tray	22.00- 37.00
☐ Compote	50.00- 65.00
☐ Creamer	21.00- 36.00
☐ Pickle dish	14.00- 20.00
☐ Pitcher, W/M	40.00- 55.00
☐ Sauce dish	10.00- 16.00
☐ Spoon holder	60.00- 75.00
☐ Sugar bowl, CVD, open	45.00- 60.00

HAMILTON (c. 1860)

☐ Castor	120.00-155.00
☐ Celery dish	55.00- 70.00
☐ Champagne glass	40.00- 55.00
☐ Compote, high, open	65.00- 80.00
☐ Cordial glass	40.00- 55.00
☐ Creamer, appl. & pressed handle	75.00- 90.00
☐ Decanter, qt.	70.00- 85.00
☐ Egg cup, DBL	20.00- 30.00
☐ Goblet	35.00- 50.00
☐ Honey	12.00- 20.00

Price Range

	Price Range
☐ Pitcher, W/M	60.00- 75.00
☐ Plate	40.00- 55.00
☐ Salt and pepper	23.00- 38.00
☐ Sauce dish	12.00- 20.00
☐ Spoon holder	30.00- 45.00
☐ Sugar bowl	70.00- 85.00
☐ Tumbler	55.00- 70.00
☐ Wine glass	50.00- 65.00

HAMILTON WITH LEAF (c. 1870)

☐ Celery vase	90.00-105.00
☐ Compote, high, low open	70.00- 85.00
☐ Cordial glass	70.00- 85.00
☐ Creamer	70.00- 85.00
☐ Egg cup	30.00- 45.00
☐ Goblet	50.00- 65.00
☐ Lamp	140.00-175.00
☐ Salt and pepper	35.00- 50.00
☐ Sauce dish	10.00- 18.00
☐ Spoon holder	50.00- 65.00
☐ Sugar bowl	75.00- 90.00
☐ Tumbler	45.00- 60.00

HAND (c. 1880)

☐ Bowl	21.00- 36.00
☐ Butter plate	40.00- 55.00
☐ Cake stand	33.00- 48.00
☐ Celery vase	27.00- 42.00
☐ Compote, CVD, opem	43.00- 58.00
☐ Creamer	27.00- 42.00
☐ Goblet	24.00- 39.00
☐ Honey	10.00- 18.00
☐ Jam jar	23.00- 38.00
☐ Pickle dish	12.00- 20.00
☐ Pitcher, W/M	52.00- 67.00
☐ Platter	24.00- 39.00
☐ Sauce dish	8.00- 16.00
☐ Sugar bowl	40.00- 55.00
☐ Wine glass	20.00- 30.00

HEART WITH THUMBPRINT
(c. 1898)

☐ Banana	18.00- 26.00
☐ Bowl	30.00- 45.00
☐ Butter plate	27.00- 42.00
☐ Carafe	43.00- 58.00
☐ Celery tray	21.00- 36.00
☐ Compote, high	43.00- 58.00
☐ Cordial glass	25.00- 40.00
☐ Creamer	25.00- 40.00

	Price Range
☐ Goblet.............	27.00- 42.00
☐ Ice bucket	45.00- 60.00
☐ Pitcher, S/W	40.00- 55.00
☐ Plate	31.00- 46.00
☐ Punch	8.00- 16.00
☐ Sauce dish	5.00- 12.00
☐ Sugar bowl	44.00- 59.00
☐ Tumbler	22.00- 32.00
☐ Vase	18.00- 26.00
☐ Wine glass	15.00- 22.00

HERRINGBONE (c. 1880)

☐ Bowl	18.00- 26.00
☐ Butter plate	43.00- 58.00
☐ Cake stand.........	25.00- 40.00
☐ Celery vase	20.00- 35.00
☐ Compote, open	18.00- 26.00
☐ Cordial glass	20.00- 30.00
☐ Creamer	22.00- 37.00
☐ Cruet, sm...........	23.00- 38.00
☐ Pickle dish	8.00- 16.00
☐ Pitcher, M/W	35.00- 50.00
☐ Plate, sq. & oval	18.00- 26.00
☐ Relish dish	8.00- 16.00
☐ Shakers, S/P........	20.00- 35.00
☐ Sauce dish	7.00- 14.00
☐ Spoon holder	16.00- 24.00
☐ Sugar, CVD, open ...	22.00- 37.00
☐ Toothpick holder	12.00- 20.00
☐ Tray, bread	20.00- 35.00
☐ Tumbler	12.00- 20.00
☐ Wine glass	10.00- 18.00

HOBNAIL FAN TOP (c. 1880)

☐ Butter dish	35.00- 50.00
☐ Celery vase	23.00- 38.00
☐ Creamer	23.00- 38.00
☐ Goblet.............	20.00- 30.00
☐ Salt, individual......	6.00- 12.00
☐ Sugar bowl	31.00- 36.00
☐ Tray...............	16.00- 24.00

Price Range

HOBNAIL OPALESCENT (c. 1880)

☐ Butter dish	65.00- 80.00
☐ Celery dish	45.00- 60.00
☐ Creamer	39.00- 54.00
☐ Cup	15.00- 22.00
☐ Pickle	20.00- 35.00
☐ Platter.............	60.00- 75.00
☐ Spoon holder	25.00- 40.00
☐ Sugar bowl, CVD	47.00- 62.00

HOBNAIL PANELLED (c. 1880)

☐ Bowl	22.00- 32.00
☐ Butter plate	26.00- 41.00
☐ Celery dish	25.00- 40.00
☐ Compote	30.00- 45.00
☐ Creamer	22.00- 32.00
☐ Goblet.............	16.00- 24.00
☐ Plate	16.00- 24.00
☐ Sauce dish	6.00- 12.00
☐ Spoon holder	15.00- 22.00
☐ Sugar bowl, CVD	25.00- 40.00
☐ Wine glass	8.00- 16.00

HOBNAIL POINTED (c. 1880)

☐ Bowl	25.00- 40.00
☐ Butter plate	30.00- 45.00
☐ Cake stand.........	30.00- 45.00
☐ Celery dish	20.00- 35.00
☐ Compote	35.00- 50.00
☐ Cordial glass	16.00- 24.00
☐ Creamer	22.00- 37.00
☐ Egg cup	18.00- 26.00
☐ Goblet.............	22.00- 37.00
☐ Inkwell	12.00- 20.00
☐ Jar	15.00- 20.00
☐ Pickle	12.00- 20.00
☐ Pitcher, W/S	27.00- 42.00
☐ Plate	16.00- 24.00
☐ Salt	6.00- 12.00
☐ Spoon holder	16.00- 24.00
☐ Toothpick holder	8.00- 16.00
☐ Tray...............	22.00- 37.00

HOBNAIL PRINTED (c. 1880)

☐ Butter dish	25.00- 40.00
☐ Celery dish	20.00- 35.00
☐ Creamer	16.00- 24.00
☐ Goblet.............	16.00- 24.00
☐ Mug..............	12.00- 20.00
☐ Jar	14.00- 20.00

	Price Range
☐ Pitcher, W	30.00- 45.00
☐ Sauce dish	6.00- 12.00
☐ Spoon holder	18.00- 26.00
☐ Sugar bowl, CVD	23.00- 38.00
☐ Tray	20.00- 35.00
☐ Tumbler	10.00- 18.00
☐ Wine glass	15.00- 22.00

HOBNAIL THUMBPRINT (c. 1880)

	Price Range
☐ Bowl	24.00- 39.00
☐ Butter plate	29.00- 44.00
☐ Celery vase	25.00- 40.00
☐ Creamer	23.00- 38.00
☐ Jar	15.00- 22.00
☐ Pitcher, W	40.00- 55.00
☐ Shakers, S/P	20.00- 30.00
☐ Spoon holder	20.00- 30.00
☐ Sugar bowl, CVD	24.00- 39.00
☐ Tray	20.00- 35.00

HOLLY (c. 1860)

	Price Range
☐ Butter plate	50.00- 65.00
☐ Cake stand	40.00- 55.00
☐ Celery, FTD	40.00- 55.00
☐ Compote, CVD	70.00- 85.00
☐ Creamer	50.00- 65.00
☐ Egg cup	60.00- 75.00
☐ Goblet	55.00- 70.00
☐ Pickle dish	8.00- 16.00
☐ Pitcher	62.00- 77.00
☐ Salt, FTD	12.00- 22.00
☐ Sauce dish	10.00- 18.00
☐ Spoon holder	25.00- 40.00
☐ Sugar bowl, CVD	45.00- 60.00
☐ Toothpick, green	20.00- 35.00
☐ Tumbler, FTD	27.00- 42.00
☐ Wine glass	35.00- 50.00

HONEYCOMB (c. 1870)

	Price Range
☐ Bottle, bitters, W	18.00- 26.00
☐ Bowl, CVD, FTD	16.00- 24.00
☐ Butter dish	24.00- 39.00
☐ Celery dish	14.00- 20.00
☐ Champagne glass . . .	20.00- 35.00
☐ Compote, CVD	40.00- 55.00
☐ Cordial glass	10.00- 18.00
☐ Creamer	20.00- 35.00
☐ Cup, custard	12.00- 20.00
☐ Decanter	25.00- 40.00
☐ Dish	8.00- 16.00

	Price Range
☐ Egg cup	14.00- 20.00
☐ Goblet	18.00- 26.00
☐ Honey dish	18.00- 26.00
☐ Jug, 3 pts	34.00- 49.00
☐ Mug	10.00- 18.00
☐ Pitcher, M	35.00- 50.00
☐ Plate	12.00- 20.00
☐ Pomade jar	10.00- 18.00
☐ Salt, FTD	18.00- 26.00
☐ Sauce dish	4.00- 8.00
☐ Shakers, S/P	18.00- 26.00
☐ Spoon holder	10.00- 18.00
☐ Sugar bowl, CVD	22.00- 37.00
☐ Tumbler, FTD	12.00- 20.00
☐ Wine jug	10.00- 18.00

HORN OF PLENTY (c. 1850)

	Price Range
☐ Bottle, perfume	45.00- 60.00
☐ Bowl	75.00- 90.00
☐ Butter dish	100.00-125.00
☐ Celery dish	95.00-110.00
☐ Champagne glass . . .	115.00-150.00
☐ Compote	140.00-175.00
☐ Cordial glass	70.00- 85.00
☐ Creamer	140.00-175.00
☐ Decanter	95.00-110.00
☐ Egg cup	40.00- 55.00
☐ Honey dish	18.00- 26.00

Price Range

	Price Range
☐ Mug	95.00-110.00
☐ Pitcher, M	265.00-300.00
☐ Plate	80.00- 95.00
☐ Relish dish	50.00- 65.00
☐ Salt, oval	23.00- 38.00
☐ Sauce dish	8.00- 16.00
☐ Spoon holder	40.00- 55.00
☐ Sugar bowl, CVD	105.00-140.00
☐ Tumbler	70.00- 85.00
☐ Wine jug	50.00- 65.00

HORSESHOE (c. 1880)

☐ Bowl	20.00- 35.00
☐ Butter dish	45.00- 60.00
☐ Cake stand	25.00- 40.00
☐ Celery, FTD	30.00- 45.00
☐ Compote	43.00- 58.00
☐ Cordial glass	33.00- 48.00
☐ Creamer	20.00- 35.00
☐ Goblet, stem	30.00- 45.00
☐ Jam jar	27.00- 42.00
☐ Muffineer	50.00- 65.00
☐ Pickle, oval	14.00- 22.00
☐ Pitcher, M	40.00- 55.00
☐ Plate	45.00- 60.00
☐ Relish dish	18.00- 26.00
☐ Salt shaker	12.00- 20.00
☐ Spoon holder	20.00- 30.00
☐ Sugar bowl, CVD	43.00- 58.00
☐ Tray	45.00- 60.00

HUBER (c. 1860)

☐ Bottle	20.00- 35.00
☐ Bowl, CVD	30.00- 45.00
☐ Butter dish	45.00- 60.00
☐ Celery vase	23.00- 38.00
☐ Champagne glass	25.00- 40.00
☐ Cordial glass	20.00- 35.00
☐ Creamer pitcher	40.00- 55.00
☐ Cup	12.00- 20.00
☐ Decanter	30.00- 45.00
☐ Egg cup	30.00- 45.00
☐ Goblet	30.00- 45.00
☐ Honey dish	18.00- 26.00
☐ Mug	18.00- 26.00
☐ Pitcher, W	40.00- 55.00
☐ Plate	20.00- 35.00
☐ Salt Shaker	18.00- 26.00
☐ Sauce dish	10.00- 16.00
☐ Spoon holder	18.00- 36.00
☐ Sugar bowl, CVD	35.00- 50.00
☐ Tumbler	20.00- 35.00
☐ Wine jug	16.00- 24.00

Price Range

HUMMING BIRD (c. 1880)

☐ Butter plate	33.00- 48.00
☐ Celery vase	25.00- 40.00
☐ Creamer, FTD	25.00- 40.00
☐ Finger bowl	16.00- 24.00
☐ Goblet	22.00- 37.00
☐ Pickle	10.00- 16.00
☐ Pitcher, W	40.00- 55.00
☐ Sauce dish	5.00- 12.00
☐ Spoon holder	20.00- 30.00
☐ Sugar bowl, CVD	30.00- 45.00
☐ Tray	22.00- 37.00
☐ Tumbler	20.00- 30.00
☐ Wine jug	23.00- 38.00

INVERTED FERN

☐ Butter, CVD	70.00- 85.00
☐ Compote	50.00- 65.00
☐ Cordial glass	35.00- 50.00
☐ Creamer	70.00- 85.00
☐ Egg cup	23.00- 38.00
☐ Goblet	32.00- 47.00
☐ Honey dish	10.00- 18.00
☐ Pitcher	215.00-250.00
☐ Plate	115.00-150.00
☐ Salt, FTD	18.00- 26.00
☐ Sauce dish	8.00- 16.00
☐ Spoon holder	32.00- 47.00
☐ Sugar bowl, CVD	60.00- 75.00
☐ Tumbler	55.00- 70.00
☐ Wine jug	50.00- 65.00

IVY IN SNOW (c. 1880)

☐ Bowl	22.00- 37.00
☐ Compote, CVD	70.00- 85.00
☐ Cordial glass	30.00- 45.00
☐ Cup/saucer	22.00- 37.00
☐ Jam jar	37.00- 52.00
☐ Pickle	14.00- 20.00
☐ Pitcher, W	60.00- 75.00
☐ Plate	22.00- 37.00
☐ Sauce dish	14.00- 20.00
☐ Spoon holder	22.00- 37.00
☐ Tumbler	25.00- 40.00
☐ Wine jug	29.00- 44.00

JACOB'S LADDER (c. 1870)

☐ Bowl	19.00- 34.00
☐ Butter plate	35.00- 50.00
☐ Cake stand	24.00- 39.00
☐ Celery dish	35.00- 50.00

	Price	Range
☐ Compote, CVD	50.00-	65.00
☐ Cordial glass	35.00-	50.00
☐ Creamer, FTD	35.00-	50.00
☐ Goblet	30.00-	45.00
☐ Honey dish	10.00-	18.00
☐ Jam jar	45.00-	60.00
☐ Mug	20.00-	35.00
☐ Pickle	20.00-	35.00
☐ Pitcher, W	45.00-	60.00
☐ Plate	20.00-	30.00
☐ Relish dish	12.00-	20.00
☐ Salt shaker	8.00-	14.00
☐ Sauce, FTD	10.00-	18.00
☐ Spoon holder	22.00-	37.00
☐ Sugar bowl, CVD	37.00-	52.00
☐ Tumbler	25.00-	40.00
☐ Wine jug	20.00-	35.00

KING'S CROWN (c. 1890)

	Price	Range
☐ Banana boat	55.00-	70.00
☐ Bowl	30.00-	45.00
☐ Bowl, oval	50.00-	65.00
☐ Bowl, punch	140.00-	175.00
☐ Butter plate	45.00-	60.00
☐ Cake stand	35.00-	50.00
☐ Castor jug, clear	10.00-	18.00
☐ Celery vase	35.00-	50.00
☐ Champagne glass	18.00-	26.00
☐ Compote	50.00-	65.00
☐ Cordial glass	12.00-	20.00
☐ Creamer	25.00-	40.00
☐ Dish, cheese	43.00-	58.00
☐ Goblet	18.00-	26.00
☐ Jar, CVD	18.00-	26.00
☐ Pitcher	50.00-	65.00
☐ Plate	20.00-	35.00
☐ Sauce dish	8.00-	16.00
☐ Shakers, S/P	30.00-	45.00
☐ Spoon holder	12.00-	20.00
☐ Sugar bowl	40.00-	55.00
☐ Toothpick holder	12.00-	20.00
☐ Tumbler	14.00-	20.00
☐ Wine jug	16.00-	26.00

LATTICE (c. 1880)

	Price	Range
☐ Bowl	15.00-	22.00
☐ Butter plate	40.00-	55.00
☐ Cake stand	45.00-	60.00
☐ Celery vase	22.00-	37.00
☐ Compote, CVD	35.00-	50.00
☐ Cordial glass	15.00-	22.00
☐ Creamer	25.00-	40.00

	Price	Range
☐ Egg cup	14.00-	20.00
☐ Goblet	20.00-	30.00
☐ Jam jar	20.00-	35.00
☐ Lamp	42.00-	57.00
☐ Pickle	10.00-	18.00
☐ Pitcher, W	35.00-	50.00
☐ Sauce dish	6.00-	12.00
☐ Shakers, S/P	18.00-	26.00
☐ Spoon holder	20.00-	30.00
☐ Sugar bowl	30.00-	45.00
☐ Tray	35.00-	50.00
☐ Wine jug	12.00-	20.00

LEAF AND DART (c. 1890)

	Price	Range
☐ Butter plate	45.00-	60.00
☐ Celery dish	40.00-	55.00
☐ Compote, CVD	43.00-	58.00
☐ Cordial glass	27.00-	42.00
☐ Creamer	40.00-	55.00
☐ Egg cup	20.00-	35.00
☐ Goblet	20.00-	30.00
☐ Lamp	45.00-	60.00
☐ Pitcher	60.00-	75.00
☐ Salt, CVD	47.00-	62.00
☐ Sauce dish	18.00-	18.00
☐ Spoon holder	30.00-	45.00
☐ Sugar bowl	30.00-	45.00
☐ Tumbler, FTD	20.00-	35.00
☐ Wine jug	25.00-	40.00

LIBERTY BELL (c. 1876)

	Price	Range
☐ Bowl, FTD	70.00-	85.00
☐ Butter, CVD	95.00-	110.00
☐ Celery dish	73.00-	88.00
☐ Compote	70.00-	85.00
☐ Creamer	90.00-	105.00
☐ Mug	240.00-	275.00
☐ Pickle dish	34.00-	49.00
☐ Plate	50.00-	65.00
☐ Platter	100.00-	135.00
☐ Relish dish	25.00-	40.00

	Price Range
☐ Shakers, S/P	23.00- 38.00
☐ Sauce, FTD	23.00- 38.00
☐ Spoon holder	70.00- 85.00
☐ Sugar bowl	85.00-100.00

LILY OF THE VALLEY (c. 1870)

	Price Range
☐ Butter plate, FTD	45.00- 60.00
☐ Cake stand	30.00- 45.00
☐ Celery dish	35.00- 50.00
☐ Compote, CVD	65.00- 80.00
☐ Cordial glass	30.00- 45.00
☐ Creamer, FTD	37.00- 52.00
☐ Cruet	37.00- 52.00
☐ Egg cup	34.00- 49.00
☐ Goblet	32.00- 47.00
☐ Pickle	16.00- 24.00
☐ Pitcher, W	30.00- 45.00
☐ Relish	14.00- 20.00
☐ Salt, CVD	37.00- 52.00
☐ Sauce dish	8.00- 14.00
☐ Spoon holder	21.00- 36.00
☐ Sugar bowl, FTD	45.00- 60.00
☐ Wine jug	45.00- 60.00

LINCOLN DRAPE (c. 1860)

	Price Range
☐ Bowl	35.00- 50.00
☐ Butter plate	80.00-100.00
☐ Celery dish	75.00- 90.00
☐ Compote	50.00- 65.00
☐ Cordial glass	27.00- 42.00
☐ Creamer	90.00-105.00
☐ Decanter	80.00- 95.00
☐ Egg cup	35.00- 50.00
☐ Goblet	60.00- 75.00
☐ Honey dish	14.00- 20.00
☐ Pitcher, W	140.00-175.00
☐ Plate	45.00- 60.00
☐ Salt shaker, FTD	19.00- 34.00
☐ Sauce dish	14.00- 20.00
☐ Spoon holder	45.00- 60.00
☐ Sugar bowl	65.00- 80.00
☐ Tumbler	25.00- 40.00
☐ Wine jug	30.00- 45.00

LOCKET ON CHAIN (c. 1890)

	Price Range
☐ Bowl	10.00- 20.00
☐ Butter dish, CVD	20.00- 35.00
☐ Cake stand	20.00- 30.00
☐ Celery dish	18.00- 26.00
☐ Compote	20.00- 35.00
☐ Creamer	18.00- 26.00
☐ Cruet	16.00- 24.00

	Price Range
☐ Goblet	14.00- 22.00
☐ Pickle	8.00- 14.00
☐ Pitcher, M	20.00- 35.00
☐ Plate	10.00- 18.00
☐ Sauce dish	6.00- 12.00
☐ Shakers, S/P	18.00- 26.00
☐ Spoon holder	12.00- 20.00
☐ Sugar bowl	22.00- 37.00
☐ Toothpick holder	18.00- 18.00
☐ Tumbler	10.00- 18.00

LOOP AND DART (c. 1860)

	Price Range
☐ Butter plate	40.00- 55.00
☐ Celery dish	35.00- 50.00
☐ Compote, FTD	30.00- 45.00
☐ Cordial glass	27.00- 42.00
☐ Creamer	45.00- 60.00
☐ Egg cup	20.00- 30.00
☐ Goblet	24.00- 39.00
☐ Pickle	10.00- 18.00
☐ Pitcher, W	55.00- 70.00
☐ Plate	50.00- 65.00
☐ Relish dish	10.00- 16.00
☐ Salt and pepper, FTD	21.00- 31.00
☐ Sauce dish	8.00- 16.00
☐ Spoon holder	30.00- 45.00
☐ Sugar bowl, CVD	45.00- 60.00
☐ Tumbler, FTD	25.00- 40.00
☐ Wine	27.00- 37.00

MAGNET AND GRAPE FROSTED LEAF (c. 1860)

	Price Range
☐ Butter plate	95.00-110.00
☐ Celery dish	105.00-140.00
☐ Champagne glass	85.00-100.00
☐ Compote	80.00- 95.00
☐ Cordial glass	105.00-140.00
☐ Creamer	80.00- 90.00
☐ Decanter	90.00-105.00
☐ Egg cup	42.00- 57.00

	Price Range
☐ Canary	45.00- 55.00
Plate	
☐ Clear	20.00- 30.00
☐ Canary	30.00- 45.00
Platter	

	Price Range
☐ Salt shaker, FTD	30.00- 45.00
☐ Sauce dish	12.00- 20.00
☐ Spoon holder	42.00- 57.00
☐ Tumbler	45.00- 60.00
☐ Wine jug	90.00-100.00

MANHATTAN (c. 1902)

☐ Bowl	10.00- 18.00
☐ Bowl, punch	65.00- 75.00
☐ Butter dish	24.00- 39.00
☐ Cake stand	25.00- 40.00
☐ Celery vase	15.00- 22.00
☐ Compote	23.00- 38.00
☐ Creamer, lg.	12.00- 20.00
☐ Dish	8.00- 16.00
☐ Goblet	0.00- 18.00
☐ Pickle	8.00- 16.00
☐ Pitcher, W	20.00- 35.00
☐ Plate	8.00- 16.00
☐ Punch cup	4.00- 8.00
☐ Sauce dish, FTD	4.00- 8.00
☐ Spoon holder	10.00- 18.00
☐ Sugar bowl, CVD	23.00- 38.00
☐ Tumbler	4.00- 8.00
☐ Water jug	12.00- 20.00

MAPLE LEAF (c. 1890)

Bowl	
☐ Clear	20.00- 30.00
☐ Canary	27.00- 43.00
Bowl, FTD	
☐ Clear	20.00- 35.00
☐ Canary	33.00- 48.00
Celery vase	
☐ Clear	25.00- 40.00
☐ Canary	40.00- 55.00
Compote, CVD	
☐ Clear	60.00- 75.00
☐ Canary	95.00-110.00
Pitcher, W	
☐ Clear	30.00- 40.00

☐ Clear	25.00- 40.00
☐ Canary	40.00- 55.00
Sauce dish, FTD	
☐ Clear	8.00- 14.00
☐ Canary	12.00- 20.00

MARQUISETTE (c. 1880)

☐ Butter dish	55.00- 70.00
☐ Celery vase	37.00- 52.00
☐ Compote, CVD	60.00- 75.00
☐ Cordial glass	33.00- 48.00
☐ Creamer	50.00- 65.00
☐ Goblet	30.00- 45.00
☐ Pickle	20.00- 35.00
☐ Pitcher	45.00- 60.00
☐ Sauce dish	10.00- 18.00
☐ Spoon holder	25.00- 40.00
☐ Sugar bowl, CVD	50.00- 65.00
☐ Wine jug	25.00- 40.00

MASCOTTE (c. 1890)

☐ Basket, cake	70.00- 85.00
☐ Bowl	12.00- 20.00
☐ Butter dish	34.00- 49.00
☐ Compote	42.00- 57.00
☐ Celery vase	27.00- 42.00
☐ Creamer	23.00- 48.00
☐ Dish	20.00- 30.00
☐ Goblet	20.00- 30.00
☐ Jar, CVD	40.00- 55.00
☐ Plate	32.00- 47.00
☐ Sauce dish	6.00- 10.00
☐ Spoon holder	20.00- 30.00
☐ Sugar bowl, CVD	20.00- 35.00
☐ Tray	33.00- 48.00

MICHIGAN (c. 1893)

	Price Range
☐ Bowl	16.00- 24.00
☐ Butter plate, CVD	21.00- 36.00
☐ Champagne glass	20.00- 35.00
☐ Creamer	20.00- 30.00
☐ Cruet	20.00- 30.00
☐ Cup	10.00- 18.00
☐ Goblet	18.00- 26.00
☐ Ice cream dish	14.00- 24.00
☐ Olive dish	10.00- 18.00
☐ Pitcher	45.00- 60.00
☐ Plate	14.00- 20.00
☐ Sauce dish	5.00- 12.00
☐ Shakers, S/P	20.00- 35.00
☐ Spoon holder	12.00- 20.00
☐ Sugar bowl, CVD	25.00- 40.00
☐ Toothpick holder	16.00- 24.00
☐ Tumbler	20.00- 30.00
☐ Water bottle	20.00- 30.00
☐ Wine jug	18.00- 26.00

MINERVA (c. 1870)

☐ Cake stand	45.00- 60.00
☐ Celery vase	35.00- 50.00
☐ Compote, CVD	70.00- 85.00
☐ Cordial glass	20.00- 30.00
☐ Creamer	40.00- 55.00
☐ Dish	25.00- 40.00
☐ Goblet	60.00- 75.00
☐ Jam jar, CVD	40.00- 55.00
☐ Pickle	40.00- 55.00
☐ Pitcher	70.00- 85.00
☐ Plate	45.00- 60.00
☐ Platter	45.00- 60.00
☐ Sauce dish, FTD	12.00- 20.00
☐ Spoon holder	20.00- 35.00
☐ Sugar bowl, CVD	30.00- 45.00

MOON AND STAR (c. 1890)

☐ Banana boat	90.00-105.00
☐ Bowl, CVD	45.00- 60.00
☐ Butter plate	60.00- 75.00
☐ Cake stand	50.00- 65.00
☐ Celery vase	40.00- 55.00
☐ Champagne glass	25.00- 40.00
☐ Cheese dish	50.00- 65.00
☐ Compote, CVD	40.00- 55.00
☐ Creamer	45.00- 60.00
☐ Cruet	60.00- 75.00
☐ Egg cup	30.00- 45.00
☐ Goblet	30.00- 45.00

	Price Range
☐ Pickle	18.00- 26.00
☐ Pitcher, W	95.00-130.00
☐ Platter	35.00- 50.00
☐ Shakers, S/P	40.00- 55.00
☐ Sauce dish, FTD	12.00- 20.00
☐ Spoon holder	20.00- 35.00
☐ Sugar bowl, CVD	55.00- 70.00
☐ Toothpick holder	15.00- 22.00
☐ Tray	50.00- 65.00
☐ Tumbler, FTD	40.00- 55.00
☐ Waste bowl	18.00- 26.00
☐ Wine jug	27.00- 42.00

NAILHEAD (c. 1885)

☐ Cake stand	18.00- 26.00
☐ Celery vase	20.00- 30.00
☐ Compote, CVD	25.00- 40.00
☐ Cordial glass	20.00- 30.00
☐ Creamer	18.00- 26.00
☐ Goblet	16.00- 24.00
☐ Pitcher, W	30.00- 45.00
☐ Plate	12.00- 20.00
☐ Sauce dish	6.00- 12.00
☐ Shakers, S/P	16.00- 24.00
☐ Spoon holder	16.00- 24.00
☐ Sugar bowl, CVD	20.00- 35.00
☐ Tumbler	16.00- 20.00
☐ Wine jug	16.00- 20.00

NEW ENGLAND PINEAPPLE (c. 1860)

☐ Bowl	80.00- 95.00
☐ Butter dish	95.00-110.00
☐ Castor bottle	23.00- 38.00
☐ Celery dish	70.00- 85.00
☐ Champagne glass	70.00- 85.00
☐ Compote, CVD	115.00-150.00
☐ Cordial glass	50.00- 65.00
☐ Cruet	70.00- 85.00
☐ Decanter	95.00-110.00
☐ Egg cup	25.00- 40.00
☐ Honey dish	15.00- 22.00
☐ Mug	70.00- 85.00
☐ Plate	80.00- 95.00
☐ Shakers, S/P, FTD	16.00- 24.00
☐ Spoon holder	35.00- 50.00
☐ Sugar bowl, CVD	90.00-105.00
☐ Tumbler	60.00- 75.00

NEW HAMPSHIRE (c. 1863)

	Price Range
☐ Butter plate	20.00- 35.00
☐ Celery vase	20.00- 30.00
☐ Champagne glass ...	15.00- 22.00
☐ Creamer	10.00- 18.00
☐ Goblet	12.00- 20.00
☐ Mug	10.00- 18.00
☐ Pitcher, M	20.00- 35.00
☐ Punch glass	8.00- 14.00
☐ Sauce dish	4.00- 8.00
☐ Sugar bowl, CVD	20.00- 35.00
☐ Toothpick holder	12.00- 20.00
☐ Tumbler	10.00- 18.00
☐ Wine jug	12.00- 20.00

NEW JERSEY (c. 1860)

	Price Range
☐ Bowl	8.00- 14.00
☐ Butter plate	35.00- 50.00
☐ Cake stand	20.00- 35.00
☐ Celery dish	10.00- 18.00
☐ Compote, CVD	20.00- 35.00
☐ Creamer	15.00- 22.00
☐ Cruet	10.00- 18.00
☐ Goblet	15.00- 22.00
☐ Jam jar	12.00- 20.00
☐ Pickle	8.00- 14.00
☐ Pitcher, S	15.00- 22.00
☐ Plate	21.00- 36.00
☐ Sauce dish	4.00- 8.00
☐ Shakers, S/P........	20.00- 35.00
☐ Spoon holder	15.00- 22.00
☐ Sugar bowl, CVD	20.00- 30.00
☐ Toothpick holder	5.00- 10.00
☐ Tumbler	75.00- 90.00
☐ Wine jug	8.00- 14.00

PALMETTE (c. 1890)

	Price Range
☐ Butter plate	20.00- 35.00
☐ Cake stand	23.00- 38.00

	Price Range
☐ Celery dish	22.00- 37.00
☐ Compote, CVD	42.00- 57.00
☐ Cordial glass	20.00- 35.00
☐ Creamer	45.00- 60.00
☐ Egg cup	18.00- 26.00
☐ Goblet	20.00- 30.00
☐ Lamp.............	40.00- 55.00
☐ Pickle	15.00- 22.00
☐ Pitcher, S	30.00- 45.00
☐ Relish dish	12.00- 20.00
☐ Sauce dish	6.00- 12.00
☐ Shakers, S/P........	35.00- 50.00
☐ Spoon holder	18.00- 26.00
☐ Sugar bowl, CVD	27.00- 42.00
☐ Tumbler	18.00- 26.00
☐ Vegetable dish......	15.00- 22.00
☐ Wine jug	18.00- 26.00

PANELLED CHERRY (c. 1888)

	Price Range
☐ Bowl	20.00- 35.00
☐ Butter, CVD	45.00- 60.00
☐ Compote, CVD	35.00- 50.00
☐ Creamer	37.00- 52.00
☐ Goblet	20.00- 35.00
☐ Pitcher, W.........	23.00- 38.00
☐ Sauce, FTD	4.00- 8.00
☐ Spoon holder	16.00- 24.00
☐ Sugar bowl, CVD	37.00- 52.00
☐ Toothpick holder	6.00- 12.00
☐ Tumbler	16.00- 24.00

PANELLED DAISY (c. 1878)

	Price Range
☐ Bowl	12.00- 20.00
☐ Butter plate, FTD	33.00- 48.00
☐ Cake stand	27.00- 42.00
☐ Celery	30.00- 45.00
☐ Compote, CVD	30.00- 45.00
☐ Creamer	35.00- 50.00
☐ Mug	20.00- 35.00
☐ Pickle dish	15.00- 22.00
☐ Relish	10.00- 18.00

	Price Range
☐ Sauce dish, FTD	10.00- 18.00
☐ Shakers, S/P	25.00- 40.00
☐ Spoon holder	20.00- 35.00
☐ Sugar bowl, CVD	40.00- 55.00
☐ Tray	37.00- 52.00

PANELLED DEWDROP (c. 1878)

☐ Butter plate	52.00- 67.00
☐ Celery vase	31.00- 46.00
☐ Compote, CVD	50.00- 65.00
☐ Cordial glass	33.00- 48.00
☐ Creamer	37.00- 52.00
☐ Goblet	27.00- 42.00
☐ Jam jar	23.00- 38.00
☐ Pickle dish	20.00- 30.00
☐ Pitcher, M	34.00- 49.00
☐ Platter	37.00- 52.00
☐ Sauce dish	8.00- 14.00
☐ Spoon holder	30.00- 45.00
☐ Sugar bowl, CVD	40.00- 55.00
☐ Tumbler	25.00- 40.00
☐ Wine jug	18.00- 26.00

PANELLED THISTLE (c. 1910)

☐ Banana plate	50.00- 65.00
☐ Bowl	12.00- 20.00
☐ Butter plate, CVD ...	25.00- 40.00
☐ Cake stand	20.00- 35.00
☐ Celery dish	15.00- 22.00

	Price Range
☐ Compote, CVD	25.00- 40.00
☐ Cordial glass	20.00- 35.00
☐ Creamer	25.00- 40.00
☐ Cruet	30.00- 45.00
☐ Egg cup	17.00- 32.00
☐ Goblet	30.00- 45.00
☐ Pitcher, lg./sm.......	45.00- 60.00
☐ Relish dish	12.00- 20.00
☐ Salt dish, FTD	18.00- 26.00
☐ Sauce dish, FTD	0.00- 18.00
☐ Shakers, S/P	35.00- 50.00
☐ Spoon holder	18.00- 26.00
☐ Sugar bowl, CVD	30.00- 45.00
☐ Toothpick holder	12.00- 20.00
☐ Tumbler	18.00- 26.00
☐ Wine jug	12.00- 20.00

PAVONIA (c. 1885)

☐ Bowl	12.00- 20.00
☐ Butter plate, CVD ...	35.00- 50.00
☐ Cake stand	23.00- 38.00
☐ Celery dish	23.00- 38.00
☐ Creamer	20.00- 35.00
☐ Compote, CVD	50.00- 60.00
☐ Goblet	22.00- 37.00
☐ Pitcher, W	60.00- 75.00
☐ Shakers, S/P	10.00- 10.00
☐ Spoon holder	18.00- 26.00
☐ Sugar bowl, CVD	35.00- 50.00
☐ Tumbler	16.00- 24.00
☐ Wine jug	25.00- 40.00

PEACOCK FEATHER (c. 1907)

☐ Butter plate, CVD ...	35.00- 50.00
☐ Cake stand	35.00- 45.00
☐ Celery dish	20.00- 30.00
☐ Compote, CVD	35.00- 45.00
☐ Creamer	35.00- 50.00
☐ Cruet	20.00- 35.00
☐ Pickle	10.00- 18.00
☐ Pitcher, W	45.00- 55.00
☐ Plate	20.00- 35.00
☐ Relish dish	8.00- 14.00
☐ Sauce dish	4.00- 8.00
☐ Shakers, S/P	25.00- 40.00
☐ Spoon holder	12.00- 20.00
☐ Sugar bowl, CVD	30.00- 45.00
☐ Tumbler	20.00- 30.00

PINEAPPLE AND FAN (c. 1891)

	Price Range
☐ Bowl, finger, punch ..	50.00- 65.00
☐ Butter plate, CVD ...	30.00- 45.00
☐ Cake stand	16.00- 24.00
☐ Celery vase	20.00- 35.00
☐ Creamer	16.00- 24.00
☐ Cup	10.00- 18.00
☐ Goblet.............	10.00- 18.00
☐ Mug	10.00- 18.00
☐ Pitcher, W..........	20.00- 30.00
☐ Plate	10.00- 18.00
☐ Sauce dish	6.00- 12.00
☐ Spoon handle.......	12.00- 20.00
☐ Sugar bowl, CVD	18.00- 26.00
☐ Tumbler	10.00- 18.00

PLEAT AND PANEL (c. 1870)

	Price Range
☐ Bowl	32.00- 47.00
☐ Butter plate, CVD ...	40.00- 55.00
☐ Cake stand	22.00- 37.00
☐ Celery vase	22.00- 37.00
☐ Compote, CVD	30.00- 45.00
☐ Creamer	30.00- 45.00
☐ Lamp.............	34.00- 49.00
☐ Marmalade jar	23.00- 38.00
☐ Pickle dish	10.00- 18.00
☐ Pitcher, M..........	45.00- 60.00
☐ Plate	18.00- 26.00
☐ Sauce dish	8.00- 14.00
☐ Shakers, S/P........	30.00- 45.00
☐ Spoon holder	18.00- 26.00
☐ Sugar bowl, CVD	37.00- 52.00

PLUME (c. 1874)

	Price Range
☐ Bowl	20.00- 30.00
☐ Butter plate, CVD ...	25.00- 40.00
☐ Cake stand	25.00- 40.00
☐ Celery dish	20.00- 35.00
☐ Compote, CVD	20.00- 30.00

	Price Range
☐ Creamer	15.00- 22.00
☐ Goblet.............	27.00- 42.00
☐ Pickle dish	10.00- 18.00
☐ Pitcher, M..........	34.00- 49.00
☐ Sauce dish	6.00- 12.00
☐ Spoon holder	18.00- 26.00
☐ Sugar bowl, CVD	27.00- 42.00
☐ Tumbler	10.00- 18.00
☐ Tray	20.00- 30.00
☐ Waste bowl	22.00- 37.00

PRESSED LEAF (c. 1881)

	Price Range
☐ Butter dish, CVD	30.00- 45.00
☐ Cake stand	45.00- 60.00
☐ Champagne glass ...	37.00- 52.00
☐ Cordial glass	18.00- 26.00
☐ Creamer	50.00- 65.00
☐ Egg cup	12.00- 20.00
☐ Goblet.............	20.00- 30.00
☐ Pickle dish	12.00- 20.00
☐ Pitcher, W..........	95.00-110.00
☐ Shakers, S/P........	35.00- 50.00
☐ Sauce dish	15.00- 22.00
☐ Spoon holder	18.00- 26.00
☐ Sugar bowl, CVD	45.00- 60.00
☐ Wine jug	40.00- 55.00

PRIMROSE (c. 1880)

	Price Range
☐ Bowl	20.00- 30.00
☐ Butter plate	35.00- 50.00
☐ Cake stand	25.00- 40.00
☐ Celery dish	20.00- 35.00
☐ Compote, CVD	37.00- 52.00
☐ Cordial glass	18.00- 26.00
☐ Creamer	25.00- 40.00
☐ Egg cup	18.00- 26.00
☐ Goblet.............	20.00- 35.00
☐ Jam jar	20.00- 30.00
☐ Pickle dish	10.00- 18.00
☐ Pitcher, M/W	37.00- 52.00
☐ Plate	20.00- 35.00

	Price	Range
☐ Platter	20.00-	35.00
☐ Sauce dish, FTD	8.00-	14.00
☐ Spoon holder	16.00-	24.00
☐ Sugar bowl, CVD	25.00-	40.00
☐ Toothpick holder	15.00-	22.00
☐ Tray	18.00-	26.00
☐ Wine jug	12.00-	20.00

PRISCILLA (c. 1890)

	Price	Range
☐ Banana plate	45.00-	60.00
☐ Bowl	45.00-	60.00
☐ Butter plate, CVD . . .	40.00-	55.00
☐ Cake stand	27.00-	42.00
☐ Celery vase	20.00-	35.00
☐ Creamer	23.00-	38.00
☐ Cruet	16.00-	24.00
☐ Cup/saucer	27.00-	42.00
☐ Goblet	20.00-	30.00
☐ Mug	10.00-	18.00
☐ Pickle dish	20.00-	30.00
☐ Plate	22.00-	37.00
☐ Spoon holder	18.00-	26.00
☐ Sugar bowl, CVD	30.00-	45.00
☐ Syrup pitcher	45.00-	60.00
☐ Tumbler	8.00-	14.00

PRISM AND FLUTE (c. 1879)

	Price	Range
☐ Butter plate	45.00-	60.00
☐ Celery dish	35.00-	50.00
☐ Cordial glass	25.00-	40.00
☐ Creamer	32.00-	47.00
☐ Egg cup	20.00-	35.00
☐ Goblet	20.00-	35.00
☐ Pickle dish	20.00-	30.00
☐ Pitcher, M	70.00-	85.00
☐ Plate	20.00-	35.00
☐ Sauce dish	8.00-	14.00
☐ Tumbler, FTD	20.00-	35.00
☐ Wine jug	8.00-	14.00

RED BLOCK (o. 1892)

	Price	Range
☐ Bowl	18.00-	26.00
☐ Butter plate	70.00-	85.00
☐ Celery vase	50.00-	65.00
☐ Cordial glass	23.00-	38.00
☐ Creamer	40.00-	55.00
☐ Dish	33.00-	48.00
☐ Pitcher	80.00-	95.00
☐ Sauce dish	10.00-	18.00
☐ Shaker, S/P	60.00-	70.00
☐ Shaker, sugar	37.00-	52.00

	Price	Range
☐ Spoon holder	24.00-	39.00
☐ Sugar bowl, CVD	40.00-	55.00
☐ Tumbler	20.00-	35.00
☐ Wine glass	20.00-	30.00

REVERSED TORPEDO (c. 1860)

	Price	Range
☐ Banana stand	90.00-	105.00
☐ Bowl	35.00-	50.00
☐ Cake plate	80.00-	95.00
☐ Compote, CVD	70.00-	85.00
☐ Pitcher, W	90.00-	105.00
☐ Sauce dish	20.00-	30.00
☐ Sugar bowl, CVD	45.00-	60.00

RIBBED IVY (c. 1858)

	Price	Range
☐ Bottle	55.00-	70.00
☐ Butter plate, CVD . . .	90.00-	105.00
☐ Compote, CVD	52.00-	67.00
☐ Cordial glass	57.00-	72.00
☐ Creamer	115.00-	150.00
☐ Egg cup	30.00-	45.00
☐ Goblet	25.00-	40.00
☐ Honey dish	12.00-	20.00
☐ Salt shaker, CVD	105.00-	140.00
☐ Sauce dish	25.00-	40.00
☐ Spoon holder	25.00-	40.00
☐ Sugar bowl, CVD	45.00-	60.00
☐ Tumbler	70.00-	85.00
☐ Wine jug	31.00-	46.00

RIBBED PALM (c. 1868)

	Price	Range
☐ Bottle	12.00-	20.00
☐ Butter plate	65.00-	80.00
☐ Celery vase	45.00-	60.00
☐ Champagne glass . . .	52.00-	67.00
☐ Cordial glass	32.00-	47.00
☐ Creamer	80.00-	95.00
☐ Egg cup	33.00-	48.00
☐ Goblet	42.00-	57.00

	Price Range
☐ Pickle dish	25.00- 40.00
☐ Plate	35.00- 50.00
☐ Salt shaker, FTD	20.00- 35.00
☐ Sauce dish	15.00- 22.00
☐ Spoon holder	25.00- 40.00
☐ Sugar bowl, CVD	30.00- 45.00
☐ Toothpick HLD	35.00- 50.00
☐ Tumbler	47.00- 62.00
☐ Wine jug	45.00- 60.00

RIBBON (c. 1867)

	Price Range
☐ Bottle	20.00- 35.00
☐ Butter plate	60.00- 75.00
☐ Cake stand	25.00- 40.00
☐ Celery dish	37.00- 52.00
☐ Cheese dish	75.00- 90.00
☐ Cordial glass	32.00- 47.00
☐ Creamer	50.00- 65.00
☐ Pitcher, lg./sm.	85.00-100.00
☐ Platter	45.00- 60..00
☐ Sauce dish, FTD	20.00- 35.00
☐ Spoon holder	22.00- 37.00
☐ Sugar bowl, CVD	60.00- 75.00
☐ Tray	70.00- 85.00

RIBBON CANDY (c. 1880)

	Price Range
☐ Butter plate, CVD	25.00- 40.00
☐ Cake stand	20.00- 35.00
☐ Celery vase	15.00- 22.00
☐ Champagne glass	25.00- 40.00
☐ Compote, CVD	18.00- 26.00
☐ Cordial glass	10.00- 16.00
☐ Creamer	12.00- 20.00
☐ Cruet	12.00- 16.00
☐ Goblet	16.00- 24.00
☐ Honey dish	10.00- 18.00
☐ Pitcher, W/M	30.00- 45.00
☐ Plate	20.00- 35.00
☐ Relish dish	8.00- 14.00
☐ Shakers, S/P	40.00- 55.00
☐ Spoon holder	15.00- 22.00
☐ Sugar bowl, CVD	20.00- 30.00
☐ Tumbler	15.00- 22.00
☐ Wine jug	16.00- 24.00

ROMAN ROSETTE (c. 1875)

	Price Range
☐ Bowl	25.00- 40.00
☐ Butter dish	37.00- 52.00
☐ Cake dish	47.00- 62.00
☐ Celery vase	27.00- 42.00
☐ Compote, CVD	34.00- 49.00
☐ Cordial glass	18.00- 26.00

	Price Range
☐ Creamer	16.00- 24.00
☐ Dish	18.00- 26.00
☐ Mug	15.00- 22.00
☐ Pickle dish	15.00- 22.00
☐ Plate	20.00- 30.00
☐ Shakers, S/P	20.00- 35.00
☐ Spoon holder	20.00- 35.00
☐ Sugar bowl, CVD	35.00- 50.00
☐ Tray	30.00- 45.00
☐ Tumbler	23.00- 38.00
☐ Wine jug	20.00- 35.00

ROSE-IN-SNOW (c. 1870)

	Price Range
☐ Bowl	20.00- 30.00
☐ Butter plate	50.00- 65.00
☐ Candy dish	30.00- 45.00
☐ Compote, CVD	65.00- 80.00
☐ Creamer	40.00- 55.00
☐ Jam jar	30.00- 45.00
☐ Pickle dish	20.00- 35.00
☐ Pitcher, W	80.00- 95.00
☐ Plate	35.00- 50.00
☐ Sauce dish	6.00- 12.00
☐ Tumbler	25.00- 40.00

ROSE SPRIG (c. 1886)

	Price Range
☐ Butter plate	35.00- 50.00
☐ Cake stand	25.00- 40.00
☐ Celery dish	20.00- 35.00
☐ Compote, CVD	32.00- 47.00
☐ Creamer	40.00- 55.00
☐ Goblet	20.00- 35.00
☐ Mug	20.00- 35.00
☐ Pickle dish	10.00- 18.00
☐ Pitcher, lg./sm.	40.00- 55.00
☐ Plate	25.00- 40.00
☐ Platter	20.00- 35.00
☐ Relish dish	8.00- 14.00
☐ Salt shaker	20.00- 30.00
☐ Sauce dish, FTD	8.00- 14.00
☐ Spoon holder	18.00- 26.00

	Price Range
☐ Sugar bowl, CVD	25.00- 40.00
☐ Tray	23.00- 38.00
☐ Tumbler	18.00- 26.00
☐ Wine jug	23.00- 38.00

ROSETTE (c. 1865)

	Price Range
☐ Butter plate, CVD ...	34.00- 49.00
☐ Cake stand	24.00- 39.00
☐ Celery dish	20.00- 35.00
☐ Compote, CVD	45.00- 60.00
☐ Cordial glass	12.00- 20.00
☐ Creamer	28.00- 43.00
☐ Goblet	21.00- 36.00
☐ Pickle dish	10.00- 16.00
☐ Pitcher, W..........	40.00- 55.00
☐ Plate	20.00- 35.00
☐ Relish dish	10.00- 16.00
☐ Sauce dish, FTD	6.00- 12.00
☐ Shakers, S/P........	30.00- 45.00
☐ Spoon holder	18.00- 26.00
☐ Sugar bowl, CVD	30.00- 45.00
☐ Tray	25.00- 40.00
☐ Tumbler	12.00- 20.00
☐ Wine jug	15.00- 30.00

SAWTOOTH (c. 1885)

	Price Range
☐ Bottle	20.00- 35.00
☐ Bowl	50.00- 65.00
☐ Butter plate	80.00- 95.00
☐ Cake stand	40.00- 55.00
☐ Celery vase	30.00- 45.00
☐ Champagne glass ...	20.00- 35.00
☐ Compote, CVD	85.00-100.00
☐ Cordial glass	47.00- 62.00
☐ Creamer	70.00- 85.00
☐ Decanter..........	55.00- 70.00
☐ Honey dish	12.00- 20.00
☐ Egg cup	27.00- 42.00
☐ Pitcher, M/W	75.00- 90.00
☐ Jug	40.00- 55.00
☐ Salt shaker, CVD	55.00- 70.00

	Price Range
☐ Sauce dish	12.00- 20.00
☐ Spoon holder	30.00- 45.00
☐ Sugar bowl, CVD	25.00- 40.00
☐ Tray	60.00- 75.00
☐ Tumbler, FTD	22.00- 37.00

SCROLL WITH FLOWERS (c. 1870)

	Price Range
☐ Butter plate	25.00- 40.00
☐ Cake stand	30.00- 45.00
☐ Celery dish	25.00- 40.00
☐ Compote, CVD	35.00- 50.00
☐ Cordial glass	20.00- 45.00
☐ Creamer	18.00- 26.00
☐ Egg cup	12.00- 20.00
☐ Goblet	22.00- 32.00
☐ Jar, CVD	20.00- 35.00
☐ Pickle dish	16.00- 24.00
☐ Pitcher, W..........	35.00- 50.00
☐ Plate	12.00- 20.00
☐ Relish	8.00- 14.00
☐ Salt shaker, FTD	10.00- 18.00
☐ Sauce dish	8.00- 14.00
☐ Shakers, S/P........	22.00- 37.00
☐ Spoon holder	18.00- 26.00
☐ Sugar bowl, CVD	20.00- 35.00
☐ Wine jug	15.00- 22.00

SHELL AND TASSEL (c. 1890)

	Price Range
☐ Bowl	20.00- 30.00
☐ Butter plate, CVD ...	45.00- 60.00
☐ Cake stand	60.00- 75.00
☐ Celery dish	40.00- 55.00
☐ Compote, CVD	35.00- 50.00
☐ Creamer	40.00- 55.00
☐ Jam jar	25.00- 40.00
☐ Pickle dish	12.00- 20.00
☐ Pitcher, W..........	50.00- 65.00
☐ Salt shaker	15.00- 22.00
☐ Sauce dish, FTD	12.00- 20.00
☐ Spoon holder	18.00- 26.00
☐ Sugar bowl, CVD	55.00- 70.00
☐ Tray	35.00- 50.00

SHERATON (c. 1880)

	Price Range
☐ Bowl	15.00- 22.00
☐ Butter plate	22.00- 37.00
☐ Cake dish	20.00- 35.00
☐ Celery dish	18.00- 26.00
☐ Compote, CVD	30.00- 45.00
☐ Creamer	16.00- 24.00
☐ Goblet	15.00- 22.00

	Price Range
Pitcher, M/W	25.00- 40.00
Sauce dish	6.00- 12.00
Spoon holder	15.00- 22.00
Sugar bowl, CVD	23.00- 38.00
Tray	12.00- 20.00
Wine jug	10.00- 18.00

SNAIL (c. 1880)

Bowl	23.00- 39.00
Butter plate, CVD	50.00- 65.00
Cake stand	45.00- 60.00
Celery dish	23.00- 38.00
Cheese dish, CVD	45.00- 60.00
Compote, CVD	55.00- 70.00
Cruet	23.00- 38.00
Goblet	35.00- 50.00
Pitcher	30.00- 45.00
Plate	32.00- 47.00
Punch glass	18.00- 26.00
Sauce dish	10.00- 18.00
Salt shaker	8.00- 14.00
Spoon holder	20.00- 35.00
Sugar bowl, CVD	35.00- 50.00
Tumbler	20.00- 35.00
Wine jug	20.00- 35.00

SPIREA BAND (c. 1885)

Bowl	16.00- 24.00
Butter plate, CVD	29.00- 44.00
Cake stand	18.00- 24.00
Celery dish	15.00- 22.00
Compote, CVD	30.00- 45.00
Cordial glass	12.00- 20.00
Creamer	12.00- 20.00
Goblet	12.00- 20.00
Pitcher, W	20.00- 35.00
Relish dish	12.00- 20.00
Sauce dish, FTD	8.00- 14.00
Shakers, S/P	18.00- 26.00
Spoon holder	12.00- 20.00
Sugar bowl, CVD	20.00- 35.00
Wine jug	10.00- 18.00

Price Range

SPRIG (c. 1880)

Butter plate, CVD	25.00- 40.00
Cake stand	35.00- 50.00
Celery dish	23.00- 38.00
Compote, CVD	40.00- 50.00
Creamer	29.00- 44.00
Goblet	22.00- 37.00
Pickle dish	8.00- 14.00
Pitcher, W	35.00- 50.00
Platter	20.00- 35.00
Sauce dish, FTD	8.00- 14.00
Spoon holder	20.00- 35.00
Sugar bowl, CVD	23.00- 38.00
Tumbler	18.00- 26.00
Wine jug	15.00- 30.00

STATES, THE (c. 1905)

Bowl	20.00- 35.00
Butter dish, CVD	20.00- 35.00
Celery dish	15.00- 22.00
Compote	20.00- 30.00
Creamer	12.00- 20.00
Goblet	20.00- 30.00
Plate	12.00- 20.00
Punch glass	8.00- 14.00
Relish dish	20.00- 30.00
Shakers, S/P	12.00- 20.00
Sugar bowl, CVD	20.00- 35.00
Toothpick holder	8.00- 14.00
Tray	10.00- 18.00
Tumbler	10.00- 18.00
Wine jug	15.00- 22.00

STEDMAN (c. 1860)

Celery dish	27.00- 42.00
Champagne glass	20.00- 35.00
Cheese dish, CVD	41.00- 56.00
Compote, CVD	60.00- 75.00
Creamer	60.00- 75.00
Decanter	40.00- 55.00

Price Range

Price Range

☐ Egg cup	20.00- 30.00
☐ Goblet	18.00- 26.00
☐ Plate	20.00- 35.00
☐ Salt shaker	10.00- 18.00
☐ Sauce dish	8.00- 14.00
☐ Spoon holder	20.00- 35.00
☐ Sugar bowl, CVD	20.00- 30.00
☐ Syrup pitcher	40.00- 55.00
☐ Tumbler	20.00- 35.00
☐ Wine jug	25.00- 40.0

STRAWBERRY (c. 1860)

☐ Butter plate	35.00- 50.00
☐ Compote, CVD	90.00-105.00
☐ Creamer	30.00- 45.00
☐ Honey bowl	12.00- 20.00
☐ Pickle dish	12.00- 20.00
☐ Pitcher	25.00- 40.00
☐ Salt shaker	8.00- 14.00
☐ Sauce dish	4.00- 8.00
☐ Spoon holder	20.00- 35.00
☐ Sugar bowl, CVD	30.00- 45.00

SUNBURST (c. 1898)

☐ Butter plate	25.00- 40.00
☐ Cake stand	20.00- 35.00
☐ Celery dish	20.00- 35.00
☐ Compote, CVD	8.00- 14.00
☐ Cordial glass	10.00- 18.00
☐ Creamer	20.00- 35.00
☐ Cruet	20.00- 30.00
☐ Egg cup	10.00- 18.00
☐ Goblet	16.00- 24.00
☐ Jam jar	20.00- 30.00
☐ Pickle dish	12.00- 20.00
☐ Pitcher, W	25.00- 40.00
☐ Plate	15.00- 22.00
☐ Salt shaker	16.00- 24.00
☐ Sauce dish	3.00- 9.00
☐ Spoon holder	16.00- 24.00
☐ Sugar bowl, CVD	23.00- 38.00

SWAN (c. 1860)

☐ Bowl	35.00- 50.00
☐ Butter plate	70.00- 85.00
☐ Celery dish	30.00- 45.00
☐ Compote	30.00- 45.00
☐ Creamer	40.00- 55.00
☐ Goblet	40.00- 55.00
☐ Pitcher, W	55.00- 70.00
☐ Sauce dish	8.00- 14.00
☐ Spoon holder	20.00- 35.00
☐ Sugar bowl, CVD	40.00- 55.00

TEARDROP AND TASSEL (c. 1890)

☐ Bowl	22.00- 32.00
☐ Butter plate, CVD	40.00- 55.00
☐ Compote, CVD	40.00- 55.00
☐ Creamer	20.00- 35.00
☐ Goblet	45.00- 60.00
☐ Pickle dish	12.00- 20.00
☐ Pitcher, W	40.00- 55.00
☐ Sauce dish	10.00- 16.00
☐ Spoon holder	24.00- 39.00
☐ Sugar bowl, CVD	35.00- 50.00
☐ Tumbler	18.00- 26.00
☐ Wine jug	35.00- 50.00

TEXAS (c. 1900)

☐ Bowl	16.00- 24.00
☐ Butter plate	25.00- 40.00
☐ Cake stand, CVD	27.00- 42.00
☐ Celery vase	18.00- 26.00
☐ Celery tray	8.00- 14.00
☐ Compote, CVD	40.00- 55.00
☐ Cruet	18.00- 26.00
☐ Goblet	20.00- 30.00
☐ Jar	10.00- 18.00
☐ Pickle dish	10.00- 18.00
☐ Pitcher	22.00- 37.00
☐ Plate	15.00- 22.00
☐ Relish dish	8.00- 14.00
☐ Sauce dish	4.00- 8.00
☐ Shaker, S/P	22.00- 32.00
☐ Spoon holder	12.00- 20.00
☐ Toothpick holder	10.00- 18.00
☐ Tumbler	10.00- 18.00
☐ Wine jug	18.00- 26.00

THISTLE (c. 1875)

	Price Range
☐ Bowl, CVD	30.00- 45.00
☐ Cake stand	40.00- 55.00
☐ Compote, CVD	35.00- 50.00
☐ Cordial glass	22.00- 37.00
☐ Creamer	35.00- 50.00
☐ Decanter	60.00- 75.00
☐ Egg cup	20.00- 30.00
☐ Pickle dish	10.00- 16.00
☐ Salt shaker, FTD	10.00- 18.00
☐ Tumbler, FTD	25.00- 40.00
☐ Wine glass	20.00- 35.00

THOUSAND EYE (c. 1888)

☐ Bowl	21.00- 36.00
☐ Butter dish	40.00- 55.00
☐ Cake stand	33.00- 48.00
☐ Celery dish	27.00- 42.00
☐ Compote, CVD	45.00- 60.00
☐ Cordial glass	18.00- 26.00
☐ Creamer	37.00- 52.00
☐ Cruet	30.00- 45.00
☐ Honey dish	12.00- 20.00
☐ Lamp	50.00- 65.00
☐ Pickle dish	18.00- 26.00
☐ Pitcher, W	37.00- 52.00
☐ Plate	20.00- 35.00
☐ Platter	25.00- 40.00
☐ Sauce dish	8.00- 14.00
☐ Shakers, S/P	21.00- 36.00
☐ Sugar bowl, CVD	40.00- 55.00
☐ Tray	40.00- 55.00

THREE FACES (c. 1878)

☐ Butter plate	25.00- 40.00
☐ Cake stand	100.00-135.00
☐ Celery dish	73.00- 88.00
☐ Champagne glass	85.00-100.00
☐ Compote, CVD	110.00-145.00
☐ Creamer	70.00- 85.00

	Price Range
☐ Goblet	45.00- 60.00
☐ Jam jar	65.00- 80.00
☐ Pitcher, M	165.00-200.00
☐ Sauce dish, FTD	20.00- 35.00
☐ Shakers, S/P	60.00- 75.00
☐ Spoon holder	55.00- 70.00

☐ Sugar bowl, CVD	85.00-100.00
☐ Tumbler	50.00- 65.00
☐ Wine jug	70.00- 85.00

THREE PANEL (c. 1888)

☐ Bowl	25.00- 40.00
☐ Butter plate	30.00- 45.00
☐ Celery dish	20.00- 30.00
☐ Compote	20.00- 35.00
☐ Creamer	30.00- 45.00
☐ Cruet	30.00- 45.00
☐ Goblet	27.00- 42.00
☐ Mug	8.00- 16.00
☐ Pitcher, W	33.00- 48.00
☐ Sauce dish, FTD	8.00- 14.00
☐ Spoon holder	16.00- 24.00
☐ Sugar bowl, CVD	25.00- 40.00
☐ Tumbler	21.00- 36.00

THUMBPRINT (c. 1860)

☐ Beer	30.00- 45.00
☐ Celery vase	70.00- 85.00
☐ Champagne glass	60.00- 75.00
☐ Compote, CVD	70.00- 85.00
☐ Cordial glass	30.00- 45.00
☐ Creamer	45.00- 60.00
☐ Decanter	85.00-100.00
☐ Egg cup	30.00- 45.00
☐ Goblet	50.00- 65.00
☐ Honey bowl	10.00- 18.00
☐ Mug	23.00- 38.00
☐ Pickle dish	20.00- 30.00
☐ Pitcher, W	85.00-100.00
☐ Shakers, S/P	25.00- 40.00

	Price Range
☐ Sauce dish	12.00- 20.00
☐ Spoon holder	34.00- 49.00
☐ Sugar bowl, CVD	85.00-100.00
☐ Tumbler, FTD	33.00- 48.00
☐ Wine glass	25.00- 40.00

TORPEDO (c. 1898)

☐ Butter plate	45.00- 60.00
☐ Cake stand	40.00- 55.00
☐ Celery vase	20.00- 35.00
☐ Compote, CVD	35.00- 50.00
☐ Creamer	25.00- 40.00
☐ Decanter...........	30.00- 45.00
☐ Goblet.............	25.00- 40.00
☐ Honey dish, CVD	30.00- 45.00
☐ Pitcher, M/W	60.00- 75.00
☐ Punch glass	18.00- 26.00
☐ Salt shaker	12.00- 20.00
☐ Sauce dish, FTD	10.00- 18.00
☐ Shakers, S/P	25.00- 40.00
☐ Spoon holder	21.00- 36.00
☐ Sugar bowl, CVD	50.00- 65.00
☐ Tumbler	30.00- 45.00
☐ Wine glass	18.00- 26.00

TREE OF LIFE (c. 1867)

☐ Bowl	10.00- 18.00
☐ Cake stand	40.00- 55.00
☐ Celery vase	30.00- 45.00
☐ Compote, CVD	70.00- 85.00
☐ Creamer	40.00- 55.00
☐ Goblet.............	55.00- 70.00
☐ Mug...............	20.00- 35.00
☐ Pitcher	12.00- 20.00
☐ Plate	16.00- 24.00
☐ Punch glass	8.00- 16.00
☐ Spoon holder	23.00- 38.00
☐ Sugar bowl, CVD	40.00- 55.00
☐ Tray...............	35.00- 50.00
☐ Tumbler, FTD	18.00- 26.00
☐ Wine jug	25.00- 40.00

	Price Range

TULIP WITH SAWTOOTH (c. 1854)

☐ Butter plate	55.00- 70.00
☐ Celery vase	30.00- 45.00
☐ Champagne glass ...	30.00- 45.00
☐ Compote, CVD	80.00- 95.00
☐ Cordial glass	25.00- 40.00
☐ Creamer	45.00- 60.00
☐ Cruet..............	50.00- 65.00
☐ Decanter...........	115.00-150.00
☐ Goblet.............	30.00- 45.00
☐ Honey dish	18.00- 26.00
☐ Pitcher, W..........	125.00-160.00
☐ Plate	32.00- 47.00
☐ Pomade jar	30.00- 45.00
☐ Salt shaker	12.00- 20.00
☐ Sauce dish	10.00- 18.00
☐ Spoon holder	23.00- 38.00
☐ Sugar bowl	70.00- 85.00
☐ Tumbler, FTD	43.00- 58.00
☐ Wine	20.00- 35.00

TWO PANEL (c. 1880)

☐ Bowl	32.00- 47.00
☐ Butter plate	25.00- 40.00
☐ Celery vase	18.00- 26.00
☐ Cordial glass	14.00- 22.00
☐ Creamer	27.00- 42.00
☐ Jam jar	20.00- 30.00
☐ Mug...............	22.00- 32.00
☐ Pickle dish	8.00- 14.00
☐ Pitcher, W..........	30.00- 45.00
☐ Platter.............	18.00- 26.00
☐ Salt shaker	3.00- 6.00
☐ Sauce dish	10.00- 18.00
☐ Shakers, S/P	18.00- 26.00
☐ Spoon holder	18.00- 26.00
☐ Sugar bowl, CVD	20.00- 35.00
☐ Tray...............	25.00- 40.00
☐ Tumbler	25.00- 40.00

VIKING (c. 1860)

☐ Bowl	20.00- 35.00
☐ Butter dish	25.00- 40.00
☐ Candleholder	12.00- 20.00
☐ Cake plate, FTD	40.00- 55.00
☐ Celery dish	22.00- 37.00
☐ Compote, CVD	35.00- 50.00
☐ Creamer	25.00- 40.00
☐ Egg cup	25.00- 40.00
☐ Goblet.............	30.00- 45.00
☐ Mug...............	35.00- 50.00
☐ Pickle	12.00- 26.00

	Price Range
☐ Pitcher, W	40.00- 55.00
☐ Platter	30.00- 45.00
☐ Salt shaker	18.00- 26.00
☐ Sauce dish, FTD	8.00- 14.00
☐ Spoon holder	20.00- 35.00
☐ Sugar bowl, CVD	40.00- 55.00
☐ Tumbler	35.00- 50.00

WAFFLE (c. 1860)

	Price Range
☐ Basket	18.00- 26.00
☐ Butter dish, CVD	50.00- 65.00
☐ Celery dish	35.00- 50.00
☐ Champagne glass . . .	45.00- 60.00
☐ Compote	45.00- 60.00
☐ Cordial glass	42.00- 57.00
☐ Creamer	70.00- 85.00
☐ Decanter	70.00- 85.00
☐ Egg cup	18.00- 26.00
☐ Goblet	70.00- 85.00
☐ Pitcher, W	85.00-100.00
☐ Plate	25.00- 40.00
☐ Salt shaker	20.00- 35.00
☐ Sauce dish	10.00- 18.00
☐ Spoon holder	40.00- 55.00
☐ Sugar bowl, CVD	70.00- 85.00
☐ Tumbler	4.00- 8.00
☐ Wine glass	18.00- 26.00

WAFFLE AND THUMBPRINT (c. 1850)

	Price Range
☐ Bowl	37.00- 52.00
☐ Butter dish	115.00-150.00
☐ Celery dish	77.00- 92.00
☐ Champagne glass . . .	35.00- 50.00
☐ Claret	75.00- 90.00
☐ Compote	95.00-110.00
☐ Creamer	90.00-105.00
☐ Decanter	18.00- 26.00
☐ Egg cup	32.00- 47.00
☐ Goblet	65.00- 80.00
☐ Relish dish	14.00- 20.00
☐ Salt shaker	21.00- 36.00
☐ Spoon holder	33.00- 48.00
☐ Tumbler, FTD	37.00- 52.00
☐ Wine jug	40.00- 55.00

WHEAT AND BARLEY (c. 1872)

	Price Range
☐ Butter dish, CVD	12.00- 20.00
☐ Cake plate	20.00- 30.00
☐ Compote, CVD	55.00- 70.00
☐ Creamer	15.00- 22.00
☐ Goblet	22.00- 37.00

	Price Range
☐ Mug	18.00- 26.00
☐ Pitcher, M	20.00- 35.00
☐ Plate	18.00- 26.00
☐ Sauce dish, FTD	8.00- 14.00
☐ Shaker, S/P	20.00- 35.00
☐ Spoon holder	14.00- 20.00
☐ Sugar bowl, CVD	30.00- 45.00
☐ Toothpick holder	15.00- 22.00
☐ Tumbler, FTD	15.00- 22.00
☐ Wine jug	8.00- 14.00

WILDFLOWER

	Price Range
☐ Bowl, CVD	18.00- 26.00
☐ Butter dish, CVD	31.00- 46.00
☐ Cake stand	30.00- 45.00
☐ Celery vase	25.00- 40.00
☐ Champagne glass . . .	25.00- 40.00
☐ Compote, CVD	40.00- 55.00
☐ Cordial glass	20.00- 35.00
☐ Creamer	18.00- 26.00
☐ Goblet	30.00- 45.00
☐ Pickle dish	20.00- 35.00
☐ Pitcher, M/W	45.00- 60.00
☐ Plate	18.00- 26.00
☐ Platter	20.00- 35.00
☐ Salt shaker	25.00- 40.00
☐ Sauce dish	8.00- 14.00
☐ Shakers, S/P	45.00- 60.00
☐ Spoon holder	20.00- 35.00
☐ Sugar bowl, CVD	25.00- 40.00
☐ Tray	30.00- 45.00
☐ Tumbler	18.00- 26.00
☐ Waste bowl	20.00- 35.00
☐ Wine jug	18.00- 26.00

WILLOW OAK (c. 1880)

	Price Range
☐ Bowl, CVD	18.00- 26.00
☐ Butter dish, CVD	50.00- 65.00
☐ Cake stand	20.00- 35.00
☐ Celery vase	25.00- 40.00
☐ Compote, CVD	31.00- 46.00
☐ Creamer	33.00- 48.00
☐ Goblet	25.00- 40.00
☐ Mug	18.00- 26.00
☐ Pitcher, M/W	40.00- 55.00
☐ Plate	12.00- 20.00
☐ Platter	20.00- 35.00
☐ Sauce dish	8.00- 14.00
☐ Shakers, S/P	25.00- 40.00
☐ Spoon holder	20.00- 30.00
☐ Sugar bowl, CVD	25.00- 40.00
☐ Tray	25.00- 40.00
☐ Tumbler	18.00- 26.00

GOLF COLLECTIBLES

While the styles have changed greatly over the years, the golf enthusiast ponders in his mind how the golf greats of the past broke par with the crude looking clubs of the past. Old clubs in good conditions are hard to come by but can still be found with a little perseverance.

Price Range

☐ Driver, Wooden shaft, c. 1910	100.00	125.00
☐ George Low Wizard 600 Putter, flanged	300.00	500.00
☐ Golf Bag, Leather, c. 1930	150.00	200.00
☐ Golf Glove, c. 1910	20.00	30.00
☐ MacGregor R. Armour Set, wood and frames, c. 1950	700.00	1200.00
☐ Marathon Wards Set, Wood and irons, c. 1922	150.00	200.00
☐ Power Bilt Driver, c. 1950	75.00	100.00
☐ Putter, wooden shaft, c. 1930	40.00	50.00
☐ Putter, Two way blade with wooden shaft, c. 1920	50.00	60.00
☐ Reuter Bulls Eye Putter	50.00	100.00
☐ Score Card, Master's Tournament	25.00	50.00
☐ The Golfer's Manual by H. B. Farnie, c. 1857	450.00	500.00
☐ Tommy Armour Wedge, 1959	100.00	150.00
☐ Wedge, Walter Hagen, c. 1930	75.00	100.00
☐ Wilson, Sam Snead Set, Woods and irons, c. 1940	300.00	350.00
☐ Wilson, R-20 Wedge, c. 1930	100.00	150.00

GREETING CARDS

☐ "Here Comes the New Year with Lots of Good Cheer." Child with Xmas tree toys, c. 1870	7.50	9.00
☐ "Merry Christmas & Happy New Year." Children romping in snow, church in background, c. 1860	2.00	3.00
☐ "A Merry Christmas to you All." Family strolling through snow-blanketed woodland, c. 1880	3.00	4.00
☐ "With the Season's Greetings." W. S. Coleman card, girl on swing (back view), c. 1890	5.00	6.00
☐ "My Lips may Give a Message." Christmas card by Kate Greenaway, young girl holding letter, c. 1880	35.00	50.00
☐ Trick fold-out Christmas card. Nativity tableau, c. 1920	3.00	5.00

VALENTINES

☐ Whitney, embossed paper in pattern, a child delivering a note to a young lady. With original embossed envelope, c. 1870	35.00	40.00
☐ Comic Valentine, the "Hat Trimmer," Elton & Co., New York, illus. of glum-looking woman sewing hat, with verse, c. 1860	20.00	25.00
☐ "Lady Killer," comic valentine by A. J. Fisher. N.Y., c. 1850	25.00	30.00
☐ Mansell Valentine in cameo embossing, two lovers walking along woodland path, c. 1845	35.00	40.00

VALENTINES

Price Range

☐ Mansell, lace paper, lovers in a park, heavily ornamented, white with silver, c. 1855	40.00	45.00
☐ Mechanical Valentine, "Such is Married Life," c. 1850	35.00	40.00
☐ Paper doll Valentine, also called "dressed Valentine," c. 1850	40.00	50.00
☐ Dobbs, "Pillar Post" Valentine, with illus. of mailbox, c. 1800	20.00	25.00
☐ Meek & Son. Gibson Girl (from photo), surrounded by lace in various ornamental patterns, cherub heads, c. 1890	50.00	55.00
☐ "Temple of Love," mother of pearl on satin background	50.00	55.00

HORSE-DRAWN CARRIAGES

The interest in carriages like all antiques date back to the earliest and most important in our history. Over recent years horse travel has experienced a new interest. Many old carriages thought to be useless, have found their way back into our hearts not as an antique but as something useful and romantic.

☐ Ambulance, Restored with bob runners, 18', c. 1900's	6000.00	7000.00
☐ Bob Sleigh, 4 passenger, slat sides, restored, c. 1905 .	900.00	1200.00
☐ Buggy, Amish, Early 1900's	800.00	1000.00
☐ Carriage Candle Lamps, 3 lights, inscribed Wm. R. Cannon, pair	450.00	550.00
☐ Carriage Foot Warmer, portable	65.00	85.00
☐ Carriage Jack	60.00	80.00
☐ Carriage Lamps, Brass, pair	350.00	450.00
☐ Coach, Brougham, Unrestored, Mfg. in New York, c. 1900	2000.00	2500.00
☐ Coach Lamps, 17" candle, restored, pair	500.00	600.00
☐ Coach, Large Victorian, unrestored	1800.00	2200.00
☐ Governess Cart, Mfg. in New England 1920, basket weave	2000.00	2500.00
☐ Hearse, Silver coach lamps, black lacquered, Mfg. in Cincinnati, Ohio, 1885	12000.00	15000.00
☐ High Carriage, Brougham, with rumble seat	4400.00	2500.00
☐ Horse Drawn 2 level pumper, Pawtucket, R. I. c. 1850 .	2400.00	2800.00
☐ Horse Tether, iron	30.00	40.00
☐ Milk Trolley, Early 1900's, restored	4800.00	5500.00
☐ Open Carriage, Canoe Victoria, with jump seat	7000.00	9000.00
☐ Phaeton, Basket, Mfg. by Brewster and Co., c. 1905, wicker and wood, restored	7000.00	10000.00
☐ Phaeton, Mfg. by Brewster and Co., c. 1898, restored, elegant, drop front	3500.00	4500.00
☐ Sleigh Cutter, Victorian style, unrestored, 2 passenger	300.00	500.00
☐ Speeding Cutter, Mfg. in Massachusetts, c. 1886	800.00	1200.00
☐ Spring Wagon, Yellow and black, Mfg. in Chester, Pa.	625.00	725.00

HORSE-DRAWN CARRIAGES

	Price	Range
☐ Sulky Racer, High wheel, restored	1400.00	1700.00
☐ Surrey, 4 passenger with fringe canopy, Mfg. in Syracuse, New york, c. 1896, restored	2500.00	3000.00
☐ Town Carriage, Brougham, Brewster and Co., New York, closed, lacquered and upholstered, c. 1895	5500.00	6500.00
☐ Whip, With bone handles	125.00	175.00

INKWELLS

Inkwells have always been an interesting collectible and most are simple and utilitarian. However, the ones most in demand are more decorative and artistic. Relatively speaking prices are still very reasonable and many bargains can still be found.

VICTORIAN SILVER INKSTAND, c. 1837 . . . . . 1000.00 - 1500.00

	Price	Range
☐ Brass, shape of kettle, Japanese, 2½" H, 19th Century	200.00	250.00
☐ Brass, cups on brass tray,6" x 9", 1900's	200.00	240.00
☐ Bronze, woman's head with flowing hair for lid	100.00	130.00
☐ Cherubs, blue and gray marble base, France, 4" H . . .	140.00	180.00
☐ Cloisonne, stone wall and tray, 7" H, 1900's	100.00	125.00
☐ Cut Glass, with sterling silver lid, 2" D	90.00	120.00
☐ Cut Glass, with eagle finial on brass lid, 19th Century	150.00	190.00
☐ Delft, windmill decor, Germany, 3" x 3½", 1800's	90.00	120.00
☐ Enameled Metal, floral designs, mottled colors, Chinese, 1800's.	100.00	140.00
☐ Milk Glass, cat on iron base, 5" H	120.00	150.00
☐ Pewter, pear with bees on tray, Kayserzinn	190.00	240.00
☐ Porcelain, boy wearing hat, French, 12", 1800's	140.00	180.00
☐ Pressed Glass, chair with cat sitting on cushion, 4" H, 19th Century	140.00	180.00
☐ Soapstone, carved dog on stand, Italian, 8" H, 18th Century	100.00	130.00
☐ Stand, bronze, crab and shell with pen tray, signed Tiffany Studios, New York, 7", 1899-1920	1900.00	2400.00
☐ Stand, iron, horse with brass cap, pen holder on back, 5"	40.00	60.00

INSULATORS

Like other glass pieces, the older the insulator, the more desirable and higher priced it is. A prime example is an old, non-thread, pin-hole insulator — this means it is over a hundred years old and valuable.

Often insulators on the same pole are different in both size and color.

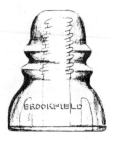   

| BROOKFIELD | HEMINGRAY | PYREX | WHITEALL TATUM |

	Price Range	
☐ A.T. & T. Co., Aqua, Single Skirt, 2 1/8" x 3 3/4", 1900 ..	5.00	9.00
☐ A.T. & T. Co., Aqua, 2 3/8" x 3 1/8"	7.00	10.00
☐ A.T. & T. Co., Aqua, 2 3/4" x 3 5/8", 2 piece	4.00	6.00
☐ A.T. & T. Co., Green, Single Skirt, 2 1/2" x 3 3/4"	4.00	7.00
☐ American Insulator Co., Double Petticoat, Aqua, 4 1/8" x 3 1/8"	9.00	12.00
☐ Armstrong, Amber, 4" x 3 1/4"	8.00	10.00
☐ Armstrong's #5, Clear, Double Petticoat, 3 1/8" x 3 3/4"	4.00	8.00
☐ A.U. PATENT, Green, 4 3/8" x 2 3/4"	29.00	35.00
☐ B.G.M. Co., Clear, 3 3/8" x 2 1/4"	15.00	20.00
☐ Barclay, Aqua, Double Petticoat, 3" x 2 1/4"	15.00	20.00
☐ Bottle Works, Aqua, 4 1/8" x 3"	45.00	60.00
☐ Brookfield, 45, Aqua, 4 1/8" x 3 1/8"	5.00	8.00
☐ Brookfield, 55, Aqua, 4" x 2 1/2"	10.00	15.00
☐ Brookfield, 83, Aqua, 4" x 3 1/8"	10.00	20.00
☐ Brookfield, Green, Double Petticoat, 3 3/16" x 3 5/8", 1865	4.00	8.00
☐ Brookfield, Dk. Olive Green, Double Petticoat, 3 3/4" x 4"	6.00	10.00
☐ B.T. Co. of Canada, Green, 3 1/2" x 2"	5.00	10.00
☐ C. & P. Til Co., Aqua, 3 1/2" x 2 3/8"	9.00	12.00
☐ C.E.N., Amethyst, 3 1/4" x 2 1/4"	30.00	40.00
☐ California, Aqua, Green, 3 3/8" x 2" .'.............	30.00	38.00
☐ California, Clear, Amethyst, 4 1/8" x 3 1/4"	4.00	6.00

INSULATORS   Price Range

☐ California, Purple, Double Petticoat, 3 3/4" x 4", CK-162	7.00	11.00
☐ Canadian Pacific, Blue, Green, Aqua, 3 5/8" x 2 3/4"	40.00	48.00
☐ Dominion 9, Amber, Aqua & Clear, 3 3/4" x 2 1/2"	1.00	3.00
☐ Gayner, Green, Double Petticoat, 3 3/16" x 3 7/8"	20.00	27.00
☐ H.G. Co., Amber, Double Petticoat, 3 1/4" x 3 3/4"	10.00	15.00
☐ H.G. Co., Petticoat, Aqua, Green, May 2, 1892	4.00	8.00
☐ Hemingray No. 2 Cable, Aqua, Green, 4" x 3 5/8"	22.00	26.00
☐ Hemingray No. 7, Aqua, Green, 3 1/2" x 2 1/2"	1.00	3.00
☐ Hemingray No. 8, Aqua, Green, 3 3/8" x 2 3/8"	12.00	16.00
☐ Hemingray No. 9, Aqua, Single Skirt, 2 1/4" x 3 1/2", May 2, 1893	—	18.50
☐ Hemingray No. 10, Clear, Single Skirt, 2 5/8" x 3 1/2"	—	14.50
☐ Hemingray No. 16, Green, Single Skirt, 2 7/8" x 4"	1.00	3.00
☐ Hemingray No. 19, Aqua, Double Petticoat, 3 1/4" x 3"	—	26.50
☐ Hemingray No. 25, Aqua, Green, 4" x 3 1/4"	10.00	14.00
☐ Hemingray No. 95, Aqua, Green, 3 5/8" x 2 7/8"	32.00	38.00
☐ Hemingray (Beehive), Green, Double Petticoat, 3 1/8" x 4 3/8"	—	16.50
☐ Fred M. Locke No. 14, Aqua, 4 3/8" x 3 1/8"	18.00	24.00
☐ Fred M. Locke No. 21, Aqua, Green, 4" x 4"	4.00	6.00
☐ Lynchburg No. 10, Aqua, Green, 3 3/8" x 2 1/4"	6.00	10.00
☐ Lynchburg, Aqua, Single Skirt, 2 1/4" x 3 5/8", #44	—	9.50
☐ Lynchburg No. 44, Aqua, 4" x 3 5/8"	4.00	7.00
☐ Maydwell 9, Clear, Aqua, 3 5/8" x 2 1/8"	4.00	7.00
☐ Maydwell #9. Clear, Single Skirt, 2 1/4" x 3 1/2"	4.00	7.00
☐ McLaughlin #9, Green, Single Skirt, 2 1/4" x 3 5/8"	—	12.50
☐ McLaughlin No. 19, Aqua, 3 3/4" x 3 1/4"	1.50	3.00
☐ Mulford & Biddle, Aqua, 3 1/4" x 2 5/8"	32.00	36.00
☐ N.E.T. & T. Co., Aqua, Green, 3 5/8" x 2 3/8"	4.00	7.00
☐ N..E.T. & T Co., Blue, 3 1/2" x 3"	10.00	15.00
☐ O.V.G. Co., Aqua, 3 1/2" x 2 1/4"	6.50	10.00
☐ Pyrex, Double Threads, 2 5/8" x 4 1/4", Carnival Glass	12.00	17.00
☐ Star, Aqua, Single Skirt, Pony, 2 3/8" x 3 1/2"	—	8.50
☐ Thomas, Brown Pottery, 2 1/2" x 1 1/8"	4.00	8.00
☐ W.F.G. Co., Green, Single Skirt, 2 3/8" x 3 5/8"	—	12.50
☐ Westinghouse, Aqua, Green, 3 1/8" x 2 3/8"	25.00	30.00
☐ Whitall Tatum, #3, Aqua, Single Skirt, 2 3/8" x 3 1/4" *	—	8.00

* In Purple (#1) - $10.00; in Red - $45.00

IRONS

The smoothing iron represents an extremely interesting and imaginative area of collectibles. Hundreds of models, ideas, and designs were developed and then discarded — all with the hope to make the unpleasant chore of ironing easier. Many older versions are still in use today in areas where electricity tricity and other conveniences are not available.

IRONS

	Price Range	
☐ Alcohol Iron, wooden handle, c. 1880	$60.00	$70.00
☐ Box Iron, with heated slug, c. 1890	40.00	50.00
☐ Box Iron, English with heated slugs, c. 1800	75.00	100.00
☐ Charcoal Iron, wooden handle, c. 1890	40.00	50.00
☐ Flat Iron, metal handle, c. 1860	25.00	35.00
☐ Flat Iron, removable handle, c. 1870	25.00	35.00
☐ Flat Iron, stone body, metal handle, c. 1850	40.00	50.00
☐ Flat Iron, wooden handle, child's, c. 1860	25.00	35.00
☐ Flat Iron, charcoal chimney vent, c. 1860	25.00	35.00
☐ Gasoline Heated Iron, wood handle, c. 1910	50.00	60.00
☐ G. E. Electric Iron, c. 1905	35.00	45.00
☐ G. E. Electric Iron, c. 1920	30.00	40.00

JARS

Jars are unusual in that they are one of the few containers that were originally sold empty. Handed down from generation to generation, there are hundreds in basements, garages, etc., waiting to be discovered.

☐ Ball Mason's Patent 1858. Handmade	25.00	30.00
☐ Ball Perfect Mason. Amber qt.....................	20.00	40.00
☐ Ball Standard. Handmade, wax sealer	25.00	30.00
☐ Banner Patent 2/9/1864; reinstated 1/22/1867	45.00	55.00
☐ Champion Patent 8/31/1869. Aqua, qt.	90.00	120.00
☐ Dandy Trade Mark. Amber, qt.....................	65.00	85.00
☐ Darling Imperial. Blue, qt.	25.00	40.00
☐ Gayner Mason. Clear, qt.	8.00	15.00
☐ Globe. Amber, qt.	25.00	40.00
☐ Hazel-Atlas Lightning Seal & E-Z Seal	10.00	15.00
☐ J & B Patent 6/14/189. Aqua, pt.	40.00	55.00
☐ Knowlton Vacuum Fruit Jar. Blue	20.00	35.00
☐ Lighting. Aqua, pt.	4.00	8.00
☐ Leotric. Clear, qt.	3.50	6.50
☐ Lynchburg Standard Mason. Aqua, qt.	10.00	20.00
☐ Mason's (CFJ Co. emblem). Improved "Trade Mark" ..	12.00	20.00
☐ Mason's Patent 11/30/1858 (Maltese Cross)	10.00	20.00
☐ Mason's Improved (Maltese Cross). Two types	9.50	15.00
☐ Mason's (Maltese Cross) Patent 11/30/1858	10.00	15.00
☐ Melville Improved. Aqua, qt.....................	15.00	30.00
☐ Pacific Mason. Zinc top, clear, qt.	12.00	22.00
☐ Porcelain lined, zinc top, aqua, qt.................	12.00	20.00
☐ Premium Coffeyville, Kas. Handmade	20.00	35.00
☐ Presto. Screw-on top, clear	3.00	6.00
☐ Putnam Glass Works. Amber, qt.	22.00	30.00
☐ Queen (The) 1875. Zinc band, aqua, qt.	18.00	24.00
☐ Ramsey Jar. Glass lid, aqua, qt.	42.00	54.00
☐ Red Key Mason. Clear or amethyst, 6½"	24.00	35.00
☐ Reid Murdock & Co. Zinc lid, clear, qt.	5.00	12.00
☐ Reliance Brand Wide Mouth Mason	4.00	8.00

JARS

	Price	Range
☐ The Smalley Self Sealer Wide Mouth	5.00	10.00
☐ C.F. Spencer's Patent 1868. Improved jar	35.00	60.00
☐ C.F. Spencer's Patent Rochester, N.Y. Qt.	35.00	60.00
☐ Sun Trademark. Green, ½ gallon	44.00	55.00
☐ Rose (The) 1920. Screw-on lid, clear	12.00	22.00
☐ Selco Surity Seal. Glass top, green or blue	8.00	12.00
☐ Scranton Jar (The). Glass stopper, aqua, qt.	42.00	55.00
☐ Schram Automatic Sealer. ½ qt.	1.50	3.00
☐ Silicon Glass 1930. Qt.	8.00	16.00
☐ Star. Zinc band with glass insert, clear, qt.	18.00	25.00
☐ Sun Trade Mark J.P. Barstow	25.00	35.00
☐ Swayzee's Improved Mason. Dark green, ½ qt.	30.00	40.00
☐ Tropical T.F. Canners	2.00	5.00
☐ True Fruit (JHS Co. emblem) Trade Mark Reb.	14.00	20.00
☐ True Seal. Glass top, clear	9.00	12.00
☐ United Drug Co. Clear, qt.	3.00	6.00
☐ Universal. Screw top, clear, qt	5.00	9.00
☐ Valne Jar. Screw-on top, aqua, qt	22.00	32.00
☐ Van Vliet (The) 1881. Green, pt.	375.00	425.00
☐ Victor Patent (The) 1899	9.00	15.00
☐ Victor Patent (The) 2/20/1900	10.00	15.00
☐ Victory 1864. Green with clear lid, qt.	120.00	150.00
☐ Wallaceburg Gem	5.00	10.00
☐ Wears, improved	8.00	16.00
☐ Weir Seal. White stoneware lid, qt	7.00	10.00

JEWELRY

The styles of today's dress encourage and enhance the use of the beautiful styles of jewelry of years gone by. With the increased value of precious metals, the prices have skyrocketed and we have a value of $250.00 per oz. of gold on which the following prices are based. Please consult our publication *The Official Price Guide to Antique Jewelry* for more prices and information.

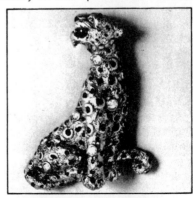

LEOPARD BROOCH, *Gold, Diamond and Black Enameled*
.... 800.00 - 1000.00

ANTIQUE GOLD EAR PENDANTS, *c. 1860* . . . . 125.00 - 200.00

DIAMOND SET, Gold and Lapis Lazuli, c. 1890 . . . . 225.00 - 300.00

BAR PINS
Price Range

☐ Agate, green gold center, filigree, 10 k. 75.00   100.00
☐ Antique Gold, platinum and diam., 59 round diam.,
   4 ct., c. 1870 . . . . 1000.00 1500.00
☐ Cameo, pink and white, 2 pearls, 10 k. 100.00   130.00
☐ Gold Leaves, 1 diam., 2 sapphires, 14 k. 115.00   165.00
☐ Lalique Glass, black onyx, 14 k. with gold 65.00   75.00
☐ Platinum, diam gold brooch, 100 round diam., 2 ct.,
   center one round diam., 1.50 ct., c. 1915 . . . . 1500.00 2000.00
☐ Platinum, diam., and octagonal onyx framed by diam.   450.00   650.00
☐ Platinum, 100 round diam., 2 ct., 1 center diam.,
   1.50 ct. 1200.00 1600.00
☐ Platinum, 1 marquise diam. and sapphire, round diam.
   stripe and chevrons of calibre French-cut diam.
   supported by a fancy link whitte gold chain 800.00 1000.00
☐ Platinum, onyx and diamond 150.00   200.00
☐ Platinum, 13 diamonds 100.00   140.00
☐ Ruby, solid gold with fancy lace work 90.00   120.00
☐ Sapphire, 2 pearls, 10 k. green gold finish 70.00   100.00
☐ Sterling Silver, 1 amethyst in center 40.00   60.00

BEADS

☐ Amber, faceted, gold plated findings, c. 1920 . . . .   120.00   150.00
☐ Amberina Glass, gold findings, c. 1925 . . . .   80.00   100.00
☐ Amethyst, full strand with silk braid cord, c. 1925 . . . . .   100.00   125.00
☐ Bohemian Crystal, fine cut silver findings, c. 1930 . . .   30.00   40.00
☐ Branch Coral, 5 strand silver findings, c. 1930 . . . .   30.00   40.00
☐ Branch Coral, 5 strand silver findings, c. 1930 . . . .   300.00   325.00
☐ Choker Seed, multi-colored elastic with silver
   findings, c. 1920 . . . .   25.00   30.00
☐ Cut Crystal, sterling fittings, long strand, c. 1925 . . . .   150.00   200.00
☐ Cut Garnet, faceted, long rope beads, c. 1925 . . . .   50.00   75.00
☐ Czechoslovakia, amethyst color, various sizes
   with gold clasp, c. 1920 . . . .   40.00   60.00
☐ Ebony, jet and silver, c. 1920 . . . .   20.00   30.00
☐ Oriental Enamel, gold design, c. 1920 . . . .   150.00   175.00
☐ Seed Beads, multi strand blue and white twisted
   and knotted, c. 1920 . . . .   60.00   80.00
☐ Venetian Glass, opalescent silver findings, c. 1920 . .   90.00   100.00

BRACELETS

☐ Antique Gold, mesh strap and pearl-set buckle,
   c. 1835 . . . .   900.00 1200.00
☐ Art Deco, carved jade plaques, strap of platinum links,
   round and baguette diamonds 6000.00 7000.00
☐ Art Deco, platinum rectangular links, 130 round and
   old-mine diamonds, 12.50 ct. 4000.00 6000.00
☐ Bangle, gold, enamel, center rings set with two
   sapphires and rubies, tiny white enamel quatrefoils,
   3 band bangle, c. 1890 . . . .   700.00   900.00

BRACELETS

Price Range

- [ ] Bangle, gold snake, rope twisted bangles, 21 k. 800.00 900.00
- [ ] Diamond, 6 round synthetic sapphires, platinum mount, geometric design, 48 old-mine diamonds, 10.75 ct., 336 old-mine diamonds, 8 ct., c. 1930 . . . . . . 7000.00 8000.00
- [ ] Diamond, marquise shaped synthetic sapphires, 5 round diam., 1.50 ct., 14 k. 600.00 700.00
- [ ] Diamond, platinum flower spray with 107 old-mine diamonds, 5 ct., white gold snake-chain bracelet 2000.00 2500.00
- [ ] Gold, ingot shaped links within brickwork borders, 21 k. 500.00 600.00
- [ ] Gold, link chain with gold ball ornaments 175.00 250.00
- [ ] Jade, gold and platinum, 18 round, oval and pear-shaped cabochons, 60 round diam., 1.75 ct. 6000.00 6500.00
- [ ] Platinum, 135 diamonds, 4 ct., openwork links, c. 1930 . . . . 1800.00 2000.00
- [ ] Platinum, strap tapering to narrower ends with numerous old-mine and rose-cut diamonds, c. 1920 . . 1500.00 1800.00
- [ ] Platinum, rectangular panel in center, 90 old-mine diam., 4.50 ct., 2 lines of calibre cut emeralds 2000.00 2500.00
- [ ] Platinum, white gold, pearl mesh work, 52 round diam., framed in pearls, c. 1915 . . . . 700.00 900.00

BROOCHES

- [ ] Antique Diamond, colored stone sword, gold and silver handle, old-mine and rose-cut diamonds, round emeralds and rubies 400.00 600.00
- [ ] Antique Diamond, 24 old-mine cut diamonds, 2.50 ct., gold topped by silver, c. 1840 . . . . 1000.00 1200.00
- [ ] Antique Gold, emerald and rose diamond, 1 large baroque emerald, crescent set with full Holland rose and old-mine diamonds 1400.00 1800.00
- [ ] Antique Gold, silver, citrine quartz, rose diamond, cartouche design, c. 1820 . . . . 550.00 750.00
- [ ] Antique Gold, silver, turquoise and diamond flower, c. 1830 . . . . 1300.00 1600.00
- [ ] Antique Gold, silver, wild flower with rose diamonds, c. 1830 . . . . 800.00 1000.00
- [ ] Antique Rose Diamond, turquoise bow-and-heart, c, 1830 . . . . 800.00 1000.00
- [ ] Antique Silver, gold and diamond flower with 8 diamonds, 3.50 ct., 1 center diamond 1.30 ct., leaves set with 22 diamonds 2 ct. 3000.00 3500.00
- [ ] Art Deco, platinum, carved crystal, 96 round and baguette diamonds, 2.25 ct. 2000.00 2500.00
- [ ] Art Nouveau, bold floral design, garnet stones, 18 k. gold, 2½ " oval, c. 1890 . . . . 300.00 350.00
- [ ] Gold, circle or irregular openwork, 22 round diamonds, 1.15 ct., 18 k. 500.00 600.00
- [ ] Gold and Citrine, set in gold 125.00 175.00

BROOCHES

	Price	Range
☐ Gold Figural, 18 k. textured gold, Incan deity style . . .	800.00	900.00
☐ Gold Pendant, leafy bow with diamonds, 1.30 ct., 37 smaller round diamonds, .90 ct.	2200.00	2500.00
☐ Gold Pendant, coral and gold cluster, 15 round diamonds, 1 ct., 1 round diamond, .95 ct., 18 d. gold . .	2500.00	3200.00
☐ Heart-Shaped, platinum, 24 round diamonds, 2.90 ct. .	1000.00	1200.00
☐ Heart-Shaped, platinum, 30 round diamonds, 2.50 ct. .	2500.00	3000.00
☐ Platinum, oval mount filigree, 37 old-mine diamonds, 2 ct., c. 1920	800.00	1000.00
☐ Platinum, diamond and sapphire circle, 16 old-mine diamonds, 2 ct., 1 old-mine diamond, 1 ct., 9 French-cut sapphires	2000.00	2500.00
☐ Platinum and Diamond Airplane, 43 round and baguette diamonds, 1.75 ct., c. 1930	3000.00	4000.00
☐ Platinum and Diamond Flower, 1 emerald-cut diamond, 1.75 ct., 57 round, square-cut marquise-shaped diamonds, 2.75 ct.	3000.00	3500.00
☐ Platinum and Diamond Pendant, mount set with 112 round, baguette and pear-shaped diamonds, 6 ct.	3000.00	3500.00
☐ Platinum and Diamond Spray, 20 round, marquise and pear-shaped diamonds, 5 ct.	3500.00	4200.00
☐ Tortoise Shell, two, oval frame, gold pique star decorations	325.00	375.00
☐ White Gold and Diamond, circular mount, 33 round diamonds, 5 ct.	1000.00	1500.00
☐ White Gold and Diamond, openwork mount, 82 round diamonds, 2 ct., 18 k. gold	500.00	600.00
☐ White Gold and Diamond Bow, looped ribbon, 66 round diamonds, 2.80 ct., 14 k. gold	800.00	1000.00
☐ Yellow and Blue Sapphire, 14 k. gold curled ribbons . .	1200.00	1500.00

CAMEO

☐ Filigree, gold frame, solid gold loop, ¾ " profile, 1½ " oval, c. 1890	200.00	225.00
☐ Goddess, etched frame, wire pendant loop, 18 k., c. 1950	85.00	100.00
☐ Goddess, with bird, pendant, 2" loop, c. 1950	400.00	450.00
☐ Gold Frame, full face, high relief, 2½ " oval, wire gold loop, c. 1880	100.00	150.00
☐ Gold Frame, high relief, 1" x 2" oval, gold loop, c. 1900	75.00	100.00
☐ House, with scene, twisted gold ribbon frame, 18 k., c. 1910	85.00	100.00
☐ Oval, full profile, high relief with full loop, c. 1880	70.00	90.00
☐ Vase, with flowers, oval, ornate frame, 14 k., c. 1910 . .	100.00	125.00

CUFF LINKS

☐ Buttons, small snap-on with mother of pearl, c. 1920 .	20.00	25.00
☐ Diamond, gold engraved initials, 18 k., c. 1890	150.00	175.00
☐ Gold, with black enamel	200.00	250.00

CUFF LINKS   Price Range

- ☐ Gold, 2 oval links, one set with jade, one set with
  a polished Chinese character 1000.00   1200.00
- ☐ Jade, plain frame, 14 k. gold, c. 1900 .... 100.00   1200.00
- ☐ Locket Style, 14 k. gold, engraved, c. 1910 .... 85.00   100.00
- ☐ Oval, gold with diamond in center, 18 k., c. 1912 ..... 120.00   130.00

EARRINGS

- ☐ Antique Gold, pendants with carved coral 125.00   175.00
- ☐ Antique Gold, silver drops set with
  42 round diamonds 800.00   1000.00
- ☐ Antique Rose Diamonds, pendants, floral motif 750.00   950.00
- ☐ Aquamarine, platinum leaf-form, 34 round diamonds,
  2.25 ct., with 2 pear-shaped aquamarines 1500.00   1700.00
- ☐ Art Deco, black enamel and chrome, c. 1920 .... 40.00   50.00
- ☐ Gold, lapis lazuli pendants, c. 1890 .... 225.00   300.00
- ☐ Gold, 12 round diamonds, 14 k. gold leaf forms 400.00   600.00
- ☐ Gold, pearl and simulated diamond pendants 175.00   225.00
- ☐ Gold Hoops, wave pattern joined by platinum links,
  86 round diamonds, 2.70 ct., 18 k. gold 1500.00   2000.00
- ☐ Jade, 14 k. gold drops, c. 1920 .... 75.00   80.00
- ☐ Opal, 14 k. gold, c. 1900 .... 90.00   100.00
- ☐ Platinum, spray form with 22 round and baguette
  diamonds, 1.90 ct., 2 larger round diamonds, 4.10 ct. . 7000.00   8000.00
- ☐ Platinum, stylized flower motif with 32 round
  diamonds, 1 ct., gold clip backs 450.00   600.00
- ☐ Silver, jet teardrop stones, c. 1900 .... 40.00   60.00

HAT PINS

- ☐ Art Deco, brass, plastic, c. 1920 .... 25.00   30.00
- ☐ Art Deco, jade, 14 k. gold, ¾", c. 1900 .... 80.00   100.00
- ☐ Art Deco, ivory, engraved, c. 1925 .... 40.00   50.00
- ☐ Art Nouveau, coral plastic stone, 10", sterling,
  c. 1910 .... 40.00   50.00
- ☐ Art Nouveau, enamel 9", silver, ornate, c. 1900 ...... 25.00   30.00
- ☐ French Design, white marble insert, large head,
  c. 1910 .... 20.00   25.00
- ☐ Victorian, aquamarine, 8½", scroll mounting ½",
  c. 1900 .... 25.00   30.00
- ☐ Victorian, turquoise, 10", gem stone, 18 k. gold,
  c. 1890 .... 90.00   110.00

NECKLACES

- ☐ Amber, round beads, 3 large, etched design, silver
  findings, c. 1920 .... 65.00   80.00
- ☐ Cultured Pearl, double strand, 73 pearls 7.9 to
  9.2 mm., oval clasp, 27 round diam., 2 ct. 1400.00   1600.00
- ☐ Cultured Pearl, single strand, with wrought gold and
  diam clasp 1200.00   1500.00
- ☐ Emerald, 28 cabochon, large cabochon emerald
  center, 570 round diamonds, 6 ct. and
  triangle-shaped, .75 ct. 8000.00   9000.00

NECKLACES

Price Range

- [ ] Lavaliere, diamond, gold and platinum pendant and chain, round and rose-cut diam., two small sapphires, supporting a round diamond, 2.10 ct. 2000.00 2400.00
- [ ] Lavaliere, platinum pendant, a pear-shaped emerald, 20 round diam., 1 ct., with 14 k. white gold chain 900.00 1000.00
- [ ] Lavaliere, platinum, pear-shaped black opal supported by a frame with numerous diamonds and fancy link chain 1000.00 1200.00
- [ ] Lavaliere, chain with scroll-shaped pendant, round diamonds, .70 ct. centering a round diamond, 1 ct., 14 k. 1200.00 1600.00
- [ ] Lavaliere, pendant with five diamonds and 1 round diamond, 1.25 ct., 14 k. white gold 1500.00 2000.00

PENDANTS

- [ ] Antique Gold, silver, emerald-cut emerald in a garland with rose diamonds and round emeralds, suspended from a jeweled bow-tied ribbon, c. 1900 . . . . 300.00 400.00
- [ ] Antique Silver, enamelled St. George on a pearl horse, emerald-set dragon supported by a simple link chain, c. 1850 . . . . 250.00 350.00
- [ ] Art Deco, sterling silver and crystal, pointed square, c. 1925 . . . . 70.00 80.00
- [ ] Cross, silver, jet gem stones, 1" H, silver loop, c. 1850 . . . . 80.00 90.00
- [ ] Heart, diamond and gold, 1½" H, 14 k., c. 1920 . . . . . . 200.00 225.00
- [ ] Opal, large drop with chain loop, 14 k., c. 1900 . . . . . . 200.00 250.00
- [ ] Victorian, etched design with two gold drops, 14 k., c. 1875 . . . . 200.00 250.00

LADIES RINGS

- [ ] Amethyst, surrounded by 26 diamonds, 2.60 ct., gold mount, border of round rubies 1500.00 2000.00
- [ ] Art Deco, two triangular black onyx, triangular diamond, platinum and diamond band 800.00 1200.00
- [ ] Art Deco, 22 round and baguette diamonds, 1.35 ct., 1 emerald cut diamond, 2.50 ct., crossover mount, 14 k. gold 5000.00 6000.00
- [ ] Art Deco, 22 baguette diamond gridwork, 1.40 ct., centering round diamond, .95 ct., 14 k. white gold 2500.00 3000.00
- [ ] Diamond and Lapis Dome, 60 round diamonds, 1.60 ct., border of marquise-shaped lapis cabochons, 14 k. gold 500.00 600.00
- [ ] Diamond and Malachite, concave oval of malachite, centered by a round diamond, 2.10 ct., 14 k. gold 3500.00 4000.00
- [ ] Diamond Ram's Head, diamond eyes, 16 round and marquise-shaped diamonds, .80 ct., 1 round diamond, 1.15 ct., 14 k. white gold 1200.00 1600.00
- [ ] Diamond and Ruby, spherical dome, round rubies, small round diamonds, 1 center round diamond, 1.90 ct., 14 k. gold, c. 1940 . . . . 3200.00 3600.00

LADIES RINGS

Price Range

☐ Gold and Diamond, centered round diamond, 1.40 ct.,
14 k. gold 1800.00 2000.00
☐ Gold and Diamond, dome mount, gold cluster with 22
round diamonds, 1 ct. 14 k. gold 600.00 700.00
☐ Gold and Diamond, gold mount, oval-faceted
diamond, 4.30 ct., 18 k. gold 6000.00 7000.00
☐ Gold and Diamond, star-form dinner ring, 9 round
diamonds, 1.30 ct., c. 1910 .... 1800.00 2200.00
☐ Gold, Diamond and Emerald, dome of rope-textured
wires, round diamonds, centering an emerald-cut
emerald, 18 k. gold 2400.00 2800.00
☐ Gold, Diamond and Platinum, domed mount with
46 round diamonds, 3.75 ct., 1 round diamond, .95 ct.,
18 k. gold 3500.00 4000.00
☐ Gold, Diamond and Sapphire, domed cluster, small
round diamonds and sapphires, centering emerald-
cut diamond, 1 ct., 18 k. gold 1500.00 2000.00
☐ Gold and Ruby, gold band textured design,
6 round rubies 1000.00 1200.00
☐ Heart-shaped Aquamarine, platinum with
2 round diamonds 400.00 550.00
☐ Platinum and Diamond, centering round diamond,
1.10 ct., 6 baguette diamonds, .40 ct. 1000.00 1400.00
☐ Platinum and Diamond, narrow band, round diamond,
1.45 ct., flanked by small round and baguette
diamonds 1000.00 1400.00
☐ Platinum and Diamond, narrow band, round diamond,
2 ct., flanked by baguette diamonds 3000.00 4000.00
☐ Platinum and Diamond, narrow band, small
diamonds, centering round diamonds, 2.35 ct. 1000.00 1400.00
☐ Platinum and Diamond, narrow band, 2 round
diamonds, .90 ct. 1600.00 1800.00
☐ Platinum and Diamond, oval panel with 9 round
diamonds, 2 ct. 1500.00 2000.00
☐ Platinum and Diamond, oval panel with 12 small
round diamonds, 60 ct., centering a round diamond,
1.15 ct. 1200.00 1600.00
☐ Platinum and Diamond, one round diamond,
1.30 ct., tiered rows of small diamonds 1800.00 2000.00
☐ Platinum and Diamond, round diamond, .90 ct.,
flanked by small round diamonds 600.00 800.00
☐ Platinum and Diamond, one round diamond, .95 ct.,
1 tapered baguette diamond 700.00 900.00
☐ Platinum and Diamond, one round diamond, 3.50 ct.,
2 baguette diamonds 6000.00 7000.00
☐ Platinum and Diamond, one round diamond, 1.70 ct.,
set with 6 marquise-shaped diamonds, .90 ct. 1000.00 1500.00
☐ Platinum, Diamond, and Sapphire, oval frame with
round and baguette diamonds, a cabochon sapphire,
2.85 ct., c. 1920 .... 800.00 1000.00

LADIES RINGS

Price Range

☐ Platinum, Diamond, and Sapphire, rectangular panel with 25 round diamonds, 1.30 ct., and calibre-cut sapphires 1000.00 1200.00

☐ Ruby and Diamond, platinum mount with a row of cabochon rubies and diamond border 600.00 800.00

☐ Ruby and Diamond Cluster, white and yellow gold mount with 9 round diamonds, 1 ct., 8 marquise-shaped rubies 700.00 900.00

☐ Sapphire and Diamond, gold mount with cushion-shaped sapphire, 10 old-mine diamonds, 2.75 ct., c. 1900 .... 1000.00 1200.00

☐ Star Sapphire and Diamond, platinum mount, numerous small diamonds centering a star sapphire, 24 ct. 1400.00 1600.00

☐ White Gold and Diamond, crossover mount, 6 old-mine diamonds, 90 ct., centering an old-mine diamond, .90 ct. 500.00 700.00

☐ White Gold and Diamond, domed mount, 88 round diamonds, 2 ct. 800.00 1000.00

☐ White Gold and Diamond, one round diamond, 1.35 ct., within a rectangular frame 800.00 1000.00

☐ White Gold and Diamond, wide band, three rows set with 24 round diamonds, 1.20 ct., centering round diamond, 1.15 ct. 2000.00 2500.00

☐ Wedding Band, platinum and diamond crossover with 42 baguette and marquise diamonds, 4.40 ct. 1800.00 2000.00

☐ Wedding Band, platinum and diamond, wide band, 30 round and baguette diamonds, 3.50 ct. 1900.00 2100.00

☐ Wedding Band, platinum and diamond, wide band, 45 round and baguette diamonds, 4.75 ct. 1200.00 1600.00

☐ Wedding Band, 48 round baguette diamonds, 1.90 ct., criss-cross motif 800.00 1000.00

☐ Wedding Band, platinum and diamond, wide open-work with 44 round diamonds, 2.60 ct. 800.00 1000.00

☐ Wedding Band, platinum and diamond, 19 round diamonds, 1.30 ct. 400.00 600.00

☐ Wedding Band, platinum and diamond, one round diamond, 1.10 ct., row of small round diamonds 2000.00 2500.00

☐ Wedding Band, platinum and diamond, 61 round diamonds, 3.50 ct. 2000.00 2500.00

☐ Wedding Band, platinum and diamond, chevron-shaped band, small round diamonds and one pear-shaped diamond, 1.50 ct. 800.00 1000.00

MEN'S RINGS

☐ Men's, cobra snake with diamond eyes, 18 k. gold, c. 1910 .... 300.00 350.00

☐ Men's diamond, gypsy mount centering round diamond, 1.95 ct., 14 k. gold 4000.00 6000.00

MEN'S RINGS

Price Range

- ☐ Men's diamond, rectangular center panel, round diamond, 1.10 ct., 14 k. gold 2400.00 2500.00
- ☐ Men's, diamond, round 1.15 ct., 18 k. yellow and white gold 2000.00 2500.00
- ☐ Men's, diamond, round 1.40 ct., 14 ct., white and gold band 1500.00 2000.00
- ☐ Men's, gold, round design, 18 diamonds .25 ct., 14 k. gold, c. 1920 . . . . 600.00 700.00
- ☐ Men's, gold nugget design, 14 k. gold, c. 1920 . . . . 200.00 250.00
- ☐ Men's, onyx, black, silver, cameo style, c. 1900 . . . . . . 100.00 145.00
- ☐ Men's, star sapphire, 7 ct., 14 k. gold 500.00 600.00
- ☐ Men's, star sapphire, silver with diamonds, c. 1910 . . 200.00 300.00
- ☐ Men's, wedding band, inlaid turquoise, 18 k. gold, c. 1930 . . . . 250.00 300.00

STICKPINS

- ☐ Brass, synthetic stone, c. 1900 . . . . 10.00 15.00
- ☐ Bug, gold with topaz, rubies and pearls, 14 k., c. 1900 . 70.00 80.00
- ☐ Bug, gold, small with safety nib, 14 k., c. 1920 . . . . 60.00 80.00
- ☐ Cross, gold, with safety nib, 14 k., c. 1920 . . . . 30.00 40.00
- ☐ Gold, with diamond, marked Tiffany, 18 k., c. 1920 . . . 200.00 250.00
- ☐ Gold, with ruby, 14 k., c. 1890 . . . . 90.00 100.00
- ☐ Gold, wire design with safety nib, 14 k., c. 1920 . . . . . . 25.00 35.00
- ☐ Gold, lapis framed by 9 round diamonds, 1.75 ct. 1100.00 1400.00
- ☐ Indian Head, 14 k. gold, c. 1910 . . . . 40.00 60.00
- ☐ Locket, for picture, 14 k. gold, c. 1900 . . . . 75.00 85.00
- ☐ Opal, 1 ct. stone, 14 k. gold, c. 1890 . . . . 100.00 120.00
- ☐ Pearl, synthetic, gold palted, safety nib, c. 1920 . . . . . 15.00 20.00
- ☐ Platinum, 1 round diamond, .45 ct., 6 round diamonds, .25 ct., c. 1920 . . . . 700.00 900.00
- ☐ Platinum, 7 round diamonds, .75 ct. and two square sapphires 325.00 400.00
- ☐ Silver, abalone shell, c. 1900 . . . . 45.00 50.00
- ☐ Silver, enamel, diamond flowers and bee, c. 1925 . . . . 150.00 175.00
- ☐ Silver, small pearl, c.1920 . . . . 40.00 50.00

LADIES WATCHES

- ☐ Ladies, Art Deco, wristwatch, enamel and gold, c. 1920 . . . . 125.00 150.00
- ☐ Ladies, Art Nouveau, worn on chain, key wind, 14 k. gold, c. 1885 . . . . 300.00 400.00
- ☐ Ladies, dress, clip style with round diamonds, 4 k. gold, c. 1920 . . . . 125.00 175.00
- ☐ Ladies, flexible bracelet pattern strap, hinged cover, 15 old-mine diamonds, 2.75 ct. 700.00 900.00
- ☐ Ladies, lapel, diamond bar brooch supporting a rectangular watch set with diamonds, watch face outlined by calibre-cut-sapphires, 78 round and baguette diamonds, 3.50 ct. 1200.00 1400.00

LADIES WATCHES

Price Range

- [ ] Ladies, pendant style, watch pin, silver with garnets, 1" oval, c. 1900 .... 70.00 100.00
- [ ] Ladies, pendant, style, with gold and diamond chips, c. 1920 .... 120.00 130.00
- [ ] Ladies, platinum and gold wristwatch, oval face, diamond set strap with calibre and round sapphires, signed Tiffany & Co., c. 1920 .... 2000.00 2500.00
- [ ] Ladies, platinum wristwatch, rectangular case, enamelled dial, diamond shoulders, 87 round and baguette diamonds, 2.60 ct. 2500.00 3000.00
- [ ] Ladies, platinum wristwatch, round, straight bracelet, 125 round diamonds, 3 ct., c. 1918 .... 3500.00 4000.00
- [ ] Ladies, platinum wristwatch, rectangular face, marquise shaped diamonds, calibre-cut sapphires, 151 round diamonds, 3 ct., c. 1920 .... 1800.00 2000.00
- [ ] Ladies, white gold wristwatch, straight bracelet, small round face, 76 round baguette diamonds, 1.85 ct., 14 k. 500.00 650.00
- [ ] Ladies, white gold wristwatch, straight bracelet, small round face, 66 round and baguette diamonds, 1.80 ct., 14 k. 800.00 1000.00

MEN'S WATCHES

- [ ] Men's, Howard, gold etched case, 14 k. gold, c. 1900 . 600.00 700.00
- [ ] Men's, Grosgraw, watch fob, black ribbon, gold engraved pendant, c. 1910 .... 40.00 50.00
- [ ] Men's, Patek Philippe, 14 k. gold, c. 1900 .... 400.00 500.00
- [ ] Men's, Waltham pocket dress watch with chain, 14 k. gold, c. 1900 .... 150.00 200.00
- [ ] Men's, Rolex stainless steel, date, sweep second hand 500.00 600.00
- [ ] Men's, Waltham Riverside, 18 k. gold, c. 1920 .... 150.00 200.00
- [ ] Men's Watch, double case 14 k. gold por. dial, engraved, c. 1850 .... 200.00 250.00

INDIAN JEWELRY

- [ ] Belt Concho, heavy silver and turquoise, c. 1880 ..... 1200.00 1500.00
- [ ] Bracelet, adjustable, turquoise, bone, coral and silver, 2" W, c. 1890 .... 500.00 600.00
- [ ] Choker, heavy turquoise nuggets, silver clasp, c. 1890 300.00 350.00
- [ ] Necklace, bear claw, turquoise, heavy silver, c. 1880 . 400.00 500.00
- [ ] Necklace, squash blossom, silver, Navajo style, heavy, c. 1900 .... 650.00 750.00
- [ ] Necklace, turquoise heishi, 6 strand, c. 1890 .... 600.00 700.00
- [ ] Ring, lady's turquoise, Zuni, square cut stones, c. 1890 .... 200.00 300.00
- [ ] Ring, man's silver and large turquoise nuggets, c. 1890 .... 200.00 300.00

MISCELLANEOUS

	Price Range	
☐ Cross, 8 amythests, 18 k. gold chain, c. 1890	250.00	300.00
☐ Cross, pearl and chain, 14 k. gold, engraved, c. 1900 .	100.00	150.00
☐ Jewel Box, bronze, enameled top, c. 1910	125.00	140.00
☐ Jewel Box, ceramic, French design, c. 1890	200.00	225.00
☐ Locket, gold engraved flowers with gold loop, c. 1880	200.00	250.00
☐ Opera Glass, shell covered on lorgnette with chain, c. 1925	200.00	250.00
☐ Pencil, 14 k. gold, c. 1920	40.00	50.00
☐ Pencil, sterling silver, c. 1925	40.00	50.00
☐ Vanity Case, Art Deco, gold plated, mother of pearl, c. 1920	125.00	150.00

JUKEBOXES

Jukebox prices are on the increase and demand is strong for pieces in good and excellent condition. These beautiful players of music are being used in more and more residential and commercial decor applications. Please consult our publication, *The Official Price Guide to Mechanical Musical Instruments* by Susan Gould for more prices and information.
Courtesy: Les Gould, S. Orange, NJ.

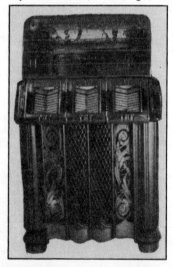

WURLITZER, *Model 1250,*
c. 1950 . . . . . . **1200.00 - 1500.00**

☐ AMI Model "A", c. 1946-8, 40 tune selections, called "Mother of Plastic," lights up, "Jewels" on front of case	1500.00	2000.00
☐ AMI "Singing Tower", c. 1941, 10 tunes, 6' H, looks like an Art Deco skyscraper	2500.00	3000.00
☐ Capehart Jukebox, c. 1930's, Early example, simple rectangular case (oak), glass panels to view mechanisism, decorative grill	500.00	750.00

JUKEBOXES

Price Range

☐ Filben "Maestro", c. 1940's, 30 tune selections, very
space age design, plastic top section 1000.00   1500.00

☐ Mills "Empress", Model 910, c. 1939, 20 tune
selections, rounded wood case, large plastic panels,
small window to view tune cards, lights up 1250.00   1750.00

☐ Mills "Throne of Music", 20 tune selections, plastic
panels, very similar in appearance to "Empress" 1000.00   1500.00

☐ Rock-Ola, "Rhythm King", c. 1937, 12 tune selections,
wood base, plain case, viewing window to see
mechanism 750.00   1250.00

☐ Rock-Ola, Style 1426, c. 1947, 20 tune, "Classic" style,
push buttons, revolving lights, plastic, viewing
window 2000.00   2500.00

☐ Seeburg, P147 (P148), c. 1947, 20 tune selections,
"Washing Machine" case style, plastic panels 1000.00   1500.00

☐ Seeburg Symphonola (early) c. 1936, 12 tune selections, rectangular plain case style, window to view
mechanism, selector dial 400.00   600.00

☐ Seeburg "Symphonola Regal", c. 1940, 20 tune selections, plastic panels, tune cards in top section (No
viewing of mechanism) 1000.00   1500.00

☐ Wurlitzer Counter Model 61, c. 1938-39, 12 tune
selections, wood base and sides, some plastic
(comes with floor stand) 750.00   1250.00

☐ Wurlitzer Model 750, c. 1937-40's, 24 tune selections,
"Classic" style, plastic panels, viewing window, push
buttons 2000.00   3000.00

☐ Wurlitzer Model 1015, c. 1946-47, 24 tune selections,
"Classic" style, revolving lights in plastic bubble
tubes, viewing window 2500.00   3000.00

☐ Wurlitzer Model 1080S, c. 1947-49, 24 tune selections,
"Classic" style, curving contours with decorated
mirrored panels, viewing window 2000.00   2500.00

☐ Wurlitzer Model 1100, c. 1948-49, 24 tune selections,
space age case style, large pointed dome-like top,
roller mechanism for tune cards, push buttons 1500.00   2000.00

Courtesy: Les Gould, S. Orange, N.J.

KITCHEN COLLECTIBLES

A large flat stone was probably the first cooking utensil. It was a bakestone, griddle, broiler, toaster and grill combined. A sharpened stick would have been needed to hold birds or other small game over the fire. Man became an accomplished toolmaker during the Bronze age. Since then a variety of very inventive and useful items have been produced for kitchen use. Please consult our publication, *From Hearth to Cookstove* by Linda Campbell Franklin for more prices and information.

"OLD TIME
MEASURES"
75.00 - 100.00

TOAST RACK
50.00 - 75.00

EGG POACHER
8.00 - 14.00

KITCHEN COLLECTIBLES

	Price Range	
☐ Apple Roasters, Tin reflecting oven with 2 or more racks	150.00	175.00
☐ Aprons, Old aprons from 1880's	1.00	10.00
☐ Bain Maries, Complete set with original pans	35.00	60.00
☐ Biscuit Cutter, tin, "White Lily Flour has no equal"	2.00	8.00
☐ Bread Knife, Scalloped or fluted cutting edge	.10	5.00
☐ Can Opener, nickeled steel, wood, 8½", L. A. & J. Edward Katzinger Company, 1940	2.00	4.00
☐ Candlestick, hogscraper stick, tin stick with push-up 1880's	8.00	20.00
☐ Chopping Knife, pivoting blade, steel, wood, 6½ x 6¼	4.00	10.00
☐ Colanders, tin 9¾" D x 3¾" H., American, 1890's	4.00	10.00
☐ Cookie Cutters, set of 4, shaped like miniature ciamond, club, spade and hearts, 1900-1920	8.00	12.00
☐ Dutch Ovens, cast iron 10", 11", 12" or 14" diameter, can be set in wood fire 1895	5.00	15.00
☐ Egg Beater, Dover, cast iron handle, and two gears, plus a small pinion gear and trimmed blades	10.00	12.00
☐ Fireless cooker, zinc, or wooden box, tin-lined	10.00	15.00
☐ Fruit Presses, tinned iron, patened June 8, 1888	2.00	8.00
☐ Graters, revolving, tin, nickel, wood, 3 grades of grater drums	8.00	16.00
☐ Ice Pick, nickel steel and steel, advertisements on side 8¾" L	4.00	8.00
☐ Ice Shredder, Tinned or nickel plated iron, adjustable for coarse or fine	2.00	7.00
☐ Juice Extractor, the dish has pouring lips and a seed barrier, glass patented 1888	4.00	10.00
☐ Match Safe, Metal or wooden, hinged cover, lined with plastic-like material	8.00	20.00
☐ Melon Ball Scoop, maple handle, brass ferrile, small 1890-1910	3.50	5.00

KITCHEN COLLECTIBLES

Price Range

☐ Mill-Grinding Machine, Hand powered, iron grinding cylinder of adjustable pressure plate 5.00	25.00
☐ Nutcracker, Alligator, brass, 12" 50.00	60.00
☐ Nutcracker, Dog, hand carved, 10" 25.00	30.00
☐ Nutcracker, Rooster, brass handles, 14" 50.00	60.00
☐ Nutmeg Grater, clamp-on "Lorraine Metal Mfg. Co." green maple top, ca 1910 .... 6.00	8.00
☐ Rolling Pin, hand turned from one piece of maple, overall 18", 1880-1900......................... 7.00	9.00
☐ Sausage Stuffer, tin or wood cylinder with small tapered funnel-like outlet, American 1870's ... 10.00	40.00
☐ Sieve, hair, woven horse-hair mesh in a wooden hoop 12.00	20.00
☐ Tea Kettle, galvanized cast iron with pit bottom and Alaska handle, c 1890 .... 30.00	60.00
☐ Toaster, Krispy Bread, polished steel with coppered iron bread rest. 10½" diameter 40.00	150.00
☐ Toasting Forks, telescoping for, 19th century steel ..	
☐ Waffle, Iron, cast iron, 8" diameter, 18½" L., 1870-1890 .... 15.00	25.00
☐ Wire Wisks, American, wooden handle, light weight ca 1870's .... .50	5.00

COFFEE MILLS

The first coffee mills were introduced in the late 1800's for domestic use.

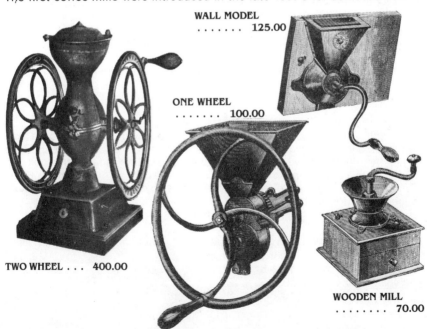

WALL MODEL
...... 125.00

ONE WHEEL
...... 100.00

TWO WHEEL ... 400.00

WOODEN MILL
.... 70.00

COFFEE MILLS

Price

- [ ] Cast Iron and Glass. Arcade 40.00
- [ ] Cast Iron. Crank top. Original red paint. Grand Union 80.00
- [ ] Cast Iron. Grinder and cup. Wall type. Tin canister 75.00
- [ ] Cast Iron. Metal container. Wall type. Universal 50.00
- [ ] Cast Iron. Two wheel "Crescent" brass hopper.
  Red paint. Floor model 475.00
- [ ] Cast Iron. Two wheel. 27" high. Elgin 350.00
- [ ] China. Wall hanging. Windmill design 90.00
- [ ] Crystal. Glass jar with tin top and spring holder. Wall type 45.00
- [ ] Iron & Glass. Wall type. Arcase 40.00
- [ ] Iron. Stubby with cap dome and urn-cup 45.00
- [ ] Iron. Two wheel. Large. Repainted. In working condition 250.00
- [ ] Iron. Two wheel. With handle. Ornate finial on dome (Eagle) 350.00
- [ ] Iron. One wheel. With crank. Cast iron & tin. Working 100.00
- [ ] Iron. Small mill. 9" high. Date early 1870's with wheels 130.00
- [ ] Iron. Wall type. With clear jar and grinder handle 35.00
- [ ] Iron. Wall type. With metal container and iron handle. 1906 . . . . 22.50
- [ ] Pine base with drawer. Cast iron handle. Lap type 45.00
- [ ] Tin with wooden bowl. Lap type 25.00
- [ ] Two wheel. Red paint. 12". Charles Parker Co. 175.00
- [ ] White iron. China jar. Delft scene. German 160.00
- [ ] Wood and iron. One drawer 80.00
- [ ] Wood and iron. One drawer. Handle on top and side 80.00
- [ ] Wood and metal. Glass insert. Golden Rule Coffee 80.00
- [ ] Wood. Brass fittings. Refinished 55.00
- [ ] Wood. Dovetailed. Iron lid and cup. Door at base 35.00
- [ ] Wood. Dovetailed. Pewter cup. Iron crank and drawer 75.00
- [ ] Wood. One wheel. One drawer 70.00
- [ ] Wood. Urn-shaped iron cup. Sliding drawers. Iron crank 40.00
- [ ] Wood. Iron cup with crank and sliding drawer 50.00
- [ ] Wooden base with drawer. Cast Iron 35.00

KNIVES

Knife collecting has existed for thousands of years, since the first cave man laid back a well chipped stone knife of a pretty color rock. Early design and styles remain basically the same as those made today. The feel and look of a fine knife is a thing of mechanical beauty. Please consult our publication *The Official Price Guide to Collector Pocket Knives* by Parker & Voyles for more prices and information.

CASE KNIVES:

PATTERN	STAMPING	YRS MADE	HANDLE	VARIATIONS	MINT PRICE
☐5488	Tested	Prior 1940	Stag		250.00
☐5488	XX	1940-54	Stag	Long Pull	200.00
☐5488	XX	1950-65	Stag		95.00
☐5488	XX	1960-65	Stag (second cut)		225.00

CASE KNIVES:

PATTERN	STAMPING	YRS MADE	HANDLE	VARIATIONS	MINT PRICE
☐5488	Transition	1964-65	Stag	XX to USA	130.00
☐5488	Transition	1964-65	Stag (second cut)	XX to USA	220.00
☐	USA	1965-70	Stag		75.00
☐	USA	1965-70	Stag (second cut)		220.00
☐	10 Dots	1970-July 70	Stag	Discontinued	110.00
☐6488	XX	1940-55	Green Bone	Long Pull	275.00
☐	XX	1940-55	Rough Black	Long Pull	150.00
☐	XX	1940-55	Red Bone	Long Pull	175.00
☐	XX	1940-55	Red Bone		85.00
☐	XX	1940-55	Bone	Long Pull	120.00
☐	Transition	1964-65	Bone	XX to USA	50.00
☐	USA	1965-70	Bone		37.00
☐	USA	1965-70	Stag (second cut)	This No. was stamped with both a 5" and 6"	220.00
☐	Transition	1969-70	Bone	USA to 10 Dots	40.00
☐	10 Dots	1970-71	Bone		35.00
☐	Dots	1970's	Bone	Discontinued	25.00
☐	Dots	1970's	Delrin	Discontinued	20.00
☐	Transitions	1970's	Bone	8 to 10 Dots	30.00

KABAR KNIVES (Length 5 3/8" closed):

PATTERN	STAMPING	HANDLE	MINT PRICE
☐61106 LG	Union in North American Shield	Bone Stag	900.00
☐61106 LG	Union Cut Co. Circle Marking	Bone Stag	725.00
☐61106 LG	Union Cut Co. Straightline Mark	Bone Stag	725.00
☐61106 LG	KA-BAR Union Cut on Rear Tang or on Second Blade	Bone Stag	675.00
☐61106	Union in North American Shield	Bone Stag	800.00
☐61106	Union Cut Co. Circle Marking	Bone Stag	650.00

KABAR KNIVES (Length 5 3/8" closed):

PATTERN	STAMPING	HANDLE	MINT PRICE
☐ 61106	Union Cut Co. Straightline Mark	Bone Stag	650.00
☐ 21106	KABAR Union Cut on Rear Tang or on Second Blade	Genuine Stag	750.00
☐ 61106	KABAR Union Cut on Rear Tang or on Second Blade	Bone Stag	600.00
☐ P1106	KA-BAR Union Cut on Rear Tang or on Second Blade	Pearl Celluloid	425.00

REMINGTON KNIVES:

PATTERN NO.	MINT PRICE	PATTERN NO.	MINT PRICE	PATTERN NO.	MINT PRICE
R-I	60.00	R-B46	90.00	R-141	120.00
R-2	60.00	R-B47	130.00	R-142	120.00
R-2	75.00	R-51	80.00	R-143	160.00
R-01	60.00	R-71	75.00	R-145	140.00
R-02	60.00	R-72	85.00	R-151	120.00
R-03	75.00	R-73	110.00	R-152	120.00
R-A1	60.00	R-75	95.00	R-153	160.00
R-C5	60.00	R-81	75.00	R-155	140.00
R-C6	60.00	R-82	85.00	R-155B	140.00
R-C7	55.00	R-83	110.00	R-155M	140.00
R-C8	55.00	R-85	95.00	R-155Z	140.00
R-C9	55.00	R-C090	70.00	R-161	120.00
R-15	100.00	R-C091	70.00	R-162	120.00
R-015	75.00	R-91	100.00	R-163	160.00
R-17	45.00	R-103	145.00	R-165	140.00
R-21	80.00	R-103ch	160.00	R-171	140.00
R-21ch	100.00	R-105	125.00	R-171	140.00
R-22	80.00	R-105A	125.00	R-173	200.00
R-23	100.00	R-105B	125.00	R-175	160.00
R-23ch	110.00	R-108ch	120.00	R-181	160.00
R-25	80.00	R-111	100.00	R-182	160.00
R-31	80.00	R-112	100.00	R-183	200.00
R-32	80.00	R-113	135.00	R-185	165.00
R-33	100.00	R-115	115.00	R-191	150.00
R-35	100.00	R-122	120.00	R-192	150.00
R-B040	75.00	R-123	160.00	R-193	200.00
R-041	74.00	R-125	140.00	R-195	175.00
R-B43	100.00	R-131	120.00	R-201	160.00
R-B44	100.00	R-132	120.00	R-202	160.00
R-B45	130.00	R-133	160.00	R-203	200.00
R-B44W	75.00	R-135	140.00	R-205	180.00

FIGHTING KNIVES:

☐ Nazi boot knife	85.00
☐ U.S. Trench knife, World War I	100.00
☐ British Sykes-Fairbairn commando knife	50.00

LABELS

It may seem odd, but some of the finest printing ever done in this country was done on labels for fruit crates—oranges, apples, pears, grapes—and for labels for other products. Many labels are extraordinarily inexpensive, and you can start a collection easily with less than $15.00.

At present, the collecting of labels is too new to have many established price guidelines. In fact, many collectors trade labels, with no money changing hands. It seems apparent, however, that certain subject matter commands higher prices than others; very desirable are Blacks, airplanes, Indians, cats, dogs, ships, etc. Most cigar, can and fruit labels bring at least $1.00 and sometimes more—up to about $12 to $15 in the case of can and fruit crate labels, and even more for rare 19th c. cigar labels. Listed first below are some typical offerings in periodicals for collectors.

	Price Range	
☐ America's Delight, Apples, Orchard Scene	1.00	1.50
☐ Azalea, Oranges, Azalea Blossoms. Florida	1.00	1.50
☐ Basketball, Lemons, Girls Playing Basketball.	5.00	6.00
☐ Black Hawk, Oranges, Indian. Riverside	18.00	20.00
☐ Blue Goose, Oranges, Large Goose. Los Angeles	2.50	3.00
☐ Corona Beauty, Lemons, Blossoms. Corona	1.00	1.50
☐ Florigold, Oranges, Coin, Indian Head. Florida	1.50	2.00
☐ Hiawatha, Oranges, Indian Brave Face	7.50	8.50
☐ Indian Belle, Grapefruit, Chief and Squaw. Porterville.	35.00	40.00
☐ Mission, Lemons, Santa Barbara Mission	7.50	8.50
☐ Rising Sun, Oranges, Sun Scene. Chicago	3.00	3.50
☐ San Francisco, Oranges, Golden Gate Bridge, Bird ..	35.00	40.00
☐ Sea Gull, Lemons, Gulls Flying	3.00	3.50
☐ Sunkist, Apples, Sunkist Emblem	20.00	25.00
☐ 50 Labels, Western Packing Houses 8" x 10"	12.00	15.00
☐ 100 Labels, Animals, Women, Children, 1920-1940 ...	10.00	12.00

MATCH BOX LABELS

Match labels are mainly a "topical" collectors' item, that is, collected for the illustration. The subjects covered by these illustrations are numerous, including animals, birds, streetcars, sports, famous persons, sailing ships, airplanes, etc. This hobby is considerably more widespread in Europe than in America. Its chief advantages are low price and the small storage space required, as a collection of many hundreds of labels can be housed in one album. The boxes themselves are rarely collected, only the labels.

☐ Ciclista Safety Matches. Man riding bicycle	2.00	3.00
☐ Gulnar Jan Safety Match. Made in Sweden. Girl in lace mantilla	1.00	1.50
☐ Ed Booher (Germany). Photo of man reading book by Vladimir Nobokov	.50	1.00
☐ Favorite Yacht, J.M. Shaska, Manchester. Arabic writing on lower portion	2.00	3.00
☐ Fosforos Hercules. Hercules fighting lion	1.00	2.00

MATCH BOX LABELS   Price Range

☐ The Kookaburra or Laughing Jackass (Sweden). "Damp proof." Illus. of birds	—	2.00
☐ Phonograph Match. Engraving of old phonograph with megaphone - No name. Three dice on label. Made in Sweden	.50	1.00
☐ Radja Stamboel. Man in military dress, wearing fez	1.00	2.00
☐ Sorbia Safety Matches. Negro head in profile	3.00	4.00
☐ The Automobile Safety Match. Four riders in car, c. 1910	5.00	6.00
☐ Three Globes Safety Match	.50	1.00
☐ Three Steamers. "Do Not Glow"	2.00	3.00

MISCELLANEOUS

☐ Art Deco, beverage labels, 50	3.50	5.00
☐ Beer Labels, 1930-1960, 100	6.00	7.00
☐ Bock Labels, all different, 25	3.00	4.00
☐ Food/Cosmetic Labels, 80 different types, 1000	15.00	16.00
☐ Pharmaceutical, Tobacco & other misc. labels, up to 11" x 14"	8.50	10.00
☐ Whiskey Labels, assorted, 100	4.00	5.00

LAMPS & LIGHTING DEVICES

Ever since the first lamp smoked and sputtered out, man has sought a less smokey, less smelly, more beautiful and more efficient artificial light. There are countless examples of lamps from the last 300 years available to collectors, and you can even start collecting some of today's lamps: many of them are quite unusual, and of good design.

MIRRORED TIN WALL SCONCES . . . . **500.00 - 600.00**

☐ Angle lamps, brass, double lacquered	120.00	225.00
☐ Art Deco Chandelier, leaded glass, signed Quezal	—	600.00
☐ Art Deco Globe, opalescent, signed, Verlys	—	360.00

LAMPS & LIGHTING DEVICES

	Price	Range
☐ Betty Lamp, tin with hanger	65.00	95.00
☐ Bradley & Hubbard, caramel shade, signed base, 24" high	450.00	600.00
☐ Carriage lamps, brass, clear glass and red reflector lenses	230.00	275.00
☐ Chandelier, Louis XV style, cut glass shade	800.00	900.00
☐ Chandelier, pewter, converted from gas, CA. 1870	—	780.00
☐ Crystal Chandelier, hand cut lead, Czecheslovakia, CA. 1925	—	1800.00
☐ Crystal Chandelier, hand cut, unusual shape, converted from candles to electric, French, CA. 1800	—	2250.00
☐ Crystal Chandelier, hand cut lead, Czech., CA 1920 ..	—	1200.00
☐ Courting lamp, pewter, clear & frosted front, 4"	65.00	95.00
☐ Gas Chandelier, hand wrought, turn of century, French	—	750.00
☐ Matching sconces, wall, pair	—	250.00
☐ Gone With the Wind lamps, umbrella shade with cupids and foliage, brass foot, 20" high	225.00	275.00
☐ Gone With the Wind lamps, grape pattern with green leaves, 22" high	425.00	500.00
☐ Gone With the Wind lamps, magnolia blossoms hand-painted, 24" high	475.00	575.00
☐ Gone With the Wind lamps, red glass with red bull's eye, 28½" high	575.00	675.00
☐ Greentown lamp, chocolate glass, 10"	425.00	475.00
☐ Hand lamp, tin, drum shape	50.00	75.00
☐ Handel lamps, all signed, Boudoir-reverse painted scene, 14" high	400.00	525.00
☐ Hanging lamps, brass with chocolate glass panels, 14"	35.00	70.00
☐ Hanging lamps, cranberry with prisms	600.00	700.00
☐ Hanging lamp, striped with canopy, 13"	110.00	170.00
☐ Hurricane lamp, 11" pair	25.00	40.00
☐ Iron Chandelier, hand wrought, floral vines, CA. 1920 .	—	750.00
☐ Matching Wall Sconces, pair	—	250.00
☐ Iron Fixture, hand wrought, Moorish influence, early 20th Century	—	375.00
☐ Jefferson, boudoir, trees	180.00	225.00
☐ Kerosene lamp, cabbage case pattern	40.00	60.00
☐ Kerosene lamp, country store fixture, brass front	90.00	150.00
☐ Kerosene lamp, green pattern, milk glass base	50.00	90.00
☐ Kerosene lamp, hanging fixture, cranberry glass with brass frame	140.00	170.00
☐ Kerosene lamp, Hobnail pattern	20.00	35.00
☐ Kerosene lamp, table, lincoln drape pattern, amber ..	80.00	125.00
☐ Kerosene lamp, table, overlay glass, 13" high	550.00	650.00
☐ Kerosene lamp, table, "Ripley Marriage Lamp"	350.00	425.00
☐ Kerosene lamp, wall , cast iron bracket, 12" high	38.00	55.00
☐ Lily, amber shades, 3 lights, bronze base	1800.00	1925.00
☐ Mac-Beth Nite Glow, ruby shade	25.00	35.00
☐ Pairpoint, Boudoir, "Puffy" rose shade with metal base, 8" deep	680.00	750.00
☐ Pairpoint, butterflies & roses, signed base and shade, 10" deep	870.00	950.00

LAMPS & LIGHTING DEVICES

	Price	Range
☐ Peg lamps, brass burner, 6"	45.00	75.00
☐ Peg lamps, ribbed glass with brass candlesticks, pair	275.00	350.00
☐ Tole Sconces, wall, French, early 20th Century, set of six	165.00 each	
☐ Sconces, wall, set of eight	135.00 each	
☐ Student lamp, single, brass font, milk glass (white) shade	260.00	325.00
☐ Student lamp, single brass font, green glass shade	260.00	325.00
☐ Student lamp, double brass, green glass shade with original chimney	430.00	520.00
☐ Student lamp, hanging double, burnished with green shade	575.00	675.00
☐ Table, "Arrow Root" leaded glass shade with bronze base, 25½" high	6800.00	7800.00
☐ Table "Dragonfly", leaded glass shade with dragon fly bodies with bronze base, 10½" high	5500.00	6000.00
☐ Table, stained glass shade with tulip bronzed copper base, 23½" high	675.00	795.00
☐ Table, leaded glass shade with green leaves and dogwood blossoms, 27" high	2650.00	3000.00
☐ Table, hybiscus, leaded shade in red, yellow, white & pink	1750.00	1900.00
☐ Table, nasturtium, amber chisled ground, signed in triplecate	500.00	650.00
☐ Tiffany, acorn, green with orange acorns shade, signed, 19" high	2400.00	2650.00
☐ Tiffany type, glass fixture, leaded fruit pattern, CA. 1910	—	1200.00
☐ Tiffany, table lamp, bronze base with leaded glass shade, acorn pattern, both pieces signed, Tiffany studios	—	3900.00
☐ Tiffany, desk lamp, signed base & shade	760.00	825.00
☐ Tiffany, floor lamp, "Damascene" shade, bronze base and lily pad feet	1900.00	2150.00
☐ Tiffany, table lamp, Kapa shell, bronze base, 12¾" high	800.00	925.00
☐ Venetian Mirror, hand cut & etched, 5' x 3' carved backing	—	1800.00
☐ Whale Oil, amethyst paneled font with marble base, 10"	250.00	325.00
☐ Whale Oil, Giant Sawtooth, 9"	90.00	110.00
☐ Whale Oil, paneled font, blue with marble base, 10"	250.00	300.00
☐ Whale Oil, tin, 7"	45.00	75.00
☐ Wicker Table with wicker shade, 19"	40.00	60.00

LIGHTING DEVICES (MINIATURE)

☐ Brass Acorn burner, 6"	40.00	70.00
☐ Brass Banquet Lamp, 10" high, jewels on base, glass with blue & white wildflowers and tendrils	150.00	300.00
☐ Brass Saucer, 4½" high, chimney sculptured, marked "1873"	20.00	45.00
☐ Brass Saucer, 2", nutmeg burner	45.00	75.00
☐ Brass Skating Lamp, 8" high, complete with link chain	35.00	70.00
☐ Bristol, blue enameled flowers, 6½"	65.00	90.00
☐ Bristol type, decorative figures on sides, hexogonal base	70.00	150.00
☐ Bull's Eye, red	40.00	80.00
☐ Clear glass base, "Nutmeg" clear glass chimney	25.00	45.00
☐ Cosmos lamp, 8" high, multi-colored floral decorations	150.00	275.00
☐ Cranberry glass, flowers on shade	325.00	425.00

LIGHTING DEVICES (MINIATURE)

	Price	Range
☐ Cranberry glass, beaded swirl, 8¾"	250.00	325.00
☐ Glow NightLamp, ribbed base & shade with original wicker holder	38.00	55.00
☐ Golden Eagle, orange body with gold & yellow trim . . .	100.00	175.00
☐ Green glass, bull's eye pattern, nutmeg burner, clear chimney	35.00	50.00
☐ Milk glass, 5½" high chimney top with fluted stem and footed base	100.00	200.00
☐ Milk glass night light, long neck & metal tank	28.00	40.00
☐ Milk glass, 8½" high, blue enamelled lillies (pair)	150.00	300.00
☐ Milk glass (white) embossed with iris, acorn burner, clear glass chimney	145.00	195.00
☐ Opalescent glass, applied feet, 8½"	375.00	450.00
☐ Opaline glass base & chimney, house scene in green acorn burner	150.00	200.00
☐ Pink milk glass, house, clear glass chimney, 4 original burners	160.00	225.00
☐ Pressed glass, daisy, kerosene	20.00	35.00
☐ Pressed glass, pineapple in basket	275.00	350.00
☐ Satin glass, diamond quilted, 6"	525.00	650.00
☐ Satin glass, petal with beading, embossed base, nutmeg burner, 9"	275.00	350.00
☐ Tin, acorn burner	10.00	20.00
☐ Tin, base & shade painted green, acorn burner, 6"	20.00	30.00

LANTERNS

During the 1700's enclosed portable candleholders (lanterns) became fashionable. They are ordinarily classified by the function for which they are used, material, or shape.

☐ Auto lamp, brass, oil burning, 14½" high	70.00	110.00
☐ Barn, Peter Gray, Boston	75.00	125.00
☐ Buggy dashboard, kerosene	15.00	25.00
☐ Candle lantern, tin, clear blown glass globe with reflector, 11" high	130.00	170.00
☐ Candle lantern, sheet metal painted black, 16¼" high	45.00	70.00
☐ Carriage, brass trim, pair	275.00	350.00
☐ Chinese junk, brass, oil	25.00	50.00
☐ Coach, Pierced, 17½"	125.00	175.00
☐ Dietz Driving Lamp with red glass in rear, 7½" high . .	90.00	130.00
☐ Kerosene lantern, brass base and top engraved "Joseph Gavett, Roxbury", 17" high	215.00	260.00
☐ Kerosene lantern, Dietz red reflector	15.00	25.00
☐ Miner's lantern, English	45.00	75.00
☐ Miner's lantern, tin & brass, Jan. 10, 1882, 5½" high . .	18.00	25.00
☐ Paul Revere type, tin with swirls	125.00	190.00
☐ Skater's lantern, brass with glass globe	55.00	80.00
☐ Ship's lantern, copper, 16" high, pair	200.00	275.00
☐ Wagon lantern, clamp on type with rear red reflector .	20.00	26.00
☐ Wood lantern, rare	135.00	175.00

LINDBERGHIANA

Charles Lindbergh was a hero to the world when he flew non-stop to Paris in his small plane, in 1927. A number of commemorative items exist which are collected by fans of Lindbergh.

	Price	Range
☐ Book, Lone Eagle	15.00	25.00
☐ Button, "Welcome Lindy"	10.00	15.00
☐ McCormick Bottles, American Portraits — Charles Lindbergh	10.00	15.00
☐ Medal, Bronze Congressional, 1928	25.00	35.00
☐ Pencil Box	15.00	20.00
☐ Postcard w/photo of Lindbergh & plane	4.00	8.00
☐ Portrait banner, "Welcome Lindbergh," cloth, 56½" x 33½"	—	225.00
☐ Stamp, Scott #1710, 13¢ multi-colored "Spirit of St. Louis" ... new	—	.26
Louis" ... used	—	.06
☐ Tapestry, New York to Paris, mint cond.	—	100.00
☐ Wheaton/Nuline Decanters, Charles Lindbergh, Blue, c. 1968	4.50	8.50

OTHER AIRPLANE COLLECTIBLES

☐ Luftwaffe Fighter Pilot Pressurized Goggles, in original case, mkd. w/eagle & swastika, 1940	—	15.00
☐ Airplane, French, chromolith, airplane, early 20th century	—	400.00

LOCKS & KEYS

Tens of thousands of varieties of antique locks and keys exist, and most can be found on the market, the greater majority in antiques shops and the rarer ones offered by dealers in ancient artifacts and auctioneers. Anyone interested in collecting rare locks should read the catalogues of major auction galleries, such as the Sotheby Parke-Bernet catalogues of Americana and European works of art.

In the following list, keep in mind that the high prices were obtained for locks and keys of an unusual or special nature. Most old locks found in antique shops fall into the class of ordinary and are worth considerably less.

It should also be noted that the demand for antique locks and keys has risen *sharply* in recent years, well ahead of most other "traditional" antiques, and that prices found in old publications are now meaningless. In fact publications only 3-4 years old have ads for locks at prices which *dealers* would now be quite willing to pay.

LOCKS & KEYS

Price Range

- ☐ Roman padlock, brass, 3¼" long, slightly twisted, green patina, average to good condition 350.00 400.00
- ☐ Portion of a Roman doorlock, 1st-2nd centuries A.D., 5 3/8ths", pitted, green patina, VG 325.00 375.00
- ☐ Medieval castle or church door lock, German or Flemish, 12th or 13th centuries, 13½ x 8¾", heavy hammered iron, some surface damage, no key 1400.00 1600.00
- ☐ Medieval gate lock, "large," iron, decorated with heads of gargoyles and griffins, other decoration, some damage but an unusual and fine specimen. (Sold at auction in England.) .... — 1800.00
- ☐ Spanish doorlock, 8 x 4½", black iron, iron studs or nailheads, some incised decoration on thin plate attached to the lock, c. 1400 .... — 900.00
- ☐ Iron castle lock, 17 x 11½", heavy iron resembling steel, thick iron bolts on a sliding frame, key present, in working condition, somewhat rusted, c. 1450-1500. — 3500.00
- ☐ Nuremberg (Germany) padlock, 7" L, barrel 5½" L, polished steel, decorated with incised hunting scene, perfect outward condition, non-working mechanism, no key, c. 1590.................................... 1500.00 1700.00
- ☐ Nuremberg padlock, 5 x 4", the barrel in the likeness of a skull, very rare, c. 1620 .... 2700.00 3000.00
- ☐ German (probably) chest lock of the 17th-century, size with bolts extended 34½ x 25", weight 62 pounds, iron and steel, one key throws ten bolts (non-working) 1800.00 2000.00
- ☐ German padlock, 5" H, V-shaped barrel, decorative design, non-working, c. 1680 .... 250.00 275.00
- ☐ American padlock, 13" L, crudely wrought iron, "cigar" design, estimated at late 18th-century, probably New England 500.00 600.00
- ☐ American padlock, mid 19th-century, approx. 5 x 4", cover over keyhole, good condition (non-working) 90.00 110.00
- ☐ American padlock, late 19th-century, heart shaped, keyhole at front................................. 50.00 70.00
- ☐ American combination padlock, 3" long, working condition, c. 1895 .... 30.00 40.00
- ☐ Roman key, 1st or 2nd century A.D., 2¼" L, simple design, green patina........................... 150.00 175.00
- ☐ Roman ring key, copper with light patina, well preserved. c. 2nd century A.D. 175.00 225.00
- ☐ German or English castle door key, brass, 14" L, heavy shank, 1200-1300 .... 250.00 275.00
- ☐ Italian palace key, iron, 9¼", late Renaissance 250.00 300.00
- ☐ Spanish door key, 12", heavy iron, ornamental, 1500-1550 .... 300.00 325.00
- ☐ European door or padlock key, 7½", well preserved, c. 1600 .... 60.00 75.00

MAGAZINES

NATIONAL GEOGRAPHIC

Certain issues of *National Geographic* are valued higher than others because they contain sought-after articles. This is quite different than the situation with most old magazines, where all issues from a given year are usually worth the same price. The November, 1914 number brings $15 on the strength of an article, "Young Russia," whereas most other 1914 issues fall in the $5-7 class. This goes for recent years, too. The December, 1969 issue, with a story on the moonwalk, fetches $10.00; other 1969 issues can be had at $1-2.

	Price Range	
☐ Volume 1, #1 (1888)	400.00	500.00
☐ Volume 1, #2	150.00	250.00
☐ March, 1898	—	40.00
☐ Most Issues 1908-1912	10.00	15.00

Bound volumes with covers intact:

☐ #1 (1888-1889), four issues	1000.00	1500.00
☐ #2 (1890-1891), five issues	300.00	400.00
☐ #3 (1891-1892), five issues	300.00	400.00
☐ #6 (1894-1895), nine issues	—	500.00

PUNCH

It should be noted that in the case of *most* magazines, especially weeklies, the sum value of individual issues from #1 to the present is higher than the value of a complete set. This is because there are relatively fewer buyers interested in full sets. With *Punch,* a full set comprises something in the range of 7,000 issues, or about 1½ tons of magazines.

☐ Volume 1, #1, 1841	20.00	25.00
☐ Random Issues, 1841-1860	—	3.00
☐ 1861-1899	—	2.00
☐ 1900-1919	—	1.50
☐ 1929-1945	—	1.00
☐ 1946 - present	.50	1.00

PLAYBOY

The problem with *Playboy* is obtaining issues in good condition. Often there are illustrations missing.

☐ Volume 1, #1, 1953	300.00	400.00
☐ Assorted Issues, 1953	—	75.00
☐ 1954-1956	25.00	50.00
☐ 1957-1960	10.00	20.00
☐ 1961-1964	4.00	10.00
☐ 1965 - present	2.00	4.00
☐ Complete Set, 1953-1978	—	3000.00

MISCELLANEOUS

ART IN AMERICA	Price	Range
☐ Volume 1, #1, 1913	—	5.00
☐ Complete Run, 1913-1978	1500.00	2000.00

ANTIQUES		
☐ Volume 1, #1, 1922	—	10.00
☐ Complete Run, 1922-1978	—	2000.00

SCRIBNERS		
☐ Volume 1, #1, 1922	5.00	7.50

THE CONNOISSEUR		
☐ Volume 1, #1, 1901	3.00	5.00
☐ Complete Run, 1901-1978	2000.00	3000.00

MAGICIAN'S MEMORABILIA

After witnessing Houdini's escape act, many parties offered challenges to him — they would nail him in a box, tie him in a bag, etc. When Houdini accepted the challenge, a special poster was printed up for display outside the theatre. A vast variety exist, not only in English but German, French, Dutch and possibly other languages.

☐ "Chung Lung Soo," colored poster, early 1900's	275.00	300.00
☐ Harry Houdini, 8" x 10" b/w photo, signed and inscribed, c. 1920	75.00	100.00
☐ Harry Houdini, small card printed with address of Houdini in holograph	25.00	30.00
☐ Harry Houdini, "challenge" poster, to be carried out on a London stage, c. 1910	40.00	50.00
☐ Kellar, 8" x 10", photo of Kellar, dressed in tophat, signed with lengthy description, c. 1910	80.00	100.00
☐ Kellar, silk hat in velvet-lined box	50.00	75.00
☐ Letterhead, "Lorenz the Miraculous Magician," w/holograph letter	40.00	50.00
☐ Matinka & Co., magic catalogue, N.Y., 1898	75.00	100.00
☐ "The Headless Countryman, c. 1910	275.00	300.00
☐ "The Second Advent of Rip Van Winkle," trick sold originally for 30 pounds, c. 1910	150.00	175.00
☐ Poster, "Bosco" the magician, color, c. 1900	85.00	125.00
☐ "Thurston the Great Magician," full color poster, four sections, 9' x 7', rare, 1914	—	1000.00
☐ Thurston, 8" x 10" b/w photo, performing trick, signed, painted, glazed wooden frame	60.00	75.00

MAPS

Although old maps are sold frequently enough on the market for price guidelines to be established on all classes of specimens, one should realize that values do fluctuate pretty regularly and are influenced by condition, the place of sale, and other factors. The prices given here are for maps in sound collector condition, meaning; no serious stains or discolorations, no tears, and with the full original margins. It would be natural to assume that a framed map would be worth more than without a frame; however, many such specimens have been trimmed down to fit their frames, and in these situations an unframed copy with full margins will certainly sell higher. The presence of *folds* is to be expected in large maps, but there should be no breakage or excessive delicacy at the folds.

EARLY MAP OF VIRGINIA .... 350.00 - 400.00

	Price Range	
☐ America, new map, by John Cary, colored outline. 20" x 23", 1806	20.00	30.00
☐ America, by D'Anville, colored, mounted on linen. 21¼" x 31¾", 1797	120.00	150.00
☐ Central America by W. R. Palmer, Washington D.C. (undated). Outline colored, 45" x 42"	70.00	90.00
☐ East India, chart by Aaron Arrowsmith. Engraved, tinted, mounted on linen, 1800	70.00	80.00
☐ England, Surrey, by Joannus Blaeu. No date (1600's), partly colored	170.00	200.00

MAPS

	Price	Range
☐ Greece, by Aaron Arrowsmith. Colored, outlined, 1824	15.00	25.00
☐ Louisiana, by J. D'Aville. 16" x 21", 1788	90.00	120.00
☐ New York, colored. 17½" x 21½", 1836	30.00	40.00
☐ North America, by J. D'Anville, colored outline. 17" x 22½", 1752	90.00	120.00
☐ North America and the West Indies, by Sayer & Bennett, colored outine. 21" x 26½", 1783	190.00	220.00
☐ North Carolina, new and accurate. 10½" x 24", 1779. .	50.00	60.00
☐ Oxford, County, by John Cary, 1797	375.00	425.00
☐ South Carolina, by William DeBrahm, two sheets, colored, total size 26½" x 48", 1757	380.00	440.00
☐ United States, by Amos Lay, colored, mounted on linen. 52" x 61", 1834	270.00	300.00
☐ United States of North America, by Aaron Arrowsmith, engraved and hand colored. 1796	290.00	320.00
☐ Venezuala, by Wilhelm Blaeu, colored. 14¾" x 19", 1640	25.00	35.00

MEDALS

The honoring of individuals often was done by the presentation of a special official medal. The interest, while somewhat limited, is most fascinating. Rare significant medals bring extremely high prices.

☐ American Presidential life saving medal, 1857	1450.00	1650.00
☐ Breast staff of the Most Noble Order of the Garter. Second quarter of the 19th century	2700.00	3000.00
☐ England. 7 Bar Naval General Service Medal (Napoleonic Wars). (Only one specimen of this medal is believed to exist.)	5000.00	5500.00
☐ Imperial Russia, order of St. Catherine the Great Martyr. Royal presentation set of diamond insignia . .	17,000.00	18,000.00
☐ Ireland. James I gold and enamel badge for the London Society, c. 1620	3800.00	4200.00
☐ Italy. Sicily. Order of St. Januarius, gold and enamel, mid 19th century	2400.00	2800.00
☐ Knight's Badge of the Order of St. Patrick. Gold. c. 1809	3000.00	3200.00
☐ Naval General Service Medal, 1793-1840. Two bars . .	1700.00	2000.00
☐ Peninsular War, Military General Service Medal (English), with eleven battle clasps	900.00	1200.00
☐ Royal National Lifeboat Institute. Gold medal (saving a life)	800.00	1200.00
☐ Star of the Most Noble Order of the Garter	1800.00	2200.00
☐ Victoria Cross, lion and crown with motto "for valour"	7400.00	8000.00

MENUS

The value of old menus depends upon their age; special circumstances; size and decorative appeal; and whether or not they bear autographs of famous persons. This is still a rather small hobby, and has not yet reached the point where values are set depending on the restaurant from which the menu comes. However, most collectors are anxious to have menus from famous restaurants and will usually pay a premium for them—say $5 for a New York "Stork Club" or (with some sports interest added) a "Jack Dempsey's." In the case of restaurants still in operation—the two just mentioned aren't— older specimens are more desirable, the older the better. Menus from still-active restaurants bring only $1 or $2 if current or fairly recent.

Valuable menus. Among the most valuable menus are those written by hand on wooden boards, which adorned the walls of early American (and foreign) taverns. The fare was simple and the prices ridiculously low by modern standards. All during the 18th-century and well into the 19th it was the custom of taverns to post menus rather than distributing printed copies to each diner. A few dishes would be listed along with beverages. Often the menu carried the establishment's name and symbol (bull & bear, etc.), along with "rules of the house" if there happened to be rooms for rent. They ranged to quite large size, sometimes a yard or more in height, and could be quite decorative. The board might be carved and the lettering handsomely painted. The *values* of board menus depends on the age, place of origin, visual appeal, and, of course, physical condition. As these factors are so variable, it is almost impossible to set price guidelines. A very rough idea of prices is as follows:

	Price Range	
☐ New England, pre-1800	500.00	1000.00
☐ New England, 1800-1850, (large size)	—	500.00
☐ New York City, pre-1800	750.00	1500.00
☐ New York City, 1800-1850, (depending on size)	500.00	1000.00
☐ Southern States, 1800-1850, with listing of many dishes	—	2000.00
☐ Old West, to 1890	500.00	5000.00

Printed wall menus, while not as valuable as those written by hand, are nevertheless very collectible and can run into several hundreds of dollars if early, decorative, etc. Specimens in the original frames, even if broken, are much preferred over modern frames.

A problem with some early menus of the "wall" type is that they do not state the place of origin—merely the establishment's name, and sometimes not even that. The collector must then search through old town directories or other records to locate it.

White House menus. The single most popular group of menus among collectors is that of special White House dinners, balls and other affairs. Menus for Presidential inaugural ball dinners are worth $25 and up, depending on the President. Their scarcity is, however, difficult to calculate. Presumably, there should be in existance just one menu for each person attending, but one never knows whether the printer ran off extra copies to sell to collectors.

MENUS

Signed menus. the value of signed menus depends on the value of the signature. These are more common than you might think; restaurants are good hunting-grounds for collectors seeking celebrity autographs, and often the only available paper is a menu. Among the most creative signed menus are those of the opera star Caruso, who often drew caricatures on them. A good caricature menu by Caruso is worth $200.

METALS

BRASS

Through the years many decorative and useful objects have been made of this alloy of copper and zinc. It is one of the most durable and versatile metals used by man.

DUTCH WALL SCONCES . . . . 450.00 - 550.00
ENGRAVED FOOT WARMER . . . . . 200.00 - 300.00

	Price	Range
☐ Anvil. 5" x 2¼"	15.00	30.00
☐ Ashtray. Art Noveau Maiden, outstretched arms, 7" x 3½"	20.00	35.00
☐ Ashtray. Shape of bulldog's head, 4½"	10.00	20.00
☐ Bell. Gong shaped alarm with trip hammer, 14"	55.00	85.00
☐ Bird Cage. Three singing birds, movable heads, 18" . .	500.00	650.00
☐ Book Ends. Pair of sailing ships, 4"	10.00	20.00
☐ Book Rack. Art Nouveau Lady and Flowers	20.00	35.00
☐ Bowl. Dragons on teak stand, 10"	10.00	20.00
☐ Bowl. Etched cow, trees and men, W. Wettemberg . . .	5.50	12.50
☐ Bowl (rice). Figures, 5"	40.00	65.00
☐ Box. Butterfly on dome lid, inlaid, 2¾"	30.00	50.00
☐ Box. Chinese dragon on lid, 4 x 3¼"	6.75	11.50
☐ Box. Lincoln Memorial, Jacoby-Benz, 5 x 3"	30.00	60.00
☐ Box. Chinese dragon on lid, 4" x 3½"	6.75	11.50
☐ Box. Lincoln Memorial, Jacoby-Benz, 5" x 3"	30.00	60.00
☐ Box. Oriental with jade trim, 2½" x 4"	12.00	32.00
☐ Box. Stamp shape of fly, 3" x 2" x 1½"	5.00	8.00

BRASS

	Price	Range
☐ Calling Card Holder. Ornate	22.00	40.00
☐ Candelabrum. Chinese, five arms, 9" x 8"	8.00	15.00
☐ Candelabrum. Detailed, four arms, removable, 5¾" x 6½"	30.00	50.00
☐ Candelabrum. Scrolls, three arms, 6¾"	5.00	8.00
☐ Candelabra Seven candles, 18"	165.00	275.00
☐ Candelabrum. Supported by two lions, three arms, 11½"	20.00	40.00
☐ Candlesticks. Beehive and diamond pattern, 12", pair	105.00	175.00
☐ Candlesticks. Engraved bases, floral design, 7½", pair	25.00	45.00
☐ Candlesticks. English, 4½"	25.00	45.00
☐ Candlesticks. Flowers and medallions, Chinese, 8¼"	8.00	15.00
☐ Candlesticks. Louis XVI, 10½", pair	130.00	200.00
☐ Candlesticks. Push-up, "The 1901", 11½"	155.00	225.00
☐ Candlesticks. Russian, footed, 10"	25.00	45.00
☐ Candlesticks. Storrar's Chester, push-up, 10", pair . . .	40.00	65.00
☐ Candlesticks. Turtle, holder sets on turtle's back, 3", pair	10.00	15.00
☐ Chestnut roaster. Brass handles, 18" long	65.00	100.00
☐ Coal Box. Ornate coal scoop, ball feet, 12" x 16" x 17"	200.00	275.00
☐ Coffeepot. Russian, long spout, 9"	60.00	110.00
☐ Compote. Three-footed base, Aral, 6" x 4"	45.00	75.00
☐ Cup. Nickel-plated, folds in 1½"	5.00	9.00
☐ Cuspidors. 12" high	60.00	100.00
☐ Desk Set. Chinese, four piece	50.00	85.00
☐ Door Bell. Fire gong 7"	35.00	60.00
☐ Door Knocker. Anchor shape, 1920	8.50	15.00
☐ Door Knocker. Deer shape, Oriental, 4¼"	10.00	20.00
☐ Door Knocker. Lady's hand shape	10.00	22.00
☐ Door Knocker. William Wordsworth bust, floral, 2½" .	30.00	55.00
☐ Ewer. Russian, turned lip, 17"	50.00	100.00
☐ Figurine. Cigarette holder in shape of a camel	4.00	8.00
☐ Fire Hose Nozzle	60.00	100.00
☐ Foot Warmer. Oval shaped	50.00	75.00
☐ Frame (easel). 6½" x 5"	5.00	8.00
☐ Frame. Heart-shaped, 2 1/8"	20.00	35.00
☐ Gong. Engraved, flowers with animals	30.00	45.00
☐ Hat Pin. Head of Indian	12.50	20.00
☐ Heel Plate. Heart-shaped cutouts	20.00	35.00
☐ Horse Head. Circled by horseshoe, 3"	20.00	25.00
☐ Humidor. China, painted cover, enameled bands	70.00	100.00
☐ Ice Tongs.	20.00	35.00
☐ Incense Burner. Chinese, small	9.00	15.00
☐ Inkwell. Crab, pewter inside well, 6" x 5"	50.00	60.00
☐ Inkwell. Devil figure, German	50.00	65.00
☐ Inkwell (double). Harvard cutting, pen rest	110.00	150.00
☐ Inkwell. Heart-shaped, 3½"	150.00	200.00
☐ Inkwell. Lid with owl's head, 11"	160.00	200.00

BRASS

	Price	Range
☐ Inkwell. Ornate, glass insert	60.00	100.00
☐ Jardiniere. 10", deer head handle	155.00	170.00
☐ Jardiniere. 8" high, 10" diameter, ball feet	60.00	90.00
☐ Jardiniere. 5" x 5"	40.00	70.00
☐ Lamp. Candlestick, 19", pair	45.00	55.00
☐ Lamp and Heater. Nautical design	75.00	100.00
☐ Letter Opener. Dog's head, 10¼"	8.50	15.00
☐ Mailbox. Combination lock	4.50	6.50
☐ Match Holder. Caricature of man	30.00	42.00
☐ Match Safe. Horseback rider	25.00	35.00
☐ Mold (spoon). Tapered wavy handle, 8"	250.00	300.00
☐ Mold (spoon). Circa 1790	275.00	325.00
☐ Nut Cracker. Parrot figure, 5½"	20.00	40.00
☐ Nut Cracker. Rooster figure	10.00	15.00
☐ Opener (bottle). Elephant figure	4.00	8.00
☐ Opener (letter). Bust of devil	3.00	4.50
☐ Opener (letter). Stork figure	4.00	6.00
☐ Pan. Iron handle, 6" x 3" x 7"	65.00	95.00
☐ Pan. Iron handle, 8" x 4" x 9"	75.00	110.00
☐ Pancake Flipper. Decorative handle	20.00	40.00
☐ Paperclip. Palmer Cox Brownie, 2½" H	25.00	30.00
☐ Paperclip. English, man reading book, 3¾"	10.00	15.00
☐ Paperweight. Dragon design, 5"	30.00	45.00
☐ Paperweight. Embossed foliage design, 4"	10.00	14.00
☐ Pitcher. 23"	250.00	285.00
☐ Pot. 3 legs, 8½" x 7"	30.00	45.00
☐ Powder Box. Painted scene, 2½"	70.00	100.00
☐ Sconce. Wall hanging, pair	80.00	100.00
☐ Sconce. Wall hanging, 2-arm, Victorian, pair	80.00	110.00
☐ Sconce. Wall hanging, 3-arm, 15½", pair	250.00	375.00
☐ Screen (fireplace). Scene of town	130.00	170.00
☐ Seal. Figure of girl, 5"	90.00	120.00
☐ Silent Butler. Embossed floral lid	10.00	20.00
☐ Snuff Bottle. Decorative	140.00	185.00
☐ Spittoon. Decorative with turquoise, coral and agates	18.00	25.00
☐ Spittoon. 11"	90.00	150.00
☐ Strainer (tea). Cupid handle	10.00	20.00
☐ Tea Caddy. Decorative, square, 5¼" x 4¼"	60.00	75.00
☐ Tea Caddy. Octagon shape, 5½"	15.00	25.00
☐ Tea Kettle. On stand	50.00	70.00
☐ Tea Kettle. Chinese motif	38.00	45.00
☐ Teapot. On stand, tapered spout	225.00	285.00
☐ Teapot. Decorative, 8"	20.00	40.00
☐ Teaspoon. Floral, Chinese	4.50	7.50
☐ Telescope. Small, extends to 7"	20.00	35.00
☐ Tieback. Decorative, pair	4.50	6.00
☐ Tray. Floral design, 10½"	24.00	29.00
☐ Tray. Raised design of an elk, 5" x 6"	45.00	55.00
☐ Tray. Oval shaped, hammered, 9½" x 15"	100.00	125.00

BRASS

		Price Range	
☐ Vase. Enamel painted, Japanese		15.00	20.00
☐ Vase. Engraved symbols, 8"		15.00	15.50
☐ Warmer (bed). 15"		155.00	170.00
☐ Whistle (conductor's). 2 barrel		10.00	15.00
☐ Whistle (steam). 13½"		38.00	50.00

COPPER

Copper has been used for many centuries as a significant metal, in cooking utensils, decorative objects, etc. All prices are for items in good condition.

MOLDED COPPER MODEL OF A
CANNON ... 600.00 - 625.00

NOTE: Reproductions are made.

		Price
☐ Bed Heater. Wooden handle, perforated design		125.00
☐ Boiler, Wash. Brass and copper with bail and handle............		50.00
☐ Burnished Copper Pan. 2 iron handles, 23" diameter, 8" deep......		60.00
☐ Candlesnuffer		4.00
☐ Candy Kettle. 12" diameter, 5½" deep on round shape, 2 handles, 3 iron feet		125.00
☐ Coal Hod. Helmet type, lacquered and polished, 16" high		175.00
☐ Coffee Pot. Pewter trim, copper body, straight spout		75.00
☐ Coffee Pot. Lacquered, 10" high		75.00
☐ Compote. Pierced open-work design		55.00
☐ Cooking Pan (cast). 12½" diameter, 6" deep, heavy iron handle		45.00
☐ Dipper. Polished and treated		70.00
☐ Dow Pot. Dutch-type, large and heavy		175.00
☐ Eagle. With heavy ball, from top of weathervane		800.00
☐ Funnel. With handle		40.00
☐ Jug. For water, with hinged cover, 8" high..................		60.00
☐ Kettle. Made for fitting into stove, 2 iron handles		125.00
☐ Kettle. 18"		150.00
☐ Kettle. 22"		160.00
☐ Kettle. 24"		175.00
☐ Milk Tank. 10 gallon capacity, handles, spout and lid		150.00
☐ Megaphone. From sailing ship, 36" tall		100.00
☐ Mold. 2¼"		24.50
☐ Mold. 6¼"		22.50
☐ Mold. 8½"		30.00

COPPER

		Price
☐	Mug. Beer	25.00
☐	Pan. 10" diameter, iron handle, 7½" long	85.00
☐	Pail. 10"	55.00
☐	Pail. 11"	65.00
☐	Pail. 16"	80.00
☐	Pail. 24"	115.00
☐	Pitcher. Small	14.50
☐	Saucepan. Covered and lacquered, iron handle, 12" long	80.00
☐	Skillet. Iron handle, 9¾" diameter pan	80.00
☐	Sap Bucket. Large with iron handles	225.00
☐	Teakettle. Early American, gooseneck spout, 12" high**	200.00
☐	Teapot. Lacquered, tin-lined, hinged spout	75.00
☐	Tray. Oval-shaped, embossed handles	75.00
☐	Umbrella Stand. Lion head handles	55.00
☐	Vase. Sterling silver inlay in floral design, circa 1900's	95.00
☐	Wash Basin. Burnished, 14" diameter, 6" deep	60.00
☐	Wash Boiler. Copper cover and iron bail handle	80.00
☐	Watercan. 15"	70.00

** Early American hallmarked teakettles — $350.00

IRONWARE

Iron has been used for centuries for useful and decorative purposes. The best factor in determining whether a piece is old or new is its condition. Iron objects showing rust, corrosion, or rough surfaces should be avoided. Collectors of early Americana who are avidly interested in collecting ironware should be careful of reproductions.

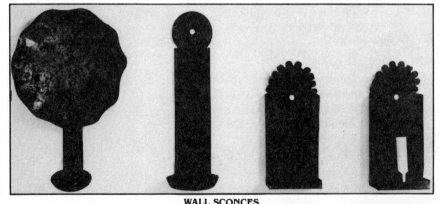

WALL SCONCES

		Price	Range
☐	Ashtray and Pipe Rest. Black & white scottie dog	15.00	18.00
☐	Ashtray. Bowling symbols	18.00	22.50
☐	Anvil. Small	8.00	10.50
☐	Bathtub. Miniature, 5½"	40.00	50.00
☐	Bedwarmer. Wooden handle, 36"	85.00	120.00
☐	Bookends. Head of A. Lincoln, bronze, 6", pair	10.00	14.00
☐	Bookends. Lions, 4", pair	15.00	18.00

IRONWARE

	Price	Range
☐ Bootjack. Bug design	3.00	5.50
☐ Bootjack. Cricket design	25.00	28.00
☐ Bootjack. Double-ended, for men's and ladies' boots	10.00	15.00
☐ Box. Treasure chest, with dividers, brass finish	18.00	22.50
☐ Bracket (shelf). Decorative, 17" x 13½", pair	15.00	20.00
☐ Broiler. Three feet, 12" diameter, early	165.00	200.00
☐ Burner (incense)	5.00	8.00
☐ Candelabra. Curved, painted holders for 5 candles	50.00	65.00
☐ Candle Snuffer. Tong type	20.00	30.00
☐ Christmas Tree Holder. 3 legs, 2-piece, North Brothers Manufacturing Co.	15.00	22.00
☐ Door Knocker. Basket of flowers	10.00	16.00
☐ Door Knocker. Parrot	14.00	18.00
☐ Door Knocker. Rose	5.00	8.50
☐ Door Latch. Leaf design, 9½" long	60.00	85.00
☐ Door Latch. Suffolk, 10 3/8"	100.00	140.00
☐ Doorstop. Aunt Jemima	18.75	25.00
☐ Doorstop. Bird	20.00	24.00
☐ Doorstop. Boston terrier	20.00	27.00
☐ Doorstop. Coach and horses, pair	15.00	24.50
☐ Doorstop. Elephant	40.00	60.00
☐ Doorstop. Sailing ship, 11"	20.00	30.00
☐ Doorstop. Sitting cat, 7"	15.00	25.00
☐ Eagle. Wings spread, 31" long, 10" high, 40 lbs.	200.00	250.00
☐ Figurine. Buffalo, 9"	20.00	30.00
☐ Figurine. Dog, 1", pair	20.00	30.00
☐ Figurine. Monkey, 3½"	15.00	20.50
☐ Flower Pot Holder. Wall hanging, 30"	20.00	30.00
☐ Fork. Long handle, 22½"	85.00	105.00
☐ Griddle. 24"	7.75	10.50
☐ Grinder. Type for table or counter	10.00	15.00
☐ Haircurling Iron	8.00	15.00
☐ Hat Rack. Six curved arms	45.00	60.00
☐ Hinge. For barn door, 42"	150.00	200.00
☐ Hinges. 15" x 17", pair	110.00	140.00
☐ Holder (rush). Spring, 20"	130.00	145.00
☐ Hook (boot). Cast iron, U.S. Cavalry	3.50	4.50
☐ Hook (meat). 8¼"	30.00	40.00
☐ Hook. Screw-in style, wall bracket, 8"	5.00	6.50
☐ Horseshoe. Large	4.75	6.50
☐ Irons. Box, cast iron with wooden handles	25.00	40.00
☐ Irons. Charcoal, wooden handle with trivot, 10"	40.00	55.00
☐ Irons. Fluting, 3 pieces	35.00	42.50
☐ Irons. Sad, engraved floral design, hollow handle	10.50	15.00
☐ Irons. Taylors, embossed #12	15.00	22.50
☐ Juicer. Landers, Frary and Clark, New Britain, Ct.	25.00	35.00
☐ Kettle. Arch handle, 3-legged, 10-quart	18.00	30.00
☐ Kettle. Round, on legs, 1813, 11"	125.00	150.00
☐ Key. 6"	5.50	8.50

IRONWARE

	Price	Range
☐ Ladle. Pouring cup	4.00	5.00
☐ Latch. Suffolk	30.00	45.00
☐ Match Holder. Two holders, animal design	20.00	30.00
☐ Match Holder. Wall hanging, floral	15.00	20.00
☐ Match Holder. Wall hanging with lid, 4¼"	20.00	25.00
☐ Milk Warmer. Long handle, footed, quart-size	25.00	40.00
☐ Muffin Pan. 8 cups	20.00	30.00
☐ Nutcracker. Alligator	15.00	19.00
☐ Nutcracker. St. Bernard	22.50	35.00
☐ Nutcracker. Marked Nestorm, England	18.00	25.00
☐ Paper Clip. Dog's head	40.00	60.00
☐ Paperweight. Ladies' figurine, 5"	30.00	45.00
☐ Paperweight. Steam engine	15.00	22.50
☐ Peeler (apple)	15.00	25.00
☐ Pot. Hinged lid, curved handle, 3½"	10.00	16.50
☐ Press (meat)	10.00	14.00
☐ Pump. Cast iron	55.00	85.00
☐ Rushlight Holder. 8"	100.00	125.00
☐ Sausage Stuffer. 13"	35.00	60.00
☐ Scraper (shoe). Dog, 12½" long	80.00	95.00
☐ Shoe (oxen). Patent 1880, pair	10.00	18.00
☐ Snow Eagle. 5"	20.00	35.00
☐ Snuffer (wick). Scissors style	24.00	28.00
☐ Spittoon. Turtle, 14"	85.00	110.00
☐ Teakettle	25.00	38.00
☐ Teapot. Japanese motif, signed, brass lid	85.00	125.00
☐ Trivet. Triangular, 26" x 12"	55.00	75.00
☐ Waffle Iron. 5" diameter, 10" handle, decorative	60.00	90.00
☐ Warmer (bed). Cut-out tin cover, Vermont	105.00	140.00
☐ Warmer (bed). Wooden handle, 36"	75.00	100.00

PEWTER

Pewter is an alloy of tin and lead, or other metals: copper antimony, or bismuth. Pewter was produced and had its greatest popularity between 1750 and 1850. The dinner plate was the chief article produced until about 1825, when china began to replace pewter in homes. After 1825 pewter was used to make other household items such as sugar bowls, coffee pots, flagons, tankards, porringers and other familiar pieces. Britannia metal is considered to be pewter. Britannia pieces are usually stamped "Jas Dixon & Son", or "Dixon".

☐ Basin. 6½" unmarked. Good condition	175.00	250.00
☐ Basin. 8" Austin, R.	250.00	375.00
☐ Basin. 8" Boardman	275.00	375.00
☐ Basin. 8" Pierse	350.00	420.00
☐ Basin. 10½" unmarked	200.00	350.00
☐ Beaker. Dixon & Son. Pint size	200.00	350.00
☐ Beaker. Griswold A.	350.00	650.00
☐ Bedpan. Boardman. Good condition	200.00	275.00

UNMARKED AMERICAN CHALICES

PEWTER UNMARKED FLAGON

	Price	Range
☐ Bowl. 8" Compton & Leonard	175.00	225.00
☐ Bowl. 8" Danforth S. Boardman T.	375.00	500.00
☐ Candlestick. 6" Dunham	150.00	250.00
☐ Candlestick. 6" J.B.	150.00	225.00
☐ Candlestick. 9" unmarked pair	275.00	375.00
☐ Candlestick. 10" unmarked pair	175.00	250.00
☐ Candlestick. Saucer-type. 8" Gleason pair	250.00	450.00
☐ Chalice. 7½" high Boardman	275.00	400.00
☐ Charger. 17" English	250.00	325.00
☐ Charger. 18" English	275.00	375.00
☐ Charger. 20" diameter English. Hallmarked	350.00	450.00
☐ Charger. 13½" Rose Mark	150.00	225.00
☐ Charger. 12" diameter. Unmarked	150.00	200.00
☐ Chocolate Pot. Swiss manufacturer. 18th century	150.00	250.00
☐ Coffee Pot. Boardman	250.00	325.00
☐ Coffee Pot. Dixon, I.	45.00	75.00
☐ Coffee Pot. 10½" high Dixon & Son. Wooden handle	150.00	275.00
☐ Coffee Pot. Dunham & Sons	275.00	350.00
☐ Coffee Pot. Gleason	275.00	350.00
☐ Coffee Pot. 9" Leonard, Reed, & Barton. Circa 1830	350.00	600.00
☐ Coffee Pot. 12" Porter, A.	450.00	575.00
☐ Coffee Pot. 10" Smith & Co.	165.00	275.00
☐ Coffee Pot. Trask, I.	500.00	650.00
☐ Coffee Urn. 14" high. Footed base. Reed & Barton	250.00	350.00
☐ Communion Set. 11" high. 2 chalices & 2 plates	1250.00	1750.00
☐ Creamers. 5½" Sheldon & Feltman	125.00	225.00
☐ Cuspidor. Oval-shaped	150.00	250.00
☐ Decanter Funnel	85.00	125.00
☐ Deep Dish. Good condition. Calder, Danforth or Barns	400.00	500.00
☐ Flagon. Unmarked	350.00	450.00
☐ Flagon. 10" high. Gleason	850.00	1500.00

PEWTER

	Price	Range
☐ Foot Warmer. Oval-shaped	100.00	200.00
☐ Inkwell. Whitcomb	60.00	120.00
☐ Inkwell. "Fish on Leaf"	275.00	400.00
☐ Ladle with wooden handle. 13" long. Unmarked	75.00	120.00
☐ Lamp. Porter Co. Burns whale oil	150.00	250.00
☐ Mugs. Curved handle. 19th century English	100.00	150.00
☐ Mug. 6" high with handle. Merey & Smith	125.00	225.00
☐ Pewter Molds. Ice cream — apple	18.50	30.00
☐ Pewter Molds. Ice cream — boxer	20.00	30.00
☐ Pewter Molds. Ice cream — carrot	8.00	20.00
☐ Pewter Molds. Ice cream — daisy	20.00	50.00
☐ Pewter Molds. Ice cream — heart	10.00	22.00
☐ Pewter Molds. Ice cream — morning glory	25.00	35.00
☐ Pewter Molds. Ice cream — orange	22.00	35.00
☐ Pewter Molds. Ice cream — pear	20.00	35.00
☐ Pewter Molds. Ice cream — potato	10.00	18.00
☐ Pewter Molds. Ice cream — Santa	35.00	50.00
☐ Pewter Molds. Ice cream — swan	20.00	35.00
☐ Pewter Molds. Ice cream — turkey	20.00	40.00
☐ Plates. 8" Austin, N.	250.00	350.00
☐ Plates. 8" diameter. Austin Richard	200.00	300.00
☐ Plates. 7½" Badger, T.	250.00	350.00
☐ Plates. 8½" Badger, T.	275.00	400.00
☐ Plates. 9" Basset, Fred	500.00	700.00
☐ Plates. 7¾" Boardman, T.	300.00	450.00
☐ Plate. 8" diameter. Wm. Calder	225.00	350.00
☐ Plate. 11" deep. Wm. Calder	250.00	400.00
☐ Plate. 8" diameter. E. Danforth & S. Danforth	300.00	600.00
☐ Plate. 8" diameter. Thomas Danforth	275.00	350.00
☐ Plate. 13¼" Wm. Danforth	400.00	600.00
☐ Plate. 8 7/8" Derby, T.S.	775.00	900.00
☐ Plate. 9" Gleason, Roswell	125.00	225.00
☐ Plate. 7" Kayserzinn	35.00	75.00
☐ Plate. 10" Kayserzinn	75.00	100.00
☐ Plate. 7¾" deep. Kill-orne, S.	350.00	475.00
☐ Plate. 13½". Flat with Eagle Mark	550.00	700.00
☐ Plate. 8" unmarked	150.00	200.00
☐ Plate. 7½" unmarked	65.00	95.00
☐ Plate. 9¾" unmarked	75.00	150.00
☐ Plate. 12" unmarked	125.00	200.00
☐ Platters. 12" Badger, T.	350.00	475.00
☐ Platter. 11" x 14" Kayserzinn	50.00	80.00
☐ Platter. 12½" x 20" Kayserzinn	125.00	200.00
☐ Platter. 17" Nekrassoff	20.00	60.00
☐ Porringer. 3" unmarked. R. Lee type handle	125.00	275.00
☐ Porringer. 4½". Heart handle. Marked I.C.	275.00	375.00
☐ Porringer. 5" Boardman	225.00	350.00
☐ Porringer. 5¼" Hamlin	450.00	600.00
☐ Porringer. 2 1/16" Lee, R.	500.00	700.00

PEWTER

	Price	Range
☐ Porringer. Heart handle. Lee, R.	225.00	350.00
☐ Shaving Mug. Richardson	95.00	110.00
☐ Spoon. Crown and Rose. Made in Holland	40.00	100.00
☐ Spoon. Dutch	8.00	15.00
☐ Spoon. Yates tablespoon	35.00	50.00
☐ Sugar & Creamer. Kayserzinn. Trumpet flower	35.00	60.00
☐ Sugar & Creamer. 4 feet. Winthrop	40.00	70.00
☐ Tankard with hinge cover. 16" high. "P. Boyd"	3000.00	4000.00
☐ Teapot. 7½" Boardman & Hart	275.00	375.00
☐ Teapot. Dixon	145.00	200.00
☐ Teapot. 7½" high. Dunham, R.	225.00	400.00
☐ Teapot. 11" Richardson, G.	525.00	650.00
☐ Teapot. 10" Savage. Hallmark	250.00	400.00
☐ Teapot. 5¾" Shaw & Fisher. England	150.00	250.00
☐ Teapot. Wilcox	175.00	300.00
☐ Trays. 12¼" x 6" Kayserzinn	60.00	100.00
☐ Tureen. 11½" poppy decor. Kayserzinn	100.00	175.00
☐ Vases. 11" Liberty & Co.	80.00	125.00
☐ Vases. 12½" Kayserzinn	75.00	150.00
☐ Wine Taster. 2 1/8" Taunton	40.00	75.00

SILVER

Silver was used extensively by the Egyptians, Assyrians, Phoenicians, Greeks and Romans. It is usually concluded by historians and archeologists that silver was among the first metals used by early man.

Since the earliest times silver, with its natural beauty, has been primarily devoted to the service of splendor. A precious metal, silver lends itself excellently to the designs of the artist and craftsman. This has helped to make it one of the best known of the noble metals. Please consult our publication, *The Official Price Guide to Silver* by Sandy Proshan for more prices and information.

SILVER SWEATMEAT BASKET AND CREAMER . . . . . 500.00 - 600.00

SILVER

☐ Artichoke Dish—Hallmark, ¾" H. X 6½" D,
London 1849-50 .... 750.00 900.00
☐ Asparagus Server—chrysanthemum pattern, Tiffany
& Co.. 350.00 400.00
☐ Basket—cake, maker's mark "S" Herbert & Co.,
Hallmark, 4", London 1753 .... 3500.00 4000.00
☐ Basket—beaded rims, Sheffield, early 1800's 400.00 450.00
☐ Basket—round with reeded handle, ornate scroll
on sides, silver plated.......................... 75.00 100.00
☐ Basket—flat dish shape of scrolled legs and handle,
fluted sides, silver plated 100.00 150.00
☐ Bibelot—sterling silver 50.00 90.00
☐ Bottle Holder—"Mappin & Webb" silver soldered,
c. 1890 .... 90.00 100.00
☐ Bowl—foliage, dome base, Gorham, 13" 500.00 900.00
☐ Brush—hair, long handle, beaded edge, scroll work,
marked "Sterling" w/matched comb 150.00 200.00
☐ Brush—military set, marked "Sterling" 150.00 200.00
☐ Brush—velvet or clothes, marked "Sterling" 90.00 125.00
☐ Bun Warmer—Mappin & Webb, 8½" x 9" x 14½" L,
Sheffield 500.00 600.00
☐ Butter Dish—dome shaped cover w/bulb handle, base
fluted w/balled feet, silver plated 75.00 100.00
☐ Butter Dish—large, scrolled silver bulb, dome shaped
cover & high curved handle, silver paged w/glass
insert 90.00 100.00
☐ Butter Dish—wide flat bowl w/circular drop-sided
cover, silver plated 50.00 75.00
☐ Cake Basket—rectangular, shell border, handle
engraved w/name Baldwin & Gardiner, 1815, Mass ... 3500.00 4000.00
☐ Candelabrum—maker's mark "J.A." 2800.00 3000.00
☐ Candle Snuffer & Tray—sterling silver, maker's mark
"Thomas Robbins" on snuffer, "John Hawkes" on
tray, Hallmark, Tary, 9½" W, London 1823-24 .... 500.00 600.00
☐ Candlestick—silver, maker's mark "William
Chawner", Hallmark, London 1771-72, pair 1800.00 2000.00
☐ Candlestick—deep bowl w/curved feather handle,
straight candle support, silver plated 50.00 75.00
☐ Candlestick—ornately cut, sculptured base & stem,
cylindrical holder, silver plated 75.00 90.00
☐ Candlestick—w/snuffer and tray, hat shape, Sheffield 170.00 200.00
☐ Candlestick—bedroom, silver-gilt, maker's mark
"Paul de Lamerie", Hallmark, 5¾" x 3¼" H, set of 4,
London c. 1748-49............................ 8000.00 10,000.00
☐ Candlestick—Bobeche, 12", Sheffield, pair 350.00 450.00
☐ Candlestick—globe base, round baluster stem, shell
ornament in relief, Sheffield, c. 1830, pair.......... 850.00 1000.00
☐ Candlestick—telescopic, Sheffield, c. 1800, pair..... 400.00 500.00
☐ Candlestick—silver, Hallmark, maker's mark
"Liberty & Co.", pair, Birmingham 1906-07 .... 900.00 1000.00

SILVER

	Price	Range
☐ Candy Dish—wide flat plate w/handsome leaf and scroll design on outer edges, silver plated	30.00	50.00
☐ Cane Top—carved indian chief, sterling silver, figural	125.00	150.00
☐ Card Carrying Case—electroplated silver panel gilt, inscribed "Ellington Mason & Co., 1852"	100.00	120.00
☐ Castor Set—five bottles, matched, covered group, silver plated	250.00	325.00
☐ Cheese Dish—etched crystal glass, sterling rim w/sterling cutter, c. 1900	75.00	90.00
☐ Cheese Dish—mark of "Edward Wakelin", Hallmark, 14" W, London 1760	1350.00	1500.00
☐ Cigarette Box—pressed glass w/sterling rim, Russian, c. 1920	225.00	250.00
☐ Cigarette Box—with golf ball and club on lid, Sheffield	40.00	50.00
☐ Clock—travel, eight-day, case made by Gorham	125.00	150.00
☐ Coaster—wine, floral borders w/wooden base, Sheffield, 4 pieces, c. 1821	350.00	450.00
☐ Coffee Percolator—large, double handled urn shape w/spigot & faucet, flat base & scrolled sides, silver plated	170.00	200.00
☐ Coffee Pot—bulbous shape, vines and sprays of flowers, scalloped edge & urn finial, Gorham & Co., 10" H	1700.00	2000.00
☐ Coffee Pot—8 cup, light scroll work, Sheffield, c. 1800	500.00	550.00
☐ Coffee Pot—Sheffield, c. 1850	1000.00	1100.00
☐ Coffee Pot—sterling silver, French, Paris 1809-19	1500.00	1600.00
☐ Coffee & Tea Set—hammered finish, teapot, coffee pot, tea kettle on lamp stand, sugar bowl, creamer and waste bowl, all with claw type feet, plain tray w/molded border	3100.00	3800.00
☐ Cooler—wine or champagne, w/handles, Sheffield . . .	600.00	650.00
☐ Cream Ladle—waterlily pattern, Unger Bros	80.00	90.00
☐ Cruet Set—plated stand & caps, Baccarat swirl pattern glass, c. 1890	80.00	90.00
☐ Cruet Set—plated stand & caps, crystal bottles, c. 1900	75.00	90.00
☐ Cruet Stand—silver w/glass bottles, maker's mark "C.C.", Hallmark, 5 7/8" W, London 1810-11	400.00	500.00
☐ Cup—child's, "Tom the Piper's Son" nursery rhyme engraved on side, reeded handle, silver plated	40.00	50.00
☐ Cup—Christening, silver, designed by "R. Redgrave, R.A.", Hallmark, London 1865	400.00	500.00
☐ Cup—silver, Hallmark, London 1623-24	4800.00	5000.00
☐ Cup—squat w/scrolled overlay, silver plated	40.00	50.00
☐ Cup & Cover—two-handled, maker's mark "James Dixon & Son", Hallmark, Sheffield, c. 1850-60	1000.00	1200.00
☐ Decanter—crystal, English, c. 1890	50.00	70.00

SILVER

Price Range

- [ ] Desserts or Sherberts—sterling base, screw-in etched crystal bowl, set of 4 .... 100.00 130.00
- [ ] Dish—entree and cover, Caldwell, c. 1900 .... 100.00 125.00
- [ ] Dish—entree with reversible cover, oval, Gorham Co. . 200.00 225.00
- [ ] Dish—pierced, handled, Sheffield 20.00 30.00
- [ ] Dish Ring—silver, English, 10¼" W, c. 1730, very rare 800.00 1000.00
- [ ] Dispenser—maple syrup, (VSA) blown glass metal top, c. 1900 .... 55.00 75.00
- [ ] Egg Cup Set—stand & 6 cups, Gale & Son, American coin silver, 1860's, unusual 650.00 1000.00
- [ ] Entree Dish—flared handles, wooden grips w/cover, Sheffield 450.00 500.00
- [ ] Ewer—etched, crystal w/plated top & 2 matching table vases, Polish, c. 1890 .... 250.00 300.00
- [ ] Ewer—pear shape w/flower, foliage & butterflies on domed foot, S. Kirk & Son, c. 1850 .... 1300.00 1500.00
- [ ] Ewer—silver, Hallmark, London 1849-59, maker's mark "Joseph & Albert Savony" 1200.00 1500.00
- [ ] Flatware—engraved "G", Gorham Co., 94 pieces 1700.00 2000.00
- [ ] Flatware—Etruscan pattern, Gorham, service for 12, 83 pieces 1500.00 1600.00
- [ ] Fork—berry or oyster, long prongs, fancy chased or gilt, various patterns marked "Sterling" 30.00 40.00
- [ ] Forks—oyster or pickle, short, gilt or enameled prongs, various patterns marked "Sterling" 30.00 40.00
- [ ] Forks—serving, cold meat or salad, curved prongs, various patterns marked "Sterling" 100.00 150.00
- [ ] Forks—serving, cold meat or cake, straight prongs, various patterns marked "Sterling" 125.00 175.00
- [ ] Glove Stretcher—Art Nouveau, sterling silver 40.00 60.00
- [ ] Goblets—water or wine, etched designs, flared rims, Sheffield, pair, 1790's to 1800 .... 350.00 500.00
- [ ] Grape Shears—Tiffany & Co., c. 1852 .... 125.00 150.00
- [ ] Ice Cream Scoops—chrysanthemum pattern, Tiffany & Co., pair, Sterling............................. 300.00 400.00
- [ ] Inkstand—silver, Hallmark, maker's mark "Robert Hennell", London, 1790's 600.00 800.00
- [ ] Jam Pot—cobalt liner and four feet, Sheffield, 3½" H 125.00 150.00
- [ ] Jewel Box—silver plated 40.00 60.00
- [ ] Jug—hot water w/wine coasters, engraved w/crest, loose lid, Sheffield 500.00 600.00
- [ ] Jug—silver, panel-gilt, Hallmark, London 1881-82, maker's mark "J. Aldwinkle & James Slater" 475.00 575.00
- [ ] Jugs—milk, two "goats & bee" forged marks, Hallmark, London, 4½" H., pair, late 19th Century ... 700.00 750.00
- [ ] Kettle—stand & spirit burner, silver plated copper, designed by "Arthur Dixon for Birmingham Guild of Handicraft", c. 1905-10......................... 650.00 750.00
- [ ] Knife Rest—andiron shape, Gorham 50.00 60.00

SILVER

Price Range

☐ Knives—various patterns, marked "Sterling"
Large fish/ice cream slices 100.00 180.00
☐ Labels—wine, silver, English, (George III), set, rare,
late 18th & 19th Century, ... 800.00 1000.00
☐ Labels—wine & spirits, silver, English, set,
late 18th & 19th Century 900.00 1100.00
☐ Ladle—medallion top, "H. & S.", 12" 250.00 300.00
☐ Ladle—pierced, beaded handle, Sheffield, c. 1890 ... 50.00 100.00
☐ Ladle—punch, silver bowl, whalebone handle,
English, 18th Century 250.00 350.00
☐ Ladle—punch, silver, rosewood handle, Hallmark,
London 1731-41 .... 300.00 400.00
☐ Ladle—punch, impressed, Geissler & Delong, 12" ... 350.00 400.00
☐ Ladle—soup, Fiddle pattern, engraved w/initial "H",
solid silver, 14 3/8", c. 1810 .... 400.00 500.00
☐ Magnifying Glass—converted sterling silver handle .. 30.00 40.00
☐ Match Safe—U.S., c. 1895 .... 125.00 150.00
☐ Match Safe—U.S., c. 1896 .... 125.00 150.00
☐ Meat Platter—beaded edge w/cover, scrolled handles,
Sheffield, c. 1820 .... 500.00 600.00
☐ Mirror—hand, floral embossing, sterling silver 75.00 120.00
☐ Mirror—hand, foral pattern, marked "Sterling" 250.00 300.00
☐ Mirror—hand, beaded edge w/scroll work, marked
"Sterling" 125.00 150.00
☐ Muffineer—octagonal, Sheffield, 8¼" H 125.00 150.00
☐ Mug—child's, Tift & Whiting, c. 1850 .... 200.00 250.00
☐ Mug—cylindrical form w/leaf capped scrolled handle,
Gardiner, 3½" H, c. 1815 .... 225.00 275.00
☐ Mug—silver, maker's mark "Langlands & Robertson",
Hallmark, New Castle 1785 .... 500.00 600.00
☐ Mug—silver, panel-gilt, maker's mark "Storr &
Mortimer", Hallmark, 4" H, London 1810 .... 500.00 60.00
☐ Mug—two pear shape w/foliate feet & scroll handles,
R. & W. Wilson, both engraved, circa 1831, 3½"
and 3 5/8" 250.00 300.00
☐ Napkin Ring—embossed cow jumping over moon,
Gorham 80.00 90.00
☐ Perfume Bottle—travel, marked "800 Italy" 40.00 50.00
☐ Picture Frame—Art Nouveau, sterling silver 150.00 200.00
☐ Pin Cushion—sterling silver 75.00 100.00
☐ Pin Tray—Art Nouveau, sterling silver 75.00 100.00
☐ Pitcher—water, baluster shape, embossed
w/grapevine, scroll handle, Baldwin Gardiner,
10¾", c. 1830, 1815 .... 1150.00 1300.00
☐ Pitcher—water, baluster body, embossed w/grape-
vine, monogrammed, scroll twig handle, Gorham Co.,
15¼", c. 1900 .... 650.00 750.00
☐ Plate—etched crystal w/sterling rim, c. 1920 .... 45.00 55.00

SILVER

	Price Range	
☐ Porringer—bulbous body & domed center, John Burt, 5 1/8" D, c. 1720	3000.00	4000.00
☐ Porringer—domed center, pierced flat handle w/initials Jonathan Clarke, 5", c. 1760	2850.00	3000.00
☐ Purse—beaded, Art Nouveau motif top, sterling silver	55.00	75.00
☐ Salt—pedestal, Sheffield, pair	60.00	70.00
☐ Salt Cellars—crystal on plated base, English, c. 1890, pair	60.00	80.00
☐ Salt Cellars—silver, Hallmark, London 1695-96, 2½" H, pair	1350.00	1500.00
☐ Salt & Pepper Holders—blue glass linings w/tray, footed, Sheffield, 1790's, pair	170.00	200.00
☐ Salt & Pepper Shakers—crystal and sterling silver	30.00	50.00
☐ Salver—silver, maker's mark "JA", Hallmark, London 1823-24	2800.00	3000.00
☐ Salver—beaded rim, engraved crest, decorated feet, Sheffield, 14½" D, c. 1780	500.00	600.00
☐ Sauce Boats—leaf-capped scroll handles, rims w/palmettes on pedestal base, Gorham Co., 5 5/8", c. 1872	900.00	1000.00
☐ Sauce Bowls—silver, maker's mark "B.E.", Hallmark, arms engraved, pair, London 1751-52	1000.00	1200.00
☐ Sauce Torene & Cover—grapevine & shell borders, 8¼" L, pair, c. 1815	700.00	800.00
☐ Sconces—silver, Hallmark, engraved, maker's mark "John Land", pair, London 1703-04,	8500.00	10000.00
☐ Seal—figural, Art Nouveau, sterling silver	50.00	65.00
☐ Seal—set with rubies, Art Nouveau, sterling silver	70.00	85.00
☐ Seafood Forks—Mother of Pearl handles, set of 6	60.00	70.00
☐ Shoe Horn—"Tiffany", Hallmark, sterling silver	50.00	65.00
☐ Snuff Box—with mosaic top, no markings, c. 1810	750.00	900.00
☐ Sock Darner Handle—Art Nouveau, sterling silver	35.00	40.00
☐ Soap Dish—travel, Art Nouveau, sterling silver	50.00	65.00
☐ Spoon—berry or salad serving, various patterns, marked "Sterling"	140.00	150.00
☐ Spoon—BonBon, various patterns marked "Sterling"	20.00	40.00
☐ Stirrup Cup—silver, mark of "W. Barwash & R. Sibley", Hallmark, London 1827, 5¾" H	5900.00	6000.00
☐ Sugar Bowl—low w/domed cover, long curved handles, silver plated	30.00	45.00
☐ Sugar Coaster—cut crystal, sterling silver	25.00	35.00
☐ Tankard—cylindrical form, domed cover, urn finial w/ scroll handle, Jonathan Clarke, 8½" H, c. 1750	6800.00	7000.00
☐ Tankard—blown crystal & sterling, c. 1890	60.00	75.00
☐ Tankard—silver, marker's mark "W. Shaw & W. Priest", Hallmark, 6¼" H, London 1756-57	2000.00	2500.00
☐ Tankard—silver, maker's mark "Anthony Nelme", Hallmark, London 1698, 7" H., base 4 5/8"	8000.00	10000.00
☐ Tea & Coffee Service—silver, Hallmark, maker's mark "Robert Hennell", London 1790's	4000.00	5000.00

SILVER

	Price Range	
☐ Tea & Coffee Service—silver, Hallmark, maker's mark "S.G. Sissons", London 1872	3000.00	4000.00
☐ Tea Caddy—silver, Hallmark, London 1831-32	1350.00	2000.00
☐ Teapot—high bulbous neck, curved feet & spout, sculptured top, silver plated	75.00	120.00
☐ Teapot—silver, Hallmark, marker's mark "TW, WM", London 1830	500.00	600.00
☐ Teapot—silver, Hallmark, maker's mark "John Hardman & Co.", Birmingham, 1861-62	900.00	1000.00
☐ Teapot—silver, maker's mark "A Fogelberg", Hallmark, 5" H, London 1778-79	1000.00	1500.00
☐ Tea Set—4 pieces, Sheffield, c. 1821	2900.00	3400.00
☐ Tea Set—teapot, covered sugar bowl, creamer and waste bowl, lioness finial on covers of teapot & sugar, first three by Colin Forbes, waste bowl by Garret Eoff, c. 1890	1800.00	2000.00
☐ Tea Service—silver, wooden knobs & handles, designed & made by "Christian Dell" at metal workshop of Bauhaus, 1925	2000.00	2500.00
☐ Tea Service—creamer, sugar bowl and teapot, Victorian design, silver plated	90.00	120.00
☐ Thermometer—desk, Art Nouveau, sterling silver	50.00	70.00
☐ Tongs—shell ends, Rockwell, c. 1839	100.00	150.00
☐ Tray—calling card, Art Nouveau, sterling silver	250.00	300.00
☐ Tray—16" x 25", ornate handles, fine scroll work center, fluted legs, oval shape, Sheffield, solid, c. 1880	1200.00	1500.00
☐ Tray—20" x 30", for tea service, ornate, pierced floral patterns at center, oval shape, Sheffield, solid, c. 1790	2500.00	3000.00
☐ Vanity Table Box—sterling silver	60.00	70.00
☐ Vase—blown crystal, plated base, Polish, c. 1880	50.00	70.00
☐ Wagner Cup—silver, maker's mark "Jas. Walker", Hallmark, height, 6 7/8", Dublin 1706-08	3500.00	4000.00
☐ Wallet—pocket, leather lined w/memo page, Art Nouveau, sterling silver, rare	500.00	600.00
☐ Warmer—for entire dish, Sheffield, c. 1790	500.00	600.00
☐ Water Pitcher—curved, squat design w/tiny floral decorations, wide neck & flared mouth, reinforced handle, silver plated	50.00	80.00
☐ Water Set—scrolled pitcher w/stand, curved feet, mounted handle which swivels at center, two goblets, silver plated	100.00	150.00
☐ Water Set—high pitcher w/floral decorations and reeded handle, covered with sculptured goblet, silver plated	90.00	130.00
☐ Wine Coolers—tub shaped with ring handles, engraved, Sheffield, 5¾" Hc. 1790	1500.00	2000.00

TIN & TOLEWARE

Tin, as you know, is really sheet iron coated with a layer of tin, which doesn't rust. Toleware is really painted or lacquered tin, but often in advertisements you will see any tin item described as tole. Both are highly collectible, and tole is a bit more expensive.

ASSORTED TINWARE . . . . 200.00 - 275.00

		Price Range	
☐	Biscuit Tin, English, 8 volumes of books, 6¼" H	84.00	100.00
☐	Candy Tin, simulated wood, 5¾" Dia.	21.00	25.00
☐	Cigarette Tin, jewel box shape, State Express brand, 3½" H	25.00	30.00
☐	Comb Case, tin, eagle in relief	15.00	20.00
☐	Cradle, tin, painted green, yellow, red	—	600.00
☐	Footwarmer, rectangular, heart-percing	100.00	120.00
☐	Spice Set, round, 8 containers, nutmeg rasp, brown . .	80.00	130.00
☐	Tin Bed Warmer, wooden handle	120.00	130.00
☐	Tin Tea Caddies, simulated inlaid wood, 5", pr.	70.00	75.00
☐	Tole Eeling Lamp, 3-wick, 19th century	40.00	60.00
☐	Tole Spice Set, 6 containers, brass-handled, tin box . .	40.00	60.00
☐	Tole Store Canister, "Mustard", porcelain knob, 9" H	115.00	130.00

MILITARIA

Militaria, a word which embraces the entire range of military collectibles, is one of the most rapidly growing of all fields of collecting. Spurred on by an increasing interest in military history, particulary in the Nazi era and World War II, it has become a multi-million dollar business. It is not at all uncommon for items to double or triple in value as many years as interest grows in areas where only a limited number of artifacts is available. Although the supply is limited the variety is great, from a cloth shoulder patch or metal cap badge selling for a dollar or two to a Nazi field marshall's baton put up at auc-

MILITARIA

tion at a reverse bid of $25,000 or Herman Goerling's Luftwaffe wedding
sword auctioned at a starting bid of $60,000. Currently, in addition to Nazi
items, there is a growing interest in Imperial German helmets (pickelhauben)
with a consequent increase in prices. The following is a sampling of a variety
of militaria with *typical* current prices. These prices reflect the latest sales at
international auctions, at militaria shows and dealers' lists. Please consult
our publication *The Official Price Guide to Military Collectibles* by Col. R.
Rankin for more prices and information.

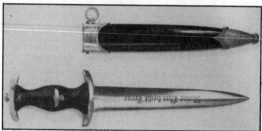

SS LEADER'S DAGGER
150.00 - 175.00

STEEL HELMET M35
45.00 - 50.00

BRITISH
Price

- ☐ Volunteer officer's Waterloo pattern shako, circa 1810 . . . . 1650.00
- ☐ Victorian period brass Albert pattern 7th Dragoon Guards helmet . 400.00
- ☐ Canadian officer's helmet, 26th Middlesex Light Infantry,
  circa 1880. . . . . 175.00
- ☐ Officer's lancer cap (shapska), 16th Queen's Lancers 200.00
- ☐ World War I and World War II steel helmet 10.00
- ☐ Post World War II steel helmet 15.00
- ☐ Paratrooper helmet 20.00
- ☐ Georgian officer's gorget, engraved "G.R." 125.00
- ☐ Victorian officer's full dress sabretache, Royal Artillery 225.00
- ☐ Shoulder belt plate, Royal Marines, circa 1854 . . . . 165.00
- ☐ Shoulder belt plate, Gordon Highlanders, circa 1881 . . . . 300.00
- ☐ Victorian standard, 1st Life Guards 650.00
- ☐ Edward VII officer's broadsword, King's Own Scottish Boarderers. 300.00
- ☐ 1788 pattern Ligh Cavalry officer's saber 350.00
- ☐ General and staff officer's sword, 1822 pattern 125.00
- ☐ Officer's sword, Royal Horse Guards, circa 1832 . . . . 650.00

FIGHTING KNIVES
- ☐ Nazi boot knife 85.00
- ☐ U.S. Trench knife, World War I 100.00
- ☐ British Sykes-Fairbairn commando knife 50.00

FIREARMS
- ☐ German Model 96, 9mm broom handle Mauser 360.00
- ☐ German Luger, more common models 400.00

FIREARMS

- [ ] Rare 7.63mm caliber Model 1893 Brochardt automatic pistol in leather covered case. Red felt lining. With shoulder stock, oil bottle, cleaning rod and key to case. This pistol is the forerunner of the famous German Luger 5000.00
- [ ] British Webley & Scott Model 1912 Royal Navy .455 caliber pistol . 260.00
- [ ] American .45 caliber Government Model 1911 Army automatic . . . 275.00
- [ ] American .45 caliber Government Model 1911 Navy automatic 500.00
- [ ] Colt Model 1905 .38 caliber Marine Corps revolver 450.00
- [ ] Springfield Model 1903 rifle with rod bayonet 2500.00
- [ ] Springfield Model 1903 rifle, pre-World War I manufacturer 300.00
- [ ] German Mauser rifle, World War II, various manufacturers 125.00
- [ ] German World War I Mauser "Butcher Knife" 40.00
- [ ] German World War I Mauser "Butcher Knife" with saw tooth back 50.00
- [ ] German World War I ersatz models 15.00
- [ ] Nazi police dress bayonet with stag grips (Coppel) 135.00
- [ ] Nazi 2nd Model Luftwaffe (Peck) 110.00
- [ ] Nazi Army dress (Spitzer) 30.00
- [ ] Nazi Model 98 service 20.00
- [ ] British No. 4 spike 4.00
- [ ] U.S. 1903 Springfield, bright blade, pre-World War I manufacturer . 30.00

FRENCH

- [ ] Other ranks shako, 54th Infantry Regiment, circa 1800 . . . . .1475.00
- [ ] Cuirassier helmet, circa 1840, other ranks 400.00
- [ ] Cuirassier sword, circa 1812 . . . . 260.00
- [ ] World War I steel helmet, infantry insigne 35.00
- [ ] World War II steel helmet, no insigne 20.00

IMPERIAL GERMAN

- [ ] Bavarian Hartschiere (Archers of the Guard) gala helmet with lion crest. The most sought after & ornate of all Imperial German helmets 5500.00
- [ ] Guard du Corps, officer's helmet with eagle crest 3000.00
- [ ] Guard du Corps, officer's helmet with spike 2500.00
- [ ] Saxon Garde-Rieter, officer's helmet with lion crest , ...3500.00
- [ ] Brunswick Infantry Regiment No. 92, 1st Battalion, officer's helmet 1300.00
- [ ] Swartzburg infantry officer's helmet 1200.00
- [ ] Bavarian Chevauleger officer's helmet, Model 1868 . . . . 400.00
- [ ] Saxon infantry officer's helmet, circa 1910 . . . . 350.00
- [ ] Prussian other ranks grenadier helmet, circa 1856 . . . . 350.00
- [ ] Hesse artillery officer's helmet, circa 1910 . . . . 550.00
- [ ] Prussian other ranks infantry helmet, brass trim, circa 1910 . . . . . . 90.00
- [ ] Prussian other ranks infantry helmet, gray metal trim, circa 1915 . . 65.00
- [ ] Prussian Jager officer's shako, line battalion 300.00
- [ ] Prussian Jager other ranks shako, line battalion 135.00
- [ ] Bavarian airship officer's shako 750.00
- [ ] Prussian Uhlan officer's lance cap (tschapka), line regiment 300.00
- [ ] Other ranks grenadier cap (grenadiermutze) Guard Grenadiers #1 .1800.00
- [ ] Prussian officer's 1st Life Guards Hussar busby (pelzmutze) 750.00
- [ ] Prussian officer's hussar busby, line regiments 500.00

IMPERIAL GERMAN   Price

- [ ] Other ranks tropical helmet, circa 1914 . . . . 300.00
- [ ] Steel trench helmet, Model 15 . . . . 65.00
- [ ] Officer's sword, circa 1910, typical line regiment sword 125.00
- [ ] Silk flag, bullion trim of veteran's organization 750.00
- [ ] Framed original oil portrait of Wilhelm II, circa 1902 . . . . 1000.00
- [ ] Mettlach regimental stein, Grenadier Regiment #2 . . . . 425.00

NAZI GERMANY

- [ ] Steel helmet M35 . . . . 45.00
- [ ] Police helmet 65.00
- [ ] Luftschulz, third pattern 85.00
- [ ] Fire police helmet 65.00
- [ ] Africa Corps tropical helmet 85.00
- [ ] Paratrooper helmet 225.00
- [ ] Police officer's shako 225.00
- [ ] Other ranks police shako 100.00
- [ ] Other ranks *rural* police shako, complete with plume 130.00
- [ ] Motorcyclist crash helmet, complete with insigne 200.00
- [ ] Navy officer's cap, typical, not flag officer 175.00
- [ ] Army officer's cap, typical, not general officer 125.00
- [ ] Army other ranks cap, typical 90.00
- [ ] KSKK other ranks "coffee can" type 225.00
- [ ] Luftwaffe officer's sword (SMF) 225.00
- [ ] Army officer's sword (Eickhorn) 125.00
- [ ] Navy officer's sword (Horster) 350.00
- [ ] Army medical officer's dagger 400.00
- [ ] 1st Model Luftwaffe officer's dagger (Halter) 165.00
- [ ] 2nd Model Luftwaffe officer's dagger (Horster) 155.00
- [ ] Labor Corps dagger (Alcoso) 325.00
- [ ] SS Leader's dagger (Puma) 150.00
- [ ] SS cuff band, bevo, marked "Gotz von Berlichmgen" 85.00
- [ ] "AFRICA" cuff band, with palm tree at each end 55.00
- [ ] Volkstrum arm band, printed 5.00
- [ ] RAD gorget with chain hallmarked 325.00
- [ ] RAD flag pole finial 135.00
- [ ] RAD standard (flag) 800.00
- [ ] Infantry standard, silk and bullion, iron cross, swastika design . . . 4600.00
- [ ] Political leader's gorget, without chain 175.00
- [ ] Original pastel painting by Adolf Hitler, authenticated 4000.00
- [ ] Soldier's pay book (soldbuch) 20.00
- [ ] NSDAP party membership book 40.00
- [ ] Paratrooper's jump log book 20.00
- [ ] Honorary citizenship certificate on genuine parchment conferring
      citizenship of town of Gutzkow on Adolf Hitler 225.00
- [ ] Letter from Herman Goering to his wife on official prisoner of war
      stationary, dated February 18, 1946 . . . . 1250.00
- [ ] Hitler Youth membership badge, circa 1932, enameled,
      hallmarked 20.00
- [ ] Police overcoat dress chevron 3.00
- [ ] Silver tray, Adolph Hitler, over 100 troy ounces, made by Wellner,
      has Nazi eagle, swastika, initials A.H. 7000.00

RUSSIAN

Price

☐ Other ranks dress helmet, Imperial Horse Guards, circa 1914 . . . . . 4000.00
☐ Other ranks helmet, Imperial 95th Infantry, Crimean War 650.00
☐ World War I steel helmet, with Imperial Eagle insigne 150.00
☐ Dragoon saber, Model 1881 . . . . 200.00
☐ Pioneer falchion, circa 1827 . . . . 125.00

UNITED STATES

☐ Enlisted artilleryman's hat, circa 1858 . . . . 300.00
☐ Enlisted man's bell top shako, circa 1810-1815 . . . . 500.00
☐ Enlisted man's militia shako, unknown unit, circa 1830 . . . . 150.00
☐ Extremely rare officer's helmet of the elite First City Troop of Philadelphia, circa 1840.
The most beautiful of all American helmets 1000.00
☐ Enlisted man's cavalry helmet, circa 1881 . . . . 150.00
☐ Enlisted man's foot troops helmet, circa 1881 . . . . 100.00
☐ Marine Corps enlisted man's helmet, circa 1898 . . . . 175.00
☐ Army enlisted man's cork summer helmet 75.00
☐ Army officer's helmet, circa 1881, 9th Infantry 150.00
☐ World War I steel helmet 20.00
☐ Modified World War I helmet (early World War II use) 10.00
☐ World War II helmet with liner 15.00
☐ Recruiting poster, Civil War, no illustration, Army 100.00
☐ Recruiting poster, Civil War, color illustration, Army 175.00
☐ Recruiting poster, Civil War, plain, Marine Corps 75.00
☐ Recruiting poster, Civil War, plain, Navy 75.00
☐ Recruiting posters, World War I, Army/Navy/Marine Corps . . 50.00
☐ Recruiting posters, World War II, Army/Navy/Marine Corps 15.00
☐ Cutlass, Revolutionary War 500.00
☐ Infantry officer's sword, Revolutionary War 500.00
☐ Cavalry saber 160.00

FLAGS & STANDARDS

☐ Standard of the British 1st Life Guards, c. 1890. Crimson silk damask banner with gold fringe. Gold bullion regimental badge in center with crowned "V" on one side and a crowned "R" on the other (Victoria Regina). Gold bullion battle honors "DETTINGEN, RENINSULA, WATERLOO, EGYPT 1882, TEL-EL-KEBIR" under regimental badge. Mounted on original fluted staff. Finial is lion standing on a crown. Bullion flag cords with tassels 800.00

☐ Nazi Naval Flag. Red cloth field with printed black anchor upon which is superimposed a white disk and black swastika. 15x22 inches 50.00

☐ Nazi Infantry Standarte. Crimson color silk flag with hand embroidered brown eagle in center holding black swastika, all within a silver wreath and centered on a black Iron Cross with white and black edges. A black swastika appears in each corner of the flag. 48x48 inches 5500.00

FLAGS & STANDARDS Price

☐ Nazi Reichs Labor Service Flag (RAD). Red cloth flag with large canted black swastika in center. Superimposed on the center of the swastika is a large embroidered circle of leaves with the RAD shovel (spade) badge on a white background in the center. The top left corner bears the name "Peter Muhlenberg" in silver thread. Three sides of the flag trimmed in silver fringe. 45x49 inches 350.00

☐ Nazi Panzer Standarte. Field of pink color silk. Finely embroidered brown eagle within silver embroidered wreath, all superimposed upon a black Iron Cross outlined in black and white. A black swastika outlined in white is in each corner. Silver fringe. 20x36 inches 4000.00

☐ Imperial German Standarte of a Jager zu Pferde Regiment. All hand sewn. A green Matlese cross occupies the field. There are white rays between the arms of the cross. In the center of the cross is the so-called eagle of Frederick the great in black. There is a gold flaming grenade centered at the center of each arm of the cross. A gold wreath of oak and laurel leaves encircles the eagle, with a gold and red clown above. 12x12 inches 1500.00

☐ Flag of the U.S. 91st AAA AW Battalion. Flag of red silk with large American eagle in the center with brown body, white head and tail, holding green laurel leaves in the right talon and white arrows in the left. Gold triangular device on a red and blue shield superimposed upon the breast of the eagle. A winged bomb appears within the triangular device. A scroll under the eagle bears the legend "NINETY FIRST AAA AW BATTALION." 36x48 inches. 650.00

MODEL SOLDIERS

Model soldiers are closely related to, but not identical with, "toy" soldiers. The difference is this, that while both are miniature representations of soldiers, so-called "toy" soldiers were manufactured by commercial companies or professional toymakers for sale on the open market, whereas model soldiers were built by collectors as a hobby for their amusement, seldom for sale.

It seems only fair, however, to include in this pricing guide some early examples, which may indeed have been manufactured for commercial sale as toys. Nevertheless they rank as works of art, and are the predecessors of modern model-making.

☐ Figure of a soldier in American revolutionary dress, 14" high, carved wood, mounted on a wooden stand, original paint, repaired, probably New England c. 1830 . . . . 800.00 1000.00

☐ Soldier in British army dress of the Napoleonic period, 9½" high, plush body with carved and painted face and hands, holding a rifle made of brass or copper, good condition, probably American, c. 1870 . 350.00 500.00

MODEL SOLDIERS   Price

☐ Soldier in U.S. calvary dress, Mexican war period,
sculptured wood, size not given, arms move, head
turns, slight damage, apparently contemporary . . . . .   —   1500.00

MOVIE MEMORABILIA

FAN MAGAZINES

Movie "fan magazines." "The older the better" is usually the view of collectors with regard to motion picture fan magazines. The earlier magazines are
scarcer because of (a) smaller printings and (b) loss over the years. However,
the value of any individual *issue* depends to some extent on the articles it
contains and the star or stars pictured on its cover, there being a much
greater demand for material on some stars than on others.

	Price	Range
☐ Fan magazines prior to 1930	7.50	20.00 per issue
☐ Fan magazines prior to 1931-1935	5.00	10.00 per issue
☐ Fan magazines prior to 1936-1940	4.00	8.00 per issue
☐ Fan magazines prior to 1941-1945	2.50	7.50 per issue
☐ Fan magazines prior to 1946-1950	2.00	5.00 per issue
☐ Fan magazines prior to 1951-1955	1.00	3.00 per issue

Fan magazines published after 1955 have little collector appeal (most can be
obtained from dealers in backdate magazines for around $1) except those
carrying articles on Elvis Presley, Marilyn Monroe or other "cult"-figure stars.
By the same token, a magazine of the 1930's that would normally fetch $4 or
$5 will bring $20 or more with a Jean Harlow or Judy Garland cover.

MISCELLANEOUS   Price Range

☐ Helmets, worn by "extras" in Biblical movies of the 1950's	35.00	50.00
☐ Library Table, gold-leaf motif used in a number of Warner Bros. productions	450.00	500.00
☐ lobby Card, film "The Tall Men" starring Jane Russell	45.00	50.00
☐ Lobby Card, film "This is Cinerama,"	75.00	85.00
☐ Photo, 8" x 10", B/W, signed and inscribed	35.00	50.00
☐ Review, movie "The Wizard of Oz," clipped from the Chicago Tribune, 1939	5.00	7.50
☐ Scrapbook, 300 items pertaining to Vivion Loigh, including six autographed pieces	250.00	275.00
☐ Scrapbook, 175 pieces pertaining to Tab Hunter, with one 8x10 color photo inscribed & signed	155.00	170.00
☐ Seat, Roxy Theater, New York, plush covered	350.00	375.00
☐ Shoes, worn by Gene Kelly in "An American in Paris," Pr.	175.00	200.00
☐ Special Eyeglasses, distributed to patrons of 3-D movies, plastic or cello lenses with cardboard frames, 1950's	5.00	10.00
☐ Ticket Stub, Radio City Music Hall, 1940's	250.00	500.00
☐ Wig, worn by Debbie Reynolds	135.00	150.00

Courtesy: Movieworld Museum, Los Angeles, CA.

MUSIC

One of the largest segments of music interest is represented by the country music enthusiast. The popularity has grown throughout the years. Demand is very strong not only for the famous but the many less popular stars will command high prices. Please consult our publication *The Official Guide to Collectible Rock Records* by Randal C. Hill for more prices and information.

JOHNNY CASH

RECORDINGS:

	VG	MINT
☐ Big Memphis Marainey, *Call Me Anything,* Sun #184 .	3.00	3.50
☐ Charlie Rich, *Big Man/Rebound,* Philips Inter. #3542 .	2.00	4.00
☐ Charlie Rich, *There's Another Place I Can't Go/I Need Your Love,* Phillips Inter. #3584	2.00	3.00
☐ Conway Twitty, *I Need Your Lovin'/Born to Sing the Blues,* Mercury #71086	5.00	8.00
☐ Conway Twitty, *Double Talk Baby/Why Can't I Get Through To You,* Mercury#71384	6.00	10.00
☐ G. L. Crockett, *Did U Ever Love Somebody,* Checker #1121	3.00	3.50
☐ Harmonica Frank, *Howlin Tomcat,* Chess #1494	3.00	3.50
☐ Harmonica Frank, *Rockin Chair Boogie,* Sun #205	3.00	3.50
☐ Roy Orbison, *Sweet and Innocent/Seems to Me,* RCA #7381	3.50	6.00
☐ Roy Orbison, *Almost Eighteen/Jolie, RCA #7447*	5.00	8.00

L P's

☐ **Merle Travis,** *Back Home,* Capitol	35.00	40.00
☐ *Ira and Charles, The Louvin Brothers,* MGM	60.00	70.00
☐ *Ranch House Favorites* by Bob Wills and His Texas Playboys, 10", MGM	40.00	45.00

COUNTRY

COUNTRY MUSIC MEMORABILIA:

	Price Range	
☐ Bradley Kincaid, 4" x 5" b/w photo signed	10.00	12.00
☐ Carson Robeson, 8" x 10" b/w photo signed & holograph letter	10.00	15.00
☐ Carson Robeson, guitar, c. 1945	—	500.00
☐ Chet Atkins, 8" x 10" b/w photo signed	5.00	7.50
☐ Dolly Parton, 8" x 10" b/w photo signed	7.50	10.00
☐ Eddie Arnold, autograph on program of "The Grand Old Opry," c. 1955	10.00	12.50
☐ Ernest Tubb, guitar and original leather strap	—	150.00
☐ Gene Autry, spurs, silver plated, pair	—	150.00
☐ Grandpa Jones, 8" x 10" b/w photo, signed, c. 1970 ..	5.00	7.50
☐ Hank Williams, magazine article signed & inscribed .	—	75.00
☐ Jimmie Rodgers, 8" x 10" b/w photo, sepia, unsigned	—	40.00
☐ Roy Acuff, necktie, c. 1940	—	125.00
☐ Roy Rogers, scrapbook of 200 photos, unsigned clippings, etc.	—	145.00
☐ W. Lee O'Daniel, typed letter signed to Lyndon Johnson	—	100.00
☐ W. Lee O'Daniel, three-foot-long pen used to sign legislation as U.S. Senator from Texas	—	200.00
☐ W. Lee O'Daniel, typed letter signed to Sam Rayburn, mentioning President Roosevelt, with framed photo of O'Daniel	—	250.00

MISCELLANEOUS

☐ Book, "Stars of Country Music", autographed by Johnny Cash, Porter Waggoner, Dolly Parton and several others	—	175.00
☐ Cassette Tape, Perry Como television program featuring Hank Snow as guest star, c. 1950	15.00	20.00
☐ Collection, 300 pieces of sheet music, 1950-1965	80.00	85.00
☐ Poster, "The Grand Old Opry", advertising, late 1940's	—	50.00
☐ Scrapbook, 14" x 17", leather bound, 600 clippings, photos and other misc. items including 30 autographed pieces on country music stars of the pre-1950 era	—	800.00

JAZZ

The collecting of jazz memorabilia had its beginnings in the night clubs and bistros of New Orleans, New York and elsewhere, where, from as early as the 1920's, the walls were often lined with inscribed photographs of the stars who performed there. Around 1950, "jazz collecting" began to take on interest as a hobby with private collectors. Many of the old-time jazz greats were still alive at that time, and ambitious collectors succeeded in obtaining from them a variety of personal mementos. Though no special cash value was then attached to much of this material, the growth of jazz-memorabilia collecting has rendered it quite valuable today.

BENNY GOODMAN

JAZZ

RECORDINGS

78's (records in average condition)

	Price Range	
☐ Benny Goodman, with Ben Pollack & his Orch., *Waitin' for Katie,* Victor, 1927	7.50	10.00
☐ Benny Goodman, with Ted Lewis & his Band, *Dip Your Brush in Sunshine,* Columbia, 1931	15.00	20.00
☐ Benny Goodman, with the Charleston Chasers, *Basin Street Blues,* Columbia, 1931	20.00	25.00
☐ Benny Goodman, with the Benny Goodman Quintet, *Pick-a-Rib,* Victor, 1938	5.00	10.00
☐ Billie Holiday, with Benny Goodman & his Orch., *Your Mother's Son-in-Law,* Columbia, 1933	25.00	30.00
☐ Billie Holiday, with Teddy Wilson & his Orch., *What a Little Moonlight Can Do,* Brunswick, 1935	10.00	15.00
☐ Billie Holiday, with Teddy Wilson & his Orch., *Miss Brown to You,* Brunswick, 1935	12.50	15.00
☐ Billie Holiday, & her Orch., *God Bless the Child,* Okeh, 1941	5.00	10.00
☐ Bix Beiderbecke, with the Wolverines, *Copenhagen,* Gennett, 1924	—	100.00
☐ Bix Beiderbecke, with Jean Goldkette, *Clementine (from New Orleans),* Victor, 1927	12.50	15.00
☐ Bix Beiderbecke, with Frankie Trumbauer & his Orch., *Riverboat Shuffle,* Okeh, 1927	40.00	50.00
☐ Bix Beiderbecke, with Paul Whiteman & his Orch., *Because My Baby Don't Mean "Maybe" Now,* Okeh, 1928	15.00	20.00
☐ Coleman Hawkins, with Fletcher Henderson & his Orch., *The Dicty Blues,* Vocalion, 1923	20.00	25.00
☐ Coleman Hawkins, with the Mound City Blue Blowers, Hello, Lola, Victor, 1929	20.00	25.00
☐ Coleman Hawkins, with Fletcher Henderson & his Orch., *Underneath the Harlem Moon,* Columbia, 1932	17.50	20.00
☐ Coleman Hawkins, with Lionel Hampton & his Orch., *Dinah,* Victor, 1939	5.00	10.00

JAZZ

	Price	Range
☐ Duke Ellington, with his Orch., *Creole Love Call,* Victor, 1927	10.00	15.00
☐ Duke Ellington, with the Jungle Band, *Mood Indigo,* Brunswick, 1930	10.00	15.00
☐ Duke Ellington, with his Orch., *Rockabye River,* Victor, Victor, 1946	3.00	5.00
☐ Earl Hines, *Chicago Rhythm,* Victor, 1929	25.00	30.00
☐ Jelly Roll Morton, *Muddy Water Blues,* Paramount, 1923	—	200.00
☐ Louis Armstrong, Hot #5, *Who's It,* Okeh, 1926	—	50.00

L P's

☐ Dave Bailey Sextet, *Gettin' Into Somethin',* Epic	20.00	25.00
☐ James Clay and David "Fathead" Newman, *The Sound of the Wide Open Spaces,* Riverside	15.00	18.00
☐ Stan Getz Quintet, *Jazz at Storyville,* 10", Roost	20.00	25.00
☐ Paul Nero, *Jam Session,* 10", Skylark	60.00	70.00

JAZZ MEMORABILIA:

☐ Bessie Smith, signed photos, rare	75.00	100.00
☐ Buddy Rich, set of drumsticks, said to have been used by him	—	50.00
☐ Charlie Parker, signed photo, rare	50.00	75.00
☐ Coleman Hawkins, front page of *Billboard* Magazine signed by him	12.50	15.00
☐ Count Basie, inscribed photograph	4.00	5.00
☐ Count Basie, piano stool, said to have been used by him, mahogany covered in green leatherette, sold w/autographed photo	—	125.00
☐ Duke Ellington, signed photograph	15.00	20.00
☐ Duke Ellington, signed hotel menu, c. 1940	7.50	10.00
☐ Harry James, trumpet, original velvet-lined wooden box, good condition	—	400.00
☐ Harry James, signed photograph	5.00	10.00
☐ Harry James, signature on record sleeve	3.50	5.00
☐ Jimmie Dorsey, signed photograph	11.50	15.00
☐ Jimmie Dorsey, cancelled check endorsed by him (from a recording company)	15.00	20.00
☐ Jimmie Dorsey, two scrapbooks, 16" x 12" containing 700 (approx.) clippings from newspapers, some signed photos	—	350.00
☐ Jimmie & Tommie Dorsey, photo of both signed by both	27.50	30.00
☐ Louis Armstrong, signed photo	10.00	15.00
☐ Louis Armstrong, 11" x 13" color photo from newspaper, signed	—	250.00
☐ Louis Armstrong, ceramic statuette, modern	12.00	15.00

ROCK 'N ROLL

One of the most popular of all hobbies, rock 'n' roll memorabilia is enormous in its scope, ranging from recordings to magazines to fan-club bulletins, to autographed photos, clothing, and, in extreme cases, even locks of hair. So strong is fan interest that memorabilia of certain rock stars can sell for higher prices than items relating to Presidents of the U.S.

Fan interest is centered basically on the major rock celebrities of the 1950's and early 1960's, but later material does have its market. There is also a demand for items of obscure personalities, who made perhaps one hit recording and then faded from the limelight.

ELVIS PRESLEY

ELVIS PRESLEY

45's	VG	MINT
☐ Mystery Train/I Forgot to Remember to Forget, RCA #6357	8.00	15.00
☐ That's All Right/Blue Moon of Kentucky, RCA #6380	8.00	15.00
☐ Good Rockin' Tonight/I Don't Care If The Sun Don't Shine, RCA #6381	8.00	15.00
☐ Milkcow Blues Boogie/You're a Heartbreaker, RCA #6382	8.00	15.00
☐ Baby Let's Play House/I'm Left, You're Right, She's Gone, RCA #6383	8.00	15.00
☐ Heartbreak Hotel/I Was The One (1), RCA #6420	2.50	5.00
☐ I Want You, I Need You, I Love You/My Baby Left Me (3), RCA #6540	2.50	5.00
L P's		
☐ Elvis Presley (double-pocket), RCA #1254	60.00	100.00
☐ Elvis Presley (24), RCA #747	6.00	12.00
☐ Heartbreak Hotel (76), RCA #821	7.00	12.00
☐ Elvis Presley (55), RCA #830	7.00	12.00
☐ The Real Elvis, RCA #940	7.00	12.00
☐ Anyway You Want Me, RCA #965	7.00	12.00
☐ Love Me Tender (35), RCA #4006	6.00	12.00

	VG	MINT
ELVIS PRESLEY		
☐ *Elvis, Vol. 1 (6)*, RCA #992	6.00	12.00
☐ *Elvis, Vol. 2 (47)*, RCA #993	7.00	12.00
☐ *Strictly Elvis*, RCA #994	7.00	12.00
☐ *Loving You, Vol. 1*, RCA #1-1515	7.00	12.00
☐ *Loving You, Vol. 2*, RCA #2-1515	7.00	12.00
BUDDY HOLLY		
45's		
☐ *Love Me/Blue Days, Black Nights*, Decca #29854	15.00	25.00
☐ *Modern Don Juan/You Are My One Desire*, Decca #30166	12.00	20.00
☐ *That'll Be The Day/Rock Around With Ollie Vee*, Decca #30534	15.00	25.00
☐ *Love Me/ You Are My One Desire*, Decca #30543	8.00	15.00
☐ *Girl On My Mind/Ting-A-Ling*, Decca #30650	12.00	20.00
☐ *Worlds Of Love/Mailman Bring Me No More Blues*, Coral #61852	18.00	30.00
☐ *Peggy Sue/Everyday (3)*, Coral #61885	1.50	3.50
☐ *I'm Gonna Love You Too/Listen To Me*, Coral #61947 .	3.00	5.00
☐ *Rave On/Take Your Time (37)*, Coral #61985	2.00	4.00
☐ *Early In The Morning/Now We're One (32)*, Coral #62006	2.00	4.00
☐ *Heartbeat/Well... All Right (82)*, Coral #62051	3.00	4.50
☐ *It Doesn't Matter Anymore/Raining in My Heart (13)*, Coral #62074	1.50	3.00
☐ *Peggy Sue Got Married/Crying, Waiting, Hoping*, Coral #62134	6.00	10.00
☐ *True Love Ways/That Makes It Tough*, Coral #62210 . .	6.00	10.00

	Price Range	
ROCK 'N' ROLL MEMORABILIA		
☐ Bill Haley, autographed sheet music, *Shake, Rattle & Roll*	10.00	15.00
☐ Bobby Darin, scrapbook of his career items, few signed colored photos, 1950's	130.00	150.00
☐ Bobby Sherman, coloring book, pub. in 1971 for 59¢ . .	5.00	7.50
☐ Buddy Holly, all items scarce because of his early death... autographed photographs	—	25.00
☐ Buddy Knox, signed tear sheet, *Cashbox* magazine showing his recording, *Party Doll*, c. 1956	—	25.00
☐ Chuck Berry, three signed photos, two unsigned photos, one signed in purple ink	20.00	25.00
☐ Connie Francis, autographed magazine article	6.00	7.50
☐ Connie Francis, holograph postcard, six lines	—	8.50
☐ Connie Francis, signed LP album cover	7.50	10.00
☐ The Diamonds, 8" x 10" b/w photo, signed by all members, notes on back	15.00	20.00
☐ Fats Domino, collection of 36 original phonograph records along with 16 signed photos/other items, in leather-bound albums, soiled	—	400.00
☐ Fats Domino, signed 8" x 10" b/w photo, seated at piano	3.00	5.00

ROCK 'N ROLL MEMORABILIA

	Price Range	
☐ Lloyd Price, signed 5" x 7" b/w photo	—	3.00
☐ Pat Boone, signed 8" x 10" b/w photos	2.00	3.00
☐ Pat Boone, signed phonograph records, Dot label . . .	10.00	12.00

SHEET MUSIC

The collector of sheet music should first of all understand that values depend not only on composer and composition but the cover illustration, and in many cases this — the cover illustration — proves the most influential factor. Many collectors buy these items for framing and are interested only in the artwork. Thus, the best hunting ground for them is printshops, where they can be found both framed and unframed.

☐ *Dundreary's Brother Sam,* by J. E. Carpenter, cover by Concanen & Lee, published by Metzler, 1865	150.00	200.00
☐ *I'm a Ship Without a Rudder,* composed by Frank Vernon, published by Hopwood	100.00	150.00
☐ *Many a Time,* written & composed by Arthur West, sung by Harry Freeman	40.00	60.00
☐ *Oh, Come With Me,* written by Richard Ryan, published by R. Cocks & Co.	10.00	12.00
☐ *Prince Albert's Marching Band,* as performed by the Military Bands, rider in military dress on cover	7.50	10.00
☐ *See-Saw Waltz,* composed by A. G. Crowe, published by Metzler	10.00	12.00
☐ *The Calendar Polka,* D. Smith, 1884	10.00	12.00
☐ *The Crystal Palace Quadrille,* published by G. H. Davidson	7.50	10.00
☐ *The Excursion Train,* sung by E. Marshall, published by J. Williams	80.00	100.00
☐ *The Great Eastern Polka* (about an ocean liner)	12.50	15.00
☐ *The Gorilla Quadrille,* composed by C. H. R. Marriott, published by J. Williams, Gorilla leading band on cover, 1870's	140.00	160.00
☐ *Two in the Morning,* sung with the Greatest Applause by Mr. W. Randall, published by Duff & Stewart	80.00	100.00
☐ *Wait for the Turn of the Tide,* written & sung by Mr. Harry Clifton, 1860's	12.00	15.00
☐ *Who's That Tapping at the Garden Gate?,* composed by S. W. New, published by Hutchings & Romer	7.50	10.00

MUSIC BOXES
(Cylinder & Disc)

To determine the value of music boxes, the governing factors are: the maker, length of cylinder, quality and arrangement of music, condition and decoration of case and works, also special features; eg. bells, butterflies, coin-operated, changer, etc. Prices are for very good to excellent condition.

Courtesy: Les Gould, S. Orange, NJ.

REGINE METAL DISC,
Numbered, w/27 Discs,
c.1880.. 1800.00 - 2000.00

MUSIC BOXES
CYLINDER-TYPE:

	Price Range	
☐ Paillard Vaucher Fils. 13" cylinder, 6 bells with bird strikers, inlaid box, lever wind	1350.00	1500.00
☐ Organ Music Box. Plays 13" cylinder, 8 tunes, has bellows. Unusual	850.00	1000.00
☐ Mermod Frere. Circa 1896, 10 tune orchestral box. Outside crank wind, 13½" cylinder, bells, drums, castanets and mandolin oak case with some carving, brass handles, coin operated	1850.00	2000.00
☐ Mermod Freres Box. Two 8" brass cylinders, plays 12 tunes, originally coin operated. "Peerless Forte Piccolo"	—	1150.00
☐ Carved Mahogany Case. Three round bells with hammer strikers, plays 10 separate tunes	—	625.00
☐ Drum and Bell Box. Polished inlaid rosewood case with drum and 6 fine-tuned bells with manual controls. 14" cylinder, Swiss made, plays 12 tunes	—	675.00
☐ Mermod Freres Double-Cylinder Box. Beautifully polished and matched rosewood, walnut and ebony woods. Complete with dial, tune-selector and safety lock. Contains 6 separate tunes on each 13" cylinder........................	—	600.00
☐ Double-cylinder Box. Multiple carvings on polished mahogany case. Wide, flared legs, plays 6 tunes on each of two fat cylinders, over 1 hour playing time	—	800.00
☐ Double Dawkins Cylinder Box. Seven separate cylinders. Each cylinder is brass and over 11" long. Hand-polished golden wood box has container for storage of spare cylinders	—	2000.00

MUSIC BOXES

Price Range

☐ Twenty-Tune Cylinder Box. Large, polished mahogany box contains two 10" brass cylinders, each with 10 separate tunes. Finest Swiss manufacturer . . . . — 750.00

Disc-Music Boxes

☐ Adler Disc Music Box. Scrolled Victorian case, 18¾" disc, coin-operated . . . . — 1800.00

☐ Britannia Music Box. Lever-wound machine with 9¼" discs, table model . . . . — 425.00

☐ Regina Table Model. 20 ¾" discs, double comb, mahogany case, short bedplate . . . . — 2000.00

☐ Monopol Disc Music Box. Double-comb machine which plays Monopol 13" discs. Cabinet has drawer for storage of spare discs. Fine German manufacturer . . . . — 600.00

☐ Olympia Disc Music Box. Single-comb table machine with 15½" discs. Contained in hand-carved mahogany grained case . . . . — 1150.00

☐ Same as 15 except with double comb . . . . — 1300.00

☐ Polyphon Deluxe Bell Box. Hand-rubbed and polished walnut case surrounding precision machine playing 14 ½" discs. Cover is richly inlaid in polished lighter wood. 12 tuned saucer bells, 18½" x 17" x 25", circa 1900 . . . . — 1750.00

☐ Stella Disc Music Box. Mahogany-cased table model, uses 9½" discs . . . . — 450.00

☐ Symphonion Disc Music Box. Unusual design housed in lower portion of 7" x 12" clock. Top-mounted music box plays 4½" discs . . . . — 525.00

☐ Polyphone Upright Music Box. German, glass front, walnut case, 64" high. Plays 35 discs, 20" diameter, coin operated . . . . — 2500.00

☐ Symphonion Disc Music Box. circa 1880's, small decorated case, plays 6" discs 250.00 350.00

☐ Polyphone Disc Music Box. Takes 19 5/8" discs, coin operated, upright walnut case, glass front . . 3000.00 3250.00

☐ Regina Floor Model. Bow front, glass door, oak or mahogany, 15" discs, automatic changer, coin-operated with 12 discs 4700.00 5000.00

☐ Symphonion Table Model. circa 1880's, case slightly carved, plays 15½" discs, beautiful original engraving inside cover 850.00 1000.00

☐ Symphonion Floor Model. circa 1880's, takes 25¼" discs, storage case in bottom, burled walnut, carved case, 20 discs 2700.00 3000.00

Courtesy Less Gould, South Orange, N.J.
Many thanks to Frank Morrello for his help.

MUSICAL INSTRUMENTS

Even if you have a stone ear, and can't play any instrument at all, you can collect beautiful musical instruments. There may not be too much room in your closet or your living room for pianos or organs, but there is a great variety of instruments made all over the world, in many materials, to choose from.

SQUARE PIANO, *Clemente & Co., London,*
c. 1830 . . . . **400.00 - 700.00**

	Price Range	
☐ Accordian, Made in Germany	125.00	225.00
☐ Clarinet, Wm. Nuernberger, German, silverplate	45.00	50.00
☐ Clavichord, Heidelberg, Rosewood Case, Four tapered legs, 1957	900.00	1400.00
☐ Cornet, Klemm & Bro., Philadelphia, mid 19th Century, Brass body with nickel mounts	300.00	450.00
☐ Drums, Chinese, Bodies of painted wood, set of 4	100.00	150.00
☐ Dulcimer, Italian, 18th Century, Fruitwood body, 19 strings	500.00	700.00
☐ Fife, rosewood & brass, 16" L., c. 1850-70	85.00	100.00
☐ Flute, Henry Hill, carved ivory, six keyed	450.00	500.00
☐ Guitar, Naples, Rosewood fingerboard, 1891	550.00	700.00
☐ Harmonica, Brass plates, 1875	50.00	100.00
☐ Harp, Swiss, Enamel and gold, 19th Century	2000.00	3000.00
☐ Helicon, Henry Pourcelle, Paris, 19th Century, Brass body with three pistonvalves	800.00	950.00
☐ Mandolin, Gibson F-4, 1910, mint	1500.00	1600.00
☐ Melodeon, Rosewood Case, Carved stand, 1900	150.00	250.00
☐ Oboe, Klenig, ivory, three keyed, 18th Century	6000.00	7100.00
☐ Rollmonica, plus 3 rolls	50.00	75.00
☐ Tenor Saxophone, Buescher & Co., Elkhart, Indiana, Brass body, and brass mounts, 1935	800.00	1000.00
☐ Ukelele, Arthur Godfrey, plastic	20.00	25.00
☐ Viola, German, 1 piece back, 18th Century	300.00	450.00
☐ Violin, Hungarian, 1 piece back, Red brown color	200.00	300.00

MUSICAL INSTRUMENTS
PIANOS

	Price	Range
☐ Baby Grand, Smith, New York	8000.00	10000.00
☐ Grand, Broadwood, 7½'	2000.00	3000.00
☐ Grand, Chickering Ampico-A, 5'4"	4900.00	5000.00
☐ Grand, Concert, Baldwin, 9' L	9500.00	10000.00
☐ Grand, Emerson, Rosewood	3200.00	4200.00
☐ Grand, Steinway, Duo-Art Player, walnut, 1929	—	13500.00
☐ Grand, Steinway, Carved	3800.00	4800.00
☐ Grand, Steinway, 1940s	4000.00	5000.00
☐ Grand, Square, Hallett & Cumston, c. 1860s	2500.00	3000.00
☐ Oak Grand, Emerson, carved, new strings & hammers	4500.00	
☐ Player, Aeolian-Duo-Art, upright, c. 1905	1800.00	2000.00
☐ Player, Coin Operated	2500.00	3500.00
☐ Player, Lindeman	1000.00	2000.00
☐ Player, Steinway	1800.00	2800.00
☐ Square, Mahogany case with carved fleur De Lys, 1830	400.00	700.00
☐ Upright, H. C. Bayes	1000.00	1500.00

ORGANS

☐ Gem roller organ, 3 rolls	350.00	400.00
☐ Esteyreed, full pedal keyboard	2500.00	3000.00
☐ Loring & Blake	700.00	1000.00
☐ Mason & Hamlin, Church	3200.00	3800.00
☐ Pump, Estey, 1880s	1000.00	1200.00

NAPKIN RINGS AND HOLDERS

Napkin rings and holders at place settings were originally only intended to be functional. As years went on, they were made of a variety of metals, generally semi-precious, in a variety of ornate shapes and forms.

RUSTIC BOYS
150.00 - 200.00

FLORAL MOTIF
50.00 - 60.00

CROSSED RIFLES
150.00 - 175.00

NAPKIN HOLDERS

	Price Range	
☐ Angel with butterfly	110.00	120.00
☐ Bulldog guarding ring	75.00	82.50
☐ Cherub with bird, flowers on side, square ring, silverplate	90.00	95.00
☐ Cherubs. Two playing, Meriden	35.00	42.50
☐ Chick looking over ring	90.00	95.00
☐ Crossed rifles, each side engraved ring, silver plate	155.00	175.00
☐ Cupid with flute	120.00	145.00
☐ Dog chasing car	125.00	145.00
☐ Dog on each side of ring, Toronto Silver plate Co.	120.00	135.00
☐ Eagle, resilvered, 4" high	125.00	175.00
☐ Fans on either side, ring above ballfooted base	130.00	145.00
☐ Floral engraving, solid silver, ornate	50.00	60.00
☐ Foxes and bird in nest	90.00	100.00
☐ Girl with pigtail pushing ring, William Rogers	215.00	250.00
☐ Horseshoe and ring	59.00	70.00
☐ Kangaroo on leaf	52.00	65.00
☐ Kate Greenaway. Boy smiling, hands behind sailor hat	145.00	170.00
☐ Kate Greenaway. Girl with dog, engraved flowers	65.00	75.00
☐ Kate Greenaway. Girl holding gun	150.00	170.00
☐ Kitten batting air beside ring	75.00	80.00
☐ Kitten pulling cart	132.00	140.00
☐ Laughing child in nightgown	110.00	125.00
☐ Leaf base with acorn	55.00	65.00
☐ Owls. Mother and owlettes on fancy footed base	225.00	250.00
☐ Peacock seated on ring	175.00	200.00
☐ Rabbit. Ornate design, silver plate	65.00	95.00
☐ Rabbit. Sitting at side of ring	40.00	45.00
☐ Ring and toothpick	65.00	75.00
☐ Rose and leaf, on both sides. Leaf engraving, silver plate	85.00	120.00
☐ Rustic Boys. Each side of square ring, silver plate	150.00	200.00
☐ Squirrel. Fancy design on ring, original condition	125.00	175.00
☐ Sunflower. Leaves on sides, Meriden	35.00	50.00
☐ Swan on oval base	125.00	145.00
☐ Turtles with ring on back	110.00	120.00
☐ Violin	62.00	75.00
☐ Water lily. Rogers	33.00	42.50
☐ Wine barrel on leaves and twigs	33.00	42.50
☐ Wishbone. "Best Wishes." 4 ball feet, Wilcox	30.00	35.00
☐ Woman on side of floral engraving	125.00	175.00

NAUTICAL GEAR

The sea and its ships have always been fascinating to people in all walks of life. Listed below are some examples of fast growing nautical collectibles.

COMPASS IN CASE
200.00 - 250.00

BRASS SEXTANT
350.00 - 400.00

	Price Range	
☐ Anchor, sailing ship, 500 lbs.	375.00	525.00
☐ Bell, brass	25.00	60.00
☐ Binnacles (container holding a ship's compass), usually brass	275.00	500.00
☐ Chest, sea, canvas on lid, ship painting	475.00	625.00
☐ Clock, brass, 7" deep, Seth Thomas	140.00	210.00
☐ Compasses, in case, on gimbals	90.00	275.00
☐ Figurehead, carved, painted wood, 19th century, 32" high	1200.00	1500.00
☐ Globe, covered with linen, 28" long, circa 1875	265.00	450.00
☐ Gold Scales (with small weights)	65.00	200.00
☐ Guinea Scales (English scale used to weigh gold coins)	100.00	150.00
☐ Helmet, brass and copper, deep sea, 17"	600.00	750.00
☐ Hydrometers, in case with weights and thermometer .	55.00	110.00
☐ Ivory or Boxwood Rules (used for measuring and drafting).	25.00	80.00
☐ Lamp, copper with brass & copper, keep sea, 17"	600.00	750.00
☐ Lantern, brass top, copper	40.00	65.00
☐ Octants (Hadley Quadrant), ebony, in case (used for ship's navigation)	300.00	500.00
☐ Pocket Scales.	45.00	125.00
☐ Porthole, brass, 8" deep	25.00	50.00
☐ Sextants (brass, in case), late 19th to 20th century . . .	280.00	365.00
☐ Ship's Telegraph.	275.00	450.00
☐ Slide Rules	50.00	525.00
☐ Sovereign Scales (English scale used to weigh coins)	40.00	55.00

NAUTICAL GEAR

	Price	Range
☐ Telescope, brass, English 19th century, with case, 19¼"	250.00	300.00
☐ Telescopes (long glass)	85.00	250.00
☐ Telescopes on stand (astronomical) or marine	300.00	2000.00

OCEANLINER MEMORABILIA

☐ Ashtray, ceramic	8.00	10.00
☐ Candy Container, tin, UNITED STATES	8.00	10.00
☐ Deck Plan, FRANCE	—	5.00
☐ Deck Plan, EUROPA	—	5.00
☐ Menu, QUEEN ELIZABETH Farewell Dinner, 1941 . . .	—	5.00
☐ Menu, SWEDISH-AMERICAN LINES, 1941	—	4.00
☐ Menu, RED STAR LINE, handprinted, 1900	—	8.00
☐ Officer's Hat	—	20.00

Items from the TITANIC are worth at least four times as much as a comparable item from another ship. Many items from the Titanic are invaluable.

NAVAJO BLANKETS

Woven on looms by women, Navajo—and a few other tribal—blankets are America's earliest textiles. They are sometimes fabulously expensive, and are incredibly beautiful. Beware of really cheap ones—they are probably not old, and not even made in America, let alone by the Indians.

☐ Chief's Blanket woven with nine spot pattern of deep red, black, brown, orange and white rectangles enclosing geometric motifs with background stripe in black and white	800.00	1100.00
☐ Germantown Wearing Blanket woven with a Chief's 3rd Phase nine spot pattern of red, white and blue diamonds each having a cross in the center and black and white stripe background	1300.00	1500.00
☐ Wearing Blanket woven in handspun and Germantown yarn with a Chief's 4th Phase nine spot pattern of red and blue. Black diamonds enclose green and yellow geometric motifs	1100.00	1400.00

NEEDLEWORKING TOOLS

While some people collect finished needlework, such as embroidery, lace, crewel, samplers, etc., others are fascinated by the dainty tools used to create the thread-and-fabric gems.

☐ Basket, wicker, 12"	18.00	22.00
☐ Darner, glass, red	24.00	28.00
☐ Darner, glove, sterling silver	35.00	40.00

NEEDLEWORKING TOOLS

	Price	Range
☐ Darner, sock, brown	25.00	30.00
☐ Needle case, brass	10.00	15.00
☐ Needle case, carved ivory	30.00	35.00
☐ Needle case, sterling silver	22.00	26.00
☐ Needle case, tortoiseshell	70.00	80.00
☐ Pincushion, ivory, pedestal base	35.00	45.00
☐ Pincushion, sterling silver	90.00	110.00
☐ Pincushion, patchwork, 8" square	12.00	15.00
☐ Scissors, Embroidery, stork, silver plate, 3"	25.00	30.00
☐ Sewing Bird, brass	40.00	45.00
☐ Sewing Bird, iron, 6"	30.00	35.00
☐ Sewing Bird, sterling silver, 6"	40.00	45.00
☐ Sewing Bird, brass, clamp-on, large w/cushion	—	150.00
☐ Sewing Machine, Singer, heavy duty	170.00	250.00
☐ Sewing Machine, White, early 1900's, Cleveland, Ohio	100.00	150.00
☐ Spinning Wheel, Norwegian, paint decorated, small	150.00	200.00
☐ Spool Cabinet, Eureka, walnut, 22 drawers, 16 w/glass	—	750.00
☐ Spool Cabinet, Brooks, 4-drawer	250.00	300.00
☐ Tape Measure, clock	60.00	70.00
☐ Tape Measure, duck and hen	30.00	40.00
☐ Tape Measure, owl	20.00	25.00
☐ Tape Measure, rabbit	28.00	35.00
☐ Tape Measure, vault	20.00	25.00
☐ Tape Measure, figural turtle, sterling, brass enamel	45.00	55.00
☐ Tape Measure, papoose, original box	10.00	15.00
☐ Tatting Shuttle, tortoiseshell	10.00	15.00
☐ Thimble, brass	12.00	16.00
☐ Thimble, celluloid	5.00	8.00
☐ Thimble, gold with leather case	70.00	90.00
☐ Thimble, sterling silver	35.00	40.00
☐ Thimble, tortoise shell and sterling silver	85.00	100.00
☐ Thimble, engraved bird, large size, 14k gold	—	75.00
☐ Thimble Holder, wooden acorn with hinged leaf top	40.00	45.00
☐ Thimble Holder, celluloid, w/thread holder	10.00	15.00

NURSERY COLLECTIBLES

There is everything from baby bottles to rattles for the juvenilia collector.

ABC PLATES:

	Price
☐ Biblical Scene, Samuel and Eli, 8" D	32.00
☐ Black Children, 7" D	45.00
☐ Boys, Reading a letter, 5" D	32.00
☐ Capitol, Washington, D.C., 7¼" D	32.00
☐ Cat and Kittens, 7¼" D	35.00
☐ Clockface Center, 8" D	52.00
☐ Dancing Master, 7¼" D	30.00

CARRIAGE

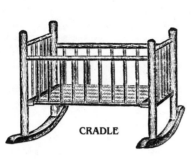

CRADLE

ABC PLATES

	Price
☐ Dog In Center, 6½" D	38.00
☐ Eagle In Center, Tin, 3" D	25.00
☐ Elephant In Center, 6" D	38.00
☐ Farm Scene, Haywagon and oxen, 4" D	38.00
☐ Fisherman In Pond, 8 3/8" D	42.00
☐ Football Scene, 7¼" D	35.00
☐ Hi Diddle Diddle, Tin, 8" D	38.00
☐ Horse Race Scene, 7" D	38.00
☐ Hunting Scene, 8½" D	40.00
☐ Ice Cream, 7½" D	38.00
☐ Kitten and Puppy in Pitcher, 7" D	28.00
☐ Little Bear, 7¼" D	42.00
☐ Little Bo Peep, Glass, 7" D	35.00
☐ Little Miss Muffet, 6¼" D	36.00
☐ Man and Dog Sliding, 7" D	40.00
☐ Mary Had a Little Lamb, Tin, 7" D	38.00
☐ Mother, Daughter and Verse, 7" D	38.00
☐ Pigs-In-Pen, Pewter, 6¼" D	62.00
☐ Potter's Art, 6¼" D	35.00
☐ Punch and Judy, 7" D	55.00
☐ Robinson Crusoe, 7" D	42.00
☐ Rosaline, 8½" D	80.00
☐ Sign Language	250.00
☐ Soccer Scene, 7¼" D	38.00
☐ Star In Center, Glass 6" D	30.00
☐ Sunbonnet Babies	150.00
☐ Titmouse, 7" D	32.00
☐ Tom the Piper's Son, Alphabet border, 6¾" D	30.00
☐ Who Killed Cock Robin, Tin, 7" D	38.00
☐ Youth and Maiden, Gothic attire, 5¾" D	35.00

MISCELLANEOUS:

☐ Baby Bottles, Cylindrical, 20th C.		8.00
☐ Baby Bottles, Egyptian	—	900.00
☐ Baby Bottles, Silver	—	850.00
☐ Baby Bottles, Turtle and tube, 19th C.	—	25.00

MISCELLANEOUS   Price Range

- [ ] Bassinet, wicker, decorated 130.00 160.00
- [ ] Bed, baby, wicker, feather mattress 140.00 180.00
- [ ] "Bubby Pots" with long spout ....   —   250.00
- [ ] Cradles, pine, spindles, 36" 90.00   120.00
- [ ] Cup, Peter Pan, engraved ....   —   75.00
- [ ] Highchair, oak, decorated 60.00   80.00
- [ ] Lantern, child's, brass, battery operated, wire handle, 10" 25.00 35.00
- [ ] Rocker, child's, painted black with flower motif 90.00 130.00

OPERA MEMORABILIA

Note: The collecting of opera memorabilia centers mainly upon photographs of stars, past and present. As opera stars have alwys had a considerable "fan" following, their pictures exist in large numbers. It should be noted, though, that *signed* photos of some stars are scarce, while *holograph letters* of stars whose pictures are common can be very hard to get.

There is also a market among collectors for oddments and miscellania of opera, including playbills, scores, posters, even tickets. Their age, the place of origin, and other circumstances influence their cash value. A playbill (or program) from opening night of the new Metropolitan Opera House, New York (1965), would, for example, be considerably more valuable than a program from the same house dated a week later. Relics of defunct opera houses are generally worth more than those still in operation.

- [ ] Enrico Caruso, caricature by Caruso, ink on drawing paper, figure of man in topcoat carrying a cane, signed 145.00 155.00
- [ ] Enrico Caruso, 8" x 10" b/w photo in costume from "The Girl of the Golden West," wearing six-gallon hat and leather vest, signed 80.00 110.00
- [ ] Enrico Caruso, check for $800 endorsed by Caruso, bank stamp slightly obliterating signature, good specimen 75.00 100.00
- [ ] Enrico Caruso, poster of the Metropolitan Opera House advertising Caruso in "I Pagliacci" 60.00 80.00
- [ ] Enrico Caruso, pair of typed letters signed by Caruso, one one hotel stationary written while on tour in Mexico, dealing with opera roles, etc. 200.00 250.00
- [ ] Enrico Caruso, 5" x 7" b/w photo (from a magazine) signed and a larger portrait, unsigned, framed along with a phonograph record in a simple gold-plated metal frame against a background of dark blue silk .. 325.00 375.00
- [ ] Ezio Pinza, holograph letter signed, 1932, sent from Milan, dealing with preparations for an operatic role . 25.00 30.00
- [ ] Ezio Pinza, small b/w photo signed and inscribed with a brief sentiment 15.00 25.00
- [ ] Metropolitan Opera House, 6" x 6" fragment of curtain from the "old" Metropolitan Opera House, New York (closed 1964), framed with identifying card in a frame of polished oak, overall size 12" x 17" 75.00 100.00

OPERA MEMORABILIA   Price Range

☐ Metropolitan Opera House, seat from the "old" Metropolitan Opera House, velvet covered, worn, good condition overall 325.00   375.00

☐ Metropolitan Opera Houe, brick from the facade of the "old" Metropolitan Opera House, mounted on a teakwood stand 75.00   125.00

☐ Metropolitan Opera House bills, most bills prior to 1915 (that is, posters carrying announcements of operas to be performed, with listing of cast, conductor, etc., but *not illustrated*)* 25.00   50.00

☐ Metropolitan Opera House bills, most bills 1915-30 .. 20.00   35.00

☐ LaScala Opera House bills, Milan, Italy, most bills 1900-1920 .... 35.00   75.00

☐ Beverly Sills, large poster of the New York City opera, picturing her in roles from the "three queens," signed by her in Magic Marker, c. 1975 .... 10.00   15.00

☐ Beverly Sills, 11" x 14" b/w photo of her as Mary Stuart, pasted on heavy cardboard, signed & inscribed (auction price) .... —   65.00

* *The values of bills vary depending on the operas and the stars named; Caruso bills invariably go higher than others.*

ORIENTALIA

Oriental collectibles are very much on the increase. The interest stemming from the fine artistic to the very mysterious, all of which seems to exude from this particular area. With the China door opening look for this whole category to continue its upward trend.

JADE URN

CINNABAR AND LACQUER SNUFF BOTTLE

ORIENTALIA
MAJOR DYNASTIES AND PERIODS
CHINA:

Shang Dynasty	c. 1523-1027 B.C.
Chou Dynasty	1027- 221 B.C.
Spring and Autumn Period	770- 475 B.C.
Warring States Period	481- 221 B.C.
Ch'in Dynasty	221- 206 B.C.
Han Dynasty	206 B.C.-A.D. 220
Three Kingdoms	A.D. 220-A.D. 280
Six Dynasties Period	A.D. 280-A.D. 589
Northern Wei	A.D. 385-A.D. 535
Northern Ch'i	A.D. 550-A.D. 577
Northern Chou	A.D. 557-A.D. 581
Sui Dynasty	A.D. 589-A.D. 618
T'ang	A.D. 618-A.D. 906
Five Dynasties	A.D. 907-A.D. 959
Sung Dynasty	A.D. 906-A.D. 1280
Yuan Dynasty	A.D. 1280-A.D. 1368
Ming Dynasty	A.D. 1368-A.D. 1643
Ch'ing Dynasty	A.D. 1644-A.D. 1912

JAPAN:

Jomon period	1000 B.C.- 200 B.C.
Yayoi period	200 B.C.-A.D. 500
Tumulus or Great Tomb period	A.D. 300-A.D. 700
Asuka period	A.D. 552-A.D. 645
Early Nara period	A.D. 645-A.D. 710
Nara period	A.D. 710-A.D. 794
Early Heian period	A.D. 794-A.D. 897
Heian or Fujiwara period	A.D. 897-A.D. 1185
Kamakura period	A.D. 1185-A.D. 1392
Ashikaga or Muromachi period	A.D. 1392-A.D. 1573
Momoyama period	A.D. 1573-A.D. 1615
Tokugawa period	A.D. 1615-A.D. 1868

CHINESE FURNITURE

	Price Range	
☐ Altar Table, Hardwood, rectangular top, carved and pierced end supports, 29" x 50"	1000.00	1400.00
☐ Altar Table, Hardwood, rectangular top, roll-over ends with straight carved legs, 36" x 5'6"	1400.00	1900.00
☐ Armchairs, Rectangular back panel painted with landscape, solid seat and straight legs, lacquered red and gold on brown ground, 19th century, pair	1800.00	2200.00
☐ Armoire, Red lacquered, rectangular cabinet with two red and gold doors on hardwood frame stand, 6' x 39½"	2200.00	2600.00
☐ Bed, Elaborate vermillion lacquered frame and canopy with figural panels, 7'4" x 7'4"	3000.00	3500.00

CHINESE FURNITURE

Price Range

☐ Cabinet, Rosewood, front enclosed with cupboard doors, carved fruitwood exotic birds and flowering bushes, 4'5" x 40" 475.00 575.00
☐ Chair, Side, carved Rosewood, solid back panel with bird and flowering branches, 19th century 225.00 325.00
☐ Club Chairs, Upholstered in black velvet, set of 4 .... 275.00 375.00
☐ Desk, Pedestal, carved wood, rounded corners, 3 drawers, deep relief with figural panels, 32" x 5'3" ... 1200.00 1800.00
☐ Dressing Table, Rectangular top, 3 drawers, above two pedestals with 3 drawers each. Drawer fronts lacquered in red and gold, 30" x 4'6" 500.00 600.00
☐ Floor Lamp, Hardwood, elaborately carved with pierced bracket supports and dragon-carved feet, 6'5" 150.00 225.00
☐ Panel, Lacquered red with gold, carved flowers, figures and precious objects, 4'6" x 45" 450.00 550.00
☐ Table, Console, rectangular hardwood top inset with blue and white porcelain plaque, straight legs with carved feet, 33½" H x 4'2½" L 2000.00 2500.00
☐ Table, Low circular, decorated in red and black lacquer with figures and scrollwork, 16" H x 31" D 450.00 550.00
☐ Table, Writing, black and gold lacquered, rectangular top with drawers and pair of cupboards on straight legs, 32" x 51" 2200.00 2800.00

CHINESE JADE

☐ Beaker, White jade bronze-form, slender ku with raised median knop, wood stand 5½" H 900.00 1200.00
☐ Bowl, Gray and brown jade dragon, 2 handles, wood stand, 5¾" D 250.00 300.00
☐ Brush Washer, Dark green jade, cluster of clouds, wood stand, 4¾" L 550.00 650.00
☐ Cats, White and gray, reclining in playful manner, 1¾" L 650.00 750.00
☐ Jade Elephant, Gray and brown, supporting on its back a small bronze form 150.00 200.00
☐ Jade Lotus, Grayish-white, undercut branches of blossoms and leafage, 4" L 325.00 400.00
☐ Jadelte Dragon Buckle, Paird of Ch'ih lung amid lotus scrolls in grayish-white, 4¾" L 2600.00 3400.00
☐ Jadeite Pendant, Small mottled apple green, carved and pierced with stems of leafage and tendrils, gold link, 1½" H 1800.00 2400.00
☐ Tripod Censer, White jade, Ch'ien Lung Period, petal-molded rim and three stump feet, wood stand, 5¼" D 2400.00 3200.00
☐ Vases, Lavender and Fei-ts'ui Jadeite miniature, green mottling and brown flecking, wood stand, 3" H, pair 575.00 675.00

CHINESE PAINTING

Price Range

- [ ] Birds and Flowering Branches, Hanging scroll, ink on silk, signed, late 15th-16th century, 36¼" x 14" 3500.00 4500.00
- [ ] Cat, Rock and Flowers, Hanging scroll, ink, tones of red, green, lilac, pink and white on silk, signed, 19th century, 48¼" x 13" 900.00 1200.00
- [ ] Ducks, Lotus and Millet, Hanging scroll, ink, tones of red and green on silk, signed, 105½" x 59½" 2400.00 3400.00
- [ ] Mountain Landscape with Travelers, Hanging scroll, ink, tones of red, green and blue on silk. K'ang Hsi period, signed, 77" x 40¼" 900.00 1400.00
- [ ] Nomadic Hunting Scene, Hanging scroll, ink, tones of red, yellow, green, grown, black and white on silk, framed, 18th century, 63" x 31¾" 700.00 1000.00
- [ ] Portrait of Lan Ts'Ai-Ho, Hanging scroll, ink, tones of red, green and white on silk. K!ang Hsi period, 44 1/2" x 19 5/8" 450.00 550.00
- [ ] Portrait of Lu Hsing, Hanging scroll, ink, silk. Character inscription, nineteen seals, 89 1/2" x 41 5/8" 800.00 1200.00
- [ ] Portrait of Shou Lao, Hanging scroll, ink, silk. Character inscription, nineteen seals, 89 1/2" x 41 5/8" 800.00 1200.00
- [ ] Rams, Three San Yang, hanging scroll, ink, tones of red and white on silk. Late 17th-18th century, 18 1/4" x 11 3/8" 375.00 475.00
- [ ] River Landscape with Scholar and Attendant, Hanging scroll, tones of green, red and white on silk. Late 16th-17th century, 47 1/2" x 20 1/8" 2200.00 3200.00
- [ ] Scholar Holding a Rock, Hanging scroll, ink, tones of blue and red, dated 1645, signed, 51¾" x 20¾" 1200.00 1800.00
- [ ] Spring Plowing, Handscroll, ink, tones of red, green and blue on silk, signed with seals, 18th century, 7¼" x 68¾" 550.00 650.00

CHINESE SNUFF BOTTLES

- [ ] Blue-Flecked, Animal mask, loop handles on edges with stopper 200.00 250.00
- [ ] Blue and White, With matching saucer, landscape scene, stopper and fitted box 400.00 500.00
- [ ] Double Overlay Glass, Milk white body, overlaid in yellow relief with a tasselled pi disc on either side with stopper 1000.00 1500.00
- [ ] Gilt-Bronze, Ear of maize with husk curled revealing the kernels with stopper 300.00 400.00
- [ ] Gold Fleck, Flattened form, black metal with gold markings and stopper 40.00 70.00
- [ ] Green Glass, Flattened form, foot and handles with dotted ju-i outline, a yin-yang medallion on both sides with stoper 700.00 850.00

CHINESE SNUFF BOTTLES

	Price Range	
☐ Interior-Painted Glass, Scene of a figure on horse firing an arrow at a bird and leading Chu Ko-liang and attendant through a snowy landscape, signed and dated 1900 with stopper	1000.00	1500.00
☐ Jade, Dot and grain pattern with stopper	300.00	400.00
☐ Jasper, Simulated, flattened form on oval foot in tones of brown, yellow and red with stopper	150.00	200.00
☐ Macaroni Agate, Pale brown translucent stone with stopper	650.00	750.00
☐ Overlay Glass, Opaque lemon yellow metal, red relief with bat above peaches with stopper	400.00	500.00
☐ Porcelain, Moulded pear shape, scaly dragon with stopper	300.00	450.00
☐ Red Overlay, Flattened form with fruiting peach trees growing from rocks with stopper	250.00	350.00
☐ Rock Crystal, Children playing beside rocks and bamboo, dated 2nd summer, 1968, with stopper	600.00	700.00
☐ White Jade, Standing on oval foot with saucer, stopper and fitted box	450.00	550.00
☐ Yi-Hsing, Oval foot, enamelled with house and landscape in blue and green tones with stopper	1200.00	1500.00
☐ Yi-Hsing, Side decorated with prunus blossom, reverse with bamboo, flat circular form with stopper .	1000.00	1200.00

JAPANESE NETSUKE

☐ Figure of Sennin, Bisque, porcelain figure standing and a gourd on his shoulder, unsigned	175.00	225.00
☐ Flower, Ebony, form of an open flower, silver studs in the center, 19th century, unsigned	225.00	300.00
☐ Horn Ashtray, Bowl formed by dragon with metal inlaid eyes, unsigned	425.00	500.00
☐ Karako, Wood figure, youth beating on drum, 19th century, unsigned	300.00	375.00
☐ Mask, Man smiling wearing a soft cap, 19th century, signed	100.00	150.00
☐ Mask, Wood carving, open mouth and protruding inlaid eyes, one larger mask and one smaller, unsigned	275.00	325.00
☐ Monkey, Feet crossed forming himotoshi, arms across eyes, "see no evil", 19th century, signed	350.00	425.00
☐ Mother and Child, Slender woman bare-footed wearing a kimono, holding baby boy in her arms, 19th century, unsigned	350.00	400.00
☐ Mother and Children, Wood group, woman with child strapped to her back and holding a smaller child in her arms, signed	150.00	225.00
☐ Rat Group, Adult and two smaller rats munching on berries, 19th century, unsigned	600.00	700.00
☐ Snake, Ebony, coiled about itself, textured skin, inlaid horn eyes, 11th century, unsigned	550.00	600.00

JAPANESE NETSUKE

	Price	Range
☐ Turtle, Wooden group, adult turtle on lotus leaf with two smaller turtles on its back, 19th century, signed .	2000.00	2500.00
☐ Tiger, Wood, seated with its head turned backwards, tail across the back, 19th century, signed	625.00	675.00
☐ Wood Group Playing Co., Hermits both wearing garments seated on oval base on either side of go aboard, 19th century, signed	400.00	475.00

JAPANESE IVORY NETSUKE

☐ Buddha, Solid, seated with pendulous earlobes and loose robes, nose worn away, 18th century, unsigned	175.00	250.00
☐ Cat, Wearing a bib, looking into discarded paper lantern while mouse escapes, 19th-20th century, signed	400.00	500.00
☐ Erotic Group, Amorous man and woman, unsigned . .	425.00	525.00
☐ Figure of a Sennin, Puzzled expression with hand on his head, 18th century, unsigned	325.00	400.00
☐ Hotei, Seated with one knee raised, wearing loose robe, holding tama in palm, 18th century, signed	700.00	800.00
☐ Hunter, Wearing short belted tunic and straw hood, carries sword and smiling monkey, 18th century	700.00	800.00
☐ Kinko, seated on carp, reading form a scroll, wearing robe and soft cap, 19th century, signed	375.00	475.00
☐ Marine Cluster, Two fish, a squid and an octopus, eyes are inlaid horn, 19th century, signed	525.00	625.00
☐ Mask Cluster, Depicting No Drama characters, 19th century, signed	475.00	575.00
☐ Okame Mask, Chubby face with black hair and two black dots on her forehead, 19th century, signed	275.00	325.00
☐ Puppy, Playing with rump in air, inlaid eyes, carved ear, signed	475.00	575.00
☐ Sake Cup, Three characters seated back to back, 19th century, signed	625.00	725.00
☐ Sage, Seated, wearing a skull cap and leaning against a table, 18th century, unsigned	325.00	425.00
☐ Tennin, Angel in flight beating on drum, signed	525.00	625.00
☐ Wolf, Forepaw resting on skull, 19th century, signed .	175.00	250.00

OWLS

Owls have appeared on objects since the Romans put them on their coins. Owls are symbols of wisdom, and have thus appealed to scholars. Sometimes owls are seen perched on top of a skull — a sculpture guaranteed to inspire a poet, maybe, to frighten most of us.

	Price
☐ Book Ends, Rookwood, tan glaze, pair	105.00
☐ Book Rack, expanding, cast brass, 2 owls	35.00
☐ Doorstop, carved wood w/glass, 1920's	20.00
☐ Fairy Lamp, bisque, owl face, glass eyes, 4½" H	150.00
☐ Inkwell, alabaster, owl on pile of books, 19th century	110.00

OWLS Price

☐ Jar, Atterbuy opal glass, inserted red eyes, 7" H 125.00
☐ Painting, primitive, 2 owls, late 19th century 100.00
☐ Stickpin, gold, 2 diamond chip eyes, 14k 125.00

PAPER MONEY

While some people prefer to collect coins, because anything made of precious metals has some intrinsic value, other collectors are fascinated by the splendid printing techniques—the engraving and the colors of paper money. They collect by date and are very aware of all kinds of things which most people would never notice, such as signatures, and minor differences in design. Please consult our publication, *The Official Blackbook Price Guide of United States Paper Money* for more prices and information.

ONE DOLLAR NOTES (1918) FEDERAL RESERVE BANK NOTES (Large Size)

BANK & CITY	GOV'T SIGNATURES	BANK SIGNATURES	A.B.P.	GOOD	V. FINE	UNC.
☐ Phila.	Teehee-Burke	Hardt-Passmore	6.00	12.00	25.00	100.00
☐ Phila.	Teehee-Burke	Dyer-Passmore	6.50	12.50	30.00	75.00
☐ Phila.	Elliot-Burke	Dyer-Passmore	7.50	15.00	35.00	90.00
☐ Phila.	Elliot-Burke	Dyer-Norris	4.50	10.00	25.00	65.00
☐ Cleveland	Teehee-Burke	Baxter-Fancher	4.50	10.00	20.00	55.00
☐ Cleveland	Teehee-Burke	Davis-Fancher	5.00	10.00	25.00	65.00
☐ Cleveland	Elliott-Burke	Davis-Fancher	4.50	10.00	20.00	55.00
☐ Richmond	Teehee-Burke	Keesee-Seay	7.00	14.00	27.50	80.00
☐ Richmond	Elliott-Burke	Keesee-Seay	7.00	14.00	27.50	80.00
☐ Atlanta	Teehee-Burke	Pike-McCord	4.50	10.00	25.00	65.00
☐ Atlanta	Teehee-Burke	Bell-McCord	7.50	15.00	40.00	90.00
☐ Atlanta	Teehee-Burke	Bell-Wellborn	6.50	12.50	25.00	75.00
☐ Atlanta	Elliott-Burke	Bell-Wellborn	6.50	12.50	25.00	75.00
☐ Chicago	Teehee-Burke	McCloud-McDougal	4.50	10.00	20.00	55.00
☐ Chicago	Teehee-Burke	Cramer-McDougal	6.00	12.00	25.00	65.00
☐ Chicago	Elliott-Burke	Cramer-McDougal	4.50	1000	20.00	55.00
☐ St. Louis	Teehee-Burke	Attebery-Wells	7.50	15.00	35.00	150.00
☐ St. Louis	Teehee-Burke	Attebery-Biggs	7.50	15.00	30.00	125.00
☐ St. Louis	Elliott-Burke	Attebery-Biggs	6.40	12.50	30.00	80.00

ONE DOLLAR NOTES (1918—Large Size)

BANK & CITY	GOV'T SIGNATURES	BANK SIGNATURES	A.B.P.	GOOD	V. FINE	UNC.
☐ St. Louis	Elliott-Burke	White-Biggs	6.50	12.50	30.00	85.00
☐ Minneapolis	Teehee-Burke	Cook-Wold	12.00	20.00	60.00	250.00
☐ Minneapolis	Teehee-Burke	Cook-Young	50.00	100.00	500.00	1000.00
☐ Minneapolis	Elliott-Burke	Cook-Young	12.00	20.00	60.00	200.00
☐ Kan. City	Teehee-Burke	Anderson-Miller	6.00	12.00	25.00	100.00
☐ Kan. City	Elliott-Burke	Anderson-Miller	6.00	12.00	30.00	125.00
☐ Kan. City	Elliott-Burke	Helm-Miller	6.00	12.00	25.00	75.00
☐ Dallas	Teehee-Burke	Talley-VanZandt	6.50	12.50	30.00	95.00
☐ Dallas	Elliott-Burke	Talley-VanZandt	17.50	30.00	100.00	450.00
☐ Dallas	Elliott-Burke	Lawder-VanZandt	6.50	12.50	30.00	150.00
☐ San Fran.	Teehee-Burke	Clerk-Lynch	6.50	12.50	25.00	100.00
☐ San Fran.	Teehee-Burke	Clerk-Calkins	6.50	12.50	25.00	80.00
☐ San Fran.	Elliott-Burke	Calkins	6.50	12.50	30.00	125.00
☐ San Fran.	Elliott-Burke	Ambrose-Calkins	6.50	12.50	30.00	125.00

FIVE DOLLAR NOTES (1914) FEDERAL RESERVE BANK NOTES (Large Size)
Series of 1914 with Blue Treasury Seal and Blue Numbers.

SERIES	CITY	SIGNATURES	SEAL	A.B.P.	GOOD	V. FINE	UNC.
☐ 1914	Boston	Burke-McAdoo	Blue	6.00	10.00	15.00	75.00
☐ 1914	Boston	Burke-Glass	Blue	7.50	15.00	20.00	85.00
☐ 1914	Boston	Burke-Houston	Blue	6.00	10.00	16.50	75.00
☐ 1914	Boston	Burke-Houston	Blue	6.00	10.00	16.50	75.00
☐ 1914	Boston	White-Mellon	Blue	6.00	10.00	16.50	75.00
☐ 1914	New York	Burke-McAdoo	Blue	6.00	10.00	16.50	75.00
☐ 1914	New York	Burke-Glass	Blue	6.50	12.50	20.00	75.00
☐ 1914	New York	Burke-Houston	Blue	6.00	10.00	16.50	75.00
☐ 1914	New York	White-Mellon	Blue	6.00	10.00	16.50	75.00
☐ 1914	Phila.	Burke-McAdoo	Blue	6.00	10.00	16.50	75.00
☐ 1914	Phila.	Burke-Glass	Blue	6.50	12.50	20.00	80.00
☐ 1914	Phila.	Burke-Houston	Blue	6.00	10.00	16.50	75.00
☐ 1914	Phila.	White-Mellon	Blue	6.00	10.00	16.50	80.00
☐ 1914	Cleveland	Burke-McAdoo	Blue	6.00	10.00	16.50	80.00
☐ 1914	Cleveland	Burke-Glass	Blue	6.00	12.50	20.00	85.00
☐ 1914	Cleveland	Burke-Houston	Blue	6.00	10.00	16.50	75.00
☐ 1914	Cleveland	White-Mellon	Blue	6.00	10.00	16.50	75.00
☐ 1914	Richmond	Burke-McAdoo	Blue	6.50	12.50	20.00	80.00
☐ 1914	Richmond	Burke-Glass	Blue	6.50	12.50	20.00	100.00
☐ 1914	Richmond	Burke-Houston	Blue	6.50	12.00	17.50	80.00
☐ 1914	Richmond	White-Mellon	Blue	6.50	12.00	17.50	75.00
☐ 1914	Atlanta	Burke-McAdoo	Blue	6.00	10.00	16.50	75.00
☐ 1914	Atlanta	Burke-Glass	Blue	7.50	15.00	25.00	100.00
☐ 1914	Atlanta	Burke-Houston	Blue	6.00	10.00	16.50	75.00
☐ 1914	Atlanta	White-Mellon	Blue	6.00	10.00	16.50	75.00
☐ 1914	Chicago	Burke-McAdoo	Blue	6.00	10.00	16.50	75.00
☐ 1914	Chicago	Burke-Glass	Blue	6.50	12.50	20.00	85.00
☐ 1914	Chicago	Burke-Houston	Blue	6.00	10.00	16.50	75.00
☐ 1914	Chicago	White-Mellon	Blue	6.00	10.00	16.50	75.00
☐ 1914	St. Louis	Burke-McAdoo	Blue	6.00	10.00	16.50	75.00
☐ 1914	St. Louis	Burke-Glass	Blue	6.50	12.50	20.00	90.00
☐ 1914	St. Louis	Burke-Houston	Blue	6.00	10.00	16.50	35.00

TEN DOLLAR NOTES (1914) BLUE SEALS & NUMBERS (Large Size)

	CITY	SIGNATURES	SEAL	A.B.P.	V. FINE	UNC.
☐	Boston	Burke-McAdoo	Blue	15.00	30.00	60.00
☐	Boston	Burke-Glass	Blue	20.00	40.00	70.00
☐	Boston	Burke-Houston	Blue	15.00	30.00	60.00
☐	Boston	White-Mellon	Blue	15.00	30.00	60.00
☐	New York	Burke-McAdoo	Blue	15.00	30.00	60.00
☐	New York	Burke-Glass	Blue	20.00	40.00	70.00
☐	New York	Burke-Houston	Blue	15.00	30.00	60.00
☐	New York	White-Mellon	Blue	15.00	30.00	60.00
☐	Philadelphia	Burke-McAdoo	Blue	15.00	30.00	60.00
☐	Philadelphia	Burke-Glass	Blue	15.00	30.00	60.00
☐	Philadelphia	Burke-Houston	Blue	15.00	30.00	60.00
☐	Philadelphia	White-Mellon	Blue	15.00	30.00	60.00
☐	Cleveland	Burke-McAdoo	Blue	15.00	30.00	60.00
☐	Cleveland	Burke-Glass	Blue	15.00	30.00	60.00
☐	Cleveland	Burke-Houston	Blue	15.00	30.00	60.00
☐	Cleveland	White-Mellon	Blue	15.00	30.00	60.00
☐	Richmond	Burke-McAdoo	Blue	15.00	30.00	60.00
☐	Richmond	Burke-Glass	Blue	15.00	30.00	60.00
☐	Richmond	Burke-Houston	Blue	15.00	30.00	60.00
☐	Richmond	White-Mellon	Blue	15.00	30.00	60.00
☐	Atlanta	Burke-McAdoo	Blue	15.00	30.00	60.00
☐	Atlanta	Burke-Glass	Blue	20.00	40.00	70.00
☐	Atlanta	Burke-Houston	Blue	15.00	30.00	60.00
☐	Atlanta	White-Mellon	Blue	15.00	30.00	60.00
☐	Chicago	Burke-McAdoo	Blue	15.00	30.00	60.00
☐	Chicago	Burke-Glass	Blue	15.00	30.00	60.00
☐	Chicago	Burke-Houston	Blue	15.00	30.00	60.00
☐	Chicago	White-Mellon	Blue	15.00	30.00	60.00
☐	St. Louis	Burke-McAdoo	Blue	15.00	30.00	60.00
☐	St. Louis	Burke-Glass	Blue	15.00	30.00	60.00
☐	St. Louis	Burke-Houston	Blue	15.00	30.00	60.00
☐	St. Louis	White-Mellon	Blue	15.00	30.00	60.00
☐	Minneapolis	Burke-McAdoo	Blue	15.00	30.00	60.00
☐	Minneapolis	Burke-Glass	Blue	15.00	30.00	60.00
☐	Minneapolis	Burke-Houston	Blue	15.00	30.00	60.00
☐	Minneapolis	White-Mellon	Blue	15.00	30.00	60.00
☐	Kansas City	Burke-McAdoo	Blue	15.00	30.00	60.00
☐	Kansas City	Burke-Glass	Blue	20.00	40.00	70.00
☐	Kansas City	Burke-Houston	Blue	15.00	30.00	60.00
☐	Kansas City	White-Mellon	Blue	15.00	30.00	60.00
☐	Dallas	Burke-McAdoo	Blue	15.00	30.00	60.00
☐	Dallas	Burke-Glass	Blue	15.00	30.00	60.00
☐	Dallas	Burke-Houston	Blue	15.00	30.00	60.00
☐	Dallas	White-Mellon	Blue	15.00	30.00	60.00
☐	San Francisco	Burke-McAdoo	Blue	15.00	30.00	60.00
☐	San Francisco	Burke-Glass	Blue	20.00	40.00	70.00
☐	San Francisco	Burke-Houston	Blue	15.00	30.00	60.00
☐	San Francisco	White-Mellon	Blue	15.00	30.00	60.00

PAPERWEIGHTS

The name paperweight does not do justice to this fascinating area of collectibles. Paperweights are not only functional but they represent an interesting art form. Some are made of beautiful brilliant glass and in the past only the wealthy collected paperweights — today anyone can enjoy collecting them.

DOGWOOD, STATE FLOWER
SERIES, *Francis Dyer
Whittemore, Jr.*
.... 250.00 - 350.00

BACCARAT, LORRAINE,
FRANCE, "STRAWBERRIES"
.... 400.00 - 500.00

	Price Range	
☐ Baccarat, millefiorm canes on ground	130.00	150.00
☐ Baccarat, mushroom double overlay	260.00	290.00
☐ Baccarat, pansy	425.00	475.00
☐ Banford, pendant, animal figures	50.00	75.00
☐ Clichy, millefiori canes on turquoise ground	550.00	600.00
☐ Clichy, star garlands on rose cane	1400.00	1600.00
☐ D'Albret, cameo of Jenny Lind	80.00	100.00
☐ D'Albret, Prince Charles, the Prince of Wales	85.00	100.00
☐ Fruit Weight, white ground	400.00	450.00
☐ Lundberg Studios, butterfly	55.00	75.00
☐ Lundberg Studios, sunflower	55.00	75.00
☐ Perthshire, millefiori, factory signature in cane	35.00	40.00
☐ Perthshire, millefiori, with 6 clusters of canes	110.00	130.00
☐ Stankard, wild rose, single flower	260.00	300.00
☐ Stankard, yellow meadowreath, single flower	260.00	300.00
☐ St. Louis, flower with 5 petals, orange ground	225.00	250.00
☐ St. Louis, red cherries on white basket	360.00	400.00
☐ St. Louis, white dahlia, mauve ground	220.00	260.00
☐ Whittemore, iris, Tennessee state flower	370.00	400.00
☐ Whittemore, wild prairie rose, North Dakota state flower	420.00	460.00

Courtesy: L.H. Selman, Santa Cruz, CA.

PENNY ARCADE COLLECTIBLES

Price Range

☐ Ticket, "Admit One to George C. Tillyou's Steeple-
case," Coney Island, Brooklyn, New York, c. 1940 .... 2.00 3.00
☐ Baseball game, electric. "Deposit 2¢." Cast-lead
pitcher throws ball, player pushes button to activate
batsman, "Fielders" include Cochrane, Gehrig,
Simmons and other stars of c. 1930 .... 4000.00 5000.00
☐ "Test Your Strength" machine. Deposit 1¢. Squeeze
handles 500.00 750.00
☐ "Fortune Teller" machine (sometimes called "Gypsy
Fortune Teller"). Nearly life-size half-length figure of
a woman, dark gown. Deposit 2¢. Woman moves
hand, takes card with printed fortune, passes it to
person 2000.00 3000.00
☐ Flip-picture machine. Deposit 5¢, turn crank, look in
viewer; pictures flip to give the appear of a movie.
World War I era (but these were still in use as late
as the 1960's) 900.00 1000.00
☐ Wooden duck from shooting gallery, target painted on
side, 8" long, c. 1940 .... 10.00 15.00

PENS AND PENCILS

Writing instruments are the hand-held implements which for centuries have recorded man's thoughts and mirrored his technical ingenuity. Specimens of writing brushes and pens date back over 4,000 years.

A few words of advice for the novice collector who wishes to write with the items in his collection. Buy as perfect examples as you can afford. All mechanical pencils should operate and fountain pens should have smooth writing nibs because spare parts and repairs are very difficult to obtain. There are probably less than 100 professionally skilled writing instrument repair persons practicing their trade in the United States today.

It is recommended that serious collectors join the national organization created to assist them: The Pen Fancier's Club, Post Office Box 413, Clearwater, Florida 33517. Mr. Cliff Lawrence, the National President, has written an excellent reference text, *Fountain Pens — History, Repair, and Current Values,* which is available through the club. Members receive a monthly newsletter, can purchase small lots of rubber sacs for their pens, and can participate in the Pen Trading Post in addition to communicating with their fellow collectors.

PARKER PENS

PENS AND PENCILS
ABBREVIATIONS FOR DESCRIPTION, METHOD OF FILLING, AND CONDITION

BC	- barrel and cap	M	- mint condition (like new)
BF	- button actuated filler	MBL	- marble-like plastic
CBHR	- chased black hard rubber	O	- overlay
E	- excellent condition	P	- poor condition
ED	- eyedropper filled	PF	- plunger filled
F	- fair condition	R	- ribbon
G	- good condition		(ladies model/ring on top)
GF	- gold filled	S	- sterling silver
GL	- gold-like (or plated)	SBHR	- smooth black hard rubber
GS14	- 14kt solid gold	SL	- silver-like (or plated)
GS18	- 18kt solid gold	T	- trim
HR	- hard rubber		(clip, decorative bands, etc.)
LF	- lever actuated filler	W	- working condition

Example · 1899 Parker No. 20 pen, SBHR-ED-EW would be a Model 20 fountain pen manufactured by the Parker Pen Company; shown in their 1899 catalog; with a barrel and cap made from smooth black hard rubber; filled by removing the front of the pen and dropping ink into the barrell with an eyedropper; and in excellent working condition.

	Price
☐ 1899 Parker No. 20 pen, SBHR-ED-EW	25.00
☐ 1903 Moore Non-Leakable pen, CBHR-ED-EW	36.00
☐ 1904 Diamond Point pen, CBHR-"coin-filler"-EW	25.00
☐ 1905 Laughlin pen, SO-ED-EW	40.00
☐ 1905 F.H. Mooney pen, GFO-EW	30.00
☐ 1913 Waterman No. 12-1/2 "PSF" pen, SBHR-SLT-LF-FW	20.00
☐ 1913 Waterman No. 52V pen, CBHR-SLT-LF-MW	20.00
☐ 1913 Waterman No. 52V-1/2 R-pen, CBHR-SLT-LF-MW	20.00
☐ 1913 Waterman No. 54 pen, CBHR-SLT-LF-EW	30.00
☐ 1914 Waterman No. 52 pen, CBHR-SLT-LF-GW	12.00
☐ 1915 Parker No. 48 R-pen, GFBC-BF-E	50.00
☐ 1915 Waterman No. 52V pen, CBHR (unusual pocket clip starts with globe on cap top)-SLT-LF-MW	30.00
☐ 1915 Waterman No. 452-1/2V R-pen, SO-FW................	28.00
☐ 1917 Waterman No. 52 pen, CBHR (wide clip)-SLT-LF-EW	20.00
☐ 1917 Waterman No. 54 pen, CBHR-SLT-LF-MW	20.00

PENS AND PENCILS

Price

☐ 1918 Wahl pen, SO-ED-GW	25.00
☐ 1918 Waterman No. 55 pen, CBHR-SLT-LF-MW	65.00
☐ 1918 Waterman No. 454 pen and pencil, S (floral engraving) LF-EW	175.00
☐ 1919 Sheaffer R-pen, GFBC-LF-E (scratched section)	10.00
☐ 1920 Dunn pen, black with red barrel end-GLT	5.00
☐ 1920 Eversharp pencil, SL-EW	5.00
☐ 1920 Sheaffer R-pencil, GF-EW	8.00
☐ 1920 Waterman No. 52V pen, CBHR (original price sticker) SLT-LF-MW	20.00
☐ 1920 Waterman No. 52V pen, CBHR-SLT-LF-MW	18.00
☐ 1920 Waterman No. 52V pen, CBHR-SLT-LF-EW	15.00
☐ 1920 Waterman No. 52-1/2V R-pen, SBHR-GLT-LF-GW	10.00
☐ 1921 Sheaffer R-pencil, S-GW	8.00
☐ 1922 Parker Duofold Jr., pen, red HR-initial model-BF-E	50.00
☐ 1922 Wahl pen, GFBC-LF-EW	10.00
☐ 1922 Waterman No. 52 pen, CBHR-SLT-LF-EW	16.00
☐ 1923 Conklin pen, SBHR-"crescent filler"-GLT-F with E nib	8.00
☐ 1923 Moore No. L-92 pen, SBHR-GLT-MW	30.00
☐ 1923 Parker Duofold Jr., pen, red-HR-BF-E	35.00
☐ 1923 Parker Duofold "Bid Red" pen, red-HR-BF-MW	90.00
☐ 1923 Shaeffer "White Dot" pen, green jade-GLT-LF-GW	50.00
☐ 1923 Wahl Eversharp pen and pencil, GF-LF-M	18.00
☐ 1923 Wahl Eversharp R-pen and pencil, GF-LF-M (in box)	15.00
☐ 1923 Wahl Eversharp R-pencil, GF-EW	5.00
☐ 1923 Wahl pen, GF-LF-EW	35.00
☐ 1923 Waterman No. 7 pen, red ripple HR-GLT-wide clip-LF-EW	65.00
☐ 1923 Waterman No. 55 pen, red ripple HR-GLT-wide clip-LF-GW	50.00
☐ 1924 Parker Duofold Jr., pen, red HR-GLT-BF-EW	30.00
☐ 1924 Parker Duofold Special pen, red HR-GLT-BF-MW	40.00
☐ 1924 Parker Duofold "Big Red" pen, red HR-GLT-BF-GW	50.00
☐ 1924 Sheaffer "White Dot" R-pen, green jade-GLT-LF-GW	15.00
☐ 1924 Sheaffer "White Dot" R-pen, green jade-GLT-LF-MW	25.00
☐ 1924 Wahl pen, GF-LF-GW	8.00
☐ 1924 Wahl Eversharp R-pencil, EW	6.00
☐ 1924 Wahl Eversharp pencil, S(floral engraving)-MW	25.00
☐ 1924 Waterman No. 52 pen, red ripple HR-GLT-wide clip-LF-EW	20.00
☐ 1925 Conklin Endura R-pen, green MBL-GLT-LF-MW	25.00
☐ 1925 Conklin Endura R-pen, brown MBL-GLT-LF-EW	22.00
☐ 1925 Parker Duofold Jr., pen, red HR-BF-EW	30.00
☐ 1925 Sheaffer "White Dot" pen, green jade-GLT-LF-EW	40.00
☐ Sheaffer "White Dot" pen, black-GLT-LF-EW	45.00
☐ 1925 Sheaffer "White Dot" R-pen, black-GLT-LF-MW	18.00
☐ 1925 Sheaffer pen, green jade-GLT-LF-EW with lifetime nib	10.00
☐ 1925 Wahl pen, GF-LF-EW	12.00
☐ 1926 Marxton pen, green MBL-GLT-GW	8.00
☐ 1926 Parker pencil, green jade-GLT-GW	10.00
☐ 1926 Sheaffer "White Dot" large pen, pearl & black -GLT-LF-EW	65.00
☐ 1926 Sheaffer "White Dot" small pen, pearl & black-GLT-LF-EW	27.00

PENS AND PENCILS
Price

- [ ] 1926 Sheaffer pen, green jade-LF-EW 15.00
- [ ] 1926 Wahl R-pen, S with GF-LF-MW 30.00
- [ ] 1926 Wahl pen, GF-LF-roller clip 22.00
- [ ] 1926 Waterman No. 5 pen, red ripple HR-GLT-LF-EW 16.00
- [ ] 1927 Chilton pen, SBHR-GLT-PF-E 12.00
- [ ] 1927 Grieshaber pen, pearl & black-EW 45.00
- [ ] 1927 Parker Duofold Sr., pen, green jade-BF-EW 50.00
- [ ] 1927 Parker Duofold Jr., pen, green jade-BF-EW 25.00
- [ ] 1927 Sheaffer "White Dot" pen, green jade-GLT-LF-MW 65.00
- [ ] 1927 Wahl Eversharp "Big Boy" pencil, wood grain-GLT-EW . . 8.00
- [ ] 1927 Waterman No. 5 pen, black-SLT-LF-EW 15.00
- [ ] 1928 Wahl Eversharp "Gold Seal" pen & pencil,
  pearl & black-GLT-MW 50.00
- [ ] 1929 Parker Lady Duofold pen, pearl & black MBL-GLT-BF-EW 22.00
- [ ] 1929 Parker Lady Duofold pen, red-BF-EW 30.00
- [ ] 1929 Parker Lady Duofold pen, green jade-BF-pocket clip-EW . 25.00
- [ ] 1929 Waterman Lady Patricia pen, S-LF-GW 40.00
- [ ] 1929 Waterman Lady Patricia pen, onyx & terra cotta
  GLT-LF-EW 15.00
- [ ] 1930 Parker Lady Duofold Streamlined pen, green
  MBL-GLT-BF-MW 20.00
- [ ] 1930 Sheaffer "White Dot" R-pen, pearl & black MBL,
  GLT-LF-GW 20.00
- [ ] 1930 Sheaffer "White Dot" Streamlined pen, black-GLT-LF-EW 50.00
- [ ] 1930 Sheaffer R-pen, pearl & black-LF-EW 25.00
- [ ] 1930 Wahl Eversharp R-pen, pearl & black MBL-GLT-LF-EW . . . 10.00
- [ ] 1930 (Wahl) Eversharp "Gold Seal" pencil, pearl & black
  GLT-EW 15.00
- [ ] 1930 Waterman No. 5 pen, black-GLT-GW 10.00
- [ ] 1931 Eversharp Doric pen, black-EW 12.00
- [ ] 1931 Parker Duofold Streamlined pen, burgandy
  MBL-GLT-BF-EW 25.00
- [ ] 1931 Parker Duofold "Big Red" pen, red-BF-EW 35.00
- [ ] 1931 Parker Duofold pen, green jade-BF-MW 25.00
- [ ] 1931 Parker Duofold pencil, green jade-MW 12.00
- [ ] 1931 Sheaffer "White Dot" combination pen & pencil,
  black-GLT-LF 40.00
- [ ] 1931 Sheaffer "White Dot" pen, green MBL-GLT-LF-GW 15.00
- [ ] 1932 Parker Duofold Streamlined pen, black-GLT-BF-EW 35.00
- [ ] 1932 Parker Parkette pen, black-GLT-LF-FW 2.00
- [ ] 1932 Sheaffer pen, green jade-GLT-LF-EW 10.00
- [ ] 1932 Waterman No. 92V pen, burgandy pearl MBL-GLT-LF-EW 8.00
- [ ] 1933 Chilton pen, black-GLT-EW 25.00
- [ ] 1933 Parker Vacumatic pen, burgandy-GLT-BF-G 5.00
- [ ] 1933 Parker Parkette pen, red & silver MBL-GLT-LF-EW 4.00
- [ ] 1933 Waterman No. 5 pen & pencil, black-GLT-LF-EW 25.00
- [ ] 1934 Parker Vacumatic pen, burgandy & black-GLT-BF-EW . . . 25.00
- [ ] 1935 Eversharp Midget pen, green MBL-GLT-E 4.00
- [ ] 1935 Parker Duofold pen, green & black-GLT-BF-EW 10.00

PENS AND PENCILS

Price

- [ ] Sheaffer desk pen with "Pen used by President Roosevelt to sign Guffey-Snyder Coal Bill Aug. 30, 1935" engraved on it.... 25.00
- [ ] 1935 Waterman No. 94 pen, green & brown MBL-GLT-LF-EW .. 15.00
- [ ] 1936 Cameleon two-nib pen, salmon-GLT-EW 25.00
- [ ] 1936 Packard combination pen and pencil, red MBL-LF-GLT-MW-boxed................................ 5.00
- [ ] 1936 Parker Duofold pen, green & black-SLT-BF-EW 6.00
- [ ] 1936 Parker Challenger pen, green MBL-LF-EW 7.00
- [ ] 1936 Ronson Penciliter, rodium plate & green MBL-EW 25.00
- [ ] 1936 Sheaffer "White Dot" pen & pencil, red & black-GLT-LF-GW 35.00
- [ ] 1936 Sheaffer "White Dot" pen, black-GLT-LF-EW 45.00
- [ ] 1936 Wahl Oxford pen, green jade-GLT-EW 8.00
- [ ] 1936 Waterman No. 3V pen, red & gray MBL-SLT-LF-EW...... 5.00
- [ ] 1936 Waterman No. 92 pen & pencil, red & green MBL-GLT-LF-GW 12.00
- [ ] 1937 Parker Vacumatic pen, blue & black, GLT-BF-MW....... 22.00
- [ ] 1937 Sheaffer pen, green & black-GLT-LF-EW 10.00
- [ ] 1937 Sheaffer "White Dot" pen, black-GLT-LF-GW 8.00
- [ ] 1937 Sheaffer "White Dot" pen, silver & black-SLT-LF-EW 50.00
- [ ] 1938 Parker Duofold pen, gold & black-GLT-BF-EW 6.00
- [ ] 1938 Sheaffer pen, grey & black-SLT-LF-GW 5.00
- [ ] 1938 Waterman No. 32 pen, black-SLT-LF-GW 3.00
- [ ] 1939 Parker "Blue Diamond" Major Vacumatic, silver & black-BF-MW................................ 15.00
- [ ] 1939 Parker Challenger pen, pearl MBL-LF-MW 7.00
- [ ] 1939 Sheaffer "White Dot" pen, gold 7 black-GLT-PF-EW 12.00
- [ ] 1939 Waterman No. 32X pen, black-SLT-LF 6.00
- [ ] 1940 Parker Challenger pen, green MBL-LF-GW 4.00
- [ ] 1940 Sheaffer "White Dot" Crest pen & pencil, black-LF-EW .. 25.00
- [ ] 1940 Waterman pen, black-SLT-LF-EW.................... 2.00
- [ ] 1940 Waterman pen, black-GLT-LF-EW.................... 5.00
- [ ] 1942 Parker Vacumatic pen, black-GLT-BF-EW (unique blind cap) 20.00
- [ ] 1942 Parker "Blue Diamond" "51" pen, black-GF, cap-BF-EW . 15.00
- [ ] 1942 Parker "Blue Diamond" "51" pen, blue-S cap-BF-EW 12.00
- [ ] 1942 Sheaffer Crest Triumph pen, black-GF, cap-PF-GW 12.00
- [ ] 1942 Sheaffer "White Dot" Triumph lady's pen, gray & black-SLT-PF-EW 20.00
- [ ] 1942 Sheaffer "White Dot" Triumph pen, green & black-GLT-PF-EW 15.00
- [ ] 1942 Sheaffer "White Dot" Triumph pen, silver & black-SLT-PF-GW 12.00
- [ ] 1942 Sheaffer "White Dot" pen, green & black-GLT-PF-GW ... 5.00
- [ ] 1943 Eversharp "64" pen & pencil, black-GS14 caps-LF-MW-boxed 55.00
- [ ] 1943 Eversharp "64" pen & pencil, black-GS14 caps LF-MW 32.00
- [ ] 1943 Parker "Blue Diamond" "51" pen, gray-S cap BF-MW.... 25.00

PENS AND PENCILS
Price

- [ ] 1943 Sheaffer "White Dot" Triumph pen, black-GS14 band on cap-PF-GW 12.00
- [ ] 1944 Parker "Blue Diamond" Vacumatic pen, blue & black-GLT-BF-MW 20.00
- [ ] 1944 Parker "Blue Diamond" Vacumatic pen, gold & black-GLT-BF-MW 9.00
- [ ] 1944 Parker "Blue Diamond" "51" pen, black-stainless cap-BF-EW 12.00
- [ ] 1944 Sheaffer "White Dot" Triumph Tuckaway pen, black-GLT-PF-GW 12.00
- [ ] 1945 Eversharp Skyline pen, green-GF cap-LF-EW 9.00
- [ ] 1945 Eversharp Skyline pen, gray-GF cap-LF-EW............ 8.00
- [ ] 1945 Eversharp Skyline pen, black-GLT-LF-EW 5.00
- [ ] 1945 Eversharp Skyline pen, burgundy-LF-EW 5.00
- [ ] 1945 Eversharp Skyline pen, black-green & black cap-LF-EW .. 5.00
- [ ] 1945 Parker "Blue Diamond" Vacumatic pen, silver & black-SLT-E 12.00
- [ ] 1945 Parker "Blue Diamond" "51" pen, green-stainless cap-BF-EW 12.00
- [ ] 1945 Parker Vacumatic pen, green & black-BF-MW 8.00
- [ ] 1945 Sheaffer "White Dot" Crest Triumph pen, black-GF cap-LF-MW 20.00
- [ ] 1945 Sheaffer Tuckaway pen & pencil, green & black-LF-MW .. 20.00
- [ ] 1946 Parker Vacumatic pen & pencil, green & black-BF-MW-boxed 15.00
- [ ] 1946 Sheaffer "White Dot" Crest Triumph pen, blue-GF cap-MW 25.00
- [ ] 1946 Sheaffer "White Dot" pen, black-GLT-LF-GW 10.00
- [ ] 1946 Sheaffer "White Dot" Sentinel Triumph Deluxe pen, pencil, and stratowriter, blue-chrome & GF caps-PF-EW 30.00
- [ ] 1946 Sheaffer "White Dot" Tuckaway, blue-chrome & GF cap-PF-MW 15.00
- [ ] 1946 Sheaffer "White Dot" Triumph pen, blue-GLT-PF-MW-price sticker 18.00
- [ ] 1946 Sheaffer "White Dot" Triumph pen, brown-GLT-PF-MW-price sticker 15.00
- [ ] 1946 Sheaffer "White Dot" pen, black-GLT-GW 10.00
- [ ] 1946 Waterman pen, gray MBL-SLT-LT-GW 5.00
- [ ] 1947 Sheaffer "White Dot" Tuckaway, black-GF cap-PF-EW .. 18.00
- [ ] 1947 Sheaffer "White Dot" Triumph pen, brown-SL & GF cap-PF-MW 22.00
- [ ] 1947 Waterman pen, black-SL & GL cap-LF-EW 6.00
- [ ] 1948 Parker "51" Special pen, gray-chrome cap-EW 5.00
- [ ] 1948 Sheaffer "White Dot" Triumph pen, SL & GF cap-PF-FW . 8.00
- [ ] 1949 Parker "21" pen & pencil, blue-stainless caps-EW 10.00
- [ ] 1949 Parker "21" pen, blue-stainless cap-MW 5.00
- [ ] 1949 Waterman pen, brown-SL & GL cap-LF-EW 5.00
- [ ] 1950 Parker "21" pen, blue-stainless cap-EW............... 6.00

PENS AND PENCILS

Price

- [ ] 1950 Sheaffer "White Dot" Triumph pen,
  black-SL & GF cap-EW 8.00
- [ ] 1950 Sheaffer "White Dot" Triumph pen,
  maroon-SL & GF cap-EW 8.00
- [ ] 1950 Sheaffer pen, blue-GLT-LF EW 4.00
- [ ] 1950 Sheaffer pen "White Dot" pen, black-GLT-PF-EW 6.00
- [ ] 1951 Sheaffer "White Dot" TM pen,
  black-SL & GFT
  cap-PF-EW 8.00
- [ ] 1951 Sheaffer "White Dot" TM pen,
  maroon-SL & GFT cap-PF-EW 8.00
- [ ] 1951 Sheaffer TM pen, maroon-GLT-EW 4.00
- [ ] 1953 Sheaffer Snorkel pen, black-GLT-MW-boxed 9.00
- [ ] 1953 Sheaffer "White Dot" Snorkel pen,
  black-GS14 cap band-PF-GW 15.00
- [ ] 1954 Sheaffer "White Dot" Snorkel pen,
  maroon-GLT-PF-G 4.00
- [ ] 1954 Sheaffer Snorkel pen, maroon-GLT-PF-GW 3.00
- [ ] 1954 Sheaffer Snorkel pen, maroon-GLT-PF-EW 4.00
- [ ] 1954 Sheaffer "White Dot" Snorkel pen,
  maroon-SL & GFT cap-PF-EW 10.00
- [ ] 1954 Sheaffer "White Dot" Snorkel pen,
  gray-GLT-PF-EW 8.00
- [ ] 1955 Waterman C.F. (cartridge) pen & ballpoint
  blue-GF caps-G 9.00

Courtesy of George S. James, Chapter President, Washington, D.C. Chapter
Pen Fancier's Club, P.O. Box 7122, Washington, D.C. 20044

PHARMACY ITEMS

Price Range

- [ ] Roman pharmacy vial, brown glass, 3½" L, narrow,
  well formed, 2nd-3rd cent. A.D. 25.00   35.00
- [ ] Roman pharmacy jar, cloudy whitish glass with
  bubbles and sand particles, 4" tall, 2nd-3rd cent. A.D.   50.00   60.00
- [ ] Mortar & pestle, English, the mortar carved from a
  solid block of wood, 7½" H, 15th century 150.00   200.00
- [ ] Pharmacist's ledger book, Roxbury, Mass., kept from
  September 1831 to March 1832, 162 pp., marbled
  boards with morocco spine 30.00   35.00
- [ ] Scrapbook containing pharmacists' advertisements
  clipped from newspapers of 1780-1830, mostly New
  England, about 800 items, the album bound in pink
  cowhide 300.00   400.00
- [ ] American pharmacist's sign, rectangular wood, a
  white ground with black hand-lettering, listing
  products and services, a few prices, c. 1840 . . . .   450.00   500.00

PHONOGRAPHS AND ROLLER ORGANS

At the same time that Thomas Edison was introducing the phonograph to the world (the original machine was patented in 1878), there were many other types of mechanical music machines already popular (e.g. many varieties of music boxes and roller organs as well as combinations of the two, etc.). As a matter of fact, the phonograph (among other things) was a great factor in the decline in manufacture and popularity of these other machines. Many years later Radio and the Depression of the 1930's were to do the same thing to the wind-up phonograph and especially the player piano. But while the wind-up phonograph was at its peak hundreds of styles, shapes and manufacturers in America and Europe were to produce what is now a very collectible and enjoyable commodity. From just after the turn of the century to the 1930's the phonograph and its musical rival for the family parlor, the player piano, enjoyed a tremendous popularity. The player piano was manufactured by hundreds of companies in endless variations as were the rolls to play on it, with great artists of the period producing performances for the rolls as well as records. Examples include Scott Joplin, Gershwin, Berlin, and on and on. Players are beginning to enjoy the revival the phonograph has had for some time. Just to complete this very brief history, it should be noted that with the advent of electricity, the player was to grow into one of the most complex mechanical musical devices ever known. Coin-operated machines with many instruments in all sizes up to the enormous band organs for amusement parks, have never been equaled for their complexity, craftsmanship and beauty. *Courtesy: Les Gould, S. Orange, NJ.*

	Price Range	
☐ Columbia "Eagle" Graphophone. 1898-1900, Model B, plays 2-minute records, nickel horn, key-wind	175.00	250.00
☐ Columbia Graphophone. 1897, Model Q, plays 2-minute records, wax cylinders, metal horn	175.00	250.00
☐ Columbia Graphophone. 2nd Series, 1898, plays 2-minute records, metal horn, key-wind	150.00	200.00
☐ Edison Amberola 30. 1910-1916, oak case, inside horn, plays 4-minute blue amberol records, diamond stylus	150.00	250.00
☐ Edison Fireside Edition. Model "A", 1910-1914, plays 2-minute cylinders, wooden cygnet horn, sapphire	275.00	400.00
☐ Edison Fireside Phonograph. 1906-1910, plays 2 and 4-minute records, wood base, morning glory horn and crane, painted horn	250.00	350.00
☐ Edison Gem Phonograph. 1906, plays 2-minute wax cylinders, cast iron case on wooden base . . .	200.00	325.00
☐ Edison Home Phonograph. 1898-1910, plays 2 and 4-minute records, metal cygnet horn	250.00	350.00

PHONOGRAPHS

Price Range

- ☐ Edison Maroon Gem. 1916-1918, plays 2 and 4-minute records, 24" morning glory horn (very rare) 350.00 550.00
- ☐ Edison Standard Phonograph. 1898-1908, wooden base, 10" tin horn, 18" brass bell, plays 2-minute records 225.00 325.00
- ☐ Victor Type E Disc Phonograph. Rear mounted horn, black enameled with brass bell, 8" turntable, plays 78 rpm records, circa 1902 . . . . . . 375.00 425.00
- ☐ Victor Table Phonograph. 1908-1916, plays 78 rpm records, oak wood cabinet 50.00 125.00
- ☐ Victor III. 1902, double spring, plays 78 rpm records on 10" turntable 350.00 450.00
- ☐ Edison & Other Manufacturers. Record cylinders rareties and famous names (Caruso, Sousa, etc.) . 1.00 3.00
- ☐ Edison Home-Suitcase Type. 1888-1891, suitcase type latches and large scroll decal on cover, plays 2-minute cylinder records, with painted morning glory horn and crane 300.00 425.00
- ☐ Pathe. Cylinder phonograph made in France, plays 3" diameter cylinder records, some models come with adaptors for smaller cylinders, aluminum horn 200.00 275.00
- ☐ Edison Standard—Suitcase Type. 1897-1901, square top style with suitcase latches, no decal on case, plays 2-minute cylinders, early model . . . 250.00 375.00
- ☐ Columbia Graphophone—Type AA. 1908, permanent reproducer, plays 2-minute cylinders smallest Columbia phono with enclosed works . . 275.00 350.00
- ☐ Portable Phonographs. Circa 1920's-1930's. There were several types of portable phonographs made to look like a box or folding camera of this period. They play 78 rpm records. All parts (i.e., reproducer, crank, tone arm, "horn", and turntable) fit inside the case for travel. They were quite small 150.00 250.00
- ☐ Edison Diamond Disc. Floor and table models circa 1915. Plays thick Edison 80 rpm disc records. Internal horn 120.00 150.00
- ☐ Cylinder Record Cabinets. Many styles and sizes were made to house the cylinder records within their boxes. May have wooden or cardboard pegs 150.00 350.00
- ☐ Concert Roller Organ. Circa 1889's. Plays wooden cobs with iron pins, hand crank (no spring), with 12 cobs 250.00 400.00
- ☐ Gem Roller Organ. Same type but with cheaper case 200.00 350.00
- ☐ Celestina Roller Organ. Circa 1880's, plays paper rolls, hand crank, several times on paper roll, with three rolls 300.00 400.00

PHONOGRAPHS

Price Range

☐ Same as above. Slightly different case and
decals (see color section) 300.00 400.00
☐ Helikon. Circa 1900, German reed organette,
hand crank, plays cardboard discs 6¾" diameter,
many types and slight variations in styles made
with six discs 175.00 200.00
☐ Rol Monica. Circa 1925-1928. Harmonica installed
in "genuine bakelite" case. Plays small paper
rolls which come in striped boxes. By blowing in
or out on mouth piece while turning crank one
produces music. The Playasax works on the
same principle and there are others too 75.00 100.00
☐ Zonophone. Circa 1900-1910. Universal Talking
Machine Manufacturing Co. 10" turntable, plays
78 rpm records, read mounted, large brass bell
horn, oak case, slotted crank 700.00 850.00
☐ Zonophone Standard. Circa 1901. Same maker as
#26. 7" turntable, plays 78 rpm records. Front
mounted bell horn, single spring motor, oak case 550.00 700.00
☐ Edison Triumph. Model D, circa 1908. Oak case,
plays 2 and 4-minute cylinder records. Model C
reproducer plays 2-minute records. Model H reproducer plays 4-minute cylinder records 325.00 450.00
☐ Edison Amberola V. Circa 1912-1913. Single
spring motor with automatic stop. Plays 4-minute
blue amberol records, mahogany caes, telescopic
tube connected to reproducer. Earlier than model
shown in #4 .... 350.00 450.00
☐ Cabinetto Roller Organ. Walnut case, plays paper
roll. Case has detailed stenciling. Larger than
organs shown in #22 and #23.

PHOTOGRAPHICA

The first camera manufactured for sale was designed by Daguerre and made
by Giroux and was first produced in Paris in 1839. Estimates show that from
15 to 20,000 different brands of cameras have been marketed and almost all
are eminently collectible, including the ubiquitous Kodak Brownie, of which
an estimated 30,000,000 were produced. Age is not a criterion of value; some
cameras dated 1900 and before are worth only a few dollars, some 1950-era
cameras sell in the hundreds. And the key word is "sell" not rarity; enlargers
and projectors, for instance, though sometimes rare, with few exceptions do
not command high prices from collectors at the moment.

We have given a range of retail prices since condition, rarity, historical value,
presence of an instruction manual and/or original box, market availability —
all affect price. Prices have been compiled from actual sales or trades — not
"asking prices" or isolated dealer offerings — at photographic historical

BOX CAMERAS

society shows, mail orders, flea markets, auctions, antique shows. Most dealers will expect to pay less than the quoted figures.

	Price Range	
☐ Adlake, 4" x 5" 1897	70.00	90.00
☐ Blair, Weno Hawkeye, No. 6	50.00	70.00
☐ Blair, Weno Hawkeye, No. 7	30.00	45.00
☐ Blair, Baby Hawkeye	140.00	175.00
☐ Brownie, No. 1, circa 1900	40.00	65.00
☐ Bullit, No. 4, 4" x 5" plate	55.00	85.00
☐ Bullseye, No. 4	55.00	70.00
☐ Conley, 4" x 5"	30.00	65.00
☐ Cyclone, Magazine type	40.00	80.00
☐ Diamond Postcard Gun Camera	425.00	475.00
☐ Errtee Photo Button camera, circa 1920	650.00	850.00
☐ Eureka (Kodak) No. 2	40.00	60.00
☐ Flexo (Eastman Kodak)	45.00	60.00
☐ Harvard, Pinhole all metal	180.00	220.00
☐ Hicro Color box camera (Kodak)	55.00	90.00
☐ Kamaret (Blair Camera Company)	320.00	420.00
☐ Kewpie, Conley 2, 3, 3A	20.00	35.00
☐ Keystone Ferrotype camera	120.00	150.00
☐ Kodak, First made, 1888	2200.00	3200.00
☐ Kodak, No. 4, 1890	275.00	375.00
☐ Kodak, Ordinary, models B, C	460.00	660.00
☐ Kodak, Speed, No. 1A	110.00	140.00
☐ Mandel Ette Camera, circa 1921	45.00	65.00
☐ New York, Ferrotype Co., camera, circa 1906	140.00	170.00
☐ Panorama Kodak, No. 1 Model D, circa 1900	70.00	150.00
☐ Premo, Film pack	45.00	60.00
☐ Ray Box, circa 1895	45.00	60.00
☐ Seneca Scout, circa 1916	14.00	24.00
☐ Turret Panoramic Camera, circa 1904	275.00	310.00
☐ Vive Tourist Mag. Plate box, circa 1895	55.00	75.00
☐ Wonder Automatic Cannon, circa 1908	360.00	525.00

CARTES DE VISITE

☐ Architectural Scene	2.00	4.00
☐ Civil War Historical Figure	10.00	50.00
☐ Lincoln	40.00	60.00
☐ Theatrical personality	12.00	35.00
☐ Tom Thumb Family	14.00	20.00
☐ Unidentified Personal Portrait	1.00	4.00

DAGUERREOTYPE CASE

☐ Abstract Rose	50.00	70.00
☐ Angel with Trumpet	30.00	65.00
☐ Civil War Theme	30.00	75.00
☐ Daniel in the Lion's Den	150.00	240.00
☐ Gypsy Fortune Teller	85.00	115.00
☐ Holy Family	180.00	225.00
☐ Horse Race	220.00	240.00

DAGUERREOTYPE CASE

	Price	Range
☐ Indian Chief	30.00	55.00
☐ Landing of Columbus	450.00	700.00
☐ Lion with Nude Lady	55.00	80.00
☐ Mary and Her Little Lamb	45.00	90.00
☐ Scroll, Constitution and the Law	45.00	85.00
☐ Washington Crossing Delaware	385.00	700.00

PROJECTORS

☐ Simplex, Multi-exposure, circa 1914	1800.00	2000.00
☐ Tourist, Multiple, 750 shot, circa 1914	2600.00	3200.00
☐ B & L 300	260.00	325.00
☐ Kodak, Model A, 16mm	90.00	120.00

TINTYPE

☐ Black Woman in Fancy Dress	18.00	30.00
☐ Family Portrait, Victorian	16.00	25.00
☐ Man and Gun	18.00	30.00
☐ Swimmers in Bathing Suits	14.00	20.00
☐ Three Men on Horseback	7.00	18.00

35mm CAMERAS

☐ Agfa & Ansco Memo, Vertical camera	40.00	60.00
☐ Argus A	14.00	30.00
☐ Argus K	105.00	140.00
☐ Compass, Kern, Le Coultre & Cie, circa 1938	800.00	1200.00
☐ Kodak, Ektra — interchangeable lenses	240.00	325.00
☐ Kodak 35, circa 1938	18.00	25.00
☐ Kodak Vollenda, Radionar, circa 1932	40.00	65.00
☐ Leica A, circa 1925, Elmax	4300.00	5000.00
☐ Leica A, 1926	300.00	600.00
☐ Leica C, 1929	3700.00	4700.00
☐ Leica D, 1932 (Body only)	160.00	275.00
☐ Leica III, 1933	110.00	150.00
☐ Leica IIIA, 1935	85.00	125.00
☐ Leica IIIB, 1937	120.00	150.00
☐ Leica IIIC, 1940	110.00	160.00
☐ Simplex, Multi-exposure,	1800.00	2000.00
☐ Tourist, Multiple, 750 shot, circa 1914	2600.00	3200.00
☐ Universal Mercury I, circa 1939	28.00	45.00
☐ Universal Mercury II, circa 1938	28.00	45.00
☐ Zeiss, Contaflex, circa 1936	550.00	700.00
☐ Zeiss, Contax I with Tessar, circa 1932	160.00	275.00
☐ Zeiss, Contax II, circa 1936	90.00	125.00
☐ Zeiss, Contax III with built in meter	100.00	150.00

HIDDEN CAMERAS

☐ Ansco Vanity — made up box, circa 1927	800.00	1200.00
☐ Ensign Pocketbook, circa 1926	2400.00	3000.00
☐ Gray's Patent Vest Camera	1500.00	2000.00
☐ Krause Photo Revolver, circa 1920	1400.00	1900.00
☐ Petal — Octagon shape	90.00	125.00
☐ Photoret — Round, circa 1897	325.00	600.00

HIDDEN CAMERAS   Price Range

☐ Pocket Presto Camera, circa 1896 .... 750.00   900.00
☐ Pocket Ticka Camera 110.00   150.00
☐ Tom Thumb with Original Box 1400.00   1850.00

MOTION PICTURE CAMERAS

☐ Bell & Howell Filmo Model 70 DA, 25mm 70.00   150.00
☐ Bell & Howell Filmo Model 75, circa 1928 .... 50.00   80.00
☐ Camex Reflex Zoom, 8mm 70.00   150.00
☐ Cine-Kodak, Model K, 25mm 30.00   50.00
☐ Simplex — Pocket movie camera, 25mm 12.00   20.00

MISCELLANEOUS

☐ Album, Bird and Floral Blue plush................ 50.00   60.00
☐ Album, Black leather embossed, gold clasp 25.00   40.00
☐ Album, Brown leather, Brass fasteners, Gold leaf 230.00   250.00
☐ Album, Music box, Brass trim 85.00   100.00
☐ Album, Red plush, musical 125.00   140.00
☐ Ambrotype, Civil War soldier holding revolver 80.00   95.00
☐ Ambrotype, Entertainment personality............. 100.00   300.00
☐ Ambrotype, Girl with doll 30.00   65.00
☐ Ambrotype, Historical figure 100.00   350.00
☐ Ambrotype, Military leader 100.00   350.00
☐ Ambrotype, Niagara Falls, Full plate 180.00   340.00
☐ Ambrotype, Outdoor Scene 150.00   250.00
☐ Ambrotype, School class picture 150.00   250.00
☐ Ambrotype, Young man picking apples 95.00   110.00

PLAYING CARDS

Whatever you do, please don't play with your collection. Cards are only valuable if in very good condition, and of course, you want to have all the cards in a deck. The most valuable of all are 18th and 19th century, hand-painted cards—worth up to several hundred dollars a deck.

☐ Chicago World Fair, deck, c. 1934 .... 10.00   15.00
☐ Civil War Pack, The Union Playing Cards, American Card Co., N.Y. 2-color, eagles, stars, flags, shields, suits.................................... 400.00   665.00
☐ Dec, 52 cards, Andrew Dougherty, tiny picture of card in two corners, c. 1870 .... 86.00   145.00
☐ Deck, Andrew Dougherty, N.Y., Owen Jones Arts & Crafts back design, c. 1880 .... 35.00   115.00
☐ Deck, 36 cards, 2 info. cards, The Game of Kings, Adams, N.Y., Englishe monarchs, 1845 .... 152.00   225.00
☐ Fleet Wing Gasoline, advertising, c. 1910 .... 10.00   15.00
☐ French Suited Pack, L.I. Cohen, large size, gold trim, mint 152.00   226.00
☐ Flinch Cards, c. 1910 .... 18.00   20.00

PLAYING CARDS

	Price	Range
☐ Gypsy Witch, fortune telling deck	6.00	10.00
☐ Hard-a-Port-Cut Plug, tobacco give-aways, 52 plus joker, complete set, late 1880's	120.00	275.00
☐ Panama Souvenir Cards, 53 plus info cards, USPC., real photos, c. 1908	27.00	60.00
☐ Uncle Sam's Cabinet, 1901	20.00	30.00
☐ Vanity Fair Transformation Deck, U.S.P.C. Co., America's first true transformation deck, 1895	300.00	475.00
☐ Victory Playing Cards, Arrco, Chicago, Uncle Sam (King), Statue of Liberty (Queen), Soldier and Sailor (Jacks), Hitler & Mussolini (Joker), 1945	120.00	150.00

POLICE MEMORABILIA

For those who like to collect something different and unusual, why not try
Police Memorabilia. While most items are difficult to find, if you are diligent
in your search, you will turn up some unique finds.

	Price	Range
☐ Badge, first worn by New York City Police, brass 1845-1857	90.00	120.00
☐ Police Baton, exquisitely grained rosewood, solid ivory sections hand carved, solid gold shield inscribed "Presented to Sgt. William McCarthy - June 8, 1901", original silk cord and tassel	180.00	240.00

POLICE EQUIPMENT

	Price	Range
☐ Winter Hat	45.00	55.00
☐ Summer Hat	45.00	55.00
☐ Day Stick	8.00	12.00
☐ Shield, municipal police badge, 1875-1889	24.00	30.00
☐ Night Stick	14.00	18.00
☐ Rosewood Baton for Parade	18.00	24.00
☐ Belt and Frog	30.00	40.00
☐ Nippers	8.00	12.00
☐ New Style Handcuffs	18.00	25.00

Courtesy: Detective Alfred J. Young
Curator, NYC Police Academy Museum

POLITICAL SOUVENIRS

You can take sides in any election during your lifetime, and you can also collect the myriad varieties of political memorabilia available to collectors today, some of which dates back to events in the 18th century! Buttons, ribbons and tokens are especially important, but other things such as handkerchiefs, pocket knives, neckties, flags, banners, and—from more recent times—bumper stickers and even mailings, all have value to collectors. Buttons with pictures of two candidates are known as "jugates" to collectors.

CAMPAIGN BUTTONS

	Price	Range
☐ Barker - Donnley	65.00	75.00
☐ Bryan - Sewall	25.00	30.00
☐ Bryan - Watson	70.00	80.00
☐ Coolige - Dawes	20.00	25.00
☐ Cleveland	10.00	15.00
☐ Davis - Bryan	200.00	300.00
☐ Debs - Stedman	—	166.00
☐ Dewey - Warren	18.00	25.00
☐ FDR - Garner	25.00	35.00
☐ FDR - Curley, 1932, "Work & Wages"	—	80.00
☐ FDR - Truman	40.00	50.00
☐ Foster - Gitlow	120.00	160.00
☐ Grant - Colfax	45.00	55.00
☐ Hancock	75.00	85.00
☐ Harrison	80.00	90.00
☐ Hoover - Curtis	35.00	45.00
☐ Hughes - Fairbanks	45.00	55.00
☐ Hughes - Fairbanks, ornate brass	—	233.00
☐ Landon - Knox	30.00	40.00
☐ McClellan	50.00	60.00
☐ McKinley	20.00	25.00
☐ Seymour - Blair	55.00	65.00
☐ Smith - Robinson	40.00	45.00
☐ Taft - Sherman	10.00	15.00
☐ T. Roosevelt - Fairbanks	15.00	20.00

CAMPAIGN BUTTONS

Price Range

☐ T. Roosevelt - Johnson	500.00	600.00
☐ Truman - Barkley	50.00	60.00
☐ Willkie - McNary	40.00	50.00
☐ Wilson - Marshall	15.00	20.00

CAMPAIGN RIBBONS

☐ Abraham Lincoln, 1860	275.00	325.00
☐ Andrew Jackson, 1828	400.00	450.00
☐ Clay & Frelinghuysen, 1844	275.00	325.00
☐ James Buchanan, 1856	60.00	75.00
☐ Jefferson Davis, 1861	475.00	525.00
☐ Seymour & Blair, 1868	350.00	400.00

CAMPAIGN TOKENS

☐ Abraham Lincoln, 1860	25.00	35.00
☐ Andrew Jackson, 1828	30.00	40.00
☐ Benjamin Harrison, 1888	10.00	15.00
☐ Franklin, 1852	20.00	25.00
☐ George McClellan, 1864	20.00	25.00
☐ Grover Cleveland, 1884-88-92	10.00	15.00
☐ Henry Clay, 1844	15.00	20.00
☐ Horace Greeley, 1872	20.00	25.00
☐ Horatio Seymour, 1868	20.00	25.00
☐ James GArfield, 1880	10.00	15.00
☐ John Bell, 1860	25.00	35.00
☐ John Breckinridge, 1860	90.00	110.00
☐ John C. Fremont, 1864	45.00	50.00
☐ Lewis Cass, 1848	90.00	110.00
☐ Martin Van Buren, 1836	20.00	25.00
☐ Millard Fillmore, 1856	20.00	25.00
☐ R. B. Hayes, 1876	50.00	55.00
☐ S. J. Tilden, 1876	50.00	55.00
☐ Stephen Douglas, 1860	35.00	40.00
☐ U.S. Grant, 1868	20.00	25.00
☐ William Henry Harrison, 1840	10.00	15.00
☐ Winfield Scott, 1852	20.00	25.00
☐ Winfield S. Hancock, 1880	10.00	15.00
☐ Zachary Taylor, 1848	25.00	30.00

MISCELLANEOUS

☐ Bryan, Wm. Jennings, tin tray, 13" x 16", worn	—	40.00
☐ Harrison & Reform sulfide brooch	175.00	200.00
☐ Hayes, ferrotype badge, c. 1876	210.00	300.00
☐ Roosevelt - Cox Watch Fob, c. 1919	—	50.00
☐ Taft - Sherman Postcard, colored, embossed	10.00	12.50

PORCELAIN AND POTTERY

Not until the later part of the eighteenth century were Westerners able to make fine porcelain. The movement of porcelain in the East and its rise in the West gave porcelain its other name of China — which it was given in the seventeenth century.

The porcelain pieces most in demand are from the eighteenth century and are very expensive. However, every once in a while every porcelain collector makes a great discovery because even the experts become confused over what is real and what is fake. Buying fine porcelain should begin at a fine shop or reputable dealer.

AMPHORA FIGURAL VASE, *c. 1900* . . . . 300.00 - 400.00

AMPHORA EWER . . . . 200.00 - 300.00

ART POTTERY

AMPHORA:

	Price Range	
☐ Vase, 6½" Black birds in flight against pale green ground. Factory mark, 1900	260.00	410.00
☐ Vase, 6½" Roughly textured body with iridescent copper glaze and applied with variegated circular bosses. Factory mark, 1903	260.00	410.00
☐ Vase, 6¾" Pink and green floral bosses, 1900	160.00	260.00
☐ Vase, 8½" Deep blue body, green and gilt leafage tendrils terminating in scrolling handles, 1915	210.00	360.00
☐ Vase, 8½" Gilt spider webs above butterflies against an iridescent blue and green ground. Factory mark, 1905	310.00	510.00
☐ Vase, 11½" Butterflies on the base below four stylized cranes. Factory mark, after 1918	260.00	410.00
☐ Vase, 13½" Colorful rooster incorporating stylized eggs and flowers against a textured deep ochre ground. Factory mark, 1915	210.00	360.00

ROOKWOOD POTTERY:

☐ Basket, 14" Hi-glaze with spiders and webs. Much gold, by Albert R. Valentien, 1882	640.00	680.00
☐ Bookends, 1925, Standing Rooks (molded) with blue matt finish	120.00	140.00
☐ Bookends, 1934, Standing Elephants (molded) with cream matt finish	100.00	130.00
☐ Clock, Seated panther next to clock (electric) hi-glaze green, 1957	160.00	190.00
☐ Ewer, 5" Standard brown glaze. Yellow floral decoration	965.00	1025.00
☐ Ewer, 8" Orange hi-glaze ground with fruiting leafy branches. Factory mark and artist signed, 1897	130.00	180.00
☐ Paperweight, Standing thoroughbred horse. Natural colors, 1922	100.00	140.00
☐ Plaque, Vellum glaze, scenic. E. T. Hurley, original frame 5" x 8", 1916	840.00	900.00
☐ Plate, 8" Nature flowering dogwood on hi-glaze salmon colored background. No artist signature, 1887	140.00	180.00
☐ Vase, 6" Vellum glaze, all over scenic by Ed Dier, 1912	390.00	440.00
☐ Vase, 6" Vellum glaze (matt finish) floral rim pattern by E. T. Hurley, 1910	130.00	160.00
☐ Vase, 8" Standard brown glaze. Mistletoe and berries decoration. Artist signed, 1899	180.00	210.00
☐ Vase, 8" Standard brown glaze with two handles. Portrait of a cavalier by Sturgis Laurence, 1897	1090.00	1150.00
☐ Vase, 8" Cream matt finish. All over molded Mexican scene	35.00	45.00
☐ Vase, 8½" Yellow poppy and green leafage. Factory mark and artist signed, 1902	160.00	210.00

ROOKWOOD POTTERY   Price Range

- ☐ Vase, 10" Iris glaze (hi-glaze with pastel colors)
  flowering crocus. Artist J. D. Wareham, 1901 . . . .   515.00   555.00
- ☐ Vase, 12" Gray body with calla lillies and leafage
  Factory mark and artist signed, 1904 . . . .   160.00   210.00
- ☐ Vase, 19½" Monumental, trumpet neck with printed
  roses and leafage in orange and green. Factory mark
  and artist signed, 1889 . . . . 1000.00 1500.00

ROSEVILLE POTTERY:

- ☐ Bushberry, 12", Handled basket, brown 60.00   80.00
- ☐ Donetello, Jardiniere and pedestal 380.00   430.00
- ☐ Donetello, Jardiniere and pedastal 380.00   430.00
- ☐ Falline, 9" Vase 80.00   100.00
- ☐ Ferrella, Console bowl with attached flower frog 90.00   120.00
- ☐ Jonquil, 10" Handled basket, brown 30.00   38.00
- ☐ Ming Tree, Hanging basket, green 70.00   85.00
- ☐ Mock Orange, 6" Experimental vase, high glaze, black
  shading to rose and back to black. Experimental
  marks on base. (Wee flake) 85.00   105.00
- ☐ Pine Cone, 15" Vase, brown 80.00   100.00
- ☐ Rozanne Azurine Mug, Hi-glaze blues and whites.
  Blackberry decoration. Artist signed Myers 510.00   560.00
- ☐ Rozanne Della Robbia, 8" three-color vase with carved
  cherries 880.00   950.00
- ☐ Rozanne Egypto, Covered inkwell 150.00   200.00
- ☐ Rozanne Olympic, 14" Tall vase with black transfer
  decor of Greek muses on hi-glaze red ground. Broken
  & repaired top) 680.00   740.00
- ☐ Rozanne Royal Light Tankard Pitcher. Grey shading
  cream. Blackberry decor. Artist signed 220.00   260.00
- ☐ Rozanne, 8" Standard brown glaze, two-handled vase.
  Jonquils. Excellent art work, uncrazed, artist signed . 155.00   185.00
- ☐ Roseville, Creamware "Good Night" candleshield . . . 215.00   255.00

WELLER POTTERY:

- ☐ Art Nouveau, 8" Matt finish vase with full length
  figure of blond woman 65.00   75.00
- ☐ Eocean, Mug, Hi-glaze with mushrooms 125.00   155.00
- ☐ Eocean, 12" Hi-glaze vase, bird in cherry tree. Artist:
  E. Roberts 740.00   790.00
- ☐ Eocean, 14" Hi-glaze vase, cabbage roses. No artist . . 165.00   195.00
- ☐ Eocean, 9" Hi-glaze vase, pansey decor. Grey
  background. No artist 90.00   110.00
- ☐ Figural, Aunt Jemima teapot 85.00   105.00
- ☐ Figural, Seated wood elf with natural colors 365.00   395.00
- ☐ Figural, Crouched frog, life-size with natural colors . .   50.00   80.00
- ☐ Figural, Pop-eye dog, small 100.00   130.00
- ☐ Figural, Pop-eye dog, large 365.00   395.00
- ☐ Figural, Life-size rabbit with natural colors 365.00   395.00

WELLER POTTERY   Price Range

☐ Figural, Squirrel, twice life-size with natural colors.
Has chip on ear................................... 460.00   500.00
☐ Glendale (Molded line), 8" Vase, molded design of
birds, nests and eggs in pastel background......... 60.00   80.00
☐ Jap Birdimal, 10" Hi-glaze vase with Geisha girl by
tree. Green background. Signed Rhead 780.00   850.00
☐ Jap Birdimal, 10" Hi-glaze vase. Scenic squeeze bag
trees and full moon. All in various shades of blue 255.00   295.00
☐ Louwelsa, Brown glaze mug with berry decor. Artist
signed 80.00   100.00
☐ Louwelsa, 8" Blue vase. Leaf decoration 340.00   380.00
☐ Louwelsa, 10" Brown glaze vase with floral decor. No
artist signature.................................. 90.00   120.00
☐ Louwelsa, 12" Brown glaze vase of St. Bernard Dog.
Artist: Blake 840.00   900.00
☐ Rosemont (Molded line), 10" Hi-glaze vase with black
background. Brightly colored birds molded all over... 100.00   140.00
☐ Sabrinian, 8" Vase with sea horse handles. Pale
lavender colors................................. 65.00   85.00
☐ Warwick (Molded line), 8" Handled basket 25.00   35.00
☐ Warwick, 10" Vase 20.00   25.00
☐ Wild Rose, 8" Handled basket.................... 12.00   18.00

MISCELLANEOUS POTTERY:

☐ Boch Keramis, 9¼" Vase, stylized birds, blossoms
and leafage in blue, pink and green against a cream
ground. Factory mark, 1925 .... 160.00   210.00
☐ Cowan, Queen of Hearts Whiskey jug.............. 140.00   160.00
☐ Fulper, 6" Vase. Green crystaline 45.00   65.00
☐ Fulper, 10" Vase. Mirror black ....·............. 135.00   165.00
☐ Grueby, 8" Vase with molded design. All green color . 540.00   590.00
☐ Hampshire, Oil lamp. Green 240.00   290.00
☐ Longwy, 13¼" Lamp base, crackle glaze with nude
female figure with two peacocks in tones of blues and
grays against turquoise ground, Ca 1925 .... 260.00   480.00
☐ Longwy, 10½" Vase, paneled shouldered vessel
molded and decorated with a narrow band of stylized
flowers. Factory mark, 1925...................... 160.00   210.00
☐ Newcomb, 5" Vase. Sculpted floral border by Henriet-
ta Bailey 365.00   400.00
☐ Newcomb, 8" Matt finish vase. Scenic, full moon with
Spanish moss in trees 440.00   500.00
☐ Newcomb, Hi-glaze scenic mug with 3 black cats 1180.00 1280.00
☐ Zsolnay, Bowl, 5¼" shallow with irregular rim and
deep oxblood interior with fish swimming against a
deep blue lustred ground. Factory mark, 1900 .... 360.00   410.00
☐ Zsolnay, Vase, 7¼" conical body with turquoise and
gold swirls against a deep blue ground. Factory mark,
1900 .... 180.00   260.00

MISCELLANEOUS POTTERY   Price Range

☐ Zsolnay, Vase, 11¼" inverted pyriform vessel with
   blue and gray - green body molded at the base with
   leafage continuing into the body and neck. Factory
   mark, 1900 . . . .   460.00   610.00
☐ Zsolnay, Vase, 17 1/8" lustred green leafage and
   grasses against a textured blue ground. Factory
   mark, 1900 . . . .   360.00   510.00

BELLEEK

This china has been made in Ireland and other European countries for many
years. It is a very thin china with creamy yellow glaze that appears wet. It was
first produced in 1857, however, it was made in the United States last century
by several firms.

☐ Animal, white bird, 2nd black mark 90.00   120.00
☐ Basket, 3 strand, 1st mark, 11" 540.00   590.00
☐ Basket, purse, 2nd black mark, 6" 215.00   245.00
☐ Bowls, oval, green trim, 2nd black mark 145.00   175.00
☐ Bowls, shamrock, 2nd black mark, 4½" 40.00   60.00
☐ Bowls, shell, 1st black mark 95.00   135.00
☐ Bowls, willet, brown, yellow roses, 8¼" 45.00   65.00
☐ Box, heart shaped, swirls & floral design, 6½" 130.00   160.00
☐ Card Tray, floral & butterfly decor, 4" square 170.00   200.00
☐ Centerpiece, 1st black mark, 7 x 10" 540.00   590.00
☐ Coffee Set, coffee pot, creamer, covered sugar bowl
   with 2 cups & saucers, gold bands, Lenox 290.00   340.00
☐ Cracker Jar, diamond pattern, 2nd black mark 220.00   260.00
☐ Creamer, Echinus pattern, 1st black mark, 3¼" 120.00   150.00
☐ Creamer, Figural, swan, black mark, 3¼" 75.00   90.00
☐ Creamer, harp, shamrock pattern,
   2nd black mark, 3½" 60.00   80.00
☐ Creamer, shamrock pattern, 2nd black mark 45.00   65.00
☐ Creamer, shell, 2nd black mark 60.00   80.00
☐ Creamer, toy, 2nd black mark 60.00   80.00
☐ Cups & Saucers, artichoke, Farmer's, 1st black mark .   135.00   165.00
☐ Cups & Saucers, dragon, 1st black mark 80.00   100.00
☐ Cups & Saucers, Erne, 2nd black mark 80.00   100.00
☐ Cups & Saucers, harp, shamrock, 3rd black mark 80.00   90.00
☐ Cups & Saucers, hexagon, 3rd black mark 35.00   50.00
☐ Cups & Saucers, tridacna, 1st black mark 40.00   50.00
☐ Cups & Saucers, Willets, demitasse, white body,
   gold handle 80.00   100.00
☐ Figurine, affection, 1st black mark, 14½" 1000.00   1150.00
☐ Figurine, leprechaun, green mark, 4½" 40.00   50.00
☐ Figurine, sea horse & shell, 1st black mark, 4" 200.00   230.00
☐ Figurine, swan, 1st black mark 85.00   100.00
☐ Figurine, woman & man, black mark, 7½" pair 155.00   175.00
☐ Egg holder, Ott & Bruver, gold bamboo, dolphin handle   85.00   105.00
☐ Goblet, pink trim, 1st black mark 50.00   70.00

BELLEEK

	Price	Range
☐ Honey Pot, shamrock, 2nd black mark	140.00	170.00
☐ Kettle, shamrock, 2nd black mark	120.00	140.00
☐ Marmalade Jar, shamrock, basketweave pattern, 3rd black mark, 4½"	40.00	55.00
☐ Match Holder, Little Red Riding Hood, 3½"	80.00	100.00
☐ Muffineer, Lenox, 7"	40.00	55.00
☐ Mug, Ceramic Art Co., Indian wearing headdress, titled "Many Horns", signed, 1901, 5½"	160.00	190.00
☐ Mug, grasses, green mark	12.00	16.00
☐ Mug, nut pattern, 2nd black mark, 2½"	80.00	100.00
☐ Mug, portrait of Cavalier, signed, 5½"	70.00	85.00
☐ Mug, yellow corn & husk, Palette mark, 5"	60.00	80.00
☐ Pitcher, bacchus & grape, green mark, 6"	42.00	52.00
☐ Pitcher, Cider, beaded handle with florals, Ceramic Art Co.	115.00	145.00
☐ Pitcher, Ivy, rope handle, 1st black mark, 5"	85.00	105.00
☐ Pitcher, lemonade, grapes & leaves, Ceramic Art Co.	70.00	90.00
☐ Pitcher, Neptune, 3rd black mark	70.00	90.00
☐ Plates, grass, 1st black mark	28.00	38.00
☐ Plates, shamrock, basketweave, 6¼"	35.00	45.00
☐ Plates, Willets, wild flowers with gold trim, 7½"	38.00	48.00
☐ Salt, pink trim, 1st mark	40.00	50.00
☐ Salt, shamrock, 2nd black mark	15.00	25.00
☐ Salt, shell & coral, 2nd black mark	38.00	48.00
☐ Sugar & Creamer, echinus, 2nd black mark	80.00	100.00
☐ Sugar & Creamer, Mask, 3rd black mark	70.00	90.00
☐ Sugar & Creamer, Neptune, 2nd black mark	80.00	100.00
☐ Sugar & Creamer, shamrock, 2nd black mark	80.00	100.00
☐ Sugar & Creamer, shell, 3rd black mark	70.00	90.00
☐ Sugar & Creamer, tangerine trim, black mark	50.00	70.00
☐ Teapots, cone, 2nd black mark	145.00	175.00
☐ Teapots, Neptune, 2nd black mark	145.00	175.00
☐ Teapots, shamrock, 3rd black mark	95.00	115.00
☐ Tea Sets, Limpet, black mark	825.00	925.00
☐ Tea Sets, Neptune, 2nd black mark	300.00	325.00
☐ Tea Sets, shamrock, 2nd black mark	280.00	310.00
☐ Tea Sets, Tridacna, 2nd black mark, 7 pieces	290.00	340.00
☐ Trays, bread, Limpet, 3rd black mark	60.00	80.00
☐ Trays, bread, Neptune, 3rd black mark	70.00	90.00
☐ Trinket Box, acorn pattern, 3rd black mark	130.00	150.00
☐ Tub, butter, shamrock, 2nd black mark	25.00	35.00
☐ Vases, Aberdeen, flowers, 3rd black mark	100.00	125.00
☐ Vases, green shamrocks, 3rd green mark, 5½"	25.00	35.00
☐ Vases, Mermaid with child	340.00	390.00
☐ Vases, shell, 2nd black mark	145.00	175.00
☐ Vases, Willets, hand painted poppies, 11"	90.00	110.00
☐ Vases, Willets, lemon tree, 11½"	100.00	130.00
☐ Vases, Willets, purple peacocks, 12"	120.00	150.00

LENOX WASHINGTON WAKEFIELD, TEAPOT, SUGAR AND CREAMER
. . . . 125.00 - 175.00

CHINESE EXPORT DEEP SERVING DISH, c.1770 . . . 325.00 - 350.00

BENNINGTON WARES

Bennington Wares were made in Bennington, Vermont, and much of it was in imitation of English Rockingham wares. Typical are the mottled glazes. Many people lump all American mottled-brown and yellow glazed wares under the name Bennington, but not by any stretch of imagination could all the attributed wares have been produced there without at least a million employees! The major names involved are Norton, Fenton, and United States Pottery.

	Price Range	
☐ Cuspidor, flint enamel glaze, 1849	120.00	140.00
☐ Cuspidor, Rockingham glaze, 1849 mark	55.00	70.00
☐ Cuspidor, Rockingham, small	35.00	—
☐ Candlestick, flint enamel glaze, 7" H	290.00	310.00
☐ Picture frame, scalloped edges, Rockingham glaze ..	300.00	315.00
☐ Pie plate, Rockingham glaze	70.00	80.00
☐ Vase, parian, grapes & tendrils, c. 1858	55.00	65.00

BOEHM

Edward Marshall Boehm made superior hand porcelain sculptures. Most of his work was inspired by nature in the forms of birds and flowers. Mr. Boehm died in 1969 and his work has been carried on at the Boehm Studios in Trenton, New Jersey.

☐ American Redstarts	1550.00	1650.00
☐ Catbird	1200.00	1300.00
☐ Koala Bear Cub...............................	440.00	490.00
☐ Mourning Doves	850.00	925.00
☐ Road Runner	2850.00	2950.00
☐ Sugarbirds	6225.00	7225.00
☐ Swan Centerpiece (Malvern)	1925.00	2025.00
☐ Towhee	1375.00	1475.00
☐ Tree Creepers (Malvern)	3175.00	3275.00
☐ Western Bluebirds	4825.00	4925.00
☐ Yellow Daisies	600.00	650.00
☐ Young American Eagle.........................	980.00	1040.00

CHINESE EXPORT PORCELAIN

Most export porcelain was made in the Kiangsi, about 600 miles from the port of Canton. A variety of raw materials from this area was used in the production of this fine porcelain. Usually a Chinese symbol was used in the design. Prices fluctuate depending on age.

☐ Bowl, Fitzhugh pattern green, circa 1820, 9½"	690.00	740.00
☐ Bowl, Hawthorne, 14½".........................	260.00	300.00
☐ Bowl, "Manderine Palette" with blossoms and butterflies, circa 1780, 11¾"	725.00	775.00
☐ Cup & Saucer, coffee, Famille Rose, circa 1750, pair ..	690.00	740.00
☐ Cup & Saucer, Fitzhugh pattern blue	48.00	58.00
☐ Dishes, Fitzhugh pattern, orange, 9½" deep, pair	390.00	460.00

CHINESE EXPORT PORCELAIN

	Price Range	
☐ Garniture Set, 3 covered balustur vases & pair beakers, dragons, 19th Century, set	950.00	1200.00
☐ Jug, Blue Willow pattern, 19th Century, 9 1/8" high ...	370.00	420.00
☐ Plate, cloak & spade center, 10" deep.............	70.00	85.00
☐ Plate, Judgement in Paris in iron red, circa 1750, 9¼" deep	580.00	650.00
☐ Platter, Fitzhugh pattern, blue, 1800, 18 7/8", naked ..	270.00	325.00
☐ Punch Bowl, "Grisaille" decor, hunt scene with naked lady, circa 1780, 14" deep	1450.00	1650.00
☐ Rice Bowl, "Famille Rose", covered, circa 1860......	35.00	45.00
☐ Tea Cup, Armorial decor, applied handle, 19th Century 2" high.......................................	55.00	75.00
☐ Tray, two ladies & scenery, 5½" x 7½"	120.00	150.00
☐ Tureen & Cover, Pagodas in river, rectangular shape, diaper border, circa 1770, 14 1/8".................	925.00	1025.00
☐ Vase, elephant head handles, dolphin, bronze, 4¼" ..	190.00	240.00
☐ Vase, Geisha woman in garden, teakwood base, Temple, 11".......................................	250.00	300.00
☐ Warming Dish, "Bird & Butterfly", orange, 9½" deep .	290.00	340.00

COLLECTIBLE PLATES (1895-1978)

Stimulated by the ancient custom of Christmas plates, the Copenhagen-based firm of Bing and Grondahl produced the first modern collector plate in 1895. Collector plates remained relatively obscure until 1965.

As a recent phenomenon in the world of collecting, plates have weathered a cycle of "boom and bust". Attempts to cash in on the success boom created by the early issues of the Franklin Mint, The Hamilton Mint, Lalique, Veneto Flair, Seven Seas, Count Agazzi, and others saw the proliferation of many "quickie" issues of limited artistic appeal and questionable status as limited edition collectible plates.

Those issues that have survived have done so on the strength of their artistic and creative appeal. The companies that presently produce these plates find that the market is healthy and receptive.

Plates made of precious metals have also risen in intrinsic value due to the worldwide increase in the price of silver and gold.

These plates should, however, be acquired primarily for their appeal as collectible plates; the value of the metal content should remain a secondary consideration.

BAYREUTHER (Germany)	Price		Price
☐ 1967 Christmas, Stifskirche...95.00		☐ 1969 Father's Day, Rhine Castle	50.00
☐ 1968 Christmas, Kappelkirche.30.00		☐ 1970 Father's Day, Castle Pfalz...............	12.00
☐ 1969 Christmas, Christkindlemarkt..........18.00		☐ 1971 Father's Day Castle Heidelberg...........	15.00
☐ 1970 Christmas, Chapel in Oberndorf 15.00		☐ 1972 Father's Day Castle Hohenschwangau 15.00	
☐ 1971 Christmas, Toys for Sale..............13.00		☐ 1973 Father's Day, Castle Katz	30.00
☐ 1972 Christmas, Trumpeters ..18.50			
☐ 1973 Christmas, Snow Scene .20.00			

BAYREUTHER (Germany)

	Price
☐ 1969 Mother's Day, Mother & Children	50.00
☐ 1970 Mother's Day Mother & Children	15.00
☐ 1971 Mother's Day, Mother & Children	15.00
☐ 1972 Mother's Day, Mother & Children	20.00
☐ 1973 Mother's Day, Mother & Children	16.50
☐ 1976 Mother's Day	24.00
☐ 1977 Mother's Day	24.00
☐ 1978 Mother's Day	27.50
☐ 1971 Thanksgiving	12.75
☐ 1972 Thanksgiving	15.00
☐ 1973 Thanksgiving	18.00
☐ 1974 Thanksgiving	24.50
☐ 1975 Thanksgiving	18.00
☐ 1978 Thanksgiving	27.50

ALL PRICES ARE FOR MINT CONDITION.

BELLEEK (Ireland)

☐ 1970 An'l, Castle Caldwell	100.00
☐ 1971 An'l., Celtic Cross	35.00
☐ 1973 An'l. (Illus.)	40.00
☐ 1974 An'l., Devenish Island	50.00
☐ 1975 An'l., Christmas	40.00
☐ 1976 An'l., Christmas	42.50
☐ 1977 An'l., Christmas	55.00
☐ 1978 An'l., Christmas	56.50

BING & GRONDAHL (Denmark)

The oldest and original producer of Limited Edition Christmas Plates

☐ 1895 Christmas (Illus.)	2500.00
☐ 1896	1750.00
☐ 1897	1000.00
☐ 1898	650.00
☐ 1899	1000.00
☐ 1900	750.00
☐ 1901	300.00
☐ 1902	280.00
☐ 1903	225.00
☐ 1904	120.00
☐ 1905	100.00
☐ 1906	80.00
☐ 1907	75.00
☐ 1908	60.00
☐ 1909	75.00
☐ 1910	60.00
☐ 1911	80.00
☐ 1912	80.00
☐ 1913	80.00
☐ 1914	72.50
☐ 1915	100.00

BING & GRONDAHL

	Price
☐ 1916	70.00
☐ 1917	65.00
☐ 1918	50.00
☐ 1919	70.00
☐ 1920	60.00
☐ 1921	60.00
☐ 1922	60.00
☐ 1923	60.00
☐ 1924	50.00
☐ 1925	60.00
☐ 1926	50.00
☐ 1927	75.00
☐ 1928	50.00
☐ 1929	70.00
☐ 1930	70.00
☐ 1931	80.00
☐ 1932	60.00
☐ 1933	60.00
☐ 1934	60.00
☐ 1935	60.00
☐ 1936	60.00
☐ 1937	70.00
☐ 1938	100.00
☐ 1939	125.00
☐ 1940	115.00
☐ 1941	200.00
☐ 1942	150.00
☐ 1943	145.00
☐ 1944	105.00
☐ 1945	100.00
☐ 1946	60.00
☐ 1947	75.00
☐ 1948	60.00
☐ 1949	90.00
☐ 1950	80.00
☐ 1951	70.00
☐ 1952	50.00
☐ 1953	60.00
☐ 1954	80.00
☐ 1955	60.00
☐ 1956	110.00
☐ 1957	115.00
☐ 1958	100.00
☐ 1959	130.00
☐ 1960	170.00
☐ 1961	110.00
☐ 1962	60.00
☐ 1963	125.00
☐ 1964	40.00
☐ 1965	42.00
☐ 1966	32.50
☐ 1967	30.00
☐ 1968	25.00
☐ 1969	20.00

BING & GRONDAHL	Price
☐ 1970	14.50
☐ 1971	20.00
☐ 1972	18.00
☐ 1973	22.00
☐ 1974	20.00
☐ 1975	25.00
☐ 1976	25.00
☐ 1977	30.00
☐ 1969 Mother's Day Dog & Puppies	300.00
☐ 1970 Mother's Day Bird & Chicks	25.00
☐ 1971 Mother's Day Cat & Kittens	10.00
☐ 1972 Mother's Day Mare & Foal	13.50
☐ 1973 Mother's Day Duck & Ducklings	12.50
☐ 1974 Mother's Day Bear & Cub	15.00
☐ 1975 Mother's Day Doe & Fawn	13.00
☐ 1976 Mother's Day	21.00
☐ 1977 Mother's Day	22.00

FRANKOMA (America)

☐ 1965 Christmas, Goodwill Towards Men	175.00
☐ 1966 Christmas, Bethlehem Shepherds	75.00
☐ 1967 Christmas, Gifts for the Christ Child	40.00
☐ 1968 Christmas, Flight into Egypt	7.50
☐ 1969 Christmas, Laid in a Manger	6.50
☐ 1970 Christmas, King of Kings	6.00
☐ 1971 Christmas, No Room in the Inn	6.50
☐ 1972 Christmas, Seeking the Christ Child	6.00
☐ 1973 Christmas, The Annunciation	6.00
☐ 1974 Christmas	6.00
☐ 1975 Christmas	6.00
☐ 1977 Christmas	6.00

HAVILAND & CO. (America/France)

☐ 1970 Christmas	140.60
☐ 1971 Christmas	40.00
☐ 1972 Christmas	30.00
☐ 1973 Christmas	30.00
☐ 1974 Christmas	30.00
☐ 1974 Mother's Day	30.00

HAVILAND & CO.	Price
☐ 1975 Mother's Day	29.00
☐ 1975 Mother's Day	29.00
☐ 1976 Christmas	15.00
☐ 1976 Mother's Day	30.00

LALIQUE (GLASS) (France)

☐ 1965 Annual	1400.00
☐ 1966 Annual	200.00
☐ 1967 Annual	125.00
☐ 1968 Annual	70.00
☐ 1969 Annual	70.00
☐ 1970 Annual	60.00
☐ 1971 Annual	60.00
☐ 1972 Annual	48.00
☐ 1973 Annual	47.50
☐ 1974 Annual	48.00
☐ 1975 Annual	60.00
☐ 1976 Annual	100.00

LENOX BOEHM (America)

☐ 1970 Wood Thrush	250.00
☐ 1971 Gold Finches	125.00
☐ 1972 Blue Birds	75.00
☐ 1972 Bird of Peace	360.00
☐ 1973 Meadowlark	50.00
☐ 1973 Eagle	175.00
☐ 1974 Hummingbird	50.00

MOSER (GLASS) (Czechoslovakia)

☐ 1970 Christmas, Hradcany Castle, lavender	150.00
☐ 1971 Christmas, Karlstein Castle, pale green	75.00
☐ 1972 Christmas, Old Town Hall	85.00
☐ 1973 Christmas, Capricorn	90.00
☐ 1971 Mother's Day	125.00
☐ 1972 Mother's Day	85.00
☐ 1973 Mother's Day	90.00

PORSGRUND (Norway)

☐ 1968 Christmas, Church Scene	165.00
☐ 1969 Christmas, Three Kings	20.00
☐ 1970 Christmas, Road to Bethlehem	12.50
☐ 1971 Christmas, A Child is Born	25.00
☐ 1972 Christmas, Hark, the Herald Angels Sing	17.50
☐ 1973 Christmas, Promise of the Savior	22.00
☐ 1971 Father's Day, Father & Son Fishing	7.50
☐ 1972 Father's Day, Cookout	7.00
☐ 1973 Father's Day	12.50

PORSGRUND

	Price
☐ 1970 Mother's Day, Mare & Foal	10.00
☐ 1971 Mother's Day, Boy & Geese	10.00
☐ 1972 Mother's Day, Doe & Fawn	8.00
☐ 1973 Mother's Day	10.00
☐ 1974 Christmas	35.00
☐ 1974 Christmas Delux	55.00
☐ 1974 Father's Day	11.50
☐ 1976 Christmas	23.00
☐ 1977 Mother's Day	15.00

ROSENTHAL (Germany)

	Price
☐ 1968 Christmas, in Bremen	200.00
☐ 1969 Christmas, Rothenburg on the Tauber	65.00
☐ 1970 Christmas, Cologne on the Rhine	125.00
☐ 1971 Christmas, Garmisch-Partenkirchen	100.00
☐ 1972 Christmas, Midnight Mass	46.50

ROYAL COPENHAGEN (Denmark)

	Price
☐ 1908	1500.00
☐ 1909	140.00
☐ 1910	125.00
☐ 1911	135.00
☐ 1912	115.00
☐ 1913	130.00
☐ 1914	114.00
☐ 1915	110.00
☐ 1916	85.00
☐ 1917	78.00
☐ 1918	80.00
☐ 1919	73.00
☐ 1920	67.50
☐ 1921	65.00
☐ 1922	65.00
☐ 1923	70.00
☐ 1924	80.00
☐ 1925	70.00
☐ 1926	70.00
☐ 1927	120.00
☐ 1928	75.00
☐ 1929	60.00
☐ 1930	60.00
☐ 1931	65.00
☐ 1932	65.00
☐ 1933	80.00
☐ 1934	85.00
☐ 1935	125.00
☐ 1936	130.00
☐ 1937	135.00
☐ 1938	240.00

ROYAL COPENHAGEN

	Price
☐ 1939 (Illus.)	240.00
☐ 1940	365.00
☐ 1941	330.00
☐ 1942	355.00
☐ 1943	450.00
☐ 1944	145.00
☐ 1945	360.00
☐ 1946	140.00
☐ 1947	220.00
☐ 1948	125.00
☐ 1949	140.00
☐ 1950	155.00
☐ 1951	225.00
☐ 1952	100.00
☐ 1953	100.00
☐ 1954	115.00
☐ 1955	225.00
☐ 1956	140.00
☐ 1957	90.00
☐ 1958	110.00
☐ 1959	100.00
☐ 1960	135.00
☐ 1961	125.00
☐ 1962	150.00
☐ 1963	60.00
☐ 1964	50.00
☐ 1965	50.00
☐ 1966	48.00
☐ 1967	30.00
☐ 1968	22.00
☐ 1969	25.00
☐ 1970	23.00
☐ 1971	23.00
☐ 1972	20.00
☐ 1973	24.00
☐ 1974	22.00
☐ 1975	27.50
☐ 1976	22.00
☐ 1977	20.00

MOTHER'S DAY PLATES

	Price
☐ 1971 Mother's Day, Mother & Child	50.00
☐ 1972 Mother's Day, Mother & Children	16.50
☐ 1973	18.00
☐ 1974	18.00
☐ 1975	20.00
☐ 1976	20.00
☐ 1977	25.00

WEDGWOOD (England)

	Price
☐ 1969 Christmas	275.00
☐ 1970 Christmas	25.00
☐ 1971 Christmas	30.00
☐ 1972 Christmas	40.00

WEDGWOOD	Price
☐ 1973 Christmas	45.00
☐ 1974 Christmas	40.00
☐ 1975 Christmas	45.00
☐ 1976 Christmas	40.00
☐ 1977 Christmas	50.00

ROYALE (Germany)

	Price
☐ 1969 Christmas	42.50
☐ 1970 Christmas	15.00
☐ 1971 Christmas	20.00
☐ 1972 Christmas	22.50
☐ 1973 Christmas	31.50

ROYALE	Price
☐ 1974 Christmas	29.00
☐ 1975 Christmas	24.00
☐ 1976 Christmas	30.00
☐ 1977 Christmas	31.50
☐ 1970 Mother's Day	35.00
☐ 1971 Mother's Day	15.00
☐ 1973 Mother's Day	32.50
☐ 1974 Mother's Day	30.00
☐ 1975 Mother's Day	26.00
☐ 1976 Mother's Day	30.00
☐ 1977 Mother's Day	30.00

FIESTA WARE

Fiesta Ware was first produced by the Laughlin Pottery in 1936, designed by Fred Rhead, an English potter. The most outstanding feature of this pottery is its very festive colors.

	Price Range	
☐ Ash Tray, basketweave, experimental flowers in relief	30.00	35.00
☐ Ash Tray, yellow, 1936	10.00	14.00
☐ Candleholders, blue, 1936, pair	40.00	60.00
☐ Candleholders, yellow, pair	25.00	30.00
☐ Carafe, 3 pt., old ivory, 1941	22.00	28.00
☐ Chop Plates, dark blue, 13", 1936	4.50	8.50
☐ Chop Plates, yellow, 6"	4.50	5.00
☐ Coffee Pot, red, 1936	22.00	26.00
☐ Compartment Plates, turquoise, 10½", 1941	4.50	8.50
☐ Cup and Saucer, red	9.00	12.00
☐ Cup and Saucer, yellow	7.00	9.00
☐ Dessert Bowl, chartreuse, 6", 1941	3.50	6.50
☐ Dessert Plate, yellow, 6"	4.50	5.00
☐ Dinner Plate, rose, 10", 1936	2.50	3.50
☐ Egg Cups, red, 1941	12.00	16.00
☐ Fruit Bowl, rose, 5½", 1939	2.25	4.25
☐ Juice Tumblers, ivory, turquoise, yellow	7.00	8.00
☐ Ice Pitcher, 2 qt., red	16.00	25.00
☐ Mug, red	20.00	25.00
☐ Mug, turquoise	15.00	20.00
☐ Mug, yellow	15.00	20.00
☐ Platter, turquoise, 12", 1939	4.25	8.25
☐ Relish Tray, green base, red center, multi-color inserts	30.00	35.00
☐ Relish Tray, old ivory, 1939	24.00	32.00
☐ Salad Bowl, yellow, 7 5/8", 1939	6.00	10.00
☐ Salt and Pepper, blue, 1937	3.25	5.25
☐ Sauceboat, green, 1939	6.00	10.00
☐ Sugar and Creamer, red, 1941	8.00	12.00
☐ Tea Pot, large, red, 1936	20.00	25.00
☐ Utility Tray, yellow, 1941	4.25	6.25
☐ Vase, old ivory, 10", 1936	4.25	6.25
☐ Water Pitcher, disc, green	14.00	18.00

FIESTA WARE

Price Range

☐ Water Tumblers, green and turquoise 2.75   3.00
☐ Water Tumblers, red 3.75   4.25

HAVILAND

Production of Haviland was begun in the mid 19th century in Limoges, France by Americans. The background history is confusing because of the various partnerships of brothers involved, etc. It continues in production today.

☐ Bone Dish, white. 10.00   15.00
☐ Bowl, Coromandel pattern, Limoges, 9¼ x 10¾" 38.00   48.00
☐ Bowl, vegetable, covered, Miami 30.00   40.00
☐ Bowl, vegetable, covered, St. Lazarre 30.00   40.00
☐ Butter Dish, Miramar pattern, Limoges, with cover . . . 50.00   60.00
☐ Butter Pats, Princess 6.00   9.00
☐ Cake Plate, green leaf, gold trim, Charles Field
   Haviland, 12" 24.00   34.00
☐ Chocolate Pot, blue-green flowers, leaves, gold trim . . 60.00   70.00
☐ Coffee Pot, moss rose, 8" 40.00   50.00
☐ Cup & Saucer, bouillon, Miami 6.00   9.00
☐ Cup & Saucer, Marquis pattern 18.00   24.00
☐ Cup & Saucer, Princess 16.00   22.00
☐ Cup & Saucer, Ranson, gold trim, bouillon 26.00   32.00
☐ Decanter, floral decor with stopper,
   Haviland-Limoges, 9". 42.00   52.00
☐ Gravy Boat, Greek pattern, American 30.00   35.00
☐ Gravy Boat, silver anniversary 38.00   45.00
☐ Hatpin Holder, blue flowers, signed 25.00   35.00
☐ Ice Cream Set, platter with 6 plates, blue & white 95.00   135.00
☐ Plate, apple blossom pattern, 9" D 8.00   14.00
☐ Plate, bread & butter, Frontenac 6.00   9.00
☐ Plate, morning glory pattern, 8½" D 22.00   28.00
☐ Plate, Princess pattern, 9½" D 22.00   28.00
☐ Plate, luncheon, Frontenac, 8½" 8.00   14.00
☐ Plate, luncheon, Princess 8.00   12.00
☐ Plate, luncheon, yellow & pink carnations,
   Charles Field Haviland. 4.50   8.50
☐ Platter, Greek pattern, Theodore Haviland, 13" 26.00   32.00
☐ Platter, Ranson pattern, 11½" D 36.00   42.00
☐ Relish Dish, violets, Theodore Haviland 22.00   28.00
☐ Salad Plate, Ranson pattern with gold, Haviland & Co. 4.50   8.50
☐ Soup Plate, Cambridge pattern, Theodore Haviland . . 9.00   12.00
☐ Soup Tureen, pink florals with gold trim, Haviland . . . 90.00   130.00
☐ Sugar Bowls, Ranson, covered, white 36.00   42.00
☐ Sugar & Creamer, Limoges, covered, autumn leaves. . 50.00   60.00
☐ Sugar & Creamer, white background, floral
   with gold trim 60.00   70.00
☐ Teapot, Cupid, gold trim, Charles Field Haviland, 5" H 60.00   70.00
☐ Tea Set, moss rose pattern, set 140.00   160.00
☐ Tray, dessert, Limoges, 11 x 8" 26.00   36.00
☐ Vase, peacock, brown & black, signed, 10 x 11½" H . . 310.00   360.00

HAVILAND

	Price	Range
☐ Vegetable Dish, Limoges, pink roses	30.00	35.00
☐ Vegetable Dish, Princess pattern, handled	36.00	46.00
☐ Vegetable Dish, Ranson pattern, covered...........	36.00	46.00
☐ Vegetable Dish, St. Lazarre pattern, covered, Haviland & Co., France	30.00	38.00

HUMMEL FIGURES

☐ #88/I "Heavenly Protection," 6¾ths", mark CM	750.00	800.00
☐ #99, "Eventide," 4¾ths", mark FB	150.00	200.00
☐ #119, "Little Thrifty," 5", mark FB	150.00	200.00
☐ #129, "Bandleader," 5¼", mark CM	135.00	150.00
☐ #135, "Soloist," 4¾ths", mark FB	100.00	150.00
☐ #141/X, "Apple Tree Girl," 29", mark unrecorded	6500.00	7000.00

LENOX

Lenox got its start on May 18, 1889, when it was incorporated in the State of New Jersey under the name of Ceramic Art Company. Jonathan Coxon, Sr., was the president of the new company, and Walter Scott Lenox was the secretary-treasurer. Walter Lenox eventually bought out his partner's interest, and renamed the company Lenox, Inc.

Over 4,000 different shapes have been made, as well as several thousands decorating styles, which gives the collector a huge area to cover. In addition to the factory-decorated items, blanks were sold to be decorated by home artists. As of this date, no fakes or forgeries of Lenox china have been noted, making it a safe collectible and sound investment. Repairs are usually easy to spot, since it is difficult to match the creamy Lenox color.

Lenox, Inc. continued to produce their fine china, both dinnerware and giftware, and they also now make crystal, bone china, oven-ware, and a variety of other items.

At least 15 different marks have been noted, the most desirable being the C.A.C. wreath mark in all its variations.

Please consult our publication *Official Price Guide to Lenox China* by Dorothy Robinson for more prices and information.

Dinnerware: **Price**

☐ Bread and Butter Plate, Ming pattern	10.00
☐ Bread and Butter Plate, J-34 pattern	7.00
☐ Cup and Saucer, demitasse, Mandarin pattern...................	20.00
☐ Cup and Saucer, demitasse, Hawthorn pattern, white	15.00
☐ Cup and Saucer, demitasse, Hawthorn pattern, eggshell thin, C.A.C. brown palette mark	45.00
☐ Cup and Saucer, demitasse, Monticello pattern..................	15.00
☐ Cup and Saucer, full size, Washington/Wakefield	28.00
☐ Cup and Saucer, full size, Alaris pattern	19.00
☐ Cup and Saucer, full size, Apple Blossom, coral & white	21.00
☐ Cup and Saucer, full size, Trellis	17.00
☐ Cup and Saucer, full size, Virginian	35.00
☐ Cup and Saucer, full size, blue dot enamel work................	30.00
☐ Cup and Saucer, bouillon, K344B pattern	15.00
☐ Cup and Saucer, bouillon, Ming	20.00
☐ Dinner Plate, Belvidere	17.00

Dinnerware   Price

☐ Dinner Plate, Mandarin 22.00
☐ Dinner Plate, Beltane, yellow and white 20.00
☐ Dinner Plate, Washington/Wakefield 20.00
☐ Luncheon Plate, Pinehurst Blue 10.00
☐ Luncheon Plate, Pagoda, blue and white 12.00
☐ Salad Plate, Monterey 9.00
☐ Salad Plate, Trio 8.00
☐ Salad Plate, S-62 .... 10.00
☐ Sugar and Creamer, Ming 75.00
☐ Sugar and Creamer, Priscilla 65.00
☐ Teapot, Cattail 30.00
☐ Teapot, sugar and creamer, Washington/Wakefield 150.00
☐ Vegetable Bowl, S-34 pattern 30.00

Figurines:

☐ Crinoline, perfect 350.00
☐ Floradora, perfect 375.00
☐ Mistress Mary, perfect 350.00
☐ Mistress Mary, minor damage to lace ruffles and tips of fingers ... 275.00
☐ Natchez Belle, minor damage to lace 335.00
☐ Southern Belle, perfect 350.00
☐ Twin, girl, perfect 100.00
☐ Twin, boy, perfect 125.00
☐ Twins, pair, undecorated and unmarked 100.00

Giftware and Novelty Items:

☐ Angel Candle Holder, white 50.00
☐ Ashtray, Rotary seal in middle 10.00
☐ Ashtray, small teardrop shape, green with gold 9.00
☐ Ashtray, large, pheasant design 30.00
☐ Bird, small, blue 25.00
☐ Bird, small, white 20.00
☐ Bird, large, flower holder, pink 30.00
☐ Bird, large, brown, holes for flower arranging 45.00
☐ Candlestick, 9", gold trim, pair 35.00
☐ Candlestick, 4", Grecian style, blue and white, pair 28.00
☐ Candy Dish, covered, white with gold trim 25.00
☐ Candy Dish, dark green, melon-ribbed, covered 38.00
☐ Candy Dish, coral and white, 6" diameter 19.00
☐ Candy Dish, white with gold trim, 8" long 15.00
☐ Cigarette Urn, gray with platinum trim 10.00
☐ Cigarette Lighter, gold trim 20.00
☐ Compote, Ming pattern 50.00
☐ Dog, running Schnauzer, white 40.00
☐ Dog, standing bulldog, white bisque 125.00
☐ Elephant, large, white 150.00
☐ Horn of Plenty, small, white and coral 25.00
☐ Llama, white 90.00
☐ Pitcher, hammered finish, mask spout, light green 90.00
☐ Pitcher, bulbous bottom, 6", pink and white 30.00

Giftware and Novelty Items

	Price
☐ Shell Bonbon, 6", ink with white	20.00
☐ Swan, 2", pink	20.00
☐ Swan, 2", white with gold, C.A.C. mark	30.00
☐ Swan, medium, Lenox Rose design	42.00
☐ Swan, medium, coral	25.00
☐ Toby Mug, William Penn, white	125.00
☐ Vase, swan handles, white with gold trim	32.00
☐ Vase, tall cylinder, sea horse decoration	25.00
☐ Vase, square base, fluting, white	30.00
☐ Vase, square base, fluting, white and green	40.00
☐ Vase, bud, one handle, gold wheat design	24.00
☐ Vase, square, raised flower design	30.00
☐ Wall Pocket, white bisque	50.00

Hand-Painted Items (Factory Artists)

☐ Fern Pot, 9" diameter with separate strainer, small h.p. flowers with gold trim, pink palette mark, C.A.C.	150.00
☐ Mug, 5", monochromatic browns, monk scene, C.A.C. wreath mark	120.00
☐ Plate, 9", fish, signed Morley	75.00
☐ Plate, 9", grapes, signed Nosek	35.00
☐ Stein, sterling lid and thumbrest, golfer, monochromatic greens, C.A.C.	200.00
☐ Tobacco Jar, Canada geese in flight, blue skys, clouds, green grass and swamp plants, signed Morley, Lenox wreath pink	350.00
☐ Vase, 14", plume handles, roses in shades of pink and gold, signed Marsh, C.A.C.	325.00
☐ Vase, covered, ceramic parts made in four sections separated by bronze connectors, bronze pineapple finial, decoration on china is garlands of flowers on white ground, circa 1898	275.00
☐ Vase, 8", portrait of springer spaniel, signed Bakery, Lenox wreath mark	225.00
☐ Vase, 10", flowering poppies, air-brushed brown background, signed Morley, C.A.C. wreath mark	350.00
☐ Whiskey Jug, fruit design, C.A.C. mark	175.00

Hand-Painted Items (Non-Factory Artists):

☐ Cornucopia, roses all over	75.00
☐ Covered Box, poppy design, nicely done	75.00
☐ Pin Tray, blue background, butterflies, 7" long	25.00
☐ Salt Dip, small roses	10.00
☐ Teaset, orange flowers with gold, 3 pieces	100.00
☐ Vase, 14", green background, roses on both sides, gold handles, C.A.C. palette mark	150.00
☐ Vase, 10", slightly rounded shape, no handles, orchid decoration	75.00
☐ Vase, 10", irridescent peacocks, dreadful art work	60.00

Please note that there is a considerable price spread on non-factory done items, since they could have been painted by anyone from an amateur with grandiose delusions to professional artists. Home-decorated items can usually be identified quickly from the inferior art work — lack of depth, crudely done designs, and over-zealous use of gold. As a rule, non-factory-decor-

Hand Painted Items (Non-Factory)

ated items will have the artist's palette mark. There are many exceptions to this, however, and the collector will have to rely on his/her own judgement regarding the quality of the art work.

Lenox Liners in Silver Holders:	Price
☐ Bouillons, C.A.C. liners, hand-painted gold and green ribbons, Gorham holders, set of 6	360.00
☐ Bouillons, C.A.C. liners, hand-painted flowers with raised gold paste, set of 8	500.00
☐ Bouillons, plain gold trim, Gorham holders, set of 12	240.00
☐ Butter Tub, plain gold trim, openwork holder	35.00
☐ Casserole with cover, hand-painted flowers, two-handled sterling holder, crack in bottom of dish	150.00
☐ Demitasse Cups and Saucers, raised gold paste flowers, Tiffany "Chrysanthemum" holders and saucers, set of 6	500.00
☐ Demitasse Cups and Saucers, plain gold trim on liners, International holders and saucers, set of 8	160.00
☐ Ramekins, C.A.C., hand-painted liners with raised gold work and flowers, Gorham holders each weighing 7 Troy oz., set of 6	600.00
☐ Ramekins, plain gold trim, openwork Reed and Barton holders, set of 12	360.00
☐ Salt Dip, plain gold trim liner, openwork holder	18.00
☐ Sauce Bowl, C.A.C. mark, hand-painted flowers, two-handled silver holder, footed	75.00
☐ Sherbert, plain gold trim, scalloped rim, Shreve & Company holder, Art Nouveau silver holder	50.00
☐ Sherbert, plain gold trim, openwork Gorham holder	30.00

Silver Overlay

☐ Biscuit Jar, white	100.00
☐ Bowl, 9" diameter, cherry blossom design	125.00
☐ Bowl, 10" diameter, skimpy silver	60.00
☐ Candlesticks, 6", white, pair	75.00
☐ Candy Dish, shell shape, C.A.C. mark	60.00
☐ Coaster, oxblood, Lenox wreath mark, has been made over into necklace on silver chain	60.00
☐ Compote, small, white, average silver	35.00
☐ Honey Pot, bees covered with silver	60.00
☐ Hot Water Pot, white with ornate silver, bottom covered with silver so mark can't be seen but shape verifiable as Lenox	65.00
☐ Luncheon Plate, 9", simple bands of silver	15.00
☐ Mustard Pot, cobalt, C.A.C. mark	95.00
☐ Tea Tile, turquoise	75.00
☐ Teaset, five piece (coffeepot, teapot, sugar, creamer, tray), white with cherry blossom design	425.00
☐ Teaset, four piece (coffeepot, teapot, sugar, creamer), minor damage inside lip of sugar, cobalt with heavy silver, C.A.C. mark, teapot has infuser	400.00
☐ Teaset, small, cobalt, C.A.C. mark on one piece only, other pieces unmarked	110.00

Silver Overlay   Price

☐ Vase, 4", cobalt with heavy silver, C.A.C. mark 85.00
☐ Vase, 6", shading from orange-brown to dark olive green, ornate
   silver work, C.A.C. mark 125.00

NIPPON

Nippon porcelain was made by the Noritake Company, Ltd. in Nagoya, Japan until 1921. It was then decided that all Japanese wares bear the English word Japan. There is much controversy over the marks used in Nippon wares. The hand-painted pieces of good quality are rising in price.

	Price	Range
☐ Ashtray, warrior on horseback	20.00	30.00
☐ Basket, florals & pink ribbons with gold, 4" wide	25.00	35.00
☐ Basket, scenic, handled, 10 x 6½"	20.00	30.00
☐ Berry set, house scene, 5 pieces	40.00	50.00
☐ Bottle, perfume, pink roses	50.00	60.00
☐ Bowl, basketweave with peanuts, 7½"	90.00	100.00
☐ Bowl, blue with ruffled top, 2 swans	90.00	100.00
☐ Bowl, blue & yellow grapes, vine handles, 11"	280.00	320.00
☐ Bowl, fluted, windmill scene	20.00	25.00
☐ Bowl, folded and rippled rim, blossoming roses, green maple leave mark, 7"	65.00	75.00
☐ Bowl, scalloped rim, florals in coral pink, 11"	80.00	90.00
☐ Bowl, sunset, lake scene, pierced handles, 10"	40.00	50.00
☐ Bowl, violets, 9½"	18.00	25.00
☐ Bowl, windmill scene, handled, 5"	18.00	25.00
☐ Bowl, women in garden, gold & red, 9"	50.00	60.00
☐ Box, biscuit, mosque scene, covered, bisque finish . .	130.00	140.00
☐ Box, floral, covered with gold trim, 3"	10.00	15.00
☐ Box, oriental scene on cover, matte finish, 4½" high x 8" deep, green wreath mark	140.00	160.00
☐ Butter Pat, floral, 5 pieces	16.00	20.00
☐ Candlesticks, yellow flowers with green leaves, black base, 8½" high, blue maple leaf mark, pair	.100.00	120.00
☐ Cheese Dish, rose decor with gold trim	24.00	30.00
☐ Chocolate Set, pink cherry blossom, green wreath mark, 29 pieces	400.00	450.00
☐ Cigarette Box, enameled horse head, bisque finish, covered	55.00	65.00
☐ Cookie Jar, scenic decor with blue & green shaded ground, 8½" high	160.00	190.00
☐ Creamer & Sugar, farm & water scene, green "M" in wreath mark	48.00	55.00
☐ Cup & Saucer, demitasse, pink & blue floral	16.00	20.00
☐ Cup & Saucer, pink roses, gold scroll	12.00	16.00
☐ Cup & Saucer, white, floral, green mark	7.00	10.00
☐ Dish, lake scene with swans & lily pad, 7¼" oval, maple leaf mark	65.00	70.00
☐ Dish, mayonnaise, yellow & gold flowers, 3 pieces . . .	22.00	30.00
☐ Dresser Tray, violets	16.00	20.00
☐ Egg Warmer, floral, gold trim on white background, with four cups, green wreath mark	80.00	90.00

NIPPON

	Price	Range
☐ Ewer, pink roses with gold beading, blue maple leaf mark	40.00	45.00
☐ Ginger Jar, rose decor with gold trim	20.00	25.00
☐ Hair Receiver, floral on blue background	32.00	38.00
☐ Hatpin Holder, desert scene, bisque finish	24.00	30.00
☐ Humidor, green, white & gold floral decor, enameled maple leaf mark	155.00	185.00
☐ Lemonade Set, floral decor, pitcher & mugs	130.00	150.00
☐ Match Holder, farm house scene, green "M" mark	40.00	55.00
☐ Mayonnaise Bowl, blue & gold trim, 2 pieces	18.00	24.00
☐ Mayonnaise Set, rising sun mark, 3 pieces	18.00	24.00
☐ Mustache Cup & Saucer, scenic, green wreath mark	125.00	150.00
☐ Napkin Ring, floral decor, gold trim	35.00	45.00
☐ Nut Bowl, basketweave with black walnuts, 7½" deep	90.00	110.00
☐ Peanut Set, peanuts & vines, bowl 8¼" long, with 5 bowls	155.00	185.00
☐ Pitcher, bulbous, grape pattern, 6"	55.00	65.00
☐ Pitcher, bulbous, sparrow flying thru blossoms, 9½" high	155.00	175.00
☐ Pitcher, tankard, pink, white & deep rose chrysanthemums, green border, 11" high	210.00	260.00
☐ Planter, Indian in canoe, green "M" in wreath mark	60.00	75.00
☐ Planter, ship decor, jeweled, 7¼" square, green wreath mark	130.00	150.00
☐ Plaque, Indian portrait, 7¾", green "M" in wreath mark	105.00	135.00
☐ Plaque, lion & lioness, 10¾" in relief	400.00	425.00
☐ Plaque, scenic, blue maple leaf, 9"	55.00	65.00
☐ Plate, orange poppies on brown background, blue maple leaf mark, 11" deep	155.00	175.00
☐ Plate, red roses with green border, 10"	28.00	38.00
☐ Rose Bowl, pink & white, gold decorations, 5½" x 3"	38.00	48.00
☐ Salt & Pepper, floral & gold	12.00	16.00
☐ Sugar Shaker, gold beading with poppies	30.00	45.00
☐ Sugar & Creamer, pink roses, gold trim, cover	20.00	30.00
☐ Sugar & Creamer, pink blossoms, gold trim, green "M" mark	25.00	35.50
☐ Tea Set, sailboat scene, 3 pieces	90.00	110.00
☐ Teapot, child's face in relief, covered, 3¼" high	3750.00	4500.00
☐ Tray, desert scene, 10½" x 7"	40.00	45.00
☐ Tray, flowers & parrot on limb, green wreath mark	60.00	80.00
☐ Urn, desert scene, 10½" x 7"	40.00	45.00
☐ Vase, camel scene, 6-sided, 9¼"	90.00	100.00
☐ Vase, deep blue, handpainted, green mark, 10"	90.00	100.00
☐ Vase, Egyptian animals & people, 9"	70.00	90.00
☐ Vase, lake scene, green wreath mark, 6"	35.00	45.00
☐ Vase, pedestal base, gold drapery swags on cobalt blue background, 8"	80.00	100.00
☐ Vase, red & white roses, gold beading, maple leaf mark, 7" x 9"	120.00	150.00

NORITAKE

Noritake china is still being produced in Japan today. Large quantities have been exported to this country. A favorite pattern with collectors is Azalea.

	Price Range	
☐ Ashtray, pine cones, Nortake-Nippon mark	37.50	42.00
☐ Basket, Azalea pattern	70.00	80.00
☐ Bonbon, Azalea pattern	22.00	30.00
☐ Bowl, cereal	12.00	16.00
☐ Butter Tub, with liner, Azalea pattern	25.00	30.00
☐ Cake Set, ivory with black & gold trim, blue urn with flowers	50.00	70.00
☐ Chocolate Set, hand painted, green mark, 11 pieces . .	40.00	50.00
☐ Condiment Set, Azalea pattern, 5 pieces	25.00	35.00
☐ Creamer, Sahara	15.00	20.00
☐ Cup & Saucer, Azalea pattern	9.00	15.00
☐ Dinner Set, Hanover, 64 pieces	300.00	350.00
☐ Egg Cup, Azalea pattern	15.00	20.00
☐ Gravy Boat, Azalea pattern, with attached stand	27.40	32.00
☐ Inkwell, Figural clown	25.00	36.00
☐ Hatpin Holder, forget-me-nots	7.00	10.00
☐ Lemon Plate, Azalea pattern	13.00	16.00
☐ Mayonnaise Set, bowl, underplate, ladle, rose decor, 3 pieces	18.00	24.00
☐ Mustard Jar, with spoon, Azalea pattern	30.00	45.00
☐ Pitcher, milk, Azalea pattern	80.00	90.00
☐ Plate, Azalea pattern, 7½" D	4.00	6.00
☐ Plate, dinner, Azalea pattern	8.00	14.00
☐ Plate, square, Azalea pattern	2750.00	3200.00
☐ Plate, soup, Azalea pattern, green mark, 7½"	10.00	12.00
☐ Plate, tree at lake, 6"	20.00	25.00
☐ Platter, Azalea pattern, 12" oval	22.00	25.00
☐ Platter, Azalea pattern, 14" oval	30.00	35.00
☐ Relish Dish, Azalea pattern, 4 section, handled, 9" . . .	42.50	50.00
☐ Sauce Dish, Azalea pattern 6" D	5.00	8.00
☐ Soup Bowl, Azalea pattern	8.00	12.00
☐ Spooner, Azalea pattern	38.00	48.00
☐ Syrup & Underplate, white roses, gold trim	32.00	38.00
☐ Tea Set, Azalea pattern, 15 pieces	90.00	100.00
☐ Teapot, tree in meadow pattern	4250.00	4850.00
☐ Toothpick Holder, Azalea pattern	65.00	75.00
☐ Tray, tree at lake pattern	20.00	25.00
☐ Tureen, gold handles, floral holder	25.00	35.00
☐ Urn, rose decor with gold, two handles	75.00	85.00
☐ Vase, fan shaped, tree in the meadow pattern	4250.00	5000.00
☐ Vase, gold handles, pink roses, 3" H	10.00	15.00
☐ Vase, lavender, 4 handles, green wreath mark, 8½" pr.	24.00	30.00
☐ Vase, sunset lake scene, gold rim, red 7 wreath, 8" . . .	24.00	30.00
☐ Vegetable Bowl, Azalea pattern, covered, handled, green mark, 9"	30.00	35.00

MUSTACHE CUPS WITH SAUCERS

The Victorian Era (1880-1900) introduced mustache cups, during this period they grew increasingly popular. Somewhat different from standard drinking mugs or glasses, they were constructed with a separate piece inserted along one rim of the cup to keep the gentleman's mustache out of his drink. "Left-handed" cups made for left-handed men are the scarcest and most valuable. Reproductions are readily available and the buyer should purchase from a reputable dealer to insure authenticity. Prices are for Good Condition with matching saucer.

	Price
☐ Austrian-designed. Multi-colored floral decoration	56.00
☐ Bavarian. Medallion of pink roses, gold scroll work Marked Royal Bavarian China — Germany. PMB	45.00
☐ Bird with floral, gold trim	30.00
☐ Civil war drum decor. Left-handed. C. 1860	165.00
☐ Cup and attached saucer, Worcester	85.00
☐ Daniel Webster's birthplace	70.00
☐ Floral design, gold, beaded edge and foot	42.50
☐ Floral design, lavender flowers (Carlsbad)	40.00
☐ Floral design, blue forget-me-nots and roses	50.00
☐ Floral design, lavender and pink assorted flowers	40.00
☐ Floral design, red roses with gold trim on cup	42.50
☐ Hand painted floral, French	50.00
☐ Inscribed, "John Summer, 1883"	60.00
☐ Inscribed, "Think of Me", white, pink and gold	50.00
☐ Raised floral design, Germany	25.00
☐ Silver Plated, cup & saucer set	30.00
☐ Swirled cup & saucer, "Papa" lettered on side	50.00
☐ Pink Lustre Ware cup & saucer, inscribed panel	65.00
☐ Victorian porcelain, pink lustre	30.00

STERLING OR "COIN" DOUBLE PRICE — LEFT-HANDED CUPS DOUBLE PRICE.

ROYAL BAYREUTH

Royal Bayreuth was made in Tettau, Germany, since 1794. The popularity of this porcelain remains high and prices are rising constantly.

	Price	Range
☐ Ashtray, clown, blue mark	125.00	135.00
☐ Ashtray, elk, blue mark	70.00	80.00
☐ Bill, hand-painted farm scene	38.00	45.00
☐ Berry Bowl, roses, gold trim, blue mark, 4¼"	55.00	60.00
☐ Bonbon, pink & white roses, footed blue mark	4850.00	5500.00
☐ Bowl, Brittany girl, blue mark, 6¼"	40.00	45.00
☐ Bowl, Dutch girl, house, blue sky & white clouds, 9'½"	170.00	180.00
☐ Bowl, poppy, blue mark, 8 x 4½"	55.00	65.00
☐ Bowl, tomato, 9½"	115.00	125.00
☐ Box, black & tan, covered, pin roses, 4 x 5"	70.00	80.00
☐ Box, card, men at table with dancing, green, blue mark	70.00	75.00
☐ Box, "Little Bo Peep", green, blue mark	115.00	125.00
☐ Candlestick, goosegirl & geese, blue mark, 4½"	50.00	55.00

ROYAL BAYREUTH

	Price	Range
☐ Celery, lobster, 13 x 5"	70.00	75.00
☐ Cracker Set, bowl & pitcher, lobster	200.00	210.00
☐ Creamer, apple	75.00	80.00
☐ Creamer, bear	100.00	110.00
☐ Creamer, butterfly, blue mark	155.00	165.00
☐ Creamer, clown, red mark	120.00	130.00
☐ Creamer, devil & cards	80.00	90.00
☐ Creamer, eagle, blue mark	85.00	95.00
☐ Creamer, pig	105.00	115.00
☐ Creamer, strawberry	75.00	85.00
☐ Creamer, water buffalo	95.00	105.00
☐ Cup & Saucer, demitasse, devil & dice	60.00	70.00
☐ Cup & Saucer, demitasse, Murex	70.00	75.00
☐ Dish, candy, clown, blue mark	150.00	160.00
☐ Dish, lettuce, blue mark, 7 x 5½"	28.50	32.00
☐ Hair Receiver, barnyard scene, blue mark	75.00	85.00
☐ Hatpin Holder, owl, black mark	220.00	230.00
☐ Hatpin Holder, red poppy, blue mark	150.00	160.00
☐ Match Holder, penguin, hanging type	80.00	90.00
☐ Mustard Jar, rose, covered with original spoon	140.00	150.00
☐ Nappy, swans on lake, handled, oval	35.00	40.00
☐ Pitchers, Brittany girl decor, 5¼"	70.00	75.00
☐ Pitchers, clown, red	180.00	190.00
☐ Pitchers, devil & cards	180.00	190.00
☐ Pitchers, hunting scene, 7½"	80.00	90.00
☐ Pitchers, milk, monkey, blue mark	120.00	130.00
☐ Pitchers, milk, poppy, blue mark	130.00	140.00
☐ Pitchers, milk, tavern scene	120.00	130.00
☐ Pitchers, water, Murex	130.00	140.00
☐ Plates, devil & cards, 7"	100.00	110.00
☐ Plates, leaf with handle, 5½"	65.00	70.00
☐ Plates, little girl with dog	85.00	95.00
☐ Salt & Pepper, grape, blue mark	100.00	110.00
☐ Shakers, conch, pair	80.00	90.00
☐ Shakers, grapes	60.00	70.00
☐ Shakers, lobster	105.00	115.00
☐ Sugar & Creamer, hunter & dogs	90.00	100.00
☐ Sugar & Creamer, lobster	125.00	115.00
☐ Tea Set, apple	200.00	220.00
☐ Tea Set, tomato, blue mark, 3 pieces	155.00	175.00
☐ Toothpick Holder, deer head	65.00	75.00
☐ Tray, pink roses, green, 10 x 7"	75.00	85.00
☐ Vase, cows grazing, green	65.00	75.00
☐ Vase, Dutch scene, 5½"	65.00	75.00
☐ Vase, girls and ship scene, 3½"	45.00	55.00
☐ Vase, "Little Bo Peep", handles, 2½"	85.00	95.00
☐ Vase, man with dogs, 7"	155.00	165.00
☐ Vase, polar bear in snow, blue mark, 5"	60.00	70.00
☐ Vase, rose tapestry, 2 gold handles, 3"	100.00	110.00

ROYAL COPENHAGEN

Royal Copenhagen has been produced in Denmark since 1771 and is still being made. The factory was under royal operation for a time. Items were imported into the United States from the late 1800's to the early 1900's.

	Price Range	
☐ Ashtray, Langelinie	60.00	70.00
☐ Bonbon	30.00	35.00
☐ Bottle, Fredercksborg castle on front, crown on back, 10"	70.00	80.00
☐ Bowl, green & gray with gold, square, 6 x 3"	3250.00	4000.00
☐ Coffee Pot, gold edge & handles with underglazed decor	150.00	170.00
☐ Dish, shape of leaf, blue flowers and handle, 9"	14.00	20.00
☐ Figurines, baby duckling, 4½" H	28.00	35.00
☐ Figurines, cat, sitting, gray & white, 5½" H	45.00	55.00
☐ Figurines, dog, Dachshund laying down, 3¼" H	55.00	65.00
☐ Figurines, girl with large goose, 9½" H	140.00	160.00
☐ Figurines, Pup sitting, tan & brown, 3½" H	48.00	55.00
☐ Figurines, Siamese cat laying with head & forepaw raised, 4" H	62.50	70.00
☐ Figurines, stag, brown tones	90.00	100.00
☐ Figurines, young boy holding pig, 6½" H	85.00	90.00
☐ Inkwell, with tray, 6 x 8½" L....................	90.00	100.00
☐ Plate, commemorative, soldiers, ships & flag	95.00	105.00
☐ Plate, fruit center, pink border, 8"	24.00	30.00
☐ Plate, portrait of Josephine, 1923, 10¾"	78.00	85.00
☐ Plate, portraits of Napoleon, Josephine, Pauline Bonapart & husband, set of 4, 10¾" D	245.00	265.00
☐ Plate, soup, blue & white with open chain edge, green mark, 7¾"	30.00	35.00
☐ Platters, gray & white, gold, 8 x 12"	70.00	80.00
☐ Platters, blue & white, 9 x 12"	70.00	80.00
☐ Platters, blue & white, 12 x 16"	100.00	110.00
☐ Sugar & Creamer, doll's, pink roses, Crown mark	34.00	40.00
☐ Soup Tureen, with cover & underplate, blue, 1897 mark, 18" L	170.00	190.00
☐ Tray, blue & white floral, 6 x II"	25.00	35.00
☐ Tray, crackleware, gold edge, green, 8¼" D	35.00	45.00
☐ Vases, blue gray, white flowers, 5"	30.00	35.00
☐ Vases, fuchsia flowers, leaves, 9½"	90.00	100.00
☐ Vases, green crackle with gold decorations, 12", pair .	230.00	250.00
☐ Vases, Rhodadendron, 10"	90.00	100.00
☐ Vases, ship decor, 8"	75.00	85.00

ROYAL DOULTON

☐ "The Football Scrimmage" (four frogs). by George Tinworth, 4½" H, c. 1885	600.00	700.00
☐ Figure of a reaper by Leslie Harradine, 7½" H, c. 1910	400.00	500.00
☐ Queen Victoria by John Broad. 11¾"	300.00	400.00

ROYAL DOULTON

	Price	Range
☐ Humoresque by Tinworth. "Play Goers" (mice watching a puppet show). 4¾ths", c. 1884	350.00	400.00
☐ Figure of Sidney Carton (Dickens character) by Leslie Harradine, 10½", c. 1912	150.00	175.00
☐ "Motherhood" by Leslie Harradine, 5", c. 1912	100.00	120.00
☐ Woman in 18th century dress with basket of flowers by John Broad, c. 1919	100.00	150.00

SHAVING MUGS
(INCLUDING OCCUPATIONAL MUGS)

As an essential toiletry utensil, the shaving mug held soap and a softbristled brush used to make lather. Occupational mugs were stored at the local barber shop and had the owner's name and occupation inscribed on the outside.

All prices are for ORIGINAL ITEMS in Good Condition

	Price
☐ Accordion	145.00
☐ Anchor. With owner's name inscribed	90.00
☐ Anvil, Tongs and Hammer................................	125.00
☐ Arc Light	130.00
☐ Architect's Insignia	110.00
☐ Athlete. High Jumper	150.00
☐ Athlete. Track Star	150.00
☐ Automobile. Early	155.00
☐ Baker	145.00
☐ Baggage Master with Truck and Car	145.00
☐ Bakery Wagon, Driver and Horse	150.00
☐ Barber	130.00
☐ Barber Shop...	210.00
☐ Bartender...	135.00
☐ Baseball Player	175.00
☐ Baseball with Bats	140.00
☐ Beer Bottle & Glasses around Barrel of Beer	120.00
☐ Beer Mug	110.00
☐ Beer Wagon with Horse and Driver	165.00
☐ Bicycle...	145.00
☐ Bill Poster	165.00
☐ Billiard Players	160.00
☐ Blacksmith Shoeing Horse.............................	130.00
☐ Boiler Maker at Work.................................	130.00
☐ Bookkeeper	115.00
☐ Bookmaker at Work (Bookbinding).......................	145.00
☐ Bowler. Men in bowling alley	160.00
☐ Brakeman Operating Brake	140.00
☐ Brewmaster	185.00
☐ Brick Layer..	125.00
☐ Bridge, Steel	140.00
☐ Buggy, Horse & Driver	100.00
☐ Butcher Killing Steer	100.00
☐ Cabinet Maker	160.00

SHAVING MUGS

Price

- [ ] Caboose 95.00
- [ ] Camera 175.00
- [ ] Carpenter at Table 165.00
- [ ] Carpenter at Work 100.00
- [ ] Cigar Store 110.00
- [ ] Clothing Store & Cigar Store 110.00
- [ ] Coal Miner at Work 130.00
- [ ] Cooper at Work Making Barrels 155.00
- [ ] Cowboys Lassoing Steer with Name. Limoges 190.00
- [ ] Dentist Pulling Teeth 185.00
- [ ] Dentist with False Teeth 170.00
- [ ] Doctor Tending Patient (Rare) 255.00
- [ ] Drug Store 125.00
- [ ] Druggist at Work 120.00
- [ ] Drum 100.00
- [ ] Engine in Station 120.00
- [ ] Fire Steam Engine 195.00
- [ ] Flour and General Store 110.00
- [ ] Furniture Store 120.00
- [ ] Grocery Store and Clerk 120.00
- [ ] Guns, Crossed Rifles and Targets 120.00
- [ ] Hardware Store 120.00
- [ ] Hatter at Work 140.00
- [ ] Hotel Register 110.00
- [ ] Horse Drawn Hearse 260.00
- [ ] Hunter, Shooting at Birds, Pointer Dog 125.00
- [ ] Ice Wagon, Horse and Driver 135.00
- [ ] Jewelry Store 120.00
- [ ] Jockey 145.00
- [ ] Judge 200.00
- [ ] Livery Stable 150.00
- [ ] Livery Stableman 135.00
- [ ] Locomotive 135.00
- [ ] Mail Wagon 110.00
- [ ] Marble Cutter at Work 125.00
- [ ] Milk Wagon, Horse and Driver 125.00
- [ ] Minister in Pulpit 210.00
- [ ] Motorman and Conductor 130.00
- [ ] Musicians 100.00
- [ ] Painter at Work 135.00
- [ ] Photographer 175.00
- [ ] Piano Player 110.00
- [ ] Plasterer 105.00
- [ ] Plumber 120.00
- [ ] Policeman 160.00
- [ ] Printer Setting Type 100.00
- [ ] Prizefighter (Rare) . . . . —
- [ ] Restaurant and Bar 110.00
- [ ] Roller Skater 100.00

SHAVING MUGS

	Price
☐ Sawmill	140.00
☐ Sheep Shearer	100.00
☐ Shoe Dealer	100.00
☐ State Senator	145.00
☐ Steamship	135.00
☐ Surveyor	140.00
☐ Tailor, with Assistant	150.00
☐ Tailor, with Scissors & Yardstick	130.00
☐ Taxi Driver	135.00
☐ Teacher Class of "1898"	105.00
☐ Telegrapher	110.00
☐ Telephone	120.00
☐ Tobacco Store	120.00
☐ Tow Truck and Driver (Old Type Truck)	145.00
☐ Tug Boat	185.00
☐ Umbrella	100.00
☐ Undertaker (Very Rare)	450.00
☐ Whiskey Wagon	160.00

REPRODUCTIONS ARE MADE.

STAFFORDSHIRE

	Price	Range
☐ Bottle, scent, decorated, 18th Century	380.00	420.00
☐ Bottle, scent, 18th Century	360.00	400.00
☐ Bowl, flowers and castles, 12" H	60.00	90.00
☐ Box, trinket, spaniel	50.00	70.00
☐ Cat, black and white, 7½" H, pair	140.00	170.00
☐ Cat, salt-glazed, 7½" H	550.00	600.00
☐ Cottage, with people	25.00	35.00
☐ Dog, greyhound, 10" H, pair	190.00	220.00
☐ Dog, poodle, 6" H, pair	90.00	120.00
☐ Figurine, girl praying	80.00	100.00
☐ Figurine, G. Gordon, 17½" H	120.00	140.00
☐ Figurine, Mrs. Punch sitting on goat	75.00	100.00
☐ Figurine, Queen Victoria, c. 1850	80.00	100.00
☐ Figurine, Robin Hood, 12"	70.00	100.00
☐ Figurine, Wallace	90.00	120.00
☐ Figurine, Victoria and Albert, 7½" H, pair	640.00	670.00
☐ Group, lion and leopard	170.00	200.00
☐ Group, lovers, 12" H	80.00	110.00
☐ Hen, carmel nest, 7" H	140.00	170.00
☐ Inkwell, girl with dog	90.00	220.00
☐ Jug, decorated with bands of checks, c. 1760	300.00	330.00
☐ Jug, milk, blue and white	60.00	80.00
☐ Lion, standing with one foot on ball, pair	190.00	220.00
☐ Pitcher, cherubs, 6¼" H	45.00	60.00
☐ Pitcher, water, Corean, c. 1850	90.00	120.00
☐ Plate, Boston Statehouse, blue, 9¼" H	325.00	350.00
☐ Snuff Box, 3¼" W, c. 1765	170.00	190.00
☐ Snuff Box, voyeurs, 3¼" W, c. 1765	800.00	850.00

STEINS

Steins, those half-litre, one litre, two litre, etc. containers for drinking beer or ale, are quite popular collectibles. Among the most desirable are those made by the German firm Mettlach. The numbers after the Mettlach listings refer to style numbers, and are often found on the bottom of the steins.

	Price	Range
☐ Art Nouveau, Copper and brass, Germany, 14" H	75.00	100.00
☐ Bacchus, Silver, Sheffield, 11½" H	475.00	550.00
☐ Character, Monkey, drunken, Musterschutz, 1 litre ...	325.00	375.00
☐ Crying Radish, Musterschutz, 3/10 litre	350.00	425.00
☐ David and Goliath, Handle with four finger holes, 1/2 litre	450.00	550.00
☐ Firefighting Scene with pewter top, 1/2 litre	250.00	300.00
☐ Glass, Farm scene with pewter lid, 1/2 litre	40.00	45.00
☐ Happy Turnip, Musterschutz, 3 litre	375.00	450.00
☐ Ivory, Battle scene, carved, 13¾" H	1800.00	2200.00
☐ Lithophanes, Clown, 1/2 litre	325.00	375.00
☐ Lithophanes, German scene, 6½" H	75.00	100.00
☐ Mettlach, No. 1527, 1/2 litre	460.00	500.00
☐ Mettlach, No. 1648, pewter lid, 1/2 litre	270.00	300.00
☐ Mettlach, No. 1675, Heidelberg, 1/2 lire	425.00	475.00
☐ Mettlach, No. 2002, Munich, 1/2 litre	325.00	375.00
☐ Mettlach, No. 2038, Black Forest, 4 litre	3500.00	3800.00
☐ Mettlach, No. 2131, 1 litre	395.00	—
☐ Mettlach, No. 2136, Brewmaster, 1/2 litre	275.00	325.00
☐ Mettlach, No. 2181, Pug, 1/2 litre	275.00	325.00
☐ Mettlach, No. 2388, Pretzel, 1/2 litre	390.00	460.00
☐ Mettlach, No. 2958, Bowling, 16" H	625.00	700.00
☐ Mettlach, No. 3085, Etched, 1/2 litre		
☐ Monk, Gesetzlicht, 1/2 litre	140.00	190.00
☐ Pewter, Kazserzinn, 10" H	150.00	180.00
☐ Puss In Boots, 6½" H	40.00	50.00
☐ Regimental, 18th Infantry, 1 litre	250.00	325.00
☐ Regimental, Franco-Prussian War, 1 litre	250.00	325.00
☐ Schlitz Beer, ceramic, 7½" H	20.00	30.00
☐ Singing Pig, Musterschutz, 1/4 litre	250.00	325.00
☐ Stoneware, Warriors battling, pewter lid, 1 litre	75.00	100.00
☐ Tower, Pewter lid, Geschuta, 1/2 litre	230.00	290.00
☐ Town Scene, Pewter lid. 1/2 litre	240.00	280.00

TOBY JUGS

Toby Jugs were used as beer and ale mugs in early times both in England and in the United States.

	Price
☐ Allerton, cobalt blue with copper trim, Toby 4" high	22.50
☐ Cat, 9" high	145.00
☐ Delft, Man with Beard, marked on lid, 9" high	465.00
☐ Delft, Man Taking Snuff with Bug on Nose, 11" high	575.00
☐ King Louis, blue and white, 7" high	110.00

TOBY JUGS

Price

- [ ] MacArthur, Douglas, 3¾" high 35.00
- [ ] Royal Doulton, Ard of Earing 340.00
- [ ] Royal Doulton, best is not too good 320.00
- [ ] Royal Doulton, brown hat and shirt, white wig,
      blue jacket, with glass, 3¾" high............................ 105.00
- [ ] Royal Doulton, Cap 'n Cuttle 160.00
- [ ] Royal Doulton, Fat Boy, 4¼" high 160.00
- [ ] Royal Doulton, Fortune Teller * 210.00
- [ ] Royal Doulton, Gladiator * 210.00
- [ ] Royal Doulton, Guardsman 22.00
- [ ] Royal Doulton, Huntsman, 8" high........................... 75.00
- [ ] Royal Doulton, Lawyer 32.50
- [ ] Royal Doulton, Lobsterman 20.00
- [ ] Royal Doulton, Old Charley, 8¼" high....................... 185.00
- [ ] Royal Doulton, Parson Brown "A"* 37.50
- [ ] Royal Doulton, Parson Brown 180.00
- [ ] Royal Doulton, Sir John Falstaff, 6" high 85.00
- [ ] Royal Doulton, Ugly Duchess * 70.00
- [ ] Royal Doulton, Uncle Tom Cobbleigh, large 310.00
- [ ] Royal Doulton, Winston Churchill, 3¾" high ..... : 20.00
- [ ] Royal Doulton, Toby, seated on wine keg, Ca. 1850, 15" high 265.00
- [ ] Royal Doulton, Beefeater * 65.00
- [ ] Royal Doulton, Captain Hook * 220.00
- [ ] Royal Doulton, Drake * 90.00
- [ ] Royal Doulton, Falconer 50.00
- [ ] Royal Doulton, Jockey * 95.00
- [ ] Royal Doulton, Johnny Appleseed * 185.00
- [ ] Royal Doulton, Lord Nelson * 210.00
- [ ] Royal Doulton, Robin Hood * 105.00
- [ ] Staffordshire, Admiral Nelson, blue coat, white breeches
      yellow and maroon coat, Ca. 1830, 11" high 620.00
- [ ] Staffordshire, Falstaff, green coat........................ 175.00
- [ ] Staffordshire, Hearty Good Fellow, Ca. 1820, 9" high....... 125.00
- [ ] Staffordshire, Herbert Hoover, 7" 90.00
- [ ] Staffordshire, John Bull, with separate hat lid, 11" high 80.00
- [ ] Staffordshire, King Louis, blue and white 110.00
- [ ] Staffordshire, man seated, tricorn hat, 8" high 440.00
- [ ] Staffordshire, Scottie 50.00
- [ ] Staffordshire, Sleeper, 6" high 45.00
- [ ] Staffordshire, Snuff Taker with removable hat lid, 14" high 140.00
- [ ] Wedgwood, Coachman, 7" high............................... 110.00
- [ ] Wedgwood, Lord Chamberlain, Toby 7" high 130.00
- [ ] Wedgwood, Preacher, 7" high 110.00
- [ ] Wedgwood, Professor, Toby, 7" high........................ 110.00
- [ ] Wedgwood, Tax Collector, Toby, 7" high.................... 110.00
- [ ] Wedgwood, Town Crier, Toby, 7" high 130.00

* DISCONTINUED ITEM

WEDGWOOD

	Price Range	
☐ Black basalt plaque, blacksmiths at work, Athene in chariot watching, 10"	500.00	600.00
☐ Black basalt bust of the poet John Milton, 13½", c. 1780	1800.00	2000.00
☐ Candelabra with cornucopia, Pair, 12½", blue and white jasper	500.00	600.00
☐ Statue of a female, 17", on stand, basalt, c. 1774	1000.00	1200.00
☐ Cupids struggling for a Heart. Earthernware, 15½", c. 1770	1800.00	2000.00
☐ Figure "Charity." Modeled by Mrs. Landre, 1768, 8½", colored earthenware, c. 1768	400.00	500.00

POSTCARDS

Postcards have been a popular collectible since their inception in the 19th century. Then, people pasted their pretty postcards (along with other colorfully-printed paper items) into scrapbooks. Today, collectors are more careful, and keep their prizes—many worth $10, $15 or even more—in plastic "sleeves." The best sources for postcards are paper and postcard shows, with as many as 150 dealers all in one place, and through the mail. The prices below are listed by subject, primarily. The really expensive cards are artist cards, and certain cards of complicated construction.

☐ Airplanes, Early	2.50	3.00
☐ Angels Flying	2.00	2.25
☐ Automobiles, Early	2.50	3.00
☐ Aviation	10.00	12.00
☐ Billikens	6.50	7.50
☐ Boats, Naval	2.00	2.25
☐ Boats, Sailing	2.00	2.25
☐ California, Early	2.00	2.25
☐ Celebrated Posters	7.00	9.00
☐ Chickens and Chicks	1.75	2.25
☐ Christmas	6.00	8.00

POSTCARDS

	Price	Range
☐ Churches	1.50	1.75
☐ Colored Folks	7.00	9.00
☐ Comics	2.00	2.50
☐ Coronation	7.00	9.00
☐ Courthouses, Early	3.00	4.50
☐ Disasters (Hurricanes, Tornadoes, Fires)	3.00	3.50
☐ Dressing Dolls	12.00	15.00
☐ Easter, Animals	2.00	2.25
☐ Easter, Birds	2.00	2.25
☐ Empire	8.00	10.00
☐ Exposition, 19th Century	3.00	3.50
☐ Fairs	4.25	4.75
☐ Floral Designs	1.50	1.75
☐ Gelatin	2.25	3.00
☐ Greetings	1.75	2.00
☐ Hall Manufacturing	2.25	2.75
☐ Hallowe'en	6.00	8.00
☐ Horseshoes	2.25	2.75
☐ Indians	2.50	3.00
☐ Jamestown Exposition	10.00	12.00
☐ Leather	2.00	2.50
☐ Louis Wain's Cats	17.00	20.00
☐ Newspaper Comics	2.00	2.50
☐ Parades, 19th Century	2.00	2.25
☐ Patriotic Theme	2.00	2.25
☐ Presidents, Before 1915	4.00	5.00
☐ Roses	1.50	1.75
☐ Santa Claus, Whitney	3.50	4.00
☐ St. Patrick	2.00	2.25
☐ Sunbonnet Baby	5.00	6.00
☐ Swinging Dolls	12.00	15.00
☐ Thanksgiving	2.00	2.25
☐ Train Wrecks	2.00	2.25
☐ U.S. Army	12.00	15.00
☐ Waterfalls, Early	2.50	3.00

POSTERS

What is a poster? It's artwork done on paper rather larger than typing paper, plus some words to advertise something or tell you about something. There are theatre posters, circus posters (some of which are incredibly large), art show posters, military enlisting posters, patriotic posters, and many others. Many kinds of printing techniques are used by poster designers—including wood blocks, lithographs, silk screens, and photographs.

☐ Back Our Girls Over There, Y.M.C.A., Clarence Underwood	30.00	40.00
☐ Be A U.S. Marine, James Montgomery Flagg	45.00	55.00
☐ Blood or Bread, Raleigh	20.00	30.00

POSTERS

	Price	Range
☐ Broadside, Bonnie & Clyde, 1930's	10.00	15.00
☐ Broadside, various Pa. sales, woodcuts, late 19th century	15.00	20.00
☐ Buy Liberty Bonds, Anon	20.00	30.00
☐ Enlist, Laura Brey	40.00	50.00
☐ Fight World Famine, Anon	30.00	40.00
☐ Get Under This Fighting Top, Raymond Bannister....	25.00	35.00
☐ Going, Going, Gone, Anon	12.00	20.00
☐ Help, Red Cross, Anon	15.00	25.00
☐ Hold Up Your End, W. B. King	20.00	30.00
☐ Join the Air Service, Anon	75.00	100.00
☐ Keep Him Free, Buy War Savings Stamps, Charles Livingston Bull	40.00	50.00
☐ Let's End It, Quick With Liberty Bonds, Maurice Ingres	50.00	70.00
☐ Men Wanted for the Army, M. P. Whelan............	60.00	70.00
☐ New York State Fair, Art Deco, c. 1922	60.00	80.00
☐ Re-Enlist Now, Cushing	20.00	30.00
☐ Remember Belguim, Buy Bond, Fourth Liberty Loan, Ellsworth Yourn	25.00	35.00
☐ "Roar of the Crowd", Joe Lewis, movie broadside, c. 1930	8.00	10.00
☐ Saturday Evening Post, advertising poster, 1940's ...	20.00	25.00
☐ Sears, Roebuck & Co., advertising slide show (1898) on Alaska gold fields, illus. lady & miner	40.00	50.00
☐ Sow the Seeds of Victory, James Montgomery Flagg.	60.00	70.00
☐ Theatre Lobby Poster, litho, "The Old Homestead"...	70.00	90.00
☐ Wake Up America, James Montgomery Flagg	60.00	70.00
☐ Welcome Home Our Victors, Anon	20.00	30.00
☐ You Can Help, Red Cross, W. T. Benda	15.00	25.00

PRINTS

As defined by the prestigious Print Council of America, a print is "a work of art", and must fulfill these requirements: (1) creation of the master image by the artist alone on the plate, stone, wood block or other material; (2) the execution of the print by the artist himself or pursuant to his directions; and (3) approval of the work by the artist himself.

It is possible today to gather good works of art at a fraction of the cost of the originals through prints, but do be careful of the "reproductions" such as are printed in calendars and books on art. Please consult our publication *The Official Price Guide to Collector Prints* by Ruth Pollard for more prices and information.

KEY TO CODING

s/n - signed & numbered   u/s - unsigned
s/o - signed only   s/s - with state seal
i/o - initialed only   rem - remarqued print

CURRIER & IVES PRINTS (OLD)

To help collectors, we have listed below the best fifty large and small folios and have identified each with the appropriate Cunningham number. Those titles followed by an asterick are known to appear on more than one composition.

AMERICAN HUNTING SCENES — *"A Good Chance"*

THE BEST FIFTY (SMALL FOLIO):	#	Price Range	
☐ The Express Train*	1790	700.00	800.00
☐ American Railroad Scene — Snowbound*	187	750.00	900.00
☐ Beach Snipe Shooting	445	900.00	1100.00
☐ Ice-Boat Race on the Hudson	3021	900.00	1200.00
☐ Central Park in Winter	953	600.00	800.00
☐ The Star of the Road	5701	150.00	175.00
☐ The High Bridge at Harlem, N.Y.*	2810	200.00	250.00
☐ Maple Sugaring, Early Spring in the Northern Woods	3975	400.00	500.00
☐ Shakers Near Lebanon	5475	500.00	600.00
☐ Winter Sports — Pickerel Fishing	6747	700.00	850.00

THE BEST FIFTY (SMALL)

	Price	Range
☐ The American Clipper Ship Witch of the Wave . 115	600.00	800.00
☐ Gold Mining in California 2412	500.00	600.00
☐ The Great International Boat Race 2623	750.00	900.00
☐ Wild Turkey Shooting. 6677	350.00	400.00
☐ Perry's Victory on Lake Erie 4754	350.00	400.00
☐ Washington at Mount Vernon, 1797 6515	200.00	275.00
☐ The Whale Fishery. "Laying On". 6626	900.00	1000.00
☐ Chatham Square, New York 1020	400.00	475.00
☐ Water Rail Shooting* 6567	475.00	550.00
☐ The Sleigh Race* 5554	450.00	500.00
☐ Franklin's Experiment* 2128	250.00	350.00
☐ Washington Crossing the Delaware* 6523	250.00	300.00
☐ American Homestead Winter 172	350.00	500.00
☐ Washington Taking Leave of the Officers of his Army 6547	200.00	250.00
☐ Steamboat Knickerbocker. 5727	250.00	300.00
☐ Kiss Me Quick!* 3349	200.00	250.00
☐ One the Mississippi Loading Cotton 4607	200.00	225.00
☐ Bound Down the River 627	325.00	375.00
☐ American Whalers Crushed in the Ice 205	600.00	750.00
☐ Dartmouth College* 1446	950.00	1200.00
☐ Terrific Combat Between the Monitor, 2 Guns, and the Merrimac, 10 Guns* 5996	350.00	400.00
☐ General Francis Marion. 2250	175.00	225.00
☐ Art of Making Money Plenty 275	150.00	175.00
☐ Honorable Abraham Lincoln* 2895	150.00	200.00
☐ General George Washington (with cape)* 2261	90.00	120.00
☐ Black Bass Spearing 543	1100.00	1300.00
☐ Early Winter 1652	1200.00	1500.00
☐ Woodcock Shooting* 6773	450.00	500.00
☐ "Dutchman" and "Hiram Woodruff" 1640	500.00	600.00
☐ Great Conflagration at Pittsburgh, Pa. 2581	400.00	450.00
☐ Bear Hunting, Close Quarters* 446	1200.00	1500.00
☐ The Destruction of Tea at Boston Harbor. 1571	500.00	700.00
☐ Cornwallis is Taken 1258	225.00	300.00
☐ Landing of the Pilgrims at Plymouth, 11th Dec., 1620* 3435	150.00	200.00
☐ The Great Fight for the Championship 2613	250.00	300.00
☐ Benjamin Franklin* 499	150.00	200.00
☐ Noah's Ark* 4494	100.00	150.00
☐ Black Eyed Susan* 551	100.00	125.00
☐ The Bloomer Costume* 574	150.00	175.00
☐ The Clipper Yacht "America"* 1173	700.00	900.00

THE BEST FIFTY (LARGE FOLIO):

☐ Husking 3008	1500.00	1800.00
☐ American Forest Scene—Maple Sugaring 157	3000.00	3500.00
☐ Central Park Winter—The Skating Pond 954	2800.00	3000.00
☐ Home to Thanksgiving. 2882	7000.00	8000.00
☐ Life of a Hunter—A Tight Fix* 3522	12000.00	15000.00

THE BEST FIFTY (LARGE)

Price Range

☐ Life on the Prairie—The Buffalo Hunt	3527	5500.00	6000.00
☐ The Lightning Express Trains Leaving the Junction	3535	4800.00	5000.00
☐ Peytona and Fashion	4763	7000.00	8000.00
☐ The Rocky Mountains—Emigrants Crossing the Plains	5196	6500.00	7500.00
☐ Trolling for Blue Fish	6158	2000.00	2500.00
☐ Whale Fishery—The Sperm Whale in a Flurry ..	6628	800.00	900.00
☐ Winter in the Country—The Old Grist Mill	6738	5000.00	5500.00
☐ American Farm Scenes No. 4 (Winter)	136	1500.00	2000.00
☐ American National Game of Baseball	180	7500.00	10000.00
☐ American Winter Sports—Trout Fishing on Chatequgay Lake	210	1750.00	2000.00
☐ Mink Trapping—Prime	4139	7500.00	8000.00
☐ Preparing for Market	4870	1200.00	1400.00
☐ Winter in the Country—Getting Ice	6737	4750.00	5200.00
☐ Across the Continent—Westward the Course of Empire Takes Its Way	33	7500.00	9000.00
☐ Life on the Praire—The Trappers Defense	3528	5500.00	6000.00
☐ The Midnight Race on the Mississippi	4116	1500.00	2000.00
☐ The Road—Winter	5171	5500.00	6000.00
☐ Summer Scenes in New York Harbor	5876	1200.00	1500.00
☐ Trotting Cracks at the Forge	6169	1500.00	1750.00
☐ View of San Francisco	6469	3750.00	4000.00
☐ Wreck of the Steamship "San Francisco"	5492	3700.00	4200.00
☐ Taking the Back Track "A Dangerous Neighborhood"	5961	5000.00	5500.00
☐ American Field Sports—Flush'd	149	800.00	1000.00
☐ American Hunting Scenes—A Good Chance ..	174	1000.00	1500.00
☐ American Winter Scenes—Morning	208	2000.00	2500.00
☐ Autumn in New England—Cider Making	322	2000.00	2500.00
☐ Catching a Trout—"We Hab You Now, Sar" ...	845	600.00	700.00
☐ Clipper Ship "Nightingale"	1159	5500.00	7000.00
☐ The Life of a Fireman—The Race	3519	800.00	900.00
☐ Mac and Zachary Taylor—Horse Race	3848	500.00	600.00
☐ New England Winter Scene	4420	3500.00	4000.00
☐ Rail Shooting on the Delaware	5054	3500.00	4000.00
☐ Snowed Up—Ruffled Grouse—Winter	5581	2600.00	2750.00
☐ Surrender of General Gurgoyne at Saratoga ...	5907	3000.00	3500.00
☐ Surrender of Cornwallis at Yorktown	5906	3000.00	3500.00
☐ Clipper Ship "Red Jacket"	1165	3500.00	4500.00
☐ American Winter Sports—Deer Shooting on the Shattagee	209	1750.00	2000.00
☐ The Bark "Theoxana"	371	1300.00	1600.00
☐ The Cares of a Family	814	1500.00	1800.00
☐ The Celebrated Horse Lexington	887	1600.00	1800.00
☐ Grand Drive—Central Park	2481	1750.00	2000.00
☐ The Great Fire at Chicago	2615	1200.00	1500.00
☐ Landscape, Fruit and Flowers	440	700.00	800.00

THE BEST FIFTY (LARGE) Price Range

- [ ] The Life of a Fireman—
The Metropolitan System 3516   800.00   900.00
- [ ] The Splendid Naval Triumph on the Mississippi   5659   400.00   500.00

DAYBREAK *by Maxfield Parrish*

MAXFIELD PARRISH

☐ Aladdin and the Lamp, 10" x 12"	70.00	90.00
☐ Ancient Trees (large oak tree by lake)	80.00	100.00
☐ Brazen, The Boatman, 10" x 12"	40.00	50.00
☐ Brown & Bigelow Landscape (the village church) 24" x 27"	40.00	50.00
☐ Cadmus Sowing the Dragons Teeth, 10" x 12"	40.00	50.00
☐ Circes Palace (Maiden standing on porch)	40.00	50.00
☐ Community Plate, 11" x 13", 1918	20.00	30.00
☐ Dawn (Maiden sitting on rock) Mazda print	40.00	45.00
☐ Daybreak, large size	110.00	125.00
☐ Djer-Kiss (Maiden on swing in forest) 10½" x 14"	40.00	60.00
☐ Dreaming, large size	275.00	325.00
☐ Duchess at Prayer, illustration for L'Allegro, 10" x 15" 1901	20.00	30.00
☐ Ecstacy, Large Edison Mazda Calendar	325.00	375.00
☐ Errant Pan, The (Pan sitting by stream) 6" x 8"	20.00	30.00
☐ Evening (Nude sitting in lake), 13" x 17"	80.00	100.00
☐ Garden of Allah (3 maidens sitting in garden), medium size	60.00	70.00
☐ Garden of Opportunity, The (Prince and princess) ...	40.00	60.00
☐ Golden Hours (Maidens in forest) Large Edison Mazda Calendar	180.00	210.00
☐ Hilltop (youths sitting on mountain), medium size House of Art	180.00	210.00
☐ His Christmas Dinner (Tramp having dinner)	40.00	60.00
☐ Isola Bella Scene, 9" x 10"	15.00	20.00

MAXFIELD PARRISH

Price Range

- [ ] Lampseller of Bagdad, The (Maiden on steps) Mazda Calendar 180.00 210.00
- [ ] Little Princess, The (Princess sitting by fountain) 15.00 20.00
- [ ] Lute Players, large size, House of Art 290.00 310.00
- [ ] Morning (Maiden sitting on rock) 13" x 16" 90.00 110.00
- [ ] Night Call (Bare breasted girl in surf) 6" x 8" 20.00 30.00
- [ ] Old Romance (Nude sitting in pool) 6" x 8" 20.00 30.00
- [ ] Pandora's Box (Maiden sitting by large box) 40.00 50.00
- [ ] Pipe Night (Comical men with pipes and coffee urns sitting facing each other at table) 9" x 12½" 20.00 30.00
- [ ] Potpourri (Nude in garden picking flowers) 15.00 30.00
- [ ] Providing it By the Book (2 gents at table) 15.00 20.00
- [ ] Sandman, The (Sandman with full moon) 6" x 7½" .. 25.00 35.00
- [ ] Shepherd with Sheep, 8½" x 13½" 15.00 20.00
- [ ] Sinbad and Cyclops, 10" x 12" 30.00 40.00
- [ ] Singing Tree, The; 10" x 12" 30.00 50.00
- [ ] Stars, House of Art, large size (nude sitting on rock) .. 290.00 310.00
- [ ] Story of Phoebus, 8" x 10", 1901 .... 15.00 20.00

WAR CHIEF *by Rance Hood*

INDIAN PRINTS
RANCE HOOD:

- [ ] War on the Plains .... s/n 215.00 245.00
- [ ] War Chief .... s/n 80.00 100.00

JEROME TIGER: Price Range

- ☐ The Coming Weather .... n/o   575.00   650.00
- ☐ Observing the Enemy .... n/o   790.00   680.00
- ☐ The Guiding Spirit........................... n/o   375.00   425.00
- ☐ The Mighty Stickballer .... n/o   875.00   950.00
- ☐ Seminole.................................. n/o   140.00   170.00
- ☐ Trail of Tears.............................. n/o   330.00   380.00
- ☐ Stick Baller .... n/o   330.00   380.00

JAPANESE PRINTS

Although we treasure Japanese colored woodblock prints, many of them were as common and part of the popular culture as today's pop posters. The Japanese prints most desired are the "Ukiyo-ye" or "passing world" (every-day world) prints beginning in the 17th century. Many gifted artists did prints. An expert is needed to accurately translate the words appearing in Japanese prints — some are signatures and some describe the scene.

HIROSADA
- ☐ Actor With Sword 70.00   90.00

HIROSHIGE I
- ☐ Cliffs At Konotai And Tonegawa, 1856 ....   230.00   300.00
- ☐ Harbor At Shinagawa, 1855 ....   230.00   300.00
- ☐ View of Mt. Fuji, 1856 ....   210.00   260.00
- ☐ Villagers In Akabone On A Snowy Day 250.00   300.00

HIROSHIGE II
- ☐ Women With Parasols, 1862 ....   70.00   90.00

HOKUSAI
- ☐ Snowy Morning In Koishikawas 100.00   150.00

KUNISADA
- ☐ Mother And Child, 1830 ....   140.00   200.00

KUNIYOSHI, YASUO
- ☐ Cafe, Signed, Dated '35' 1600.00 2000.00
- ☐ Circus Girl With Plumed Hat, Signed, 1933 ....   900.00 1400.00
- ☐ Pears and Grapes, Signed, 1928 ....   1000.00 1200.00
- ☐ So. Berwick, Maine, Signed, 1934 ....   350.00   500.00
- ☐ Summer, Signed 1100.00 1400.00

SADAYOSHI   Price   Range
☐ Farmer With Hoe, 1850 ....   70.00   100.00

TOYOKURI
☐ Kabuki Actor, 1820 ....   300.00   375.00

YOSHIDA, HIROSHI
☐ Avenue of Cherry Trees, 1935 ....   170.00   220.00

YOSHITSUYA
☐ Puzzle Print, 1849 ....   70.00   100.00

WARWICKSHIRE STEEPLECHASE AWAITING START
by Henry Koehler

NATURE & PORTRAIT PRINTS
CAROLYN BLISH:

☐ Roadside Daisies	....	s/n	155.00	185.00
☐ Wonderment	....	s/n	165.00	195.00
☐ Shore Birds	....	s/n	175.00	195.00
☐ Misty Sea	....	s/n	110.00	130.00

ANNE O. DOWDEN:

☐ Flowering Dogwood	....	s/o	35.00	45.00
☐ Goldenrod	....	s/o	35.00	45.00
☐ Wildflowers of the Plains	....	s/o	35.00	45.00
☐ Spring Flowers/Autumn Flowers	....	s/o	45.00	55.00
☐ Mushrooms (portfolio of six)	....	s/o	65.00	90.00
☐ Yellow Bouquet	....	s/o	55.00	75.00
☐ Flame Azalea/Piedmont Azalea	....	s/o	35.00	45.00
☐ Plumleaf Azalea	....	s/o	35.00	45.00

ANNE O'DOWDEN

			Price Range	
☐ Hybrid Tea Roses/Old Roses	s/o	50.00	70.00
☐ Carolina Roses/Cherokee Rose	s/o	35.00	45.00

BEN HAMPTON:

☐ Reflecting Sycamores	s/n	90.00	110.00
	s/o	65.00	85.00
☐ Sorghum Mill	s/n	120.00	140.00
	s/o	90.00	110.00
☐ Carolina Haze	s/n	225.00	275.00
	s/o	140.00	170.00
☐ Bridgeport Ferry	s/n	160.00	190.00
	s/o	90.00	110.00
☐ Sunday Morning	s/n	165.00	185.00
	s/o	115.00	145.00
☐ Gentle Mist	s/n	115.00	145.00
	s/o	90.00	110.00
☐ Appalachian Spring	s/n	365.00	400.00
	s/o	290.00	320.00
☐ Sand Mountain Cabin	s/n	365.00	385.00
☐ The Stump	s/n	190.00	220.00
☐ Claude's Creek	s/n	190.00	220.00
☐ The Good Earth	s/n	285.00	325.00
☐ Monument to an Era	s/n	880.00	940.00

JIM HARRISON:

☐ Disappearing America	s/n	475.00	525.00
☐ American Byways	s/n	115.00	145.00
☐ Rural Delivery	s/n	90.00	110.00
☐ Fallow & Forgotten	s/n	65.00	75.00
☐ Dr. Pepper	s/n	80.00	110.00

BRETT HARPER:

☐ Petunia Power	s/n	35.00	45.00
☐ Zinnia	s/n	35.00	45.00
☐ Mellow Yellow	s/n	40.00	60.00

EDIE HARPER:

☐ Noazark	s/n	130.00	160.00
☐ Jonah	s/n	80.00	100.00
☐ Dan's Den	s/n	75.00	95.00
☐ Tree House	s/n	70.00	85.00

EDNA HIBEL:

☐ Kristina & Child No. 1	s/n	440.00	475.00
☐ Kristina & Child No. 2	s/n	190.00	320.00
☐ Kristina & Child No. 3	s/n	190.00	320.00
☐ Wedding of David and Bathsheba	s/n	585.00	650.00

LASZLO ISPANKY:

			Price Range
☐ Lady of Mirrors	s/n	500.00	550.00
☐ Pegasus	s/n	640.00	700.00
☐ Deluxe	s/n	1100.00	1300.00
☐ Standard		380.00	430.00
☐ Blossom	s/n	400.00	450.00

HENRY KOEHLER:

☐ Warwickshire Steeplechase Awaiting Start	s/n	50.00	70.00
☐ Racing Colors (portfolio of four)	s/n	90.00	120.00
☐ Riva Ridge	s/o	65.00	85.00

IKKI MATSUMOTO:

☐ Sandpipers	s/n	1000.00	1200.00
☐ Pelican	s/n	80.00	110.00
☐ Blue Heron	s/n	140.00	170.00
☐ Go Fly a Kite	s/n	90.00	110.00
☐ Rainbow Drops	s/n	120.00	150.00
☐ Stranger on the Beach	s/n	90.00	110.00
☐ Butterfly Tree	s/n	70.00	90.00

LE ROY NEIMAN:

☐ Match Point	s/n	1900.00	2100.00
☐ Tiger	s/n	2450.00	2650.00
☐ Stock Market	s/n	2475.00	2650.00
☐ Leopard	s/n	2900.00	3200.00
☐ Hockey Player	s/n	1450.00	1600.00
☐ Lion Pride	s/n	2450.00	2600.00
☐ Roulette	s/n	2175.00	2300.00
☐ Love Story	s/n	1150.00	1300.00
☐ Trotters	s/n	700.00	800.00

NORMAN ROCKWELL:

☐ Spelling Bee	s/n	2950.00	3150.00
☐ Blacksmith Shop	s/n	2950.00	3150.00
☐ Family Tree	s/n	1950.00	2150.00
☐ Shuffelton's Barbershop	s/n	2400.00	2650.00
☐ Doctor and Doll	s/n	3950.00	4200.00
☐ Girl at Mirror	s/n	1950.00	2175.00
☐ Freedom from Fear	s/n	1775.00	1900.00
☐ Freedom from Want	s/n	1600.00	1825.00
☐ Freedom of Speech	s/n	1750.00	1900.00
☐ Freedom of Religion	s/n	1625.00	1825.00
☐ Marriage License	s/n	2300.00	2600.00
☐ Lincoln	s/n	3975.00	4200.00
☐ Ichabod Crane	s/n	2150.00	2375.00
☐ Tom Sawyer Folio	s/n	9900.00	11000.00
☐ Huck Finn Folio	s/n	11775.00	13000.00

NORMAN ROCKWELL

		Price	Range
☐ Poor Richard's Almanac	s/n	8750.00	10000.00
☐ Summer Stock (in Japan)	s/n	1700.00	1825.00
☐ The Rivals	s/n	1450.00	1650.00
☐ Puppy Love (portfolio of 4)	s/n	5550.00	6500.00
☐ April Fool	s/n	2775.00	3250.00
☐ See America First	s/n	2450.00	2800.00
☐ Benjamin Franklin	s/n	2900.00	3200.00
☐ Day in the Life of a Boy	s/n	2150.00	2350.00
☐ Football Hero	s/n	850.00	975.00
☐ She's My Baby	s/n	1000.00	1250.00
☐ Young Lincoln	s/n	4450.00	4700.00
☐ Young Spooners	s/n	1350.00	1500.00
☐ Boy on Stilts	s/n	775.00	975.00
☐ Sports Portfolio	s/n	4450.00	4700.00
☐ Can't Wait	s/n	1150.00	1300.00

MANABU SAITO:

☐ Spring Flowers	s/n	90.00	120.00
☐ Tulips/Daffodils	s/n	70.00	90.00
☐ Cinnamon Fern	s/n	80.00	110.00
☐ Apple	s/o	15.00	35.00

IRENE SPENCER:

ETCHINGS

☐ Hills of Home	s/n	380.00	430.00
☐ Summer Afternoon	s/n	290.00	320.00
☐ Dear Child	s/n	280.00	320.00
☐ Yesterday, Today and Tomorrow	s/n	690.00	750.00
☐ Smoke Dreams	s/n	1950.00	2150.00

LITHOGRAPHS

☐ Secrets	s/n	950.00	1100.00
☐ First Kiss	s/n	425.00	475.00
☐ Mother's Here	s/n	140.00	170.00
☐ L'Envoi	s/n	85.00	105.00
☐ Hug Me	s/n	680.00	750.00
☐ Miracle	s/n	490.00	550.00

BOB TIMBERLAKE:

☐ My Yankee Drum	s/n	120.00	140.00
☐ Rowboat	s/n	425.00	475.00
☐ Mr. Garrison's Slab Pile	s/n	1470.00	1600.00
☐ The Alexander Long House	s/n	380.00	440.00
☐ May	s/n	140.00	170.00
☐ Daily Sunning	s/n	215.00	250.00
☐ Morning Sun	s/n	220.00	250.00
☐ Another World (etching)	s/n	975.00	1125.00

MARY VICKERS: Price Range

LITHOGRAPHS

☐ Age of Innocence	s/n	180.00	220.00
☐ Brother & Sister	s/n	180.00	220.00
☐ Climbing	s/n	90.00	110.00
☐ Embrace	s/n	115.00	145.00
☐ Face to the Wind	s/n	140.00	170.00
☐ Flight of Fancy	s/n	140.00	170.00
☐ Guitar Solo	s/n	140.00	170.00
☐ Rag Doll	s/n	180.00	220.00
☐ Reflections	s/n	115.00	135.00
☐ Sharing	s/n	190.00	220.00
☐ Sunshine 'n Sand	s/n	140.00	170.00
☐ Together	s/n	110.00	140.00
☐ Two Children in Field	s/n	140.00	170.00
☐ Water Babies	s/n	220.00	250.00

ETCHINGS

☐ Alice	s/n	90.00	110.00
☐ Autumn Bouquet	s/n	140.00	170.00
☐ Breath of Spring	s/n	140.00	170.00
☐ Dawn	s/n	60.00	80.00
☐ First Grade	s/n	45.00	55.00
☐ Good Times	s/n	170.00	200.00
☐ Lunch Ready Mom	s/n	165.00	195.00
☐ Janine	s/n	165.00	195.00
☐ Lovers	s/n	115.00	135.00
☐ October	s/n	180.00	220.00
☐ One More Game	s/n	180.00	220.00
☐ Patience	s/n	90.00	110.00
☐ Secret Path	s/n	90.00	110.00
☐ Someday	s/n	115.00	135.00
☐ Sound of Music	s/n	115.00	135.00
☐ Tattered Hero	s/n	140.00	170.00
☐ Together We're Stronger	s/n	125.00	145.00
☐ Yesterday's Tomorrow	s/n	180.00	220.00

DALHART WINDBERG:

☐ Autumn Memories	s/n	165.00	195.00
	s/o	90.00	110.00
☐ Sunday Outing	s/n	65.00	85.00
☐ Autumn's Way	s/n	140.00	170.00
☐ Spring's Way	s/n	90.00	110.00
☐ Summer's Way	s/n	90.00	110.00
☐ Winter's Way	s/n	90.00	110.00

WELLINGTON WARD, JR.:

☐ Port and Starboard Watch	s/n	65.00	85.00
☐ The Doryman	s/n	50.00	70.00

NAVAJO MADONNA *by Olaf Wieghorst*

WESTERN ART

JAMES BAMA:

		Price Range	
☐ Ken Hinder, Working Cowboy	s/n	65.00	85.00
☐ Shoshone Chief	s/n	105.00	125.00
☐ Chuck Wagon in the Snow	s/n	70.00	80.00
☐ Sage Grinder	s/n	110.00	140.00

FRANK McCARTHY:

☐ Long Column	s/n	215.00	245.00
☐ The Long Sentinel	s/n	360.00	400.00
☐ The Hunt	s/n	165.00	195.00
☐ The Survivor	s/n	80.00	100.00
☐ Smoke was their Ally	s/n	90.00	110.00
☐ Returning Raiders	s/n	120.00	140.00
☐ Sioux Warriors	s/n	110.00	130.00
☐ The Beaver Man	s/n	110.00	140.00
☐ The Warrior	s/n	110.00	140.00
☐ Vignette Series No. 3	s/n	90.00	110.00

RAY SWANSON:

☐ Chatting at Chilchinbitoh	s/n	90.00	110.00

OLAF WIEGHORST:

☐ Buffalo Scout	s/n	140.00	170.00
☐ California Wrangler	s/n	140.00	170.00
☐ Missing in the Round-up	s/n	140.00	170.00
☐ Navajo Madonna	s/n	950.00	1100.00
☐ Packing In	s/n	140.00	170.00
☐ Corralling in the Cavvy	s/n	140.00	170.00

RANDY STEFFEN:

☐ Indians of the Plains (portfolio of two)	s/n	95.00	110.00
☐ Indians of the Plains (portfolio of four)	s/n	85.00	115.00

BLACK BEAR *by Harris Antis*

WILDLIFE ART

Price Range

ROBERT ABBETT:

☐ Bobwhites and Pointer	s/n	125.00	175.00
☐ First Season	s/n	100.00	150.00

HARRY ANTIS:

☐ Whitetail Buck	s/n	40.00	60.00
	s/o	30.00	50.00
☐ Doe and Fawns	s/n	40.00	60.00
☐ Black Bear	s/n	40.00	60.00
	s/o	60.00	80.00
☐ Chipmunk	s/n	20.00	40.00
	s/o	20.00	30.00
☐ Cougar	s/n	400.00	450.00
☐ Bobcat	s/o	65.00	85.00
☐ Timber Wolf	s/n	80.00	110.00
	s/o	65.00	85.00
☐ Bear Cubs	s/n	30.00	50.00
☐ Old American	s/n	40.00	60.00
☐ Proud American	s/n	60.00	80.00

HARRY ANTIS

		Price	Range
☐ Cardinal	s/o	40.00	60.00
☐ Saw-Whet	s/n	40.00	60.00
☐ Patriarch	s/n	300.00	350.00

GUY COHELEACH:

☐ Golden Eagle	s/n	350.00	400.00
☐ Great Blue Heron	s/n	115.00	145.00
☐ Striped Bass	s/o	40.00	60.00
☐ Purple Gallinule	s/o	30.00	50.00
☐ Snowy Egrets	s/n	275.00	325.00
	u/s	225.00	275.00
☐ Barn Swallow	s/o	50.00	70.00
☐ American Elk	s/o	45.00	65.00
☐ Grizzly Bear	s/o	50.00	70.00
☐ Peregrine Falcon	s/o	70.00	90.00
☐ Leopard	s/n	475.00	525.00
☐ Wood Thrush	s/o	40.00	60.00
☐ Elephant	s/n	105.00	140.00
☐ African Lion	s/o	80.00	100.00
☐ Leopard Stare	s/n	170.00	210.00
☐ Kaola Bear	s/o	90.00	120.00
☐ Wapiti Stag	s/n	140.00	180.00
☐ Snow Leopard	s/n	250.00	300.00
☐ The Chase	s/o	85.00	125.00
☐ Winter Cardinals	s/o	90.00	110.00
☐ Jungle Jaguar	s/o	140.00	165.00
☐ Clouded Leopard	s/o	105.00	135.00
☐ Screech Owls	i/o	140.00	160.00
☐ Cats of the Americas	i/o	155.00	175.00
☐ Fox Den	s/n	300.00	350.00
	s/o	250.00	300.00
☐ Black Bear Cubs	i/o	60.00	80.00
☐ Long Billed Marshwren	i/o	40.00	60.00
☐ Tiger Head	i/o	175.00	225.00
☐ The Lookout	s/n	350.00	400.00
	s/o	300.00	350.00
☐ Bicentennial Eagle	s/n	180.00	225.00
	s/o	140.00	170.00
☐ Racoons	s/o	130.00	170.00
☐ Dusk-Stone lithograph	s/n	420.00	470.00
☐ Dawn-Stone lithograph	s/n	460.00	510.00
☐ Reflections-Stone lithograph	s/n	280.00	330.00
☐ Long Eared Owl	s/n	750.00	825.00
☐ Species	s/n	660.00	710.00
☐ Black Watch	s/n	130.00	170.00
	s/o	95.00	125.00
☐ Mountain Stalk (Snow Leopard)	s/n	140.00	170.00
	s/o	100.00	130.00
☐ Whitetail Deer	s/n	65.00	90.00
	s/o	50.00	70.00

DON RICHARD ECKELBERRY:

Price Range

☐ Barred Owl	u/s	140.00	170.00
☐ White-eared Puffbird	s/o	40.00	60.00
☐ Blue-gray Tanager	s/o	30.00	60.00
☐ Mallard Drakes Rising	s/n	85.00	115.00
	s/o	70.00	90.00
☐ Spruce Grouse	s/o	40.00	60.00
☐ Mottled Owl	s/o	50.00	75.00
☐ Black Ducks over the Marsh	s/o	65.00	95.00
☐ Woodcock and Young	s/o	40.00	65.00
☐ Alert and Ready	s/o	40.00	65.00
☐ (White Gryfalcon)	s/n	115.00	150.00
	s/o	85.00	130.00
☐ Cardinal	s/o	50.00	70.00
☐ Meadowlark	s/o	60.00	80.00

IMOGENE FARNSWORTH:

☐ Bengal Tiger	s/n	375.00	425.00
	s/o	230.00	280.00
☐ African Lion	s/n	90.00	120.00
	s/o	30.00	50.00
☐ Giraffe	s/n	70.00	90.00
	s/o	30.00	50.00
☐ Tiger	s/n	140.00	170.00
☐ African Lioness & Cubs	s/n	90.00	120.00
☐ Cheetah Head	s/n	50.00	70.00
☐ African Leopard	s/n	135.00	165.00
☐ Bengal Cubs	s/n	50.00	70.00

CHARLES FRACÉ:

☐ African Lion	s/o	165.00	195.00
☐ Tiger	s/o	165.00	195.00
☐ Golden Eagle	s/n	115.00	135.00
☐ Raccoon	s/o	110.00	125.00
☐ Giant Panda	s/o	70.00	90.00
☐ Lion Cub	s/o	80.00	105.00
☐ Northern Goshawk	s/o	90.00	115.00
☐ Tiger Cub	s/o	90.00	110.00
☐ Snow Leopard	s/n	775.00	825.00
☐ Snow Leopard (remarqued)	s/n	525.00	575.00
☐ Screech Owls	s/o	50.00	70.00
☐ Morris the Cat	s/o	75.00	95.00
☐ White Tiger	s/n	140.00	170.00
☐ White Tiger (remarqued)	s/n	180.00	220.00
☐ Oscelot Kittens	s/o	65.00	85.00
☐ Canada Lynx	s/o	70.00	90.00

ALBERT EARL GILBERT:

		Price Range	
☐ Cardinals on Apple Blossom		650.00	750.00
☐ Orange Blossom		180.00	240.00

GENE GRAY:

☐ Eastern Gray Squirrel	s/o	100.00	130.00
☐ American Red Fox	s/n	115.00	140.00
	s/o	125.00	160.00
☐ Wildcat	s/n	375.00	410.00
	s/o	360.00	400.00
☐ Striped Skunk	s/n	80.00	100.00
	s/o	70.00	90.00
☐ Eastern Cottontail Rabbit	s/n	60.00	85.00
	s/o	55.00	75.00
☐ Eastern Belted Kingfisher	s/n	60.00	80.00
	s/o	50.00	70.00
☐ Cougar	s/n	70.00	80.00
☐ Screech Owl	s/n	40.00	60.00
	s/o	25.00	35.00
☐ Raccoon	s/n	85.00	110.00
	s/o	80.00	95.00
☐ American Otter	s/n	40.00	60.00
	s/o	25.00	35.00

DAVID HAGERBRAUMER:

☐ October Evening	s/n	775.00	850.00
☐ Placid Marsh-Black Ducks	s/n	775.00	850.00
☐ Woodlot Covey Bob-white Quail	s/n	775.00	825.00
☐ Canvasbacks, Green Wing Tail		825.00	900.00
☐ Hill Country Gobblers-Turkey	s/n	325.00	375.00
☐ Over the Ridge-Pheasants	s/n	225.00	275.00
☐ Widgeon	s/n	280.00	330.00

HISTORICAL SERIES NO. 2:

☐ The Old Duck Camp Mallard	s/n	115.00	140.00
☐ Afternoon Squall Canada Geese	s/n	115.00	140.00

RAY HARM:

☐ American Butterflies	s/o	45.00	60.00
☐ American Eagle	s/n	325.00	375.00
	s/o	235.00	265.00
☐ Bald Eagle	s/o	625.00	675.00
☐ Baltimore Oriole	s/o	145.00	175.00
☐ Belted Kingfisher	s/o	65.00	85.00
☐ Blue Jay	s/o	80.00	100.00
☐ Bobcat	s/o	425.00	475.00
☐ Kentucky Wildcat	s/n	440.00	470.00
☐ Brown Thrasher	s/o	65.00	85.00

RAY HARM

		Price	Range
☐ California Ground Squirrel	s/o	45.00	55.00
☐ Cardinal (Dogwood)	s/o	340.00	380.00
☐ Cardinal (Sunflower)	s/o	140.00	170.00
☐ Carolina Wren	s/o	70.00	90.00
☐ Downy Woodpecker	s/o	45.00	60.00
☐ Eagle and Osprey	w/n	1950.00	2100.00
☐ Eastern Bluebird	s/o	90.00	110.00
☐ Eastern Bobwhite	s/o	280.00	320.00
☐ Evening Grosbeak	s/o	55.00	70.00
☐ Feeder Group	s/o	75.00	95.00
☐ Flicker	s/o	70.00	85.00
☐ Great Horned Owl	s/n	125.00	155.00
	s/o	110.00	130.00
☐ House Wren	s/o	55.00	75.00
☐ Impala	s/o	75.00	95.00
☐ Indigo Bunting	s/o	60.00	75.00
☐ Kentucky Wildcat (Bobcat)			
☐ Bobcat	s/n	425.00	475.00
☐ Kentucky Wildcat	s/n	425.00	475.00
☐ Kestrel (Sparrow Hawk)	s/o	45.00	60.00
☐ Lazuli Bunting	s/o	30.00	40.00
☐ Mallard	s/o	70.00	85.00
☐ Mockingbird	s/o	100.00	120.00
☐ Mountain Lion	s/n	100.00	115.00
	s/o	80.00	100.00
☐ Ovenbird	s/o	30.00	40.00
☐ Pelicans	s/n	140.00	170.00
☐ Pileated Woodpecker	s/o	90.00	105.00
☐ Raccoon (family)	s/n	280.00	320.00
☐ Red Fox	s/n	115.00	140.00
	s/o	90.00	110.00
☐ Reticulated Giraffe	s/n	115.00	140.00
	s/o	90.00	110.00
☐ Roadrunner	s/o	55.00	75.00
☐ Robin	s/o	150.00	180.00
☐ Ruffed Grouse	s/o	70.00	85.00
☐ Scarlet Tanager	s/o	155.00	165.00
☐ Screech Owl		50.00	60.00
☐ Spring Wildflowers (set of 6)		90.00	110.00
☐ Upland Birds	s/n	95.00	110.00
☐ Vermillion Flycatcher	s/o	30.00	40.00
☐ White Throated Sparrow	s/o	30.00	40.00
☐ Wild Turkey	s/n	120.00	135.00
	s/o	90.00	110.00
☐ Yellow-billed Cuckoo	s/o	60.00	70.00
☐ Yellow-headed Blackbird	s/o	55.00	65.00

CHARLES HARPER:

			Price Range	
☐ Hungry Eyes	s/n	225.00	275.00	
☐ Ladybug	s/n	180.00	220.00	
☐ Water Spider	s/n	300.00	350.00	
☐ Cardinal on Corn	w/n	225.00	275.00	
☐ Crayfish Molting	s/n	65.00	85.00	
☐ Puffin	s/n	50.00	60.00	
☐ Red-bellied Woodpecker	s/n	55.00	65.00	
☐ Ladybug Lovers	s/n	55.00	70.00	
☐ Bear in the Birches	s/n	200.00	240.00	
☐ Wedding Feast	s/n	60.00	75.00	
☐ Pelican in a Downpour	s/n	125.00	150.00	
☐ Wood Duck	s/n	115.00	140.00	
☐ Family Owlbum	s/n	75.00	95.00	
☐ Watermelon Moon	s/n	180.00	230.00	
☐ Tall Tail	s/n	65.00	85.00	
☐ Chipmunk	s/n			
☐ Cool Cardinal	s/n	140.00	170.00	
☐ Bluebirds in the Bluegrass	s/n	65.00	80.00	
☐ Birdwatcher	s/n	110.00	130.00	
☐ Birds of a Feather	s/n	80.00	100.00	
☐ Love from Above	s/n	165.00	195.00	
☐ Devotion in the Ocean	s/n	70.00	90.00	
☐ Cornprone	s/n	75.00	95.00	
☐ Down Under Down Under	s/n	70.00	80.00	
☐ Skipping School	s/n	85.00	100.00	

J. FENWICK LANSDOWNE:

☐ Screech Owl		325.00	375.00
☐ Barred Owl	s/n	140.00	170.00
☐ Wood Ducks	s/n	100.00	130.00
☐ Pintail Ducks	s/n	110.00	140.00

RALPH McDONALD:

☐ Whitetail & Descending Canvasbacks	s/n	90.00	110.00
☐ The Raccoons	s/n	90.00	110.00
	s/o	70.00	85.00
☐ Largemouth Bass	s/n	45.00	55.00
☐ The Tennessee Mockingbird	s/s	140.00	170.00
☐ Whitetail Deer	s/n	95.00	110.00
☐ The Bobwhite Quail	s/n	70.00	80.00
☐ Screech Owl	s/o	70.00	80.00
☐ The Cardinal	s/o	45.00	55.00

BICENTENNIAL SERIES OF 5 PRINTS:

☐ American Bald Eagle	s/n	325.00	375.00
☐ American Wild Turkey	s/n	65.00	85.00
☐ American Bald Eagle (1776 Series)	s/n	80.00	95.00
☐ Great Horned Owl	s/n	60.00	70.00
☐ Walker's Pond (Wood Ducks)	s/n	315.00	375.00

CLAY McGAUGHY:

			Price Range	
☐ Bachelor	s/n	120.00	135.00
	s/o	90.00	110.00
☐ Birds of a Feather	s/n	115.00	135.00
	s/o	90.00	110.00
☐ Follow the Leader	s/n	120.00	135.00
☐ Intruder	s/n	115.00	135.00
☐ Checkin' In	s/n	120.00	135.00
☐ Loafers	s/n	115.00	135.00

PETER PARNALL:

☐ Richardson's Owl	s/n	110.00	120.00
☐ Pygmy Owl	s/n	95.00	115.00
☐ Buffalo Sun	s/n	165.00	185.00
☐ Bee	s/n	165.00	185.00
☐ Coyote Pups	s/n	75.00	95.00
☐ Frog	s/n	70.00	85.00
☐ Goldfinch	s/n	65.00	85.00
☐ Sea Otters	s/n	115.00	125.00
☐ Sperm Whale	s/n	115.00	135.00
☐ Butterfly	s/n	70.00	80.00

ROGER TORY PETERSON:

☐ Baltimore Oriole	s/n	275.00	325.00
☐ Flicker	s/n	275.00	325.00
☐ Great Horned Owl	s/n	775.00	850.00
☐ Bobwhite	s/n	350.00	400.00
☐ Snowy Owls	s/n	585.00	625.00
☐ Golden Eagle	s/n	215.00	245.00
☐ Bluebird	s/n	115.00	135.00

MAYNARD REECE:

☐ Mallards (Stone Lithograph)		575.00	650.00
☐ Bobwhites (Stone Lithograph)		580.00	640.00
☐ Pheasant Country	s/n	125.00	145.00
☐ Late Afternoon Mallards	s/n	275.00	325.00
☐ Buffleheads (color edition)	s/n	380.00	430.00
☐ Solitude-Whitetail Deer	s/n	140.00	170.00
☐ Wooded Seclusion Turkey	s/n	115.00	135.00
☐ Mallards Dropping In	s/n	145.00	165.00
☐ Winging South Canada Geese	s/n	245.00	275.00
☐ Courtship Flight Pintails	s/n	115.00	135.00
☐ Dark Sky - Mallards	s/n	140.00	170.00
☐ Autumn Trio - Ring-necked Pheasants	s/n	120.00	140.00

JOHN A. RUTHVEN: **Price Range**

AQUATINT SERIES

☐ Carolina Paraquet	s/n	975.00	1100.00
☐ Passenger Pigeon	s/n	825.00	900.00
☐ Ivory Billed Woodpecker	s/n	475.00	525.00
☐ Bengal Tiger	s/n	140.00	170.00

NORTH AMERICAN SERIES

☐ Ruddy Ducks	s/n	165.00	195.00
☐ Redheaded Woodpecker	s/n	165.00	195.00
☐ New York State Bluebird	s/n	140.00	170.00
☐ Fox Family	s/n	480.00	540.00

AMERICANA SERIES

☐ Roadrunner	s/n	140.00	170.00
☐ Herring Gulls	s/n	140.00	170.00
☐ Great Horned Owl	s/n	165.00	195.00

GEORGE TOWN SERIES

☐ Cinnamon Teal	s/n	45.00	55.00
☐ Fox Masque	s/n	45.00	55.00

REGAL SERIES

☐ Red Fox	s/n	780.00	830.00

MASTERPIECE SERIES

☐ Gray Fox	s/n	245.00	275.00

JOHN A. RUTHVEN SERIES

☐ Ruffed Grouse Plate 1	s/n	1200.00	1350.00

INITIAL SERIES

☐ Pheasant	s/n	325.00	375.00
☐ Wild Turkey	s/n	325.00	375.00
☐ Quail	s/n	325.00	375.00
☐ Wood Duck	s/n	140.00	170.00
☐ Ruffed Grouse	s/n	240.00	270.00

COMMISSIONS

☐ Eagle to the Moon	s/n	975.00	1100.00

RICHARD EVANS YOUNGER:

☐ American Eagle	s/n	140.00	170.00
	s/o	115.00	135.00
☐ Beach Preps	s/n	45.00	55.00
☐ Bobcat (on ground)	s/o	140.00	170.00
☐ Canada Goose (in flight)	s/n	65.00	85.00

RICHARD EVANS YOUNGER

		Price Range	
☐ Cheetah	s/n	140.00	170.00
	s/o	90.00	110.00
☐ Chimpanzee	s/o	40.00	50.00
☐ Mourning Dove	s/o	40.00	60.00
☐ Rufous-thighed Falconets	s/o	40.00	60.00
☐ Yearling	s/o	70.00	85.00

PRINTING COLLECTIBLES

Often people with some connection with the printing trade collect the tools of the trade—everything from measuring sticks to printing press.

☐ Brass Ink Can, screw top, c. 1910	30.00	40.00
☐ Brass Rule, pica and inches	12.00	15.00
☐ Gutenberg Press, miniature, wood, 7" x 10" x 13"	825.00	850.00
☐ Ives Printing Press, c. 1897	150.00	175.00
☐ Type Drawers, regularly and irregularly-spaced compartments, 16½" x 11"	5.00	6.00
☐ Wooden Type, various sizes, letters less than punctuation marks	1.00	10.00

PUPPETS

Though the making of puppets is an ancient art, it is rare for early specimens to come upon the market. In fact, few truly early puppets are preserved, even in museums, probably because the materials from which they were constructed did not lend themselves to preservation. Nothing remains of Greek or Roman puppets. Many Egyptian dolls in clay or wood do exist, but these do not qualify as puppets in the modern understanding of the word. The oldest European puppets likely to be found on the antiques market date from the 18th century. Most are of Italian manufacture, though it is often not possible to accurately judge the country of origin of a puppet. (The French antiques shops are, incidentally, much better hunting grounds for antique puppets than those of America; but prices are high.) Many puppets which appear very old are in fact no earlier than the middle 1800's, due to primitive or "folk" craftsmanship, old designing methods, and (often) lots of abuse. The style of *costume* is not a good indicator of a puppet's age, many being purposely clothed in outdated fashions to suit special requirements. Puppets for a Shakespearean play are attired in Elizabethan dress, but no one except a beginner would suspect they were manufactured in 1600.

But the puppet collector does not look only for age. A very old puppet may be valuable on grounds of age, but one of much more recent date can be even more valuable. Materials, craftsmanship, originality, background and other factors all enter the picture, and all must be interpreted according to the specimen at hand. Of *all* considerations, theatrical fame counts most. The sale of a celebrated puppet, such as the original Charlie McCarthy or Howdy Doody, would excite great interest, even though these are 20th century creations of no special brilliance in design or workmanship.

PUPPETS

Also of interest for reasons other than antiquity or beauty are the products of well-known puppeteers. There are many collectors who would pay dearly for an original by Bil Baird or other modern puppet makers (the Baird puppets are not made personally by Baird but by a team of workers, including five wood-carvers, in a factory-like operation; nevertheless their appeal to collectors is to, say, a painting from the studio of DaVinci.

Any puppet that has appeared in a television program is desirable for that reason alone, even if poorly designed and constructed.

The physical size of puppets is rarely an influence on their value. Large puppets are more expensive to construct. Anyone who orders a lifesize puppet from a puppet-maker will pay $3,000 to $5,000 for it, possibly more; but its value to collecotrs may be less, as not many collectors have the space to store or display large specimens.

Nor does style have more than a minimal effect on value. The four most common types of puppets are: marionettes (operated by strings); hand puppets; rod puppets; and ventriloquist dummies, the last being of fairly recent development. All other factors being equal, a good marionette would probably outsell a good speciman of the other varieties, but factors are never equal and the puppet market is, to say the least, unpredictable. Strict guidelines can never to set on prices because every puppet is different from another, excepting those mass-produced for the toy market. There are few private collectors, especially in America (Europe is the headquarters of puppet-making, puppet collecting, and everything else to do with puppets). When a collection is sold, most of the buyers are dealers in antique dolls.

At the present time, Oriental puppets are just coming into popularity with American collectors. Their beauty and craftsmanship merit higher prices than are now being obtained. Within a very few years, they are likely to outsell most or all western puppets. Fine puppets are still being made in the Orient — not those sold in "Chinatown" stops but the puppets used in Japanese theatrical productions.

When buying old puppets, take care to see that all component parts are original or (at least) old. With some specimens this is not the case, and of course the value of such puppets is not comparable to those which have not been rebuilt or improved. The costume, if any, should also be old. Some signs of wear are inevitable. Much better to have marks of age than for the face, hands, etc., to be repainted. Repainting greatly reduces the value and may even render the specimen valueless to collectors.

Puppet heads. Heads without bodies are frequently offered for sale. These are collectible, but the price should not be nearly so high as for a complete specimen. Anyone purchasing a puppet head should not attempt to reconstruct the body, unless intending it for theatrical use.

It is vital to stress that the prices given below are for specific specimens sold on the market or offered for sale, except where the word "estimate" is given. A similar specimen might sell considerably higher or lower, depending on circumstances. Estimates are given for puppets of which there is no sales record, but whose value can be judged in light of collector interest, rarity, etc.

MARIONETTES

	Price Range	
☐ Man with round face, bulging eyes, in tuxedo, 37" tall, American, carved and painted wooden face, 20th C. .	700.00	800.00
☐ Fish carved and painted wood, moveable lower jaw, fins and tail, "about two feet long"	450.00	500.00
☐ Figure of Satan, papier-mache head, garishly painted, the body made of red plush, wooden shoes, carved wooden pitchford, 29" tall, some damage, 20th C. . . .	600.00	700.00
☐ Howdy Doody, the original puppet used when the TV program first appeared on the air (1948)	10000.00	20000.00
☐ Howdy Doody, replica of the TV puppet, reduced size (about 12"), sold in toy stores in the early 1950's	50.00	75.00
☐ Figure in the likeness of a skeleton, painted wood, 16½" tall, two strings missing, some paint worn off face, Mexican (?), first half of the 20th C.	350.00	400.00
☐ "Buffalo Bill," 46" tall, composition head, dressed in western outfit, belt with two guns, one hand missing, signs of wear	1250.00	1300.00
☐ "Black Sambo," composition head and hands, 11½" tall, checkered shirt, brown striped pants, brown jacket, in original box with 78 r.p.m. phonograph record, American, circa 1947	50.00	75.00
☐ Figure of a dragon, entirely of wood, green, purple & other colors, prominent eyes, 56" long, Chinese, 20th C.	750.00	1000.00
☐ Figure of a woman, possibly a princess, silk attire in multi colors, composition head, Japanese, modern . .	60.00	70.00

HAND PUPPETS (puppets in which the hand is inserted into the puppet through a sleeve, rather than being operated by strings, rods or other means)

☐ Policeman, old style uniform and hat, the head carved of balsa wood, traces of paint and gilding, very worn, American, first quarter of the 20th C.	125.00	150.00
☐ Punch, long crooked nose, red cheeks, brightly colored costume, porcelain head and hands, chipped, probably English, mid-Victorian	800.00	1000.00
☐ Oliver J. Dragon of the "Kukla, Fran & Ollie" television program, the original puppet made and used by Burr Tilstrom, 1940's . . . . (estimated)	5000.00	6000.00
☐ Figure of an old woman, wearing long dress and apron, carved wood head, painted (the painting may not be original), French or Swiss, late 18th or early 19th C.	500.00	600.00

ROD PUPPETS

☐ Man on a horse, stuffed bodies, papier-mache heads, also some components in other materials, one of the rods missing, soiled, but generally in good condition . 275.00 300.00

☐ Monkey with smiling face, long arms, total height 21", rods attached to arms 200.00 300.00

VENTRILOQUIST "DUMMIES"

☐ The average price of a newly or recently made ventriloquist dummie, large enough for theatrical use (height at least 36" with a head 3/4ths life-size or larger). The price is higher for those with special features, such as moveable eyelids, eyeballs that can be moved from side to side, etc. 350.00 500.00

☐ The original Charlie McCarthy dummie of radio fame, head of carved wood. For a long while Edgar Bergen worked with just a single model of Charlie, then made another in case something happened to the first .... (estimated) 20000.00 30000.00

☐ The original Jerry Mahoney used by Paul Winchell, head of carved wood. Jerry was by far the best-designed of all the "famous" puppets, with many special features .... (estimated) 5000.00 6000.00

☐ Jerry Mahoney, composition head and hands, 32" tall, wearing suit and white shirt, American, c. 1950 ..... 150.00 175.00

(in original suitcase-like carrying case with photograph record) 250.00 300.00

☐ Jerry Mahoney, composition head and hands, 21" tall, a smaller but otherwise exact replica of the above, American, c. 1950 (Was not sold with phonograph record.) 75.00 100.00

QUILTS

Quilts were the thrifty housewife's answer to a prayer: how to use up scraps of cloth too small for clothing. They are pieced, appliqued, quilted, embroidered, and come with names for the patterns. These patterns are named in all the standard quilt collector's books. Right now, Amish quilts seem to have the greatest potential value, although a magnificent appliqued quilt (shown on the cover of the book *The Flowering of American Folk Art*) recently (1979) sold for a reported $20,000 to $25,000.

☐ Amish Single Irish Chain Doll's Quilt, all wool with maroon, navy blue and gray patches and zigzag quilting 325.00 425.00

☐ Appliqued Calico Quilt with pink, red, yellow and green flowers 325.00 425.00

PIECED COTTON QUILT, *Flower Basket Pattern* . 400.00 - 500.00

QUILTS

☐ Appliqued Cotton Quilt with orange and green appliques on white ground with swag border	225.00	375.00
☐ Comforter, crazy quilt design, wood pieces joined with many embroidering stitches, 1914	—	85.00
☐ Crazy quilt in satin & velvet, dated 1892	—	425.00
☐ Crazy quilt, wool, 68" x 80"	—	40.00
☐ Crib quilt, pink & brown calico, 33" x 41"	—	195.00
☐ Double Irish Chain Quilt in red, white and blue	80.00	120.00
☐ Double Irish Chain Quilt with arch design, hand quilted in red and white	150.00	225.00
☐ Double wedding ring, scalloped edges, 78" x 67", unused	—	110.00
☐ Lavender and White appliqued Quilt, center panel with sunburst and S scroll, white cotton ground with leaf and flower quilting	60.00	100.00
☐ Nine Patch pattern, machine-quilted, c. 1890	—	135.00
☐ Patchwork Quilt, hand embroidered silk on velvet	100.00	150.00
☐ Pieced Amish Cotton Basket Quilt with blue and black patches dated 1918	375.00	575.00
☐ Pieced Amish Cotton and Wool Basket Quilt with maroon, rust, green, blue, purple wool and cotton patches forming baskets	350.00	450.00
☐ Pieced Amish Satin, cotton and wool crib quilt in the Trip Around the World pattern with maroon, gray, black, blue, magenta and rust patches with a navy blue border	325.00	425.00
☐ Pieced Amish Variable Star cotton and sateen quilt with black and shocking pink patches	225.00	275.00
☐ Pieced Calico and Chintz Friendship Quilt with red, green, brown, blue, and orange print and solid calico with chintz patches in the Square pattern	525.00	725.00
☐ Pieced Calico Bow Tie Quilt with blue, red, brown, maroon and black calico patches with cubes of white cotton	225.00	325.00

QUILTS

☐ Pieced Calico Crib Quilt with pink, yellow, black and green calico patches with square quilting 225.00 275.00

☐ Pieced Calico Philadelphia Pavement Quilt with yellow, orange, pink, red and green calico patches ... 175.00 225.00

☐ Pieced Calico Pinwheel Quilt with red, brown, yellow and black calico patches 150.00 250.00

☐ Pieced Calico Quilt in the Star of the East pattern with brown, pink and blue calico patches on white cotton ground 175.00 275.00

☐ Pieced Calico Quilt, Variable Star pattern with various colored patches on white ground 75.00 150.00

☐ Pieced Calico Star of Bethlehem Quilt with red, blue, orange, green, and pink calico patches on white cotton ground 225.00 325.00

☐ Pieced Calico Zig Zag Quilt with red, brown, green, blue, purple, pink and gray calico patches and red and white gingham check border 225.00 325.00

☐ Pieced Cotton and Calico "Sawtooth Diamond" Quilt, pink calico patches on deep blue ground 225.00 325.00

☐ Pieced Cotton and Sateen Amish Quilt in the Old Maid's Puzzle in various shades of red, rust and black patches 200.00 300.00

☐ Pieced Cotton Quilt, Flower Basket pattern, with brown and beige patches on white ground. Diagnol and zig zag quilting 400.00 500.00

☐ Pieced Cotton Quilt, handmade pyramid design on white background 75.00 125.00

☐ Pieced Cotton Quilt with Texas Star. Stars in green, gold and orange 75.00 125.00

☐ Pieced Mennonite Calico Ocean Waves Quilt with pink, blue, red, gray and green calico and cotton patches with wide pink 250.00 300.00

☐ Pieced trapunto, pair, green/white, late 19th C. ...... — 650.00

☐ Tulip applique, red/green/gray/white, c. 1880 .... — 145.00

☐ Tumbling Blocks, silk & velvet .... — 200.00

☐ Victorian Crazy Quilt with variously shaped velvet and silk colored patches embroidered with leaves, pansies, and petunias 1600.00 2100.00

☐ Wool quilt with log cabin design, 19th C. 175.00 200.00

RADIO PREMIUMS

Radio premiums are items given away by radio stations, the more avidly collected ones falling into the 1935-45 era. Usually there was some sort of sponsor tie-in; the listener sent a boxtop, label, etc., with his request, and sometimes a small charge was made also. Seldom do these items bear the radio station names, as they were designed to be given away by networks comprising numerous stations across the country.

RADIO PREMIUMS Price Range

☐ The Lone Ranger Finger Ring, All zinc, adjustable, portrait of the Lone Ranger, c. 1947 (This price is for a sound specimen. Many are broken.)	5.00	6.00
☐ Card with Photo of Roy Rogers & His Singing Group, "The Sons of the Pioneers," facsimile signature, small, B/W, c. 1945	2.00	2.50
☐ Booklet, "Cooking Hints from Betty Crocker," wrapper, unpaged, c. 1938	.50	1.00
☐ Booklet, "Breakfast Ideas from General Mills," four-color cover, wrappers, some recipes but mainly promotional material on various cereal products, c. 1940	.75	1.00
☐ Membership card in the Gene Autry fan club, small photo of Gene Autry with facsimile signature, place for recipient to write in name and address, late 1940's	3.00	4.00
☐ "Little Orphan Annie" decoder ring. One of the classic radio premiums, c. 1936 (Millions must have been distributed but, as with other premiums, few survive.)	—	50.00

RADIO RECEIVERS

The listings given below are for receivers manufactured before 1930. Although post-1930 receivers are collected, they fall mainly into the class of "nostalgia" and "furniture" and are not primarily sought as examples of pioneer receiving instruments.

☐ A.C. Dayton Co. Crystal set, 1923	90.00	110.00
☐ A.C. Dayton Co. Super Six, 1924	120.00	130.00
☐ Adams-Morgan. Paragon Regen, 1921	180.00	200.00
☐ Adams-Morgan. R10 Short Wave, 1921	225.00	250.00
☐ Crosley. VI, 1922	250.00	300.00
☐ Crosley. X, 1922	175.00	200.00
☐ Crosley. Pup, 1925	275.00	300.00
☐ Crosley. 5-38, 1926	175.00	200.00
☐ DeFrost. D6, 1923	275.00	300.00
☐ DeFrost. D10, 1923	350.00	400.00
☐ DeFrost. Everyman (crystal), 1923	175.00	225.00
☐ Federal. 58DX, 1922	375.00	400.00
☐ Federal. 57DX, 1922	350.00	400.00
☐ Federal. 61DX, 1923	375.00	400.00
☐ Freshman. Masterpiece, 1924	225.00	250.00
☐ Grebe. CR6, 1919	400.00	500.00
☐ Grebe. CR5, 1921	200.00	300.00
☐ Grebe. Synchrophase, 1925	375.00	400.00
☐ Magnavox. TRF-5, 1925	225.00	250.00
☐ Philco. 551, 1928	115.00	120.00
☐ Philco. 525, 1929	75.00	100.00

RADIO RECEIVERS

	Price	Range
☐ RCA. Radiola X, 1925	375.00	400.00
☐ RCA. Radiola 26, 1925	400.00	500.00
☐ RCA. Radiola, 1923	140.00	150.00
☐ RCA. Radiola special, 1923	140.00	160.00
☐ RCA. Aeriola Jr. (crystal), 1922	120.00	130.00

RAILROADIANA

Some railroad buffs know the timetables of their favorite lines by heart. This only goes to prove how dedicated and enthusiastic railroad collectors can be. Everything is collected—from the tools, badges, caps and uniforms of the railroad men (linemen, switchmen, conductors and porters), to things used on the train, such as tableware, headrest linens, etc.

☐ Ashtray, Floor model, Brass	80.00	100.00
☐ Badge, Police	60.00	90.00
☐ Bell, Brass, 12"	500.00	600.00
☐ Buttons, Uniform	4.00	6.00
☐ Cuspidor, Maine Central	20.00	30.00
☐ Dish, Pacific Railroad, Silver	20.00	35.00
☐ Glass, Bar, Erie Railroad	15.00	20.00
☐ Key, Switch, Brass	10.00	15.00
☐ Key, Switch, New York Central	10.00	15.00
☐ Lantern, Caboose, Wabash	40.00	60.00
☐ Lantern, Switch, Missouri Central	60.00	80.00
☐ Passes, New York Central	16.00	22.00
☐ Pin, Conductor's, Enamel inlay	15.00	20.00
☐ Plates, Tin, 13 of them	35.00	—
☐ Postcards, Railroad scenes	1.50	6.00
☐ Punch, Conductor's	10.00	15.00
☐ Ring, Conductor's, Enamel, 10 KG	35.00	40.00
☐ Scrapbook, Magazine pictures, patches, postcards	55.00	—
☐ Sign, Atlantic Coast Line, Round, 34"	20.00	25.00
☐ Sign, Crossing, pre-1900	30.00	—
☐ Ticket Holder, Wood	30.00	40.00
☐ Track Maul, 5 to 10 pounds	6.00	10.00
☐ Tumbler, New York Central	4.00	6.00
☐ Tumbler, Pennsylvania Railroad	2.00	4.00

RAZORS

They may be scared to try their razors on their own five-o'clock shadows, but razor collectors are thrilled when they find a razor with a patent date or a name that they don't already have. Straight and folding razors are collected, as well as various Gillette traveling razors in kits, with a head which unscrews. These go fo $5 on up. Also, look out for the numerous types of sharpeners. . . from strops to patented grinding wheels as small as a pack of cigarettes.

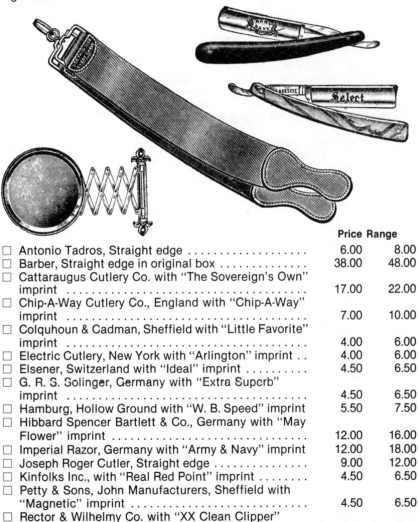

	Price	Range
☐ Antonio Tadros, Straight edge	6.00	8.00
☐ Barber, Straight edge in original box	38.00	48.00
☐ Cattaraugus Cutlery Co. with "The Sovereign's Own" imprint	17.00	22.00
☐ Chip-A-Way Cutlery Co., England with "Chip-A-Way" imprint	7.00	10.00
☐ Colquhoun & Cadman, Sheffield with "Little Favorite" imprint	4.00	6.00
☐ Electric Cutlery, New York with "Arlington" imprint . .	4.00	6.00
☐ Elsener, Switzerland with "Ideal" imprint	4.50	6.50
☐ G. R. S. Solinger, Germany with "Extra Superb" imprint	4.50	6.50
☐ Hamburg, Hollow Ground with "W. B. Speed" imprint	5.50	7.50
☐ Hibbard Spencer Bartlett & Co., Germany with "May Flower" imprint	12.00	16.00
☐ Imperial Razor, Germany with "Army & Navy" imprint	12.00	18.00
☐ Joseph Roger Cutler, Straight edge	9.00	12.00
☐ Kinfolks Inc., with "Real Red Point" imprint	4.50	6.50
☐ Petty & Sons, John Manufacturers, Sheffield with "Magnetic" imprint	4.50	6.50
☐ Rector & Wilhelmy Co. with "XX Clean Clipper" imprint	4.50	6.50

RAZORS   Price Range

☐ Reuter Bros. 3.50   5.50
☐ Robeson Shur Edge, New York with "The Nugget"
   imprint 4.50   6.50
☐ Simmons Hardware Co. with "Hornet" imprint 4.50   6.50
☐ Simmons Hardware Co. with "Royal Keen Kutter"
   imprint 12.00   15.00
☐ Sterling Razor Works with "Rattler" imprint 3.50   5.50
☐ Victory Hone Co., Iowa with "Victory Hollow #1"
   imprint 3.50   5.50
☐ Winchester, Straight edge 50.00   60.00
☐ Witte Hardware Co., Mo. with "Witte's Rattler" 3.50   5.50

REDWARE

This is probably the most common of all early pottery which was first made in the 1600's. The red glazed material was readily available and was used for the making of bricks and roof tiles — a true part of our early history.

☐ Bean Pot, brown, covered, 2 handles 30.00   35.00
☐ Bed Pan, brown design, manganese splotching 80.00   100.00
☐ Candle Sconce, yellow and green, clear glaze 275.00   325.00
☐ Flask, dark brown, glaze, 6" H 75.00   100.00
☐ Jar, green with brown splotches, 2 handles, 10½" H . 100.00   125.00
☐ Jug, brown glaze, ovoid, 2 handles 70.00   100.00
☐ Loaf Pan, brown splotches, glaze 140.00   170.00
☐ Pitcher, milk, spotted glaze, 15½" D 55.00   85.00
☐ Spittoon, speckled glaze 90.00   120.00

ROGERS GROUPS

Rogers was to the late Victorian what Goebel Hummel is to some collectors today, although the Rogers pieces were closer to real art sculpture than are Hummel figurines. The groups of plaster figures were posed in vignettes illustrative of scenes from history, from family life and from politics. They are all sort of yellow-brown, dead white, black or polychrome and could be found in almost any American parlor at the turn of the century.

☐ Balcony 675.00   775.00
☐ Bubbles 500.00   600.00
☐ Charity Patient 540.00   610.00
☐ Checker Players 600.00   700.00
☐ Chess 650.00   700.00
☐ Coming to the Parson 600.00   700.00
☐ Country Post Office 600.00   700.00
☐ Fairy's Whispers 425.00   500.00
☐ Fetching the Doctor 650.00   750.00
☐ Fighting Bob 500.00   550.00

ONE MORE SHOT
600.00 - 750.00

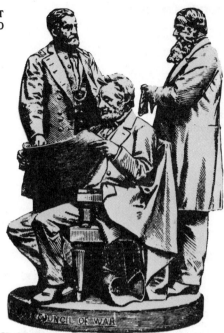

COUNCL OF WAR
1100.00 - 1400.00

ROGERS GROUP

	Price	Range
☐ First Love	400.00	475.00
☐ First Ride	600.00	700.00
☐ Football	1000.00	1400.00
☐ Fugitive Story	750.00	850.00
☐ Going for the Cows	475.00	575.00
☐ Hide & Seek	650.00	750.00
☐ Home Guard	700.00	800.00
☐ Mail Day	625.00	700.00
☐ Miles Standish	330.00	430.00
☐ Neighboring Pews	650.00	750.00
☐ One More Shot	625.00	775.00
☐ Peddler at the Fair	675.00	775.00
☐ Playing Doctor	575.00	675.00
☐ Politics	550.00	650.00
☐ Referee	600.00	700.00
☐ Rip Van Winkle Returned	540.00	640.00
☐ Romeo & Juliet	475.00	575.00
☐ School Days	675.00	775.00
☐ Slave Auction	1300.00	1700.00
☐ Slave Market	1400.00	1700.00
☐ Taking the Oath	675.00	775.00
☐ Tap on the Window	475.00	575.00
☐ Traveling Magician	425.00	500.00
☐ Village Schoolmaster	700.00	800.00
☐ Washington	950.00	1050.00

ROGERS GROUP   Price Range
- ☐ Watch on the Santa Maria 550.00   600.00
- ☐ Wounded Scout 900.00   1200.00
- ☐ Wrestler 1000.00   1200.00

ROYAL COLLECTIBLES

A document from the reign of William The Conquerer of England (1027-1087) endorsed with his sign, on vellum, would sell for $100,000-$150,000, even though William was illiterate and signed all his letters and documents with an "X" which had to be witnessed to be official. His "autograph," if it can be called that, is extremely rare, only one specimen being in the Brittish Museum.)

- ☐ Elizabeth I (1559-1603), document on vellum, 7x4½", unsigned but bearing a well-impressed specimen of her Great Seal, the queen on horseback on one side, seated on a throne on the other, small portion missing, cracked, attached to the document with a braided cord made of silken twine of various colors, enclosed in a folding **Price** fleece-lined case 1000.00
- ☐ Elizabeth II, 8x10 b/w photo signed and inscribed 500.00
- ☐ Elizabeth II, Christmas card with her photo, signed by her & Philip . 250.00
- ☐ Henry VII (1757-1509), letter signed, the body in secretary's hand, concerning affairs in Spain, on paper, well preserved 800.00
- ☐ Henry VII, specimen of his Great Seal, no document attached, yellow wax, cracked and with a large portion missing, set into a leatherette folding case 85.00
- ☐ Henry VIII (1485-1547), document signed, vellum, 1532, on appointment of a treasurer, genuine signature, upper portion of the document stained, seal missing 750.00
- ☐ Henry VIII, genuine signature removed from a letter or document, vellum, framed 500.00
- ☐ Henry VIII, for documents bearing the Great Seal but not his signature 750.00
- ☐ Henry VIII, for signed documents bearing a reasonably well preserved specimen of the Great Seal 1500.00
- ☐ Henry VIII, large document on vellum, eight membranes, each measuring about 13x18, signed with his notorious wooden stamp (he hated signing his name and had a stamp made for the purpose), several small seals of bishops and various officials in different colors of wax, fairly well preserved in a morocco-baked box, 1519 .... 850.00
- ☐ Louis XIV of France, signature removed from a document or letter, paper, good specimen 200.00
- ☐ Richard II (1367-1400), document on vellum in his name but not bearing his signature, 14x8½", signed by several officials, seal missing, mouse chewed at corner 350.00
- ☐ Richard II, document on vellum from his reign, not bearing his signature but carrying a specimen of his seal in orange wax, about ¼ missing, contained in a protective case of heavy cardboard with hinges, covered with plastic 600.00

BRASS RUBBINGS

Price

☐ Brass rubbing, King Ethelred of the West Saxons, died 871, brass effigy dating from 1440. 14½" 65.00

☐ Brass rubbing, Lady Katherine Howard, one of Henry VIII's wives, 1535, 38" 250.00

(A note on brass rubbing: the values of these collectors' items, which have a very long history, are variable depending on the quality of paper used to make the rubbing and the skill with which the work was executed. A specimen on good-quality paper by a master at the craft will usually fetch twice as much, or more, than the average. Many rubbings are on poor paper and, while well executed, are not very desirable to collectors as they can scarcely be handled without the risk of damage.)

RUGS

HOOKED

Most experts feel that hooked rugs, if they didn't originate in America, reached their peak as an art here. The earliest ones known in America go back to about 1820, and most examples sold today are either very late 19th century, early 20th, or are quite recent examples done on the (excellent) patterns of such designers as Pearl McGown. The most desirable rugs are those which were designed by the rug hooker and are unique; in addition, figural subjects are more valuable than abstract geometrics or florals.

	Price Range	
☐ American 19th Century American eagle and shield in shades of grey and brown with a floral and leaf border, 30" x 5'2"	525.00	725.00
☐ American 19th Century depicting a lion lying between leaf and scrolling design in tones of blue, yellow, grey and red. 30" x 56½"	425.00	625.00
☐ American 19th Century with dog on grass in shades of red, brown, green and tan. 38" x 59"	225.00	325.00
☐ American 19th Century with two lions surrounded by leaves and flowers. 30½ x 5'1"	525.00	725.00
☐ American Floral 19th Century with center of flowers and leaves, S-scroll devices in center on yellow ground	325.00	525.00
☐ American Geometric in strips of brown, yellow, grey and blue. 53" x 10'3"	225.00	325.00
☐ American Pictorial with animals on tan ground with tones of brown, red, beige, navy blue and black. 21" x 33"	125.00	225.00
☐ American Pictorial with ducks, geese, stag and deer in landscape setting with beige, orange, green, blue, brown fabric. 21¼" x 42"	200.00	300.00
☐ American Pictorial with horse surrounded by vines in tan, mauve, green and black fabric. 19" x 39¾"	175.00	275.00
☐ American Pictorial with vessel flying the American flag in red, white and blue fabric. 29¼" x 45"	200.00	300.00

HOOKED - AMERICAN FLAG

ORIENTAL - KAZAK

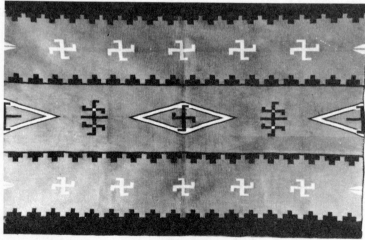

NAVAJO

HOOKED

Price Range

- American Runner flowers and leaves in center surrounded by squares. 25" x 20" 225.00 325.00
- American Floral in tones of beige and black with garlands of green, red and yellow flowers, large 1525.00 2025.00
- American Geometric, red, black, yellow, green, 2' x 3', 1890's 45.00 60.00
- American, Flag motif .... 600.00 —
- Often sold by the same dealers are rag rugs (sold according to size and good coloring from about $40 to several hundred for long runners) and the so-called "penny" rugs and "tongue" rugs, made up of large discs of wool, or tongue-shaped pieces of wool, sewed in overlapping layers like shingles, and embroidered. These rugs sell for upwards of $70, and those with unusual embroidering — beyond the usual featherstitching — of animals or stars or flags or hearts go for upwards of $200.00

ORIENTAL

There is only one way to buy oriental rugs — and that is through recognized authoritative dealers who know what they are doing and who are willing to tell you what they know. Among the most affordable "orientals" (a loose term covering rugs not only from the Orient, but form all of the Near, Far and Middle East) are the Kilim rugs, easily recognized because with each change of color there is a small gap or break in the weaving. Oriental rugs are either knotted or tied, or woven. Beware of contemporary oriental-style rugs sold in stores (most notoriously on New York's Fifth Avenue) to the unsuspecting. Get help before buying an oriental rug.

- Afghan Hatchli Rug, Holbein border and double "E" border. 6'8" x 4'2" 500.00 700.00
- Belouchistan Rug, Brown ground with geometric designs in brown, navy and red. 9'3" x 5'2" 750.00 850.00
- Chinese Rug, Rust ground with good luck symbol and lotus. 12' x 9' 1000.00 1500.00
- Daghestan Rug, Ivory with flowerheads and geometric designs, red border. 4'6" x 3'2" 2000.00 2500.00
- Greek Island Silk and Metallic Thread Embroidery, beige field embroidered with flowers and blossoming vines. 6' x 3'3" 400.00 600.00
- Hereke Rug, Ivory with floral medallion and stars. 16' x 12'8" 9000.00 10000.00
- Heriz Rug, Rust with salmon medallion and ivory spandrels. 13' x 10'8" 1800.00 2400.00
- Kirman Rug, Red ground, sunburst medallion with floral spandrels. 11'7" x 9' 2000.00 2600.00

ORIENTAL RUGS

	Price Range	

☐ Makal Carpet, Flower latticework, rust ground with blue border. 24' x 14' 2000.00 3000.00

☐ Salor Bagface, Red with Salor guls within geometric border. 4' x 1'3" 850.00 1100.00

☐ Sarouk Carpet, Red ground, floral sprigs, blue border. 11'6" x 9' 1200.00 1600.00

☐ Silk Embroidered Turcoman Bagface. 2'8" x 1'9" 150.00 250.00

☐ Spanish Rug, Yellow with flower medallions. 12'8" x 9'8" 800.00 1200.00

☐ Turkish Embroidery, Gold metallic thread, arch design, red felt ground. 6'2" x 3'2" 700.00 1100.00

☐ Turkish Felt Embroidery. 4'10" x 4'10" 200.00 300.00

☐ Veramin Rug, Blue field with latticework. 10' x 7' 3000.00 3600.00

☐ Yomud Bagface, Brown with two Kespie guls. 3'8" x 1'8" 800.00 1000.00

☐ Yomud Rug, Burgundy with five rows of guls within a sunburst border. 13' x 8'5" 2000.00 2500.00

NAVAJO

☐ 33" x 49" Germantown yarn in green, yellow, purple & white on red, c. 1910 .... 1300.00 1500.00

☐ 34" x 51" Native yarn analine dyed in red, black, white, orange, yellow, green, with addition of Germantown yarn, c.1900 .... 1800.00 2000.00

☐ 36" x 52" 4-ply yarn in green, white, brown and purple on red, c. 1900 .... 1500.00 1800.00

☐ 38" x 60" Crystal rug, grey center panel, black border, black and white figures, 1890's 3500.00 5000.00

☐ 43" x 62" Crystal rug (New Mexico), black & white figures on red ground, 1890's 5000.00 6000.00

☐ 45" x 65" Serape possibly from Bosque Redondo, orange, light and dark blue, green and yellow on gray bands. Zigzag figures in other colors, c. 1890 .... 2500.00 3000.00

☐ 52" x 68" Serape, late terraced style, indigo blue, white, red, c. 1890 .... 3500.00 3800.00

☐ 54" x 72" Serape, white and indigo blue on two-ply red ground, c. 1880 .... 7000.00 8000.00

☐ 68" x 56" Terraced style, black, white, indigo blue, red, c. 1875 .... 3600.00 4000.00

☐ 72" x 60" White, black, blue, red, c. 1910 .... 5000.00 6000.00

☐ 74" x 52" black and white alternating stripes, c. 1900 . 4000.00 5000.00

SPACE & SCIENCE FICTION

You may be surprised to learn that science fiction is over 100 years old, even if it didn't have that name. However, most "Sci-Fi" collectors concentrate on printed matter from the last 35 years or so. Because of a certain overlap, with supernatural beings able to jump over tall buildings, and strange lapses in natural laws, we have grouped the pulp magazines with the Sci-Fi periodicals. Please consult our publication *The Official Price Guide to Comic and Science Fiction Books* by Michael Resnick for more prices and information.

© Continental Publications

© Street and Smith

© Street and Smith

PULP MAGAZINES

	Price	Range

THE AVENGER (1939-1942)

	Price	Range
☐ Vol. 1, #1	15,00	25.00
☐ Vol. 1, #2 - Vol. 6, #6	12.50	17.50
☐ Vol. 2, #1 - Vol. 2, #6	10.00	15.00
☐ Vol. 3, #1 - Vol. 3, #6	8.00	12.50
☐ Vol. 4, #1 - Vol. 4, #6	6.00	10.00

CAPTAIN FUTURE (1940-1944)

☐ Vol. 1, #1	10.00	15.00
☐ Vol. 1, #2 - Vol. 2, #3	8.00	12.50
☐ Vol. 3, #1 - Vol. 4, #3	6.00	10.00

DOC SAVAGE (1933-1949)

☐ Vol. 1,	115.00	150.00
☐ Vol. 1, #2 - Vol. 2, #4	20.00	32.50
☐ Vol. 2, #5 - Vol. 4, #4	14.00	20.00
☐ Vol. 4, #6 - Vol. 8, #4	6.00	10.00
☐ Vol. 10, #5 - Vol. 14, #4	5.00	8.00
☐ Vol. 31, #1	4.50	7.00

FLASH GORDON STRANGE ADVENTURES MAGAZINE (1936)

☐ Vol. 1, #1	90.00	120.00

	Price	Range

THE SHADOW (1931-1949)

	Price	Range
☐ Vol. 1, #1	175.00	250.00
☐ Vol. 1, #2 - Vol. 1, #5	75.00	100.00
☐ Vol. 3, #3 - Vol. 4, #2	37.50	60.00
☐ Vol. 12, #3 - Vol. 16, #2	17.50	30.00
☐ Vol. 20, #1 - Vol. 23, #6	14.00	25.00
☐ Vol. 28, #1 - Vol. 31, #6	12.00	20.00
☐ Vol. 40, #1 - Vol. 43, #6	8.00	12.50
☐ Vol. 46, #5 - Vol. 48, #4	5.50	9.00
☐ Vol. 52, #5 - Vol. 54, #4	4.00	7.00

THE SPIDER (1933-1943)

	Price	Range
☐ Vol. 1, #1 - Vol. 1, #2	32.50	55.00
☐ Vol. 1, #3 - Vol. 1, #4	40.00	65.00
☐ Vol. 4, #1 - Vol. 7, #3	37.50	60.00
☐ Vol. 11, #1 - Vol. 13, #4	28.00	45.00
☐ Vol. 17, #1 - Vol. 19, #4	22.50	35.00
☐ Vol. 23, #1 - Vol. 25, #4	15.00	25.00
☐ Vol. 26, #1 - Vol. 28, #4	12.50	20.00
☐ Vol. 29, #1 - Vol. 30, #2	10.00	15.00

WU FANG (1935-1936)

	Price	Range
☐ Vol. 1, #1	67.00	110.00
☐ Vol. 1, #2 - Vol. 1, #4	60.00	100.00

COMIC SPACE BOOKS

	Price	Range
☐ Air Wonder Stories (1929-30) Vol. 1, #1	15.00	25.00
☐ Amazing Detective Tales (1930) Vol. I, #6	17.50	30.00
☐ Amazing Stories (1926-present) Vol. I, #1	60.00	90.00
☐ Amazing Stories Annual (1927) Vol. 1, #1	70.00	100.00
☐ Amazing Stories Quarterly (1928-34) Vol. 1, #1	10.00	15.00
☐ A. Merritt Fantasy Magazine (1949-50) Vol. I, #1	2.50	4.00
☐ Astonishing Stories (1940-43) Vol. I, #1	5.00	8.00
☐ Astounding Stories (1930-present) Vol. I, #1	220.00	300.00
☐ Authentic Science Fiction (1951-57) #1	6.00	10.00
☐ Avon Fantasy Reader (1947-52) #1	2.50	4.00
☐ Avon Science Fiction Reader (1951-52) #1-#3	2.00	3.00
☐ Avon Science Fiction and Fantasy Reader (1953) #1-#2	2.00	3.00
☐ Beyond Fantasy Fiction (1953-55) Vol. I, #1	2.50	4.00
☐ Bizarre Mystery Magazine (1965-66) Vol. I, #1	3.00	4.50
☐ Comet Stories (1940-41) Vol. I, #1	3.00	5.00
☐ Cosmic Stories (1941) Vol. 1, #1	3.00	4.00
☐ Cosmos Science Fiction and Fantasy Magazine (1953-54) Vol. 1, #1	2.00	3.00
☐ Cosmos (1976-77) Vol. 1, #1	1.00	1.50
☐ Coven 13 (1969-71) Vol. I, #1	1.25	2.00

COMIC SPACE BOOKS

		Price	Range
☐ Dime Mystery Magazine (1932-50) Vol. I, #1		6.00	10.00
☐ Dream World (1957) Vol. 1, 1		2.50	4.00
☐ Dynamic Science Fiction (1952-54) Vol. I, #1		1.50	2.50
☐ Dynamic Science Stories (1939) Vol. I, #1		3.50	5.00
☐ Erie Mysteries (1938-39) Vol. I, #1		15.00	25.00
☐ Famous Fantastic Mysteries (1939-53) Vol. I, #1		8.00	12.50
☐ Famous Science Fiction (1966-69) Vol. I, #1		2.50	4.00
☐ Fantastic (1952-present) Vol. I, #1		2.00	3.00
☐ Fantastic Adventures (1939-53) Vol. I, #1		4.00	7.50
☐ Fantastic Novels Magazine (1940-41 and 1948-51) Vol. 1, #1		6.00	10.00
☐ Fantastic Science Fiction (1952) Vol. I, #1		1.25	2.00
☐ Fantastic Story Quarterly (1950-55) Vol. I, #1		1.50	2.50
☐ Fantastic Universe (1953-60) Vol. I, #1		2.50	4.00
☐ Fantasy Book (1947-51) Vol. I, #1		1.00	1.50
☐ Fantasy Fiction (1950) Vol. I, #1		2.00	3.00
☐ Fantasy Magazine (1953) Vol. I, #1		1.50	2.50
☐ Fear (1960) Vol. I, #1		1.25	2.00
☐ Forgotten Fantasy (1970-71) Vol. I, #1		1.25	2.00
☐ Future Fiction (1939-43 and 1950-60) Vol. I, #1 (1939)		4.50	7.50
☐ Galaxy Science Fiction (1950-present) Vol. I, #1		2.25	3.50
☐ Galileo (1976-present) Vol. I, #1		1.00	1.50
☐ Gamma (1963-65) Vol. I, #1		1.25	2.00
☐ Ghost Stories (1926-32) Vol. 1, #1		10.00	15.00
☐ Golden Fleece (1938-39) Vol. I, #1		12.00	17.50
☐ Horror Stories (1935-41) Vol. I, #1		50.00	75.00
☐ Imagination Stories of Science and Fantasy (1950-58) Vol. I, #1		1.50	2.50
☐ Imaginative Tales (1954-58) #1		1.25	2.00
☐ Infinity Science Fiction (1955-58) Vol. I, #1		1.25	2.00
☐ International Science Fiction (1967-68) Vol. I, #1		1.00	1.50
☐ Isaac Asimov's Science Fiction (1977-present) Vol. I, #1		1.25	2.00
☐ Magazine of Fantasy and Science Fiction (1949-present) Vol. I, #1		2.50	4.00
☐ Magazine of Horror and Strange Stories (1963-65) Vol. I, #1		2.50	4.00
☐ Magic Carpet Magazine (1933-34) Vol. 3, #1		65.00	100.00
☐ Marvel Science Stories (1938-41 and 1950-52) Vol. I, #1		6.00	10.00
☐ Mind, Inc. (1929-31) Vol. I, #1		95.00	130.00
☐ Miracle Science and Fantasy Stories (1931) Vol. I, #1		40.00	65.00
☐ The Mysterious Traveler Magazine (1951-52) Vol. I, #1		2.00	3.00
☐ New Worlds Science Fiction (American Reprints—1960) Vol. I, #1-Vol. 1, 5		.60	1.00
☐ Odyssey Science Fiction (1976-77) Vol. I, #1		.60	1.00

COMIC SPACE BOOKS

	Price	Range
☐ Orbit Science Fiction (1953-54) Vol. I, #1	1.00	1.50
☐ Oriental Stories (1930-32) Vol. I, #1-Vol. 2, #3	65.00	100.00
☐ Other Worlds Science Stories (1949-57) Vol. I, #1	2.25	3.50
☐ Out of This World Adventures (1950) Vol. I, #1 . . .	3.00	5.00
☐ Planet Stories (1939-55) Vol. I, #1	10.00	15.00
☐ Rocket Stories (1953) Vol. I, #1	2.00	3.00
☐ Satellite Science Fiction (1956-59) Vol. I, #1	2.00	3.00
☐ Saturn Magazine of Fantasy and Science		
Fiction (1957-58) Vol. I, #1	1.25	2.00
☐ Science Fiction (1939-41 and 1943) Vol. I, #1	3.00	4.50
☐ Science Fiction Adventures (1956-58) Vol. 1, #6 .	1.50	2.50
☐ Science Fiction Digest (1954) Vol. I, #1	1.25	2.00
☐ Science Fiction Plus (1953) Vol. I, #1	2.50	4.00
☐ Science Fiction Quarterly (1940-43) #1	4.50	7.50
☐ Science Fiction Stories (1953-60) 1953	1.50	2.00
☐ Science Stories (1953-54) #1	1.25	2.00
☐ Science Wonder Stories (1929-30) Vol. 1, #1	15.00	25.00
☐ Science Wonder Quarterly (1929-30) Vol. I, #1 . . .	8.00	12.50
☐ Scientific Detective Monthly (1930) Vol. I, #1	17.50	30.00
☐ Shock (1948) Vol. I, #1	3.00	5.00
☐ Shock (1960) Vol. I, #1	1.25	2.00
☐ Sinister Stories (1940) Vol. I, #1	6.00	10.00
☐ Space Science Fiction (1952-53) Vol. I, #1	1.50	2.50
☐ Space Science Fiction Magazine (1957) Vol. I, #1	1.00	1.50
☐ Space Stories (1952-53) Vol. I, #1	1.25	2.00
☐ Space Travel (1958) Vol. 5, #4-Vol. 5, #6	.60	1.00
☐ Spaceway Science Fiction (1953-55) Vol. 1, #1 . .	1.25	2.00
☐ Speed Mystery Stories (1943) Vol. 1, #1	2.50	4.00
☐ Spicy Mystery Stories (1934-42) Vol. I, #1	35.00	50.00
☐ Star Science Fiction (1958) Vol. I, #1	1.00	1.50
☐ Startling Mystery Magazine (1940) Vol. I, #1	20.00	30.00
☐ Startling Stories (1939-55) Vol. I, #1	6.00	10.00
☐ Stirring Science Stories (1941-42) Vol. I, #1	4.00	6.00
☐ Strange Stories (1939-41) Vol. I, #1	15.00	25.00
☐ Strange Tales (1931-33) Vol. I, #1	55.00	80.00
☐ Super-Science Fiction (1956-59) Vol. I, #1	1.25	2.00
☐ Super-Science Stories (1940-43 and 1949-51)		
Vol. 1, #1	4.50	7.50
☐ Suspense (1951-52) Vol. 1, #1	1.25	2.00
☐ Tales of Magic and Mystery (1927-28) Vol. 1, #1 .	50.00	75.00
☐ Tales of the Frightened (1957) Vol. I, #1	20.00	30.00
☐ Ten-Story Fantasy (1951) Vol. I, #1	1.50	2.50
☐ Terror Tales (1934-41) Vol. 1, #1	50.00	75.00
☐ The Thrill Book (1919) Vol. I, #1	650.00	1000.00
☐ Thrilling Mystery (1935-39) Vol. 1, #1	15.00	25.00
☐ Thrilling Mystery (1935-39) Vol. I, #1	15.00	25.00
☐ Thrilling Mysteries, Vol. I, #1	50.00	75.00
☐ Thrilling Wonder Stories (1936-55) Vol. 8, #1	4.50	7.50
☐ Tops in Science Fiction (1953) Vol. I, #1	1.00	1.50

COMIC SCIENCE BOOKS

	Price	Range
☐ Two Complete Science Adventure Books (1950-54) Vol. 1, #1	1.50	2.50
☐ Uncanny Stories (1941) Vol. I, #1	13.00	20.00
☐ Uncanny Tales (1938-40) Vol. 2, #4	20.00	30.00
☐ Unearth (1976-present) Vol. I, #1	.60	1.00
☐ Universe Science Fiction (1953-55) #1	1.00	1.50
☐ Unknown (1939-43 and 1948) Vol. I, #1	12.00	17.50
☐ Vanguard Science Fiction (1958) Vol. I, #1	1.25	2.00
☐ Venture Science Fiction (1958) Vol. I, #1	1.25	2.00
☐ Vertex (1973-75) Vol. I, #1-Vol. 3, #2	1.00	1.50
☐ Vision of Tommorrow (1969-70) Vol. I, #1	.75	1.25
☐ Vortex Science Fiction (1953) Vol. I, #1	1.00	1.50
☐ Wierd Mystery (1970-72) All issues	.60	1.00
☐ Weird TerrorTales (1970) Vol. I, #1	2.25	3.50
☐ Weird Tales (1923-54 and 1973-74) Vol. I, #1	400.00	600.00
☐ Wonder Stories (1930-36, 1957 and 1963) Vol. 2, #1	8.00	12.50
☐ Wonder Stories Annual (1950-53) Vol. I, #1	1.25	2.00
☐ Worlds Beyond (1950-51) Vol. I, #1	1.00	1.50
☐ Worlds of Fantasy (1968 and 1970) Vol. I, #1	1.00	1.50
☐ Worlds of IF (1952-74) Vol. I, #1	2.00	3.00
☐ Worlds of Tommorrow (1963-67 and 1970-71) Vol. I, #1	1.00	1.50

SCOUTING COLLECTIBLES

They should give a badge for collecting scouting materials! Everything from cloth badges and to metal neckerchief rings, from tools to backpacks, from uniforms to manuals are collected, and while Boy Scout collectors are a bit more numerous, Girl Scout collectors are remembering where those cookies came from.

☐ Air Scout Manual, 1942	10.00	12.00
☐ Bookmark, Boy Scout, metal	6.00	10.00
☐ Boy Scout Diaries, 1917	20.00	25.00
☐ Cup, collapsible, Girl Scout	6.00	10.00
☐ Gavel, Boy Scout	3.50	5.50
☐ Neckerchief, red, National Jamboree, 1935	100.00	120.00
☐ Pocket Patch, leather, World Jamboree 1951	60.00	70.00
☐ Pocket Patch, woven, World Jamboree, 1955	20.00	25.00
☐ Sash, cloth badges, Boy Scout, 1940's	45.00	55.00
☐ Sterling Ring, adjustable, National Jamboree, 1953	20.00	25.00

SCRIMSHAW

Scrimshaw — carved whale ivory — is the work of scrimshanders, seamen who carved useful objects and decorated pieces from bits of whalebone and from teeth. Certain whales are, fortunately, protected now, and only old scrimshaw is legally sold. Many imitations are made — not only of bone and teeth of unprotected species of animals, but even of plastic.

ENGRAVED WHALE TEETH AND WALRUS TUSK

	Price Range	
☐ Bust of Man, 4" H	90.00	120.00
☐ Cane, Dove on knob, brass tip, 38" H	250.00	350.00
☐ Carpenter's Square, Teakwood handle	100.00	150.00
☐ Corset Stays, Whale bone, home scenes, 14" L	100.00	150.00
☐ Hammer, dolphin on handle, 7" L	180.00	230.00
☐ Horn, 19th C., 10'"L	100.00	150.00
☐ Napkin Holder with cats	35.00	45.00
☐ Pie Crimper, Fancy with rosewood handle	130.00	160.00
☐ Walrus' Tusk, Cribbage Board	625.00	725.00
☐ Walrus' Tusk, Dagger, 10" L	50.00	75.00
☐ Walrus' Tusk, Indians, 6" L	375.00	450.00
☐ Walrus' Tusk, Mother and child on swing, 11" L	200.00	275.00
☐ Whale's Tooth, Crucifix, 6" L	140.00	190.00
☐ Whale's Tooth, Eagle and flag, 5" L	325.00	400.00
☐ Whale's Tooth, Sperm whale	450.00	525.00
☐ Whale's Tooth, Whaling scene, 5" L	475.00	575.00
☐ Whale's Tooth, Young woman with long curls, 6½" L	1800.00	2200.00

SHAKER CRAFTS & FURNITURE

The Shakers, a religious sect with early 19th century origins in England, have a long history in America. They were committed to an anti-worldly life, and showed their devotion to God and the spiritual life by finding their own ways of doing everything. The Shakers were great furniture makers, and they sought perfection and purity in their designs, which were simpler and more useful and well-made than practically any other furniture. They also made goods for sale to the world outside their communities, including not only furniture but baskets, boxes, drying racks for food and clothing, medicines, herbs and seeds. Everything from wall cupboards to seed-packet printed la-labels are collectible.

	Price Range	
☐ Almanac, 1885	40.00	50.00
☐ Basket, double handle, 7"	90.00	120.00
☐ Basket, cover, red-painted handle	225.00	—
☐ Basket, draining	80.00	—
☐ Bonnet, Woven with straw	80.00	110.00
☐ Box, 8½" oval	80.00	110.00
☐ Box, 10½" oval	90.00	140.00
☐ Box, pincushion	150.00	200.00
☐ Box, sewing	175.00	225.00
☐ Comb, wood	20.00	25.00
☐ Bucket, wood with handle and lid, 12"	100.00	125.00
☐ Bucket, 1 gallon, dove-tailed, fair condition	11.00	—
☐ Sap Bucket, Enfield, N.H.	42.00	—
☐ Clothes Hanger	40.00	70.00
☐ Clothes Hanger, 6 peg	50.00	—
☐ Comb, wood	20.00	25.00
☐ Dust Pan	30.00	60.00
☐ Foot Stool, decorated	175.00	225.00
☐ Hay Winder w/rope	35.00	
☐ Jelly cupboard, red stained wood, c. 1890	500.00	—
☐ Pegboard, wood	140.00	180.00
☐ Plantation Desk	300.00	—
☐ Rack, Spice Dryer	140.00	180.00
☐ Rocker, ladderback, mushrooms arms, splint seat	425.00	—
☐ Soap Shaver	95.00	—
☐ Spinning Wheel	130.00	170.00

SHIP MODELS

	Price
☐ American cargo ship "Explorer," 27" in length, masts and sails, mounted on a metal base, well preserved except for portions of the rigging, c. 1880	700.00
☐ American gunner "Victory," 41" in length, meticulous workmanship, some detail work damaged, overall well preserved, mounted on a new stand made of polished walnut, c. 1900	1400.00

CHINESE EXPORT CARVED IVORY PLEASURE BOAT,
Early 19th Century, 9½"H . . . .   700.00 - 800.00

SHIP MODELS

Price

☐ American battleship "Kentucky," 19" long, the hull carved from a solid block of wood, painted, traces of original paint, one mast restored, the sails not original, mounted on a wooden platform painted deep blue, c. 1870 . . . . 900.00

☐ American battleship "Maine," 24" long, the guns made of real brass, figures of seamen in carved wood, tins and crates on board, the work of a master modeler, c. 1890 . . . . .2000.00

☐ English battleship "Great Harry," 57" long, brass guns, made largely of oak, some components of other wood, gilded work with most of the original gliding intact, rare model, probably English or Scottish, of a ship dating to the 16th C., c. 1810 . . . . .4500.00

☐ English liner "Titanic," 32" long, wood and metal painted in various shades of grey, mounted on wooden stand, American or English, recent 750.00

☐ English liner "Queen Mary," 55" long, wood and metal, scale built by a modelist down to the smallest detail, rubber life preservers, scale-built lifeboats, etc. Mounted on a copper and wood stand with engraved nameplate, c. 1940 . . . . .3500.00

☐ English schooner "Admiral V," 26" long, c. 1900 . . . . 375.00

☐ German-built model of an unnamed sailing ship, 15th C. design, well detailed, weathered wood, wormholes, some parts restored, unmounted, c. 1750-1800 . . . . .1650.00

☐ Model of an early Viking sailing ship, 10th or 11th C. A.D., 31" long, wood and canvas, probably German (not entirely accurate in design), c. 1860 . . . . .1500.00

☐ Model of an unnamed 17th C. Dutch merchant vessel, 63" long, well scaled, mermaid figurehead painted & gilded, contained in a very large half-box painted with waves, sea serpents, etc. (weight 600 pounds overall), probably Dutch, c. 1890 . . . . .5000.00

SIGNS

Signs come in all sizes, shapes, ages and types. Anyone who says he collects signs is normally a specialist in one type, it being impossible to make a comprehensive collection of them all. Below are listed prices for signs of a variety of descriptions, yet there are many other kinds not mentioned.

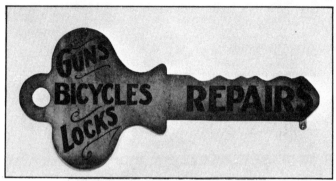

LOCKSMITHS TRADE SIGN,
Painted Tin, 32"L . 250.00 - 300.00

	Price Range	
☐ Standing sign, "BUS STOP," iron on shaft, set into weighted iron base, American, c. 1950	75.00	100.00
☐ Wooden sign, English, shield shape, 37x26", a black ground with painted symbol of "fox and hare," no lettering, remains of hooks, faded, the wood rotted and split in several places. (Identifying names should not be expected on English signs of this early a date; nor should they be referred to as "tavern signs," a name often but mistakenly given them. Usually, such signs belonged to the house to which they were attached, and were not the invention or property of any business being conducted there, though of course such business did become identified with the signs.) c. 1500	1200.00	1500.00
☐ Wooden sign, English, rectangular, approx. 26x19", a reddish ground painted with heraldic emblem and motto in Latin, hardware missing, the wood well preserved, the paint somewhat eroded, c. 1580	700.00	1000.00
☐ Wooden sign, American, rectangular with shaped crest, silhouette portrait of George Washington in black against what was apparently a cream ground (worn away), lettered "The George," New England, possibly Massachusetts, c. 1820	1500.00	2000.00
☐ Wooden sign, American, shaped like a teapot, 31" tall, lettered "Henry Blackwell's," partially repainted, good condition, c. 1840	800.00	1000.00

SIGNS

☐ Wooden sign, American, in the shape of a cigar, 8½ feet in length (approx. size), gaudily painted, some incised surface work, made of one plank of wood, c. 1880 . . . .   1400.00   1600.00

☐ Wooden sign, American, in the likeness of a pair of spectacles, about six feet in width, painted light grey, original hangings attached, the wood mildewed, c. 1880 . . . .   1000.00   1500.00

☐ Wooden sign, American or English, in the likeness of a pig, 54" in width, painted in various shades of pink and red, advertising a butcher's shop, fixtures missing, slightly defective, c. 1870 . . . .   900.00   1200.00

☐ Wooden sign, American, in the likeness of a high laced boot, 78x51", painted brown and black, used either for a cobbler's shop or a shoe store, c. 1890 . . . .   1500.00   1800.00

☐ Wooden sign, American, in the likeness of a molar tooth, approx. 43x41", painted in white, yellow and dark grey, used over a dentist's office. (Guess who buys most signs of this kind. Collectors? No, dentists!) c. 1870 . . . .   2500.00   3000.00

SILHOUETTES

Put simply, silhouettes are cut-out paper profiles of heads, half-figures or full-figures of people, animals, and sometimes including articles of furniture or costume accessories such as parasols. They are almost always cut from black paper and place on white or cream paper backgrounds. Occasionally, silhouette-like portraits are done with watercolor to create the same effect. One of the most desirable names of all is that of Augustin Edouart, a freehand (as opposed to those aided by strong light casting a shadow) cutter. He cut something close to 250,000 silhouettes in his life, and at least 10,000 of those were done during a 10-year stay in America. Many of those were lost when a ship carrying them went down at sea. Edouart died in 1861. A good number of single profiles by anonymous or unknown silhouettists are available for between $90 and $180.

☐ Aaron Burr, bust portrait, black watercolor. Signed Jos. Wood, dated 1812. 3" x 2¾" 300.00   350.00

☐ Alexander Hamilton, bust portrait wearing frilled stock. Signed J. W. Jarvis, dated 1804. 4½" x 3½" . . .   400.00   500.00

☐ Charles Carroll of Carrollton, holding trowel and cane, dated 1828. 13" x 10¾" 200.00   300.00

☐ Couple in double frame, 19th C. . . . .   230.00   —

☐ Double Portrait of Gentleman and Lady, full length figures. Signed Augn. Edouart Fecit, dated 1844. 9" x 7 1/8" 175.00   250.00

PORTRAIT SILHOUETTES *of Gov. and Mrs. S. W. Kearney,*
c.1847 . . . . 400.00 - 500.00

SILHOUETTES

☐ Gentleman Wearing Top Hat, landscape setting. Signed Aug. Edouart Fecit, dated 1829. 8 7/8" x 6 5/8"	225.00	275.00
☐ Gov. Robert Young Hayne and Mr. Dorothy M., water-color bust protraits, black heads. Signed S. L. Lyon, dated 1834. 4 1/2" x 3 3/8"	125.00	200.00
☐ Hon. Henry Clay, bust portrait, inscribed J. W. Jarvis, dated 1810, 8" x 6¼"	75.00	125.00
☐ Miss Elizabeth Frobiser, Clad in Bonnet, dress and white pantalettes. Signed Frith, dated 1821	250.00	300.00
☐ Portrait Group, 19th C., two adults, six children	˙175.00	225.00
☐ Portrait Group, Edouart, 2 adults, 2 children	525.00	550.00
☐ Portrait Group, watercolor, two gentlemen and a lady, landscape setting. Signed Cath. Ludlow, dated 1777. 8 3/4" x 9 7/8"	700.00	800.00
☐ Rev. Henry Jackson, top hat and carrying walking stick. Signed W. H. Brown, dated 1840, 9 3/8" x 6 3/4" .	200.00	275.00
☐ The Vegetable Huckster, watercolor. Signed G. Atkinson, dated 1838. 8¾" x 11"	200.00	250.00
☐ Watercolor Portrait of Gen. Andrew Jackson, head in black. Signed S. L. Waldo, dated 1820, 5¼" x 3¾" . . .	575.00	675.00
☐ Young Girl, posed with hoop, dated 1840. 7½" x 5¼"	150.00	200.00

SPORTS EQUIPMENT

Sports equipment need not be old to be valuable. Modern or current items used by star players have substantial value, *if it can be proven* that they were indeed used by such players. The fraudulent sale of sports equipment, said to have belonged to professional players but in fact nothing but common factory items, has become widespread. The collector is advised to obtain these collectors' items directly from the players, their descendants, or reliable dealers. Blind ads placed in hobby newspapers, those carrying nothing but postal box addresses, should be considered suspect.

SPORTS EQUIPMENT

Note: Most of the prices given are for items of which there is a record of actual sales. Some, however, are estimates, based on collector interest and the value of similar material.

	Price Range	
☐ Baseballs of the 1920's, ...	5.00	10.00
☐ Baseball bats manufactured prior to 1910 (1860's-1870's, would be worth more)	25.00	30.00
☐ Baseball shoes, 1910, reasonable wear, spikes intact	50.00	60.00
☐ Baseball uniform, modern, ...	50.00	100.00
☐ Baseball uniform, 1940's, not including stockings or shoes	150.00	175.00
☐ Baseball uniform, turn of the century, not including stockings or shoes	300.00	325.00
☐ Baseball uniform, modern, *known to have been worn* (at least once) by a star major league player	300.00	500.00
☐ Baseball uniform, any age, known to have been worn by a Hall of Fame player	—	1000.00
☐ Baseball uniform, known to have been worn by Babe Ruth	—	5000.00
☐ Baseman's mit, c. 1910	75.00	100.00
☐ Catcher's chest protector, c. 1905	180.00	200.00
☐ Catcher's glove, late 1800's, ...	100.00	150.00
☐ Catcher's mask, similar to one advertised in 1902 catalogue	45.00	50.00
☐ Fielder's glove, c. 1890	75.00	100.00
☐ Fielder's glove, Early Wynn model, 1950's	15.00	20.00
☐ Fielder's glove, Larry Doby model, 1950's	15.00	20.00
☐ First baseman's glove, c. 1930	50.00	60.00
☐ First baseman's glove, Gil Hodges model, 1950's	25.00	30.00
☐ Football dating before 1900, depending on condition. (It should be noted that prices on such items as footballs, basketballs and other inflated sports balls vary according to whether or not they can be inflated to a point where they resemble the original shape.)	25.00	75.00
☐ Football of the 1930's	10.00	15.00
☐ Football known to have been thrown for a touchdown pass by Norm Van Brocklin, Los Angeles Rams, c. 1952	200.00	225.00
☐ Football used in the first year of the American Football League (shaped slightly differently from National League ball)	75.00	100.00
☐ Football kicking tee, hard rubber, c. 1950	4.00	6.00

STAMPS

Stamp collectors number in the millions, and they have brethern and sisters all over the world. There are many ways of collecting stamps — by country, by denomination, and even by subject. The latter is called topical stamp collecting, and there are hundreds of subjects listed as categories; everything from cats, horses and dogs to paintings, religion and airplanes. Most experienced stamp collectors agree that there is little chance of brand new commemorative stamps ever being worth much more than face value, but don't worry — there are millions of others to choose from. Please consult our publication *The Official Black Book Price Guide of United States Postage Stamps* by Tom Hudgeons for more prices and information.

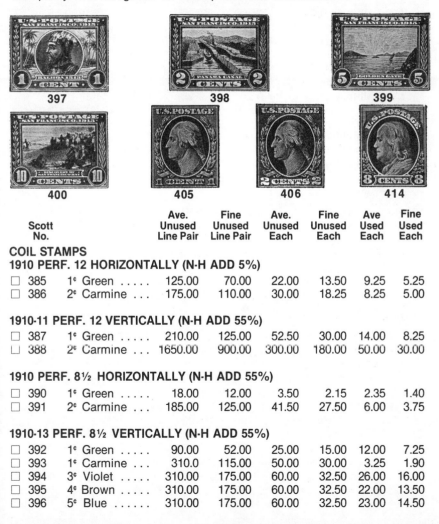

397 398 399

400 405 406 414

Scott No.		Ave. Unused Line Pair	Fine Unused Line Pair	Ave. Unused Each	Fine Unused Each	Ave Used Each	Fine Used Each
COIL STAMPS							
1910 PERF. 12 HORIZONTALLY (N-H ADD 5%)							
☐ 385	1¢ Green	125.00	70.00	22.00	13.50	9.25	5.25
☐ 386	2¢ Carmine . . .	175.00	110.00	30.00	18.25	8.25	5.00
1910-11 PERF. 12 VERTICALLY (N-H ADD 55%)							
☐ 387	1¢ Green	210.00	125.00	52.50	30.00	14.00	8.25
☐ 388	2¢ Carmine . . .	1650.00	900.00	300.00	180.00	50.00	30.00
1910 PERF. 8½ HORIZONTALLY (N-H ADD 55%)							
☐ 390	1¢ Green	18.00	12.00	3.50	2.15	2.35	1.40
☐ 391	2¢ Carmine . . .	185.00	125.00	41.50	27.50	6.00	3.75
1910-13 PERF. 8½ VERTICALLY (N-H ADD 55%)							
☐ 392	1¢ Green	90.00	52.00	25.00	15.00	12.00	7.25
☐ 393	1¢ Carmine . . .	310.0	115.00	50.00	30.00	3.25	1.90
☐ 394	3¢ Violet	310.00	175.00	60.00	32.50	26.00	16.00
☐ 395	4¢ Brown	310.00	175.00	60.00	32.50	22.00	13.50
☐ 396	5¢ Blue	310.00	175.00	60.00	32.50	23.00	14.50

STAMPS 1913 PERF. 12	Ave. Unused Line Pair	Fine Unused Line Pair	Ave. Unused Each	Fine Unused Each	Ave. Used Each	Fine Used Each
PANAMA-PACIFIC ISSUE (N-H ADD 60%)						
☐ 397 1¢ Green	72.00	45.00	17.50	10.50	1.75	1.00
☐ 398 2¢ Carmine . . .	75.00	45.00	18.50	12.00	.75	.45
☐ 399 5¢ Blue	300.00	175.00	68.00	40.00	11.50	6.50
☐ 400 10¢ Orange Yellow	500.00	300.00	125.00	72.00	20.00	12.00
☐ 400A 10¢ Orange . . .	775.00	465.00	180.00	110.00	14.00	8.25
1914-15 PERF. 10 (N-H ADD 60%)						
☐ 401 1¢ Green	82.00	45.00	19.50	11.50	6.25	3.50
☐ 402 2¢ Carmine . . .	235.00	140.00	55.00	32.50	1.65	.90
☐ 403 5¢ Blue	650.00	400.00	175.00	95.00	13.50	7.75
6 404 10¢ Orange . . .	4000.00	2250.00	925.00	550.00	52.00	30.00
1912-14 PERF. 12 (N-H ADD 40%)						
☐ 405 1¢ Green	17.00	10.75	4.00	2.50	.10	.06
☐ 406 2¢ Carmine . . .	13.00	7.25	3.00	1.80	.10	.06
☐ 407 7¢ Black	195.00	150.00	50.00	28.00	5.75	3.50
1912 IMPERFORATE (N-H ADD 40%)						
☐ 408 1¢ Green	4.25	3.10	1.10	.80	.50	.38
☐ 409 2¢ Carmine . . .	4.80	3.50	1.20	.90	.50	.38
1912 PERF. 8½ HORIZONTALLY (N-H ADD 50%) COIL STAMPS						
☐ 410 1¢ Green	25.00	15.50	4.50	3.00	2.55	1.50
☐ 411 2¢ Carmine . . .	23.00	14.00	5.50	3.50	2.75	1.65
1912 PERF. 8½ VERTICALLY (N-H ADD 50%)						
☐ 412 1¢ Green	68.00	40.00	23.00	14.00	4.50	2.75
☐ 413 2¢ Carmine . . .	150.00	80.00	40.00	23.00	.45	.30
1912-14 SINGLE LINE WATERMARK "U.S.P.S." PERF 12 (N-H ADD 45%)						
☐ 414 8¢ Olive Green .	72.50	45.00	17.50	10.50	1.25	.75
☐ 415 9¢ Salmon Red	100.00	57.50	23.00	14.00	12.00	6.85
☐ 416 10¢ Orange Yellow	80.00	45.00	18.00	11.00	.22	.15
☐ 417 12¢ Claret Brown	70.00	40.00	16.50	10.00	3.25	2.00
☐ 418 15¢ Gray	150.00	90.00	34.00	20.00	2.75	1.65
☐ 419 20¢ Ultramar . .	350.00	210.00	82.50	50.00	14.00	8.25
☐ 420 30¢ Orange Red	275.00	165.00	70.0	38.50	13.00	7.25
☐ 421 50¢ Violet	1350.00	775.00	310.00	190.00	13.00	7.75
1912 DOUBLE LINE WATERMARK (N-H ADD 50%)						
☐ 422 50¢ Violet	625.00	375.00	150.00	90.00	12.00	7.25
☐ 423 $1 Violet Black	1525.00	825.00	360.00	210.00	50.00	30.00

STAMPS

Scott No.		Ave. Unused Block	Fine Unused Block	Ave. Unused Each	Fine Unused Each	Ave Used Each	Fine Used Each
1914-15 SINGLE LINE WATERMARK "U.S.P.S." PERF. 10 (N-H ADD 55%)							
☐ 424	1¢ Green	9.25	5.50	2.25	1.40	.12	.07
☐ 425	2¢ Carmine ...	7.35	4.75	1.90	1.10	.10	.06
☐ 426	3¢ Deep Violet..	32.50	19.50	7.75	4.75	1.25	.72
☐ 427	4¢ Brown	82.00	52.00	20.00	20.00	12.00	.38
☐ 428	5¢ Blue	50.00	31.00	11.50	7.10	.42	.25
☐ 429	6¢ Orange	90.00	55.00	22.00	1.10	.70	
☐ 430	7¢ Black	175.00	92.50	38.50	23.50	4.00	2.50
☐ 431	8¢ Olive Green.	92.00	55.00	22.00	13.25	1.50	.90
☐ 432	9¢ Salmon Red.	125.00	72.50	29.00	17.50	8.00	4.75
☐ 433	12¢ Orange Yellow	82.00	50.00	19.50	12.00	.18	.10
☐ 434	11¢ Dark Green.	57.50	34.00	13.50	8.25	5.00	3.00
☐ 435	12¢ Claret Brown	58.00	35.00	14.00	8.25	3.75	2.25
☐ 435a	12¢ Copper Red	58.00	35.00	14.00	8.25	3.75	2.25
☐ 437	15¢ Gray	300.00	185.00	72.00	45.00	5.50	3.35
☐ 438	20¢ Ultramar ..	450.00	275.00	110.00	65.00	3.50	2.10
☐ 439	30¢ Orange Red	600.00	365.00	150.00	90.00	10.00	5.75
☐ 440	50¢ Violet	1975.00	1200.00	450.00	275.00	13.00	7.35

STEVENGRAPHS

Thomas Stevens of England produced silk woven bookmarks in 1854. He produced his first Stevengraph (framed silk woven picture) in 1874.

BOOKMARKS

	Price Range	
☐ Birthday Blessings	65.00	75.00
☐ Centennial, Washington	140.00	180.00
☐ Coach Scene	70.00	100.00
☐ Daughter	30.00	40.00
☐ Flowers and Verse	55.00	75.00
☐ Happy New Year	30.00	40.00
☐ Home Sweet Home	110.00	150.00
☐ Little Bo-Peep	45.00	55.00
☐ Merry Christmas	50.00	70.00
☐ Moses in the Bullrushes	90.00	120.00
☐ Remember Me	35.00	55.00
☐ To A Dear Friend	40.00	60.00
☐ Unchanging Love	20.00	30.00

STEVENGRAPHS

☐ Are You Ready	120.00	140.00
☐ Buffalo Bill	475.00	525.00
☐ Called To The Rescue	200.00	250.00
☐ Card, Birthday Greeting	30.00	50.00

STEVENGRAPHS

	Price	Range
☐ Crystal Place	250.00	300.00
☐ Death Of Nelson	180.00	220.00
☐ Finish	140.00	180.00
☐ First Touch	325.00	375.00
☐ For Life Or Death	225.00	275.00
☐ Fourth Bridge	325.00	375.00
☐ Full Cry	225.00	275.00
☐ Good Old Days	275.00	325.00
☐ Home Sweet Home	100.00	125.00
☐ Lady Godiva Procession	150.00	200.00
☐ Last Lap	225.00	275.00
☐ Louisiana Purchase	125.00	175.00
☐ Madonna And Child	475.00	525.00
☐ Meet, The	200.00	250.00
☐ Mrs. Cleveland	275.00	300.00
☐ Present Time	325.00	375.00
☐ Procession	150.00	175.00
☐ To The Rescue	125.00	150.00
☐ Water Jump	150.00	175.00

STOCK CERTIFICATES

☐ Acme Uranium Mines, Inc. Delaware, used 1950's. Allegorical Vignette of female and two males	2.25	2.75
☐ Boston Chamber of Commerce Realty Trust. Massachusetts, used 1923, 1924. Vignette of old office building showing people and automobiles	2.25	2.75
☐ Buffalo Iron Company. Tennessee. Proxy used with battleship revenue stamp affixed, 1900's	2.25	3.00
☐ Citizens National Bank in Gastonia. Gastonia, North Carolina, unissued. Eagle with outspread wings.	1.75	2.50
☐ Eames Petroleum Iron Company. New York, 1882, used. Allegorical vignette representing New York	6.00	7.00
☐ Fidelity Fund, Inc. Massachusetts, used, early 1960's. Vignette features the statue of the mariner located at Gloucester, Massachusetts	2.25	3.00
☐ International Resistance Company. Delaware, used early 1960's. Vignette showing rocket, radar antenna, etc. representative of company's business.	3.25	4.00
☐ Louisville Railway Company. Used early 1890's. Two vignettes. Streetcar and female holding lightning bolts. Right edge trimmed close.	8.00	9.00
☐ National Tool Company. Ohio, used 1940's. Eagle with outstretched wings	1.25	1.75
☐ New England Gas and Electric Association. Used 1940's. Topless female flanked by power lines on the left and gas storage tanks on the right	2.75	3.25

STOCK CERTIFICATES

Price Range

☐ New York, Ontario and Western Railway Company. New York, used 1920's. Vignette of steam engine pulling freight cars. 8.00   9.25

☐ Philadelphia Rapid Transit Company. Pennsylvania, used 1930's. Vignette of double deck bus flanked by elevated train and trolley car. 5.75   6.75

☐ Thirteenth and Fifteenth Streets Passenger Railway Company of Philadelphia. Used 1930's. Two horses at top, small girl at bottom. 5.75   6.75

☐ United Motor Clubs, Inc. Unissued. Style used in the 1930's. Eagle with brown borders. Delaware. 3.25   4.00

☐ Virginia, City of Norfolk. City street paving bonds. Used, 1873. Green border, vignette of capitol building.   9.50   11.00

☐ West End Street Railway Company. Massachusetts, used early 1920's. Vignette of woman and Indian, rather small. Brown border. 3.75   4.50

STONEWARE

☐ Batter Pitcher, blue floral design on grey ground, 10" H 200.00   240.00

☐ Bottle, grey, inscribed E. C. Boynton, 10" H 30.00   40.00

☐ Bowl, blue and greyware, 8" 35.00   45.00

☐ Butter Crock, cobalt blue on white ground, 7½" D . . .   90.00   130.00

☐ Canning Jar, cobalt blue, 8" H 25.00   35.00

☐ Crock, blue floral design with handles, 10½" H 70.00   100.00

☐ Crock, blue snowflake design on grey ground, inscribed F. H. Cowden, Harrisburg 60.00   75.00

☐ Crock, blue sunflower on grey ground, inscribed O.L. & A.K. Ballard, Burlington, VT, 3 gal., 10½" H 70.00   100.00

☐ Ewer, grey, cobalt with handles, 8" H 50.00   70.00

☐ Flask, cobalt blue leaf sprays on upper body, 8½" H .   200.00   240.00

☐ Jar, blue grape cluster on grey ground, inscribed A. K. Ballard, Burlington, VT, 2 gal., 11" H 75.00   100.00

☐ Jar, deep blue with flowers on grey ground, J. Heister, Buffalo, NY, 3 gal., 13½" H 50.00   70.00

☐ Jar, grey and blue, Rice's Landing, PA, 3 gal., 13" H . .   70.00   100.00

☐ Jug, cobalt blue bird on grey, Whites, Utica, 1 gal., 10½" H 70.00   100.00

☐ Jug, cobalt blue floral with handles, 1800's, 10" H . . .   40.00   50.00

☐ Jug, cobalt blue leaves on grey, ovoid, I. Seymour, Troy, NY, 2 gal., 13¼" H 40.00   50.00

☐ Jug, cobalt blue leaf decor on grey, ovoid, 1 gal., 9½" H 35.00   50.00

STONEWARE JUGS AND VESSELS

STONEWARE

	Price	Range
☐ Jug, cobalt blue plant design on grey, ovoid, Gilson & Co., Reading, PA, 13" H	70.00	90.00
☐ Jug, impressed tulip, applied handle, ovoid, c. 1800 . .	190.00	240.00
☐ Pitcher, butterfly, 10" H	45.00	55.00
☐ Pitcher, cobalt blue flower on tan ground, applied handle, 8½" H	180.00	240.00
☐ Pitcher and Jug, cobalt blue flowers on grey ground, White's, Binghamton, 19th century	275.00	325.00
☐ Salt Box, blue and grey, embossed salt on front, 6" D	45.00	55.00
☐ Spittoon, blue on grey	30.00	40.00
☐ Water Cooler, urn form, flared top, impressed birds, cobalt blue on grey, Summerset Potters Works, 3 gal., 16" H	1300.00	1600.00

TELEPHONES

"Hello! Give me Central!" And anything else to do with telephones. Yes, collectors specialize in telephones and many are also interested in old telegraph equipment. Alexander Graham Bell invented the first really practical telephone in 1875, and it was patented in 1877, but the word "telephony" had been used 14 years before in a lecture on sending and receiving sounds in Frankfort, Germany.

☐ Bell, Brass receiver	100.00	150.00
☐ Candlestick, Brass dial	60.00	100.00
☐ Candlestick, Brass, Stromberg	110.00	160.00

	Price	Range
☐ Desk, Dial 1920's	40.00	60.00
☐ Lineman's Monitor	25.00	30.00
☐ Portable, Forest Service, Model C, no cranks, pair ...	35.00	—
☐ Wall, Kellogg	160.00	200.00
☐ Wall, Stromberg Carlson	140.00	190.00
☐ Wall, Walnut case, 1900's	160.00	200.00
☐ Wall, Western Electric	90.00	140.00
☐ Wall, oak, 20"	90.00	150.00
☐ Wall, oak, carved, 23"	130.00	200.00

THEATRICAL MEMORABILIA

☐ Poster of the Riverside Theater, New York, advertising Burns & Allen comedy team, c. 1938	40.00	50.00
☐ 8x10 b/w photo, signed & inscribed, of DeWolf Hopper (famous for his readings of "Casey at the Bat"), c. 1900. Sepia photo	50.00	75.00
☐ Silk scarf worn by Katherine Hepburn, in an early role, c. 1938	100.00	150.00
☐ Set of seven scrapbooks, 8½xll inches, containing 1,600 items pertaining to the English music halls of 1900-1920, with signed and (in some cases) inscribed photographs of actors, actresses, singers, and other entertainers, along with playbills, clippings, tickets and miscellaneous memorabilia	900.00	1000.00
☐ Card signed by Agnes Morehead, 1940's	5.00	10.00
☐ Large poster advertisement of the B.F. Keith Circuit theaters, listing twelve acts, along with addresses of the Keith theatres in various parts of the country, worn along folds, lightly damp-stained, framed in an oak frame, glazed	70.00	80.00
☐ Poster from the Palace Theater, New York, advertising Judy Garland, covered in protective cellophane, one corner creased	250.00	275.00

THEATRICAL MEMORABILIA

	Price	Range
☐ Walking stick used by Nigel Bruce, along with a pocket photo of him in a typical role and two letters from the owner of this memorabilia to a collector	100.00	125.00
☐ Collection of curtain fragments (ranging in size from 3x3 to about 8x8") from various U.S. vaudeville playhouses, 17 in all, each matted in heavy colored cardboard with identifying card, the whole contained in a specially constructed wooden box covered in pink velvet and fitted with brass hinges and catches. Soiled .	350.00	400.00
☐ Collection of 167 posters and lobby cards from U.S. vaudeville and legitimate playhouses, mostly 1910-30, mostly New York, good condition, a few duplicates . .	1700.00	1750.00
☐ 8x10 b/w photo, signed, of Alfred Hitchcock	25.00	30.00
☐ Holograph letter, signed, of David Belasco	30.00	40.00
☐ Collection of 14 typed letters signed and 3 holograph letters signed from Alfred Lunt, 1953-1961, all to the same correspondent	150.00	160.00
☐ 8x10 b/w photo, signed & inscribed, of Lynn Fontanne, costumed as Queen Elizabeth, matted and framed . .	70.00	80.00
☐ Poster advertising Lew Dockstadter Minstrels, 17x26", lightly damp stained, rare, c. 1922	100.00	110.00
☐ Pair of green silk gloves worn by Celeste Holm	65.00	75.00

TOBACCO COLLECTIBLES

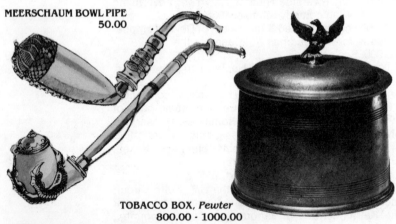

MEERSCHAUM BOWL PIPE
50.00

TOBACCO BOX, *Pewter*
800.00 - 1000.00

CIGAR BANDS

☐ D.W.G. Corp. Custom Made. Detroit, Michigan. Silhouette of woman holding flower.	.75	1.00
☐ El Generalisimo Arzeno y Rodriguez. Man in military hat, embossed seals at sides	1.00	1.50
☐ El Kairo, man wearing Egyptian headdress	1.25	1.75

CIGAR BANDS

	Price	Range
☐ El Rajah - no other wording - man in Indian (Asian) headgear,	1.00	1.25
☐ Glorias de Guillermo 11. Very wide band in oval shape, embossed, portrait	10.00	15.00
☐ Her Majesty Alexandra Victoria, Elias Rojas, made in Tenerife. Large half-length portrait with motto "God Save the Queen"	9.50	11.00
☐ Jockey Club La Corona, "rolled in U.S.A.," horses' head	.75	1.00
☐ Judge Schemanske. Detroit, Michigan. Embossed	1.75	2.25
☐ King Edward VII, Hoja La Rica. Wide label with portrait	7.00	8.00
☐ King Solomon, wide label, attractive, portrait with scroll, swords and shield	3.00	5.00
☐ Mi Carmen, maker C. Fernandez	.75	1.00
☐ Regalia Coronation, 1902, portrait of Edward VII	10.00	15.00
☐ Robert Walker, portrait of man in 18th century garb	1.75	2.25
☐ Triunfos de J. Canalejas. Portrait	4.75	5.50

MISCELLANEOUS · U.S. PRESIDENTS

☐ Abraham Lincoln, the 16th President. Portrait	10.00	15.00
☐ Grover Cleveland, band	7.50	10.00
☐ John Tyler, band	9.50	11.00
☐ Millard Fillmore, band	7.50	10.00
☐ R. B. Hayes, band	7.50	10.00

TOBACCO JARS & HUMIDORS

Made of wood, china, pottery, iron and other metals, the Tobacco Jar was generally a combination humidor and pipe holder. Frequently, it was not only functional but also quite ornately decorated. Sculptured heads, figures or animals were quite common. Prices are for ORIGINAL JARS in good condition.

☐ Arab, wearing headdress, 7" high	55.00	60.00
☐ Boy, 6¾" Bisque	55.00	60.00
☐ Buffalo, Pottery, Dedare Ware	175.00	200.00
☐ Bulldog, Bristol Ware tan colored ceramic	50.00	55.00
☐ Devils Head, color red, bee on side of head	45.00	52.50
☐ Elephant, Majolica pottery	85.00	95.00
☐ Egyptian Queen, exotic face, 4" high, very colorful	70.00	75.00
☐ Frog with pipe	80.00	95.00
☐ Girl's Face, with light hair, hat functions as cover	75.00	85.00
☐ Human Skull	85.00	95.00
☐ Indian Chief 5"	55.00	65.00
☐ Indian Chief, Majolica, feathered headdress 10" high	80.00	95.00
☐ Jester with Dog, Staffordshire, 9½" high	225.00	255.00
☐ Jockey, colored boy with cap, Majolica, 4½" high	100.00	110.00

TOBACCO JARS AND HUMIDORS

	Price	Range
☐ Lion's Head, Austrian Hallmarks	45.00	55.00
☐ Man, seated on chair, Staffordshire china, 8" high	80.00	90.00
☐ Man, with derby hat, pipe in mouth, Austrian	45.00	55.00
☐ Man, with skull cap, English pottery	85.00	90.00
☐ Monk, fat, with laughing face, Bisque chinaware	50.00	65.00
☐ Monkey Head, sports cap and pipe, Majolica	85.00	95.00
☐ Monkeys, face on lid and around base	125.00	145.00
☐ Old Salt Sea Captain, with cap and pipe (illus.)	75.00	85.00
☐ Owl, Majolica pottery, 7" high	50.00	60.00
☐ Pipes on Cover, pink and green pottery (illus.)	60.00	75.00
☐ Pirate, shirt and hat, Majolica pottery	85.00	95.00
☐ Ram's Head, Majolica ware	80.00	90.00
☐ Royal Bayreuth, tapestry ware, cows in field	250.00	260.00
☐ Sea Captain, pipe in mouth, Majolica pottery	85.00	95.00

PIPES

Puff, puff! Some collectors of pipes don't smoke, but they are attracted to pipes for the fine workmanship and interesting use of materials exhibited in them. Even women collect pipes.

☐ Briar, Bull's head, glass eyes	30.00	—
☐ Delft, Blue and White	15.00	20.00
☐ Elk's Head, 6" L	50.00	60.00
☐ Lady, Victorian, 6" L	40.00	50.00
☐ Lion, Devouring Prey, 12" L	60.00	80.00
☐ Meerschaum, German, late 19th C., mk'd Arthur Schneider, Leipzig, 18" L	—	3500.00
☐ Meerschaum, Deer, 14" L	240.00	270.00
☐ Meerschaum, Deer pursued by dog, 9" L	100.00	130.00
☐ Meerschaum, Running deer, leather case, amber stem	95.00	—
☐ Meerschaum, Floral Design, Silk lined leather case	80.00	100.00
☐ Meerschaum, Fu Man Chu	190.00	220.00
☐ Meerschaum, Horse's Head, 9½" L	60.00	80.00
☐ Meerschaum, Monk's Head, 6" L	40.00	50.00
☐ Meerschaum, Suede Bowl, Leather case	60.00	80.00
☐ Meerschaum, Wolf, Amber Stem	90.00	110.00
☐ Opium, Chinese Figures, 14" L	60.00	80.00
☐ Opium, Cloisonne, 15" L	240.00	280.00
☐ Panther's Head, 10" L	40.00	50.00
☐ Porcelain, German, Painted decor	40.00	50.00
☐ Porcelain, Landscape Decor, Handpainted	100.00	120.00
☐ Pugs, Two on Stem	25.00	35.00
☐ Water, Cloisonne, 10" L	130.00	160.00
☐ Water, Snakeskin Bowl	120.00	150.00

TOOLS

Interest in old tools has been primarily a masculine activity. However, it is now developing into a more universal collectible. Most of these early tools were handmade out of basic necessity and show ingenuity and resourcefulness. Hand tools, basically woodworking, are the most popular. Generally the price of tools is rising steadily. *Courtesy: Charles Colt, New York, NY.*

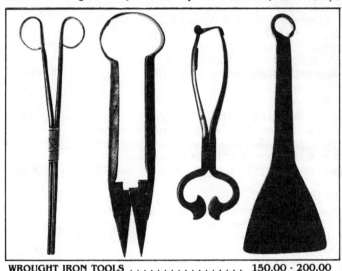

WROUGHT IRON TOOLS . . . . **150.00 - 200.00**

AUGERS: Price Range

☐ Hand forged, stem is Y-shaped at hickory handle, 24" long, 1¼" deep, 1850's 12.00   15.00

☐ Hand forged, crude hickory handle, unreadable mark, 15" long, 1¼" deep, 1850's 10.00   12.00

☐ Stamped #5, no manufacturer's mark, well-shaped hickory handle, 15" long, 1½" deep, circa 1880 . . . . . .   8.00   10.00

BRACES:

☐ Walnut with brass trim, English mark, bit spring broken, 1810-1830 . . . .   75.00   90.00

☐ Metal and wood, set screw holds bits (hand turned handles), 1840-1860 . . . .   25.00   40.00

☐ Metal and wood, set screw holds bits, 1880-1900 . . . . .   15.00   25.00

CHISELS:

☐ Marked "Charles Buck—Cast Steel", brass ferrille, blade 7/8" wide, maple with leather, handle striking surface, 1900-1920 . . . .   6.00   8.00

☐ Common, hand-forged, from file, 6½" long blade, iron ferrille, 1840-1860 . . . .   7.00   9.00

☐ Corner, hand-forged, each side 11" wide, blade 7¼" long, iron collar on handle, 1810-1883 . . . .   18.00   21.00

Price Range

CLAMPS:
☐ All wood, two "bolts", 5" jaw, marked "William
J. Hood, maker, Valley Falls, R.I.", 1860-1880 . . . .   12.00   15.00

DRAW KNIFE:
☐ Cooper's, tangs bent through handles, brass ferrilles,
1830-1850 . . . .   10.00   12.00
☐ Leather working "Snell & Atherton", #5, all metal
scraper, circa 1870 . . . .   12.00   15.00
☐ Open scorp, brass ferrilles, 19th century 12.00   15.00
☐ Wagon maker's "Ohio Tool Co." #9 — 9" blade,
egg-shaped handles, maple, circa 1870 . . . .   12.00   15.00

HAMMERS:
☐ Caulking, slotted head, iron wings, 1880's 12.00   15.00
☐ Cobbler's, marked "Steel drop forged champion"
handle replaced 1920's 4.00   6.00
☐ Cobbler's or upholstery "Made in Germany", hand
forged tool, steel 165", unusually angled head, 1920's   6.00   8.00

HAT BRIM TRIMMER:
☐ Tool used to cut felt to make hats, has adjustable
blade holder that slides away from curved base so
that brim can be cut to 2"-5" width as desired, maple
with brass-locking nuts, 19th century 25.00   30.00

HATCHETS:
☐ LL beam, 9" straight handle, blade 2½" wide, 1920. . .   10.00   12.00
☐ Plumb, boy scout holster, 10½" curved handle, blade
3" wide, 1920 . . . .   6.00   8.00

HOOK:
☐ Hay, hand-wrought, hickory handle, 9th century 4.00   6.00

KNIVES:
☐ For trimming hooves, 1890-1910 . . . .   2.00   3.00
☐ May, brass ferrilles, on both handles, 1860-1880 . . . . .   15.00   18.00

LEVELS:
☐ All metal, cast iron decorative body, 18" x 2½" x 1",
circa 1910 . . . .   18.00   22.00
☐ #2 stamped on butt, horizontal & vertical bubbles
working, mahogany, 28" x 3¼" x 1¼", circa 1880 . . . .   50.00   55.00

	Price	Range

LEVELS:
- ☐ "Stratton Brothers, Greenfield, Mass." with eagle logo on brass plate, brass corners .... 25.00 — 30.00

PLANES:
- ☐ All wood except blade, carpenter's plane, Boech, 12", 19th century .... 12.00 — 15.00
- ☐ All wood except blade, "Horn" plane, European, Boech, 19th century .... 15.00 — 18.00
- ☐ All wood except blade, Ohio Tool Co., joining plane, Boech, 26" long, 19th century .... 15.00 — 18.00
- ☐ All wood except blade, toothing plane, Boech, 19th century .... 15.00 — 18.00
- ☐ Metal and wood Stanley Rule and Level Co., #33, 28" long, 1900-1910............................ 20.00 — 25.00
- ☐ Molding plane, "E.T. Burrones & Co., Portland, Me" printed on side of plane. "Use this tool for fitting Burrowes Patent Sliding Screens" .... 25.00 — 30.00
- ☐ Molding plane, fancy with brass plow planes, etc..... 45.00 — 50.00
- ☐ Molding plane, standard, generally priced, up to 1½" wide .... 9.00 — 12.00

RULERS, FOLDING:
- ☐ Chapin Stephens Co., brass trim all around stamped "JRP", 19th century .... 18.00 — 20.00
- ☐ Ivory, 24", 19th century...................... 45.00 — 50.00
- ☐ Lufkin, #651, brass trim, marked "Boxwood — Made in England" .... 7.00 — 9.00
- ☐ Lufkin, pat'd, 12/3/18, brass trim, marked "Boxwood", stamped "Maguire", 1918 .... 10.00 — 12.00
- ☐ Stanley, #66½, brass at hinges and end, "Warranted Boxwood", 36" long, 19th century .... 8.00 — 10.00
- ☐ Stanley, #68, brass trim on hinges and ends, "Boxwood", circa 1900........................ 7.00 — 9.00

SAWS:
- ☐ Backsaw, Wright & Co. on blade, 11" long, extra heavy back, Boech handle, circa 1890 .... 10.00 — 12.00
- ☐ Keyhole, W.B. Sears & Co. on blade, 7" long, "C.B." stamped on maple handle, brass bolts, circa 1890 ... 8.00 — 10.00

SCALES:
- ☐ Lumber, J. Chatillon & Son, New York in yellow paint, "200", black, 19th century .... 35.00 — 45.00
- ☐ Steel yard, reversible, two hooks on "Heavy" measure, hand forged, 1810-1830 .... 18.00 — 22.00

SCRAPER:

Price Range

☐ Unusual, paint or wood scraper, 3½" chestnut, turned
handle, "W.S. Thompson", 19th century stamped in
3-sided U-shaped blade, handmade, 19th century 20.00 25.00

SCREW DRIVERS:

☐ Clockmaster's, brass ferrille, Boelh handle, marked
"Sargent, Cast Steel", circa 1890 .... 7.00 9.00
☐ Primitive Yankee model 15.00 18.00
☐ Winchester, wood handle 8.00 10.00

SCRIBE — MARKING GAUGES:

☐ Boelh with brass facing and trim.................. 8.00 10.00
☐ Handmade, all Boelh, 8" hand-stamped inches and
numbers 6.00 8.00
☐ Handmade, Boelh and mahogany, no inches 6.00 8.00
☐ Rosewood with brass facings and trim............. 20.00 25.00

SHOVELS:

☐ Carved from one piece, maple or chestnut, grain
shovel, 1840-1880 .... 12.00 15.00
☐ Snow shovel, handmade, wood with tin trim,
20th century 10.00 15.00

T SQUARES:

☐ Rosewood handle, brass plate and 4 leaf clover inlay,
blade 12" x 2 1/8", "JM" carved in handle, 1870-90.... 15.00 18.00
☐ Rosewood handle, brass plate and 3 pointed
diamond, inlay, blade 7½" x 1 3/4", stamped "OWO",
1890-1910 .... 12.00 15.00
☐ Rosewood handle, "Miller's Falls, Made in U.S.A.",
#1438, 8" x 1 1/2", brass plate, circa 1920 .... 8.00 10.00

WRENCHES:

☐ Monkey, A-1, pat'd., '00 & '08, miniature, 2" opening,
circa 1910 .... 4.00 6.00
☐ Wagon wrench, hand forged, curved body,
circa 1840-1850 .... 8.00 10.00

TOYS

The number of toy collectors around the world is astronomical. The demand
of fine toys far exceeds the supply. The Museum of Yesterday's Toys in St.
Augustine, Florida houses one of the finest toy collections in the world and
certainly is worth visiting. Please remember, as with most antique purchases,
consult a reputable dealer.

SHEFFIELD FARMS HORSE-DRAWN WOODEN MILK WAGON

PRISCILLA SIDE-PADDLE WHEELER

RAGGEDY ANDY

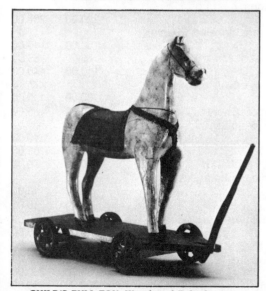

CHILD'S PULL TOY, Wood and Polychrome

ROLY-POLY, Papier-Mache

TOYS

Price Range

☐ Airplane, "Dare-Devil Flyer," with hanger, with plane, with blimp, 10" tall, Marx	80.00	110.00
☐ Airplane, "Cross-Country Flyer," plane/airship/tower, 19" long, Marx	100.00	140.00
☐ Airplane, U.S. Marines, single wing airplane, tin, mech., 17" x 17," circa 1930	85.00	110.00
☐ Airplane, Ford Tri-Motor plane, pressed steel, 25" x 24"	110.00	140.00
☐ Airplane, cast iron, single wing plane, 4" long	50.00	65.00
☐ Airplane, cast iron single wing, early 1900's	25.00	35.00
☐ Airplane, World War II fighter, Marx, tin, mech., wind up	10.00	13.00
☐ Airplane, "Sea Gull," propeller turns, 1930's	40.00	50.00
☐ Alabama Coon Jigger, tin, windup, Lehmann	140.00	155.00
☐ Alligator, tin	30.00	40.00
☐ Amos & Andy, "Fresh Air Taxi," tin mech., Marx	400.00	460.00
☐ Amos & Andy, tin mech., figure, 12", walks	450.00	550.00
☐ Andy Gump, mech., Tootsietoy	150.00	170.00
☐ Auto, car pulling trailer, tin, pull toy, 1930's	40.00	50.00
☐ Auto, Lehmann's autobus, miniature, 1903	575.00	625.00
☐ Auto, Mercedes, tin, mech., windup, early 1900's	200.00	250.00
☐ Auto, Buick, Brougham, Tootsietoy, convertible, 6" ..	120.00	140.00
☐ Auto, Pontiac, 6½" 1928	190.00	220.00
☐ Auto Speedway, windup, Japanese	8.00	12.00
☐ Auto, 4 door sedan, tin mech., with driver, 7" long Lehmann, circa 1910	235.00	265.00
☐ Auto, "Model T" Ford, 7" long, cast iron, Arcade, ca. 1918	225.00	265.00
☐ Auto, "Service Car," cast iron, nickeled wheels, 5" Long, Hubley 1930's	100.00	140.00
☐ B.O. Plenty & Sparkle, tin mech., Marx	65.00	85.00
☐ Balky Mule, Lehmann	110.00	140.00
☐ Balky Mule, tin, mech./clown driver, 7¼" long, Lehmann	80.00	110.00
☐ Barnacle Bill in barrel, windup, Chein	75.00	85.00
☐ Battleship, friction motor, 16" long, Dayton, ca. 1920's	100.00	140.00
☐ Battleship, tin, 1920's	40.00	55.00
☐ Bears, "Teddy" miniature by Stuff,2½"	50.00	70.00
☐ Big parade," soldiers, trucks, ambulances, 24" long, Marx	95.00	115.00
☐ Bird, tin, windup, Marx	7.00	10.00
☐ Black Mammy, windup, Lindstrom	40.00	50.00
☐ Boat, metal, Marx	4.00	6.00
☐ Boat, submarine, German, 9"	40.00	50.00
☐ Bojangles, wood, Negro, tin base	20.00	30.00
☐ Buck Rogers, rocket Police Patrol, tin mech.	180.00	230.00
☐ Buggy with driver, cast iron, medium size, Hubley ...	390.00	450.00

TOYS

	Price	Range
☐ Bus, cast iron, Arcade mfg. Company, 1920's	120.00	145.00
☐ Bus, Double Decker, tin, mech., 8½" long, Lehmann, 1910	370.00	410.00
☐ Cannon, cast iron, caps, 1900's	40.00	50.00
☐ Carriage, Baby, split reed, 24"H	120.00	140.00
☐ Cap Pistol, small, non mech., Patent 1887	55.00	75.00
☐ Cat, iron shaft, stuffed	75.00	90.00
☐ Charley Weaver, Bartender, battery operated	40.00	70.00
☐ Charlie Chaplin, tin mech., figure, 9", German Walks .	100.00	145.00
☐ Charlie McCarthy, Mortimer Snerd car, tin mech., Marx	200.00	250.00
☐ Charlie McCarthy, tin mech., Marx, car	180.00	210.00
☐ Charlie McCarthy, tin mech., figure, Marx walks	70.00	100.00
☐ Circus, clown with barrel, wooden, Schoenhert	50.00	65.00
☐ Circus, Lion cage, tin, 2 lions & driver, 7½" x 12"	115.00	135.00
☐ Circus, ringmaster, wooden, Schoenhert	80.00	100.00
☐ Circus, lady performer, Schoenhert	80.00	105.00
☐ Circus Wagon, 2 horses, one Lion, Hubley 1906	425.00	500.00
☐ Circus Wagon, 2 Horses, two lions, 9½" long, Hubley	500.00	575.00
☐ "Corn Shooter" pistol, cast iron	40.00	60.00
☐ Cow, calfskin, on platform, moos when pulled, 10" long	75.00	95.00
☐ Crane, mechanical, windup, lithographed, 11½"H ...	70.00	85.00
☐ Dick Tracy, car in garage, original box	65.00	75.00
☐ Dinosaurs, multi-jointed, 13" L, 1930's	10.00	14.00
☐ Ditcher, tin, Kenton	400.00	500.00
☐ Dollhouse, tin, lithographed, 8 rooms, 1930's	65.00	75.00
☐ Donkey, Schoenhut, jointed, 8"	45.00	55.00
☐ Drum, tin with wooden sticks, 1940's	20.00	25.00
☐ Drummer Boy, windup, Chein	14.00	18.00
☐ Duck, wooden, pull toy, Germany	5.00	7.00
☐ Dumbbells, Wooden, 1 lb., 1900's	5.00	9.00
☐ Dump Truck, cast iron, red, Arcade, 1928	270.00	310.00
☐ Dump Truck, cast iron & tin, donkey, Harris, 1906	225.00	275.00
☐ Dump Truck, cast iron, medium size Arcade, 1920's	200.00	275.00
☐ Elephant Jumbo, wooden with tin legs	65.00	85.00
☐ Felix, wooden pull toy with 2 mice, Nifty toys	70.00	100.00
☐ Felix, "Speedy Felix" wooden roadster with bellows, Nifty Toys	70.00	110.00
☐ Felix, Bowler, bowling game, Nifty Toys	55.00	75.00
☐ Felix on 3 wheeled Scooter, mech. 7" Nifty Toys	25.00	45.00
☐ Felix, sparkler, squeeze mech., Felix's head, Nifty ...	25.00	45.00
☐ Felix, Wagon, wooden pull toy, Nifty Toys	25.00	45.00
☐ Ferris Wheel, windup, with bell, Chein	45.00	55.00
☐ Fountain, steam operated, brass finished engine, 1892, 9"H	190.00	230.00
☐ Fred Flintstone & Dino the Dinosaur, battery operated	35.00	45.00

TOYS

	Price	Range
☐ Fire Engine Hook & Ladder, 3 horses, Harris, circa 1903	500.00	575.00
☐ Fire Engine, pumper, with boiler, 3 horses, Hubley, ca. 1910	400.00	475.00
☐ Fire Truck, steel, medium, Buddy "L," 1930's	100.00	150.00
☐ Fire Hose Wagon, cast iron, 2 horse & driver, 14"L, Hubley, ca 1915	340.00	390.00
☐ Frog, tin mechanical, jumps	70.00	85.00
☐ G.I. Joe, with pups, tin, mech.	50.00	60.00
☐ Gas Range, cast iron, eagle, worn paint, 4½"	28.00	32.00
☐ Garage, tin, 2 windup cars	150.00	175.00
☐ Grasshoppers, wooden, hand carved, 1960's	10.00	14.00
☐ Gun, cap, Buffalo Bill, 7½"	6.00	8.50
☐ Gun, water, atom, Ray pistol	30.00	45.00
☐ Ham & Sam, tin, mech., windup, Strauss, 1920's	230.00	260.00
☐ Happy Hooligan, tin mech., figure, 5", Chein walks	100.00	145.00
☐ Happy Hooligan, tin, mech.	145.00	160.00
☐ Harold Lloyd, tin mech., figure, 11" walks	340.00	390.00
☐ Hatchet, hand forged, 1900's, 11"	18.00	22.00
☐ Hay Wagon, wooden with 2 horses, 14" long, 1896	175.00	230.00
☐ Hose, reel, wagon, cast iron, 2 horses, 2 firemen, Wilkens, 1880, 15" L	550.00	700.00
☐ Howdy Doody Band, tin mech.	125.00	175.00
☐ Hurdy-Gurdy, wooden, musical disc., late 1800's	240.00	270.00
☐ Ice Box, cast iron, worn paint, with cube of ice, 5"	35.00	45.00
☐ Ice Wagon & Horse, wooden, "Silver Moon," ca. 1920, 22" L	200.00	275.00
☐ Ice Wagon, 2 horses, 10" L, iron	250.00	310.00
☐ Jack-in-the-Box, clown, wood box	25.00	40.00
☐ Jack-in-the-Box, tin, mech.	150.00	170.00
☐ Jockey & Horse, pull, cast iron wheels, 10"	65.00	75.00
☐ Joe Penner, tin mechanical, windup, lithographed, by Marx, 8" H	300.00	340.00
☐ Joe Penner & Goo Goo the Duck, tin mech. Marx	260.00	310.00
☐ Lamp, Tootsietoy	20.00	24.00
☐ Lariat, Cisco kid, Humming	20.00	24.00
☐ Lassie, dancing, tin, windup, Lindstrom	30.00	50.00
☐ "Leapin Lena," tin mech., car, 5½" L	100.00	140.00
☐ Li'l Abner Band, mech., windup, Unique mfg. co., NJ	250.00	290.00
☐ Li'l Abner Band, tin mechanical	180.00	230.00
☐ Light House, tin mechanical, man in boat, 12" H	100.00	140.00
☐ Lone Ranger, tin mechanical, windup, lithographed, mark	110.00	130.00
☐ Lone Ranger, tin mechanical, with lasso and horse	80.00	110.00
☐ Mail truck, tin mechanical, windup, 1920's	70.00	80.00
☐ Man, playing billiards, mechanical, tin	120.00	140.00
☐ Man Sawing Wood, mechanical, tin, 5" L	100.00	140.00
☐ Marine, Negro, mechanical, 5"	20.00	25.00

TOYS
                                 Price Range

	Price	Range
☐ Mickey Mouse Drummer, tin mechanical	180.00	230.00
☐ Mickey Mouse Circus, pull toy, tumbling Mickey & Minnie	100.00	140.00
☐ Mickey Mouse Sparkler, mechanical, Nifty toys	60.00	80.00
☐ Mickey Mouse Acrobat, squeeze, 12"	50.00	70.00
☐ Milton Berle Crazy Car	60.00	75.00
☐ Monkey, windup, Japanese	9.00	12.00
☐ Mortimer Snerd, tin mechanical, Marx	50.00	70.00
☐ Monkey on Tricycle, tin mechanical, 1905	170.00	210.00
☐ Monkey "Tippo" climbing, tin mechanical 1930	50.00	80.00
☐ Motorcycle, windup, Japanese	9.00	12.00
☐ Noah's Ark, wooden, pull toy, lithographed paper on wood	50.00	65.00
☐ Organ, child's, hand	90.00	110.00
☐ Piano, upright, with music holder & bench, Schoenhut, 19½" x 22"	70.00	90.00
☐ Piano, pictures of angles, Schoenhut 16 x 11"	125.00	145.00
☐ Pinocchio, acrobat	135.00	155.00
☐ Pluto, dog, Marx 1930	15.00	25.00
☐ Pool Player, Lechmann, 14½"	70.00	90.00
☐ Popeye on Roof, tin mechanical, Marx	200.00	250.00
☐ Popeye & Olive on Roof, tin mechanical, Marx	100.00	140.00
☐ Popeye in airplane, tin mechanical, marx	170.00	210.00
☐ Popeye & Cart with Parrot, tin mechanical	150.00	200.00
☐ Popeye & Punching Bag, tin mechanical Chein	145.00	185.00
☐ Popeye Band, tin mechanical, Chein	110.00	140.00
☐ Popeye Rollover, tin	85.00	115.00
☐ Popeye, roller skater, tin, windup	80.00	90.00
☐ Porky Pig, tin mechanical, figure, Marx	80.00	110.00
☐ Preacher, in pulpit, mechanical, Ives	675.00	725.00
☐ Puzzle, cardboard train, Milton Bradley, Mass. 1900's	25.00	35.00
☐ Racer, cast iron with driver, early 1900's	95.00	145.00
☐ Railroad Station, Lithographed tin with water tower and crane on bridge	25.00	35.00
☐ Rattles, wooden, Germany 1900's pr.	20.00	30.00
☐ Refrigerator, Pretty Maid, Marx, 4½" x 3"	20.00	30.00
☐ Reindeer & Santa Sled, 2 reindeer with original Santa, Hubley, ...	450.00	575.00
☐ Roller Coaster, windup, tin, Chein	50.00	60.00
☐ Roly Poly, clown, tin, Chein	45.00	55.00
☐ Sam the Gardner, Marx	15.00	20.00
☐ Sandy, tin mechanical	50.00	70.00
☐ Sewing Machine, black with floral scroll, Germany, original box	35.00	45.00
☐ Sewing Machine, 10" L, nickel plated	80.00	110.00
☐ Skates, leather back & strap, 1910	50.00	75.00
☐ Space Ship, Buck Rogers	300.00	350.00
☐ Spelling Boards, wood, pat. 1886	60.00	90.00

TOYS

	Price	Range
☐ Stage, honeymooners, Jackie Gleason, 1955	20.00	25.00
☐ Steam Engine, mechanical, alcohol burner	100.00	150.00
☐ Steam Engine, V. or H., electrical	100.00	150.00
☐ Steam Engine, Alcohol burner, iron-brass	200.00	260.00
☐ Steam Roller, tin, Buddy L, 1930's, 12½"	75.00	100.00
☐ Stove, iron, cook	80.00	100.00
☐ Streetcar, tin, pulltoy, Lehmann, 1890's, 8" L	110.00	160.00
☐ Superman Rollover Tank, tin, mechanical	70.00	100.00
☐ Superman Rollover Air Plane, tin, mechanical, 6"	100.00	140.00
☐ Teddy Bear, Miniature	35.00	40.00
☐ Touring Car, tin, mechanical, 4 door, Bing	275.00	375.00
☐ Train, American Flyer, No. 2, cast iron, windup	130.00	160.00
☐ Train, Buddy L, Standard gauge, 5 cars	1200.00	1400.00
☐ Train, Lionel Steam, No. 384 with tender	180.00	230.00
☐ Train, Lithograph on wood, 3 piece, 1850's	170.00	220.00
☐ Train, Lithograph on tin, 1800's	275.00	350.00
☐ Train, Trolley, lithograph, Chein, 8" L	200.00	225.00
☐ Trolley, "Hill Climber," tin 15" L, friction motor	180.00	230.00
☐ Truck, produce, iron, Mack, 5"	55.00	65.00
☐ Truck, tin, Howard Johnson's, 1950's	35.00	45.00
☐ Truck, White rubber wheels, 9" L..................	75.00	95.00
☐ Truck, Wrecker, Keystone	90.00	140.00
☐ Typewriter, Symplex	16.00	20.00
☐ Typewriter, Tom Thumb	25.00	35.00
☐ Uncle Wiggily Car, tin, mechanical	100.00	140.00
☐ Wagons, tin, pull toy, early 1900's	90.00	110.00
☐ Wagons, horse driver, Northwestern	25.00	35.00
☐ Washing Machines, Marx	30.00	40.00
☐ Wheelbarrow, wooden, 1920's 18" L	15.00	25.00
☐ Whirligigs, soldier, 19th century, 28" H	800.00	900.00
☐ Whistle, wooden rabbits, 1930's, 8½" pr.	20.00	30.00
☐ Yellow cab, cast iron, Arcade, 1925, 8"	250.00	300.00
☐ Zeppelin, steel, 28" L	80.00	110.00
☐ "Zig Zag," tin, mechanical 2 drivers	325.00	400.00

TRAMP ART

Literally the work of itinerants of the late 19th and early 20th centuries, tramp art is easily identified by common characteristics. Most of it was put together with glued or nailed layers of cigar box wood, notched or cut with zigzag edges, and "stepped" in such a way as to give depth to the piece — the same depth which would have existed if heavier, thicker lumber had been used. The most common pieces are boxes of various sorts... many made on a "base" of a complete cigar box. There are some extremely large pieces, too, such as secretaries and kneehole desks and hutch compartments.

☐ American eagle statuette, 14" tall, wingspan not stated, carved from wood, the feathers indicated by incised lines, possibly western Pennsylvania origin, c. 1870, very good specimen	450.00	500.00

TRAMP ART

Price Range

☐ American eagle statuette, 9½" tall, wingspan 16", carved from wood, the wings carved separately and attached, not traces of paint, rough workmanship, c. 1870 . . . .   300.00   315.00

☐ Birdcage, 14" high, constructed of matchsticks, twigs and other materials, domed top with ring for hanging, well preserved, late 19th C. 270.00   300.00

☐ Birdcage, 27" high, twelve perches, constructed of thin galvanized & other wire, matchsticks, etc., c. 1870 . . . .   400.00   450.00

☐ Jewel chest, 14 x 12 x 5 inches, made of planks of several different kinds (and thicknesses) of wood, joined with glue and nails, the lid opening on English-style hinges, covered over in seashells, the interior lined with green felt, somewhat damaged, c. 1910 . . .   125.00   150.00

☐ Jewel chest, 10 x 8 x 4½ inches, made of pine slats, incised carving of birds on lid, columns at the sides constructed from matchsticks, good condition, c. 1880 . . . .   150.00   175.00

☐ Jewel chest, 11½ x 8 x 6¼ inches, the interior compartmented, made of sheet tin partially painted, traces of tar or similar substance at the joins, c. 1880   85.00   100.00

☐ Jewel chest, large size, 18 x 13 x 7 inches, mahogany (apparently cut down from the top of a discarded dining table), decorated with incised lines, some attempt at relief carving *which may be modern,* c. 1900 . . . . . .   150.00   175.00

☐ Jewel (or other) box, made from a cardboard cigar box, the lid and exterior sides covered with matchsticks to form decorative patterns, c. 1910 . . . .   65.00   75.00

☐ Mirror in frame, overall size 8 x 6 inches, the frame made of tree branches, wooden plank at the back, burn holes at the back, good condition otherwise, c. 1880 . . . .   75.00   100.00

☐ Pencil box, made of orange-crate wood, glued, the top section sliding, painted in shades of red and green with foilage decorations in other colors, some incised linework done with jackknife or similar tool, good condition, c. 1900 . . . .   35.00

☐ Pocket mirror, oval, 4", probably a fragment of wall mirror set into a discarded photo mount, c. 1870 or earlier (one of the favorite "throw-aways" used by tramp artists were broken mirrors, which could be sawn or otherwise cut down) 75.00   100.00

☐ Small box, 6 x 4 inches, made of several hundred wooden dowels glued together, geometrical pattern at the top also formed by dowels, c. 1880 . . . .   235.00   250.00

☐ Small box, 5 x 4 inches, lid missing, carved entirely from a solid block of wood, decorative work at the sides, traces of gilding, some damage, c. 1870 . . . . . .   100.00   125.00

TRAMP ART   Price Range

☐ Small box, 5 x 4½ inches, sliding lid (broken), the box
   made of thin wood, the lid of wood set with a mirror,
   c. 1890 ....   95.00   100.00

TRIVETS

☐ "Odd Fellows." Horseshoe shape, clasped hands
   with eagle above, early 25.00   30.00
☐ "Jenny Lind." Fine large trivet with full figure
   portrait, c. 1850 ....   30.00   40.00
☐ Small trivet. Horseshoe shape, c. 1890 ....   10.00   15.00
☐ Wedge shape. c. 1894 ....   10.00   15.00
☐ Geometric design. c. 1890 ....   5.00   7.50
☐ Trailing Vine or lattice work. Wedge shaped.   5.00   6.00

TYPEWRITERS

☐ Blickensderfer, with case, c. 1890 ....   30.00   40.00
☐ Blickensderfer, wooden case, c. 1880 ....   60.00   70.00
☐ Corona, portable, folding, c. 1900 ....   30.00   40.00
☐ Corona, office model, c. 1910 ....   65.00   75.00
☐ Merritt, wooden case, c. 1890 ....   100.00   110.00
☐ Oliver, office model, c. 1910 ....   60.00   70.00
☐ Underwood, office, c. 1920 ....   60.00   70.00

UMBRELLAS

☐ American, late 18th century, diameter when opened
   41", length of handle 34", handle made of walnut 350.00   400.00
☐ English, mid 18th century, diameter when opened
   43", length of handle 35", handle made of ebony
   fitted with silver plate, ivory knob 500.00   600.00
☐ French, high domed model, dia. 35½", length of
   handle 39", handle of cherrywood, c. 1800 ....   700.00   300.00
☐ American, dia. when opened 39", length of handle
   33½", handle made of pine, c. 1820 ....   70.00   90.00
☐ American, the cover painted in a floral pattern, dia.
   39", length of handle 35½", handle made of oak,
   c. 1850 ....   250.00   300.00
☐ English or Irish, Victorian, the cover knitted in shades
   of pink, light blue and green, floral pattern 100.00   150.00
☐ American, men's umbrella sold by Sears Roebuck
   & Co., in good workable condition, c. 1900 ....   15.00   20.00

VACUUM CLEANERS

	Price Range	
☐ Bissel, hand sweeper	25.00	30.00
☐ Bissell, Grand Rapids, hand sweeper	40.00	50.00
☐ General Electric, electric, 110 volt	50.00	60.00
☐ Thuro Electric, 110 volt, c. 1910	75.00	85.00
☐ Wardway Electric, 110 volt, c. 1922	40.00	50.00
☐ Wardway, hand sweeper	15.00	20.00

WEATHER VANES

Weather vanes indicate wind direction and are made in the form of objects, i.e., animals, birds, etc.

	Price
☐ American Eagle with spread wings mounted on wooden block	495.00
☐ Automobile. Open roadster. Intricate detail. Heavy copper gilded gold leaf. 26" long, full bodied	350.00
☐ Automobile. Open top. Complete with goggled old green patina navigator and driver. Heavy copper, full bodied, 24"	550.00
☐ Banneret and Scroll. 3' long. Ornately gilded copper	50.00
☐ Beaver. Quebec. Made of tin, 1860	800.00
☐ Cannon. Mounted on spoked gun carriage. Reinforced barrel and stand. Copper	135.00
☐ Chicken. Old decorations made of tin with iron rods	675.00
☐ Cow. 9½" long. Mounted on 20½" arrow	100.00
☐ Cow. 42" long. Short-horned Jersey. Scrolled direction indicators	110.00
☐ Crowing Cock. 28½". Made of copper	725.00
☐ Deer. 50" long. Running buck with curved antlers. Full bodied. copper, old green patina with traces of old gilt	200.00
☐ Dragon. 54" long. Winged beast with snake-like tail. Crouching on stand above scrolled direction indicators	150.00
☐ Eagle. Hollow copper, spreadwing, 24" W, 19th C.	800.00
☐ Eagle. 5' wing span. Clawed feet resting on ball, old green patina	125.00
☐ Eagle. Perched on sphere. Cast iron with directional lettering	700.00
☐ Fish. 26" long. Made of copper	725.00
☐ Fiske Running Horse. Black hawk #201, 33" L	2500.00
☐ Flag. Unfurled 48-star banner with pointed standard	95.00
☐ Fox. 30" long. Running. Scrolled pointers. Copper, full bodied	145.00
☐ Goose. 23" wing span. Cast Iron	425.00
☐ Greyhound. 30" long. Long-legged animal standing on reinforced pedestal. ¾ full bodied. Green patina	135.00
☐ Heraldic arrow with lions. Wrought iron with scrolling base	195.00
☐ Horse & Arrow. Gold Globe	200.00
☐ Horse. Copper & wrought iron directional atop milk glass ball	340.00
☐ Horse & Rider. Hollow copper, directional roof finial	1700.00
☐ Locomotive with Tender. 5' long. Large model of late 19th century railroad machine. Full bodied, copper	270.00
☐ Lion. 4' long. Large head with carved mane. Copper. ¾ full bodied	180.00

WEATHER VANES

Price

☐ Race Horse with Jockey. 32" long. Kentucky thoroughbred, thoroughbred, full bodied, copper 195.00
☐ Sailing Vessel. Painted green 200.00
☐ Standing Indian. Original zinc finish. Single direction indicator.

WOODENWARE

Many beautifully made wooden items contribute to this broad category of "woodenware". With the rising prices of rare wood these items are also rapidly rising in price.

	Price Range	
☐ Apple Butter Scoop	50.00	100.00
☐ Apple Tray. Old red stain	18.00	25.00
☐ Barber Pole, Hanging. 22" long (original decorations)	—	250.00
☐ Baskets. Peck measure	20.00	30.00
☐ Bellows. Pine	—	55.00
☐ Boot Jack	20.00	30.00
☐ Bowls. 6" x 2½" burl, maple	150.00	250.00
☐ Bowls. 9½" x 4¾"	100.00	150.00
☐ Bowls. 12" diameter. Turned maple	14.00	20.00
☐ Bowls. 14" maple	35.00	70.00
☐ Bowls. 14" x 23" (original paint)	75.00	150.00
☐ Bowls. 15" diameter. Burl (refinished)	275.00	400.00
☐ Bowls. 16" diameter. Maple (old)	175.00	275.00
☐ Bowls. 17" diameter, 7" high. Burl (walnut)	350.00	400.00
☐ Bowls. 22" long, 8" deep (turned)	100.00	200.00
☐ Bread Board. "Give Us This Day"	55.00	90.00
☐ Bread Board. 11" deep. Maple	40.00	55.00
☐ Bread Peels (48" long paddle for taking bread out of oven)	—	55.00
☐ Bread Trough	—	150.00
☐ Brooms. Birch	—	30.00

ASSORTED WOODENWARE

WOODENWARE

	Price Range	
☐ Brooms. Fireplace	—	16.50
☐ Brooms. Long handle, kitchen	—	30.00
☐ Butter Churn	100.00	175.00
☐ Butter Churn with lid and dasher refinished	100.00	150.00
☐ Butter Molds. Cow	40.00	70.00
☐ Butter Molds. Flowers and leaves	—	40.00
☐ Butter Molds. Large round with leaf design	30.00	45.00
☐ Butter Molds. Round, pineapple	45.00	75.00
☐ Butter Molds. Sheaf of wheat	55.00	75.00
☐ Butter Molds. Paddle	—	40.00
☐ Butter Molds. Paddle with handle and bowl	7.00	15.00
☐ Butter Molds. Prints	—	75.00
☐ Butter Molds. Tubs	—	75.00
☐ Cabbage Cutter	110.00	140.00
☐ Cabbage Cutting Board	35.00	50.00
☐ Candle Box	55.00	80.00
☐ Carrying Yoke	—	28.50
☐ Cheese Drainer	80.00	100.00
☐ Cheese Ladle	30.00	50.00
☐ Cheese Press. 1883	275.00	400.00
☐ Chopping Bowl	—	50.00
☐ Chopping Knife	—	30.00
☐ Church Rail	70.00	85.00
☐ Cider Press	—	75.00
☐ Cigar Humidor	35.00	75.00
☐ Clothes Drying Rack	35.00	50.00
☐ Clothes Mangler	—	75.00
☐ Clothes Pins	—	3.50
☐ Clothesline Winder	—	18.50
☐ Collection Box	55.00	80.00
☐ Cookie Roller	14.00	20.00
☐ Cookie Spoon	—	25.00
☐ Cranberry Rake	70.00	110.00
☐ Cream Skimmer	35.00	55.00

WOODENWARE

	Price	Range
☐ Curd Knife. 20"	55.00	75.00
☐ Darning Egg. With handle	10.00	20.00
☐ Dippers	60.00	80.00
☐ Document Box	120.00	145.00
☐ Dough Box	75.00	120.00
☐ Dough Box. With cover	95.00	150.00
☐ Drinking Cup	30.00	50.00
☐ Eating Spoons (refinished)	6.00	12.00
☐ Eating Spoons (rough)	4.00	8.00
☐ Egg Cups	55.00	75.00
☐ Flour Scoop	—	35.00
☐ Flour Sifter	—	20.00
☐ Foot Warmer. For charcoal	60.00	90.00
☐ Funnel	—	50.00
☐ Grater	—	12.50
☐ Hasty Pudding Stick	—	10.00
☐ Herb Box. With cover	25.00	45.00
☐ Hobby Horse. 41" long, 33" high. In swing standard	—	120.00
☐ Keeles Tubs	—	40.00
☐ Knife Boxes. Pine (as had)	—	32.50
☐ Knife Boxes. Pine (refinished)	45.00	65.00
☐ Knife Boxes. Walnut (refinished)	60.00	80.00
☐ Knife Boxes. Walnut (rough)	30.00	50.00
☐ Knife Tray	30.00	40.00
☐ Ladle	—	30.00
☐ Lemon Squeezer	18.00	30.00
☐ Letter Writing Box (refinished)	—	65.00
☐ Maple Syrup Stirrer	—	8.50
☐ Meat Pounder	—	12.50
☐ Mixing Bowl	—	80.00
☐ Mortar and Pestles (Lignum Vitae)	85.00	110.00
☐ Mortar and Pestles (Maple)	60.00	80.00
☐ Noggins	90.00	150.00
☐ Nutcracker. 11½"	30.00	45.00
☐ Ox Yokes. With bows	90.00	120.00
☐ Ox Yokes. Without bows	60.00	90.00
☐ Pantry Box. With cover	25.00	75.00
☐ Pepper Mills	—	75.00
☐ Pie Crimper. 5½"	35.00	65.00
☐ Pie Lifter	8.00	16.00
☐ Pill Box	—	30.00
☐ Pitch Fork (four tine)	—	42.50
☐ Pitch Fork (two tine)	—	32.00
☐ Plates	—	24.00
☐ Platter	—	36.00
☐ Potato Masher	8.00	16.00
☐ Propeller Airplane	95.00	135.00
☐ Rolling Pin (Lignum, Vitae)	—	55.00
☐ Rolling Pin (Mahogany inserts)	—	45.00

WOODENWARE

	Price	Range
☐ Rolling Pin (Maple with handles)	30.00	55.00
☐ Rum Keg (rundlet)	40.00	75.00
☐ Salt Box. Hanging pine. Pennsylvania Dutch type (refinished)	—	85.00
☐ Salt Box. 5½" x 6¼" x 6" high. Covered pine (refinished)	50.00	75.00
☐ Sap Bucket	30.00	45.00
☐ Sap Bucket. 11½" diameter. Handle added (refinished)	—	24.50
☐ Sausage Gun (not wood, but very popular)	—	40.00
☐ Sewing Box	20.00	35.00
☐ Shovel. Grain, all wood, large	100.00	140.00
☐ Sieve. Wooden mesh (as had)	—	18.50
☐ Sieve. Horse-hair mesh	—	25.00
☐ Soap Dish	40.00	70.00
☐ Soap Scoop	50.00	75.00
☐ Soap Stick	—	6.50
☐ Spatula	—	12.50
☐ Spice Box. Oval	35.00	45.00
☐ Spice Box. Round	45.00	55.00
☐ Spoon Holder	20.00	30.00
☐ Stamp Box	20.00	45.00
☐ Sugar Box	—	30.00
☐ Sugar Bin	120.00	160.00
☐ Sugar Bucket. With cover	45.00	65.00
☐ Sugar Bucket. Without cover	30.00	45.00
☐ Sugar Sifter	—	20.00
☐ Sugar Scoop	—	30.00
☐ Sugar Tub	50.00	75.00
☐ Swigglers	—	40.00
☐ Tankards. With cover	—	50.00
☐ Tankards. With Toddy Hole	—	60.00
☐ Towel Rack. Pine	75.00	100.00
☐ Utensil Rack. Pine with wrought iron hooks	45.00	75.00
☐ Wagon Jack. Wood	175.00	250.00
☐ Wagon Seat	65.00	150.00
☐ Wagon Wheel (different sizes)	130.00	160.00
☐ Walking Stick	65.00	110.00
☐ Wall Bucket	—	32.50
☐ Washboards. Slat	—	35.00
☐ Washboards. Spool	—	60.00
☐ Washtub	—	80.00
☐ Washtub. Scrubbing stick	—	8.50
☐ Water Bucket	30.00	45.00
☐ Water Pump	—	34.50
☐ Whetstone. Foot operated	—	155.00
☐ Wooden Bench. Small	35.00	55.00

COLLECTIBLE REFERENCE INDEX

HOW TO USE THIS INDEX: Locate the particular *item* or *subject category* in question in the alphabetical listing below.

BECOME AN EXPERT

The **HOUSE OF COLLECTIBLES** *publishes the largest selling, most comprehensive, up-to-date* **OFFICIAL PRICE GUIDES** *on collectibles.*

KEEPING UP WITH THE EXPANDING MARKET IN COLLECTIBLES-IS OUR BUSINESS. Our series of OFFICIAL PRICE GUIDES covers virtually every facet of collecting with subjects that range from ANTIQUES to ZEPPELIN STAMPS. Each volume is devoted to a particular subject and is written by an expert in that field. The information is presented in an organized, easily understood format with the utmost care given to accuracy. This comprehensive approach offers valuable information to both the novice and the seasoned collector.

Send for our latest catalog or contact your local bookseller.

BUY IT ● USE IT ● BECOME AN EXPERT

"Exclusive Publishers of Official Price Guides"

773 Kirkman Road, No. 120, Orlando, Florida 32811
Phone (305) 299-9343